Direct3D ShaderX

Vertex and Pixel Shader Tips and Tricks

Edited by Wolfgang F. Engel

Wordware Publishing, Inc.

Library of Congress Cataloging-in-Publication Data
Direct3d ShaderX : vertex and pixel shader tips and tricks / edited by
Wolfgang F. Engel.
  p. cm.
Includes bibliographical references and index.
 ISBN 1-55622-041-3
1. Computer games--Programming.   2. Three-dimensional display systems.
3. Direct3D.   I. Engel, Wolfgang F.
 QA76.76.C672 D57 2002
 794.8'15265--dc21

2002006571

ISBN 1-55622-041-3

10 9 8 7 6 5 4 3 2 1
0502

RenderMan is a registered trademark of Pixar Animation Studios.
krass engine is a trademark of Massive Development.
3D Studio Max is a registered trademark of Autodesk/Discreet in the USA and/or other countries.
GeForce is a trademark of NVIDIA Corporation in the United States and/or other countries.
Some figures in this book are copyright ATI Technologies, Inc., and are used with permission.
Other product names mentioned are used for identification purposes only and may be trademarks of their respective companies.

All inquiries for volume purchases of this book should be addressed to Wordware Publishing, Inc., at the above
address. Telephone inquiries may be made by calling:

(972) 423-0090

Contents

Part 1: Introduction to Shader Programming

Fundamentals of Vertex Shaders 4
Wolfgang F. Engel

Basic Shader Development with Shader Studio 149

John Schwab

Part 2: Vertex Shader Tricks

Vertex Decompression in a Shader 172
Dean Calver

viii   Contents

Part 3: Pixel Shader Tricks

Non-Photorealistic Rendering with Pixel and Vertex Shaders 319

Drew Card and Jason L. Mitchell

Animated Grass with Pixel and Vertex Shaders 334

John Isidoro and Drew Card

Texture Perturbation Effects 337

John Isidoro, Guennadi Riguer, and Chris Brennan

A Non-Integer Power Function on the Pixel Shader **383**
Philippe Beaudoin and Juan Guardado

Bump Mapped BRDF Rendering **405**
Ádám Moravánszky

Real-Time Simulation and Rendering of Particle Flows **414**
Daniel Weiskopf and Matthias Hopf

Foreword

With the advent of Microsoft® DirectX® version 8.0, the revolution of programmable graphics had arrived. With vertex shaders for the programmable geometry pipeline and pixel shaders for the programmable pixel pipeline, the control over geometry and pixels was handed back to the developer. This unprecedented level of control in the graphics pipeline means graphics developers, once they have mastered the basics of shaders, now have the tools to generate new, as yet unheard-of, effects. Wolfgang and his contributors have selected shader topics that they believe will help to open wide the doors of illumination on shaders and the programmable pipeline. Read on, be illuminated, and learn how to create your own effects using the programmable graphics pipeline.

Phil Taylor
Program Manager
Windows Graphics & Gaming Technologies
Microsoft Corporation

Acknowledgments

Like any book with a number of authors, this one has its own history. In late autumn of 2000, I was very impressed by the new capabilities that were introduced with DirectX 8.0 by Microsoft and NVIDIA. At Meltdown 2001 in London, I met Philip Taylor for the first time and discussed with him the idea to write an entire book dedicated to vertex and pixel shader programming. We had a good time thinking about a name for the book, and it was this discussion that led to the title: *Direct3D ShaderX*.

Philip was one of the driving spirits who encouraged me to start this project, so I was very glad when he agreed to write the foreword without hesitation. Jason L. Mitchell from ATI, Juan Guardado from Matrox, and Matthias Wloka from NVIDIA (I met Matthias at the Unterhaltungs Software Forum in Germany) were the other driving spirits who motivated their colleagues to contribute to the book.

During a family vacation, I had the pleasure to get to know Javier Izquierdo (nurbs1@hotmail.com) who showed me some of his artwork. I was very impressed and asked him if he would create a ShaderX logo and design the cover of the book. His fantastic final draft formed the basis of the cover design, which shows in-game screen shots of *AquaNox* from Massive Development. These screen shots were sent to me by Ingo Frick, the technical director of Massive and a contributor to this book. *AquaNox* was one of the first games that used vertex and pixel shaders extensively.

A number of people have enthusiastically contributed to the book:

David Callele (University of Saskatchewan), Jeffrey Kiel (NVIDIA), Jason L. Mitchell (ATI), Bart Sekura (People Can Fly), and Matthias Wloka (NVIDIA) all proofread several of these articles.

A big thank you goes to the people at the Microsoft Direct3D discussion group (http://DISCUSS.MICROSOFT.COM/archives/DIRECTXDEV.html), who were very helpful in answering my numerous questions.

Similarly, a big thank you goes to Jim Hill from Wordware Publishing, along with Wes Beckwith, Alan McCuller, and Paula Price. Jim gave me a big boost when I first brought this idea to him. I had numerous telephone conferences with him about the strategic positioning of the book in the market and the book's progress, and met him for the first time at GDC 2002 in San Jose.

I have never before had the pleasure of working with so many talented people. This great teamwork experience will be something that I will never forget, and I am very proud to have had the chance to be part of this team.

My special thanks goes to my wife, Katja, and our infant daughter, Anna, who had to spend most evenings and weekends during the last five months without me, and to my parents who always helped me to believe in my strength.

Wolfgang F. Engel

Direct3D ShaderX

Vertex and Pixel Shader Tips and Tricks

Part 1

This introduction covers the fundamentals of vertex shader and pixel shader programming. You will learn everything here necessary to start programming vertex and pixel shaders from scratch for the Windows family of operating systems. Additionally, there is a tutorial on Shader Studio, a tool for designing vertex and pixel shaders.

Fundamentals of Vertex Shaders

This article discusses vertex shaders, vertex shader tools, and lighting and transformation with vertex shaders.

Programming Vertex Shaders

This article outlines how to write and compile a vertex shader program.

Introduction to Shader Programming

Fundamentals of Pixel Shaders

This article explains the pixel shader architecture, describes various pixel shader tools, and gives an overview of basic programming.

Programming Pixel Shaders

This article takes a look at writing and compiling a pixel shader program, including texture mapping, texture effects, and per-pixel lighting.

Basic Shader Development with Shader Studio

The creator of Shader Studio explains how to use this tool for designing vertex and pixel shaders.

Fundamentals of Vertex Shaders

Wolfgang F. Engel

We have seen ever-increasing graphics performance in PCs since the release of the first 3dfx Voodoo cards in 1995. Although this performance increase has allowed PCs to run graphics faster, it arguably has not allowed graphics to run <u>much</u> better. The fundamental limitation thus far in PC graphics accelerators has been that they are mostly fixed-function, meaning that the silicon designers have hard-coded specific graphics algorithms into the graphics chips, and as a result, game and application developers have been limited to using these specific fixed algorithms.

For over a decade, a graphics technology known as RenderMan® from Pixar Animation Studios has withstood the test of time and has been the professionals' choice for high-quality photorealistic rendering.

Pixar's use of RenderMan in its development of feature films such as *Toy Story* and *A Bug's Life* has resulted in a level of photorealistic graphics that have amazed audiences worldwide. RenderMan's programmability has allowed it to evolve as major new rendering techniques were invented. By not imposing strict limits on computations, RenderMan allows programmers the utmost in flexibility and creativity. However, this programmability has limited RenderMan to software implementations.

Now, for the first time, low-cost consumer hardware has reached the point where it can begin implementing the basics of programmable shading similar to RenderMan with real-time performance.

The principal 3D APIs (DirectX and OpenGL) have evolved alongside graphics hardware. One of the most important new features in DirectX graphics is the addition of a programmable pipeline that provides an assembly language interface to the transformation and lighting hardware (vertex shader) and the pixel pipeline (pixel shader). This programmable pipeline gives the developer a lot more freedom to do things that have never before been seen in real-time applications.

Shader programming is the new and real challenge for game-coders. Face it...

What You Need to Know/Equipment

You need a basic understanding of the math typically used in a game engine, and you need a basic to intermediate understanding of the DirectX Graphics API. It helps if you know how to use the Transform & Lighting (T&L) pipeline and the SetTextureStageState() calls. If you need help with these topics, I recommend working through an introductory level text first, such as *Beginning Direct3D Game Programming*.

Your development system should consist of the following hardware and software:

- DirectX 8.1 SDK
- Windows 2000 with at least Service Pack 2 or higher or Windows XP Professional (the NVIDIA shader debugger only runs on these operating systems)
- Visual C/C++ 6.0 with at least Service Pack 5 (needed for the DirectX 8.1 SDK) or higher
- More than 128 MB RAM
- At least 500 MB of hard drive storage
- A hardware-accelerated 3D graphics card. To be able to get the maximum visual experience of the examples, you need to own relatively new graphics hardware. The pixel shader examples will only run properly on GeForce3/4TI or RADEON 8x00 boards at the time of publication.
- The newest graphics card device driver

If you are not the lucky owner of a GeForce3/4TI, RADEON 8x00, or an equivalent graphics card (that supports shaders in hardware), the standardized assembly interface will provide highly tuned software vertex shaders that AMD and Intel have optimized for their CPUs. These software implementations should jump in when there is no vertex shader capable hardware found. There is no comparable software-emulation fallback path for pixel shaders.

Vertex Shaders in the Pipeline

The diagram on the following page shows the source or polygon, vertex, and pixel operations levels of the Direct3D pipeline in a very simplified way.

On the source data level, the vertices are assembled and tessellated. This is the high-order primitive module, which works to tessellate high-order primitives such as N-Patches (as supported by the ATI RADEON 8500 in hardware), quintic Béziers, B-splines, and rectangular and triangular (RT) patches.

A GPU that supports RT-Patches breaks higher-order lines and surfaces into triangles and vertices.

Note: It appears that, beginning with the 21.81 drivers, NVIDIA no longer supports RT-Patches on the GeForce3/4TI.

A GPU that supports N-Patches generates the control points of a Bézier triangle for each triangle in the input data. This control mesh is based on the positions and normals of the original triangle. The Bézier surface is then tessellated and evaluated, creating more triangles on chip [Vlachos01].

 Note: The N-Patch functionality was enhanced in Direct3D 8.1. There is more control over the interpolation order of the positions and normals of the generated vertices. The new D3DRS_POSITIONORDER and D3DRS_NORMALORDER render states control this interpolation order. The position interpolation order can be set to either D3DORDER_LINEAR or D3DORDER_CUBIC.

 Note: The normal interpolation order can be set to either D3DORDER_LINEAR or D3DORDER_ QUADRATIC. In Direct3D 8.0, the position interpolation was hard-wired to D3DORDER_CUBIC and the normal interpolation was hard-wired to D3DORDER_LINEAR.

 Note: If you use N-Patches together with programmable vertex shaders, you have to store the position and normal information in input registers v0 and v3. That's because the N-Patch tessellator needs to know where this information is to notify the driver.

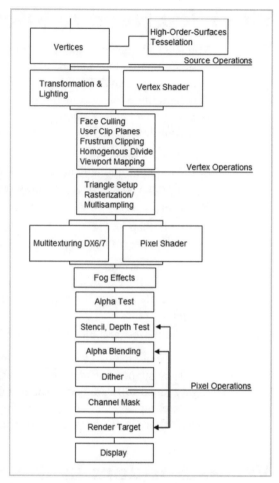

Figure 1: Direct3D pipeline

The next stage shown in Figure 1 covers the vertex operations in the Direct3D pipeline. There are two different ways of processing vertices:

1. The "fixed-function" pipeline. This is the standard Transform & Lighting (T&L) pipeline, where the functionality is essentially fixed. The T&L pipeline can be controlled by setting render states, matrices, and lighting and material parameters.

2. Vertex shaders. This is the new mechanism introduced in DirectX 8. Instead of setting parameters to control the pipeline, you write a vertex shader program that executes on the graphics hardware.

Our focus is on vertex shaders. It is obvious from the simplified diagram in Figure 1 that face culling, user clip planes, frustum clipping, homogenous divide, and viewport mapping operate on pipeline stages after the vertex shader. Therefore, these stages are fixed and can't be controlled by a vertex shader. A vertex shader is not capable of writing to vertices other than the one it currently shades. It is also not capable of creating vertices; it generates one output vertex from each vertex it receives as input.

So what are the capabilities and benefits of using vertex shaders?

Why Use Vertex Shaders?

If you use vertex shaders, you bypass the fixed-function pipeline or T&L pipeline. But why would you want to skip them?

The hardware of a traditional T&L pipeline doesn't support all of the popular vertex attribute calculations on its own, and processing is often job-shared between the geometry engine and the CPU. Sometimes, this leads to redundancy.

There is also a lack of freedom. Many of the effects used in games look similar to the hard-wired T&L pipeline. The fixed-function pipeline doesn't give the developer the freedom he needs to develop unique and revolutionary graphical effects. The procedural model used with vertex shaders enables a more general syntax for specifying common operations. With the flexibility of the vertex shaders, developers are able to perform operations including:

- Procedural geometry (cloth simulation, soap bubble [Isidoro/Gosselin])
- Advanced vertex blending for skinning and vertex morphing (tweening) [Gosselin]
- Texture generation [Riddle/Zecha]
- Advanced keyframe interpolation (complex facial expression and speech)
- Particle system rendering [Le Grand]
- Real-time modifications of the perspective view (lens effects, underwater effects)
- Advanced lighting models (often in cooperation with the pixel shader) [Bendel]
- First steps to displacement mapping [Calver]

There are many more effects possible with vertex shaders, some that have not been thought of yet. For example, a lot of *SIGGRAPH* papers from the last couple of years describe graphical effects that are realized only on SGI hardware so far. It might be a great challenge to port these effects with the help of vertex and pixel shaders to consumer hardware.

In addition to opening up creative possibilities for developers and artists, shaders also attack the problem of constrained video memory bandwidth by executing on-chip on shader-capable hardware. Take, for example, Bézier patches. Given two floating-point values per vertex (plus a fixed number of values per primitive), one can design a vertex shader to generate a position, a normal, and a number of texture coordinates. Vertex shaders even give you the ability to decompress compressed position, normal, color, matrix, and texture coordinate data and to save a lot of valuable bandwith without any additional cost [Calver].

There is also a benefit for your future learning curve. The procedural programming model used by vertex shaders is very scalable. Therefore, the adding of new instructions and new registers will happen in a more intuitive way for developers.

Vertex Shader Tools

As you will soon see, you are required to master a specific RISC-oriented assembly language to program vertex shaders because using the vertex shader is taking responsibility for programming the geometry processor. Therefore, it is important to get the right tools to begin to develop shaders as quickly and productively as possible.

I would like to present the tools that I am aware of at the time of publication.

NVIDIA Effects Browser 2/3

NVIDIA provides its own DirectX 8 SDK, which encapsulates all its tools, demos, and presentations on DirectX 8.0. All the demos use a consistent framework called the Effects Browser.

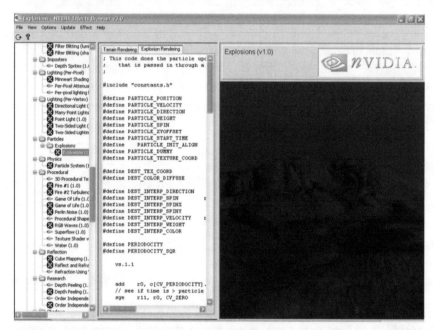

Figure 2: NVIDIA Effects Browser

The Effects Browser is a wonderful tool for testing and developing vertex and pixel shaders. You can select the effect you would like to see in the left column. The middle column gives you the ability to see the source of the vertex and/or pixel shader. The right column displays the effect.

Not all graphics cards will support all the effects available in the Effects Browser. GeForce3/4TI will support all the effects. Independent of your current graphic card preferences, I recommend downloading the NVIDIA DirectX 8 SDK and trying it out. The many examples, including detailed explanations, show you a variety of the effects possible with vertex and pixel shaders. The upcoming NVIDIA Effects Browser 3 will provide automatic online update capabilities.

NVIDIA Shader Debugger

Once you use it, you won't live without it. The NVIDIA Shader Debugger provides you with information about the current state of the temporary registers, input streams, output registers, and constant memory. This data changes interactively while stepping through the shaders. It is also possible to set instruction breakpoints as well as specific breakpoints.

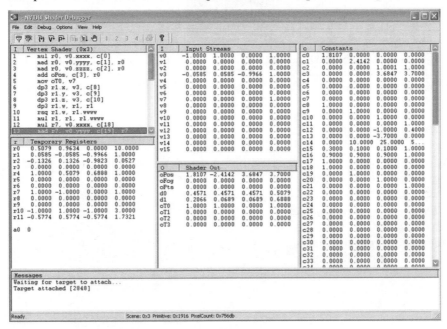

Figure 3: NVIDIA Shader Debugger

A user manual that explains all the possible features is provided. You need at least Windows 2000 with Service Pack 1 to run the Shader Debugger because debug services in DX8 and DX8.1 are only supplied in Windows 2000 and higher. It is important that your application uses software vertex processing (or you have switched to the reference rasterizer) at run time for the debugging process.

Note: You are also able to debug pixel shaders with this debugger, but due to a bug in DirectX 8.0, the contents of t0 are never displayed correctly and user-added pixel shader breakpoints will not trigger. DirectX 8.1 fixes these issues, and you receive a warning message if the application finds an installation of DirectX 8.0.

Shader City

You can find another vertex and pixel shader tool, along with source code, at http://www.palevich.com/3d/ShaderCity/. Designed and implemented by Jack Palevich, Shader City allows you to see any modification of the vertex and/or pixel shaders in the small client window in the upper-left:

The results of a modification of a vertex and/or pixel shader can be seen after they are saved and reloaded. In addition, you are able to load index and vertex buffers from a file. The source code for this tool might help you to encapsulate Direct3D in an ActiveX control, so go ahead and try it.

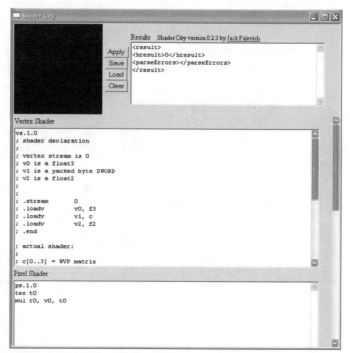

Figure 4: Jack Palevich Shader City

Vertex Shader Assembler

To compile a vertex shader ASCII file (for example, basic.vsh) into a binary file (for example, basic.vso), you must use a vertex shader assembler. As far as I know, there are two vertex shader assemblers: the Microsoft vertex shader assembler and the NVIDIA vertex and pixel shader macro assembler. The latter provides all of the features of the vertex shader assembler plus many other features, whereas the vertex shader assembler gives you the ability to also use the D3DX effect files (as of DirectX 8.1).

NVIDIA NVASM — Vertex and Pixel Shader Macro Assembler

NVIDIA provides its vertex and pixel shader macro assembler as part of its DirectX 8 SDK. NVASM has very robust error reporting built into it. It not only tells you what line the error was on, but it is also able to backtrack errors. Good documentation helps you get started. NVASM was written by *Direct3D ShaderX* author Kenneth Hurley, who provides additional information in his article [Hurley]. We will learn how to use this tool in one of the upcoming examples in the next article.

Microsoft Vertex Shader Assembler

The Microsoft vertex shader assembler is delivered in the DirectX 8.1 SDK in C:\dxsdk\bin\DXUtils.

Note: The default path of the DirectX 8 SDK is c:\mssdk. The default path of the DirectX 8.1 SDK is c:\dxsdk.

If you call vsa.exe from the command line, you will get the following options:

```
usage: vsa -hp012 <files>
-h : Generate .h files (instead of .vso files)
-p : Use C preprocessor (VisualC++ required)

-0 : Debug info omitted, no shader validation performed
-1 : Debug info inserted, no shader validation performed
-2 : Debug info inserted, shader validation performed. (default)
```

I haven't found any documentation for the vertex shader assembler. It is used by the D3DXAssembleShader*() methods or by the effect file method D3DXCreateEffectFromFile(), which compiles the effect file.

If you want to be hardware vendor-independent, you should use the Microsoft vertex shader assembler.

Shader Studio

John Schwab has developed a tool that will greatly aid in your development of vertex and pixel shaders. Whether you are a beginner or an advanced Direct3D programmer, this tool will save you a lot of time by allowing you to get right down to development of any shader without actually writing any Direct3D code. Therefore, you can spend your precious time working on what's important, the shaders.

The tool encapsulates a complete vertex and pixel shader engine with a few nice ideas. For a hands-on tutorial and detailed explanation, see [Schwab]. The newest version should be available online at www.shaderstudio.com.

Figure 5: John Schwab's Shader Studio: phong lighting

NVLink 2.x

NVLink is a very interesting tool that allows you to:

■ Write vertex shaders that consist of "fragments" with #beginfragment and #endfragment statements. For example:

```
#beginfragment world_transform
dp4 r_worldpos.x, v_position, c_world0
dp3 r_worldpos.y, v_position, c_world1
dp4 r_worldpos.z, v_position, c_world2
#endfragment
```

■ Assemble vertex shader files with NVASM into "fragments"

■ Link those fragments to produce a binary vertex shader at run time

NVLink helps you to generate shaders on demand that will fit into the end users' hardware limits (registers/instructions/constants). The most attractive feature of this tool is that it will cache and optimize your shaders on the fly. NVLink is shown in the NV Effects Browser:

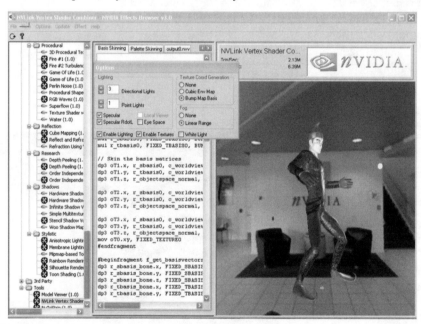

Figure 6:
NVLink

You can choose the vertex shader capabilities in the dialog box and the resulting vertex shader will be shown in output0.nvv in the middle column.

Note: The default path of the DirectX 8 SDK is c:\mssdk.
The default path of DirectX 8.1 SDK is c:\dxsdk.

NVIDIA Photoshop Plug-ins

You will find on NVIDIA's web site two frequently updated plug-ins for Adobe Photoshop: NVIDIA's Normal Map Generator and Photoshop Compression plug-in.

The Normal Map Generator can generate normal maps that can be used, for example, for Dot3 lighting. The plug-in requires DirectX 8.0 or later to be installed. The dynamic preview window, located in the upper-left corner, shows an example light that is moved with the Ctrl + left mouse button. You are able to clamp or wrap the edges of the generated normal map by selecting or deselecting the Wrap check box. The height values of the normal map can be scaled by providing a height value in the Scale entry field.

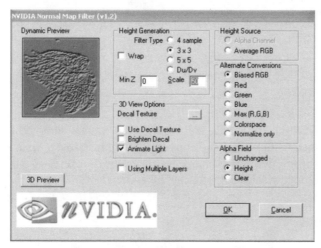

Figure 7: NVIDIA Normal Map Generator

There are different options for height generation:

- Alpha Channel — Use alpha channel
- Average RGB — Average R, G, B
- Biased RGB, h = average (R, G, B) — Average of whole image
- Red — Use red channel
- Green — Use green channel
- Blue — Use blue channel
- Max — Use max of R, G, B
- Colorspace, $h = 1.0 - [(1.0 - r) * (1.0 - g) * (1.0 - b)]$

This plug-in also works with layers. The software's readme.txt file provides you with more information about its features.

Another Adobe Photoshop plug-in provided by NVIDIA is the Photoshop Compression plug-in. It is used by choosing <Save As> in Adobe Photoshop and then the <DDS> file format. The following dialog provides a wide variety of features:

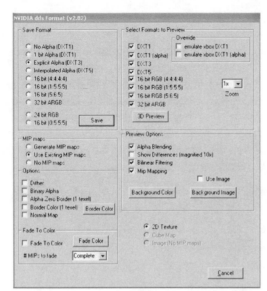

Figure 8: NVIDIA Compression plug-in

A 3D preview shows the different quality levels that result from different compression formats. This tool can additionally generate mip-maps and convert a height map to a normal map. The provided readme file is very instructive and explains the hundreds of features of this tool. As the name implies, both tools support Adobe Photoshop 5.0 and higher.

Diffusion Cubemap Tool

Kenneth Hurley wrote a tool that helps you produce diffusion cube maps. It aids in the extraction of cube maps from digital pictures. The pictures are of a completely reflective ball. The program also allows you to draw an exclusion rectangle to remove the picture taker from the cube map.

To extract the reflection maps, first load in the picture and use the mouse to draw the ellipse enclosed in a rectangle. This rectangle should be stretched and moved so that the ellipse falls on the edges of the ball. Then set which direction is associated with the picture in the menu options. The following screen shots use the –X and –Z direction:

Figure 9: Negative X sphere picture

Figure 10: Negative Z sphere picture

The cube maps are generated with the Generate menu option. The program, the source code, and much more information can be found in [Hurley].

DLL Detective with Direct3D Plug-in

Ádám Moravánszky wrote a tool called DLL Detective. It is not only very useful as a performance analysis tool but also for vertex and pixel shader programming:

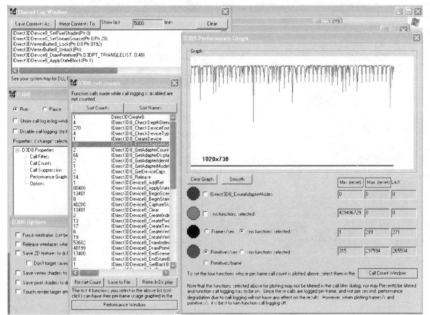

Figure 11: Ádám Moravánszky's DLL Detective

It is able to intercept vertex and pixel shaders, disassemble them, and write them into a file. A lot of different graphs show the usage of the Direct3D API under different conditions to help find performance leaks. You can even suppress API calls to simulate other conditions. To impede the parallelism of the CPU and GPU usage, you can lock the rendertarget buffer.

DLL Detective is especially suited for instrumenting games or any other applications which run in full-screen mode, preventing easy access to other windows (like DLL Detective, for example). To instrument such programs, DLL Detective can be configured to control instrumentation via a multimonitor setup and even from another PC over a network.

The full source code and compiled binaries can be downloaded from Ádám Moravánszky's web site at http://n.ethz.ch/student/adammo/DLLDetective/index.html.

3D Studio Max 4.x/gmax 1.1

The new 3D Studio Max 4.x gives a graphic artist the ability to produce vertex shader code and pixel shader code while producing models and animations.

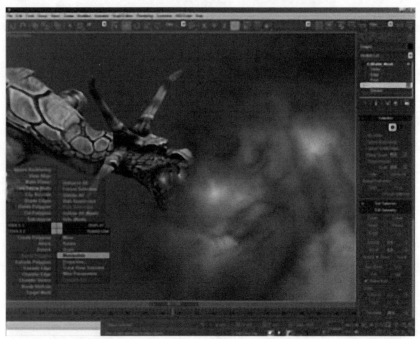

Figure 12: 3D Studio Max 4.x/gmax 1.1

A WYSIWYG view of your work will appear by displaying multitextures, true transparency, opacity mapping, and the results of custom pixel and vertex shaders.

gmax is a derivative of 3D Studio Max 4.x that supports vertex and pixel shader programming. However, the gmax free product does not provide user interface to access or edit these controls. Find more information at www.discreet.com.

Vertex Shader Architecture

Let's get deeper into vertex shader programming by looking at a graphical representation of the vertex shader architecture:

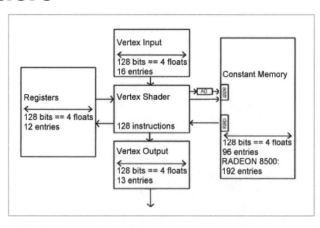

Figure 13: Vertex shader architecture

All data in a vertex shader is represented by 128-bit quad-floats (4x32-bit):

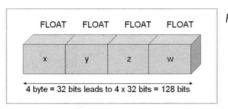

Figure 14: 128 bits

A hardware vertex shader can be seen as a typical SIMD (Single Instruction Multiple Data) processor, as you are applying one instruction and affecting a set of up to four 32-bit variables. This data format is very useful because most of the transformation and lighting calculations are performed using 4x4 matrices or quaternions. The instructions are very simple and easy to understand. The vertex shader does not allow any loops, jumps, or conditional branches, which means that it executes the program linearly — one instruction after the other. The maximum length of a vertex shader program in DirectX 8.x is limited to 128 instructions. Combining vertex shaders to have one to compute the transformation and another to compute the lighting is impossible. Only one vertex shader can be active at a time, and the active vertex shader must compute <u>all</u> required per-vertex output data.

A vertex shader uses up to 16 input registers (named v0-v15, where each register consists of 128-bit (4x32-bit) quad-floats) to access vertex input data. The vertex input register can easily hold the data for a typical vertex: its position coordinates, normal, diffuse and specular color, fog coordinate, and point size information with space for the coordinates of several textures.

The constant registers (constant memory) are loaded by the CPU before the vertex shader starts executing parameters defined by the programmer. The vertex shader is not able to write to the constant registers. They are used to store parameters such as light position, matrices, procedural data for special animation effects, vertex interpolation data for morphing/key frame interpolation, and more. The constants can be applied within the program and can even be addressed indirectly with the help of the address register a0.x, but only one constant can be used per instruction. If an instruction needs more than one constant, it must be loaded into one of the temporary registers before it is required. The names of the constant registers are c0-c95 or, in the case of the ATI RADEON 8500, c0-c191.

The temporary registers consist of 12 registers used to perform intermediate calculations. They can be used to load and store data (read/write). The names of the temporary registers are r0-r11.

There are up to 13 output registers (vertex output), depending on the underlying hardware. The names of the output registers always start with o for output. The vertex output is available per rasterizer, and your vertex shader program has write-only access to it. The final result is yet another vertex, a vertex transformed to the "homogenous clip space." The following table is an overview of all available registers.

Registers	Number of Registers	Properties
Input (v0-v15)	16	RO1
Output (o*)	GeForce 3/4TI: 9; RADEON 8500: 11	WO
Constants (c0-c95)	vs.1.1 Specification: 96; RADEON 8500: 192	RO1
Temporary (r0-r11)	12	R1W3
Address (a0.x)	1 (vs.1.1 and higher)	WO (W: only with mov)

An identifier of the streaming nature of this vertex shader architecture is the read-only input registers and the write-only output registers.

High-Level View of Vertex Shader Programming

Only one vertex shader can be active at a time. It is a good idea to write vertex shaders on a per-task basis. The overhead of switching between different vertex shaders is smaller than, for example, a texture change. So if an object needs a special form of transformation or lighting, it will get the proper shader for this task. Let's build an abstract example:

You are shipwrecked on a foreign planet. Dressed in your regular armor, armed only with a jigsaw, you move through the candlelit cellars. A monster appears, and you crouch behind one of those crates that one normally finds on other planets. While thinking about your destiny as a hero who saves worlds with jigsaws, you start counting the number of vertex shaders for this scene.

There is one for the monster to animate it, light it, and perhaps to reflect its environment. Other vertex shaders will be used for the floor, the walls, the crate, the camera, the candlelight, and your jigsaw. Perhaps the floor, the walls, the jigsaw, and the crate use the same shader, but the candlelight and the camera might each use one of their own. It depends on your design and the power of the underlying graphic hardware.

Note: You might also use vertex shaders on a per-object or per-mesh basis. If, for example, a *.md3 model consists of, let's say, ten meshes, you can use ten different vertex shaders, but that might harm your game performance.

Every vertex shader-driven program must run through the following steps:

- Check for vertex shader support by checking the D3DCAPS8::VertexShaderVersion field.
- Declare the vertex shader with the D3DVSD_* macros to map vertex buffer streams to input registers.
- Set the vertex shader constant registers with SetVertexShaderConstant().
- Compile previously written vertex shader with D3DXAssembleShader*() (this could be precompiled using a shader assembler).
- Create a vertex shader handle with CreateVertexShader().
- Set a vertex shader with SetVertexShader() for a specific object.
- Delete a vertex shader with DeleteVertexShader().

Check for Vertex Shader Support

It is important to check the installed vertex shader software or hardware implementation of the end-user hardware. If there is a lack of support for specific features, then the application can fall back to a default behavior or give the user a hint as to what he might do to enable the required features. The following statement checks for support of vertex shader version 1.1:

```
if( pCaps->VertexShaderVersion < D3DVS_VERSION(1,1) )
    return E_FAIL;
```

The following statement checks for support of vertex shader version 1.0:

```
if( pCaps->VertexShaderVersion < D3DVS_VERSION(1,0) )
    return E_FAIL;
```

The D3DCAPS8 structure caps must be filled in the startup phase of the application with a call to GetDeviceCaps(). If you use the common files framework provided with the DirectX 8.1 SDK, this is done by the framework. If your graphics hardware does not support your requested vertex shader version, you must switch to software vertex shaders by using the D3DCREATE_SOFTWARE_VERTEXPROCESSING flag in the CreateDevice() call. The previously mentioned optimized software implementations made by Intel and AMD for their respective CPUs will then process the vertex shaders.

Supported vertex shader versions are:

Version	Functionality
0.0	DirectX 7
1.0	DirectX 8 without address register a0
1.1	DirectX 8 and DirectX 8.1 with one address register a0
2.0	DirectX 9

The only difference between levels 1.0 and 1.1 is the support of the a0 register. The DirectX 8.0 and DirectX 8.1 reference rasterizer and the software emulation delivered by Microsoft and written by Intel and AMD for their respective CPUs support version 1.1. At the time publication, only GeForce3/4TI and RADEON 8500-driven boards support version 1.1 in hardware. No known graphics card supports vs.1.0-only at the time of publication, so this is a legacy version.

Vertex Shader Declaration

You must declare a vertex shader before using it. This declaration can be called a static external interface. An example might look like this:

```
float c[4] = {0.0f,0.5f,1.0f,2.0f};
DWORD dwDecl0[] = {
  D3DVSD_STREAM(0),
  D3DVSD_REG(0, D3DVSDT_FLOAT3 ),       // input register v0
  D3DVSD_REG(5, D3DVSDT_D3DCOLOR ),     // input Register v5
                                        // set a few constants
  D3DVSD_CONST(0,1),*(DWORD*)&c[0],*(DWORD*)&c[1],*(DWORD*)&c[2],*(DWORD*)&c[3],
  D3DVSD_END()
};
```

This vertex shader declaration sets data stream 0 with D3DVSD_STREAM(0). Later, SetStreamSource() binds a vertex buffer to a device data stream by using this declaration. You are able to feed different data streams to the Direct3D rendering engine this way.

> **Note:** For example, one data stream could hold positions and normals, while a second held color values and texture coordinates. This also makes switching between single-texture rendering and multitexture rendering trivial: Just don't enable the stream with the second set of texture coordinates.

You must declare which input vertex properties or incoming vertex data has to be mapped to which input register. D3DVSD_REG binds a single vertex register to a vertex element/property from the vertex stream. In our example, a D3DVSDT_FLOAT3 value should be placed in the first input register, and a D3DVSDT_D3DCOLOR color value should be placed in the sixth input register. For example, the position data could be processed by the input register 0 (v0) with D3DVSD_REG(0, D3DVSDT_FLOAT3) and the normal data could be processed by input register 3 (v3) with D3DVSD_REG(3, D3DVSDT_FLOAT3).

How a developer maps each input vertex property to a specific input register is only important if one wants to use N-Patches because the N-Patch tessellator needs the position data in v0 and the normal data in v3. Otherwise, the developer is free to define the mapping as he sees fit. For example, the position data could be processed by the input register 0 (v0) with D3DVSD_REG(0, D3DVSDT_FLOAT3), and the normal data could be processed by input register 3 (v3) with D3DVSD_REG(3, D3DVSDT_FLOAT3).

> **Note:** In contrast, the mapping of the vertex data input to specific registers is fixed for the fixed-function pipeline. d3d8types.h holds a list of #defines that predefine the vertex input for the fixed-function pipeline. Specific vertex elements such as position or normal must be placed in specified registers located in the vertex input memory. For example, the vertex position is bound by D3DVSDE_POSITION to Register 0, the diffuse color is bound by D3DVSDE_DIFFUSE to Register 5, etc. Here's the complete list from d3d8types.h:
>
> ```
> #define D3DVSDE_POSITION 0
> #define D3DVSDE_BLENDWEIGHT 1
> #define D3DVSDE_BLENDINDICES 2
> #define D3DVSDE_NORMAL 3
> #define D3DVSDE_PSIZE 4
> #define D3DVSDE_DIFFUSE 5
> #define D3DVSDE_SPECULAR 6
> #define D3DVSDE_TEXCOORD0 7
> #define D3DVSDE_TEXCOORD1 8
> #define D3DVSDE_TEXCOORD2 9
> #define D3DVSDE_TEXCOORD3 10
> #define D3DVSDE_TEXCOORD4 11
> #define D3DVSDE_TEXCOORD5 12
> #define D3DVSDE_TEXCOORD6 13
> #define D3DVSDE_TEXCOORD7 14
> #define D3DVSDE_POSITION2 15
> #define D3DVSDE_NORMAL2 16
> ```

The second parameter of D3DVSD_REG specifies the dimensionality and arithmetic data type. The following values are defined in d3d8types.h:

```
// bit declarations for _Type fields
#define D3DVSDT_FLOAT1 0x00 // 1D float expanded to (value, 0., 0., 1.)
#define D3DVSDT_FLOAT2 0x01 // 2D float expanded to (value, value, 0., 1.)
#define D3DVSDT_FLOAT3 0x02 // 3D float expanded to (value, value, value, 1.)
```

```
#define D3DVSDT_FLOAT4 0x03 // 4D float

// 4D packed unsigned bytes mapped to 0. to 1. range
// Input is in D3DCOLOR format (ARGB) expanded to (R, G, B, A)
#define D3DVSDT_D3DCOLOR 0x04

#define D3DVSDT_UBYTE4 0x05 // 4D unsigned byte
// 2D signed short expanded to (value, value, 0., 1.)
#define D3DVSDT_SHORT2 0x06
#define D3DVSDT_SHORT4 0x07 // 4D signed short
```

Note: GeForce3/4TI doesn't support D3DVSDT_UBYTE4, as indicated by the D3DVTXPCAPS_NO_VSDT_UBYTE4 caps bit.

D3DVSD_CONST loads the constant values into the vertex shader constant memory. The first parameter is the start address of the constant array to begin filling data. Possible values range from 0-95 or, in the case of the RADEON 8500, from 0-191. We start at address 0. The second number is the number of constant vectors (quad-float) to load. One vector is 128 bits long, so we load four 32-bit FLOATs at once. If you want to load a 4x4 matrix, you would use the following statement to load four 128-bit quad-floats into the constant registers c0-c3:

```
float c[16] = (0.0f, 0.5f, 1.0f, 2.0f,
               0.0f, 0.5f, 1.0f, 2.0f,
               0.0f, 0.5f, 1.0f, 2.0f,
               0.0f, 0.5f, 1.0f, 2.0f);
D3DVSD_CONST(0, 4), *(DWORD*)&c[0],*(DWORD*)&c[1],*(DWORD*)&c[2],*(DWORD*)&c[3],
        *(DWORD*)&c[4],*(DWORD*)&c[5],*(DWORD*)&c[6],*(DWORD*)&c[7],
        *(DWORD*)&c[8],*(DWORD*)&c[9],*(DWORD*)&c[10],*(DWORD*)&c[11],
        *(DWORD*)&c[12],*(DWORD*)&c[13],*(DWORD*)&c[14],*(DWORD*)&c[15],
```

D3DVSD_END generates an END token to mark the end of the vertex shader declaration. Another example is:

```
float c[4] = {0.0f,0.5f,1.0f,2.0f};
DWORD dwDecl[] = {
D3DVSD_STREAM(0),
D3DVSD_REG(0, D3DVSDT_FLOAT3 ),     //input register v0
D3DVSD_REG(3, D3DVSDT_FLOAT3 ),     // input register v3
D3DVSD_REG(5, D3DVSDT_D3DCOLOR ),   // input register v5
D3DVSD_REG(7, D3DVSDT_FLOAT2 ),     // input register v7
D3DVSD_CONST(0,1),*(DWORD*)&c[0],*(DWORD*)&c[1],*(DWORD*)&c[2],*(DWORD*)&c[3],
D3DVSD_END()
};
```

Data stream 0 is set with D3DVSD_STREAM(0). The position values (value, value, value, 1.0) might be bound to v0, the normal values might be bound to v3, the diffuse color might be bound to v5, and one texture coordinate (value, value, 0.0, 1.0) might be bound to v7. The constant register c0 gets one 128-bit value.

Set the Vertex Shader Constant Registers

You will fill the vertex shader constant registers with SetVertexShaderConstant() and get the values from these registers with GetVertexShaderConstant():

```
// Set the vertex shader constants
m_pd3dDevice->SetVertexShaderConstant( 0, &vZero, 1 );
m_pd3dDevice->SetVertexShaderConstant( 1, &vOne, 1 );
m_pd3dDevice->SetVertexShaderConstant( 2, &vWeight, 1 );
m_pd3dDevice->SetVertexShaderConstant( 4, &matTranspose, 4 );
m_pd3dDevice->SetVertexShaderConstant( 8, &matCameraTranspose, 4 );
m_pd3dDevice->SetVertexShaderConstant( 12, &matViewTranspose, 4 );
m_pd3dDevice->SetVertexShaderConstant( 20, &fLight, 1 );
m_pd3dDevice->SetVertexShaderConstant( 21, &fDiffuse, 1 );
m_pd3dDevice->SetVertexShaderConstant( 22, &fAmbient, 1 );
m_pd3dDevice->SetVertexShaderConstant( 23, &fFog, 1 );
m_pd3dDevice->SetVertexShaderConstant( 24, &fCaustics, 1 );
m_pd3dDevice->SetVertexShaderConstant( 28, &matProjTranspose, 4 );
```

SetVertexShaderConstant() is declared as

```
HRESULT SetVertexShaderConstant(
  DWORD Register,
  CONST void* pConstantData,
  DWORD ConstantCount);
```

As stated earlier, there are at least 96 constant registers (RADEON 8500 has 192) that can be filled with four floating-point values before the vertex shader is executed. The first parameter holds the register address at which to start loading data into the vertex constant array. The last parameter holds the number of constants (4 x 32-bit values) to load into the vertex constant array. So in the first row above, vZero will be loaded into register 0, matTranspose will be loaded into registers 4 through 7, matViewTranspose will be loaded into registers 12 through 15, registers 16 through 19 are not used, fLight is loaded into register 20, and registers 25 through 27 are not used.

Note: So what's the difference between D3DVSD_CONST used in the vertex shader declaration and SetVertexShaderConstant()? D3DVSD_CONST can be used only once, while SetVertexShaderConstant() can be used before every DrawPrimitive*() call.

We have learned how to check the supported version number of the vertex shader hardware, how to declare a vertex shader, and how to set the constants in the constant registers of a vertex shader unit. Next we shall learn how to write and compile a vertex shader program.

Write and Compile a Vertex Shader

Before we are able to compile a vertex shader, we must write one. I would like to give you a high-level overview of the instruction set first and then give further details of vertex shader programming in the next article, "Programming Vertex Shaders."

The syntax for every instruction is:

```
OpName dest, [-]s1 [,[-]s2 [,[-]s3]] ;comment
e.g.
mov r1, r2
mad r1, r2, -r3, r4 ; contents of r3 are negated
```

There are 17 different instructions:

Instruction	Parameters	Action
add	dest, src1, src2	add src1 to src2 (and the optional negation creates substraction)

dp3	dest, src1, src2	three-component dot product
		
		`dest.x = dest.y = dest.z = dest.w =`
		`(src1.x * src2.x) + (src1.y * src2.y) + (src1.z * src2.z)`

dp4	dest, src1, src2	four-component dot product
		
		`dest.w = (src1.x * src2.x) + (src1.y * src2.y) + (src1.z *`
		`src2.z) + (src1.w * src2.w);`
		`dest.x = dest.y = dest.z = the scalar result of dp4`
		
		What is the difference between dp4 and mul? dp4 produces a scalar product and mul is a component by component vector product.

dst	dest, src1, src2	The dst instruction works like this: The first source operand (src1) is assumed to be the vector (ignored, d*d, d*d, ignored) and the second source operand (src2) is assumed to be the vector (ignored, 1/d, ignored, 1/d).
		
		Calculate distance vector:
		
		`dest.x = 1;`
		`dest.y = src1.y * src2.y`
		`dest.z = src1.z`
		`dest.w = src2.w`
		
		dst is useful to calculate standard attenuation. Here is a code snippet that might calculate the attenuation for a point light:
		
		`; r7.w = distance * distance = (x*x) + (y*y) + (z*z)`
		`dp3 r7.w, VECTOR_VERTEXTOLIGHT,`
		`VECTOR_VERTEXTOLIGHT`
		`; VECTOR_VERTEXTOLIGHT.w = 1/sqrt(r7.w)`
		`; = 1/||V|| = 1/distance`
		`rsq VECTOR_VERTEXTOLIGHT.w, r7.w`
		`...`
		`; Get the attenuation`
		`; d = distance`
		`; Parameters for dst:`
		`; src1 = (ignored, d * d, d * d, ignored)`
		`; src2 = (ignored, 1/d, ignored, 1/d)`
		`;`
		`; r7.w = d * d`
		`; VECTOR_VERTEXTOLIGHT.w = 1/d`
		`dst r7, r7.wwww, VECTOR_VERTEXTOLIGHT.wwww`
		`; dest.x = 1`
		`; dest.y = src0.y * src1.y`
		`; dest.z = src0.z`
		`; dest.w = src1.w`
		`; r7(1, d * d * 1 / d, d * d, 1/d)`
		`; c[LIGHT_ATTENUATION].x = a0`
		`; c[LIGHT_ATTENUATION].y = a1`
		`; c[LIGHT_ATTENUATION].z = a2`
		`; (a0 + a1*d + a2* (d * d))`
		`dp3 r7.w, r7, c[LIGHT_ATTENUATION]`
		`; 1 / (a0 + a1*d + a2* (d * d))`
		`rcp ATTENUATION.w, r7.w`
		`...`
		`; Scale the light factors by the attenuation`
		`mul r6, r5, ATTENUATION.w`

Instruction	Parameters	Action

expp	dest, src.w	Exponential 10-bit precision
		
		--- 	
		
		``
		float w = src.w;
		float v = (float)floor(src.w);
		dest.x = (float)pow(2, v);
		dest.y = w - v;
		// Reduced precision exponent
		float tmp = (float)pow(2, w);
		DWORD tmpd = *(DWORD*)&tmp & 0xffffff00;
		dest.z = *(float*)&tmpd;
		dest.w = 1;
		``
		
		--- 	
		
		Shortcut:
		``
		dest.x = 2 **(int) src.w
		dest.y = mantissa(src.w)
		dest.z = expp(src.w)
		dest.w = 1.0
		``

lit	dest, src	Calculates lighting coefficients from two dot products and a power.
		
		--- 	
		
		To calculate the lighting coefficients, set up the registers as shown:
		
		src.x = N*L; the dot product between normal and direction to light
		src.y = N*H; the dot product between normal and half vector
		src.z = ignored; this value is ignored
		src.w = specular power; the value must be between –128.0 and 128.0
		
		--- 	
		
		usage:
		``
		dp3 r0.x, rn, c[LIGHT_POSITION]
		dp3 r0.y, rn, c[LIGHT_HALF_ANGLE]
		mov r0.w, c[SPECULAR_POWER]
		lit r0, r0
		``
		
		--- 	
		
		``
		dest.x = 1.0;
		dest.y = max (src.x, 0.0, 0.0);
		dest.z= 0.0;
		if (src.x > 0.0 && src.w == 0.0)
		  dest.z = 1.0;
		else if (src.x > 0.0 && src.y > 0.0)
		  dest.z = (src.y)src.w
		dest.w = 1.0;
		``
		
		--- 	
		
		Shortcut:
		``
		dest.x = exponent((int)src.w)
		dest.y = mantissa(src.w)
		dest.z = log2(src.w)
		dest.w = 1.0
		``

Instruction	Parameters	Action

logp	dest, src.w	Logarithm 10-bit precision
		
		--- 	
		<pre>float v = ABSF(src.w);
		if (v != 0)
		{
		    int p = (int)(*(DWORD*)&v >> 23) - 127;
		  dest.x = (float)p; // exponent
		  p = (*(DWORD*)&v & 0x7FFFFF)
			0x3f800000;
			  dest.y = *(float*)&p; // mantissa;
			  float tmp = (float)(log(v)/log(2));
			  DWORD tmpd = *(DWORD*)&tmp & 0xffffff00;
			  dest.z = *(float*)&tmpd;
			  dest.w = 1;
			}
			else
			{
			  dest.x = MINUS_MAX();
			  dest.y = 1.0f;
			  dest.z = MINUS_MAX();
			  dest.w = 1.0f;
			}</pre>

mad	dest, src1, src2, src3	`dest = (src1 * src2) + src3`
max	dest, src1, src2	`dest = (src1 >= src2)?src1:src2`
min	dest, src1, src2	`dest = (src1 < src2)?src1:src2`
mov	dest, src	move Optimization tip: Question every use of mov, because there might be methods that perform the desired operation directly from the source register or accept the required output register as the destination.

mul	dest, src1, src2	set dest to the component by component product of src1 and src2
		<pre>; To calculate the Cross Product (r5 = r7 X r8),
		; r0 used as a temp
		mul r0,-r7.zxyw,r8.yzxw
		mad r5,-r7.yzxw,r8.zxyw,-r0</pre>

nop		do nothing

rcp	dest, src.w	<pre>if(src.w == 1.0f)
		{
		    dest.x = dest.y = dest.z = dest.w = 1.0f;
		}
		else if(src.w == 0)
		{
		    dest.x = dest.y = dest.z = dest.w = PLUS_INFINITY();
		}
		else
		{
		    dest.x = dest.y = dest.z = m_dest.w = 1.0f/src.w;
		}</pre>Division:
		<pre>; scalar r0.x = r1.x/r2.x
		RCP r0.x, r2.x
		MUL r0.x, r1.x, r0.x</pre>

Instruction	Parameters	Action

rsq	dest, src	reciprocal square root of src
		(much more useful than straight "square root"):
		<pre>float v = ABSF(src.w);
		if(v == 1.0f)
		{
		    dest.x = dest.y = dest.z = dest.w = 1.0f;
		}
		else if(v == 0)
		{
		    dest.x = dest.y = dest.z = dest.w = PLUS_INFINITY();
		}
		else
		{
		    v = (float)(1.0f / sqrt(v));
		    dest.x = dest.y = dest.z = dest.w = v;
		}</pre>Square root:
		<pre>; scalar r0.x = sqrt(r1.x)
		RSQ r0.x, r1.x
		MUL r0.x, r0.x, r1.x</pre>

sge	dest, src1, src2	dest = (src1 >=src2) ? 1 : 0
		useful to mimic conditional statements:
		<pre>; compute r0 = (r1 >= r2) ? r3 : r4
		; one if (r1 >= r2) holds, zero otherwise
		SGE r0, r1, r2
		ADD r1, r3, -r4
		; r0 = r0*(r3-r4) + r4 = r0*r3 + (1-r0)*r4
		; effectively, LERP between extremes of r3 and r4
		MAD r0, r0, r1, r4</pre>

slt	dest, src1, src2	dest = (src1 < src2) ? 1 : 0

You can download this list as a Word file from www.shaderx.com. Check out the SDK for additional information.

The Vertex Shader ALU is a multithreaded vector processor that operates on quad-float data. It consists of two functional units. The SIMD Vector Unit is responsible for the mov, mul, add, mad, dp3, dp4, dst, min, max, slt, and sge instructions. The Special Function Unit is responsible for the rcp, rsq, logp, expp, and lit instructions. Most of these instructions take one cycle to execute, although rcp and rsq take more than one cycle under specific circumstances. They take only one slot in the vertex shader, but they actually take longer than one cycle to execute when the result is used immediately because that leads to a register stall.

Application Hints

rsq, for example, is used in normalizing vectors to be used in lighting equations. The exponential instruction expp can be used for fog effects, procedural noise generation (see the NVIDIA Perlin Noise example on the companion CD), behavior of particles in a particle system (see the NVIDIA Particle System example on the companion CD), or to implement a system for how objects in a game are damaged. You will use it when a fast-changing function is necessary. This is contrary to the use of logarithm functions with logp, which are useful if extremely slow growth is necessary (also they grow pretty fast at the beginning). A log function can be the inverse of an exponential function, meaning it undoes the operation of the exponential function.

The lit instruction deals by default with directional lights. It calculates the diffuse and specular factors with clamping based on N * L and N * H and the specular power. There is no attenuation involved, but you can use an attenuation level separately with the result of lit by using the dst instruction. This is useful for constructing attenuation factors for point and spot lights. The min and max instructions allow for clamping and absolute value computation.

Complex Instructions in the Vertex Shader

There are also complex instructions that are supported by the vertex shader. The term "macro" should not be used to refer to these instructions because they are not simply substituted like a C-preprocessor macro. You should think carefully before using these instructions. If you use them, you might lose control over your 128-instruction limit and possible optimization path(s). On the other hand, the software emulation mode provided by Intel or by AMD for their processors is able to optimize a m4x4 complex instruction (and perhaps others now or in the future). It is also possible that in the future, some graphics hardware may use gate count to optimize the m4x4. So, if you need, for example, four dp4 calls in your vertex shader assembly source, it might be a good idea to replace them by m4x4. If you have decided to use an m4x4 instruction in your shader, you should not use a dp4 call on the same data later because there are slightly different transformation results. If, for example, both instructions are used for position calculation, z-fighting could result:

Macro	Parameters	Action	Clocks
expp	dest, src1	Provides exponential with full precision to at least 1/220	12
frc	dest, src1	Returns fractional portion of each input component	3
log	dest, src1	Provides log2(x) with full float precision of at least 1/220	12
m3x2	dest, src1, src2	Computes the product of the input vector and a 3x2 matrix	2
m3x3	dest, src1, src2	Computes the product of the input vector and a 3x3 matrix	3
m3x4	dest, src1, src2	Computes the product of the input vector and a 3x4 matrix	4
m4x3	dest, src1, src2	Computes the product of the input vector and a 4x3 matrix	3
m4x4	dest, src1, src2	Computes the product of the input vector and a 4x4 matrix	4

You are able to perform all transform and lighting operations with these instructions. If it seems to you that some instructions are missing, rest assured that you can achieve them through the existing instructions. For example, the division of two numbers can be accomplished with a reciprocal and a multiply. You can even implement the whole fixed-function pipeline by using these instructions in a vertex shader. This is shown in the NVIDIA NVLink example on the companion CD.

Putting It All Together

Now let's see how these registers and instructions are typically used in the vertex shader ALU.

In vs.1.1, there are 16 input registers, 96 constant registers, 12 temporary registers, 1 address register, and up to 13 output registers per rasterizer. Each register can handle 4x32-bit values. Each 32-bit value is accessible via an x, y, z, and w subscript. That is, a 128-bit value consists of an x, y, z, and w value. To access these register components, you must add .x, .y, .z, and .w at the end of the register name. Let's start with the input registers.

Using the Input Registers

The 16 input registers can be accessed by using their names, v0 - v15. Typical values provided to the input vertex registers are:

- Position (x,y,z,w)
- Diffuse color (r,g,b,a) — 0.0 to +1.0
- Specular color (r,g,b,a) — 0.0 to +1.0
- Up to eight texture coordinates (each as s, t, r, q or u, v, w, q) but normally four or six, depending on hardware support
- Fog (f,*,*,*) — value used in fog equation
- Point size (p,*,*,*)

You can access the x-component of the position with v0.x, the y-component with v0.y, and so on. If you need to know the green component of the RGBA diffuse color, you check v1.y. You may set the fog value, for example, into v7.x. The other three 32-bit components, v7.y, v7.z, and v7.w, would not be used. The input registers are read only. Each instruction may access only one vertex input register. Unspecified components of the input register default to 0.0 for the x, y, and z components and to 1.0 for the w component. In the following example, the four-component dot product between each of c0-c3 and v0 is stored in oPos:

```
dp4 oPos.x , v0 , c0
dp4 oPos.y , v0 , c1
dp4 oPos.z , v0 , c2
dp4 oPos.w , v0 , c3
```

Such a code fragment is usually used to map from projection space into clip space with the help of the already concatenated world, view, and projection matrices. The four component dot product performs the following calculation:

```
oPos.x = (v0.x * c0.x) + (v0.y * c0.y) + (v0.z * c0.z) + (v0.w * c0.w)
```

Given that we use unit length (normalized) vectors, it is known that the dot product of two vectors will always range between [−1, 1]. Therefore, oPos will always get values in that range. Alternatively, you could use:

```
m4x4 oPos, v0 , c0
```

Don't forget to use those complex instructions consistently throughout your vertex shader because as discussed earlier, there might be slight differences between dp4 and m4x4 results. You are restricted to using only one input register in each instruction.

All data in an input register remains persistent throughout the vertex shader execution and even longer. That means they retain their data longer than the lifetime of a vertex shader. So it is possible to reuse the data of the input registers in the next vertex shader.

Using the Constant Registers

Typical uses for the constant registers include:

- Matrix data — quad-floats are typically one row of a 4x4 matrix
- Light characteristics (position, attenuation, etc.)
- Current time
- Vertex interpolation data
- Procedural data

There are 96 quad-floats (or in the case of the RADEON 8500, 192 quad-floats) for storing constant data. This reasonably large set of matrices can be used, for example, for indexed vertex blending, more commonly known as "matrix palette skinning."

The constant registers are read only from the perspective of the vertex shader, whereas the application can read and write into the constant registers. The constant registers retain their data longer than the life-time of a vertex shader, so it is possible to reuse this data in the next vertex shader. This allows an app to avoid making redundant SetVertexShaderConstant() calls. Reads from out-of-range constant registers return (0.0, 0.0, 0.0, 0.0).

You can use only one constant register per instruction, but you can use it several times. For example:

```
; the following instruction is legal
mul r5, c11, c11 ; The product of c11 and c11 is stored in r5
; but this is illegal
add v0, c4, c3
```

A more complicated-looking, but valid, example is:

```
; dest = (src1 * src2) + src3
mad r0, r0, c20, c20 ; multiplies r0 with c20 and adds c20 to the result
```

Using the Address Register

You access the address registers with a0 to a*n* (more than one address register should be available in vertex shader versions higher than 1.1). The only use of a0 in vs.1.1 is as an indirect addressing operator to offset constant memory.

```
c[a0.x + n] ; supported only in version 1.1 and higher
; n is the base address and a0.x is the address offset
```

Here is an example using the address register:

```
...
//Set 1
mov a0.x,r1.x
m4x3 r4,v0,c[a0.x + 9];
m3x3 r5,v3,c[a0.x + 9];
...
```

Depending on the value that is stored in temporary register r1.x, different constant registers are used in the m4x3 and m3x3 instructions. Please note that register a0 only stores whole numbers and no fractions (integers only) and that a0.x is the only valid component of a0. Further, a vertex shader may write to a0.x only via the mov instruction.

> **Note:** Beware of a0.x if there is only a software emulation mode; performance can be significantly reduced [Pallister].

Using the Temporary Registers

You can access the 12 temporary registers using r0 to r11. Here are a few examples:

```
dp3 r2, r1, -c4 ; A three-component dot product: dest.x = dest.y = dest.z =
                ; dest.w = (r1.x * -c4.x) + (r1.y * -c4.y) + (r1.z * -c4.z)
...
mov r0.x, v0.x
mov r0.y, c4.w
mov r0.z, v0.y
mov r0.w, c4.w
```

Each temporary register has single write and triple read access. Therefore, an instruction could have the same temporary register as a source three times. Vertex shaders cannot read a value from a temporary register before writing to it. If you try to read a temporary register that was not filled with a value, the API will give you an error message while creating the vertex shader (== CreateVertexShader()).

Using the Output Registers

There are up to 13 write-only output registers that can be accessed using the following register names. They are defined as the inputs to the rasterizer; the name of each register is preceded by a lowercase "o." The output registers are named to suggest their use by pixel shaders.

Name	Value	Description
oDn	2 quad-floats	Output color data directly to the pixel shader. Required for diffuse color (oD0) and specular color (oD1).
oPos	1 quad-float	Output position in homogenous clipping space. Must be written by the vertex shader.
oTn	up to 8 quad-floatsGeforce 3: 4RADEON 8500: 6	Output texture coordinates. Required for maximum number of textures simultaneously bound to the texture blending stage.
oPts.x	1 scalar float	Output point-size registers. Only the scalar x-component of the point size is functional.
oFog.x	1 scalar float	The fog factor to be interpolated and then routed to the fog table. Only the scalar x-component is functional.

Here is a typical example that shows how to use the oPos, oD0, and oT0 registers:

```
dp4 oPos.x , v0 , c4    ; emit projected x position
dp4 oPos.y , v0 , c5    ; emit projected y position
dp4 oPos.z , v0 , c6    ; emit projected z position
dp4 oPos.w , v0 , c7    ; emit projected w position
mov oD0, v5             ; set the diffuse color
mov oT0, v2    ; outputs the texture coordinates to oT0 from input register v2
```

Using the four dp4 instructions to map from projection to clip space with the already concatenated world, view, and projection matrices was shown above. The first mov instruction moves the content of the v5 input register into the color output register, and the second mov instruction moves the values of the v2 register into the first output texture register.

Using the oFog.x output register is shown in the following example:

```
; Scale by fog parameters :
; c5.x = fog start
; c5.y = fog end
; c5.z = 1/range
; c5.w = fog max
dp4 r2, v0, c2              ; r2 = distance to camera
sge r3, c0, c0              ; r3 = 1
add r2, r2, -c5.x           ; camera space depth (z) - fog start
mad r3.x, -r2.x, c5.z, r3.x ; 1.0 - (z - fog start) * 1/range
                            ; because fog=1.0 means no fog, and
                            ; fog=0.0 means full fog
max oFog.x, c5.w, r3.x      ; clamp the fog with our custom max value
```

Having a fog distance value permits more general fog effects than using the position's z or w values. The fog distance value is interpolated before use as a distance in the standard fog equations used later in the pipeline.

Every vertex shader must write at least to one component of oPos, or you will get an error message by the assembler.

Note: Optimization tip: Emit to oPos as early as possible to trigger parallelism in the pixel shader. Try to reorder the vertex shader instructions to make this happen.

All iterated values transferred out of the vertex shader are clamped to [0..1]. That means any negative values are cut off to 0 and the positive values remain unchanged. If you need signed values in the pixel shader, you must bias them in the vertex shader by multiplying them with 0.5 and adding 0.5, and then re-expand them in the pixel shader by using _bx2.

Swizzling and Masking

If you use the input, constant, and temporary registers as source registers, you can swizzle the .x, .y, .z, and .w values independently of each other. If you use the output and temporary registers as destination registers, you can use the .x, .y, .z, and .w values as write masks. Here are the details:

Swizzling (only source registers: vn, cn, rn)

Swizzling is very useful for efficiency, where the source registers need to be rotated (like cross products). Another use is converting constants such as (0.5, 0.0, 1.0, 0.6) into other forms, such as (0.0, 0.0, 1.0, 0.0) or (0.6, 1.0, -0.5, 0.6).

All registers that are used in instructions as source registers can be swizzled. For example:

```
mov R1, R2.wxyz;
```

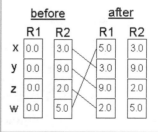

Figure 15: Swizzling

The destination register is R1, where R could be a write-enabled register like the output (o*) or any of the temporary registers (r). The source register is R2, where R could be an input (v), constant (c), or temporary register (source registers are located on the right side of the destination register in the instruction syntax).

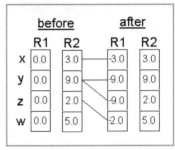

Figure 16: Swizzling #2

The following instruction copies the negation of R2.x into R1.x, the negation of R2.y into R1.y and R1.z, and the negation of R2.z into R1.w. As shown, all source registers can be negated and swizzled at the same time:

```
mov R1, -R2.xyyz
```

Masking (only destination registers: *on, rn*)

A destination register can mask which components are written to it. If you use R1 as the destination register (actually any write-enabled registers : o*, r), all the components are written from R2 to R1. If you choose, for example,

```
mov R1.x, R2
```

only the x component is written to R1, whereas

```
mov R1.xw, R2
```

writes only the x and w components of R2 to R1. No swizzling or negation is supported on the destination registers.

Here is the source for a three-vector cross-product:

```
; r0 = r1 x r2 (3-vector cross-product)
mul r0, r1.yzxw, r2.zxyw
mad r0, -r2.yzxw, r1.zxyw, r0
```

This is explained in detail in [LeGrand].

The following table summarizes swizzling and masking:

Component Modifier	Description
R.[x][y][z][w]	Destination mask
R.xwzy (for example)	Source swizzle
–R	Source negation

Since any source can be negated, there is no need for a subtract instruction.

Guidelines for Writing Vertex Shaders

The most important restrictions you should remember when writing vertex shaders are the following:

■ They must write to at least one component of the output register oPos.

■ There is a 128 instruction limit.

■ Every instruction may source no more than one constant register (e.g., add r0, c4, c3 will fail).

- Every instruction may source no more than one input register (e.g., `add r0, v1, v2` will fail).

- There are no C-like conditional statements, but you can mimic an instruction of the form `r0 = (r1 >= r2) ? r3 : r4` with the sge instruction.

- All iterated values transferred out of the vertex shader are clamped to [0..1].

There are several ways to optimize vertex shaders. Here are a few rules of thumb:

- See [Pallister] for information on optimizing software vertex shaders. It also helps on optimizing vertex shaders running in hardware.

- When setting vertex shader constant data, try to set all data in one SetVertexShaderConstant() call.

- Stop and think before using a mov instruction; you may be able to avoid it.

- Choose instructions that perform multiple operations over instructions that perform single operations:

```
mad r4,r3,c9,r4
mov oD0,r4
==
mad oD0,r3,c9,r4
```

- Collapse (remove complex instructions like m4x4 or m3x3 instructions) vertex shaders before thinking about optimizations.

- A rule of thumb for load-balancing between the CPU/GPU: Many calculations in shaders can be pulled outside and reformulated per-object instead of per-vertex and put into constant registers. If you are doing some calculation, which is per-object rather than per-vertex, then do it on the CPU and upload it on the vertex shader as a constant, rather than doing it on the GPU.

Note: One of the most interesting methods to optimize your application's bandwidth usage is the usage of compressed vertex data [Calver].

Now that you have an abstract overview of how to write vertex shaders, I would like to mention at least three different ways to compile one.

Compiling a Vertex Shader

Direct3D uses bytecodes, whereas OpenGL implementations parse a string. Therefore, the Direct3D developer needs to assemble the vertex shader source with an assembler. This might help you find bugs earlier in your development cycle, and it also reduces loadtime.

I see three different ways to compile a vertex shader:

- Write the vertex shader source into a separate ASCII file (for example, test.vsh) and compile it with a vertex shader assembler into a binary file (for example, test.vso). This file will be opened and read at game startup. This way, not every person will be able to read and modify your vertex shader source.

Note: Don't forget that NVLink can link together already compiled shader fragments at run time.

■ Write the vertex shader source into a separate ASCII file or as a char string into your *.cpp file, and compile it "on the fly" while the app starts up with the D3DXAssembleShader*() functions.

■ Write the vertex shader source in an effect file and open this effect file when the app starts up. The vertex shader can be compiled by reading the effect files with D3DXCreateEffectFromFile(). It is also possible to precompile an effect file. This way, most of the handling of vertex shaders is simplified and handled by the effect file functions.

Note: Another way is to use the opcodes shown in d3dtypes.h and build your own vertex assembler/disassembler.

Let's review what we have examined so far. After we checked the vertex shader support with the D3DCAPS8::VertexShaderVersion field, we declared a vertex shader with the D3DVSD_* macros. Then we set the constant registers with SetVertexShaderConstant() and wrote and compiled the vertex shader.

Now we need to get a handle to call it.

Create a Vertex Shader

The CreateVertexShader() function is used to create and validate a vertex shader:

```
HRESULT CreateVertexShader(
 CONST DWORD* pDeclaration,
 CONST DWORD* pFunction,
 DWORD* pHandle,
 DWORD Usage);
```

This function takes the vertex shader declaration (which maps vertex buffer streams to different vertex input registers) in pDeclaration as a pointer and returns the shader handle in pHandle. The second parameter pFunction gets the vertex shader instructions compiled by D3DXAssembleShader() / D3DXAssembleShaderFromFile() or the binary code precompiled by a vertex shader assembler. With the fourth parameter, you can force software vertex processing with D3DUSAGE_SOFTWAREPROCESSING. It must be used when D3DRS_SOFTWAREVERTEXPROCESSING is set to TRUE. By setting the software processing path explicitly, vertex shaders are simulated by the CPU by using the software vertex shader implementation of the CPU vendors. If a vertex shader-capable GPU is available, using hardware vertex processing should be faster. You must use this flag or the reference rasterizer for debugging with the NVIDIA Shader Debugger.

Set a Vertex Shader

You set a vertex shader for a specific object by using SetVertexShader() before the DrawPrimitive*() call of this object. This function dynamically loads the vertex shader between the primitive calls.

```
// set the vertex shader
m_pd3dDevice->SetVertexShader( m_dwVertexShader );
```

The only parameter you must provide is the handle of the vertex shader created by CreateVertexShader(). The overhead of this call is lower than a SetTexture() call, so you are able to use it often.

Vertex shaders are executed with SetVertexShader() as many times as there are vertices. For example, if you try to visualize a rotating quad with four vertices implemented as an indexed triangle list, you will see in the NVIDIA Shader Debugger that the vertex shader runs four times before the DrawPrimitive*() function is called.

Free Vertex Shader Resources

When the game shuts down or when the device is changed, the resources used by the vertex shader must be released. This must be done by calling DeleteVertexShader() with the vertex shader handle:

```
// delete the vertex shader
if (m_pd3dDevice->m_dwVertexShader != 0xffffffff)
{
  m_pd3dDevice->DeleteVertexShader( m_dwVertexShader );
  m_pd3dDevice->m_dwVertexShader = 0xffffffff;
}
```

Summary

We have now stepped through the vertex shader creation process on a high level. Let's summarize what was shown so far:

- To use vertex shaders, you must check the vertex shader support of the hardware vertex shader implementation installed on the end-user's computer with the D3DCAPS8::VertexShaderVersion field.

- You must declare which input vertex properties or incoming vertex data have to be mapped to which input register. This mapping is done with the D3DVSD_* macros. You are able to fill the constant registers of the vertex shader with values by using the provided macros or by using the SetVertexShaderConstant() function.

- After you have prepared everything this way and you have written a vertex shader, you are able to compile it, retrieve a handle to it by calling CreateVertexShader(), and prepare it for execution by using SetVertexShader().

- To release the resources that are allocated by the vertex shader you should call DeleteVertexShader() at the end of your game.

What Happens Next?

In the next article, "Programming Vertex Shaders," we will start writing our first vertex shader. We will also discuss basic lighting algorithms and how to implement them.

References

[Bendel] Steffen Bendel, "Smooth Lighting with ps.1.4," *Direct3D ShaderX: Vertex and Pixel Shader Tips and Tricks*, (Wordware Publishing, Inc., 2002).

[Calver] Dean Calver, "Vertex Decompression in a Shader," *Direct3D ShaderX*.

[Gosselin] David Gosselin, "Character Animation with Direct3D Vertex Shaders," *Direct3D ShaderX*.

[Hurley] Kenneth Hurley, "Photorealistic Faces with Vertex and Pixel Shaders," *Direct3D ShaderX*.

[Isidoro/Gosselin] John Isidoro and David Gosselin, "Bubble Shader," *Direct3D ShaderX*.

[Le Grand] Scott Le Grand, "Compendium of for Vertex Shaders," *Direct3D ShaderX*.

[Pallister] Kim Pallister, "Optimizing Software Vertex Shaders," *Direct3D ShaderX*.

[Riddle/Zecha] Steven Riddle and Oliver C. Zecha, "Perlin Noise and Returning Results from Shader Programs," *Direct3D ShaderX*.

[Schwab] John Schwab, "Basic Shader Development with Shader Studio," *Direct3D ShaderX*.

[Vlachos01] Alex Vlachos, Jörg Peters, Chas Boyd, and Jason L. Mitchell, "Curved PN Triangles," ACM Symposium on Interactive 3D Graphics, 2001 (http://www.ati.com/na/pages/resource_centre/dev_rel/CurvedPNTriangles.pdf).

Additional Resources

A lot of information on vertex shaders can be found at the web sites of NVIDIA (developer.nvidia.com), ATI (www.ati.com), and various others. I would like to name a few:

Author	Article	Published at
Richard Huddy	Introduction to DX8 Vertex Shaders	NVIDIA web site
Erik Lindholm, Mark J Kilgard, Henry Moreton	SIGGRAPH 2001 — A User Programmable Vertex Engine	NVIDIA web site
Evan Hart, Dave Gosselin, John Isidoro	Vertex Shading with Direct3D and OpenGL	ATI web site
Jason L. Mitchell	Advanced Vertex and Pixel Shader Techniques	ATI web site
Philip Taylor	Series of articles on shader programming	http://msdn.microsoft.com/directx
Keshav B. Channa	Geometry Skinning / Blending and Vertex Lighting	http://www.flipcode.com/tutorials/tut_dx8shaders.shtml
Konstantin Martynenko	Introduction to Shaders	http://www.reactorcritical.com/review-shadersintro/review-shadersintro.shtml

Acknowledgments

I'd like to recognize a couple of individuals that were involved in proofreading and improving this paper (in alphabetical order):

- David Callele (University of Saskatchewan)
- Jeffrey Kiel (NVIDIA)
- Jason L. Mitchell (ATI)

Programming Vertex Shaders

Wolfgang F. Engel

In this article, a very simple program that shows a rotating quad will evolve into a more sophisticated application showing a Bézier patch class with a diffuse and specular reflection model and featuring a point light source. The example applications are all built on each other in such a way that most of the code in the previous example is reused. This way, the explanation of the features stays focused on the advancements of the specific example.

RacorX

RacorX displays a green color that is applied to the quad evenly. This example demonstrates the usage of the common files framework provided with the DirectX 8.1 SDK and shows how to compile vertex shaders with the D3DXAssembleShader() function.

As with all the upcoming examples, which are based on the common files, <Alt>+<Enter> switches between the windowed and full-screen mode, <F2> gives you a selection of the usable drivers, and <Esc> will shut down the application.

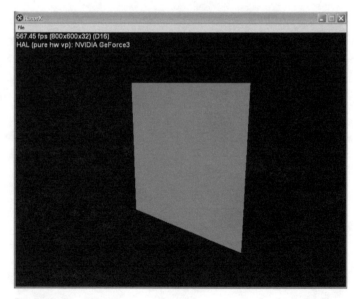

Figure 1: RacorX

First let's take a look at the files you need to compile the program:

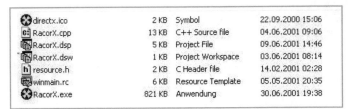

Figure 2: Directory content

The source file is RacorX.cpp, the resource files are winmain.rc and resource.h, the icon file is directx.ico, and the executable is RacorX.exe. The remaining files are for the use of the Visual C/C++ 6 IDE.

To compile this example, you should link it with the following *.lib files:

- d3d8.lib
- d3dx8dt.lib
- dxguid.lib
- d3dxof.lib
- winmm.lib
- gdi32.lib
- user32.lib
- kernel32.lib
- advapi32.lib

Most of these *.lib files are COM wrappers. The d3dx8dt.lib is the debug version of the Direct3DX static link library.

Note: The release Direct3DX static link library is called d3dx8.lib. There is also a *.dll version of the debug build called d3dx8d.dll in the system32 directory. It is used by linking to the d3dx8d.lib COM wrapper.

All of these *.lib files have to be included in the Object/libary modules entry field. This is located at Project->Settings on the Link tab:

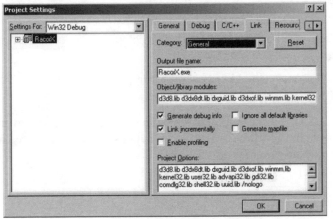

Figure 3: Project Settings dialog

The provided Visual C/C++ 6 IDE workspace references the common files in a folder with the same name.

They were added to the project by selecting Project->Add To Project->Files:

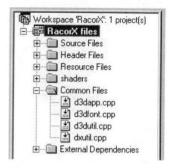

Figure 4: Workspace

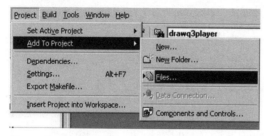

Figure 5: Adding files to a project

The Common Files Framework

The common files framework helps you get up to speed because:

- It helps to avoid how-tos for Direct3D in general, so the focus of this text is the real stuff.
- It's common and is a tested foundation, which helps reduce the debug time.
- All of the Direct3D samples in the DirectX SDK use it. Learning time is very short.
- Its window mode makes debugging easier.
- Self-developed production code could be based on the common files, so knowing them is always an advantage.

A high-level view of the common files shows 14 *.cpp files in C:\DXSDK\samples\Multimedia\Common\src.

These files encapsulate the basic functionality you need to start programming a Direct3D application. The most important, d3dapp.cpp, contains the class CD3DApplication. It provides seven functions that can be overridden and used in the main *.cpp file of any project in this introduction:

- virtual HRESULT OneTimeSceneInit() { return S_OK; }
- virtual HRESULT InitDeviceObjects() { return S_OK; }
- virtual HRESULT RestoreDeviceObjects() { return S_OK; }
- virtual HRESULT DeleteDeviceObjects() { return S_OK; }
- virtual HRESULT Render() { return S_OK; }
- virtual HRESULT FrameMove(FLOAT) { return S_OK; }
- virtual HRESULT FinalCleanup() { return S_OK; }

All that has to be done to create an application based on this framework code is to create a new project and new implementations of these overridable functions in the main source file. This is also shown in all Direct3D examples in the DirectX SDK.

RacorX uses these framework functions in RacorX.cpp. They can be called the public interface of the common files framework.

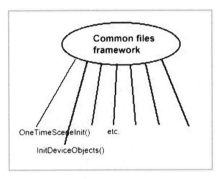

The following functions are called in the following order in RacorX.cpp at startup:

- ConfirmDevice()
- OneTimeSceneInit()
- InitDeviceObjects()
- RestoreDeviceObjects()

While the application is running, the framework calls:

- FrameMove()
- Render()

in a loop.

If the user resizes the window, the framework will call:

- InvalidateDeviceObjects()
- RestoreDeviceObjects()

If the user presses F2 or clicks File->Change Device and changes the device by choosing, for example, another resolution or color quality, the framework will call:

- InvalidateDeviceObjects()
- DeleteDeviceObjects()
- InitDeviceObjects()
- RestoreDeviceObjects()

If the user quits the application, the framework will call:

- InvalidateDeviceObjects()
- DeleteDeviceObjects()
- FinalCleanup()

There are matching functional pairs. InvalidateDeviceObjects() destroys what RestoreDevice-Objects() has built up, and DeleteDeviceObjects() destroys what InitDeviceObjects() has built up. The FinalCleanup() function destroys what OneTimeSceneInit() built up.

The idea is to give every functional pair its own tasks. The OneTimeSceneInit()/Final-Cleanup() pair is called once at the beginning and at the end of a life cycle of the game. Both are used to load or delete data that is not device-dependent. A good candidate might be geometry data. The target of the InitDeviceObjects()/DeleteDeviceObjects() pair is, like the name implies, data that is device-dependent. If the already loaded data has to be changed when the device changes, it should be loaded here. The following examples will load, create, or destroy their vertex buffer and index buffers and their textures in these functions.

The InvalidateDeviceObjects()/RestoreDeviceObjects() pair has to react to the changes of the window size. So, for example, code that handles the projection matrix might be placed here. Additionally, the following examples will set most of the render states in RestoreDeviceObjects().

Now back to RacorX. As shown in "Fundamentals of Vertex Shaders," the following list tracks the life cycle of a vertex shader:

■ Check for vertex shader support by checking the D3DCAPS8::VertexShaderVersion field.

■ Declare the vertex shader with the D3DVSD_* macros to map vertex buffer streams to input registers.

■ Set the vertex shader constant registers with SetVertexShaderConstant().

■ Compile an already written vertex shader with D3DXAssembleShader*() (alternatively: could be precompiled using a shader assembler).

■ Create a vertex shader handle with CreateVertexShader().

■ Set a vertex shader with SetVertexShader() for a specific object.

■ Free vertex shader resources handled by the Direct3D engine with DeleteVertexShader().

We will walk step by step through this list in the following pages.

Check for Vertex Shader Support

The supported vertex shader version is checked in ConfirmDevice() in RacorX.cpp:

```
HRESULT CMyD3DApplication::ConfirmDevice( D3DCAPS8* pCaps,
                                          DWORD dwBehavior,
                                          D3DFORMAT Format )
{
 if( (dwBehavior & D3DCREATE_HARDWARE_VERTEXPROCESSING ) ||
     (dwBehavior & D3DCREATE_MIXED_VERTEXPROCESSING ) )
   {
    if( pCaps->VertexShaderVersion < D3DVS_VERSION(1,1) )
       return E_FAIL;
   }
 return S_OK;
}
```

If the framework has already initialized hardware or mixed vertex processing, the vertex shader version will be checked. If the framework initialized software vertex processing, the software implementation provided by Intel and AMD jumps in and a check of the hardware capabilities is not needed.

The globally available *pCaps* capability data structure is filled with a call to GetDeviceCaps() by the framework. pCaps->VertexShaderVersion holds the vertex shader version in a DWORD. The macro D3DVS_VERSION helps with checking the version number. For example, the support of at least vs.2.0 in hardware will be checked with D3DVS_VERSION(2,0).

After checking the hardware capabilities for vertex shader support, the vertex shader has to be declared.

Vertex Shader Declaration

Declaring a vertex shader means mapping vertex data to specific vertex shader input registers; therefore, the vertex shader declaration must reflect the vertex buffer layout because the vertex buffer must transport the vertex data in the correct order. The one used in this example program is very simple. The vertex shader will get the position data via *v0*.

```
// shader decl
DWORD dwDecl[] =
{
    D3DVSD_STREAM(0),
    D3DVSD_REG(0, D3DVSDT_FLOAT3 ), // D3DVSDE_POSITION,0
    D3DVSD_END()
};
```

The corresponding layout of the vertex buffer looks like this:

```
// vertex type
struct VERTEX
{
    FLOAT x, y, z; // The untransformed position for the vertex
};
// Declare custom FVF macro.
#define D3DFVF_VERTEX (D3DFVF_XYZ)
```

The position values will be stored in the vertex buffer and bound through the SetStream-Source() function to a device data stream port that feeds the primitive processing functions (this is the Higher-Order Surfaces (HOS) stage or directly the vertex shader, depending on the usage of HOS; see the Direct3D pipeline in Figure 1 in the previous article).

We do not use vertex color here, so no color values are declared.

Set the Vertex Shader Constant Registers

The vertex shader constant registers have to be filled with a call to SetVertexShaderConstant(). In this example, set the material color in RestoreDeviceObjects() in *c8*:

```
// set material color
FLOAT fMaterial[4] = {0,1,0,0};
m_pd3dDevice->SetVertexShaderConstant(8, fMaterial, 1);
```

SetVertexShaderConstant() is declared like:

```
HRESULT SetVertexShaderConstant (DWORD Register,
                                 CONST void* pConstantData,
                                 DWORD ConstantCount);
```

The first parameter provides the number of the constant register that should be used; in this case, it is *8*. The second parameter stores the 128-bit data in that constant register, and the third parameter gives you the ability to use the following registers as well. A 4x4 matrix can be stored with one SetVertexShaderConstant() call by providing 4 in ConstantCount. This is done for the clipping matrix in FrameMove():

```
// set the clip matrix
...
m_pd3dDevice->SetVertexShaderConstant(4, matTemp, 4);
```

This way, the c4, c5, c6, and c7 registers are used to store the matrix.

The Vertex Shader

The vertex shader that is used by RacorX is very simple:

```
// reg c4-7 = WorldViewProj matrix
```

```
// reg c8 = constant color
// reg v0 = input register
const char BasicVertexShader[] =
"vs.1.1                //Shader version 1.1 \n"\
"dp4 oPos.x, v0, c4 //emit projected position \n"\
"dp4 oPos.y, v0, c5 //emit projected position \n"\
"dp4 oPos.z, v0, c6 //emit projected position \n"\
"dp4 oPos.w, v0, c7 //emit projected position \n"\
"mov oD0, c8           //material color = c8 \n";
```

It is used inline in a constant char array in RacorX.cpp. This vertex shader incorporates the vs.1.1 vertex shader implementation rules. It transforms from the concatenated and transposed world, view, and projection matrix to the clip matrix or clip space with the four dp4 instructions and kicks out into a oD0 green material color with mov.

As shown above, the values of the c4-c7 constant registers are set in FrameMove(). These values are calculated by the following code snippet:

```
// rotates the object about the y-axis
D3DXMatrixRotationY( &m_matWorld, m_fTime * 1.5f );
// set the clip matrix
D3DXMATRIX matTemp;
D3DXMatrixTranspose( &matTemp , &(m_matWorld * m_matView * m_matProj) );
m_pd3dDevice->SetVertexShaderConstant(4, matTemp, 4);
```

First the quad is rotated around the y-axis by the D3DMatrixRotationY() call, then the concatenated matrix is transposed and stored in the constant registers c4-c7. The source of the D3DMatrixRotationY() function might look like:

```
VOID D3DMatrixRotationY(D3DMATRIX * mat, FLOAT fRads)
{
  D3DXMatrixIdentity(mat);
  mat._11 =  cosf(fRads);
  mat._13 = -sinf(fRads);
  mat._31 =  sinf(fRads);
  mat._33 =  cosf(fRads);
}
=
cosf(fRads) 0 -sinf(fRads) 0
0           0  0           0
sinf(fRads) 0  cosf(fRads) 0
0           0  0           0
```

fRads equals the amount you want to rotate about the y-axis. After changing the values of the matrix this way, we transpose the matrix by using D3DXMatrixTranspose(), so its columns are stored as rows. Why do we have to transpose the matrix?

A 4x4 matrix looks like this:

```
a b c d
e f g h
i j k l
m n o p
```

The formula for transforming a vector (v0) through the matrix is:

```
dest.x = (v0.x * a) + (v0.y * e) + (v0.z * i) + (v0.w * m)
dest.y = (v0.x * b) + (v0.y * f) + (v0.z * j) + (v0.w * n)
dest.z = (v0.x * c) + (v0.y * g) + (v0.z * k) + (v0.w * o)
dest.w = (v0.x * d) + (v0.y * h) + (v0.z * l) + (v0.w * p)
```

So each column of the matrix should be multiplied with each component of the vector.
Our vertex shader uses four dp4 instructions:

```
dest.w = (src1.x * src2.x) + (src1.y * src2.y) +
         (src1.z * src2.z) + (src1.w * src2.w)
dest.x = dest.y = dest.z = unused
```

The dp4 instruction multiplies a row of a matrix with each component of the vector. Without transposing, we would end up with:

```
dest.x = (v0.x * a) + (v0.y * b) + (v0.z * c) + (v0.w * d)
dest.y = (v0.x * e) + (v0.y * f) + (v0.z * g) + (v0.w * h)
dest.z = (v0.x * i) + (v0.y * j) + (v0.z * k) + (v0.w * l)
dest.w = (v0.x * m) + (v0.y * n) + (v0.z * o) + (v0.w * p)
```

which is wrong. By transposing the matrix, it looks like this in constant memory:

```
a e i m
b f j n
c g k o
d h l p
```

So the 4 dp4 operations would now yield:

```
dest.x = (v0.x * a) + (v0.y * e) + (v0.z * i) + (v0.w * m)
dest.y = (v0.x * b) + (v0.y * f) + (v0.z * j) + (v0.w * n)
dest.z = (v0.x * c) + (v0.y * g) + (v0.z * k) + (v0.w * o)
dest.w = (v0.x * d) + (v0.y * h) + (v0.z * l) + (v0.w * p)
```

or

```
oPos.x = (v0.x * c4.x) + (v0.y * c4.y) + (v0.z * c4.z) + (v0.w * c4.w)
oPos.y = (v0.x * c5.x) + (v0.y * c5.y) + (v0.z * c5.z) + (v0.w * c5.w)
oPos.z = (v0.x * c6.x) + (v0.y * c6.y) + (v0.z * c6.z) + (v0.w * c6.w)
oPos.w = (v0.x * c7.x) + (v0.y * c7.y) + (v0.z * c7.z) + (v0.w * c7.w)
```

which is exactly how the vector transformation should work.

dp4 gets the matrix values via the constant register c4-c7 and the vertex position via the input register v0. Temporary registers are not used in this example. The dot product of the dp4 instructions is written to the oPos output register, and the value of the constant register c8 is moved into the output register oD0, which is usually used to output diffuse color values.

Compile a Vertex Shader

The vertex shader that is stored in a char array is compiled with a call to the following code snippet in RestoreDeviceObjects():

```
// Assemble the shader
rc = D3DXAssembleShader( BasicVertexShader , sizeof(BasicVertexShader) -1,
                    0 , NULL , &pVS , &pErrors );
if ( FAILED(rc) )
{
  OutputDebugString( "Failed to assemble the vertex shader, errors:\n" );
  OutputDebugString( (char*)pErrors->GetBufferPointer() );
  OutputDebugString( "\n" );
}
```

D3DXAssembleShader() creates a binary version of the shader in a buffer object via the ID3DXBuffer interface in *pVS*:

```
HRESULT D3DXAssembleShader(
  LPCVOID pSrcData,
  UINT SrcDataLen,
  DWORD Flags,
  LPD3DXBUFFER* ppConstants,
  LPD3DXBUFFER* ppCompiledShader,
  LPD3DXBUFFER* ppCompilationErrors
);
```

The source data is provided in the first parameter, and the size of the data length in bytes is provided in the second parameter. There are two possible flags for the third parameter:

```
#define D3DXASM_DEBUG 1
#define D3DXASM_SKIPVALIDATION 2
```

The first one inserts debug info as comments into the shader and the second one skips validation. This flag can be set for a working shader.

Via the fourth parameter, an ID3DXBuffer interface can be exported to get a vertex shader declaration fragment of the constants. To ignore this parameter, it is set to NULL here. In case of an error, the error explanation would be stored in a buffer object via the ID3DXBuffer interface in pErrors. To see the output of OutputDebugString(), the debug process in the Visual C/C++ IDE must be started with F5.

Create a Vertex Shader

The vertex shader is validated and a handle for it is retrieved via a call to CreateVertexShader() in m_dwVertexShader. The following lines of code can be found in RestoreDeviceObjects():

```
// Create the vertex shader
rc = m_pd3dDevice->CreateVertexShader( dwDecl, (DWORD*)pVS->GetBufferPointer(),
                                       &m_dwVertexShader, 0 );
if ( FAILED(rc) )
{
  OutputDebugString( "Failed to create the vertex shader, errors:\n" );
  D3DXGetErrorStringA(rc,szBuffer,sizeof(szBuffer));
  OutputDebugString( szBuffer );
  OutputDebugString( "\n" );
}
```

CreateVertexShader() gets a pointer to the buffer with the binary version of the vertex shader via the ID3DXBuffer interface. This function gets the vertex shader declaration via dwDecl, which maps vertex data to specific vertex shader input registers. If an error occurs, its explanation is accessible via a pointer to a buffer object that is retrieved via the ID3DXBuffer interface in pVS->GetBufferPointer(). D3DXGetErrorStringA() interprets all Direct3D and Direct3DX HRESULTS and returns an error message in szBuffer.

It is possible to force the usage of software vertex processing with the last parameter by using the D3DUSAGE_SOFTWAREPROCESSING flag. It must be used when the D3DRS_SOFTWAREVERTEXPROCESSING member of the D3DRENDERSTATETYPE enumerated type is TRUE.

Set a Vertex Shader

The vertex shader is set via SetVertexShader() in the Render() function:

```
// set the vertex shader
m_pd3dDevice->SetVertexShader( m_dwVertexShader );
```

The only parameter that must be provided is the handle to the vertex shader. This function executes the vertex shader as often as there are vertices.

Free Vertex Shader Resources

Vertex shader resources must be freed with a call to:

```
if ( m_dwVertexShader != 0xffffffff )
{
  m_pd3dDevice->DeleteVertexShader( m_dwVertexShader );
  m_dwVertexShader = 0xffffffff;
}
```

This example frees the vertex shader resources in the InvalidateDeviceObjects() framework function; this must happen if a window size or a device changes.

Non-Shader Specific Code

The non-shader specific code of RacorX deals with setting render states and the handling of the vertex and index buffer. A few render states have to be set in RestoreDeviceObjects():

```
// z-buffer enabled
m_pd3dDevice->SetRenderState( D3DRS_ZENABLE, TRUE );
// Turn off D3D lighting, since we are providing our own vertex shader lighting
m_pd3dDevice->SetRenderState( D3DRS_LIGHTING, FALSE );
// Turn off culling, so we see the front and back of the quad
m_pd3dDevice->SetRenderState( D3DRS_CULLMODE, D3DCULL_NONE );
```

The first instructions enable the z-buffer (a corresponding flag has to be set in the constructor of the Direct3D framework class so that the device is created with a z-buffer).

The fixed-function lighting is not needed, so it is switched off with the second statement. To see both sides of the quad, backface culling is switched off with the third statement.

The vertex and index buffer is created in InitDeviceObjects():

```
// create and fill the vertex buffer
// Initialize vertices for rendering a quad
VERTEX Vertices[] =
{
// x y z
{ -1.0f,-1.0f, 0.0f, },
{ 1.0f,-1.0f, 0.0f, },
{ 1.0f, 1.0f, 0.0f, },
{ -1.0f, 1.0f, 0.0f, },
};

m_dwSizeofVertices = sizeof (Vertices);
// Create the vertex buffers with four vertices
if( FAILED( m_pd3dDevice->CreateVertexBuffer( 4 * sizeof(VERTEX),
        D3DUSAGE_WRITEONLY , sizeof(VERTEX), D3DPOOL_MANAGED, &m_pVB ) ) )
  return E_FAIL;
```

```
// lock and unlock the vertex buffer to fill it with memcpy
VOID* pVertices;
if( FAILED( m_pVB->Lock( 0, m_dwSizeofVertices, (BYTE**)&pVertices, 0 ) ) )
  return E_FAIL;
memcpy( pVertices, Vertices, m_dwSizeofVertices);
m_pVB->Unlock();
// create and fill the index buffer
// indices
WORD wIndices[]={0, 1, 2, 0, 2, 3};

m_wSizeofIndices = sizeof (wIndices);

// create index buffer
if(FAILED (m_pd3dDevice->CreateIndexBuffer(m_wSizeofIndices, 0,
        D3DFMT_INDEX16, D3DPOOL_MANAGED, &m_pIB)))
  return E_FAIL;

// fill index buffer
VOID *pIndices;
if (FAILED(m_pIB->Lock(0, m_wSizeofIndices, (BYTE **)&pIndices, 0)))
  return E_FAIL;
memcpy(pIndices, wIndices, m_wSizeofIndices);
m_pIB->Unlock();
```

The four vertices of the quad are stored in a VERTEX structure, which holds for each vertex three FLOAT values for the position.

By using the flag D3DFMT_INDEX16 in CreateIndexBuffer(), 16-bit variables are used to store the indices into the wIndices structure. So the maximum number of available indices is 64 K. Both buffers use a managed memory pool with D3DPOOL_MANAGED, so they will be cached in the system memory.

Note: D3DPOOL_MANAGED resources are read from the system memory, which is quite fast, and are written to the system memory and then uploaded to wherever the non-system copy has to go (AGP or VIDEO memory). This upload happens when the resource is unlocked. There are always two copies of a resource, one in the system and one in the AGP or VIDEO memory. This is a less efficient but bullet-proof way. It works for any class of driver and must be used with unified memory architecture boards. Handling resources with D3DPOOL_DEFAULT is more efficient. In this case, the driver will choose the best place for the resource.

Note: Why do we use a vertex buffer at all? The vertex buffer can be stored in the memory of your graphic card or AGP, where it can be accessed very quickly by 3D hardware, so a copy between system memory and the graphic card/AGP memory can be avoided. This is important for hardware that accelerates transformation and lighting. Without vertex buffers, a lot of bus traffic would happen by transforming and lighting the vertices.

Note: Why do we use an index buffer? You will get maximum performance when you reduce the duplication in vertices transformed and sent across the bus to the rendering device. A non-indexed triangle list, for example, achieves no vertex sharing, so it's the least optimal method because DrawPrimitive*() is called several times. Using indexed lists or strips reduces the call overhead of DrawPrimitive*() methods (reducing DrawPrimitve*() methods is also called batching) and because of the reduction of vertices to send through the bus, it saves memory bandwidth. Indexed strips are more hardware cache-friendly on newer hardware than indexed lists.

The performance of index processing operations depends heavily on where the index buffer exists in memory. At the time of pubication, the only graphic cards that support index buffers in hardware are the RADEON 8x00 series.

Summary

RacorX shows a simple vertex shader together with its infrastructure. The shader is inlined in RacorX.cpp and compiled with D3DXAssembleShader(). It uses four dp4 instructions for the transformation of the quad and only one material color.

The upcoming examples are built on this example, and only the functional additions will be shown on the following pages.

RacorX2

The main difference between RacorX and RacorX2 is the compilation of the vertex shader with NVASM. Whereas the first example compiles the vertex shader with D3DXAssembleShader() while the application starts up, RacorX2 uses a precompiled vertex shader.

To add the NVIDIA vertex and pixel shader assembler, you have to do the following steps:

■ Create a directory (for example, <C:\NVASM>:) and unzip nvasm.exe and the documentation into it.

■ Show your Visual C++ IDE path to this exe with Tools->Options->Directories and choose Executable files from the Show directories for drop-down list.

■ Add the path to NVASM <C:\NVASM>.

Now the dialog box should look like this:

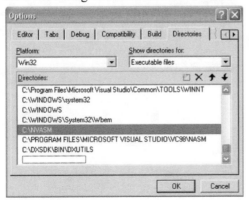

Figure 7: Integrating NVASM into Visual C/C++

■   Additionally, you have to tell every vertex shader file in the IDE that it has to be compiled with NVASM. The easiest way to do that is by looking into the example RacorX2. Just fire up your Visual C++ IDE by clicking on RacorX.dsp in the RacorX2 directory. Click on the FileView tab of the Workspace dialog and then on Shaders to view the available shader files. A right-click on the file basic.vsh should show you a pop-up. Click on Settings. The settings of your project might look like this:

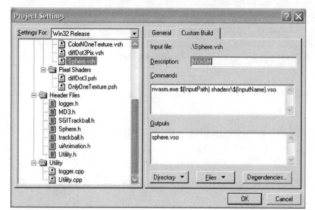

Figure 8: Custom Build options for Vertex Shader files

■   The entry in the Commands field is nvasm.exe $(InputPath) shaders\$(InputName).vso.

In the Outputs field entry, I use the input name as the name for the output file with an *.vso extension. The output directory should be the shaders directory. *Direct3D ShaderX* author Kenneth Hurley is the author of NVASM. Read more in [Hurley].

The output of NVASM in the build window of your Visual C/C++ IDE should look like this:

```
-----------------------Configuration: RacorX - Win32 Debug--------------
NVASM
**** NVASM 1.37, Copyright (C) 2000 NVIDIA Corporation ***
------ Assembly successful, 12 lines assembled, 0 errors, 0 warnings

RacorX.exe - 0 error(s), 0 warning(s)
```

Figure 9: NVASM output

The vertex shader is provided in its own ASCII file called basic.vsh. After compilation, a binary object file with the name basic.vso is created in the shaders directory:

Figure 10: Directory content of RacorX2

Create a Vertex Shader

Because of the already compiled vertex shader, the creation of the vertex shader has to be done in a different way than in the previous example. This happens in the InitDeviceObjects() function:

```
//shader decl
DWORD dwDecl[] =
{
  D3DVSD_STREAM(0),
  D3DVSD_REG(0, D3DVSDT_FLOAT3 ), // input register 0
  D3DVSD_END()
};

// loads a *.vso binary file, already compiled with NVASM and
// creates a vertex shader
if (FAILED(CreateVSFromCompiledFile (m_pd3dDevice, dwDecl,"shaders/basic.vso",
&m_dwVertexShader)))
    return E_FAIL;
```

CreateVSFromCompiledFile() opens and reads in the binary vertex shader file and creates a vertex shader. The source of this function can be found at the end of the RacorX.cpp file in the RacorX2 directory:

```
//-------------------------------------------------------------------------
// Name: CreateVSFromBinFile
// Desc: loads a binary *.vso file that was compiled by NVASM
// and creates a vertex shader
//-------------------------------------------------------------------------
HRESULT CMyD3DApplication::CreateVSFromCompiledFile (IDirect3DDevice8*
                                                     m_pd3dDevice,
                                                     DWORD* dwDeclaration,
                                                     TCHAR* strVSPath,
                                                     DWORD* m_dwVS)
{
  char szBuffer[128]; // debug output
  DWORD* dwpVS; // pointer to address space of the calling process
  HANDLE hFile, hMap; // handle file and handle mapped file
  TCHAR tempVSPath[512]; // temporary file path
  HRESULT hr; // error

if( FAILED( hr = DXUtil_FindMediaFile( tempVSPath, strVSPath ) ) )
  return D3DAPPERR_MEDIANOTFOUND;

hFile = CreateFile(tempVSPath, GENERIC_READ,0,0,OPEN_EXISTING,
                   FILE_ATTRIBUTE_NORMAL,0);
if(hFile != INVALID_HANDLE_VALUE)
{
  if(GetFileSize(hFile,0) > 0)
  hMap = CreateFileMapping(hFile,0,PAGE_READONLY,0,0,0);
  else
  {
    CloseHandle(hFile);
  return E_FAIL;
  }
}
else
  return E_FAIL;
```

```
// maps a view of a file into the address space of the calling process
dwpVS = (DWORD *)MapViewOfFile(hMap, FILE_MAP_READ, 0, 0, 0);

// Create the vertex shader
hr = m_pd3dDevice->CreateVertexShader( dwDeclaration, dwpVS, m_dwVS, 0 );
if ( FAILED(hr) )
{
  OutputDebugString( "Failed to create Vertex Shader, errors:\n" );
  D3DXGetErrorStringA(hr,szBuffer,sizeof(szBuffer));
  OutputDebugString( szBuffer );
  OutputDebugString( "\n" );
return hr;
}

  UnmapViewOfFile(dwpVS);
  CloseHandle(hMap);
  CloseHandle(hFile);

  return S_OK;
}
```

DXUtil_FindMediaFile(), a helper function located in the framework file dxutil.cpp, returns the path to the already compiled vertex shader file. CreateFile() opens and reads the existing file:

```
HANDLE CreateFile(
  LPCTSTR lpFileName,                    // file name
  DWORD dwDesiredAccess,                 // access mode
  DWORD dwShareMode,                     // share mode
  LPSECURITY_ATTRIBUTES lpSecurityAttributes, // SD
  DWORD dwCreationDisposition,           // how to create
  DWORD dwFlagsAndAttributes,            // file attributes
  HANDLE hTemplateFile                   // handle to template file
);
```

Its first parameter is the path to the file. The flag GENERIC_READ specifies read access to the file in the second parameter. The following two parameters are not used because file sharing should not happen and the file should not be inherited by a child process. The fifth parameter is set to OPEN_EXISTING. This way, the function fails if the file does not exist. Setting the sixth parameter to FILE_ATTRIBUTE_NORMAL indicates that the file has no other attributes. A template file is not used here, so the last parameter is set to 0. Please consult the Platform SDK help file for more information.

CreateFileMapping() creates or opens a named or unnamed file-mapping object for the specified file:

```
HANDLE CreateFileMapping(
  HANDLE hFile,                          // handle to file
  LPSECURITY_ATTRIBUTES lpAttributes,    // security
  DWORD flProtect,                       // protection
  DWORD dwMaximumSizeHigh,               // high-order DWORD of size
  DWORD dwMaximumSizeLow,                // low-order DWORD of size
  LPCTSTR lpName                         // object name
);
```

The first parameter is a handle to the file from which to create a mapping object. The file must be opened with an access mode compatible with the protection flags specified by the flProtect parameter. We have opened the file in CreateFile() with GENERIC_READ, therefore we use

PAGE_READONLY here. Other features of CreateFileMapping() are not needed, so we set the rest of the parameters to 0. MapViewOfFile()maps a view of a file into the address space of the calling process:

```
LPVOID MapViewOfFile(
  HANDLE hFileMappingObject,  // handle to file-mapping object
  DWORD dwDesiredAccess,      // access mode
  DWORD dwFileOffsetHigh,     // high-order DWORD of offset
  DWORD dwFileOffsetLow,      // low-order DWORD of offset
  SIZE_T dwNumberOfBytesToMap // number of bytes to map
);
```

This function only gets the handle to the file-mapping object from CreateFileMapping() and the access mode FILE_MAP_READ. The access mode parameter specifies the type of access to the file view and, therefore, the protection of the pages mapped by the file. Other features are not needed; therefore, the rest of the parameters are set to 0.

CreateVertexShader() is used to create and validate a vertex shader. It takes the vertex shader declaration (which maps vertex buffer streams to different vertex input registers) in its first parameter as a pointer and returns the shader handle in the third parameter. The second parameter gets the vertex shader instructions of the binary code precompiled by a vertex shader assembler. With the fourth parameter, you can force software vertex processing with D3DUSAGE_SOFTWAREPROCESSING.

As in the previous example, OutputDebugString() shows the complete error message in the output debug window of the Visual C/C++ IDE, and D3DXGetErrorStringA() interprets all Direct3D and Direct3DX HRESULTS and returns an error message in szBuffer.

Summary

This example showed the integration of NVASM to precompile a vertex shader and how to open and read a binary vertex shader file.

RacorX3

The main improvement of RacorX3 over RacorX2 is the addition of a per-vertex diffuse reflection model in the vertex shader. This is one of the simplest lighting calculations, which outputs the color based on the dot product of the vertex normal with the light vector.

RacorX3 uses a light positioned at (0.0, 0.0, 1.0) and a green color.

As usual, we are tracking the life cycle of the vertex shader.

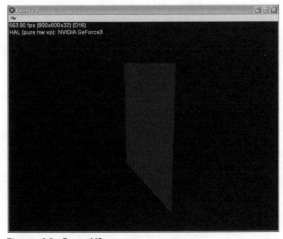

Figure 11: RacorX3

Vertex Shader Declaration

The vertex shader declaration has to map vertex data to specific vertex shader input registers. In addition to the previous examples, we need to map a normal vector to the input register v3:

```
// vertex shader declaration
DWORD dwDecl[] =
{
  D3DVSD_STREAM(0),
  D3DVSD_REG(0, D3DVSDT_FLOAT3 ), // input register #1
  D3DVSD_REG(3, D3DVSDT_FLOAT3 ), // normal in input register #4
  D3DVSD_END()
};
```

The corresponding layout of the vertex buffer looks like this:

```
struct VERTICES
{
  FLOAT x, y, z;      // The untransformed position for the vertex
  FLOAT nx, ny, nz;   // the normal
};
// Declare custom FVF macro.
#define D3DFVF_VERTEX (D3DFVF_XYZ|D3DFVF_NORMAL)
```

Each vertex consists of three position floating-point values and three normal floating-point values in the vertex buffer. The vertex shader gets the position and normal values from the vertex buffer via v0 and v3.

Set the Vertex Shader Constant Registers

The vertex shader constants are set in FrameMove() and RestoreDeviceObjects(). This example uses a more elegant way to handle the constant registers. The file const.h that is included in RacorX.cpp and diffuse.vsh gives the constant registers names that are easier to remember:

```
#define CLIP_MATRIX 0
#define CLIP_MATRIX_1 1
#define CLIP_MATRIX_2 2
#define CLIP_MATRIX_3 3
#define INVERSE_WORLD_MATRIX    4
#define INVERSE_WORLD_MATRIX_1 5
#define INVERSE_WORLD_MATRIX_2 6
#define LIGHT_POSITION 11
#define DIFFUSE_COLOR 14
#define LIGHT_COLOR 15
```

In FrameMove(), a clipping matrix and an inverse world matrix are set into the constant registers:

```
HRESULT CMyD3DApplication::FrameMove()
{
  // rotates the object about the y-axis
  D3DXMatrixRotationY( &m_matWorld, m_fTime * 1.5f );
  // set the clip matrix
  m_pd3dDevice->SetVertexShaderConstant(CLIP_MATRIX, &(m_matWorld *
                                    m_matView * m_matProj), 4);
  D3DXMATRIX matWorldInverse;
```

```
D3DXMatrixInverse(&matWorldInverse, NULL, &m_matWorld);
m_pd3dDevice->SetVertexShaderConstant(INVERSE_WORLD_MATRIX,
                                        &matWorldInverse,3);

return S_OK;
}
```

Contrary to the previous examples, the concatenated world, view, and projection matrix, which is used to rotate the quad, is not transposed here. This is because the matrix will be transposed in the vertex shader, as shown below.

To transform the normal, an inverse 4x3 matrix is sent to the vertex shader via c4-c6.

The Vertex Shader

The vertex shader is a bit more complex than the one used in the previous examples:

```
; per-vertex diffuse lighting
#include "const.h"
vs.1.1
; transpose and transform to clip space
mul r0, v0.x, c[CLIP_MATRIX]
mad r0, v0.y, c[CLIP_MATRIX_1], r0
mad r0, v0.z, c[CLIP_MATRIX_2], r0
add oPos, c[CLIP_MATRIX_3], r0
; transform normal
dp3 r1.x, v3, c[INVERSE_WORLD_MATRIX]
dp3 r1.y, v3, c[INVERSE_WORLD_MATRIX_1]
dp3 r1.z, v3, c[INVERSE_WORLD_MATRIX_2]
; renormalize it
dp3 r1.w, r1, r1
rsq r1.w, r1.w
mul r1, r1, r1.w
; N dot L
; we need L vector towards the light, thus negate sign
dp3 r0, r1, -c[LIGHT_POSITION]
mul r0, r0, c[LIGHT_COLOR]          ; modulate against light color
mul oD0, r0, c[DIFFUSE_COLOR]       ; modulate against material
```

The mul, mad, and add instructions transpose and transform the matrix provided in c0-c3 to clip space. As such, they are nearly functionally equivalent to the transposition of the matrix and the four dp4 instructions shown in the previous examples. There are two caveats to bear in mind: The complex matrix instructions like m4x4 might be faster in software emulation mode and v0.w is not used here. oPos.w is automatically filled with 1.

These instructions should save the CPU cycles used for transposing.

The normals are transformed in the following three dp3 instructions and then renormalized with the dp3, rsq, and mul instructions.

You can think of a normal transform in the following way: Normal vectors (unlike position vectors) are simply directions in space, and as such they should not get squished in magnitude, and translation doesn't change their direction. They should simply be rotated in some fashion to reflect the change in orientation of the surface. This change in orientation is a result of rotating and squishing the object but not moving it. The information for rotating a normal can be extracted from the 4x4 transformation matrix by doing transpose and inversion. A more math-related explanation is given in [Haines/Möller][Turkowski].

So the bullet-proof way to use normals is to transform the transpose of the inverse of the matrix that is used to transform the object. If the matrix used to transform the object is called M, then we must use the matrix N, below, to transform the normals of this object.

```
N = transpose( inverse(M) )
```

Note: The normal can be transformed with the transformation matrix (usually the world matrix) that is used to transform the object in the following cases:

- Matrix formed from rotations (orthogonal matrix) because the inverse of an orthogonal matrix is its transpose
- Matrix formed from rotations and translation (rigid-body transforms) because translations do not affect vector direction
- Matrix formed from rotations and translation and uniform scalings because such scalings affect only the length of the transformed normal, not its direction. A uniform scaling is simply a matrix, which uniformly increases or decreases the object's size, vs. a non-uniform scaling, which can stretch or squeeze an object. If uniform scalings are used, then the normals do have to be renormalized.

Therefore, using the world matrix would be sufficient in this example.

That's exactly what the source is doing. The inverse world matrix is delivered to the vertex shader via c4-c6. The dp3 instruction handles the matrix in a similar way as dp4.

By multiplying a matrix with a vector, each column of the matrix should be multiplied with each component of the vector. dp3 and dp4 are only capable of multiplying each row of the matrix with each component of the vector. In the case of the position data, the matrix is transposed to get the right results.

In the case of the normals, no transposition is done, so dp3 calculates the dot product by multiplying the rows of the matrix with the components of the vector. This is like using a transposed matrix.

The normal is renormalized with the dp3, rsq, and mul instructions. Renormalizing a vector means to align its length to 1. That's because we need a unit vector to calculate our diffuse lighting effect.

To calculate a unit vector, divide the vector by its magnitude or length. The magnitude of vectors is calculated by using the Pythagorean theorem:

```
x² + y² + z² = m²
```

The length of the vector is retrieved by:

```
||A|| = sqrt(x² + y² + z²)
```

The magnitude of a vector has a special symbol in mathematics. It is a capital letter with two vertical bars on each side: $\|A\|$. So dividing the vector by its magnitude is:

```
UnitVector = Vector / sqrt(x² + y² + z²)
```

The lines of code in the vertex shader that handle the calculation of the unit vector look like this:

```
; renormalize it
dp3 r1.w, r1, r1   ; (src1.x * src2.x) + (src1.y * src2.y) + (src1.z * src2.z)
rsq r1.w, r1.w     ; if (v != 0 && v != 1.0) v = (float)(1.0f / sqrt(v))
mul r1, r1, r1.w   ; r1 * r1.w
```

dp3 squares the x, y, and z components of the temporary register r1, adds them, and returns the result in r1.w. rsq divides 1 by the result in r1.w and stores the result in r1.w. mul multiplies all components of r1 with r1.w. Afterward, the result in r1.w is no longer used in the vertex shader.

The underlying calculation of these three instructions can be represented by the following formula, which is mostly identical to the formula postulated above:

```
UnitVector = Vector * 1/sqrt(x² + y² + z²)
```

Lighting is calculated with the following three instructions:

```
dp3 r0, r1, -c[LIGHT_POSITION]
mul r0, r0, c[LIGHT_COLOR]         ; modulate against light color
mul oD0, r0, c[DIFFUSE_COLOR]      ; modulate against diffuse color
```

Nowadays, the lighting models used in current games are not based on much physical theory. Game programmers use approximations that try to simulate the way photons are reflected from objects in a rough but efficient manner.

One usually differentiates between different kinds of light sources and different reflection models. The common lighting sources are called directional, point light, and spotlight. The most common reflection models are ambient, diffuse, and specular lighting.

This example uses a directional light source with a diffuse reflection model.

Directional Light

RacorX3 uses a light source in an infinite distance. This simulates the long distance that light beams have to travel from the sun. We treat these light beams as being parallel. This kind of light source is called directional light source.

Diffuse Reflection

Whereas ambient light is considered to be uniform from any direction, diffuse light simulates the emission of an object by a particular light source. Therefore, you are able to see that light falls onto the surface of an object from a particular direction by using the diffuse lighting model.

It is based on the assumption that light is reflected equally well in all directions, so the appearance of the reflection does not depend on the position of the observer. The intensity of the light reflected in any direction depends only on how much light falls onto the surface.

If the surface of the object is facing the light source, which means it is perpendicular to the direction of the light, the density of the incidental light is the highest. If the surface is facing the light source at an angle smaller than 90 degrees, the density is proportionally smaller.

The diffuse reflection model is based on a law of physics called Lambert's Law, which states that for ideally diffuse (totally matte) surfaces, the reflected light is determined by the cosine between the surface normal N and the light vector L. (See Figure 12.)

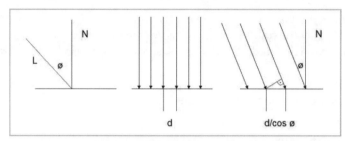

Figure 12: Diffuse lighting

The left figure shows a geometric interpretation of Lambert's Law (see also [RTR]). The middle figure shows the light rays hitting the surface perpendicularly at a distance d apart. The intensity of the light is related to this distance. It decreases as d becomes greater. This is shown in the right figure. The light rays make an angle ø with the normal of the plane. This illustrates that the same amount of light that passes through one side of a right-angle triangle is reflected from the region of the surface corresponding to the triangle's hypotenuse. Due to the relationships in a right-angle triangle, the length of the hypotenuse is d/cos ø of the length of the considered side. Thus, you can deduce that if the intensity of the incident light is $I_{directed}$, the amount of light reflected from a unit surface is $I_{directed}$ cos ø. Adjusting this with a coefficient that describes reflection properties of the matter leads to the following equation (see also [Savchenko]):

$$I_{reflected} = C_{diffuse} * I_{directed} \cos ø$$

This equation demonstrates that the reflection is at its peak for surfaces that are perpendicular to the direction of light and diminishes for smaller angles because the cosinus value is very large. The light is obscured by the surface if the angle is more than 180 or less than 0 degrees because the cosinus value is small. You will obtain negative intensity of the reflected light, which will be clamped by the output registers.

In an implementation of this model, you have to find a way to compute cos ø. By definition, the dot or scalar product of the light and normal vector can be expressed as

$$N \text{ dot } L = \|N\| \|L\| \cos ø$$

where $\|N\|$ and $\|L\|$ are the lengths of the vectors. If both vectors are unit length, you can compute cos ø as the scalar or dot product of the light and normal vector. Thus, the expression is

$$I_{reflected} = C_{diffuse} * I_{directed}(N \text{ dot } L)$$

So (N dot L) is the same as the cosine of the angle between N and L; therefore, as the angle decreases, the resulting diffuse value is higher.

This is exactly what the dp3 instruction and the first mul instruction are doing. Here is the source with the relevant part of constant.h:

```
#define LIGHT_POSITION 11
#define MATERIAL_COLOR 14


-----
dp3 r0, r1, -c[LIGHT_POSITION]
mul r0, r0, c[LIGHT_COLOR] ; modulate against light color
mul oD0, r0, c[DIFFUSE_COLOR] ; modulate against material
```

So the vertex shader registers are involved in the following way:

```
r0 = (r1 dot -c11) * c14
```

This example modulates additionally against the blue light color in c15:

```
r0 = (c15 * (r1 dot -c11)) * c14
```

Summary

RacorX3 shows the usage of an include file to give constants a name that can be remembered more easily. It shows how to normalize vectors, and although it just touches the surface in solving the problem of transforming normals, it shows a bullet-proof method to do it.

The example introduces an optimization technique that eliminates the need to transpose the clip space matrix with the help of the CPU and shows the usage of a simple diffuse reflection model that lights the quad on a per-vertex basis.

RacorX4

RacorX4 has a few additional features compared to RacorX3. First of all, this example will not use a plain quad anymore; it uses a Bézier patch class instead that shows a round surface with a texture attached to it. To simulate light reflections, a combined diffuse and specular reflection model is used.

RacorX4 uses the trackball class provided with the common files framework to rotate and move the object. You can choose different specular colors with the C key and zoom in and out with the mouse wheel.

Figure 13: RacorX4

Vertex Shader Declaration

Additionally, the texture coordinates will be mapped to input register v7.

```
// shader decl
DWORD dwDecl[] =
{
  D3DVSD_STREAM(0),
  D3DVSD_REG(0, D3DVSDT_FLOAT3 ),  // input register v0
  D3DVSD_REG(3, D3DVSDT_FLOAT3 ),  // normal in input register v3
  D3DVSD_REG(7, D3DVSDT_FLOAT2),   // tex coordinates
  D3DVSD_END()
};
```

The corresponding layout of the vertex buffer in BPatch.h looks like this:

```
struct VERTICES {
  D3DXVECTOR3 vPosition;
  D3DXVECTOR3 vNormal;
  D3DXVECTOR2 uv;
};
// Declare custom FVF macro.
#define D3DFVF_VERTEX (D3DFVF_XYZ|D3DFVF_NORMAL|D3DFVF_TEX1)
```

The third flag used in the custom FVF macro indicates the usage of one texture coordinate pair. This macro is provided to CreateVertexBuffer().

The vertex shader gets the position values from the vertex buffer via v0, the normal values via v3, and the two texture coordinates via v7.

Set the Vertex Shader Constants

The vertex shader constants are set in FrameMove() and RestoreDeviceObjects(). The file const.h holds the following defines:

```
#define CLIP_MATRIX 0
#define CLIP_MATRIX_1 1
#define CLIP_MATRIX_2 2
#define CLIP_MATRIX_3 3
#define INVERSE_WORLD_MATRIX 8
#define INVERSE_WORLD_MATRIX_1 9
#define INVERSE_WORLD_MATRIX_2 10
#define LIGHT_VECTOR 11
#define EYE_VECTOR 12
#define SPEC_POWER 13
#define SPEC_COLOR 14
```

In FrameMove() a clipping matrix, the inverse world matrix, an eye vector, and a specular color are set:

```
// set the clip matrix
m_pd3dDevice->SetVertexShaderConstant(CLIP_MATRIX,&(m_matWorld * m_matView *
        m_matProj),4);
// set the world inverse matrix
D3DXMATRIX matWorldInverse;
D3DXMatrixInverse(&matWorldInverse, NULL, &m_matWorld);
m_pd3dDevice->SetVertexShaderConstant(INVERSE_WORLD_MATRIX, matWorldInverse,3);
// stuff for specular lighting
// set eye vector E
m_pd3dDevice->SetVertexShaderConstant(EYE_VECTOR, vEyePt,1);
// specular color
if(m_bKey['C'])
{
  m_bKey['C']=0;
  ++m_dwCurrentColor;
  if(m_dwCurrentColor >= 3)
    m_dwCurrentColor=0;
}
m_pd3dDevice->SetVertexShaderConstant(SPEC_COLOR, m_vLightColor
        [m_dwCurrentColor], 1);
```

Like in the previous example, the concatenated world, view, and projection matrix are set into c0-c3 to get transposed in the vertex shader, and the inverse 4x3 world matrix is sent to the vertex shader to transform the normal.

The eye vector (EYE_VECTOR) that is used to build up the view matrix is stored in constant register c12. As shown below, this vector is helpful to build up the specular reflection model used in the upcoming examples.

The user can pick one of the following specular colors with the C key:

```
m_vLightColor[0]=D3DXVECTOR4(0.3f,0.1f,0.1f,1.0f);
m_vLightColor[1]=D3DXVECTOR4(0.1f,0.5f,0.1f,1.0f);
m_vLightColor[2]=D3DXVECTOR4(0.0f,0.1f,0.4f,1.0f);
```

In RestoreDeviceObjects(), the specular power, the light vector, and the diffuse color are set:

```
// specular power
m_pd3dDevice->SetVertexShaderConstant(SPEC_POWER, D3DXVECTOR4(0,10,25,50),1);
// light direction
D3DXVECTOR3 vLight(0,0,1);
m_pd3dDevice->SetVertexShaderConstant(LIGHT_VECTOR, vLight,1);
D3DXCOLOR matDiffuse(0.9f, 0.9f, 0.9f, 1.0f);
m_pd3dDevice->SetVertexShaderConstant(DIFFUSE_COLOR, &matDiffuse, 1);
```

As in the previous examples, the light is positioned at (0.0, 0.0, 1.0). There are four specular power values, from which one will be used in the vertex shader.

Note: To optimize the usage of SetVertexShaderConstant(), the specular color could be set into the fourth component of the light vector, which only used three of its components.

The Vertex Shader

The vertex shader handles a combined diffuse and specular reflection model:

```
; diffuse and specular vertex lighting
#include "const.h"
vs.1.1
; transpose and transform to clip space
mul r0, v0.x, c[CLIP_MATRIX]
mad r0, v0.y, c[CLIP_MATRIX_1], r0
mad r0, v0.z, c[CLIP_MATRIX_2], r0
add oPos, c[CLIP_MATRIX_3], r0
; output texture coords
mov oT0, v7
; transform normal
dp3 r1.x, v3, c[INVERSE_WORLD_MATRIX]
dp3 r1.y, v3, c[INVERSE_WORLD_MATRIX_1]
dp3 r1.z, v3, c[INVERSE_WORLD_MATRIX_2]
; renormalize it
dp3 r1.w, r1, r1
rsq r1.w, r1.w
mul r1, r1, r1.w
; light vector L
; we need L towards the light, thus negate sign
mov r5, -c[LIGHT_VECTOR]
; N dot L
dp3 r0.x, r1, r5
```

```
; compute normalized half vector H = L + V
add r2, c[EYE_VECTOR], r5 ; L + V
; renormalize H
dp3 r2.w, r2, r2
rsq r2.w, r2.w
mul r2, r2, r2.w
; N dot H
dp3 r0.y, r1, r2
; compute specular and clamp values (lit)
; r0.x - N dot L
; r0.y - N dot H
; r0.w - specular power n
mov r0.w, c[SPEC_POWER].y ; n must be between -128.0 and 128.0
lit r4, r0
; diffuse color * diffuse intensity(r4.y)
mul oD0, c[DIFFUSE_COLOR], r4.y
; specular color * specular intensity(r4.z)
mul oD1, c[SPEC_COLOR], r4.z
```

Compared to the vertex shader in the previous example program, this shader maps the texture coordinates to texture stage 0 with the following instruction:

```
; output texture coords
mov oT0, v7
```

The corresponding texture stage states set for the shading of the pixels in the multitexturing unit will be shown later in the "Non-shader Specific Code" section. The instructions that transform the normal and calculate the diffuse reflection were discussed in the previous example.

The real new functionality in this shader is the calculation of the specular reflection, which happens in the code lines starting with the add instruction.

Specular Reflection

Compared to the diffuse reflection model, the appearance of the reflection in the specular reflection model depends on the position of the viewer. When the direction of the viewing coincides, or nearly coincides, with the direction of specular reflection, a bright highlight is observed. This simulates the reflection of a light source by a smooth, shiny, and polished surface.

To describe reflection from shiny surfaces, an approximation is commonly used, which is called the Phong illumination model (not to be confused with Phong shading), named after its creator Phong Bui Tong [Foley]. According to this model, a specular highlight is seen when the viewer is close to the direction of reflection. The intensity of light falls off sharply when the viewer moves away from the direction of the specular reflection.

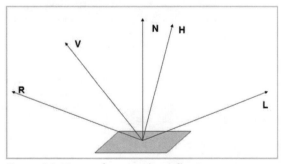

Figure 14: Vectors for specular reflection

A model describing this effect has to be aware of at least the location of the light source L, the location of the viewer V, and the orientation of the surface N. Additionally, a vector R that describes the direction of the reflection might be useful. The halfway vector H that halves the angle between L and V is discussed below.

The original Phong formula approximates the falloff of the intensity. It looks like this:

$$k_{specular} \cos^n(\beta)$$

where $k_{specular}$ is a scalar coefficient showing the percentage of the incident light reflected. ß describes the angle between R and V. The exponent n characterizes the shiny properties of the surface and ranges from 1 to infinity. Objects that are matte require a small exponent, since they produce a large, dim, specular highlight with a gentle falloff. Shiny surfaces should have a sharp highlight that is modeled by a very large exponent, making the intensity falloff very steep.

Together with the diffuse reflection model shown above, the Phong illumination model can be expressed in the following way:

$$I_{reflected} = I_{directed}((N \text{ dot } L) + k_{specular} \cos^n(\beta))$$

$\cos^n(\beta)$ can be replaced by using the mechanism of the dot or scalar product of the unit vectors R and V:

$$I_{reflected} = I_{directed}((N \text{ dot } L) + k_{specular} (R \text{ dot } V)^n)$$

This is the generally accepted phong reflection equation. As the angle between V and R decreases, the specularity rises.

Because it is expensive to calculate the reflection vector R (mirror of light incidence around the surface normal), James F. Blinn [Blinn] introduced a way to do this using an imaginary vector H, which is defined as halfway between L and V. H is therefore:

$$H = (L + V) / 2$$

When H coincides with N, the direction of the reflection coincides with the viewing direction V and a specular hightlight is observed. So the original formula

$$(R \text{ dot } V)^n$$

is expanded to

$$(N \text{ dot } ((L + V) / 2))^n$$

or

$$(N \text{ dot } H)^n$$

The complete Blinn-Phong model formula looks like:

$$I_{reflected} = I_{directed}((N \text{ dot } L) + k_{specular} (N \text{ dot } H)^n)$$

Now back to the relevant code that calculates the specular reflection:

```
; compute normalized half vector H = L + V
add r2, c[EYE_VECTOR], r5 ; L + V
; renormalize H
dp3 r2.w, r2, r2
```

```
rsq r2.w, r2.w
mul r2, r2, r2.w
; N dot H
dp3 r0.y, r1, r2
; compute specular and clamp values (lit)
; r0.x - N dot L
; r0.y - N dot H
; r0.w - specular power n
mov r0.w, c[SPEC_POWER].y ; n must be between -128.0 and 128.0
lit r4, r0
```

The add instruction adds the L and V vectors, but compared to the Blinn-Phong formula shown above, the divide by 2 is missing. This is compensated by altering the specular power value, which leads to good visual results. So this code snippet handles the following equation, which is very similar to the equation of the Blinn-Phong reflection formula:

$$(N \text{ dot } (L+V))^n$$

Although L + V is not equivalent to the half vector H, the term half vector H will be used throughout the upcoming examples.

In the vertex shader source, H is normalized in the following dp3, rsq, and mul instructions.

The reduction of the original Blinn-Phong formula reduces the number of vertex shader instructions and thus leads to a higher performance. This is a typical way to optimize vertex shader code on a functional level [Taylor]. Although L + V is not equivalent to H, the term vector H is used throughout the example source.

One of the main instructions in this piece of code is the lit instruction. It handles a lot of work in only one instruction. The following code fragment shows the operations performed by lit:

```
dest.x = 1;
dest.y = 0;
dest.z = 0;
dest.w = 1;
float power = src.w;
const float MAXPOWER = 127.9961f;
if (power < -MAXPOWER)
  power = -MAXPOWER; // Fits into 8.8 fixed point format
else if (power > MAXPOWER)
  power = -MAXPOWER; // Fits into 8.8 fixed point format
if (src.x > 0)
{
  dest.y = src.x;
  if (src.y > 0)
  {
    // Allowed approximation is EXP(power * LOG(src.y))
    dest.z = (float)(pow(src.y, power));
  }
}
```

lit returns the diffuse intensity in the y component of the destination register and the specular intensity in the z component of the destination register. If there is no diffuse light, there will be no specular light. So N dot L is only used to switch off the specular light in case there is no diffuse lighting.

> **Note:** A way to do specular lighting without the lit instruction would be to raise the specular power with a few mul instructions, like this:
> mul r3, r3, r3 ; 2nd
> mul r3, r3, r3 ; 4th
> mul r3, r3, r3 ; 8th
> mul r3, r3, r3 ; 16th

The last two instructions multiply the intensity with the diffuse and specular color components and move them into their respective output registers:

```
; diffuse color * diffuse intensity(r4.y)
mul oD0, c[DIFFUSE_COLOR], r4.y
; specular color * specular intensity(r4.z)
mul oD1, c[SPEC_COLOR], r4.z
```

Non-Shader Specific Code

This example uses the multitexturing unit to shade pixels. The proper texture stage states are set in RestoreDeviceObjects():

```
// texture settings
m_pd3dDevice->SetTextureStageState(0, D3DTSS_COLOROP, D3DTOP_MODULATE);
m_pd3dDevice->SetTextureStageState(0, D3DTSS_COLORARG1, D3DTA_TEXTURE);
m_pd3dDevice->SetTextureStageState(0, D3DTSS_COLORARG2, D3DTA_DIFFUSE);
m_pd3dDevice->SetTextureStageState( 1, D3DTSS_COLOROP, D3DTOP_DISABLE );
m_pd3dDevice->SetTextureStageState( 1, D3DTSS_ALPHAOP, D3DTOP_DISABLE );
m_pd3dDevice->SetTextureStageState( 0, D3DTSS_MINFILTER, D3DTEXF_LINEAR );
m_pd3dDevice->SetTextureStageState( 0, D3DTSS_MAGFILTER, D3DTEXF_LINEAR );
m_pd3dDevice->SetTextureStageState( 0, D3DTSS_MIPFILTER, D3DTEXF_LINEAR );
m_pd3dDevice->SetTextureStageState( 0, D3DTSS_ADDRESSU, D3DTADDRESS_CLAMP );
m_pd3dDevice->SetTextureStageState( 0, D3DTSS_ADDRESSV, D3DTADDRESS_CLAMP );
```

These texture stage states modulate the diffuse color with the texture color, disable texture stage 1, and switch on a bilinear filtering with the D3DTEXF_LINEAR flags for the D3DTSS_MINFILTER/D3DTSS_MAGFILTER texture stage states. The D3DTSS_MIPFILTER texture stage state indicates the texture filter to use between mipmap levels. By providing D3DTEXF_LINEAR, trilinear texture filtering, or mip map filtering, is switched on. The clamp texture-addressing mode applies the texture only once on the polygon and then smears the color of the edge pixels of the texture. Furthermore, all negative values become 0 and the positive values remain unchanged.

We use a Bézier patch here to build up the surface used on the source provided by *Direct3D ShaderX* author Bart Sekura. A Bézier patch is the surface extension of the Bézier curve. Whereas a curve is a function of one variable and takes a sequence of control points, the patch is a function of two variables with an array of control points. A Bézier patch can be viewed as a continuous set of Bézier curves. The Bézier patch is the most commonly used surface representation in the computer graphic (see [Skinner]). CD3DBPatch::Create() builds the Bézier patch in InitDeviceObjects() from nine control points and calculates the normals. CD3DBPatch::RestoreDeviceObjects() fills the vertex and index buffer with the data on which the m_pvVertices and m_pwIndices pointers refer.

Summary

RacorX4 shows a specular reflection model that is very similar to the Blinn-Phong reflection model. Additionally, it shows the functionality behind the lit instruction and the basics of texture mapping with a vertex shader.

RacorX5

The only improvement of RacorX5 over RacorX4 is the addition of a point light source. The light can be moved via the Home and End keys and the Left, Right, Down, and Up arrow keys. As with the previous example, the specular light can be changed with the C key.

Point Light Source

A point light source has color and position within a scene but no single direction. All light rays originate from one point and illuminate equally in all directions. The intensity of the rays will remain constant regardless of their distance from the point source,

Figure 15: RacorX5 with point light

unless a falloff value is explicitly stated. A point light is useful to simulate a lightbulb.

Note: A spot light is a light source in which all light rays illuminate in the shape of a cone. The falloff, spread, and dropoff of a spotlight are adjustable.

Light Attenuation for Point Lights

Usually, the energy from the point light that hits a surface diminishes as the distance increases. There are a few functions used to simulate the idea of attenuation in computer graphics. The simplest one might be:

$$\text{func}_{\text{Attenuation}} = 1 / d_L$$

The inverse linear falloff doesn't look as good as the inverse squared falloff:

$$\text{func}_{\text{Attenuation}} = 1 / d_L * d_L$$

This is the attenuation equation that might be used in conjunction with a directional light source. The problem with this function and a point light source is that when a light is far away, its intensity is too low, but when it is close, the intensity becomes high, leading to visual artifacts.

To get a wider range of effects, a decent attenuation equation is used:

$$\text{func}_{\text{Attenuation}} = 1 / A_0 + A_1 * d_L + A_2 * d_L * d_L$$

This is the same equation that is used by the Direct3D fixed-function pipeline to calculate the falloff of point lights. A_0, A_1, and A_2 are known as the attenuation constants. You get a radial distance falloff with $A_1 = 0$ and $A_2 > 0$ and a linear falloff with $A_1 > 0$ and $A_2 = 0$. If the light is too close to the surface, then attenuation becomes very large, making the light too bright. To avoid this, set A_0 to 1 or greater.

The attenuation at the maximum range of the light is not 0.0. To prevent lights from suddenly appearing when they are at the light range, an application can increase the light range. Or, the application can set up attenuation constants so that the attenuation factor is close to 0.0 at the light range. The attenuation value is multiplied by the red, green, and blue components of the light's color to scale the light's intensity as a factor of the distance light travels to a vertex.

To demonstrate the code used to implement this equation, the life cycle of a vertex shader is tracked in the following sections.

Compared to the previous examples, the same input register layout is used by RacorX5, but to feed the vertex shader with the attenuation data, additional constant registers have to be filled with data.

Set the Vertex Shader Constants

The three attenuation values are set in RestoreDeviceObjects():

```
; in const.h:
#define LIGHT_ATTENUATION 17
...
// Attenuation
D3DXVECTOR4 Attenuation(1.0f, 0.0f, 0.0f, 0.0f);
m_pd3dDevice->SetVertexShaderConstant(LIGHT_ATTENUATION, &Attenuation.x, 1);
```

c17.x, c17.y, and c17.z hold the A0, A1, and A2 values. The world matrix and the point light position, which is changeable with the Left, Right, Up, and Down arrow keys, are set in FrameMove():

```
// set the world matrix
m_pd3dDevice->SetVertexShaderConstant(WORLD_MATRIX,&m_matWorld,4);
...
if(m_bKey[VK_LEFT]) { m_bKey[VK_RIGHT]=0;m_vLight.x -= 1.0f * m_fElapsedTime;}
if(m_bKey[VK_RIGHT]) { m_bKey[VK_LEFT]=0;m_vLight.x += 1.0f * m_fElapsedTime;}
if(m_bKey[VK_UP]) { m_bKey[VK_DOWN]=0; m_vLight.y += 1.0f * m_fElapsedTime;}
if(m_bKey[VK_DOWN]) { m_bKey[VK_UP]=0; m_vLight.y -= 1.0f * m_fElapsedTime;}
if(m_bKey[VK_END]) { m_bKey[VK_HOME]=0; m_vLight.z += 1.0f * m_fElapsedTime;}
if(m_bKey[VK_HOME]) { m_bKey[VK_END]=0; m_vLight.z -= 1.0f * m_fElapsedTime;}
// light direction
m_pd3dDevice->SetVertexShaderConstant(LIGHT_VECTOR, m_vLight,1);
```

The world matrix is used to calculate a vector that has its origin at the position of the vertex in world space and its end point at the position of the light in world space.

The Vertex Shader

The vertex shader handles a combined diffuse and specular reflection model and the point light source. The point light's position in world space and the coordinate of the vertex in world space is used to derive a vector for the direction of the light and the distance that the light has traveled.

If you compare this vertex shader to the previous one, the only new elements are the calculation of a light vector and the calculation of the attenuation factor.

```
; diffuse and specular point light
#include "const.h"
vs.1.1
; transpose and transform to clip space
mul r0, v0.x, c[CLIP_MATRIX]
mad r0, v0.y, c[CLIP_MATRIX_1], r0
mad r0, v0.z, c[CLIP_MATRIX_2], r0
add oPos, c[CLIP_MATRIX_3], r0

; output texture coords
mov oT0, v7

; transform normal
dp3 r1.x, v3, c[INVERSE_WORLD_MATRIX]
dp3 r1.y, v3, c[INVERSE_WORLD_MATRIX_1]
dp3 r1.z, v3, c[INVERSE_WORLD_MATRIX_2]

; renormalize it
dp3 r1.w, r1, r1
rsq r1.w, r1.w
mul r1, r1, r1.w

; transpose and transform position to world space
mul r7, v0.x, c[WORLD_MATRIX]
mad r7, v0.y, c[WORLD_MATRIX_1], r7
mad r7, v0.z, c[WORLD_MATRIX_2], r7
add r7, c[WORLD_MATRIX_3], r7

; calculate vector from light position
; to vertex position in world space
add r10.xyz, c[LIGHT_VECTOR], -r7.xyz
; renormalize vector VERTEX_TO_LIGHT
; d = distance
dp3 r10.w, r10, r10   ; r10.w = d * d = (x*x) + (y*y) + (z*z)
rsq r11.w, r10.w      ; r11.w = 1/d = 1/||V|| = 1/sqrt(r7.w)
mul r11, r10, r11.w

dp3 r0.x, r1, r11 ; N dot L

; Get the attenuation
; Parameters for dst:
; src1 = (ignored, d * d, d * d, ignored)
; src2 = (ignored, 1/d, ignored, 1/d)
; r10.w = d * d
; r11.w = 1 / d
dst r4, r10.w, r11.w
; dest.x = 1
; dest.y = src0.y * src1.y
; dest.z = src0.z
```

```
; dest.w = src1.w
; r4(1, d * d * 1 / d, d * d, 1/d)
; c[LIGHT_ATTENUATION].x = a0
; c[LIGHT_ATTENUATION].y = a1
; c[LIGHT_ATTENUATION].z = a2
dp3 r7.x, r4, c[LIGHT_ATTENUATION] ; (a0 + a1*d + a2* (d * d))
rcp r7.x, r7.x                ; simplified:
                              ; if (src.w != 0.0 && src.w != 1.0)
                              ; 1 / (a0 + a1*d + a2* (d * d))
; compute normalized half vector H = L + V
add r2, c[EYE_VECTOR], r11 ; L + V

; renormalize H
dp3 r2.w, r2, r2
rsq r2.w, r2.w
mul r2, r2, r2.w
; N dot H
dp3 r0.y, r1, r2

; compute specular and clamp values (lit)
; r0.x - N dot L
; r0.y - N dot H
; r0.w - specular power n
mov r0.w, c[SPEC_POWER].y ; n must be between -128.0 and 128.0
lit r4, r0

; Scale the diffuse and specular intensity by the attenuation
mul r4, r4, r7.xxxx

; diffuse color * diffuse intensity (r4.y)
mul oD0, c[DIFFUSE_COLOR], r4.y

; specular color * specular intensity (r4.z)
mul oD1, c[SPEC_COLOR], r4.z
```

The lines, including the renormalization of the normal, should look quite familiar. The position of the vertex is then transformed to world space, which is used to calculate the light vector L in the following add instruction. L is renormalized in the following three instructions. It is important to note that this renormalization is used at the same time to get the parameters for the dst instruction. The following dp3 instruction performs the well-known diffuse reflection.

In the next paragraph, the dst, dp3, and rcp instructions calculate the attenuation factor with the formula already shown above:

$$\text{func}_{\text{Attenuation}} = 1 / A_0 + A_1 * d_L + A_2 * d_L * d_L$$

Therefore, dst gets distance * distance (squared distance) and 1 / distance via r10.w and r11.w. This instruction then performs the following calculation:

```
r4.x = 1
r4.y = d = d * d * 1 /d
r4.z = d * d
r4.w = 1 / d
```

In the next dp3 instruction, the dot product between the first three components of r4 and the attenuation constants is calculated:

```
; c[LIGHT_ATTENUATION].x = a0
; c[LIGHT_ATTENUATION].y = a1
; c[LIGHT_ATTENUATION].z = a2
```

```
dp3 r7.x, r4, c[LIGHT_ATTENUATION] ; (a0 + a1*d + a2* (d * d))
rcp r7.x, r7.x ; 1 / (a0 + a1*d + a2* (d * d))
```

The rcp instruction performs the following calculation:

```
if(src.w == 1.0f)
{
 dest.x = dest.y = dest.z = dest.w = 1.0f;
}
else if(src.w == 0)
{
 dest.x = dest.y = dest.z = dest.w = PLUS_INFINITY();
}
else
{
 dest.x = dest.y = dest.z = m_dest.w = 1.0f/src.w;
}
```

Therefore, the source value of src.w is divided through 1.0f if it is not 1.0f or 0.0f. This corresponds to the attenuation function postulated above.

The only thing left to get the point light effect is the component-wise multiplication of the attenuation factor with the diffuse and specular factors:

```
; Scale the diffuse and specular intensity by the attenuation
mul r4, r4, r7.xxxx
```

Summary

This example showed the implementation of a point light with a falloff model as used in the Direct3D fixed function pipeline. The light uses a combined diffuse and specular reflection model. To improve this example, an ambient light might be added and a number of point lights with different colors might be implemented.

What Happens Next?

This article covered basic lighting models and very basic transformations with vertex shaders. To read more on advanced transformations, see [Gosselin] and [Isidoro/Card].

The next article shows the fundamentals for using pixel shaders.

References

[Blinn] James F. Blinn and Martin E. Newell, "Texture and Reflection in Computer Generated Images," *Communications of the ACM* (1976), 19: 542-546.

[Foley] James D. Foley, Andries van Dam, Steven K. Feiner, and John F. Hughes, *Computer Graphics — Principles and Practice*, 2nd Ed. (Addison Wesley, 1996) pp. 728-731.

[Gosselin] David Gosselin, "Character Animation with Direct3D Vertex Shaders," *Direct3D ShaderX*.

[Haines/Möller] Eric Haines and Thomas Möller, "Normal Transforms," http://www.gignews.com/realtime020100.htm.

[Hurley] Kenneth Hurley, "Photorealistic Faces with Vertex and Pixel Shaders," *Direct3D ShaderX*.

[Isidoro/Card] John Isidoro and Drew Card, "Animated Grass with Pixel and Vertex Shaders," *Direct3D ShaderX*.

[RTR] Thomas Möller and Eric Haines, *Real-Time Rendering* (A. K. Peters, Ltd., 1999), p. 71.

[Savchenko] Sergei Savchenko, *3D Graphics Programming Games and Beyond* (SAMS, 2000), p. 266.

[Skinner] Michael Skinner, "Bézier Patches," http://www.gamedev.net/reference/articles/article1584.asp.

[Taylor] Philip Taylor, "Shader Optimization — Techniques to Write More Efficient Shaders," http://msdn.microsoft.com/directx.

[Turkowski] Ken Turkowski, "Properties of Surface-Normal Transformations," in Andrew Glassner (ed.), *Graphics Gems* (Academic Press, Inc., 1990), pp. 539-547, or http:/www.worldserver.com/turk/computergraphics/index.html.

Acknowledgments

I'd like to recognize the following individuals who were involved in proofreading and improving this article (in alphabetical order): David Callele (University of Saskatchewan) and Bart Sekura (People Can Fly).

Fundamentals of Pixel Shaders

Wolfgang F. Engel

The final output of any 3D graphics hardware consists of pixels. Depending on the resolution, in excess of 2 million pixels may need to be rendered, lit, shaded, and colored. Prior to DirectX 8.0, Direct3D used a fixed-function multitexture cascade for pixel processing. The effects possible with this approach were very limited, depending on the implementation of the graphics card device driver and the specific underlying hardware. A programmer was restricted on the graphic algorithms implemented by these.

With the introduction of shaders in DirectX 8.0 and the improvements of pixel shaders in DirectX 8.1, a whole new programming universe can be explored by game/demo coders. Pixel shaders are small programs that are executed on individual pixels. This is an unprecedented level of hardware control for their users.

This article shows you:

- The place and the tasks of pixel shaders in the Direct3D pipeline
- The architecture of the pixel shader unit
- Tools that help to program pixel shaders
- The ingredients for a pixel shader-driven application

The following article, "Programming Pixel Shaders," will present many pixel shader concepts and algorithms with example code.

Why Use Pixel Shaders?

Pixel shaders are, at the time of publication, supported by GeForce 3/4TI and RADEON 8500-based cards. Unlike vertex shaders, however, there is no feasible way to emulate pixel shaders using software.

The best argument for using pixel shaders is to take a look at a few demos that use them or one phrase: per-pixel non-standardized lighting. The gain in visual experience is enormous. You can use membrane shaders for balloons, skins, Kubelka-Munk shaders for translucency effects, fur/hair shaders, and new lighting formulas that lead to a totally new lighting experience. Think of a foreign planet with three moons moving faster than the two suns or with a planet surface consisting of different crystalline substances, reflecting light in different ways.

The following list should give you a glimpse of the many types of effects that are possible by using pixel shaders now:

- Single pass, per-pixel lighting (see the next section)
- True Phong shading [Beaudoin/Guardado]
- Anisotropic lighting [Isidoro/Brennan]
- Non-photorealistic rendering: cartoon shading, hatching, gooch lighting, image space techniques [Card/Mitchell]
- Per-pixel Fresnel term [Brennan]
- Volumetric effects [Kraus][Hart]
- Advanced bump mapping (self-shadowing bump maps, also known as horizon mapping)
- Procedural textures [Zecha] and texture perturbation [Isidoro/Riguer]
- Bidirectional reflectance distribution functions [Moravánsky]

There are also effects that have not yet been discovered or that are discovered but used only in scientific journals. These visual effects are waiting until they get implemented by you.

One of the biggest catches of pixel shaders is that they often have to be "driven" by the vertex shader. For example, to calculate per-pixel lighting, the pixel shader needs the orientation of the triangle, the orientation of the light vector, and, in some cases, the orientation of the view vector. The graphics pipeline shows the relationship between vertex and pixel shaders.

The diagram at right shows the DX6/7 multitexturing unit and the new pixel shader unit. On pixel shader-capable hardware, the pixel shader heightens the number of transistors on the graphic chip because it is added to the already existing DX 6/7 multitexturing hardware. Therefore, it is also functionally an independent unit that the developer can choose instead of the DX6/7 multitexturing unit.

But what happens in the 3D pipeline before the pixel shader?

A vertex leaves the vertex shader as a transformed and colored vertex. The so-called backface culling removes all triangles that are facing away from the viewer or camera. These are by default the vertices that are grouped counterclockwise. On average, half of your game world triangles will be facing away from the camera at any given time, so this helps reduce rendering time. A critical point is the usage of translucent or transparent front

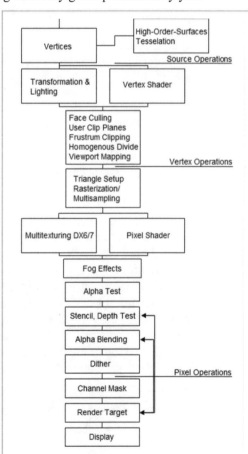

Figure1: Direct3D pipeline

triangles. Depending on what is going to be rendered, backface culling can be switched off with the D3DCULL_NONE flag.

Note: Backface culling uses the crossproduct of two sides of a triangle to calculate a vector that is perpendicular to the plane that is formed by these two sides. This vector is the face normal. The direction of this normal determines whether the triangle is front- or backfacing. Because the Direct3D API always uses the same vertex order to calculate the crossproduct, it is known whether a triangle's vertices are "wound" clockwise or counterclockwise.

Pixel Shaders in the Pipeline

User clip planes can be set by the developer, with the help of the graphics card, to clip triangles that are outside of these planes and thus reduce the number of calculations. How to set user clip planes is shown in the Direct3D 8.1 clip mirror example and in the ATI RADEON 8500 nature demo. The RADEON and RADEON 8500 support six independent user clip planes in hardware. The clip planes on the GeForce 1/2/3/4TI chips are implemented using texture stages. That means that using two user clip planes eats up one texture stage.

Note: It looks like NVIDIA no longer exposes the cap bits for these. The DirectX Caps Viewer reports MaxUserClipPlanes == 0 since the release of the 12.41 drivers.

One alternative to clip planes is shown in the TexKillClipPlanes example in the NVIDIA Effects Browser, where the pixel shader instruction texkill is used to get a functionality similar to clip planes.

Another alternative to clip planes is guard band clipping as supported by GeForce hardware [Dietrich01]. The basic idea of guard band clipping is that hardware with a guard band region can accept triangles that are partially or totally off-screen, thus avoiding expensive clipping work. There are four cap fields for guard band support in the D3DCAPS8 structure: GuardBandLeft, GuardBandRight, GuardBandTop, and GuardBandBottom. These represent the boundaries of the guard band. These values have to be used in the clipping code. Guard band clipping is handled automatically by switching on clipping in Direct3D.

Frustum clipping is performed on the viewing frustum. Primitives that lie partially or totally off-screen must be clipped to the screen or viewport boundary, which is represented by a 3D viewing frustum. The viewing frustum can be visualized as a pyramid, with the camera positioned at the tip. The view volume defines what the camera will see and won't see. The entire scene must fit between the new and far clipping planes and also be bounded by the sides, bottom, and top of the frustum. A given object in relation to the viewing frustum can fall into one of three categories [Watt92]:

- The object lies completely outside the viewing area, in which case it is discarded.
- The object lies completely inside the viewing frustum, in which case it is passed on to the homogenous divide.
- The object intersects the viewing frustum, in which case it is clipped against it and then passed on to the homogenous divide.

Translating the definition of the viewing frustrum above into homogenous coordinates gives us the clipping limits:

```
-w <= x <= w
-w <= y <= w
 0 <= z <= w
```

This would be a slow process if it had to be done by the CPU because each edge of each triangle that crosses the viewport boundary must have an intersection point calculated, and each parameter of the vertex (x,y,z diffuse r,g,b, specular r,g,b, alpha, fog, u, and v) must be interpolated accordingly. Therefore, frustum clipping is done by modern graphics hardware on the GPU essentially for free with clip planes and guard band clipping.

After frustum clipping, the homogenous or perspective divide happens. This means that the x-, y-, and z-coordinates of each vertex of the homogenous coordinates are divided by w. The perspective divide makes nearer objects larger and farther objects smaller, as you would expect when viewing a scene in reality. After this division, the coordinates are in a normalized space:

```
-1 <= x/w <= 1
-1 <= y/w <= 1
 0 <= z/w <= 1
```

Note: Why do we need this divide through w? By definition, every point gets a fourth component w that measures distance along an imaginary fourth-dimensional axis called w. For example, (4, 2, 8, 2) represents the same point as (2, 1, 4, 1). Such a w-value is useful, for example, to translate an object because a 3x3 matrix is not able to translate an object without changing its orientation. The fourth coordinate, w, can be thought of as carrying the perspective information necessary to represent a perspective transformation.

Clip coordinates are also referred to as normalized device coordinates (NDC). These coordinates are now mapped to the screen by transforming into screen space via the so-called viewport mapping. To map these NDCs to screen space, the following formula is used for a resolution of 1024x768:

```
ScreenX(max) = NDC(X) * 512 + 512
ScreenY(max) = NDC(Y) * 384 + 384
```

The minimum and maximum value of X and Y is (–1, –1) to (1, 1). When the NDCs is (–1, –1), the screen coordinates are:

```
ScreenX = -1 * 512 + 512
ScreenY = -1 * 384 + 384
```

This point lies in the upper-left corner. For example, the lower-right corner will be reached with NDCs of (1, 1). Although z and w values are retained for depth buffering tests, screen space is essentially a 2D coordinate system, so only x and y values need to be mapped to screen resolution.

Now comes the triangle setup, where the life of the vertices end and the life of the pixel begins. It computes, triangle for triangle, the parameters required for the rasterization of the triangles; among other things, it defines the pixel-coordinates of the triangle outline. This means that it defines the first and the last pixel of the triangle scan line by scan line (see Figure 2):

Then the rasterizer interpolates color and depth values for each pixel from the color and depth values of the vertices. These values are interpolated using a weighted average of the color and depth values of the edge's vertex values, where the color and depth data of edge pixels closer to a given vertex more closely approximate values for that vertex. Then the rasterizer fills in pixels for each line.

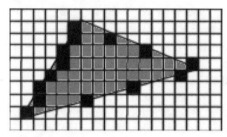 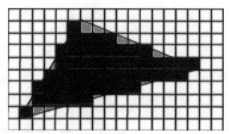

Figure 2: Triangle setup   *Figure 3: Filled triangle*

In addition, the texture coordinates are interpolated for use during the multitexturing/pixel shader stage in a similar way.

The rasterizer is also responsible for Direct3D multisampling. Because it is done in the rasterizer stage, multisampling only affects triangles and groups of triangles, not lines. It increases the resolution of polygon edges and, therefore, depth and stencil tests as well. The RADEON 7x00/GeForce 3 supports this kind of spatial anti-aliasing by setting the D3DRAS-TERCAPS_STRECHBLTMULTISAMPLE flag, but both ignore the D3DRS_MULTI-SAMPLEMASK render state to control rendering into the sub-pixel samples, whereas the RADEON 8500 is able to mask the sub-samples with a different bit pattern by using this render state. By affecting only specific sub-samples, effects like motion blur or depth of field and others can be realized.

 Note: Alternatively, motion blur and depth of field effects are possible with the help of vertex and pixel shaders; see the NVIDIA examples in the Effects Browser.

 Note: GeForce 3/4TI, RADEON 7x00, and RADEON 8500 chips have another stage in-between the triangle setup and the pixel shader. Both chips have a visibility subsystem that is responsible for z occlusion culling. In the case of ATI cards, it is called hierarchi-cal-Z. It determines if a pixel will be hidden behind a pixel rendered earlier or not. If the z occlusion culling should determine that the pixel is hidden, it will directly be discarded and it won't enter the pixel shader, thus saving the initial z-buffer read of the pixel-rendering pipeline. During scan line conversion, the screen is divided into 8x8 pixel blocks (RADEON 7x00) or 4x4 pixel blocks (RADEON 8500), and each block is assigned a bit that determines whether that block is "not cleared," meaning visible, or "cleared," meaning occluded. A quick z-check is performed on each of these blocks to determine whether any pixels in them are visible. If a pixel in a block is visible, the status bit is flipped to visible and the new z-value for that pixel is written to the z-buffer. If the block is not visible, its status bit remains set to occluded and the z-buffer isn't touched. The whole block will not be sent to the pixel shader.

Sorting objects or object groups from front to back when rendering helps z-culling to kick out pixels from the graphics pipeline very early, saving not only a write into the z-buffer (as with texkill) but also a read of the z-buffer.

The pixel shader is not involved on the sub-pixel level. It gets the already multisampled pixels along with z, color values, and texture information. The already Gouraud-shaded or flat-shaded pixel might be combined in the pixel shader with the specular color and the texture values fetched from the texture map. For this task, the pixel shader provides instructions that affect the texture addressing and instructions to combine the texture values in different ways with each other.

There are five different pixel shader standards supported by Direct3D 8.1. Currently, no pixel shader-capable graphics hardware is restricted on the support of ps.1.0. Therefore, all available hardware supports at least ps.1.1. I will not mention the legacy ps.1.0 again. ps.1.1 is the pixel shader version that is supported by GeForce 3. GeForce 4TI additionally supports ps.1.2 and ps.1.3. The RADEON 8x00 supports all of these pixel shader versions, plus ps.1.4.

Whereas the ps.1.1, ps.1.2, and ps.1.3 are, from a syntactical point of view, built on each other, ps.1.4 is a new and more flexible approach. ps.1.1-ps.1.3 differentiate between texture address operation instructions and texture blending instructions. As the name implies, the first kind of instructions is specialized and only usable for address calculations, and the second kind of instructions is specialized and only usable for color shading operations. ps.1.4 simplifies the pixel shader language by allowing the texture blending (color shader) instruction set to be used for texture address (address shader) operations as well. It differentiates between arithmetic instructions that modify color data and texture address instructions that process texture coordinate data and, in most cases, sample a texture.

Note: Sampling means looking up a color value in a texture at the specified coordinates (up to four) (u, v, w, q) while taking into account the texture stage state attributes.

One might say that the usage of the instructions in ps.1.4 happens in a more RISC-like manner, whereas the ps.1.1-ps.1.3 instruction sets are only usable in a CISC-like manner.

This RISC-like approach will be used in ps.2.0 that will appear in DirectX 9. Syntactically, ps.1.4 is compared to ps.1.1-ps.1.3, an evolutionary step into the direction of ps.2.0.

What are the other benefits of using ps.1.4?

- Unlimited texture address instructions: Direct3D 8.0 with ps.1.1 is restricted to a small number of meaningful ways in which textures can be addressed. Direct3D 8.1 with ps.1.4 allows textures to be addressed and sampled in a virtually unlimited number of ways because the arithmetic operation instructions are also usable as texture address operation instructions.
- Flexible dependent texture reads.
- RADEON 8x00 performs ps.1.4 faster than ps.1.1-ps.1.3 because the latter is emulated.
- All of the upcoming graphics hardware that will support ps.2.0 will support ps.1.4 for backward compatibility.

The next stage in the Direct3D pipeline is *fog*. A fog factor is computed and applied to the pixel using a blending operation to combine the fog amount (color) and the already shaded pixel color, depending on how far away an object is. The distance to an object is determined by its z- or w-value or by using a separate attenuation value that measures the distance between the camera and the object in a vertex shader. If fog is computed per-vertex, it is interpolated across each triangle using Gouraud shading. The MFC Fog example in the DirectX 8.1 SDK shows linear and exponential fog calculated per-vertex and per-pixel. A layered range-based fog is shown in the height fog example in the NVIDIA Effects Browser. The volume fog example in the DirectX 8.1 SDK shows volumetric fog produced with a vertex and a pixel shader and the alpha blending pipeline. As shown in these examples, fog effects can be driven by the vertex and/or pixel shader.

The *alpha test* stage kicks out pixels with a specific alpha value because these shouldn't be visible. This is, for example, one way to map decals with an alpha-mapped texture. The alpha test is switched on with D3DRS_ALPHATESTENABLE. The incoming alpha value is compared with the reference alpha value, using the comparison function provided by the D3DRS_ALPHAFUNC render state. If the pixel passes the test, it will be processed by the subsequent pixel operation; otherwise, it will be discarded.

Alpha testing does not incur any extra overhead, even if all the pixels pass the test. By tuning the reference value of alpha test appropriately to reject the transparent or almost transparent pixels, one can improve the application performance significantly if the application is memory bandwidth fill-bound. Basically, varying the reference value acts like a threshold, setting up how many pixels are going to be evicted. The more pixels being discarded, the faster the application will run.

There is a trick to drive the alpha test with a pixel shader, which is shown in the section on swizzling. The image space outlining technique in [Card/Mitchell] uses alpha testing to reject pixels that are not outlines and consequently improve performance.

The *stencil test* masks the pixel in the render target with the contents of the stencil buffer. This is useful for dissolves, decaling, outlining, or building shadow volumes [Brennan]. See the RadeonShadowShader example on the ATI web site.

The *depth test* determines whether a pixel is visible by comparing its depth value to the stored depth value. An application can set up its z-buffer, z-min, and z-max with positive z going away from the view camera in a left-handed coordinate system. The depth test is a pixel-by-pixel logical test that asks "Is this pixel in back of another pixel at this location?" If the answer is yes, that pixel gets discarded; if the answer is no, that pixel will travel further through the pipeline, and the z-buffer is updated. There is also a more precise and bandwidth-saving depth buffer form called w-buffer. It saves bandwidth by having only to send x-, y-, and z-coordinates over the bus, while the z-buffer in certain circumstances has to send all that plus z.

Note: This is the only depth buffering method used by the Savage 2000-based boards. These cards emulate the z-buffer with the help of the hardware w-buffer.

When using vertex shaders with w-buffering on a GeForce 3/4TI card, make sure the projection matrix is set in the traditional way (using SetTransform()); otherwise, w-buffering won't work correctly. (Read more in the GeForce 3 FAQ, which can be found at www.nvidia.com/developer.)

The pixel shader is able to "drive" the depth test with the texdepth (ps.1.4 only) or the texm3x2depth (ps.1.3 only) instructions. These instructions can calculate the depth value used in the depth buffer comparison test on a per-pixel basis.

The *alpha blending* stage blends the pixel's data with the pixel data already in the render target. The blending happens with the following formula:

```
FinalColor = SourcePixelColor * SourceBlendFactor +
             DestPixelColor * DestBlendFactor
```

There are different flags that can be set with the D3DRS_SRCBLEND (SourceBlendFactor) and D3DRS_DESTBLEND (DestBlendFactor) parameters in a SetRenderState() call. Alpha blending was formerly used to blend different texture values together, but today it is more efficient to do that with the multitexturing or pixel shader unit, depending on hardware support. Alpha blending is used on newer hardware to simulate different levels of transparency.

Dithering tries to fool the eye into seeing more colors than are actually present by placing different colored pixels next to one another to create a composite color that the eye will see. For example, using a blue pixel next to a yellow pixel would lead to a green appearance. That was a common technique in the days of the 8-bit and 4-bit color systems. You switch on the dithering stage globally with D3DRS_DITHERENABLE.

The *render target* is normally the backbuffer in which you render the finished scene, but it could also be the surface of a texture. This is useful for the creation of procedural textures or for reusing results of former pixel shader executions. The render target is read by the stencil test, depth test, and alpha blending stages.

To summarize the tasks of the pixel shader in the Direct3D pipeline:

- The pixel shader is fed with rasterized pixels, which means, in most cases, z-occlusion culled, multisampled, and already Gouraud-shaded pixels.

- The pixel shader receives an interpolated texture coordinate and interpolated diffuse and specular colors.

- There are mainly four flavors of pixel shaders. The ps.1.1-ps.1.3 standards are, from a syntactical point of view, a more CISC-like approach, whereas the ps.1.4 standard uses a RISC-like approach that will also be used in the upcoming ps.2.0.

- The pixel shader delivers the shaded pixel to the fog stage.

- The pixel shader is able to support or drive the consecutive Direct3D stages.

Before getting our feet wet with a first look at the pixel shader architecture, let's take a look at the currently available tools.

Pixel Shader Tools

I already introduced Shader Studio, Shader City, DLL Detective, 3D Studio Max 4.x/gmax, NVASM, the Effects Browser, the Shader Debugger, and the Photoshop plug-ins from NVIDIA in "Fundamentals of Vertex Shaders." There is one thing to remember specifically for pixel shaders: Because the GeForce 4TI supports ps.1.1-ps.1.3, it is possible that a few of the NVIDIA tools won't support ps.1.4. Additionally, there are the following pixel shader-only tools.

Microsoft Pixel Shader Assembler

The pixel shader assembler is provided with the DirectX 8.1 SDK. Like with the vertex shader assembler, it does not come with any documentation. Its output look like Figure 4 on the following page.

The pixel shader assembler is used by the Direct3DX functions that compile pixel shaders and can also be used to precompile pixel shaders.

```
C:\DXSDK\bin\DXUtils>psa.exe
Microsoft (R) Direct3D8 Pixel Shader Assembler
Copyright (C) Microsoft Corp 2000. All rights reserved.

usage: psa.exe -hp012 <files>

   -h : Generate .h files (instead of .pso files)
   -p : Use C preprocessor (VisualC++ required)

   -0 : Debug info omitted, no shader validation performed
   -1 : Debug info inserted, no shader validation performed
   -2 : Debug info inserted, shader validation performed. (default)
```

Figure 4: Pixel shader assembler output

MFC Pixel Shader

The MFC pixel shader example provided with the DirectX 8.1 SDK comes with source. It is very useful for quickly trying out pixel shader effects and debugging them. Just type in the pixel shader syntax you want to test, and it will compile at once. Debugging information is provided in the window at the bottom. If your graphics card doesn't support a particular pixel shader version, you can always choose the reference rasterizer and test all desired pixel shader versions. In the figure shown at right, the reference rasterizer was chosen on a GeForce 3 to simulate ps.1.3.

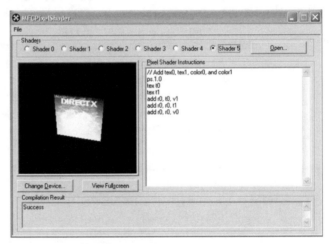

Figure 5: MFC pixel shader

ATI ShadeLab

The ATI ShadeLab helps with designing pixel shaders. After writing the pixel shader source into the entry field in the middle, the compilation process starts immediately. To be able to load the pixel shader later, it has to be saved with the Save button and loaded with the Load button.

You may set up to six textures with specific texture coordinates and the eight constant registers. The main advantage

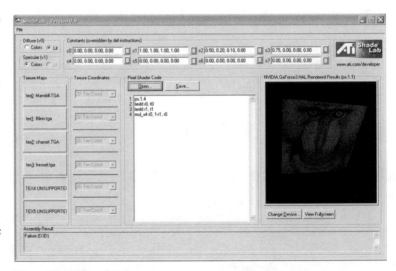

Figure 6: ATI ShadeLab

over the MFC pixel shader tool is the ability to load constant registers and textures on your own. This tool is provided on the companion CD in the Tools directory.

With that overview on the available tools in mind, we can go one step further by examining a diagram with the pixel shader workflow.

Pixel Shader Architecture

The diagram shows the logical pixel shader data workflow. The shaded field at the top left marks functionality specific for ps.1.1-ps.1.3. The shaded field at the bottom left marks functionality that is specific to ps.1.4.

On the right half of the diagram, the pixel shader arithmetic logic unit (ALU) is surrounded by four kinds of registers. The color registers stream iterates vertex color data from a vertex shader or a

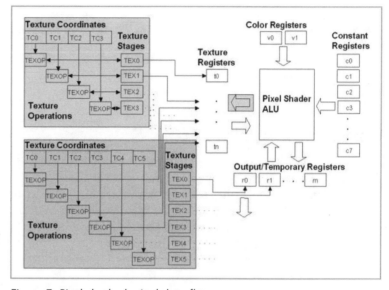

Figure 7: Pixel shader logical data flow

fixed-function vertex pipeline to a pixel shader. The constant registers provide constants to the shader that are loaded by using the SetPixelShaderConstant() function or in the pixel shader with the def instruction. The *temporary registers* rn are able to store temporary data. The r0 register also serves as the *output* register of the pixel shader.

The *texture coordinates* can be supplied as part of the vertex format or can be read from certain kinds of texture maps. Texture coordinates are full precision and range, as well as perspective correct, when used in a pixel shader. There are D3DTSS_* *texture operations* that are not replaced by the pixel shader functionality; they can be used on the textures (up to four for ps.1.1-ps.1.3 or up to six for ps.1.4). The *texture stages* hold a reference to the texture data that might be a one-dimensional (for example, in a cartoon shader), two-dimensional, or three-dimensional texture (volume textures or cube map). Each value in a texture is called a texel. These texels are most commonly used to store color values, but they can contain any kind of data desired including normal vectors for bump maps, shadow values, or general loopup tables.

Sampling occurs when a texture coordinate is used to address the texel data at a particular location with the help of the *texture registers*. The usage of the texture registers tn differ between the ps.1.1-ps.1.3 (t0-t3) and the ps.1.4 (t0-t5) implementations.

With ps.1.1-ps.1.3, the association between the texture coordinate set and the texture data is a one-to-one mapping, which is not changeable in the pixel shader. Instead this association can be changed by using the oT*n* registers in a vertex shader or by using the texture stage state flag TSS_TEXCOORDINDEX together with SetTextureStageState(), in case the fixed-function pipeline is used.

In ps.1.4, the texture data and the texture coordinate set can be used independent of each other in a pixel shader. The texture stage from which to sample the texture data is determined by the register number r*n*, and the texture coordinate set that should be used for the texture data is determined by the number of the t*n* register specified.

Let's take a closer look at the different registers shown in Figure 7:

Type	Name	ps.1.1	ps.1.2	ps.1.3	ps.1.4	Read/Write Caps
Constant Registers	c_n	8	8	8	8	RO
Texture Registers	t_n	4	4	4	6	RW / ps.1.4: RO
Temporary Registers	r_n	2	2	2	6	RW
Color Registers	v_n	2	2	2	2 in Phase 2	RO

Constant Registers (c0-c7)

There are eight constant registers in every pixel shader specification. Every constant register contains four floating-point values or channels. They are read only from the perspective of the pixel shader, so they could be used as a source register but never as destination registers in the pixel shader. The application can write and read constant registers with calls to SetPixelShaderContant() and GetPixelShaderConstant(). A def instruction used in the pixel shader to load a constant register is effectively translated into a SetPixelShaderConstant() call by executing SetPixelShader().

The range of the constant registers goes from −1 to +1. If you pass anything outside of this range, it just gets clamped. Constant registers are not usable by ps.1.1-ps.1.3 texture address instructions except for texm3x3spec, which uses a constant register to get an eye-ray vector.

Output and Temporary Registers (ps.1.1-ps.1.3: r0+r1; ps.1.4: r0-r5)

The temporary registers r0-r*n* are used to store intermediate results. The output register r0 is the destination argument for the pixel shader instruction, so r0 is able to serve as a temporary and output register. In ps.1.4, r0-r5 are also used to sample texture data from the texture stages 0-5 in conjunction with the texture registers. In ps.1.1-ps.1.3, the temporary registers are not usable by texture address instructions.

CreatePixelShader() will fail in shader preprocessing if a shader attempts to read from a temporary register that has not been written to by a previous instruction. All shaders have to write to r0.rgba the final result, or the shader will not assemble or validate.

Texture Registers (ps.1.1-ps.1.3: t0-t3; ps.1.4: t0-t5)

The texture registers are used in different ways in ps.1.1-ps.1.3 and in ps.1.4. In ps.1.1-ps.1.3, the usage of one of the t0-t3 texture registers determines the usage of a specific pair of texture data and texture coordinates. You can't change this one-to-one mapping in the pixel shader:

```
ps.1.1            // version instruction
tex t0            // samples the texture at stage 0
                  // using texture coordinates from stage 0
mov r0, t0        // copies the color in t0 to output register r0
```

tex samples the texture data from the texture stage 0 and uses the texture coordinates set that is set in the vertex shader with the oT*n* registers. In ps.1.4, having texture coordinates in their own registers means that the texture coordinate set and the texture data are independent from each other. The texture stage number with the texture data from which to sample is determined by the destination register number (r0-r5) and the texture coordinate set is determined by the source register (t0-t5) specified in phase 1.

```
ps.1.4 // version instruction
texld r4, t5
mov r0, r4
```

The texld instruction samples the map set via SetTexture (4, lpTexture) using the sixth set of texture coordinates (set in the vertex shader with oT5) and puts the result into the fifth temporary register *r4*.

Texture registers that don't hold any values will be sampled to opaque black (0.0, 0.0, 0.0, 1.0). They can be used as temporary registers in ps.1.1-ps.1.3. The texture coordinate registers in ps.1.4 are read only and, therefore, not usable as temporary registers. The maximum number of textures is the same as the maximum number of simultaneous textures supported (MaxSimultaneousTextures flag in D3D8CAPS).

Color Registers (ps.1.1-ps.1.4: v0+v1)

The color registers can contain per-vertex color values in the range 0 through 1 (saturated). It is common to load v0 with the vertex diffuse color and v1 with the specular color.

> **Note:** Using a constant color (flat shading) is more efficient than using a per-pixel Gouraud-shaded vertex color. If the shade mode is set to D3DSHADE_FLAT, the application iteration of both vertex colors (diffuse and specular) is disabled. Regardless of the shade mode, fog will still be iterated later in the pipeline.

Pixel shaders have read-only access to color registers. In ps.1.4, color registers are only available during the second phase, which is the default phase. All of the other registers are available in each of the two phases of ps.1.4.

Range

One reason for using pixel shaders is that, compared to the multitexturing unit, its higher precision is used by the pixel shader arithmetic logic unit.

Register Name	Range	Versions
cn	–1 to +1	all versions
rn	–D3DCAPS8.MaxPixelShaderValue to D3DCAPS8.MaxPixelShaderValue	all versions

Register Name	Range	Versions
tn	–D3DCAPS8.MaxPixelShaderValue to D3DCAPS8.MaxPixelShaderValue	ps.1.1-ps.1.3
	–D3DCAPS8.MaxTextureRepeat to D3DCAPS8.MaxTextureRepeat	ps.1.4
vn	0 to +1	all versions

The color register vn is 8-bit precision per channel (i.e., 8-bit red, 8-bit green, etc.). For ps.1.1 to ps.1.3, D3DCAPS8.MaxPixelShaderValue is a minimum of one, whereas in ps.1.4, D3DCAPS8.MaxPixelShaderValue is a minimum of eight. The texture coordinate registers provided by ps.1.4 use high-precision signed interpolators. The DirectX caps viewer reports a MaxTextureRepeat value of 2048 for the RADEON 8500. This value will be clamped to MaxPixelShaderValue when used with texcrd because of the usage of an rn register as the destination register. In this case, it is safest to stick with source coordinates within the Max-PixelShaderValue range. However, if tn registers are used for straight texture lookups (i.e., texld r0, t3), then the MaxTextureRepeat range should be expected to be honored by hardware.

Using textures to store color values leads to much higher color precision with ps.1.4.

High-Level View of Pixel Shader Programming

Pixel shading takes place on a per-pixel, per-object basis during a rendering pass.

Let's start by focusing on the steps required to build a pixel shader-driven application. The following list, in the sequence of execution, shows the necessary steps to build a pixel shader-driven application:

- Check for pixel shader support.
- Set texture operation flags (with D3DTSS_* flags).
- Set texture (with SetTexture()).
- Define constants (with SetPixelShaderConstant()/def).
- Pixel shader instructions.
  - Texture address instructions
  - Arithmetic instructions
- Assemble pixel shader.
- Create pixel shader.
- Set pixel shader.
- Free pixel shader resources.

The following text will work through this list step by step.

Check for Pixel Shader Support

It is important to check for the proper pixel shader support because there is no feasible way to emulate pixel shaders. If there is no pixel shader support or the required pixel shader version is not supported, there have to be fallback methods to a default behavior (i.e., the multitexturing unit or ps.1.1). The following statement checks the supported pixel shader version:

```
if( pCaps->PixelShaderVersion < D3DPS_VERSION(1,1) )
        return E_FAIL;
```

This example checks the support of the pixel shader version 1.1. The support of at least ps.1.4 in hardware might be checked with D3DPS_VERSION(1,4). The D3DCAPS structure has to be filled in the startup phase of the application with a call to GetDeviceCaps(). If the common files framework, which is provided with the DirectX 8.1 SDK, is used, this is done by the framework. If your graphics card does not support the requested pixel shader version and there is no fallback mechanism that switches to the multitexturing unit, the reference rasterizer will jump in. This is the default behavior of the common files framework, but it is not useful in a game because the REF is too slow.

Set Texture Operation Flags (D3DTSS_* flags)

The pixel shader functionality replaces the D3DTSS_COLOROP and D3DTSS_ALPHAOP operations and their associated arguments and modifiers that were used with the fixed-function pipeline. For example, the following four SetTextureStageState() calls could be handled now by the pixel shader:

```
m_pd3dDevice->SetTextureStageState( 0, D3DTSS_COLORARG1, D3DTA_TEXTURE );
m_pd3dDevice->SetTextureStageState( 0, D3DTSS_COLORARG2, D3DTA_DIFFUSE);
m_pd3dDevice->SetTextureStageState( 0, D3DTSS_COLOROP, D3DTOP_MODULATE);
m_pd3dDevice->SetTexture( 0, m_pWallTexture);
```

The following texture stage states are still observed:

```
D3DTSS_ADDRESSU
D3DTSS_ADDRESSV
D3DTSS_ADDRESSW
D3DTSS_BUMPENVMAT00
D3DTSS_BUMPENVMAT01
D3DTSS_BUMPENVMAT10
D3DTSS_BUMPENVMAT11
D3DTSS_BORDERCOLOR
D3DTSS_MAGFILTER
D3DTSS_MINFILTER
D3DTSS_MIPFILTER
D3DTSS_MIPMAPLODBIAS
D3DTSS_MAXMIPLEVEL
D3DTSS_MAXANISOTROPY
D3DTSS_BUMPENVLSCALE
D3DTSS_BUMPENVLOFFSET
D3DTSS_TEXCOORDINDEX
D3DTSS_TEXTURETRANSFORMFLAGS
```

The D3DTSS_BUMP* states are used with the bem, texbem, and texbeml instructions.

In ps.1.1-ps.1.3, all D3DTSS_TEXTURETRANSFORMFLAGS flags are available and have to be property set for a projective divide, whereas in ps.1.4, the texture transform flag D3DTTFF_PROJECTED is ignored. It is accomplished by using source register modifiers with the texld and texcrd registers.

The D3DTSS_TEXCOORDINDEX flag is valid only for fixed-function vertex processing. When rendering with vertex shaders, each stage's texture coordinate index must be set to its default value. The default index for each stage is equal to the stage index.

ps.1.4 gives you the ability to change the association of the texture coordinates and the textures in the pixel shader. The texture wrapping, filtering, color border, and mip mapping flags are fully functional in conjunction with pixel shaders.

Note: A change to these texture stage states doesn't require the regeneration of the currently bound shader because they are not available to the shader at compile time, and the driver can therefore make no assumption about them.

Set Texture (with SetTexture())

After checking the pixel shader support and setting the proper texture operation flags, all textures have to be set by SetTexture(), as with the DX6/7 multitexturing unit. The prototype of this call is:

```
HRESULT SetTexture(DWORD Stage, IDirect3DBaseTexture8* pTexture);
```

The texture stage that should be used by the texture is provided in the first parameter, and the pointer to the texture interface is provided in the second parameter. A typical call might look like this:

```
m_pd3dDevice->SetTexture( 0, m_pWallTexture);
```

This call sets the already loaded and created wall texture to texture stage 0.

Define Constants (with SetPixelShaderConstant()/def)

The constant registers can be filled with SetPixelShaderConstant() or the def instruction in the pixel shader. Similar to the SetVertexShaderConstant() call, the prototype of the pixel shader equivalent looks like this:

```
HRESULT SetPixelShaderConstant(
  DWORD Register,
  CONST void* pConstantData,
  DWORD ConstantCount
  );
```

First the constant register must be specified in Register. The data to transfer into the constant register is provided in the second argument as a pointer. The number of constant registers that have to be filled is provided in the last parameter. For example, to fill c0-c4, you might provide c0 as the Register and 4 as the ConstantCount.

The def instruction is an alternative to SetPixelShaderConstant(). When SetPixelShader() is called, it is effectively translated into a SetPixelShaderConstant() call. Using the def instruction makes the pixel shader easier to read. A def instruction in the pixel shader might look like this:

```
def c0, 0.30, 0.59, 0.11, 1.0
```

Each value of the constant source registers has to be in the range [–1.0..1.0].

Pixel Shader Instructions

Using vertex shaders, the programmer is free to choose the order of the used instructions in any way that makes sense, whereas pixel shaders need a specific arrangement of the used instructions. This specific instruction flow differs between ps.1.1-ps.1.3 and ps.1.4.

ps.1.1-ps.1.3 allow four types of instructions that must appear in the order shown in Figure 8.

This example shows a per-pixel specular lighting model that evaluates the specular power with a lookup table. Every pixel shader starts with the version instruction. It is used by the assembler to validate the instructions that follow. Below the version instruction, a constant definition could be placed with def. Such a def instruction is translated into a SetPixelShaderConstant() call when SetPixelShader() is executed.

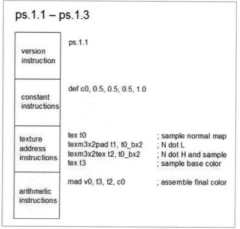

Figure 8: ps.1.1-ps.1.3 pixel shader instruction flow (specular lighting with lookup table)

The next group of instructions are the so-called texture address instructions. They are used to load data from the *tn* registers and, in ps.1.1-ps.1.3, to modify texture coordinates. Up to four texture address instructions could be used in a ps.1.1-ps.1.3 pixel shader.

In this example, the tex instruction is used to sample the normal map that holds the normal data. There must always be at least two texm* instructions:

```
texm3x2pad t1, t0_bx2
texm3x2tex t2, t0_bx2
```

Both instructions calculate the proper u/v texture coordinate pair with the help of the normal map in t0 and sample the texture data from t2 with it. This texture register holds the light map data with the specular power values. The last texture addressing instruction samples the color map into t3.

The next type of instructions are the arithmetic instructions. There could be up to eight arithmetic instructions in a pixel shader.

mad adds t2 and c0, the ambient light, multiplies the result with t3, and stores it into the output register r0.

Instructions in a ps.1.4 pixel shader must appear in the order shown in Figure 9.

This is a simple transfer function, which could be useful for sepia or heat signature effects. It is explained in detail in [Mitchell]. The

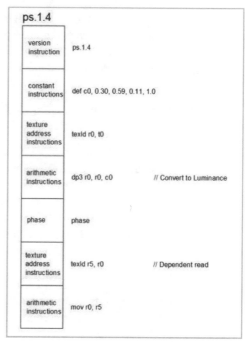

Figure 9: ps.1.4 pixel shader instruction flow (simple transfer function for sepia or heat signature effects)

ps.1.4 pixel shader instruction flow has to start with the version instruction ps.1.4. After that, as many def instructions as needed might be placed into the pixel shader code. This example sets a luminance constant value with one def.

There could be up to six texture addressing instructions used after the constants. The texld instruction loads a texture from texture stage 0 with the help of the texture coordinate pair 0, which is chosen by using t0. In the following arithmetic instructions (up to eight), color, texture, or vector data might be modified. This shader uses only the arithmetic instruction to convert the texture map values to luminance values.

So far, a ps.1.4 pixel shader has the same instruction flow as a ps.1.1-ps.1.3 pixel shader, but the phase instruction allows it to double the number of texture addressing and arithmetic instructions. It divides the pixel shader into two phases: phase 1 and phase 2. That means that as of ps.1.4, a second pass through the pixel shader hardware can be done.

Note: Another way to reuse the result of a former pixel shader pass is to render into a texture and use this texture in the next pixel shader pass. This is accomplished by rendering into a separate render target.

The additional six texture addressing instruction slots after the phase instruction are only used by the texld r5, r0 instruction. This instruction uses the color in r0, which was converted to luminance values before as a texture coordinate to sample a 1D texture (sepia or heat signature map), which is referenced by r5. The result is moved with a mov instruction into the output register r0.

Adding up the number of arithmetic and addressing instructions shown in the pixel shader instruction flow in Figure 9 leads to 28 instructions. If no phase marker is specified, the default phase 2 allows up to 14 addressing and arithmetic instructions.

Both of the preceding examples show the ability to use dependent reads. A dependent read is a read from a texture map using a texture coordinate that was calculated earlier in the pixel shader. More details on dependent reads will be presented in the next section.

Texture Address Instructions

Texture address instructions are used on texture coordinates. The texture coordinate address is used to sample data from a texture map. Controlling the u/v pair, u/v/w triplet, or u/v/w/q quadruplet of texture coordinates with address operations gives the ability to choose different areas of a texture map. Texture coordinate "data storage space" can also be used for other reasons than sampling texture data. The registers that reference texture coordinate data are useful to "transport" any kind of data from the vertex shader to the pixel shader via the oT*n* registers of a vertex shader. For example, the light or half-angle vector or a 3x2, 3x3, or 4x4 matrix might be provided to the pixel shader this way.

ps.1.1-ps.1.3 Texture Addressing

The following diagram shows the ways that texture address instructions work in ps.1.1-ps.1.3 for texture addressing:

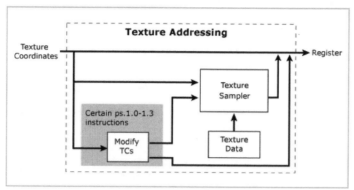

All of the texture addressing happens "encapsulated" in the texture address instructions masked with a gray field. That means results of texture coordinate calculations are not accessible in the pixel shader. The texture address instruction uses these results internally to sample the texture. The only way to get access to texture coordinates in the pixel shader is to use the texcoord instruction. This instruction converts texture coordinate data to color values so that they can be manipulated by texture addressing or arithmetic instructions. These color values could be used as texture coordinates to sample a texture with the help of the texreg2* instructions.

The following instructions are texture address instructions in ps.1.1-ps.1.3. The *d* and *s* in the Para column are the destination and source parameters of the instruction. The usage of texture coordinates is shown by parentheses around the texture register, (t0)for example.

Instruction	1.1	1.2	1.3	Para	Action
tex	x	x	x	d	Loads *tn* with color data (RGBA) sampled from the texture.

texbem	x	x	x	d, s	Transforms red and green components as du, dv signed values of the source register using a 2D bump mapping matrix to modify the texture address of the destination register.
					
					Can be used for a variety of techniques based on address perturbation such as fake per-pixel environment mapping, diffuse lighting (bump mapping), environment matting, etc.
					
					There is a difference in the usage of the texture stages between environment mapping with a pixel shader (texbem, texbeml, or bem) and environment mapping with the DX 6/7 multitexturing unit. texbem (texbeml or bem) needs the matrix data connected to the texture stage that is sampled. This is the environment map. Environment mapping with the DX 6/7 multitexturing unit needs the matrix data connected to the texture stage used by the bump map (see also the example program Earth Bump on the companion CD):
					
					------------------ 	
					`// texture stages for environment mapping`
					`// with a pixel shader:`
					`SetRenderState(D3DRS_WRAP0,D3DWRAP_U|D3DWRAP_V);`
					`// color mapSetTexture( 0, m_pEarthTexture );`
					`SetTextureStageState(0, D3DTSS_TEXCOORDINDEX, 1);`

Instruction	1.1	1.2	1.3	Para	Action
texbem (cont.)					(see below)

```
// bump map
SetTexture(1, m_psBumpMap);
SetTextureStageState(1, D3DTSS_TEXCOORDINDEX, 1);
// environment map
SetTexture(2, m_pEnvMapTexture);
SetTextureStageState(2, D3DTSS_TEXCOORDINDEX, 0);
SetTextureStageState(2, D3DTSS_BUMPENVMAT00,
                        F2DW(0.5f));
SetTextureStageState(2, D3DTSS_BUMPENVMAT01,
                        F2DW(0.0f));
SetTextureStageState(2, D3DTSS_BUMPENVMAT10,
                        F2DW(0.0f));
SetTextureStageState(2, D3DTSS_BUMPENVMAT11,
                        F2DW(0.5f));
```

texbem performs the following operations:

```
u += 2x2 matrix(du)
v += 2x2 matrix(dv)
Then sample (u, v)
```

Read more in the "Bump Mapping Formulas" section in the DirectX 8.1 SDK documentation.

Some rules for *texbem/texbeml*:

The *s* register cannot be read by any arithmetic instruction until it is overwritten again by another instruction:

```
...
texbem/l t1, t0
mov r0, t0 ; not legal
...
texbem/l t1, t0
mov t0, c0
mov r0, t0 ; legal
...
```

The s register of texbem/l cannot be read by any texture instruction except for the texbem/l instruction:

```
...
texbem/l t1, t0
texreg2ar t2, t0 ; not legal
...
texbem/l t1, t0
texbem/l t2, t0 ; legal
...
---------------------------------
; t2 environment map
; (t2) texture coordinates environment map
; t1 du/dv perturbation data
ps.1.1
tex t0 ; color map
tex t1 ; bump map
texbem t2, t1 ; Perturb and then sample the
              ; environment map.
add r0, t2, t0
```

See the *bem* instruction for the ps.1.4 equivalent. See [Weiskopf] for an interesting use of *texbem*.

Instruction	1.1	1.2	1.3	Para	Action

texbeml	x	x	x	d,s	Same as above, but applies additional luminance. Now three components of the source register are used: red, green, and blue as du, dv, and I for luminance.
					
					u += 2x2 matrix(du)
					v += 2x2 matrix(dv)
					
					Then sample (u, v) and apply luminance.
					
					See the texbem/l rules in the *texbem* section.
					
					-------------------------------- 	
					<pre>; t1 holds the color map
					; bump matrix set with the
					; D3DTSS_BUMPENVMAT* flags
					ps.1.1
					tex t0 ; bump map with du, dv, l data
					texbeml t1, t0 ; compute u, v
					               ; sample t1 using u, v
					               ; apply luminance correction
					mov r0, t1 ; output result</pre>

texcoord	x	x	x	d	Clamps the texture coordinate to the range [0..1.0] and outputs it as color. If the texture coordinate set contains fewer than three components, the missing components are set to 0. The fourth component is always 1.
					
					Provides a way to pass vertex data interpolated at high precision directly into the pixel shader.
					
					-------------------------------- 	
					<pre>ps.1.1
					texcoord t0 ; convert texture coordinates
					            ; to color
					mov r0, t0 ; move color into output
					            ; register r0</pre>

texdp3		x	x	d, s	Performs a three-component dot product between the texture coordinate set corresponding to the *d* register number and the texture data in s and replicates clamped values to all four color channels of *d*.
					
					-------------------------------- 	
					<pre>; t0 holds color map
					; (t1) hold texture coordinates
					ps.1.2
					tex t0 ; color map
					texdp3 t1, t0 ; t1 = (t1) dot t0
					mov r0, t1 ; output result</pre>

texdp3tex		x	x	d, s	Performs a three-component dot product between the texture coordinate set corresponding to the d register number and the texture data in s. Uses the result to do a 1D texture lookup in d and places the result of the lookup into d. A common application is to look up into a function table stored in a 1D texture for procedural specular lighting terms. --------------------------------

Instruction	1.1	1.2	1.3	Para	Action

texdp3tex (cont.)		x	x	d, s	```; t1 holds 1D color map```
					```ps.1.2```
					```tex t0 ; vector data (x, y, z, w)```
					
					```texdp3tex t1, t0 ; u = (t1) dot t0```
					``` ; lookup data in t1```
					``` ; result in t1```
					```mov r0, t1 ; output result```

texkill	x	x	x	s	Cancels rendering of the current pixel if any of the first three components of the texture coordinates in s is less than zero.
					
					When using vertex shaders, the application is responsible for applying the perspective transform. If the arbitrary clipping planes contain anisomorphic scale factors, you have to apply the perspective transform to these clip planes as well.
					
					`--------------------------------`
					```ps.1.1```
					```texkill t0 ; mask out pixel using```
					``` ; uvw texture coordinates < 0.0```
					```mov r0, v0```

texm3x2depth			x	d, s	Calculates together with a texm3x2pad instruction the depth value to be used in depth testing for this pixel. Performs a three-component dot product between the texture coordinate set corresponding to the d register number and the second row of a 3x2 matrix in the s register and stores the resulting w into d. After execution, the d register is no longer available for use in the shader.
					
					The benefit of a higher resolution of the depth buffer resulting from multisampling is eliminated because texm3x2depth (same with ps.1.4: texdepth) will output the single depth value to each of the sub-pixel depth comparison tests.
					
					Needs to be clamped to [0..1] w and z values or the result stored in the depth buffer will be undefined.
					
					`--------------------------------`
					```; (t1) holds row #1 of the 3x2 matrix```
					```; (t2) holds row #2 of the 3x2 matrix```
					```; t0 holds normal map```
					```ps.1.3```
					```tex t0 ; normal map```
					```texm3x2pad t1, t0 ; calculates z from row #1```
					
					```; calculates w from row #2```
					```; stores a result in t2 depending on```
					```; if (w == 0)```
					```; t2 = 1.0;```
					```; else```
					```; t2 = z/w;```
					```texm3x2depth t2, t0```

texm3x2pad	x	x	x	d, s	This instruction cannot be used by itself. It must be combined with either texm3x2tex or texm3x2depth. It performs a three-component dot product between the texture coordinate set corresponding to the d register number and the data of the s register and stores the result in d.

Instruction	1.1	1.2	1.3	Para	Action
texm3x2pad (cont.)	x	x	x	d, s	See the example shown for the texm3x2depth and texm3x2tex instructions.
texm3x2tex	x	x	x	d, s	It calculates the second row of a 3x2 matrix by performing a three-component dot product between the texture coordinate set corresponding to the d register number and the data of the s register to get a v value, which is used to sample a 2D texture. This instruction is used in conjunction with texm3x2pad, which calculates the u value.

```
; Dot3 specular lighting with a lookup table
ps.1.1
; t0 holds normal map
; (t1) holds row #1 of the 3x2 matrix (light vector)
; (t2) holds row #2 of the 3x2 matrix (half vector)
; t2 holds a 2D texture (lookup table)
; t3 holds color map
tex t0 ; sample normal
texm3x2pad t1, t0_bx2 ; calculates u from first row
texm3x2tex t2, t0_bx2 ; calculates v from second row
                      ; samples texel with u,v
                      ; from t2 (lookup table)
tex t3 ; sample base color
mul r0,t2,t3 ; blend terms
-------
; A ps.1.4 equivalent to the
; texm3x2pad/texm3x2tex pair could be
; specular power from a lookup table
ps.1.4
; r0 holds normal map
; t1 holds light vector
; t2 holds half vector
; r2 holds 2D texture (lookup table)
; r3 holds color map
texld r0, t0
texcrd r1.rgb, t1
texcrd r4.rgb, t2

dp3 r1.r, r1, r0_bx2 ; calculates u
dp3 r1.g, r4, r0_bx2 ; calculates v

phase

texld r3, t3
texld r2, r1 ; samples texel with u,v
             ; from r2 (lookup table)
mul r0, r2, r3
```

Instruction	1.1	1.2	1.3	Para	Action
texm3x3		x	x	d, s	Performs a 3x3 matrix multiply similar to *texm3x3tex*, except that it does not automatically perform a lookup into a texture. The returned result vector is placed in d with no dependent read. The .a value in d is set to 1.0. The 3x3 matrix is comprised of the texture coordinates of the third texture stage and by the two preceding texture stages. Any texture assigned to any of the three texture stages is ignored. This instruction must be used with two *texm3x3pad* instructions.

Instruction	1.1	1.2	1.3	Para	Action

texm3x3 (cont.)		x	x	d, s	`------------------------------------`
					`; (t1) holds row #1 of the 3x3 matrix`
					`; (t2) holds row #2 of the 3x3 matrix`
					`; (t3) holds row #3 of the 3x3 matrix`
					`ps.1.2`
					`tex t0 ; normal map`
					`texm3x3pad t1, t0 ; calculates u from row #1`
					`texm3x3pad t2, t0  ; calculates v from row #2`
					`texm3x3 t3, t0      ; calculates w from row #3`
					`                    ; store u, v , w in t3`
					`mov r0, t3`
					` `
					`; ps.1.4 equivalent`
					`; r1 holds row #1 of the 3x3 matrix`
					`; r2 holds row #2 of the 3x3 matrix`
					`; r3 holds row #3 of the 3x3 matrix`
					`ps.1.4`
					`def c0, 1.0, 1.0, 1.0, 1.0`
					`texld r0, t0 ; r0 normal map`
					`texcrd r1.rgb, t1 ; calculates u from row #1`
					`texcrd r2.rgb, t2 ; calculates v from row #2`
					`texcrd r3.rgb, t3 ; calculates w from row #3`
					`dp3 r4.r, r1, r0`
					`dp3 r4.g, r2, r0`
					`dp3 r4.b, r3, r0 ; store u, w, w in r4.rgb`
					`mov r0.a, c0`
					`+mov r0.rgb, r4`

texm3x3pad	x	x	x	d, s	Performs the first or second row of a 3x3 matrix multiply. The instruction cannot be used by itself and must be used with *texm3x3, texm3x3spec, texm3x3vspec,* or *texm3x3tex.*

texm3x3spec	x	x	x	d, s1, s2	Performs, together with two *texm3x3pad* instructions, a 3x3 matrix multiply. The resulting vector is used as a normal vector to reflect the eye-ray vector from a constant register in s2 and then uses the reflected vector as a texture address for a texture lookup in d.
					
					The 3x3 matrix is typically useful for orienting a normal vector of the correct tangent space for the surface being rendered. The 3x3 matrix is comprised of the texture coordinates of the third texture stage and the results in the two preceding texture stages. Any texture assigned to the two preceding texture stages is ignored.
					
					This can be used for specular reflection and environment mapping.
					
					`------------------------------------`
					`; (t1) holds row #1 of the 3x3 matrix`
					`; (t2) holds row #2 of the 3x3 matrix`
					`; (t3) holds row #3 of the 3x3 matrix`
					`; t3 is assigned a cube or volume map with`
					`; color data (RGBA)`
					`; t0 holds a normal map`
					`; c0 holds the eye-ray vector E`

Instruction	1.1	1.2	1.3	Para	Action
| texm3x3spec (cont.) | | | | | ```
ps.1.1
tex t0
texm3x3pad t1, t0 ; calculates u from row #1
texm3x3pad t2, t0 ; calculates v from row #2

; calculates w from row #3
; reflect u, v and w by the
; eye-ray vector in c0
; use reflected vector to lookup texture in t3
texm3x3spec t3, t0, c0
mov r0, t3 ; output result

; A similar effect is possible with the following
; ps.1.4 pixel shader.
; The eye vector is stored as a normalized
; vector in a cube map
ps.1.4
texld r0, t0 ; Look up normal map.
texld r1, t4 ; Eye vector through normalizer cube map
texcrd r4.rgb, t1 ; 1st row of environment matrix
texcrd r2.rgb, t2 ; 2st row of environment matrix
texcrd r3.rgb, t3 ; 3rd row of environment matrix

dp3 r4.r, r4, r0_bx2 ; 1st row of matrix multiply
dp3 r4.g, r2, r0_bx2 ; 2nd row of matrix multiply
dp3 r4.b, r3, r0_bx2 ; 3rd row of matrix multiply
dp3 r5, r4, r1_bx2 ; (N.Eye)
mov r0, r5
``` |
| texm3x3tex | x | x | x | d, s | Performs, together with two texm3x3pad instructions, a 3x3 matrix multiply and uses the result to look up the texture in d. The 3x3 matrix is typically useful for orienting a normal vector to the correct tangent space for the surface being rendered. The 3x3 matrix is comprised of the texture coordinates of the third texture stage and the two preceding texture stages. The resulting u, v, and w is used to sample the texture in stage 3. Any textures assigned to the preceding textures are ignored.<br><br>`-----------------------------------`<br>```
; (t1) holds row #1 of the 3x3 matrix
; (t2) holds row #2 of the 3x3 matrix
; (t3) holds row #3 of the 3x3 matrix
; t3 is assigned a cube or volume map with
; color data (RGBA)
ps.1.1
tex t0 ; normal map
texm3x3pad t1, t0 ; calculates u from row #1
texm3x3pad t2, t0 ; calculates v from row #2
; calculates w from row #3
; uses u, v and w to sample t3
texm3x3tex t3, t0
mov r0, t3 ; output result

; ps.1.4 equivalent
; r1 holds row #1 of the 3x3 matrix
; r2 holds row #2 of the 3x3 matrix
; r3 holds row #3 of the 3x3 matrix
``` |

Instruction	1.1	1.2	1.3	Para	Action

texm3x3tex (cont.)					```
					; r3 is assigned a cube or volume map with
					; color data (RGBA)
					ps.1.4
					texld r0, t0
					texcrd r1.rgb, t1
					texcrd r2.rgb, t2
					texcrd r3.rgb, t3
					dp3 r4.r, r1, r0 ; calculates u from row #1
					dp3 r4.g, r2, r0 ; calculates v from row #2
					dp3 r4.b, r3, r0 ; calculates w from row #3
					phase
					texld r3, r4
					mov r0, r3
					``

texm3x3vspec	x	x	x	d, s	Performs, together with two *texm3x3pad* instructions, a 3x3 matrix multiply. The resulting vector is used as a normal vector to reflect the eye-ray vector and then uses the reflected vector as a texture address for a texture lookup. It works just like texm3x3spec, except that the eye-vector is taken from the q coordinates of the three sets of 4D textures. The 3x3 matrix is typically useful for orienting a normal vector of the correct tangent space for the surface being rendered. The 3x3 matrix is comprised of the texture coordinates of the third texture stage and the results in the two preceding texture stages. Any texture assigned to the two preceding texture stages is ignored.
					
					This can be used for specular reflection and environment mapping, where the eye-vector is not constant.
					
					-- 	
					``
					; (t1) holds row #1 of the 3x3 matrix
					; (t2) holds row #2 of the 3x3 matrix
					; (t3) holds row #3 of the 3x3 matrix
					; t3 is assigned a cube or volume map with
					; color data (RGBA)
					; t0 holds a normal map
					; used for cubic bump mapping
					; the per-vertex eye vector is derived using
					; the camera position in the vertex shader
					ps.1.1
					tex t0
					texm3x3pad t1, t0 ; calculates u from row #1
					texm3x3pad t2, t0 ; calculates v from row #2
					
					; calculates w from row #3
					; calculates eye-ray vector from the q texture
					; coordinate values of t1 - t3
					; reflect u, v and w by the eye-ray vector
					; use reflected vector to lookup texture in t3
					texm3x3vspec t3, t0
					mov r0, t3 ; output result
					``

Instruction	1.1	1.2	1.3	Para	Action

texreg2ar	x	x	x	d, s	General dependent texture read operation that takes the alpha and red color components of s as texture address data (u, v) consisting of unsigned values to sample a texture at d.
					
					-- 	
					
					``ps.1.1
					tex t0 ; color map
					texreg2ar t1, t0
					mov r0, t1```

texreg2gb	x	x	x	d, s	General dependent texture read operation that takes the green and blue color components of s as texture address data (u, v) consisting of unsigned values to sample a texture at d.
					
					-- 	
					
					``ps.1.1
					tex t0 ; color map
					texreg2gb t1, t0
					mov r0, t1```

texreg2rgb		x	x	d, s	General dependent texture read operation that takes the red, green, and blue color components of s as texture address data (u, v, w) consisting of unsigned values to sample a texture at d. This is useful for color-space remapping operations.
					
					-- 	
					
					``ps.1.2
					tex t0 ; color map
					texreg2rgb t1, t0
					mov r0, t1```

All of these texture address instructions use only the t*n* registers with the exception of *tex3x3spec*, which uses a constant register for the eye-ray vector. In a ps.1.1-ps.1.3 pixel shader, the destination register numbers for texture addressing instructions had to be in increasing order.

In ps.1.1-ps.1.3, the ability to reuse a texture coordinate after modifying it in the pixel shader is available through specific texture address instructions that are able to modify the texture coordinates and sample a texture with these afterward. The following diagram shows this reliance:

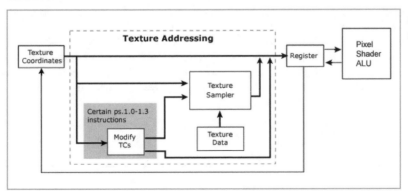

Figure 11: Dependent read in ps.1.1-ps.1.3

The texture address operations that sample a texture after modifying the texture coordinates are:

- texbem/texbeml
- texdp3tex
- texm3x2tex
- texm3x3spec
- texm3x3tex
- texm3x3vspec

The following instructions sample a texture with the help of color values as texture coordinates. If one of these color values has been changed by an instruction, the sampling happens to be a dependent read.

- texreg2ar
- texreg2gb
- texreg2rgb

Therefore, these instructions are called general dependent texture read instructions.

As already stated above, each ps.1.1-ps.1.3 pixel shader has a maximum of eight arithmetic instructions and four texture address instructions. All texture address instructions use one of the supplied slots, with the exception of texbeml, which uses one texture address slot plus one arithmetic slot.

ps.1.4 Texture Addressing

To use texels or texture coordinates in ps.1.4, you have to load them first with texld or texcrd. These instructions are the only way to get access to texels or texture coordinates. Texture coordinates can be modified after a conversion to color data via texcrd, with all available arithmetic instructions. As a result, texture addressing is more straightforward with ps.1.4.

The following instructions are texture address instructions in ps.1.4:

Instruction	Para	Action
texcrd	d, s	Copies the texture coordinate set corresponding to s into d as color data (RGBA). No texture is sampled. Clamps the texture coordinates in tn with a range of [–MaxTextureRepeat, MaxTextureRepeat] (RADEON 8500: 2048) to the range of rn [–8, 8] (MaxPixelShaderValue). This clamp might behave differently on different hardware. To be safe, provide data in the range of [–8, 8].

		A .rgb or .rg modifier should be provided to d. The fourth channel of d is unset/undefined in all cases. The third channel is unset/undefined for a projective divide with _dw.xyz (D3DTFF_PROJECTED is ignored in ps.1.4). The allowed syntax, taking into account all valid source modifier/selector and destination write mask combinations, is shown below:
		`texcrd rn.rgb, tn.xyz`
		`texcrd rn.rgb, tn`
		`texcrd rn.rgb, tn.xyw`
		`texcrd rn.rg, tn_dw.xyw`

Instruction	Para	Action

texdepth	d	Calculates the depth value used in the depth buffer comparison test for the pixel by using the r5 register. The r5 register is then unavailable for any further use in the pixel shader. *texdepth* updates the depth buffer with the value of r5.r and r5.g. The .r channel is treated as the z-value and the .g channel is treated as the w-value. The value in the depth buffer is replaced by the result of the .r channel divided by the .g channel == z/w. If the value in .g channel is zero, then the depth buffer is updated with 1.0.
		
		 texdepth is only available in phase 2.
		
		 Using this instruction eliminates the benefit of a higher resolution of the depth buffer resulting from multisampling, because *texdepth* (and *texm3x2depth*) will output the single depth value to each of the sub-pixel depth comparison tests.
		
		 `----------------------------------------`
		 ```ps.1.4```
		 ```texld r0, t0 ; samples from texture stage 0 with```
		 ``` ; texture coordinates set t0```
		 ```texcrd r1.rgb, t1 ; load texture coordinates from```
		 ``` ; t1 into r1 as color values```
		 ```add 5.rg, r0, r1 ; add both values```
		 ```phase```
		 ```texdepth r5 ; calculate pixel depth as r5.r/r5.g```
		 ```// do other color calculation here and output it to r0```

texkill	s	Cancels rendering of the current pixel if any of the first three components of the texture data (ps.1.1-ps.1.3: texture coordinates) in *s* is less than zero. You can use this instruction to implement arbitrary clipping planes in the rasterizer.
		
		 When using vertex shaders, the application is responsible for applying the perspective transform. If the arbitrary clipping planes contain anisomorphic scale factors, you have to apply the perspective transform to the clip planes as well.
		
		 texkill is only available in phase 2 and sources *rn* or *tn* registers.
		
		 `--------------------------------`
		 ```ps.1.4```
		 ```... ; include other shader instructions here```
		 ```phase```
		 ```texkill t0 ; mask out pixel using```
		 ```; uvw texture coordinates < 0.0```
		 ```mov r0, v0 ; move diffuse into r0```

texld	d, s	Loads *d* with the color data (RGBA) sampled using the texture coordinates from *s*. The texture stage number with the texture data from which to sample is determined by the number of *d* (r0-r5), and the texture coordinate set is determined by the number of *src* (t0-t5) in phase 1. *texld* is able to additionally use *rn* as s in phase 2.
		
		 The allowed syntax is:
		 ```texld rn, tn```
		 ```texld rn, tn.xyz ; same as previous```
		 ```texld rn, tn.xyw```
		 ```texld rn, tn_dw.xyw```
		 ```texld rn, rn```
		 ```texld rn, rn.xyz ; same as previous```
		 ```texld rn, rn_dz ; only valid on rn```
		 ``` ; no more than two times per shader```
		 ```texld rn, rn_dz.xyz ; same as previous```

Instruction	Para	Action

texld (cont.)		`-----------------------------------`
		`; Simple transfer function for sepia or`
		`; heat signature effects [Mitchell]`
		`; c0 holds the luminance value`
		`; t0 holds the texture coordinates`
		`; r0 holds the original image`
		`; r5 holds the 1D sepia or heat signature map`
		`ps.1.4`
		`def c0, 0.30, 0.59, 0.11, 1.0`
		`texld r0, t0`
		`dp3 r0, r0, c0`
		`phase`
		`texld r5, r0    ; dependent read`
		`mov r0, r5`
		``
		`; ps.1.2 equivalent`
		`; t0 holds the original image`
		`; t1 holds the 1D sepia or heat signature map`
		`; (t1) holds 0.30, 0.59, 0.11, 1.0`
		`ps.1.2`
		`tex t0            ; color map`
		`texdp3tex t1, t0 ; u = (t1) dot t0`
		`                 ; lookup data in t1`
		`                 ; result in t1`
		`mov r0, t1       ; output result`

In ps.1.4, there are only four texture address instructions, but, as mentioned before, all the arithmetic instructions can be used to manipulate texture address information. So there are plenty of instruments to solve texture addressing tasks.

Valid source registers for first phase texture address instructions are t*n*. Valid source registers for second phase texture address instructions are t*n* and also r*n*. Each r*n* register may be specified as a destination to a texture instruction only once per phase. Aside from this, destination register numbers for texture instructions do not have to be in any particular order (as opposed to previous pixel shader versions in which destination register numbers for texture instructions had to be in increasing order).

No dependencies are allowed in a block of tex* instructions. The destination register of a texture address instruction cannot be used as a source in a subsequent texture address instruction in the same block of texture address instruction (same phase).

Dependent reads with ps.1.4 are not difficult to locate in the source. Pseudocode of the two possible dependent read scenarios in ps.1.4 might look like:

```
; transfer function
texld    ; load first texture
modify color data here
phase
texld    ; sample second texture with changed color data as address
```

or

```
texcrd   ; load texture coordinates
modify texture coordinates here
phase
texld    ; sample texture with changed address
```

Another way to think of it is that if the second argument to a texld after the phase marker is r*n* (not t*n*), then it's a dependent read because the texture coordinates are in a temp register so they must have been computed:

```
. . . . .
phase
texld rn, rn
```

Set the first three channels of an r*n* register, which is used as a source register. This must be set before it is used as a source parameter. Otherwise, the shader will fail.

To manipulate texture coordinates with arithmetic instructions, they have to be loaded into texture data registers (ps.1.1-ps.1.3: t*n*; ps.1.4: r*n*) via texcoord or texcrd. There is one important difference between these two instructions; texcoord clamps to [0..1] and texcrd does not clamp at all.

If you compare texture addressing used in ps.1.1-ps.1.3 and texture addressing used in ps.1.4, it is obvious that the more CISC-like approach uses much more powerful instructions to address textures compared to the more RISC-like ps.1.4 approach. On the other hand, ps.1.4 offers a greater flexibility in implementing different texture addressing algorithms by using all of the arithmetic instructions compared to ps.1.1-ps.1.3.

Arithmetic Instructions

The arithmetic instructions are used by ps.1.1-ps.1.3 and ps.1.4 in a similar way to manipulate texture or color data. Here is an overview of all available instructions in these implementations:

Instruction	Arguments	Registers				Version
		v_n	c_n	t_n	r_n	
	dest			x	x	ps.1.1-ps.1.3
					x	ps.1.4
add	src0, src1	x	x	x	x	ps.1.1-ps.1.3
			x		x	ps.1.4 phase 1
		x	x		x	ps.1.4 phase 2

Performs a component-wise addition of register src0 and src1:

```
dest.r = src0.r + src1.r
dest.g = src0.g + src1.g
dest.b = src0.b + src1.b
dest.a = src0.a + src1.a
------------------------------------
; glow mapping
ps.1.1
tex t0          ; color map
tex t1          ; glow map
add r0, t0, t1 ; add the color values
                ; increase brightness lead to a glow effect
; glow mapping
ps.1.4
texld r0, t0    ; color map
texld r1, t1    ; glow map
```

Instruction	Arguments	Registers				Version
		v_n	c_n	t_n	r_n	

```
add r0, r0, r1    ; add the color values
                  ; increase brightness lead to a glow effect


---------
; detail mapping
ps.1.1
tex t0 ; color map
tex t1 ; detail map
add r0, t0, t1_bias ; detail map is add-signed to the color map
                    ; watch out for the used texture coordinates of
                    ; the detail map

; detail mapping
ps.1.4
texld r0, t0      ; color map
texld r1, t0      ; sample detail map with the texture coords of the color map
add r0, r0, r1_bias ; detail map is add-signed to the color map
```

You may increase the detail map effect by using _bx2 as a modifier in the add instruction.

Instruction	Arguments	v_n	c_n	t_n	r_n	Version
bem	dest				x	ps.1.4 phase 1
	src0		x		x	ps.1.4 phase 1
	src1				x	ps.1.4 phase 1

Apply a fake bump environment transform.

There is a difference in the usage of the texture stages between environment mapping with a pixel shader (meaning *texbem*, *texbeml*, or *bem*) and environment mapping with the DX 6/7 multitexturing unit. *bem* (*texbeml* or *texbem*) needs the matrix data connected to the texture stage that is sampled. This is the environment map. Environment mapping with the DX 6/7 multitexturing unit needs the matrix data connected to the texture stage used by the bump map (see the example code for the texbem instruction).

bem has a lot of restrictions when used in a pixel shader:

- bem must appear in the first phase of a shader (that is, before a phase marker).
- bem consumes two arithmetic instruction slots.
- Only one use of this instruction is allowed per shader.
- Destination writemask must be .rg /.xy.
- This instruction cannot be co-issued.
- Aside from the restriction that destination write mask be .rg, modifiers on source src0, src1, and instruction modifiers are unconstrained.

bem performs the following calculation:

```
(Given n == dest register #)
dest.r = src0.r + D3DTSS_BUMENVMAT00(stage n) * src1.r
                + D3DTSS_BUMPENVMAT10(stage n) * src1.g

dest.g = src0.g + D3DTSS_BUMENVMAT01(stage n) * src1.r
                + D3DTSS_BUMPENVMAT11(stage n) * src1.g


------------------------------------
```

Instruction	Arguments	Registers				Version
		v_n	c_n	t_n	r_n	

```
ps.1.4
; r2 environment map texture coordinates
; r1 du/dv perturbation data
texld r1, t1      ; bump map
texcrd r2.rgb, t2
bem r2.rg, r2, r1 ; perturb
                  ; r2.rg = tex coordinates to sample environment map
phase
texld r0, t0      ; color map
texld r2, r2      ; environment map
add r0, r0, r2
```

See the BumpEarth example program on the companion CD. See also the articles on improved environment mapping techniques, such as cube mapping [Brennan2][Brennan3] and per-fresnel term [Brennan].

		v_n	c_n	t_n	r_n	Version
cmp	dest			x	x	ps.1.2, ps.1.3
					x	ps.1.4
	src0, src1, src2	x	x	x	x	ps.1.2, ps.1.3
			x		x	ps.1.4 phase 1
		x	x		x	ps.1.4 phase 2

Conditionally chooses between src1 and src2 based on a per-channel comparison src0 >= 0.

For ps.1.2 and ps.1.3, cmp uses two arithmetic instruction slots. *CreatePixelShader()* erroneously assumes that this instruction consumes only one instruction slot. So you have to check the instruction count of a pixel shader that uses this instruction manually. Another validation problem is that in ps.1.2 and ps.1.3, the destination register of *cmp* cannot be the same as any of the source registers.

```
// Compares all four components.
ps.1.2

... fill t1, t2 and t3
// t1 holds -0.6, 0.6, 0, 0.6
// t2 holds 0, 0, 0, 0
// t3 holds 1, 1, 1, 1
cmp r0, t1, t2, t3 // r0 is assigned 1,0,0,0 based on the following:
// r0.x = t3.x because t1.x < 0
// r0.y = t2.y because t1.y >= 0
// r0.z = t2.z because t1.z >= 0
// r0.w = t2.w because t1.w >= 0
----------
// Compares all four components.
ps.1.4
texcrd r1, t1
texcrd r2, t2
texcrd r3, t3
// r1 holds -0.6, 0.6, 0, 0.6
// r2 holds 0, 0, 0, 0
// r3 holds 1, 1, 1, 1
cmp r0, r1, r2, r3 // r0 is assigned 1,0,0,0 based on the following:
// r0.x = r3.x because r1.x < 0
// r0.y = r2.y because r1.y >= 0
```

Instruction	Arguments	Registers				Version
		v_n	c_n	t_n	r_n	

```
// r0.z = r2.z because r1.z >= 0
// r0.w = r2.w because r1.w >= 0
----------
; Cartoon pixel shader
; explained in detail in [Card/Mitchell]
; c0 holds falloff 1
; c1 holds falloff 2
; c2 holds dark
; c3 holds average
; c4 holds bright
; t0 holds normal information
; t1 holds the light vector
ps.1.4
def c0, 0.1f, 0.1f, 0.1f, 0.1f
def c1, 0.8f, 0.8f, 0.8f, 0.8f
def c2, 0.2f, 0.2f, 0.2f, 1.0f
def c3, 0.6f, 0.6f, 0.6f, 1.0f
def c4, 0.9f, 0.9f, 1.0f, 1.0f

texcrd r0.xyz, t0       ; place normal vector in r0
texcrd r1.xyz, t1       ; place light vector in r1
dp3 r3, r0, r1          ; n.l
sub r4, r3, c0          ; subtract falloff #1 from n.l
cmp_sat r0, r4, c3, c2  ; check if n.l is > zero
                        ; if yes use average color
                        ; otherwise darker color
sub r4, r3, c1          ; subtract falloff #2 from n.l
cmp_sat r0, r4 c4, r0   ; check if n.l is > zero
                        ; if yes use bright color
                        ; otherwise use what is there

; ps.1.2 equivalent with less precision
ps.1.2
def c0, 0.1f, 0.1f, 0.1f, 0.1f
def c1, 0.8f, 0.8f, 0.8f, 0.8f
def c2, 0.2f, 0.2f, 0.2f, 1.0f
def c3, 0.6f, 0.6f, 0.6f, 1.0f
def c4, 0.9f, 0.9f, 1.0f, 1.0f

texcoord t0             ; place normal vector in t0
texcoord t1             ; place light vector in t1
dp3 r1, t0, t1          ; n.l
sub t3, r1, c0          ; subtract falloff #1 from n.l
cmp_sat r0, t3, c3, c2  ; check if n.l is > zero
                        ; if yes use average color
                        ; otherwise darker color
sub t3, r1, c1          ; subtract falloff #2 from n.l
cmp_sat r0, t3, c4, r0  ; check if n.l is > zero
                        ; if yes use bright color
                        ; otherwise use what is there
```

The ps.1.2 version is not able to provide the same precision as the ps.1.4 version because of *texcoord*, which clamps to [0..1]. *texcrd* does not clamp at all. It is able to handle values in the range of its source registers *rn* [−8..+8].

Instruction	Arguments	Registers				Version
		v_n	c_n	t_n	r_n	
cnd	dest			x	x	ps.1.1-ps.1.3
					x	ps.1.4
	src0				r0.a	ps.1.1-ps.1.3
	src1, src2	x	x	x	x	ps.1.1-ps.1.3
	src0, src1, src2		x		x	ps.1.4 phase 1
		x	x		x	ps.1.4 phase 2

Conditionally chooses between src1 and src2 based on the comparison r0.a > 0.5, whereas ps.1.4 conditionally chooses between src1 and src2 based on the comparison src0 > 0.5 by comparing all channels of src0.

```
// Version 1.1 to 1.3
if (r0.a > 0.5)
  dest = src1
else
  dest = src2

// Version 1.4 compares each channel separately.
for each channel in src0
{
    if (src0.channel > 0.5)
      dest.channel = src1.channel
    else
      dest.channel = src2.channel
}
-----------------------------------------
// Compares r0.a > 0.5
ps.1.1
def c0, -0.5, 0.5, 0, 0.6
def c1, 0, 0, 0, 0
def c2, 1, 1, 1, 1
mov r0, c0
cnd r1, r0.a, c1, c2 // r1 is assigned 0,0,0,0 based on the following:
// r0.a > 0.5, therefore r1.xyzw = c1.xyzw
-----------
// Compares all four components.
ps.1.4
// r1 holds -0.6, 0.5, 0, 0.6
// r2 holds 0, 0, 0, 0
// r3 holds 1, 1, 1, 1
texcrd r1, t1
texcrd r2, t2
texcrd r3, t3
cnd r0, r1, r2, r3 // r0 is assigned 1,1,1,0 based on the following:
// r0.x = r3.x because r1.x < 0.5
// r0.y = r3.y because r1.y = 0.5
// r0.z = r3.z because r1.z < 0.5
// r0.w = r2.w because r1.w > 0.5
```

See [Bendel] for an interesting usage of cnd to smooth fonts.

Instruction	Arguments	Registers				Version
		v_n	c_n	t_n	r_n	
dp3	dest			x	x	ps.1.1-ps.1.3
					x	ps.1.4
	src0, src1	x	x	x	x	ps.1.1-ps.1.3
			x		x	ps.1.4 phase 1
		x	x		x	ps.1.4 phase 2

Calculates a three-component dot product. The scalar result is replicated to all four channels:

```
dest.w = (src0.x * src1.x) + (src0.y * src1.y) + (src0.z * src1.z);
dest.x = dest.y = dest.z = dest.w = the scalar result of dp3
```

It does not automatically clamp the result to [0..1]. This instruction executes in the vector pipeline so it can be paired or co-issued with an instruction that executes in the alpha pipeline. (More on co-issuing below.)

```
dp3 r0.rgb, t0, v0
+mov r2.a, t0
```

In ps.1.1-ps.1.3, *dp3* always writes out to .rgb. In ps.1.4, you are free to choose three channels of the four rgba channels in any combination by masking the destination register.

```
; Dot3 per-pixel specular lighting
; specular power comes from a lookup table
ps.1.4
; r0 holds normal map
; t1 holds light vector
; t2 holds half vector
; r2 holds a 2D texture (lookup table)
; r3 holds color map
texld r0, t0          ; normal map
texcrd r1.rgb, t1
texcrd r4.rgb, t2

dp3 r1.r, r1, r0_bx2 ; calculates u
dp3 r1.g, r4, r0_bx2 ; calculates v

phase

texld r3, t3
texld r2, r1          ; samples texel with u,v from t2 (lookup table)
mul r0, r2, r3
```

You will find the ps.1.1 equivalent as an example for the texm3x2tex instruction. See the RacorX8 and RacorX9 examples in "Programming Pixel Shaders."

dp4	dest				x	ps.1.2, ps.1.3
					x	ps.1.4
	src0, src1	x	x	x	x	ps.1.2, ps.1.3
			x		x	ps.1.4 phase 1
		x	x		x	ps.1.4 phase 2

Calculates a four-component dot product. It does not automatically clamp the result to [0..1]. This instruction executes in the vector and alpha pipeline, so it cannot be co-issued. Unfortunately, *CreatePixelShader()* assumes that this instruction consumes only one instruction slot, although it really consumes two. So the instruction count in a pixel shader that uses *dp4* must be checked manually.

Instruction	Arguments	Registers				Version
		v_n	c_n	t_n	r_n	

Additionally, in ps.1.2 and ps.1.3, the destination register for *dp4* cannot be the same as any of the source registers. *CreatePixelShader()* will not catch a wrong usage.

A maximum of four dp4 commands are allowed in a single pixel shader.

dp4 is useful for handling 4x4 matrices or quaternions in a pixel shader. *dp4* does not seem to be useful in conjunction with most of the texture address instructions of ps.1.2 and ps.1.3 because these instructions support only matrices with three columns.

Instruction	Arguments	v_n	c_n	t_n	r_n	Version
lrp	dest			x	x	ps.1.1-ps.1.3
					x	ps.1.4
	src0, src1, src2	x	x	x	x	ps.1.1-ps.1.3
			x		x	ps.1.4 phase 1
		x	x		x	ps.1.4 phase 2

Performs a linear interpolation based on the following formula:

```
dest = src2 + src0 * (src1 - src2)
```

src0 determines the amount for the blend of *src1* and *src2*.

```
-------------------------------------------
ps.1.1
def c0, 0.4, 0.2, 0.5, 1.0
tex t0
tex t3
lrp r0, c0, t3, t0 ; the texture values of t3 and t0 are
                   ; interpolated depending on c0
-----------------------
ps.1.4
def c0, 0.4, 0.2, 0.5, 1.0
texld r0, t0
texld r3, t3
lrp r0, c0, r3, r0 ; the texture values of t3 and t0 are
                   ; interpolated depending on c0
```

[Vlachos] shows how to programmatically interpolate with *lrp* between two textures based on their normal.

Instruction	Arguments	v_n	c_n	t_n	r_n	Version
mad	dest			x	x	ps.1.1-ps.1.3
					x	ps.1.4
	src0, src1, src2	x	x	x	x	ps.1.1-ps.1.3
			x		x	ps.1.4 phase 1
		x	x		x	ps.1.4 phase 2

Performs a multiply accumulate operation based on the following formula:

```
dest = src0 * src1 + src2
```

This might be useful, for example, for dark mapping with diffuse color.

```
-------------------------------------------
; The following examples show a modulation of a light map with a color map.
; This technique is often used to darken parts of a color map. In this case
; it is called dark mapping. Additionally, a diffuse color is added.
ps.1.1
tex t0 ; color map
tex t3 ; light map
mad r0, t3, t0, v0
```

Instruction	Arguments	Registers				Version
		v_n	c_n	t_n	r_n	

```
; Dark Mapping + diffuse color
ps.1.4
texld r0, t0 ; color map
texld r3, t3 ; light map
mad r0, r3, r0, v0
```

Instruction	Arguments	v_n	c_n	t_n	r_n	Version
mov	dest			x	x	ps.1.1-ps.1.3
					x	ps.1.4
	src	x	x	x	x	ps.1.1-ps.1.3
			x		x	ps.1.4 phase 1
		x	x		x	ps.1.4 phase 2

Copies the content of the source to the destination register. Question every use of move because there might be more suitable instructions.

Instruction	Arguments	v_n	c_n	t_n	r_n	Version
mul	dest			x	x	ps.1.1-ps.1.3
					x	ps.1.4
	src0, src1	x	x	x	x	ps.1.1-ps.1.3
			x		x	ps.1.4 phase 1
		x	x		x	ps.1.4 phase 2

Performs the following operation:
```
dest = src0 * src1
```

```
; The following examples show a modulation of a light map with a color map.
; This technique is often used to darken parts of a color map. In this case
; it is called dark mapping
ps.1.1
tex t0 ; color map
tex t3 ; light map
mul r0, t0, t3

; Dark Mapping
ps.1.4
texld r0, t0 ; color map
texld r3, t3 ; light map
mul r0, r0, r3
```

nop

Performs no operation in ps.1.1-ps.1.4.

Instruction	Arguments	v_n	c_n	t_n	r_n	Version
sub	dest			x	x	ps.1.1-ps.1.3
					x	ps.1.4
	src0, src1	x	x	x	x	ps.1.1-ps.1.3
			x		x	ps.1.4 phase 1
		x	x		x	ps.1.4 phase 2

Performs the following operation:
```
dest = src0 - src1
```

```
ps.1.1
tex t0          ; color map #1
tex t1          ; color map #2
sub r0, t1, t0  ; subtract t0 from t1
```

All arithmetic instructions can use the temporary registers rn. The rn registers are initially unset and cannot be used as source operands until they are written. This requirement is enforced independently per each channel of each rn register. In ps.1.4, the tn registers cannot be used with any arithmetic instruction, so they are restricted on texture addressing instructions (exception: texdepth).

Valid source registers for first phase arithmetic instructions are rn and cn. Valid source registers for second phase arithmetic instructions are rn, vn, and cn.

The comparison of ps.1.1-ps.1.3 to ps.1.4 shows only a few differences. The ps.1.4-only instruction is bem. It substitutes the texbem and texbeml capabilities in an arithmetic operation in ps.1.4. Furthermore, the cmd and cnd instructions are more powerful in ps.1.4. The scope of the arithmetic instructions is much bigger in ps.1.4 than in ps.1.1-ps.1.3 because they are used for all texture addressing and blending tasks in ps.1.4.

As with the vertex shader, the pixel shader arithmetic instructions provide no If statement, but this functionality can be emulated with cmp or cnd.

All of the rn.a channels are marked as unset at the end of the first phase and cannot be used as a source operand until written. As a result, the fourth channel of color data will be lost during the phase transition. This problem can be partly solved by reordering the instructions. For example, the following code snippet will lose the alpha value in r3.

```
ps.1.4
...
texld r3, t3
phase
...
mul r0, r2, r3
```

The next code snippet will not loose the alpha value:

```
ps.1.4
...
phase
texld r3, t3
...
mul r0, r2, r3
```

If no phase marker is present, then the entire shader is validated as being in the second phase.

All four channels of the shader result r0 must be written.

ps.1.1-ps.1.3 and ps.1.4 are limited in different ways regarding the maximum number of source registers of the same type that can be read.

Read Port Limit

The read port limit gives you the maximum number of registers of the same register type that can be used as a source register in a single instruction.

Register Name	Version			
	ps.1.1	ps.1.2	ps.1.3	ps.1.4
cn	2	2	2	2
rn	2	2	2	3
tn	2	3	3	1
vn	2	2	2	2

The color registers have a read port limit of 2 in all versions. In the following code snippet, mad uses *v0* and *v1* as a source register:

```
ps.1.1 // Version instruction
tex t0 // Declare texture
mad r0, v0, t0, v1
```

This example exposes a readport limit of 2. The following example exposes a readport limit of 1 because *v0* is used twice:

```
ps.1.1 // Version instruction
tex t0 // Declare texture
mad r0, v0, t0, v0
```

The following pixel shader fails in ps.1.1:

```
ps.1.1
tex t0
tex t1
tex t2
mad r0, t0, t1, t2
```

It exceeds the readport limit of 2 for the texture registers. This shader won't fail with ps.1.2 and ps.1.3 because these versions have a readport limit of 3 for the *tn* registers. The functional equivalent in ps.1.4 won't fail either:

```
ps.1.4
texld r0, t0
texld r1, t1
texld r2, t2
mad r0, r0, r1, r2
```

Another example for the usage of three temporary registers in ps.1.4 in the same instruction is shown in the examples for the cmp and cnd instructions. In ps.1.4 the *tn* registers cannot be used with arithmetic instructions and none of the texture address instructions can use more than one *tn* register as a source; therefore, it is not possible to cross the readport limit of the *tn* registers in ps.1.4.

There is no write port limit because every instruction has only one destination register.

Instruction Modifiers

How instructions can be modified is best illustrated in the following diagram:

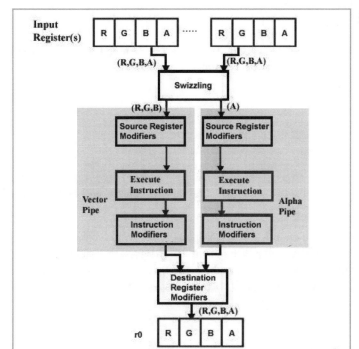

Figure 12: Pixel shader ALU

This diagram shows the parallel pipeline structure of the pixel shader ALU. The vector, or color, pipeline handles the color values and the scalar, or alpha, pipeline handles the alpha value of a 32-bit value. There are "extensions" for instructions that enable the programmer to change the way data is read and/or written by the instruction. These are called swizzling, source register modifiers, instruction modifiers, and destination register modifiers.

We will work through all instruction "extensions" shown in Figure 12 in the following sections.

Swizzling/Using Selectors

In contrast to the more powerful swizzles that can be used in vertex shaders, the swizzling supported in pixel shader is only able to replicate a single channel of a source register to all channels. This is done by so-called source register selectors.

Source Register Selectors	Syntax	ps.1.1	ps.1.2	ps.1.3	ps.1.4
Red replicate	source.r				x
Green replicate	source.g				x
Blue replicate	source.b	x	x	x	x
Alpha replicate	source.a	x	x	x	x

The .r and .g selectors are only available in ps.1.4. The following instruction replicates the red channel to all channels of the source register:

```
r1.r ; r1.rgba = r1.r
```

As shown in Figure 12, selectors are applied first in the pixel shader ALU. They are only valid on source registers of arithmetic instructions.

The .b replicate functionality is available in ps.1.1-ps.1.3 since the release of DirectX 8.1, but this swizzle is only valid together with an alpha write mask in the destination register of an instruction like this:

```
mul r0.a, r0, r1.b
```

Note: ps.1.1 does not support the .b replicate in DirectX 8.0.

This means that the .b source swizzle cannot be used with dp3 in ps.1.1-ps.1.3 because the only valid write destination masks for dp3 are .rgb or .rgba (write masks will be presented later):

```
dp3 r0.a, r0, c0.b ; fails
```

The ability to replicate the blue channel to alpha opens the door to a bandwidth optimization method, described in an NVIDIA OpenGL paper titled "Alpha Test Tricks" [Dominé01]. A pixel shader allows a dot product operation at the pixel level between two RGB vectors. Therefore, one can set one of the vectors to be (1.0, 1.0, 1.0), turning the dot product into a summation of the other's vectors components:

```
(R, G, B) dot (1.0, 1.0, 1.0) = R + G + B
```

In the following code snippet, the pixel shader instruction dp3 calculates the sum of the RGB color by replicating the scalar result into all four channels of *r1*.

```
ps.1.1
def c0, 1.0, 1.0, 1.0, 1.0
tex t0
dp3 r1, t0, c0
mov r0.a, r1.b
+mov r0.rgb, t0
```

An appropriate blending function might look like this:

```
dev->SetRenderState(D3DRS_ALPHAREF, (DWORD)0x00000001);
dev->SetRenderState(D3DRS_ALPHATESTENABLE, TRUE);
dev->SetRenderState(D3DRS_ALPHAFUNC, D3DCMP_GREATEREQUAL);
```

If the color data being rasterized is more opaque than the color at a given pixel (D3DPCMPCAPS_GREATEREQUAL), the pixel is written. Otherwise, the rasterizer ignores the pixel altogether, saving the processing required to, for example, blend the two colors.

An even more clever method to utilize the alpha test for fillrate optimization was shown by *Direct 3D ShaderX* author Dean Calver on the public Microsoft DirectX discussion forum [Calver]. He uses an alpha map to lerp three textures this way:

```
; Dean Calver
; 2 lerps from a combined alpha texture
ps.1.1
tex t0                  ; combined alpha map
tex t1                  ; texture0
tex t2                  ; texture1
tex t3                  ; texture2
mov r1.a, t0.b          ; copy blue to r1.a
lrp r0, r1.a, t2, t1    ; lerp between t1 and t2
lrp r0, t0.a, t3, r0    ; lerp between result and t3
```

The .a replicate is analogous to the D3DTA_ALPHAREPLICATE flag in the DX6/7 multitexturing unit.

> **Note:** To move any channel to any other channel, use dp3 to replicate the channel across, and then mask it out with the help of def instructions. The following pixel shader moves the blue channel to the alpha channel:
>
> ```
> ; move the red to blue and output combined
> ps.1.1
> def c0, 1.f, 0.f, 0.f, 0.f ; select red channel
> def c1, 0.f, 0.f, 1.f, 0.f ; mask for blue channel
> def c2, 1.f, 1.f, 0.f, 1.f ; mask for all channels but blue
> tex t0
> dp3 r0, t0, c0            ; copy red to all channels
> mul r0, r0, c1            ; mask so only blue is left
> mad r0, t0, c2, r0        ; remove blue from original texture and
>                          ; add red shifted into blue
> ```
>
> This trick was shown by *Direct3D ShaderX* author Dean Calver on the Microsoft DirectX discussion forum [Calver].

In ps.1.4, there are specific source register selectors for texld and texcrd:

Source Register Selectors	Description	Syntax
.xyz/.rgb	maps x, y, z to x, y, z ,z	source.xyz/source.rgb
.xyw/.rga	maps x, y, w to x, y, w, w	source.xyw/source.rga

texld and texcrd are only able to use three channels in their source registers, so these selectors provide the option of taking the third component from either the third or the fourth component of the source register. Here are two examples of how to use these selectors:

```
texld r0, t1.rgb
...
texcrd r1.rgb, t1.rga
texcrd r4.rgb, t2.rgb
```

An overview of all possible source register selectors, modifiers, and destination write masks is provided with the description of the texcrd and texld instructions above.

Source Register Modifiers

Source register modifiers are useful for adjusting the range of register data in preparation for the instruction or to scale the value.

Modifier	Syntax	ps.1.1	ps.1.2	ps.1.3	ps.1.4
Bias	r0_bias	x	x	x	x
Invert	1–r0	x	x	x	x
Negate	–r0	x	x	x	x
Scale x2	r0_x2				x
Signed Scaling	r0_bx2	x	x	x	x

All modifiers can be used on arithmetic instructions. In ps.1.1, you can use the signed scale modifier _bx2 on the source register of any texm3x2* and texm3x3* instruction. In ps.1.2 and ps.1.3, it can be used on the source register of any texture address instruction.

bias subtracts 0.5 from all components. It allows the same operation as D3DTOP_ADD-SIGNED in the DX6/7 multitexturing unit. It is used to change the range of data from 0 to 1 to –0.5 to 0.5. Applying bias to data outside this range may produce undefined results. Data outside this range might be saturated with the _sat instruction modifier to the range [0..1] before being used with a biased source register (more on instruction modifiers in the next section).

A typical example for this modifier is detail mapping, shown in the add example.

Invert inverts (1 – value) the value for each channel of the specified source register. The following code snippet uses inversion to complement the source register *r1*:

```
mul r0, r0, 1-r1 ; multiply by (1.0 - r1)
```

Negate negates all source register components by using a subtract sign before a register. This modifier is mutually exclusive with the invert modifier, so it cannot be applied to the same register.

Scale with the _x2 modifier is only available in ps.1.4. It multiplies a value by two before using it in the instruction, and it is mutually exclusive to the invert modifier.

Signed scaling with the _bx2 modifier is a combination of bias and scale, so it subtracts 0.5 from each channel and scales the result by 2. It remaps input data from unsigned to signed values. As with bias, using data outside of the range 0 to 1 may produce undefined results. This modifier is typically used in dp3 instructions. An example for this is presented with the description of the dp3 instruction above. Signed scaling is mutually exclusive with the invert modifier.

None of these modifiers change the content of the source register they are applied to. These modifiers are applied only to the data read from the register, so the value stored in the source register is not changed.

Modifiers and selectors may be combined freely. In the following example, *r1* uses the negative, bias, and signed scaling modifiers as well as a red selector:

```
-r1_bx2.r
```

With the help of the source register modifiers, per-pixel normalization is possible in the pixel shader. Per-pixel normalization can be used instead of a cubemap:

```
; Assuming v0 contains the unnormalized biased & scaled vector ( just
; like a normal map), r0 will end up with a very close to normalized
; result.
; This trick is also useful to do 'detail normal maps' by adding
; a vector to a normal map, and then renormalizing it.
dp3 r0, v0_bx2, v0_bx2 ; r0 = N . N
mad r0, v0_bias, 1-r0, v0_bx2 ; (v0_bias * (1-r0)) + v0_bx2
                             ; ((N - 0.5) * (1 - N.N)) + (N - 0.5) * 2
```

Normalization requires calculating 1/sqrt(N). This code snippet normalizes the normal vector with a standard Newton-Raphson iteration for approximating a square root. This trick was shown by Sim Dietrich in the Microsoft DirectX forum [Dietrich-DXDev].

In the first line, the normal vector N is biased and scaled by _bx2 and then multiplied with itself via a dot product. The result is stored in *r0*. In the next line, the normal is again biased and scaled and added to the inverse of *r0*. The result of this addition is multiplied with the biased normal.

There are additional modifiers specific to the texld and texcrd instructions in the ps.1.4 implementation. These modifiers provide projective divide functionality by dividing the x and y values by either the z or w values; therefore, projective dependent reads are possible in ps.1.4.

Source Register Modifiers	Description	Syntax

_dz/_db	divide x, y components by z (pseudocode):
	`if (z==0)`
	`  x' = 1.0;`
	`else`
	`  x' = x/z;`
	`if (z==0)`
	`  y' = 1.0;`
	`else  y' = y/z;`
	`// z' and w' are undefined`
		source_dz/source_db

_dw/_da	divide x, y components by w (pseudocode):
	`if (w==0)`
	`  x' = 1.0;`
	`else`
	`  x' = x/w;`
	`if (w==0)`
	`  y' = 1.0;`
	`else`
	`  y' = y/w;`
	`// z and w are undefined`
		source_dw/source_da

These modifiers provide a functional replacement of the D3DTFF_PROJECTED flag of the D3DTSS_TEXTURETRANSFORMFLAGS texture stage state flag in the pixel shader. A typical instruction would look like this:

```
texcrd r2.rg, t1_dw.xyw ; third channel unset
```

The modifier copies x/w and y/w from *t1* into the first two channels of *r2*. The third and fourth channels of *r2* are uninitialized. Any previous data written to these channels will be lost. The per-pixel perspective divide is useful, for example, for projective textures.

The restriction for the two texture addressing registers are:

texld	texcrd
_dz/_db only valid with rn (second phase)	Does not support _dz/_db
_dz/_db may be used no more that two times per shader	The fourth channel result of texcrd is unset/undefined in all cases.
The third channel is unset/undefined for the .xyw case.	
The same .xyz or .xyw modifier must be applied to every read of an individual tn register within a shader. If .xyw is being used on tn register read(s), this can be mixed with other read(s) of the same tn register using .xyw.	

Instruction Modifiers

After the swizzling of the source register channels and the modification of the values read out from a source register with source register modifiers, the instruction starts executing. As shown in Figure 12, now the instruction modifiers are applied. These are indicated as an appendix to the instruction connected via an underscore. Instruction modifiers are used to change the output of an instruction. They can multiply or divide a result or clamp a result to [0..1]:

Source Register Modifiers	Description	Syntax	ps.1.1-ps.1.3	ps.1.4
_x2	multiply by 2	instruction_x2	x	x
_x4	multiply by 4	instruction_x4	x	x
_x8	multiply by 8	instruction_x8		x
_d2	divide by 2	instruction_d2	x	x
_d4	divide by 4	instruction_d4		x
_d8	divide by 8	instruction_d8		x
_sat	clamp to [0..1]	instruction_sat	x	x

Instruction modifiers can be used only on arithmetic instructions. The _x8, _d4, and _d8 modifiers are new to the 1.4 shading model. _sat may be used alone or combined with one of the other modifiers (i.e., mad_d8_sat).

Multiplier modifiers are useful for scaling a value. Note that any such scaling reduces accuracy of results. The following examples scale the results by using _x2 or _x4:

```
ps.1.1
tex t0
tex t1
mul_x2 r0, t1, t0      ; (t1 * t0) * 2
...
mul_x2 r0, 1-t1, t0    ; t0 * inverse(t1) * 2
...
mad_x2 r0, t1, v0, t0  ; (t1 + ( v0 * t0)) * 2
...
mul_x4 r0, v0, t0      ; (v0 * t0) * 4
mul_x4 r1, v1, t1      ; (v1 * t1) * 4
add r0, r0, r1         ; (v0*t0 * 4)+(v1*t1 * 4)
```

The _x2 modifer does the same as a shift left in C/C++.

The _d2 modifer does the same as a right shift in C/C++. Here is a more complex example:

```
; Here is an example for per-pixel area lighting
ps.1.1
def c1, 1.0, 1.0, 1.0, 1.0     ; sky color
def c2, 0.15, 0.15, 0.15, 1.0 ; ground color
def c5, 0.5, 0.5, 0.5, 1.0
tex t0 ; normal map
tex t1 ; base texture
dp3_d2 r0, v0_bx2, t0_bx2       ; v0.rgb is hemi axis in tangent space
                                ; dot normal with hemi axis
```

```
add r0, r0, c5                  ; map into range
lrp r0, r0, c1, c2
mul r0, r0, t1                  ; modulate base texture
```

This pixel shader biases the hemisphere axis in v0 and scales it by 2. The same is done to the values of the normal map. dp3_bx2 divides the result through 2. The add instruction adds 0.5 to the vector of r0. lrp uses r0 as the proportion to linearly interpolate between sky color in c1 and ground color in c2.

The saturation modifer _sat clamps each component or channel of the result to the range [0..1]. It is most often used to clamp dot products, like in the code snippet:

```
dp3_sat r0, t1_bx2, r0 ; N.H
dp3_sat r1.rgb, t1_bx2, r1 ; N.L
```

The result of the dot product operation of the normal vector with the half angle vector and the result of the dot product operation of the normal and the light vector are saturated. That means the values in r0 and r1.rgb are clamped to [0..1].

Destination Register Modifiers/Masking

A destination register modifer, or write mask, controls which channel in a register is updated, so it only alters the value of the channel it is applied to.

Write masks are supported for arithmetic instructions only. The following destination write masks are available for all arithmetic instructions:

Write Mask	Syntax	ps.1.1-ps.1.3	ps.1.4
color	destination register.rgb	x	x
alpha	destination register.a	x	x
red	destination register.r		x
green	destination register.g		x
blue	destination register.b		x
arbitrary			x

In ps.1.1-ps.1.3, a pixel shader can only use the .rgb or .a write masks. The arbitrary write mask in ps.1.4 allows any set of channels in the order r, g, b, a to be combined. It is possible to choose, for example:

```
mov r0.ra, r1
```

If no destination write mask is specified, the destination write mask defaults to the .rgba case, which updates all channels in the destination register. An alternate syntax for the r, g, b, a channels is x, y, z, w.

As with the source register selectors and source register modifiers, the texld and texcrd instructions have additional write masks and write mask rules. texcrd can write only to the .rgb channels. It also supports a write mask that masks the first two channels with .rg or .xy. texld uses all four channels of the destination register. There is no alternative write mask available.

The usage of write masks is shown in the following ps.1.4 pixel shader that handles diffuse bump mapping with two spotlights (taken from the file 14_bumpspot.sha of the ATI Treasure Chest example program on the companion CD):

```
ps.1.4

def c0, 1.0f, 1.0f, 1.0f, 1.0f      ; Light 1 Color
def c1, 1.0f, -0.72f, 1.0f, 1.0f    ; Light 1 Angle scale(x) and bias(Y)
def c2, 1.0f, 1.0f, 1.0f, 1.0f      ; Light 2 Color
def c3, 0.25f, 0.03f, 1.0f, 1.0f    ; Light 2 Angle scale(x) and bias(Y)

texcrd r0.rgb, t2    ; Spot light 1 direction
texcrd r1.rgb, t4    ; Spot light 2 direction
texld r2, t1         ; Light 1 to Point vector
texld r3, t3         ; Light 2 to Point vector
texcrd r4.rgb, t1             ; Light 1 space position for attenuation
texcrd r5.rgb, t3             ; Light 2 space position for attenuation

dp3_sat r4.x, r4, r4         ; Light 1 Distance^2
dp3_sat r5.x, r5, r5         ; Light 2 Distance^2
dp3_sat r4.y, r0, r2_bx2     ; Light 1 Angle from center of spotlight
dp3_sat r5.y, r1, r3_bx2     ; Light 2 Angle from center of spotlight
mad_x4 r4.y, r4.y, c1.x, c1.y ; Light 1 scale and bias for angle
mad_x4 r5.y, r5.y, c3.x, c3.y ; Light 2 scale and bias for angle

phase

texld r0, t0    ; Base Map
texld r1, t0    ; Normal Map
texld r4, r4    ; Distance/Angle lookup map
texld r5, r5    ; Distance/Angle lookup map

dp3_sat r2.rgb, r1_bx2, r2_bx2 ; *= (N.L1)
mul_x2 r2.rgb, r2, r4.r        ; Attenuation from distance and angle
mad r2.rgb, r2, c0, c7         ; * Light Color + Ambient

dp3_sat r3.rgb, r1_bx2, r3_bx2 ; *= (N.L2)
mul_x2 r3.rgb, r3, r5.r        ; Attenuation from distance and angle
mad r3.rgb, r3, c2, r2         ; * Light 2 Color + Light 1 Color + Ambient

mul r0.rgb, r3, r0             ; Modulate by base map
+mov r0.a, c0
```

There are four different write masks used throughout this shader. These are the *.rgb*, *.x*, *.y*, and *.a* write masks. The first write mask used for the *texcrd* instructions are imperative. *texld* can't handle write masks other than .rgba, which is the same as applying no explicit write mask. The first four *dp3* and the next two mad instructions write to the first component x of the r4 register and the second component y of the r5 register. These write masks are not supported by ps.1.1-ps.1.3. The usage of the .rgb write mask in the second phase of this shader is supported by all implementations. The last two lines of this shader show the pairing of two instructions using co-issue. We will discuss instruction pairing, or "co-issuing," in the next section.

Instruction Pairing

As shown in Figure 12, there are two pipelines: one for the color data and one for the alpha data. Because of the parallel nature of these pipelines, the instructions that write color data and instructions that write only alpha data can be paired. This helps reduce the fill-rate. Only arithmetic instructions can be co-issued, with the exception of dp4. Pairing, or co-issuing, is indicated by a plus sign (+) preceding the second instruction of the pair. The following shader fragment shows three pairs of co-issued instructions:

```
 dp3_sat r1.rgb, t1_bx2, r1
+mul r1.a, r0, r0
 mul r1.rgb, r1, v0
+mul r1.a, r1, r1
 add r1.rgb, r1, c7
+mul_d2 r1.a, r1, r1
```

First, a dp3 instruction is paired with a mul, then a mul instruction with a mul, and finally an add instruction with a mul. Pairing happens in ps.1.1-ps.1.3 always with the help of a pair of .rgb and .a write masks. In ps.1.4, a pairing of the .r, .g, or .b write masks together with an .a masked destination register is possible. The line:

```
mul r1.a, r0, r0
```

only writes the alpha value of the result of the multiplication of *r0* with itself into *r1.a*.

Co-issued instructions are considered a single entity, with the result from the first instruction unavailable until both instructions are finished and vice versa. The following shader will fail shader validation:

```
ps.1.1
def c0, 1, 1, 1, 1
mov r0, v0
dp3 r1.rgb, r0, c0
+mov r0.a, r1.b
```

Note: GeForce3/4TI has a problem with co-issuing instructions in the eighth arithmetic instruction slot. It stops showing the results when a co-issue happens in the eighth arithmetic instruction, whereas the REF works as expected. The following meaningless pixel shader doesn't show a result with the driver version 28.32:

```
ps.1.1
tex t0 ; color map
tex t1 ; normal map
dp3 r0,t1_bx2,v1_bx2; ; dot(normal,half)
mul r1,r0,r0;
mul r0,r1,r1;
mul r1,r0,r0;
mul r0,r1,r1;
mul r1, r0, r0
mul r0, r1, r1
; assemble final color
mul r0.rgb,t0,r0
+mov r0.a, r1
```

If you use the REF or remove the last line, the results are as expected.

mov tries to read r1.b, but *dp3* did not write to r1.b at that time. The shader will fail because r1.b was not initialized before. This could be troublesome when r1.b is initialized before by any instruction. The validator will not catch the bug, and the results will not look as expected.

Another restriction to be aware of is the maximum number of three different register types that can be used across two co-issued instructions.

Assemble Pixel Shader

After checking for pixel shader support, setting the proper textures with SetTexture(), writing a pixel shader, and setting the needed constant values, the pixel shader has to be assembled. This is needed because Direct3D uses pixel shaders as byte-code.

Assembling the shader is helpful in finding bugs earlier in the development cycle.

At the time of publication, there are three different ways to compile a pixel shader:

- **Precompiled Shaders** — Use the pixel shader in a separate ASCII file, such as test.psh, and compile it with a pixel shader assembler (Microsoft Pixel Shader Assembler or NVASM) to produce a byte-code file which could be named test.pso. This way, not every person will be able to read and modify your source.
- **On-the-Fly Compiled Shaders** — Write the pixel shader in a separate ASCII file or as a char string into your *.cpp file and compile it "on-the-fly" while the application starts up with the D3DXAssembleShader*() functions.
- **Shaders in Effect Files** — Write the pixel shader source in an effect file and open this effect file when the application starts up. The pixel shader will be compiled by reading the effect file with D3DXCreateEffectFromFile(). It is also possible to precompile an effect file. This way, most of the handling of pixel shaders is simplified and handled by the effects file functions.

The precompiled shader should be the preferred way of compiling shaders, since compilation happens during development of the code (i.e., at the same time that the *.cpp files are compiled).

Create a Pixel Shader

The CreatePixelShader() function is used to create and validate a pixel shader:

```
HRESULT CreatePixelShader(
  CONST DWORD* pFunction,
  DWORD* pHandle
);
```

This function takes the pointer to the pixel shader byte-code in pFunction and returns a handle to the pixel shader in pHandle. A typical piece of source might look like this:

```
TCHAR Shad[255];
LPD3DXBUFFER pCode = NULL;
```

```
DXUtil_FindMediaFile(Shad, _T("environment.psh"));
if(FAILED(D3DXAssembleShaderFromFile(Shad,0,NULL, &pCode,NULL) ) )
  return E_FAIL;
if( FAILED(m_pd3dDevice->CreatePixelShader((DWORD*)pCode->GetBufferPointer(),
&m_dwPixShader) ) )
  return E_FAIL;
```

DXUtil_FindMediaFile() helps you find the ASCII file. D3DXAssembleShaderFromFile() compiles it before CreatePixelShader() returns the handle in m_dwPixShader.

The pointer pCode to the ID3DXBuffer interface is used to store the object code and return a pointer to this object code with GetBufferPointer().

Set Pixel Shader

You set a pixel shader for a specific amount of vertices by using the SetPixelShader() function before the DrawPrimitive*() call for these vertices:

```
m_pd3dDevice->SetPixelShader(m_dwPixShader);
```

The only parameter that has to be provided is the handle of the pixel shader created by CreatePixelShader(). The pixel shader is executed for every pixel that is covered by the vertices in the DrawPrimitive*() call.

Free Pixel Shader Resources

While the game shuts down or before a device change, the resources used by the pixel shader have to be freed. This must be done by calling DeletePixelShader() with the pixel shader handle like this:

```
if(m_dwPixShader)
    m_pd3dDevice->DeletePixelShader(m_dwPixShader);
```

Summary

We have walked step by step through a vertex shader creation process. Let's summarize what was shown so far:

■ First, the pixel shader support of end-user hardware has to be checked with the caps bit PixelShaderVersion.

■ All textures have to be set with SetTexture(), like with the multitexturing unit.

■ The constant values for a pixel shader have to be set afterward in the application code with the SetPixelShaderConstant() or in the pixel shader code with def.

■ There are texture address and arithmetic instructions. The scope of the texture address instruction in ps.1.1-ps.1.3 enfolds loading and changing of texture data. The scope of the texture address instructions in ps.1.4 enfolds only the loading of texture data. Changing of texture data is done in ps.1.4 and ps.1.1-ps.1.3 with the arithmetic instructions.

■ After a pixel shader is written into a source file, it has to be compiled.

■ To get a handle to a pixel shader, it has to be created with CreatePixelShader().

■ To use a pixel shader, it has to be set with a call to SetPixelShader().

■ At the end of a pixel shader-driven application, the resources occupied by the pixel shader must be freed with a call to DeletePixelShader().

What Happens Next?

In the next article, "Programming Pixel Shaders," we will start with a basic pixel shader program and discuss a few basic algorithms and how to implement them with pixel shaders.

References

[Bendel] Steffen Bendel, "Hallo World — Font Smoothing with Pixel Shaders," *Direct3D ShaderX*.

[Beaudoin/Guardado] Philippe Beaudoin and Juan Guardado, " A Non-Integer Power Function on the Pixel Shader," *Direct3D ShaderX*.

[Brennan] Chris Brennan, "Per-Pixel Fresnel Term," *Direct3D ShaderX*.

[Brennan2] Chris Brennan, "Diffuse Cube Mapping," *Direct3D ShaderX*.

[Brennan3] Chris Brennan, "Accurate Reflections and Refractions by Adjusting for Object Distance," *Direct3D ShaderX*.

[Card/Mitchell] Drew Card and Jason L. Mitchell, "Non-Photorealistic Rendering with Pixel and Vertex Shaders," *Direct3D ShaderX*.

[Calver] Dean Calver, Microsoft DirectX discussion forum, mail from Fri, 21 Sep 2001 10:00:55, http://discuss.microsoft.com/SCRIPTS/WA-MSD.EXE?A2=ind0109C&L=DIRECTXDEV&P=R25479.

[Dietrich01] Sim Dietrich, "Guard Band Clipping in Direct3D," NVIDIA web site.

[Dietrich-DXDev] Sim Dietrich, Microsoft DirectX discussion forum, mail from Tue, 14 Aug 2001 20:36:02, http://discuss.microsoft.com/SCRIPTS/WA-MSD.EXE?A2=ind0108B&L=DIRECTXDEV&P=R13431.

[Dominé01] Sébastien Dominé, "Alpha Test Tricks," NVIDIA web site.

[Hart] Evan Hart, "3D Textures and Pixel Shaders," *Direct3D ShaderX*.

[Isidoro/Brennan] John Isidoro and Chris Brennan, "Per-Pixel Strand-Based Anisotropic Lighting," *Direct3D ShaderX*.

[Isidoro/Riguer] John Isidoro and Guennadi Riguer, "Texture Perturbation Effects," *Direct3D ShaderX*.

[Kraus] Martin Kraus, "Truly Volumetric Effects," *Direct3D ShaderX*.

[Mitchell] Jason L. Mitchell, "Image Processing with Pixel Shaders in Direct3D," *Direct3D ShaderX*.

[Moravánsky] Ádám Moravánszky, "Bump Mapped BRDF Rendering," *Direct3D ShaderX*.

[Vlachos] Alex Vlachos, "Blending Textures for Terrain," *Direct3D ShaderX*.

[Watt92] Alan Watt and Mark Watt, *Advanced Animation and Rendering Techniques* (Addison Wesley, 1992).

[Weiskopf] Daniel Weiskopf and Matthias Hopf, "Real-Time Simulation and Rendering of Particle Flows," *Direct3D ShaderX*.

[Zecha] Oliver Zecha, "Perlin Noise and Returning Results for Shader Programs," *Direct3D ShaderX*.

Additional Resources

The best resource to accompany this article is the pixel shader assembler reference in the Direct3D 8.1 documentation at DirectX Graphics->Reference->Pixel Shader Assembler Reference.

A lot of valuable information on pixel shaders can be found at the NVIDIA (developer.nvidia.com) and ATI (http://www.ati.com/developer/) web sites, as well as other sites.

Author	Article	Published at
Philip Taylor	Per-Pixel Lighting	http://msdn.microsoft.com/directx
Miscellaneous	Meltdown Power Point Slides	http://www.microsoft.com/mscorp/corpevents/ \ meltdown2001/presentations.asp
Sim Dietrich	Intro to Pixel Shading in DX8	NVIDIA web site (courseware)
Sim Dietrich	DX8 Pixel Shader Details	NVIDIA web site (courseware)
Sim Dietrich	DX8 Pixel Shaders	NVIDIA web site (courseware)
Sim Dietrich	AGDC Per-Pixel Shading	NVIDIA web site (courseware)
Jason L. Mitchell	1.4 Pixel Shaders	ATI web site
Jason L. Mitchell	Advanced Vertex and Pixel Shader Techniques	ATI web site
Alex Vlachos	Preparing Sushi — How Hardware Guys Write a 3D Graphics Engine	ATI web site
Rich	Direct3D 8.0 pipeline	http://www.xmission.com/~legalize/book/
Dave Salvator	3D Pipeline Part I-III	http://www.extremetech.com and there <3D Graphics, Gaming & Audio> -> <Analysis & Tutorials>

Acknowledgments

I'd like to recognize the following individuals who were involved in proofreading and improving this article (in alphabetical order): Jason L. Mitchell (ATI), Ádám Moravánszky (Swiss Federal Institute of Technology), and Matthias Wloka (NVIDIA).

Programming Pixel Shaders

Wolfgang F. Engel

This article covers the basics of pixel shader programming. You will learn in the following pages how to code a pixel shader-driven application by using the same lighting reflection models as in "Programming Vertex Shaders." There is one big difference: This time, we will calculate light reflection on a per-pixel basis, which leads to a bumpy impression of the surface.

Most of the effects that modify the appearance of a surface in many games are calculated on a per-vertex basis. This means that the lighting/shading calculations are done for each vertex of a triangle, as opposed to each pixel that gets rendered or per-pixel. In some cases, per-vertex lighting produces noticeable artifacts. Think of a large triangle with a light source close to the surface. As long as the light is close to one of the vertices of the triangle, you can see the diffuse and specular reflection on the triangle. When the light moves toward the center of the triangle, the rendering gradually loses these lighting effects. In the worst case, the light is directly in the middle of the triangle and there is almost no effect visible on the triangle, when there should be a triangle with a bright spot in the middle.

That means that a smooth-looking object needs a lot of vertices or a high level of tesselation; otherwise, the coarseness of the underlying geometry is visible.

That's the reason the examples in "Programming Vertex Shaders" used a highly tessellated Bézier patch class — to make the lighting effect look smooth.

RacorX6

Our first example shows a directional light source with a diffuse reflection model.

Like all the previous and upcoming examples, the example on the following page is based on the common files framework provided with the DirectX 8.1 SDK (read more in "Programming Vertex Shaders"). Therefore, Alt+Enter switches between the windowed and full-screen mode, F2 gives you a selection of the usable drivers, and Esc will shut down the application. Additionally, the B key toggles diffuse lighting, the W and S keys allow zooming in and out, the left mouse button rotates the globe, the right mouse button moves the directional light, and the P key toggles between ps.1.1 and ps.1.4, if available.

The following examples won't run on graphics hardware that doesn't support pixel shaders. On hardware that is not capable of running ps.1.4, the message "ps.1.4 Not Supported" is displayed.

As in the previous three articles, we will track the life cycle of the pixel shader in the following pages.

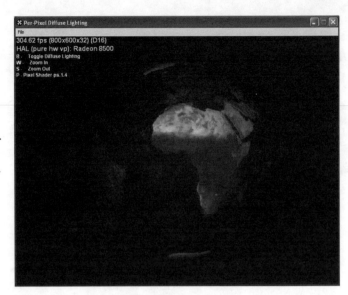

Figure 1: Per-pixel diffuse reflection

Check for Pixel Shader Support

To be able to fall back on a different pixel shader version or the multitexturing unit, the pixel shader support of the graphics hardware is checked with the following piece of code in ConfirmDevice():

```
if( pCaps->PixelShaderVersion < D3DPS_VERSION(1,4) )
    m_bPS14Available = FALSE;
if( pCaps->PixelShaderVersion < D3DPS_VERSION(1,1) )
    return E_FAIL;
```

The value in the D3DCAPS structure, which is filled by GetDeviceCaps(), corresponds to the ps.x.x instruction at the beginning of the pixel shader source. Therefore, the macro D3DPS_VERSION(1,4) checks for support of ps.1.4. If ps.1.4 is not available, the BOOL variable m_bPS14Available is set to false and the user is prevented from switching between the pixel shader versions.

Set Texture Operation Flags (with D3DTSS_* flags)

The pixel shader functionality replaces the D3DTSS_COLOROP and D3DTSS_ALPHAOP operations and their associated arguments and modifiers, but the texture addressing, bump environment, texture filtering, texture border color, mip map, and texture transform flags (except in ps.1.4: D3DTFF_PROJECTED) are still valid. The texture coordinate index is still valid together with the fixed-function T&L pipeline (read more in "Fundamentals of Pixel Shaders"). Using the D3DTEXF_LINEAR flag for the D3DTSS_MINFILTER and D3DTSS_MAGFILTER texture stage states indicates the usage of bilinear filtering of textures ("linear filtering" in Direct3D terminology). This is done in RestoreDeviceObjects() for the color map:

```
m_pd3dDevice->SetTextureStageState( 0, D3DTSS_MINFILTER, D3DTEXF_LINEAR);
m_pd3dDevice->SetTextureStageState( 0, D3DTSS_MAGFILTER, D3DTEXF_LINEAR);
```

> **Note:** Switching on mip map filtering or trilinear filtering with the following statement would be a good idea in production code:
> ```
> m_pd3dDevice->SetTextureStageState( 0, D3DTSS_MIPFILTER,
> D3DTEXF_LINEAR);
> ```

Set Texture (with SetTexture())

With proper pixel shader support and the texture stage states set, the textures are set with the following calls in Render():

```
// diffuse lighting
if(m_bBump)
{
  m_pd3dDevice->SetTexture(0,m_pColorTexture);
  m_pd3dDevice->SetTexture(1,m_pNormalMap);

  m_pd3dDevice->SetPixelShader(m_dwPixShaderDot3);
}
else
{
  //no lighting, just base color texture
  m_pd3dDevice->SetTexture(0,m_pColorTexture);
  m_pd3dDevice->SetPixelShader(m_dwPixShader);
}
```

If the user switched the diffuse lighting off, only the color texture is set. Otherwise, the color texture and the normal or bump map texture are set.

Define Constants (with SetPixelShaderConstant()/def)

We set four constant values in c33 in RestoreDeviceObjects(). These constants are used to bias the values that should be sent via the vertex shader color output register to v0 of the pixel shader:

```
// constant values
D3DXVECTOR4 half(0.5f,0.5f,0.5f,0.5f);
m_pd3dDevice->SetVertexShaderConstant(33, &half, 1);
```

In FrameMove(), the light direction, the concatenated world, view, and projection matrix, and the world matrix is set in c12, c8, and c0:

```
// light direction
D3DXVec4Normalize(&m_LightDir,&m_LightDir);
m_pd3dDevice->SetVertexShaderConstant(12, &m_LightDir, 1 ); // light direction

// world * view * proj matrix
D3DXMATRIX matTemp;
D3DXMatrixTranspose(&matTemp,&(m_matWorld * m_matView * m_matProj));
m_pd3dDevice->SetVertexShaderConstant(8, &matTemp, 4);

// world matrix
D3DXMatrixTranspose(&matTemp,&m_matWorld);
m_pd3dDevice->SetVertexShaderConstant(0, &matTemp, 4);
```

This example uses a directional light that can be moved with the right mouse button. The mouse movement is tracked via WM_MOUSEMOVE in the Windows message procedure function MsgProc().

Pixel Shader Instructions

Provided in all the upcoming examples is a very simple ps.1.1 pixel shader in diff.psh that only displays the color map. Additionally, a ps.1.1 pixel shader in diffDot3.psh and a ps.1.4 pixel shader in diffDot314.psh that are specific for the respective examples can be found in the example directory on the companion CD.

```
ps.1.1
tex t0 //sample texture
mov r0,t0

ps.1.1
tex t0                     ; color map
tex t1                     ; normal map
dp3 r1, t1_bx2, v0_bx2 ; dot(normal,light)
mul r0,t0, r1             ; modulate against base color

ps.1.4
texld r0, t0              ; color map
texld r1, t0              ; normal map
dp3 r2, r1_bx2, v0_bx2 ; dot(normal, light)
mul r0, r0, r2
```

Unlike vertex shaders, the instructions in a pixel shader need a specific ordering, which is called the instruction flow. This instruction flow differs between ps.1.1-ps.1.3 and ps.1.4.

ps.1.1-ps.1.3 allow four types of instructions, which must appear in this order:

- Version instruction: ps.1.1
- Constant instruction: def c0, 1.0, 1.0, 1.0, 1.0
- Texture address instructions: tex*
- Arithmetic instructions: mul, mad, dp3, etc.

Every pixel shader starts with the version instruction. It is used by the assembler to validate the instructions that follow. After the version instruction, a constant definition could be placed with def. Such a def instruction is translated into a SetPixelShaderConstant() call when SetPixelShader() is executed.

The next group of instructions are the texture address instructions. They are used to load data into the tn registers and additionally in ps.1.1-ps.1.3 to modify texture coordinates. Up to four texture address instructions could be used in a ps.1.1-ps.1.3 pixel shader. The ps.1.1 pixel shader uses the tex instruction to load a color map and a normal map.

Until ps.1.4, it was not possible to use tex* instructions after an arithmetic instruction. Therefore, dp3 and mul had to come after the tex* instructions. There could be up to eight arithmetic instructions in a ps.1.1 shader.

The ps.1.4 pixel shader instruction flow is a little bit more complex:

- Version instruction: ps.1.4
- Constant instruction: def c0, 1.0, 1.0, 1.0, 1.0
- Texture address instructions: tex*

- Arithmetic instructions: mul, mad, dp3, etc.
- Phase marker
- Texture address instruction
- Arithmetic instructions

A ps.1.4 pixel shader must start with the version instruction. Then as many def instructions as needed may be placed into the pixel shader. This example doesn't use constants. There can be up to six texture addressing instructions after the constants. The diffuse reflection model shader only uses two texld instructions to load a color map and a normal map.

After the tex* instructions, up to eight arithmetic instructions can modify color, texture, or vector data. This shader only uses two arithmetic instructions: dp3 and mul.

Up to this point, a ps.1.4 pixel shader has the same instruction flow as a ps.1.1-ps.1.3 pixel shader. The phase marker allows it to double the number of texture addressing and arithmetic instructions. It divides the pixel shader into two phases: phase 1 and phase 2. That means as of ps.1.4, a second pass through the pixel shader hardware can be done. Adding up the number of arithmetic and addressing instructions shown in the pixel shader instruction flow above leads to 28 instructions. If no phase marker is specified, the default phase 2 allows up to 14 addressing and arithmetic instructions.

This pixel shader doesn't need more tex* or arithmetic instructions; therefore, a phase marker is not used.

In this simple example, the main difference between the ps.1.1 and the ps.1.4 pixel shader is the usage of the tex instructions in ps.1.1 to load the texture data into t0 and t1 and the usage of the texld instruction in ps.1.4 to load the texture data into r0 and r1. Both instructions are able to load four components of a texture. Valid registers for tex are tn registers only, whereas texld accepts only rn registers as the destination registers, tn in both phases as source registers, and rn only in the second phase.

The number of the temporary destination register of texld is the number of the texture stage. The source register always holds the texture coordinates. If the source register is a texture coordinate register, the number of the tn register is the number of the texture coordinate pair. For example, texld r0, t4 samples a texture from texture stage 0 with the help of the texture coordinate set 4. In this pixel shader, the texture with the color map is sampled from texture stage 0, with the texture coordinate set 0 and the texture with the normal map is sampled from texture stage 1 with the texture coordinate set 1.

The dp3 instruction calculates the diffuse reflection with a dot product of the light and the normal vector on a per-pixel basis. This instruction replicates the result to all four channels. dp3 does not automatically clamp the result to [0..1]. For example, the following line of code needs a _sat modifier:

Note: The dot product instruction executes in the vector portion of the pixel pipeline; therefore, it can be co-issued with an instruction that executes only in the alpha pipeline:

```
   dp3 r0.rgb, t0, r0
 + mov r.a, t0, r0
```

Because of the parallel nature of these pipelines, the instructions that write color data and the instructions that write only alpha data can be paired. This helps reduce the fill-rate. Co-issued instructions are considered a single entity, since the first instruction is not available until both instructions are finished and vice versa. Pairing happens in ps.1.1-ps.1.3 always with the help of a pair of .rgb and .a write masks. In ps.1.4, a pairing of the .r, .g., or .b write masks together with an .a masked destination register is possible. Therefore, for example, dp3.r is not possible in ps.1.1-ps.1.3.

```
dp3_sat r0, t1_bx2, r0
```

The calculation of the dp3 instruction in both pixel shaders is similar to the calculation of the diffuse reflection on a per-vertex basis in RacorX3 in "Programming Vertex Shaders," although the values provided to dp3 for the per-pixel reflection model are generated in different ways.

Per-Pixel Lighting

Per-pixel lighting needs per-pixel data. High-resolution information about the normal vector is stored in a two-dimensional array of three-dimensional vectors called a bump map or normal map. Each vector in such a normal map represents the direction in which the normal vector points. A normal map is typically constructed by extracting normal vectors from a height map whose contents represent the height of a flat surface at each pixel (read more in [Dietrich][Lengyel]). This is done in the following code snippet:

```
if(FAILED(D3DXCreateTextureFromFile(m_pd3dDevice, m_cColorMap,
                                    &m_pColorTexture)))
    return E_FAIL;

LPDIRECT3DTEXTURE8 pHeightMap = NULL;
if(FAILED(D3DXCreateTextureFromFile(m_pd3dDevice,m_cHeightMap,&pHeightMap)))
    return E_FAIL;

D3DSURFACE_DESC desc;
pHeightMap->GetLevelDesc(0,&desc);
if(FAILED(D3DXCreateTexture(m_pd3dDevice, desc.Width, desc.Height, 0, 0,
                           D3DFMT_A8R8G8B8,D3DPOOL_MANAGED, &m_pNormalMap)))
    return E_FAIL;

D3DXComputeNormalMap(m_pNormalMap,pHeightMap,NULL,0,D3DX_CHANNEL_RED,10);
SAFE_RELEASE(pHeightMap);
```

D3DXCreateTextureFromFile() reads in the height map file earthbump.bmp from the media directory and provides a handle to this texture. A new and empty texture is built with D3DX-CreateTexture() with the same width and height as the height map. D3DXComputeNormal-Map() converts the height field to a normal map and stores this map in the texture map created with D3DXCreateTexture().

Note: The CreateFileBasedNormalMap() function of the DotProduct3 example from the DirectX 8.1 SDK shows how to convert a height map into a normal map with source code.

The most important function is D3DXComputeNormalMap(), which was introduced in the DirectX 8.1 SDK. It maps the (x,y,z) components of each normal to the (r,g,b) channels of the output texture. Therefore, the height map is provided in the second parameter, and the normal map is retrieved via the first parameter. This example doesn't use a paletized texture, so no palette has to be provided in the third parameter. The flags in the fourth entry field allow the user to mirror or invert the normal map or store an occlusion term in its alpha channel. The last parameter is the amplitude parameter, which multiplies the height map information. This example scales the height map data by 10.

With the help of D3DXComputeNormalMap(), we create a map with normals on a per-pixel basis, but there is still one problem left: The normals in the normal map were defined in one space based on how the textures were applied to the geometry. This is called texture space. In contrast, the light is defined in world space. The L dot N product between vectors in two different spaces will lead to unintentional results.

There are two solutions for this problem: Generate the normal maps to always be defined relative to world space, or move the light into texture space.

The second solution is the most common. On a very abstract level, it can be divided into two steps:

- A texture space coordinate system is established at each vertex.
- The direction to light vector L is calculated at each vertex and transformed into the texture space.

This is shown in the following two sections.

Establish a Texture Space Coordinate System at Each Vertex

The texture coordinates at each vertex form a coordinate system with a U (tangent), V (binormal = u x v), and W (normal) axis.

V and U are also called tangent vectors. These three vectors form a rotation/shear matrix that transforms or maps from world to texture space.

This example uses a sphere on which the textures are mapped. At different vertices of this sphere, these vectors will point in an entirely different direction. Therefore, you have to calculate these vectors for every vertex.

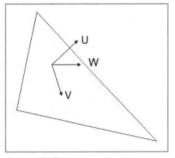

Figure 2: Texture space

To retrieve the U and V vectors, the partial derivatives of U and V relative to X, Y, and Z in world space are calculated (read more in [Dietrich][Lengyel]). This is done with the following piece of code in the LoadXFile() function in RacorX.cpp for the whole mesh:

```
// compute the normals
hr = D3DXComputeNormals(pMeshSysMem,NULL);
if(FAILED(hr))
  return E_FAIL;

// compute texture
hr = D3DXComputeTangent(pMeshSysMem,0,pMeshSysMem2,1,
                D3DX_COMP_TANGENT_NONE,TRUE,NULL);
if(FAILED(hr))
  return E_FAIL;
```

D3DXComputeNormals() computes normals for each vertex in a mesh. It uses in its first parameter a pointer to the mesh. The second parameter can be used to specify the three neighbors for each face in the created progressive mesh, which is not used here.

D3DXComputeTangent() (new in DirectX 8.1) is used to compute the tangent U vector based on the texture coordinate gradients of the first texture coordinate set in the input mesh.

```
HRESULT D3DXComputeTangent(
  LPD3DXMESH InMesh,
  DWORD TexStage,
  LPD3DXMESH OutMesh,
  DWORD TexStageUVec,
  DWORD TexStageVVec,
```

```
  DWORD Wrap,
  DWORD* pAdjacency
);
```

The first parameter must be a pointer to an ID3DXMESH interface, representing the input mesh, and the third parameter will return a mesh with the one or two vectors added as a texture coodinate set. The texture coordinate set is specified in the TexStageUVec and TexStageVVec parameters. The flag D3DX_COMP_TANGENT_NONE used in one of these parameters prevents the generation of a vector. TexStage chooses the texture coordinate set in the input mesh that will be used for the calculation of the tangent vectors.

Wrap wraps the vectors in the U and V direction if this value is set to 1, as in this example. Otherwise, wrapping doesn't happen. With the last parameter, one can get a pointer to an array of three DWORDs per face that specify the three neighbors for each face in the created mesh.

Both functions store the vectors in the mesh. Therefore, the mesh will "transport" the vectors to the vertex shader via the vertex buffer as a texture coordinate set, consisting of the three vector values.

The normal from D3DXComputeNormals() and the tangent from D3DXComputeTangent() form the two axes necessary to build the per-vertex texture space coordinate system to transform L.

Transforming L into Texture Space

After building up the U and W vectors, L is transformed into texture space in the following lines in the vertex shader:

```
; Input Registers
; v0 - Position
; v3 - Normal
; v7 - Texture
; v8 - Tangent

...

m3x3 r5, v8, c0 ; generate tangent U
m3x3 r7, v3, c0 ; generate normal W

; Cross product
; generate binormal V
mul r0, r5.zxyw, -r7.yzxw;
mad r6, r5.yzxw, -r7.zxyw,-r0;

;transform the light vector with U, V, W
dp3 r8.x, r5, -c12
dp3 r8.y, r6, -c12
dp3 r8.z, r7, -c12

// light -> oD0
mad oD0.xyz, r8.xyz, c33, c33 ; multiply by a half to bias, then add half
...
```

The tangent U produced by D3DXComputeTangent() is delivered to the vertex shader via *v8* and the normal W is provided in *v3*. To save bandwidth, the binormal is calculated via the cross product of the tangent and the normal in the vertex shader. The transform happens with the following formula:

L.x' = U dot –L
L.y' = V dot –L
L.z' = W dot –L

At the end of this code snippet, L is clipped by the output register *oD0* to the range [0..1]. That means any negative values are set to 0 and the positive values remain unchanged. To prevent the cutting off of negative values in the range of [–1..1] of v8 to [0..1], the values have to be shifted into the [0..1] range. This is done by multiplying by 0.5 and adding 0.5 in the last instruction of the vertex shader. This is not necessary for texture coordinates because they are usually in the range [0..1].

To get the values back into the [–1..1] range, the *_bx2* source register modifiers subtract by 0.5 and multiply by 2 in the pixel shader:

```
ps.1.1
tex t0                      ; color map
tex t1                      ; normal map
dp3 r1, t1_bx2, v0_bx2 ; dot(normal,light)
mul r0,t0, r1               ; modulate against base color

ps.1.4
texld r0, t0                ; color map
texld r1, t0                ; normal map
dp3 r2, r1_bx2, v0_bx2 ; dot(normal, light)
mul r0, r0, r2
```

Pixel shader instructions can be modified by an instruction modifier, a destination register modifier, a source register modifier, or a selector (swizzle modifier).

```
mov_IM dest_DM, src_SM || src_SEL
```

The instruction modifiers (IM) _x2, _x8, _d2, _d8, and _sat multiply or divide the result or, in the case of the _sat modifier, saturate it to [0..1].

The destination register modifiers (DM) .rgb, .a, and in ps.1.4 .r, .g, and .b, control which channel in a register is updated. They only alter the value of the channel to which they are applied.

The source register modifiers (SM) _bias (–0.5), 1– (invert), – (negate), _x2 (scale), and _bx2 (signed scaling) adjust the range of register data. Alternatively, a selector or swizzle modifier .r, .g, .b, and .a replicates a single channel of a source register to all channels (read more in "Fundamentals of Pixel Shaders"). Both pixel shaders use _bx2 as a source register modifier that doesn't change the value in the source register. For example, the value of v0 in the mov instruction has not changed after the execution of the following instruction:

```
mul r1, v0_bx2
```

The values that are delivered to mul for the multiplication are modified by _bx2 but not the content of the registers itself.

Both pixel shaders shown above produce a valid Lambertian reflection term with the dot product between L, which is now in texture space, and a sample from the normal map (read more in [Lengyel]).

The last two lines of the vertex shader store the texture coordinate values of the color texture in two texture coordinate output registers:

```
mov oT0.xy, v7.xy
mov oT1.xy, v7.xy
```

Sending the same texture coordinates via two texture output registers is redundant; therefore, using only one of the output registers would be an improvement. The first idea that comes to mind is setting D3DTSS_TEXCOORDINDEX as a texture stage state to use the texture coordinates of the first texture additionally for the second texture. Unfortunately, this flag is only valid for usage with the fixed-function T&L pipeline, but not for the usage with vertex shaders. With ps.1.1, there is no way to use the texture coordinates of the first texture for the second texture without sending them via *oT1* to the pixel shader a second time. The texture coordinates must be sent via one of the texture coordinate registers with the same number as the texture stage.

In a ps.1.4 pixel shader, the programmer is able to choose the texture coordinates that should be used to sample a texture in the texld instruction, as shown in the ps.1.4 pixel shader:

```
...
texld r1, t0 ; normal map
...
```

This way, the remaining texture coordinate output registers in the vertex shader can be used for other data, such as vector data.

Assemble Pixel Shader

Similar to the examples used in "Programming Vertex Shaders," the pixel shaders are assembled with NVASM or, in the case of the ps.1.4 pixel shaders, with Microsoft's psa.exe since NVASM doesn't support ps.1.4. The integration of NVASM into the Visual C/C++ IDE is done in the same way as for vertex shaders (read more in "Programming Vertex Shaders").

Create Pixel Shader

The pixel shader binary files are opened and read, and the pixel shader is created by CreatePSFromCompiledFile() in InitDeviceObjects():

```
CreatePSFromCompiledFile (m_pd3dDevice, "shaders/diffdot3.pso",
                         &m_dwPixShaderDot3);
CreatePSFromCompiledFile (m_pd3dDevice, "shaders/diff.pso", &m_dwPixShader);
CreatePSFromCompiledFile (m_pd3dDevice, "diffdot314.pso",
                         &m_dwPixShaderDot314);
```

The CreatePSFromCompiledFile() function is located at the end of RacorX.cpp:

```
//-----------------------------------------------------------
// Name: CreatePSFromBinFile
// Desc: loads a binary *.pso file
// and creates a pixel shader
//-----------------------------------------------------------
HRESULT CMyD3DApplication::CreatePSFromCompiledFile (IDirect3DDevice8*
                                                     m_pd3dDevice,
                                                     TCHAR* strPSPath,
                                                     DWORD* dwPS)
{
    char szBuffer[128];        // debug output
    DWORD* pdwPS;              // pointer to address space of the calling process
    HANDLE hFile, hMap;        // handle file and handle mapped file
    TCHAR tchTempVSPath[512];  // temporary file path
    HRESULT hr;               // error
```

```
if( FAILED( hr = DXUtil_FindMediaFile( tchTempVSPath, strPSPath ) ) )
    return D3DAPPERR_MEDIANOTFOUND;

hFile = CreateFile(tchTempVSPath, GENERIC_READ,0,0,OPEN_EXISTING,
                   FILE_ATTRIBUTE_NORMAL,0);

if(hFile != INVALID_HANDLE_VALUE)

  if(GetFileSize(hFile,0) > 0)
    hMap = CreateFileMapping(hFile,0,PAGE_READONLY,0,0,0);
  else
  {
    CloseHandle(hFile);
  return E_FAIL;
  }
}
else
  return E_FAIL;

// maps a view of a file into the address space of the calling process
pdwPS = (DWORD *)MapViewOfFile(hMap, FILE_MAP_READ, 0, 0, 0);

// Create the pixel shader
hr = m_pd3dDevice->CreatePixelShader(pdwPS, dwPS);
if ( FAILED(hr) )
{
  OutputDebugString( "Failed to create Pixel Shader, errors:\n" );
  D3DXGetErrorStringA(hr,szBuffer,sizeof(szBuffer));
  OutputDebugString( szBuffer );
  OutputDebugString( "\n" );
 return hr;
}

  UnmapViewOfFile(pdwPS);
  CloseHandle(hMap);
  CloseHandle(hFile);

  return S_OK;
}
```

This function is nearly identical to the CreateVSFromCompiledFile() function shown in "Programming Vertex Shaders." Please consult the "Create a Vertex Shader" section in the RacorX2 example section of that article for more information. The main difference is the usage of CreatePixelShader() instead of CreateVertexShader().

CreatePixelShader() is used to create and validate a pixel shader. It takes a pointer to the pixel shader byte-code in its first parameter and returns a handle in the second parameter.

> **Note:** CreatePixelShader() fails on hardware that does not support ps.1.4 pixel shaders. You can track that in the debug window after pressing F5. Therefore, the following examples indicate this with a warning message that says "ps.1.4 Not Supported." To be able to see a ps.1.4 shader running on the Reference Rasterizer (REF), the function CreatePixelShader() has to be called once again after switching to the REF. This functionality is not supported by the examples used throughout Part One.

OutputDebugString() shows the complete error message in the output debug window of the Visual C/C++ IDE, and D3DXGetErrorStringA() interprets all Direct3D and Direct3DX HRESULTS and returns an error message in szBuffer.

Set Pixel Shader

Depending on the choice of the user, three different pixel shaders might be set with SetPixelShader() in Render():

```
//diffuse lighting.
if(m_bBump)
{
  m_pd3dDevice->SetTexture(0,m_pColorTexture);
  m_pd3dDevice->SetTexture(1,m_pNormalMap);

if (m_bPixelShader)
  m_pd3dDevice->SetPixelShader(m_dwPixShaderDot314);
else
  m_pd3dDevice->SetPixelShader(m_dwPixShaderDot3);

}
else
{
  //no lighting, just base color texture
  m_pd3dDevice->SetTexture(0,m_pColorTexture);
  m_pd3dDevice->SetPixelShader(m_dwPixShader);
}
```

If diffuse lighting is switched on, the user may select with the P key between the ps.1.1 and ps.1.4 pixel shader, if supported by hardware. If diffuse lighting is switched off, the simple ps.1.1 pixel shader that only uses the color texture is set.

Free Pixel Shader Resources

All pixel shader resources are freed in DeleteDeviceObjects():

```
if(m_dwPixShaderDot3)
  m_pd3dDevice->DeletePixelShader(m_dwPixShaderDot3);
if(m_dwPixShaderDot314)
  m_pd3dDevice->DeletePixelShader(m_dwPixShaderDot314);
if(m_dwPixShader)
  m_pd3dDevice->DeletePixelShader(m_dwPixShader);
```

Non-Shader Specific Code

I used source code published by SGI as open source some years ago to emulate a virtual trackball. The file trackball.h holds an easy to use interface to the SGI code in SGITrackball.cpp.

Summary

RacorX6 shows how the pixel shader is driven by the vertex shader. All the data that is needed by the pixel shader is calculated and provided by the vertex shader. Calculating the U and W vectors, which is necessary to build up a texture space coordinate system, is done one time, while the *.x file is loaded with the D3DXComputeNormals() and D3DXComputeTangent() functions. The V vector as the binormal is calculated for every vertex in the vertex shader because it saves bandwidth. These three vectors that form a texture space coordinate system are used to transform the light vector L to texture space. L is sent through the color output register *oD0* to the pixel shader. The usage of a texture space coordinate system is the basis of per-pixel lighting and will be used throughout the upcoming example.

RacorX7

The main improvement of RacorX7 over RacorX6 is the usage of a specular reflection model instead of the diffuse reflection model used by the previous example.

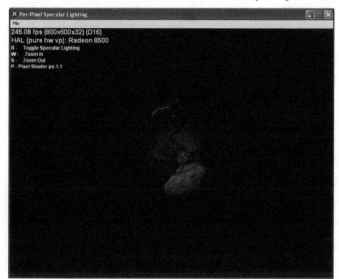

Figure 3: RacorX7 specular lighting

RacorX7 sets the same textures and texture stage states as RacorX6, but with only one additional constant.

Define Constants (with SetPixelShaderConstant()/def)

Because this example uses a specular reflection model, an eye vector must be set into *c24* in FrameMove(), as already shown in the RacorX4 example:

```
// eye vector
m_pd3dDevice->SetVertexShaderConstant(24, &vEyePt, 1);
```

This eye vector helps to build up the V vector, which describes the location of the viewer. This is shown in the next paragraph.

Pixel Shader Instructions

The pixel shader in this example calculates the specular reflection on the basis of a modified Blinn-Phong reflection model that was already used in RacorX4 in "Programming Vertex Shaders."

The following diagram visualizes the vectors involved in the common specular reflection models.

A model describing a specular reflection has to be aware of at least the location of the light source L, the location of the viewer V, and the orientation of the surface normal N. Additionally, a vector R that describes the direction of the reflection might be useful. The half way vector H was introduced by Jim Blinn to bypass the expensive calculation of the R vector in the original Phong formula.

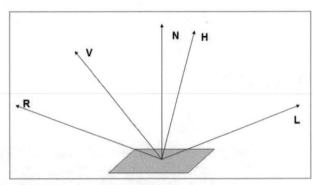

Figure 4: Vectors for specular reflection

The original Blinn-Phong formula for the specular reflection looks like this:

$$k_{specular} (N \text{ dot } H)^n)$$

whereas:

$$H = (L + V)/2$$

The simplified formula that was used in RacorX4 and used here is

$$k_{specular} (N \text{ dot } (L + V))^n)$$

Compared to the Blinn-Phong formula, the specular reflection formula used by the examples in Part 1 does not divide through L + V through 2. This is compensated by a higher specular power value, which leads to good visual results. Although L + V is not equivalent to H, the term "half vector" is used throughout the example source for this.

The calculation of the vector H works in a similar way as the calculation of the light vector L in the previous example in the vertex shader:

```
vs.1.1
...
; position in world space
m4x4 r2, v0, c0

; get a vector toward the camera/eye
add r2, -r2, c24

; normalize eye vector
dp3 r11.x, r2.xyz, r2.xyz
rsq r11.xyz, r11.x
mul r2.xyz, r2.xyz, r11.xyz

add r2.xyz, r2.xyz, -c12 ; get half angle

; normalize half angle vector
dp3 r11.x, r2.xyz, r2.xyz
rsq r11.xyz, r11.x
mul r2.xyz, r2.xyz, r11.xyz

; transform the half angle vector into texture space
dp3 r8.x,r3,r2
dp3 r8.y,r4,r2
dp3 r8.z,r5,r2

; half vector -> oD1
mad oD1.xyz, r8.xyz, c33, c33 ; multiply by a half to bias, then add half
```

The first three code blocks calculate V. The next two code blocks generate the half vector H. H is transformed into texture space with the three dp3 instructions like the light vector in the previous example, and it is stored biased in *oD1* in the same way as the light vector was transfered in the previous example.

Like in the previous example, this pixel shader is driven by the vertex shader:

```
ps.1.1
tex t0 ; color map
tex t1 ; normal map
dp3 r0,t1_bx2,v1_bx2; ; dot(normal,half)

mul r1,r0,r0;          ; raise it to 32nd power
mul r0,r1,r1;
mul r1,r0,r0;
mul r0,r1,r1;

; assemble final color
mul r0,t0,r0

ps.1.4
texld r0, t0           ; color map
texld r1, t1           ; normal map
dp3 r2, r1_bx2, v1_bx2 ; dot(normal, half)

mul r3,r2,r2           ; raise it to 32nd power
mul r2,r3,r3
mul r3,r2,r2
mul r2,r3,r3

mul r0, r0, r2
```

The pixel shader gets H via *v1* and N, as in the previous example, via a normal map. The specular power is caculated via four mul instructions. This was done in RacorX4 in "Programming Vertex Shaders" via a lit instruction in the vertex shader.

Using the mul instructions to perform the specular color leads to visible banding artifacts as shown in Figure 5.

These artifacts are a result of the small precision of the pixel shader registers and the precision loss of the H vector by shifting this vector from the range [−1..1] to [0..1] in the vertex shader and back in the pixel shader, which is necessary because the vertex shader output registers deliver only values in the range [0..1]. The only way to provide higher precision is by delivering a texture map with the specular values encoded, which is loaded in the pixel shader. This is shown below in the RacorX8 section.

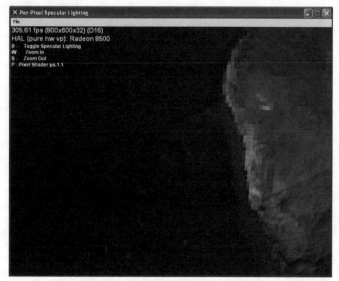

Figure 5: RacorX7 visual artifacts

Summary

RacorX7 showed one way to implement a specular reflection model. The drawback to this example is its low precision when it comes to specular power values. RacorX8 will show a way to get a higher precision specular reflection.

RacorX8

The main difference between RacorX8 and RacorX7 is the use of a lookup table to store the specular power values for the specular reflection instead of using a few mul instructions in the pixel shader. The advantage of using a lookup table is the banding is reduced. This is due to the higher value range of the lookup table compared to the solution with multiple mul instructions.

The drawback of using a lookup table as shown in this example is the need for an additional texture stage.

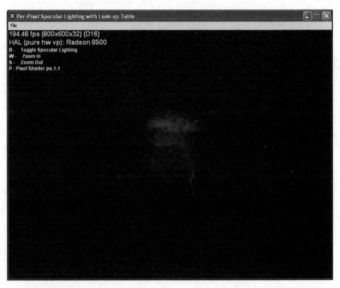

Figure 6: RacorX8 specular lighting with specular power from a lookup table

Set Texture Operation Flags (with D3DTSS_* flags)

RacorX8 sets RestoreDeviceObjects() in these two additional texture stage states for the texture map that holds the specular power values (specular map):

```
// additionally for specular table
m_pd3dDevice->SetTextureStageState( 2, D3DTSS_ADDRESSU, D3DTADDRESS_CLAMP );
m_pd3dDevice->SetTextureStageState( 2, D3DTSS_ADDRESSV, D3DTADDRESS_CLAMP );
```

With D3DTADDRESS_CLAMP flag, the texture is applied once and then the color of the edge pixel is smeared. Clamping sets all negative values to 0, whereas all positive values remain unchanged. Without the clamping, a white ring around the earth would be visible.

Set Texture (with SetTexture())

This example sets the specular power lookup table or specular map with the handle m_pLightMap16 in Render():

```
...
m_pd3dDevice->SetTexture(2, m_pLightMap16);
...
```

This lookup table is created as a texture map and filled with specular power values in the following lines:

```
// specular light lookup table
void LightEval(D3DXVECTOR4 *col, D3DXVECTOR2 *input,
               D3DXVECTOR2 *sampSize, void *pfPower)
{
  float fPower = (float) pow(input->y,*((float*)pfPower));
  col->x = fPower;
  col->y = fPower;
  col->z = fPower;
  col->w = input->x;
}
...
//
// create light texture
//
if (FAILED(D3DXCreateTexture(m_pd3dDevice, 256, 256, 0, 0,
                             D3DFMT_A8R8G8B8, D3DPOOL_MANAGED, &m_pLightMap16)))
      return S_FALSE;

FLOAT fPower = 16;
if (FAILED(D3DXFillTexture(m_pLightMap16, LightEval, &fPower)))
  return S_FALSE;
```

D3DXFillTexture() (new in DirectX 8.1) uses the user-provided function LightEval() in its second parameter to fill each texel of each mip level of the lookup table texture that is returned in the first parameter:

```
HRESULT D3DXFillTexture(
  LPDIRECT3DTEXTURE8 pTexture,
  LPD3DXFILL2D pFunction,
  LPVOID pData
);
```

This function is useful to build all kind of procedural textures that might be used in the pixel shader as a lookup table.

LightEval(), which is provided in pFunction, uses this declaration:

```
VOID (*LPD3DXFILL2D) (
  D3DXVECTOR4* pOut,
  D3DXVECTOR2* pTexCoord,
  D3DXVECTOR2* pTexelSize,
  LPVOID pData
);
```

The first parameter returns the result in a pointer to a vector. The second parameter gets a vector containing the coordinates of the texel currently being processed. In our case, this is a pointer to a 2D vector named input. The third parameter is unused in LightEval() and might be useful for providing the texel size. The fourth parameter is a pointer to user data. Here, LightEval() gets a pointer to the pfPower variable. This value is transferred via the third parameter of the D3DXFillTexture() function.

This example sets the same constants as the previous example, so we can proceed with the pixel shader source.

Pixel Shader Instructions

The vertex shader that drives the pixel shader differs from the vertex shader in the previous examples only in the last four lines:

```
; oT0 coordinates for normal map
; oT1 half angle
; oT2 half angle
; oT3 coordinates for color map
mov oT0.xy, v7.xy
mov oT1.xyz, r8
mov oT2.xyz, r8
mov oT3.xy, v7.xy
```

The texture coordinates for the normal map and the color map are stored in *oT0* and *oT3*. The half angle vector is stored as a texture coordinate in *oT1* and *oT2*. This example uses a 3x2 table of exponents, stored in the specular map in texture stage 2.

The two pixel shaders TableSpec.psh and TableSpecps14.psh calculate the u and v position and sample a texel from the specular map. After the color texture is sampled, the color value and the value from the specular map is modulated:

```
ps.1.1
; t0 holds normal map
; (t1) holds row #1 of the 3x2 matrix
; (t2) holds row #2 of the 3x2 matrix
; t2 holds the lookup table
; t3 holds color map
tex t0 ; sample normal
texm3x2pad t1, t0_bx2 ; calculates u from first row
texm3x2tex t2, t0_bx2 ; calculates v from second row
; samples texel with u,v
tex t3 ; sample base color
mul r0,t2,t3 ; blend terms

; specular power from a lookup table
ps.1.4
; r0 holds normal map
; t1 holds the half vector
; r2 holds the lookup table
; r3 holds color map
texld r0, t0
texcrd r1.rgb, t1
dp3 r1.rg, r1, r0_bx2 ; (N dot H)

phase
texld r3, t0
texld r2, r1 ; samples specular value with u, v
mul r0, r2, r3
```

In the ps.1.1 pixel shader, texm3x2pad performs a three-component dot product between the texture coordinate set corresponding to the destination register number and the data of the source register and stores the result in the destination register. The texm3x2tex instruction calculates the second row of a 3x2 matrix by performing a three-component dot product between the texture coordinate set corresponding to the destination register number and the data of the source register.

texcrd in the ps.1.4 shader copies the texture coordinate set corresponding to the source register into the destination register as color data. It clamps the texture coordinates in the destination register with a range of [–MaxTextureRepeat, MaxTextureRepeat] (RADEON 8500: 2048) to the range of the source register [–8, 8] (MaxPixelShaderValue). This clamp might behave differently on different hardware. To be safe, provide data in the range of [–8, 8].

> **Note:** Values from the output registers of the vertex shader are clamped to [0..1]; that means the negative values are set to 0, while the positive values remain unchanged. To bypass the problem of clamping, the data can be loaded in a texture into the pixel shader directly.
>
> In a ps.1.1-ps.1.3 pixel shader, the rn, tn, and cn registers can handle a range of [–1..1]. The color registers can only handle a range of [0..1]. To load data in the range [–1..1] via a texture in ps.1.1-ps.1.3 the tex tn instruction can be used. In ps.1.4, the rn registers can handle a range of [–8..8] and the tn registers can handle, in the case of the RADEON 8500, a range of [–2048..2048]. So data from a texture in the range of [–8..8] can be loaded via texcrd rn, tn; via texld rn, tn; or texld rn, rn (only phase 2) in a ps.1.4 pixel shader.

A .rgb or .rg modifier should be provided to the destination register of texcrd because the fourth channel of the destination register is unset/undefined in all cases.

The arithmetic instruction dp3 performs a three-component dot product between the two source registers. Its result is stored in r and g of r1.

Both shaders perform a dependent read. A dependent read is a read from a texture map using a texture coordinate that was calculated earlier in the pixel shader. The texm3x2pad/texm3x2tex instruction pair calculate the texture coordinate that is later used to sample a texel by the texm3x2tex instruction. In the ps.1.4 shader, the second texld instruction uses the texture coordinate that was calculated earlier in the two dp3 instructions.

It is interesting to note that the first texld instruction after the phase marker uses the same texture coordinate pair as the normal map. This reusage of texture coordinates is only possible in ps.1.4. It is also important to note that using the texm3x2pad/texm3x2tex pair to load a value from a specular map is inefficient, because both instructions calculate the same value and get the same half vector via two texture coordinate registers. Using only the texm3x2tex instruction is not possible, because this instruction can only be used together with a texm3x2pad instruction.

A more elegant solution comparable to the ps.1.4 shader is possible by using the texdp3tex instruction together with a 1D specular map, but this instruction needs ps.1.2 or ps.1.3 capable hardware.

> **Note:** You cannot change the order of the t0-t3 registers in a ps.1.1-ps.1.3 pixel shader. These registers must be arranged in this pixel shader version in numerical order. For example, setting the color map in texture stage 1 in the above ps.1.1 shader won't work. In ps.1.4, it is not necessary to order the r0-r5 or t0 and t1 registers in any way.

Summary

This example improved the specular power precision by using a specular power lookup table. The drawback of this technique is the usage of an additional texture, which may be overcome by using the alpha channel of the normal map.

RacorX9

RacorX9 combines a diffuse reflection model with the specular reflection model. It is based on RacorX6, RacorX7, and a further improved ps.1.4 shader, which gets the specular value from the alpha value of the normal map.

The main point about this example is that it handles both reflection models with the help of only two textures, so there is some room left to use additional textures for other tasks or for more per-pixel lights (see [Gosselin] for a ps.1.4 shader with three lights with falloff).

This example uses two different vertex shaders: one for the ps.1.1 and one for the ps.1.4 pixel shader. The vertex shader that feeds the ps.1.1 pixel shader named SpecDot3Pix.vsh stores the half vector in *oD1* and the light vector in *oD0*. The two texture coordinates are stored in *oT0* and *oT1*.

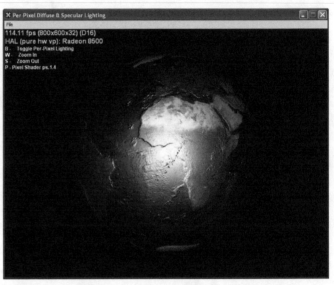

Figure 7: RacorX9 diffuse and specular lighting

```
; half vector -> oD1 ps.1.1
mad oD1.xyz, r8, c33, c33      ; multiply by a half to bias, then add half

...

; light -> oD0
mad oD0.xyz, r8.xyz, c33, c33 ; multiply a half to bias, then add half

mov oT0.xy, v7.xy
mov oT1.xy, v7.xy
```

The only difference compared to the vertex shader used in RacorX7 is the storage of an additional light vector in *oD0*. The light vector is necessary to calculate the diffuse reflection in the pixel shader in the same way as shown in RacorX6:

```
ps.1.1
tex t0                   ; color map
tex t1                   ; normal map
dp3 r0,t1_bx2,v1_bx2     ; dot(normal,half)

mul r1,r0,r0;            ; raise it to 32nd power
mul r0,r1,r1;
mul r1,r0,r0;
mul r0,r1,r1;

dp3 r1, t1_bx2, v0_bx2 ; dot(normal,light)
mad r0, t0, r1, r0
```

Heightening the specular power value with four mul instructions in the pixel shader is a very efficient method. The drawback of visible banding effects is reduced by combining the specular reflection model with a diffuse reflection model. The light vector in the dp3 instruction is used in the same way as in RacorX7.

Compared to the vertex shader above, the second vertex shader named SpecDot314.psh stores the half vector in *oT2* and *oT3* instead of *oD1* and the texture coordinates, which are used later in the pixel shader for both textures in *oT0*:

```
; half vector -> oT2/oT3 ps.1.4
mad oT2.xyz, r8, c33, c33 ; multiply by a half to bias, then add half
mad oT3.xyz, r8, c33, c33 ; multiply by a half to bias, then add half
...
; light -> oD0
mad oD0.xyz, r8.xyz, c33, c33 ; multiply a half to bias, then add half

mov oT0.xy, v7.xy
--------
; specular power from a lookup table
ps.1.4
; r1 holds normal map
; t0 holds texture coordinates for normal and color map
; t2 holds half angle vector
; r0 holds color map
texld r1, t0
texcrd r4.rgb, t2

dp3 r4.rg, r4_bx2, r1_bx2 ; (N dot H)
mov r2, r1                 ; save normal map data to r2

phase
texld r0, t0
texld r1, r4               ; samples specular value from normal map with u,v

dp3 r3, r2_bx2, v0_bx2    ; dot(normal,light)
mad r0, r0, r3, r1.a
```

The new thing in this pixel shader is the storage of the specular power value in the alpha value of the normal map. This lookup table is accessed like the lookup table in RacorX8. Therefore, the normal map is sampled a second time in phase 2.

Note: If this pixel shader tried to use the v0 color register, the two dp3 instructions would have to be moved in phase 2, but then the necessary dependent texture read done in the second texld instruction in phase 2 would not be possible. Therefore, the ps.1.4 shader wouldn't work with the half vector in v0 at all.

The lookup table is built up with the following piece of code:

```
//specular light lookup table
void LightEval(D3DXVECTOR4 *col,D3DXVECTOR2 *input,
D3DXVECTOR2 *sampSize,void *pfPower)
{
  float fPower = (float) pow(input->y,*((float*)pfPower));
  col->x = fPower;
  col->y = fPower;
  col->z = fPower;
  col->w = input->x;
}
...
```

```
//
// create light texture
//
if (FAILED(D3DXCreateTexture(m_pd3dDevice, desc.Width, desc.Height, 0, 0,
D3DFMT_A8R8G8B8, D3DPOOL_MANAGED, &m_pLightMap16)))
return S_FALSE;

FLOAT fPower = 16;
if (FAILED(D3DXFillTexture(m_pLightMap16,LightEval,&fPower)))
return S_FALSE;

// copy specular power from m_pLightMap16 into the alpha
// channel of the normal map
D3DLOCKED_RECT d3dlr;
m_pNormalMap->LockRect( 0, &d3dlr, 0, 0 );
BYTE* pDst = (BYTE*)d3dlr.pBits;

D3DLOCKED_RECT d3dlr2;
m_pLightMap16->LockRect( 0, &d3dlr2, 0, 0 );
BYTE* pDst2 = (BYTE*)d3dlr2.pBits;

for( DWORD y = 0; y < desc.Height; y++ )
{
  BYTE* pPixel = pDst;
  BYTE* pPixel2 = pDst2;

  for( DWORD x = 0; x < desc.Width; x++ )
  {
  *pPixel++;
  *pPixel++;
  *pPixel++;
  *pPixel++ = *pPixel2++;
  *pPixel2++;
  *pPixel2++;
  *pPixel2++;
  }
  pDst += d3dlr.Pitch;
  pDst2 += d3dlr2.Pitch;
}
m_pNormalMap->UnlockRect(0);
m_pLightMap16->UnlockRect(0);

SAFE_RELEASE(m_pLightMap16);
```

A specular map in m_pLightMap16 is created, as already shown in RacorX8, with the help of the LightEval() function. The values of this map are stored in the alpha values of the normal map after retrieving a pointer to the memory of both maps. The specular map is then released. This way, the ps.1.4 pixel shader only uses two texture stages, but there is a weak point in this example: The ps.1.4 pixel shader is slow compared to the ps.1.1 pixel shader. The higher precision of the specular value has its price. Using the normal map with 2048x1024 pixels for storage of the specular power slows down the graphics card. Using a smaller normal map speeds up the frame rate substantially, but on the other hand, it reduces the precision of the normals. Using specular power in an additional texture would eat up one texture stage. Using an equivalent to the ps.1.1 shader, which is shown below, won't allow us to use more than one or two lights:

```
ps.1.4
texld r0, t0          ; color map
texld r1, t1          ; normal map
dp3 r2, r1_bx2, v1_bx2 ; dot(normal, half)
```

```
mul r3,r2,r2          ; raise it to 32nd power
mul r2,r3,r3
mul r3,r2,r2
mul r2,r3,r3

dp3 r1, r1_bx2, v0_bx2 ; dot(normal,light)
mad r0, r0, r1, r2
```

One way to improve the ps.1.1 and ps.1.4 pixel shaders in this example is to store the specular power value in the alpha value of an additional smaller texture, which might add new functionality to this example. This is shown by Kenneth L. Hurley [Hurley] for a ps.1.1 shader and by Steffen Bendel [Bendel] and other *Direct3D ShaderX* authors for a ps.1.4 pixel shader.

Summary

This example has shown the usage of a combined diffuse and specular reflection model while using only two texture stages. It also demonstrates the trade-off that has to be made by using the specular power in the alpha value of a texture, but there is also an advantage: There are more instruction slots left for using more than one per-pixel light. A rule of thumb might be using up to three per-pixel lights in a scene to highlight the main objects and lighting the rest of the scene with the help of per-vertex lights.

These examples might be improved by adding an attenuation factor calculated on a per-vertex basis like in RacorX5 or by adding an attenuation map in one of the texture stages [Dietrich00][Hart].

Further Reading

I recommend reading "A Non-Integer Power Function on the Pixel Shader" by Philippe Beaudoin and Juan Guardado [Beaudoin/Guardado] to see a power function in a pixel shader that calculates a high-precision specular power value. David Gosselin implements three lights with a light falloff in [Gosselin]. Kenneth Hurley [Hurley] describes how to produce diffuse and specular maps in an elegant way with Paint Shop Pro. Additionally, he describes a ps.1.1 pixel shader that uses a diffuse and specular texture map to produce better looking diffuse and specular reflections. This pixel shader is an evolutionary step forward compared to the ps.1.1 shaders shown here. Steffen Bendel [Bendel] describes a way to produce a combined diffuse and specular reflection model in a ps.1.4 pixel shader that uses a much higher precision and leads to a better visual experience. That's the reason he called it "smooth lighting."

References

[Beaudoin/Guardado] Philippe Beaudoin and Juan Guardado, "A Non-Integer Power Function on the Pixel Shader," *Direct3D ShaderX*.

[Bendel] Steffen Bendel, "Smooth Lighting with ps.1.4," *Direct3D ShaderX*.

[Dietrich] Sim Dietrich, "Per-Pixel Lighting," NVIDIA developer web site.

[Dietrich00] Sim Dietrich, "Attenuation Maps," in *Game Programming Gems* (Charles River Media, 2000), pp. 543-548.

[Gosselin] David Gosselin, "Character Animation with Direct3D Vertex Shaders," *Direct3D ShaderX*.

[Hart] Evan Hart, "3DTextures and Pixel Shaders," *Direct3D ShaderX*.

[Hurley] Kenneth L. Hurley, "Photorealistic Faces with Vertex and Pixel Shaders," *Direct3D ShaderX*.

[Lengyel] Eric Lengyel, *Mathematics for 3D Game Programming & Computer Graphics* (Charles River Media, Inc., 2002), pp. 150-157.

Acknowledgments

I would like to thank Philip Taylor for permission to use the earth textures from the Shader workshop held at Meltdown 2001. Additionally, I would like to thank Jeffrey Kiel from NVIDIA for proofreading this article.

Epilogue

Improving this introduction is a constant effort. Therefore, I appreciate any comments and suggestions. Improved versions of this text will be published on http://www.direct3d.net and http://www.gamedev.net.

Basic Shader Development with Shader Studio

John Schwab

Introduction

Shader Studio is a tool that lets Microsoft Direct3D Version 8.1 developers experiment and design vertex and pixel shaders. By presenting most of the internal operations of the Direct3D API in a unique and intuitive form, you can spend more time designing and less time programming. When using Shader Studio, the only programming you will have to do is in the shaders themselves; geometry, transformations, textures, and states are all managed by Shader Studio.

What You Should Know

It is assumed that the user is very familiar with the architecture, structure, and especially Vertex and Pixel Shader Instruction Set of the Direct3D 8.1 API. Though this is not a requirement, it will allow you to understand the terminology and detailed aspects of Shader Studio much easier. Beginners may want to review the introductory sections on writing shaders, and then come back and explore the possibilities of shaders without having to do any Direct3D programming.

Installation

Locate the Shader Studio directory on the companion CD and run Setup.exe to install.

Directories

        Shader Studio/
                Data/
                Shaders/
                Workspaces/

Coordinate Systems

Shader Studio uses a right-handed coordinate system; future versions will allow left and right configuration. When you reset the translation and rotation, all transformation modes (see the Transformations section later in this article) default to the identity matrix for orientation and then the camera and light are translated to the coordinates. The following diagram shows how the light and camera are aligned within the coordinate system.

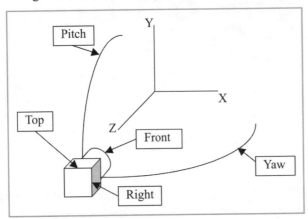

Features

Shader Studio has the following features:

Full DirectX 8.1 API shader support: Every state, texture stage, and shader capability is exposed and can be changed.

.x File mesh loading: Currently you can only load meshes using the .x file format. If your data is in a different format, there are many conversion tools and exporters available. You can find most of these tools in the extras directory of the DirectX 8.1 SDK before installation.

Automatic constants calculations: Data in the constant registers (for example, matrices, materials, and lights) can be manually edited. As this data is changed in the Shader Studio interface, it is automatically transferred to the appropriate constant registers.

Full state control: Every Direct3D render state, texture state, and all eight texture stages can be directly manipulated in the Shader Studio interface.

All capable texture formats supported: Shader Studio can load all the texture formats that Direct3D supports.

Alternate texture loading and rebinding to any stage: Any textures referenced in an .x file will be loaded automatically. You have the option to load and apply your own textures to any of the eight texture stages.

Shader declaration remapping: The declarator maps mesh format to the data entering the vertex shader. You can control how the data is formatted and to which vertex the data goes.

Dynamic vertex and pixel shader programming: The rendered view immediately displays the results of successfully compiled code. Shader Studio also displays errors from your code as you work.

Flexible shader pipeline: Shader Studio supports all combinations of shaders. You can use the fixed-function pipeline, vertex shaders only, pixel shaders only, or both vertex shaders and pixel shaders. The choice is yours.

Mesh material listing: Shader Studio provides a complete list of all material properties loaded with the mesh.

Real-time rendering preview with interactive controls: Shader Studio provides a limited set of camera, light, and object controls to change how you view the effect of your shaders. This data is exposed to the shader through the automatic constants.

Vector browser (a great debugging tool): This is a display window that converts the color values under the cursor to vector values — very useful for pixel shaders.

Effect browsing: Workspace files can be associated with the application and quickly loaded.

Code generation: To quickly start your development, the automatic code generator can create the minimal shader code for you based on the mesh format and declaration. The automatic code generator is a great way to minimize errors and eliminate the effort of repeatedly entering the same data.

Limitations

There are several items that you should be aware of before developing in Shader Studio.

- The current version of Shader Studio only allows one vertex and pixel shader to be developed at the same time. Therefore, you should be as certain as possible that you can accomplish your desired effect within this constraint.

- You may be tempted to put some *def* instructions within your vertex shader code. Currently, *def* instructions will have no effect due to the way Direct3D handles them. Instead, you must directly enter the data into the constant registers for it to be accessible by your shaders. You can, however, enter *def* instructions in your code for use by your exported shader. Pixel shaders don't have this problem.

- The current version of Shader Studio implements single pass rendering only. Shader Studio does not (at the time of publication) handle multiple rendering pass techniques.

- States in Shader Studio are considered a setting. This is because you can only set one at a time and don't have programmatic control when they are set. You may have to manually play with the states to get the effect you're looking for.

- No alternate buffer formats are exposed. Shader Studio does not, for example, support stencil operations (such as shadows) beyond what the states can do.

- The list of all material properties loaded with the mesh is read only.

Default Light

Shader Studio has one directly controllable light source. You can access its properties through the automatic constants, but there are several properties that are fixed internally. Below is a list of fixed properties in the D3DLIGHT8 structure:

- Type = spot light
- All white colors
- Maximum range
- 0 Falloff
- Constant attenuation
- 180° inner and outer cone

Controls

The primary means of controlling the objects is by mouse manipulation.

Left Button: Rotate (polar orbit) around the current center. The x-axis controls azimuth, and y-axis controls elevation.

Right Button: Translates (pans) the center relative to the camera view. With Shift down you move along the depth axis (z-camera axis).

Middle Button: Translates (dollies) the object relative to the center and controls the orbit distance.

Wheel: If you have a mouse wheel, rolling it will dolly the object in one unit increments.

Create a Vertex Shader

This section introduces the features of Shader Studio in the context of building a very simple vertex shader. The step-by-step instructions illustrate how to use Shader Studio as intended: what to do and what to avoid.

When you first start Shader Studio, you won't see anything; there is no geometry available for Shader Studio to render. Therefore, your first step is to load a mesh.

Note: Shader Studio only supports .x files. If necessary, the DirectX 8.1 SDK contains utilities to convert or export files from your favorite modeling tool to the .x file format.

Step 1: Loading a Mesh

In this exercise, you are going to use the cornell.x mesh, available on the companion CD, as a starting point. To load the file, go to the File menu and select the Load Mesh option. Change to the Data subdirectory and select the file cornell.x. Press OK to load the file. You should now see a room with a sphere and a cube suspended in midair. During the load process, the texture for the walls is automatically loaded. If you are interested, you can inspect the materials and textures in the Materials or Textures views.

 Note: You can use a mesh other than the suggested cornell.x mesh.

Step 2: Transformations

Shader Studio allows you to easily change the position and orientation of the camera, the light, and the object in the scene via the commands within the Transform menu (please refer to the "Transformations" section under "Shaders Reference" later in this article for detailed information about these controls and how they are used).

Begin with controlling the position and orientation of the camera. You must ensure that the camera transform is selected; either press Alt+C or select the Transform/Camera menu item. Use the left mouse button to orbit the scene, the right mouse button to pan, and Shift and the right mouse button or rolling wheel to dolly.

If you lose your orientation and you can't find the objects in your scene, then you can use the reset options from the Transform menu or press Alt+R to reset all positions and orientations to their default values. Experiment with the controls to become familiar with them, then set the camera view a little to the right and above the center of the scene (see the following figure).

Switch to the light with either Alt+L or select the Transform/Light menu item. The light is represented as a blue arrow. You can adjust the position and the orientation of the light using the same controls you just used with the camera.

If you don't see the light, dolly it in with the middle mouse button or wheel. Now move it to a location to the right of the camera. You should see a highlight off all the surfaces.

For the purposes of this tutorial, you do not need to alter the object transformation. For your reference, altering the object transformation modifies the world transformation matrix.

Step 3: Starting a Shader

In Steps 1 and 2, Shader Studio is rendering the scene using the Direct3D fixed-function graphics pipeline. Here is your chance to take control and create your first vertex shader.

To begin, select the View/Shaders menu item to open the Shaders dialog; you may have to move or resize your windows to make items fit. The Shaders dialog may look complicated now, but it will become very easy to use with some experience. The "Shaders Reference" section later in this article contains detailed explanations of each screen element.

Begin by selecting the Vertex tab to enable vertex shader operations. Shader Studio protects you from trying to enable defective vertex shaders; you cannot enable vertex shaders at this time because there is no vertex shader available or the current vertex shader contains invalid code.

You can enter a vertex shader by typing in the Code box or by loading a vertex shader from disk. If you are creating a new vertex shader, you can use the Default button to automatically generate some initial code for you. The initial code is based on Shader Studio's analysis of the current declarations.

You can now enable the default vertex shader to see what effect it has on the scene. The default code works, but the lighting model is very simple and most of you will want to go much farther.

Step 4: Editing Code

You can extend the vertex shader by editing the code in the Code box. Any valid changes that you make are immediately updated in the render view; errors are reported in the Status window.

To continue with the tutorial, you can now add a directional light to the scene. Change the third line of code from:

```
dp3 oD0, v3, -c2
```

to:

```
dp3 oD0, v3, -c21
```

The scene has disappeared! Actually, everything in the scene just turned black. The new code instructs the vertex processor to take the dot product of the (negation of the) vector stored in constant register 21 with the vector stored in *v3* (the current vertex normal — see the Declarations section) and store the result in output register *oD0* (the diffuse color for this vertex).

 Note: Shader Studio often refers to a specific constant register (for example, constant register 21) as a constant (for example, constant 21 or c21).

However, constant 21 is currently undefined and contains the default value of zero. To set the value of constant 21, locate row 21 in the ID column of the Constants box. Double-click the line at 21 to bring up the Constant Properties dialog box so that you can change its properties (please refer to the Constant Properties section for detailed information about this dialog box). For now, just check the Auto Set box to enable the Auto Constant which defaults to Light Direction for this constant register. Select OK and you will see that the scene is now lit by the direction of the light source. Try moving the light around to verify that the lighting equations are using only the direction of the light vector and not the position of the light.

Note: Auto Set places a comment beside constant 21 that documents the purpose of the register.

Step 5: Adding Some Color

You have now added a directional light to your scene, but what happened to the materials that are a part of the mesh? You can inspect the material definitions in the Materials view (select the View/Materials menu item). Assuming that you loaded cornell.x as directed, you will see eight materials listed along with their properties (see the "Materials" section for a detailed explanation of the material properties). In many cases, you don't need to know the properties of the materials, only that some materials have textures and some don't.

You can extend your vertex shader to include the effects of the diffuse material. Make the following changes from the third line:

```
dp3 oD0, v3, -c21
```

to:

```
dp3 r0, v3, -c21 // calculate the contribution from the light
mul oD0, r0, c23 // calculate the interaction of the light and material
```

Once again, the scene turns black. As you have probably guessed, the material isn't set at constant 23. Repeat the operations of step 4 to enable the constant. Go to ID 23 and enable the Auto Set check box (you can see that it defaults to Diffuse Material), and then select OK. The sphere and cube now display the proper colors.

Note: You can add comments to your vertex shader code using the "//" as illustrated above.

Step 6: Saving Your Work

You have made a lot of progress at this point, so you should save what you have done to disk. Since Shader Studio exposes all of Direct3D's states, it is possible to set them to an unsupported or invalid state if you're not careful, thereby producing unpredictable results. Therefore, it is always wise to save your work often.

Note: The next step in the tutorial will overwrite all of your work, so you are strongly advised to save your workspace.

To save everything to disk, select the File/Save Workspace menu item, select the location for the saved workspace (for convenience, it is best to put your workspace in the Workspaces directory), and give the workspace a meaningful name (use tutorial.sws for the current workspace).

> **Note:** Shader Studio uses absolute file references by default. Therefore, if you change any file locations at a later date, you may lose the links to files referenced in your workspace. You can change Shader Studio to use relative file references by checking the Relative File References box when saving your workspace, but a side effect of doing this is your referenced files <u>must</u> be on the same drive as the workspace.

Step 7: Loading a Vertex Shader

You are now going to load a prebuilt vertex shader into your workspace. You can continue with the current workspace or create a new workspace (select the File/New Workspace menu item). If you create a new workspace, then you must reload cornell.x.

Open the Shaders view and select the Vertex tab. Press the Load button and select Shaders/PhongPnt.vsh. Once the shader is loaded, your existing code is overwritten. Remember this when you are loading shaders!

A quick review of the code illustrates that it is significantly more complex than the code used earlier in the tutorial. This vertex shader implements the functionality of almost all features of the default fixed-function pipeline.

If you started with a new workspace, you will have a black screen again when you enable this shader. From steps 1 through 5, you will remember that you need to set the constants to have the vertex shader operate properly. Since this code is well documented, you can just assign the proper constants to their values. You can start by enabling those constants identified in the comments at the beginning of the code (C20, C23, C24, C25, C27); each of these will default to the proper auto constant.

Constant registers C0 through C3 should already be set by default to the transform auto constant. The final constant register is C4; you must manually assign the auto constant for this register. In the Constant Properties (double-click the line at C4), check the Auto Set check box, select World from the drop-down list, and close the dialog.

If you have the shader enabled, it is likely that a large portion of the scene is white. This is due to the fact that the default specular power is 0, causing most colors to approach infinity. To make the specular power more reasonable, set C26.w to 50 by manually entering this value in the Constant Properties; you can also enter a comment like "specular power" while the dialog is open.

Now, when you toggle between your vertex shader and the fixed-function pipeline (by enabling and disabling the vertex shader via the check box), you should see little difference. The difference between this vertex shader and the fixed-function pipeline is that every feature (such as attenuation) isn't implemented in this vertex shader. Of course, you can extend this shader and add support for attenuation; <u>that</u> is the power of programmable shaders in Shader Studio.

Step 8: Settings

You can do a lot with a shader, but you still need control over Direct3D's state engine. Shader Studio controls Direct3D states via the Settings dialog (select the Options/Settings menu item). The details of all the settings are beyond the scope of this article (see the Direct3D documentation for further information). Simply put, all of Direct3D's render and texture states are here and can be easily changed.

To illustrate, you can add some fog to the current scene. Start by finding the D3DRS_FOGENABLE state and open the branch to determine the current state. You should see that it is FALSE; right-click on the state information and select TRUE to enable this state. Nothing will happen yet because fog also requires several other states to be set. Next, find the D3DRS_FOGTABLEMODE state and set it to D3DFOG_EXP. The scene will go black because the two remaining states that affect the fog, the color and the density, default to unusable values and need to be changed.

First, you can get the scene back by changing the default density state from 1 to 0.05. Find the D3DRS_FOGDENSITY state and right-click, enter the value of 0.05 via the keyboard, and press Enter (or select elsewhere with the mouse). The scene is now visible, properly fogged.

You can also change the color of the fog. Locate the D3DRS_FOGCOLOR state and right-click to change the value. Notice that this state is a hex value; all of Direct3D's color values are in ARGB order, so if you want blue fog, you must enter 0x000000ff (or just FF) into the field and press Enter. The scene is now rendered with blue fog.

Note: Fog is controlled by and implemented by the fixed-function pipeline, not the vertex shader. Therefore, it is possible to mix a vertex shader with some fixed functionality by setting the appropriate states.

At this point, you have covered three of the four possible ways to change a state; the only one left is the multiple bit flags state. To see an example of this control mechanism, find the D3DRS_COLORWRITEENABLE state. This state uses a bit mask to control which colors are used. If you only want to write to the blue color component, then mask out the color components that are not blue. Right-click and remove the check marks by Alpha, Red, and Green, and then select somewhere off of the menu to confirm your changes. The scene is now rendered with only the information in the blue channel. However, the blue fog may be interfering with your perception, so try disabling the fog to verify that only the blue values are being written. Before you continue, return the mask back to its default state (all color components enabled).

Step 9: Texture Control

This step illustrates how Shader Studio controls textures. You will now add multitexturing to the scene.

Note: This step assumes that your hardware has the ability to perform multitexturing. To verify your hardware capabilities, check Options/Statistics and see how many max simultaneous textures your hardware can support. If your hardware can only support one texture you may have to switch to the (software) Reference Rasterizer (see Options/Configure).

To begin, open the View/Texture dialog. The dialog identifies the texture that was loaded with the mesh and the Set by Materials option at stage #0 (for a detailed explanation of this dialog, see the "Textures" section).

Load a new texture called Spot.bmp. Press the Load button and find the texture in the Data directory, and then click OK to load it. Once the texture is loaded, you will see most of its properties in the main area. If you want to use this new texture, you have to assign it to a texture stage.

To verify that Spot.bmp is loaded, manually set it at stage #0, thereby overriding Set by Materials and forcing this texture to be applied to all geometry with texture coordinates. Right-click on the Set by Materials option to display the list of the available options. Select the new texture (Spot.bmp). Since the Textures dialog is a modal dialog, you will have to close it (press OK) to see its changes. You should see the spot texture on all surfaces. Open the Textures dialog again and set stage #0 back to Set By Materials and assign the Spot.bmp texture to stage #1. Then close the dialog to see the change. The scene returns to its original form. Since you have set the new texture to a previously unused texture stage, you must make several changes to see it.

Open the Shaders dialog and verify that the vertex shader is enabled. Begin by adding a second set of texture coordinates so that the new texture can be mapped to the geometry. You don't need to change the geometry to do this; simply use the same data as the base texture by adding this line to the code in the vertex shader:

```
mov oT1, v7
```

You can place the new line right below this line:

```
mov oT0, v7
```

Not much will happen yet since all texturing is currently handled in the fixed-function pipeline and we haven't added a pixel shader yet.

Return to the Settings dialog, and this time select the Texture States tab; this will allow you to change the texture states. To enable Stage 1, look at the Texture settings under stage #1. The first state is D3D-TSS_COLOROP (note that stages begin at 0). Change the state to D3DTOP_MOD-ULATE, and the two textures will be blended together. A subtle property that you may not notice is that the texture filtering for the remaining stages defaults to D3D-TEXF_POINT. You might want to change the D3DTSS_MAGFILTER and D3DTSS_MINFILTER to D3DTEXF_LINEAR to make the scene look much nicer.

That concludes your introduction to the basic functionality of creating a vertex shader. The next section explains how to create more advanced effects using a pixel shader. See the following figure for the completed vertex shader.

Create a Pixel Shader

In this tutorial, you will expand on the previous tutorial by writing a pixel shader with functionality equivalent to that of the fixed-function pipeline, in the sense that a pixel shader can only handle a single material passed from the vertex shader. Even though a pixel shader follows a vertex shader in the pipeline, it is not necessarily dependent on it. In this tutorial, however, the pixel shader does depend on the vertex shader, both to reduce complexity and to illustrate Shader Studio's ability to simultaneously develop a vertex shader and a pixel shader.

Note: If you are continuing from the Vertex Shader tutorial, proceed to Step 1. If you skipped the tutorial on vertex shaders, please load the workspace vPhong.sws.

Step 1: Configuration

The pixel shader you are about to construct works with a single material. The last tutorial enabled multi-texturing; this configuration must now be modified. Select the View/Textures menu option. In the Textures dialog, configure the text stages as follows:

- Set stage #0 to the base texture env2.bmp.
- Set the remaining stages to NULL and close the Textures dialog.

The sphere and the cube are now textured because their meshes have texture coordinates and stage #0 has been configured to apply the texture env2.bmp.

You can now begin writing your pixel shader.

Step 2: Writing a Pixel Shader

To begin, open the Shaders dialog and select the Pixel tab to configure for pixel shader development. Begin with the simplest pixel shader possible; use the default code (press the Default button) and enable the pixel shader. The scene is now rendered using diffuse lighting only.

The default pixel shader code is always implemented using version 1.0 of the pixel shader specification. If you wish to develop using other versions of the pixel shader specification, you must manually change this value. To enable the functionality equivalent to the fixed-function pipeline, you must replace the default pixel shader code with the following:

```
ps.1.0
tex t0
mov r1,v1
mad r0,t0,v0,r1
```

You can verify that there is no difference between the results of the fixed-function pipeline rendering and the pixel shader rendering by enabling and disabling the pixel shader. That means both approaches are processing the same information.

Pixel shaders support local definitions for constant values because the constant values are compiled with the shader and, therefore, override any external constants defined in the Constants view. Of course, you could enter the constant value in the Constants view and the pixel shader would behave the same way. To illustrate, replace the current pixel shader with the following code:

```
ps.1.0
def c0, 1.0f, 1.0f, 1.0f, 0.0f
tex t0
mul r1,v1,c0
mad r0,t0,v0,r1
```

The local definition of c0 is used to define a new specular color that the pixel shader uses to override the specular color from the vertex shader. This is just a trivial example and is probably not practical, but you can manually adjust the constant to see the changes in the specular highlight.

Shaders Reference

This section explains all the functionality of Shader Studio's controls.

Workspace

Menu Layout

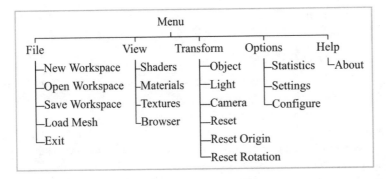

Files

■ **New Workspace**: Resets all properties in Shader Studio to their default settings.

■ **Open Workspace**: Loads an existing workspace so you can continue your work where you left off.

■ **Save Workspace**: Saves the current workspace. All states, shaders, and settings will be saved in this file. Texture files and the mesh are referenced but not saved in the workspace file itself. If you plan on sharing these workspaces, be sure to enable Relative File Referencing before saving. All referenced file paths are then saved relative to the workspace file.

■ **Load Mesh**: Loads a mesh into the workspace. If a mesh is already loaded, you will be asked to confirm before the loaded mesh is overwritten.

 Note: Relative paths to referenced files must be local to the same logical drive as the workspace. It is also efficient to have the files relatively close to the workspace.

Shaders Dialog

The principal interface for developing shader code in Shader Studio, this modeless dialog allows you to modify your code and immediately see the results in the rendering window. This dialog has many options (please refer to the following diagram); each option is discussed below.

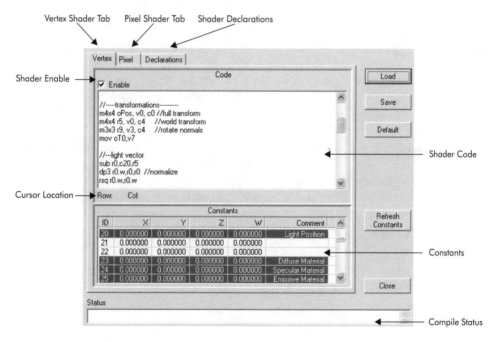

Along the right-hand side of the dialog are several buttons (Load, Save, Default, and Refresh Constants) whose use depends on the identity of the currently active tab.

- **Load and Save buttons**: These are context-dependent Load and Save functions. For example, if you're currently working on a vertex shader (the Vertex tab is active), you can only load or save a vertex shade rwhen you click the Load button or the Save button.

- **Default button**: The Default button takes the current mesh declarations and automatically creates the minimal code required for a working shader. The default code is generated using version 1.0 of the vertex shader and pixel shader specification.

- **Refresh Constants**: Refresh Constants updates the values displayed in the constants pane. Note that the values displayed are correct at the time that they are requested. However, some values are used many times during the rendering process, so the values displayed may not represent the "final" values.

- **Shader Code**: The Shader Code portion of the dialog is where you place your shader instructions. It is immediately compiled and is updated in the rendered view when successful.

Vertex Shader

A functional vertex shader requires vertex shader assembly language code, configuration of the constant registers (constants), and declarations. Shader Studio does not support the *def* instruction within vertex shader code. Instead, constants must be defined and set in the Constants view. Auto constants allows you to quickly configure the constants that are required.

The only property not within this tab is the declaration, which is processed separately (see Declarations).

Pixel Shader

For the most part, there is little difference between the Vertex Shader and Pixel Shader tabs. Pixel shaders use the pixel shader instruction set and definitions (*def* instruction) that are supported in the code. Pixel shader constants can also be controlled in the Constants view, but auto constants are not supported.

- **Constants View**: The Constants view lists all available constants, their values, and an optional comment. To access a constant, double-click to edit its properties. When editing group constants, be sure to select the base item of a group to change it or you will set the base ID of the group to the new base ID location and possibly overwrite a constant that you manually configured.

- **Vertex Constants (Auto Constants)**: A highlighted constant is controlled by the auto constants. See the "Constant Properties" section for more information.

- **Pixel Constants**: Pixel constants are identical in operation to the vertex constants except that auto constants are not supported.

- **Error Reporting**: Errors reported by the shader compiler (as you write your shader) are reported in the status bar at the bottom of the dialog.

Declarations

Declarations map the internal vertex data format of a mesh to the registers used when the mesh data enters the vertex shader. You can define any mapping that you require — from the vertex data to the registers.

To change the map for a register, right-click on the register, and then select the source and data type. In most cases, the data type should remain constant or you may get unpredictable results. Once you change the map for a register, you will most likely get an error status of "Vertex shader doesn't match declaration," unless you have already made the corresponding changes to your vertex shader code. Similarly, if you change the registers in your vertex shader code, you must also change the declarations.

If you are unsure of the internal mesh format, you can check Mesh Format in Options/Statistics to see what vertex data is present.

Note: Only stream 0 is supported, and you can't add or delete registers.

Constant Properties Dialog

The Constant Properties dialog allows you to change the behavior of a constant; you can either set the values manually or use the auto constant sets. When you enter this dialog (by double-clicking on a constant in the Shaders dialog), two values are displayed: ID and size. The size is determined by the intended purpose of the constant. Some constants, such as matrices, are composed of multiple constant registers. Other constants, such as positions, require only a single constant register. Constants that are not auto constants are assumed to require a single constant register.

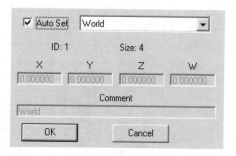

- **Values**: When the Auto Set check box is disabled, you can manually enter values in the X, Y, Z, and W data fields. You also have the option to type in a comment for this constant.
- **Auto Constant**: When the Auto Set check box is enabled, you can only select from the predefined constant sets.
- **Constant Sets**: The most common uses for the constant registers are predefined as the following constant sets.

  P = Projection matrix (Calculated from FOV, Near, and Far Clip)
  V = View matrix (Calculated from the camera, center, and dolly)
  W = World matrix (Calculated from the object; can also be an auxiliary matrix)
  T = Transformation matrix (concatenation of several matrices)
  C = Center of orbit
  D = Z dolly vector from C as *(0,0,D)*
  R_X = X rotation matrix
  R_Y = Y rotation matrix
  L_P = Light position

L_C = Center of light orbit
L_D = Z dolly vector from L_C as $(0,0,L_D)$
L_N = Normal direction of light
E_P = Eye (camera) position
E_N = Eye (camera) normalized facing direction

Note: All matrices are pre-transposed before being passed to the constant registers.

Name	Default ID	Equation
Projection	unassigned	$M_p = P$
Inverse projection	unassigned	$M_p = P^{-1}$
View	unassigned	$M_v = (\bar{C} + (R_Y \times R_X))\bar{D}$
Inverse view	4	$M_v = ((\bar{C} + (R_Y \times R_X)) - \bar{D})^{-1}$
World	unassigned	$M_W = R_Y \times R_X$
Inverse world	8	$M_W = (R_Y \times R_X)^{-1}$
Transform	0	$M_T = M_W \times M_V \times M_P$
Inverse transform	12	$M_T = (M_W \times M_V \times M_P)^{-1}$
World view	unassigned	$M_T = M_W \times M_V$
Inverse world view	16	$M_T = (M_W \times M_V)^{-1}$
Light position	20	$\bar{L}_P = (\bar{L}_C + (R_Y \times R_X))\bar{L}_D$
Light direction	21	$\bar{L}_N = R_Y \times R_X \times (0,0,-1)$
Ambient material	22	n/a
Diffuse material	23	n/a
Specular material	24	n/a
Emissive material	25	n/a
Material power	26	n/a
Eye position	27	$\bar{E}_P = M_V^{-1} \times (-\bar{C} + \bar{D})$
Eye direction	28	$\bar{E}_N = M_V^{-1} \times (0,0,-1)$

Materials Dialog

The materials loaded with the current mesh are inspected via this dialog.

The material number and its properties are displayed. The properties directly correspond to Direct3D's D3DMATERIAL8 structure.

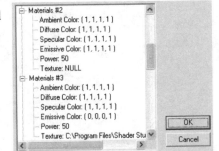

Note: You cannot change the properties of a material; they are presented here for reference only.

Textures Dialog

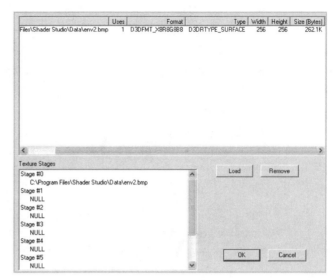

Textures are managed via this dialog. You can load and remove any number (and type) of texture(s) that Direct3D supports, with the exception of textures that are loaded by your mesh.

The Textures dialog lists the texture files and some parameters. The Texture Stages box shows which texture is applied to each texture stage. You can edit the texture stages by right-clicking the name and selecting the new texture. Texture stage #0 also allows you to set it to the default material with the Set by Material option. Choosing this option will automatically select the texture that was loaded with the mesh.

Browser

The browser is a modeless dialog that determines the color underneath the cursor position in the render view and converts the color to a signed biased value vector for display.

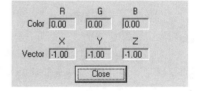

One of the best uses for this is to visualize normal maps for bump mapping. Here is an equation that converts the color to a vector.

Transformations Dialog

The positions and orientations of the light, the camera, and the geometry are represented by transformations. To adjust any transformation, choose the mode (the target for the transformation) and use the mouse to set the new position and orientation.

Object

The object mode controls the transformation information for an object. The following Auto Constants (see the Constant Properties section) are affected:

- World
- Inverse world
- Transform
- Inverse transform
- World view
- Inverse World view

Light

The light mode controls the transformation information for the light. The following Auto Constants are affected:

- Light position
- Light direction

Camera

The camera mode controls the transformation information for the scene viewpoint. The following Auto Constants are affected:

- Transform
- Inverse transform
- World view
- Inverse world view
- View
- Inverse view
- Eye position
- Eye direction

There are three ways to reset the transformations to a known state.

- **Reset**: Reset both the origin and orientation of the current transformation mode.
- **Reset Origin**: Set the translation (position) to 0,0,0.
- **Reset Rotation**: Set the orientation (rotation) to the identity matrix.

Statistics Dialog

This dialog lists various internal statistics about the current workspace.

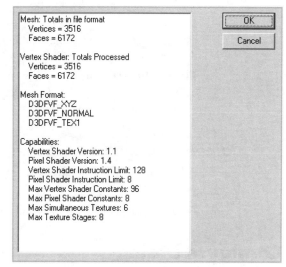

- **Mesh**: Displays how many faces and vertices are in the mesh that is currently loaded.

- **Vertex Shader**: Displays how many vertices are processed by the vertex shader.

- **Mesh Format**: Displays the Flexible Vertex Format (FVF) definition for the mesh.

- **Capabilities**: Displays the capabilities of your video card relevant to Shader Studio.

Settings Dialog

The Settings dialog presents all of Direct3D's internal states in a tree structure. Most of these internal states will not be used when you have shaders enabled, but they are all used when rendering is performed by the fixed-function pipeline.

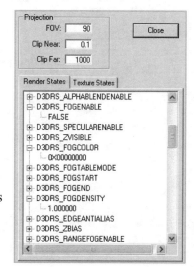

The viewport settings (the Projection block) defines the rendering window for both the fixed-function and shader pipelines (see the "Camera Projection" section for further information).

The settings are separated into render states and texture states. The texture states are further organized by stage.

The names of the states directly correspond to their respective property in Direct3D; this is also true for the states that you set. For both tabs, the mechanism for changing states is the same and will follow one of the patterns illustrated by the following state methods. In all cases, select for edit with the right mouse button or by pressing the Enter key when the state is highlighted.

State Methods

- **Single State**: This method allows selection of a single state. You are presented with a pop-up menu of possible options. Once you have made the selection, select anywhere off the pop-up menu to set the selection.

- **Bit Flags**: Bit Flags allows selection of multiple states. You are presented with a pop-up menu of possible options with a check mark

beside states that are enabled. Once you have made the selection(s),
select anywhere off the pop-up menu to set the selection(s).

- **Hex Value**: This allows entry of colors and numbers as a 32-bit value
  as an unsigned hexadecimal number. It is not necessary to type the
  "0X" before a number.

- **Float Value**: This method allows entry of floating point numbers. Be
  careful when entering these numbers; make sure they are within the
  state's respective capabilities.

Camera Projection

- Adjusts the FOV, near, and far clipping planes.
- FOV: Field Of View in degrees, can be from 0-180.
- Far must be greater than near and can be any positive number.

Configure Dialog

The Configure dialog allows you to set various internal properties for Shader Studio.

The Rendering Device selects between hardware acceleration (HAL) and the internal (Direct3D) reference software
rasterizer (REF). Be careful when changing rendering devices
— most drivers don't implement all the features of the software
rasterizer, so you could end up with errors such as invalid states or unsupported capabilities.
You should always save your work before changing the rendering device.

Assets

The following files are available on the companion CD:

Vertex Shaders
- PhongPnt.vsh

Pixel Shaders
- PhongPnt.psh

Workspaces
- vPhong.sws
- pPhong.sws
- Tutorial.sws

Meshes
- Cornell.x
- Light.x
- teapot.x

Textures
- Env2.bmp
- Spot.bmp

Further Info

To get the latest version and any other up-to-date information, please go to the Shader Studio home page at http://www.shaderstudio.com/.

Part 2

Vertex Shader Tricks

Vertex Decompression in a Shader

Dean Calver

Introduction

Vertex compression can help save two valuable resources, memory and bandwidth. As you can never have enough of either, compression is almost always a good thing. The main reasons to not use compression are if the processing time to decompress is too high or if the quality is noticeably lower than the original data (for lossy compression schemes). The methods described here are designed to avoid both problems with reasonable compression ratios.

Graphics literature has a wide range of vertex compression schemes, but most of these require a complex decompression step that cannot be executed inside a vertex shader.

Vertex Compression Overview

Our aim is to get the entire decompression step in the vertex shader itself. This rules out many of the standard compressors that require either large compression tables or access to other vertices (predictor methods). The amount of data we can use for the decompression algorithm (almost all vertex shader constant space may already be used, i.e., skinning matrices, etc.) is very limited. We generally have a few per-object constants to upload into vertex constant memory.

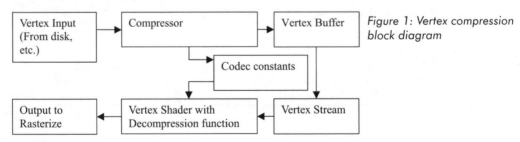

Figure 1: Vertex compression block diagram

A number of techniques can be used inside a vertex shader. These include:

■ Quantization — The simplest form of compression; we simply lose the least significant bits.

■ Scaled offset — Actually a special case of linear equations method, but limiting the equation to a scaled offset from a point.

■ Compression transform — A method that calculates linear equations to transform by where the variables (the vertex values) need less precision.

■ Multiple compression transforms — Each vertex selects from a palette of compression transforms.

■ Sliding compression transform — Extends the precision of the compression transforms by putting spare padding bytes to good use.

■ Displacement mapping and vector fields — Only for special kinds of data, but by storing geometry like a texture, we can save space.

All these compression methods rely on the same basic technique — storing the vertex components in fewer bits. Floating-point is designed with a huge dynamic range; usually we don't need much so we can save space. DirectX helps us by having a number of non-floating-point data types that are converted to floating-point before entry into the vertex shader.

Vertex Shader Data Types

As of DirectX 8.1, there are four different data types for us to work with (excluding the float data types):

■ D3DVSDT_UBYTE4 — Four unsigned 8-bit integers that map in the vertex shader in the range 0.0 to 255.0.

■ D3DVSDT_D3DCOLOR — Four unsigned 8-bit integers that map in the vertex shader in the range 0.0 to 1.0. Also, the mapping of each component into the vertex shader register is different from D3DVSDT_UBYTE4.

■ D3DVSDT_SHORT2 — Two signed 16-bit integers that map in the vertex shader in the range –32767.0 to +32768.0.

■ D3DVSDT_SHORT4 — Four signed 16-bit integers that map in the vertex shader in the range –32767.0 to +32768.0.

Some video cards don't support D3DVSDT_UBYTE4, but this isn't a problem in practice since D3DVSDT_D3DCOLOR can be used as a replacement with a few minor modifications. The two changes needed are accounting for the change in range (the vertex shader code has to multiply the incoming values by 255.0) and swapping the vertex stream components so they appear in the correct places when used. This can be achieved by either changing the input data (i.e., swapping the data in the vertex buffer and multiplying a transformation matrix by 255.0) or adding the following vertex shader code:

```
; v1 = D3DVSDT_D3DCOLOR4 to be used a D3DVSDT_UBYTE4
; c0 = <255.0, 255.0, 255.0, 255.0>
mul r0.zyxw, v1, c0          ; multiply color4 by 255 and swizzle
```

If we are going to use these types instead of standard float vector, then we are going to have to insert dummy pad values for odd vector sizes. The pad values show up a lot with vertex data because most components (positions, normals, etc.) are 3D vectors. Even with pad spaces, the new types are much smaller than floats, and often we can use these pad values to store other data.

As different vertex components have different numerical ranges and requirements, it is quite common to have varying compression methods in a single stream. We set up our stream declarations with the new types and fill vertex buffers with the packed values.

Compressed Vertex Stream Declaration Example

A lit vertex with a single uv channel format before compression:

```
D3DVSD_STREAM(0),
D3DVSD_REG( 0, D3DVSDT_FLOAT3),    // position
D3DVSD_REG( 1, D3DVSDT_FLOAT3),    // normal
D3DVSD_REG( 2, D3DVSDT_FLOAT2),    // texture coordinate
D3DVSD_END()
```

After compression, the position is stored in three signed 16-bit integers, the normal is stored in three unsigned 8-bit integers, and the texture coordinate is stored in two signed 16-bit integers. We have a signed 16-bit integer and an unsigned 8-bit integer that are unused (padding). The original size is 32 bytes, and the compressed size is 16 bytes, so we have a 50% savings.

```
D3DVSD_STREAM(0),
D3DVSD_REG( 0, D3DVSDT_SHORT4),    // position
D3DVSD_REG( 1, D3DVSDT_UBYTE4),    // normal
D3DVSD_REG( 2, D3DVSDT_SHORT2),    // texture coordinate
D3DVSD_END()
```

Basic Compression

Several simple forms of vertex compression are discussed in this section.

Quantization

The simplest form of vertex compression is to store fewer bits; as there is no floating-point format of less than 32 bits, this also implies a shift to integer or fixed-point data representation.

This has problems with almost all data sets but is a reasonable solution for data with a very limited dynamic range. The obvious candidates among standard vertex components are normalized values (normals and tangents are usually normalized for lighting calculations).

Compression

I choose a policy of clamping to a minimum and maximum range of the data type, but if this happens, we shouldn't use quantization as a compression method.

We also have to choose how many bits to use for the integer part and how many for the fractional part. This is very data-sensitive because there is no reasonable default with so few bits in total.

```
fracScale = number of bits for fractional values

Quantise( originalVal )
{
    return ClampAndFloatToInteger ( originalVal * fracScale );
}
```

Decompression

Decompression just reverses the compression process, taking the compressed values and restoring any fractional part.

```
Constants
{
    fracScale = number of bits for fractional vales
}
Decompress( compressedVal )
{
    return IntegerToFloat( compressedVal ) / fracScale
}
```

Practical Example

Normalized normals or tangents are usually stored as three floats (D3DVSDT_FLOAT3), but this precision is not needed. Each component has a range of −1.0 to 1.0 (due to normalization), ideal for quantization. We don't need any integer components, so we can devote all bits to the fractional scale and a sign bit. Biasing the floats makes them fit nicely into an unsigned byte.

For most normals, 8 bits will be enough (that's 16.7 million values over the surface of a unit sphere). Using D3DVSDT_UBYTE4, we have to change the vertex shader to multiply by 1.0/127.5 and subtract 1.0 to return to signed floats. I'll come back to the optimizations that you may have noticed, but for now, I'll accept the one cycle cost for a reduction in memory and bandwidth saving of one-fourth for normals and tangents.

Quantization vertex shader example:

```
; v1 = normal in range 0 to 255 (integer only)
; c0 = <1.0/127.5, -1.0, ???? , ????>
mad  r0, v1, c0.xxxx, c0.yyyy  ; multiply compressed normal by 1/127.5, subtract 1
```

Scaled Offset

This method produces better results than quantization by redistributing the bits to a more reasonable range for this object. By choosing a scale that covers the entire object, we ensure the object is correct to the accuracy of the quantization level.

A good candidate is to use the axis-aligned bounding box (AABB) as scale and translation vector. Each vector is defined in object space, so we use the entire compressed range to cover the AABB. This requires us to translate and then scale the input vectors. You can use either the center of the AABB or a corner. I usually use a corner, which gives each compressed vertex a range of 0.0 to 1.0.

Compression

For static objects, we determine the minimum and maximum values for each axis and use these to calculate the offset point and scales. For dynamic objects, we have to choose the maximum and minimum that will encompass all dynamic changes. We maximize our dynamic range by allowing separate scale and offset per axis.

```
DetermineScaleAndOffset()
{
    For Every Vertex
        LowerRange  = Minimum (LowerRange, Vertex)
        UpperRange  = Maximum (UpperRange, Vertex)
}

offset = LowerRange
scale = (UpperRange - LowerRange)

ScaledOffset( originalVal )
{
    scaledOffset =  (originalVal - offset) / scale;
    return FloatToInteger (scaledOffset );
}
```

Decompression

The incoming values are in the range 0.0 to 1.0. We simply have to multiply by the scale value and add the offset to get the original vertex coordinate back.

```
Constants
{
    scale = scale used in the compression
    offset = corner used in the compression
}

Decompress( compressedVal )
{
    return (IntegerToFloat( compressedVal ) * scale) + centroid
}
```

Practical Example

Texture coordinate data is a good candidate for this form of compression. 8 bits is usually too low for texture data (only enough for 1 texel accuracy with a 256x256 texture), but 16 bits is often enough (unless tiling textures often). We apply the compression and then upload the scale and offset constants into vertex constants; the scale is itself scaled by 65,535, and the offset has an additional 0.5 to convert the short back into the 0.0 to 1.0 range. We use a mad instruction to perform the decompression, so it costs us one cycle but saves us 50% in size.

Scaled offset vertex shader example:

```
; v1 = uv texture coordinate in the range -32767.0 to 32768.0 (integer only)
; c0 = <u scale / 65535.0, v scale / 65535.0, u offset + 0.5, v offset + 0.5, >
mad r0.xy, v1.xy, c0.xy, c0.zw ; multiply uv by scale and add offset
```

Compression Transform

This is the superset of the previous two compression methods. We transform our input data into a space that compresses better. With the scaled offset method, we took our uncompressed data and applied a scale and offset. This can be represented by applying a scale matrix and a translation matrix to our input vector. This method further extends the idea by applying another linear transform (i.e., a matrix).

To see why this method can produce better results than the other two, look at the case in Figure 2. We have a simple two-polygon square that is oriented at 45 degrees (A). After scaled offset compression, we might be left with (B) which has clearly been distorted by the loss of precision. While higher precision would reduce the error, we may not wish/be able to spend more precision on it. Looking at (C), it is clear that if the object was rotated by 45 degrees, the existing precision would produce an exact result.

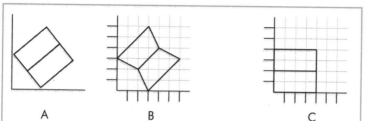

A   B   C

Figure 2: A square quantized in both the rotated and non-rotated case

The compression stage mainly consists of finding a transformation that will minimize the error when quantization occurs. The method I use is based on finding an optimal oriented bounding box for the vertices and using the basis matrix of this as my compression space. While it is possible to find better compression matrices for some objects (this method doesn't consider transforms such as shears), for most objects it finds a near-optimal linear quantization space. The compression space I usually use consists of a rotate, a scale, and a translation (a standard affine transformation), but in theory, any linear transformations could be used. A similar idea is used in image compression systems, such as MPEG, that use the DCT transform (a DCT is essentially an 8D rotation matrix).

Compression

Given a set of vertices, we want to find a compression space that minimizes the artifacts caused by the quantization. The problem has parallels in the collision detection field of trying to find an optimal oriented bounding box, so I use algorithms developed there to compute the compression transformation. It uses the vertex data from all triangles to set up a covariance matrix that we then extract the eigenvectors from.

This gives us a basis system that is aligned along the dominant axes of the data. Combined with the correct scale and translation, this gives excellent results for almost all data. From a geometrical point of view, compression transforms each input vector by the OBB basis space and then translates it so the minimum vertex in AABB space becomes the vector <0.0, 0.0, 0.0> and scales it so the maximum vertex becomes <1.0, 1.0, 1.0>.

```
CalculateRotationMatrix()
{
    n = Number of triangles
    m = vector size of data to be compressed
    p^i = 1st vertex of triangle i
    q^i = 2nd vertex of triangle i
    r^i = 3rd vertex of triangle i
```

$$\mu \; \frac{1}{3n} \sum_{i=0}^{n} \left(p^i + q^i + r^i \right)$$

$$\overline{p}^i = p^i - \mu$$
$$\overline{q}^i = q^i - \mu$$
$$\overline{r}^i = r^i - \mu$$
$$R_{jk} = \frac{1}{3n} \sum_{i=0}^{n} \left(\overline{p}_j^i \cdot \overline{p}_k^i + \overline{q}_j^i \cdot \overline{q}_k^i + \overline{r}_j^i \cdot \overline{r}_k^i \right) \quad 1 \le j, k \le m$$

```
ExtractNormalizedEigenvectors(R)

}

DetermineCompressionMatrix()
{

    CalculateRotationMatrix();

    For Every Vertex
        v' = R⁻¹ * v
        LowerRange = Minimum (LowerRange, v')
        UpperRange = Maximum (UpperRange, v')

    O = TranslationMatrix( LowerRange )
    S = ScaleMatrix( UpperRange - LowerRange )

    C = R⁻¹ * O⁻¹ * S⁻¹
}

CompressionTransform( originalVal )
{
    v = originalVal
    v" = C*v
    return FloatToInteger(v")
}
```

Decompression

We transform the incoming values by the decompression matrix. This has the effect of transforming the compressed vector from compression space back into normal space.

```
Constants
{
    D = C⁻¹
}

Decompress( compressedVal )
{
    return (IntegerToFloat( compressedVal ) * D)
}
```

Practical Example

This compression method is ideal for position data, except for huge objects. Using 16-bit data types gives 65,535 values across the longest distance of the object; in most cases, it will provide no visual loss in quality from the original float version. We have to compensate for the data type range by changing the scale and translation matrix (same as scaled offset) and then transpose the matrix (as usual for vertex shader matrices). This gives us a 25% savings in vertex size for four cycles of vertex code.

Compression transform shader example:

```
; v1 = position in the range -32767.0 to 32768.0 (integer only)
; c0 - c3 = Transpose of the decompression matrix
m4x4 r0, v1, c0    ; decompress input vertex
```

Using the same data stream from the earlier example, we can now see what the vertex shader might look like.

Compressed vertex example:

```
D3DVSD_STREAM(0),
D3DVSD_REG( 0, D3DVSDT_SHORT4),    // position
D3DVSD_REG( 1, D3DVSDT_UBYTE4),    // normal
D3DVSD_REG( 2, D3DVSDT_SHORT2),    // texture coordinate
D3DVSD_END()
```

Compressed vertex shader example:

```
; v1.xyz = position in the range -32767.0 to 32768.0 (integer only)
; v2.xyz = normal in the range 0.0 to 255.0 (integer only)
; v3.xy = uv in the range -32767.0 to 32768.0 (integer only)
; c0 - c3 = Transpose of the world view projection matrix
; c4 - c7 = Transpose of the decompression matrix
; c8 = <1.0/255.0, 1.0/255.0, 1.0/255.0, 1.0/255.0>
; c9 = <u scale / 65535.0, v scale / 65535.0, u offset + 0.5, v offset + 0.5>
m4x4    r0, v1, c4                 ; decompress compress position
mul     r1, v2, c8                 ; multiply compressed normal by 1/255
mad     r2.xy, v3.xy, c9.xy, c9.zw ; multiply uv by scale and add offset

; now the normal vertex shader code, this example just transforms
; the position and copies the normal and uv coordinate to the rasterizer
m4x4    oPos, r0, c0               ; transform position into HCLIP space
mov oT0, r2                        ; copy uv into texture coordinate set 0
mov oT1, r1                        ; copy normal into texture coordinate set 1
```

For an extra six cycles of vertex shader code, we have reduced vertex data size by 50%.

Optimizations

We can usually eliminate most of the decompression instructions, reducing the shader execution time to roughly the same as the uncompressed version.

The first optimization is noting that anywhere we are already doing a 4x4 matrix transform, we can get any of the previous compressions for free. By incorporating the decompression step into the transform matrix, the decompression will occur when the matrix vector multiply is performed (this works because all the compressions involve linear transforms). This is particularly important for position; we always do a 4x4 matrix transform (to take us from local space into HCLIP space) so we can decompress any of the above for free!

Another optimization is the usual vertex shader rule of never moving a temporary register into an output register. Wherever you are, simply output directly into the output register.

Anywhere you use quantized D3DVSDT_UBYTE4, you might as well use D3D-VSDT_D3DCOLOR instead, as it automatically does the divide by 255.0 and swizzling is free in the vertex shader. This also applies the other way; if you are scaling by a

D3DVSDT_D3DCOLOR by 255.0 (and your device supports both), use
D3DVSDT_UBYTE4.

Practical Example

By applying these three rules to the same data as before, we achieve 50% savings of memory
and bandwidth for zero cycles.

Optimized compressed vertex example:

```
D3DVSD_STREAM(0),
D3DVSD_REG( D3DVSDE_POSITION,    D3DVSDT_SHORT4),
D3DVSD_REG( D3DVSDE_NORMAL,      D3DVSDT_D3DCOLOR),
D3DVSD_REG( D3DVSDE_TEXCOORD0,   D3DVSDT_SHORT2),
D3DVSD_END()
```

Optimized compressed vertex shader example:

```
; v1.xyz = position in the range -32767.0 to 32768.0 (integer only)
; v2.xyz = normal in the range 0.0 to 255.0 (integer only) (swizzled)
; v3.xy = uv in the range -32767.0 to 32768.0 (integer only)
; c0 - c3 = Transpose of the decompression world view projection matrix
; c4 = <u scale / 65535.0, v scale / 65535.0, u offset + 0.5, v offset + 0.5>
m4x4    oPos, v1, c0           ; decompress and transform position
mad     oT0.xy, v3, c4.xy, c4.zw  ; multiply uv by scale and add offset
mov     oT1.xyz, v2.zyx        ; swizzle and output normal
```

Advanced Compression

There are several methods that extend and improve on the basic techniques described in the
previous section for special situations.

Multiple Compression Transforms

The main reason that you may not be able to use a compression transform for position is if the
object is huge but still has fine details (these are classic objects like large buildings, huge space
ships, or terrain). This technique trades vertex constant space for an increase in precision
across the object. It doesn't mix with palette skinning very well, but for static data it can
increase precision significantly.

Essentially, it breaks the object up into separate compressed areas and each vertex picks
which areas it belongs to. The main issue is making sure the compressor doesn't cause gaps in
the object.

We load the address register with the matrix to use, which we store by using a spare component (position w is usually spare with compressed data).

Note: This is the same technique used to speed up rendering of lots of small
objects (things like cubes): Every vertex is treated as if it were skinned with a single index and a weight of 1.0. This allows a single render call to have multiple
local matrices. We just use it to select compression matrices rather than local
space matrices.

Compression

The object is broken into chunks beforehand and the standard compressor is applied to each chunk, storing the chunk number in the vertex.

The exact method of breaking the object into chunks will be very data-dependent. A simple method might be to subdivide the object into equally spaced chunks; another might be to choose an area of high detail.

```
MultipleCompressionTransforms
{

    BreakObjectIntoChunks()
    For Each Chunk
        DetermineCompressionMatrix()

        compressionMatrixArray[chunkNum] = C

        For Each Vertex v in Chunk
        {
            v" = C * v
            Store FloatToInteger(v") && chunkNum
        }
}
```

Decompression

The only change from the standard compression transform decompression is to use the stored chunkNum to index into the compression matrix first.

```
Constants
{
    D[MAX_CHUNKS] = C⁻¹ [MAX_CHUNKS]
}

Decompress( compressedVal, chunkNum )
{
    return (IntegerToFloat( compressedVal ) * D[chunkNum] )
}
```

Practical Example

This compression method is good for position data, even for large objects, but isn't usable for skinned or multi-matrix objects. Each matrix takes four constants, so for equally spaced compression matrices, it quickly fills up constant space. The only extra cost is a single instruction to fill the index register.

Multiple compression transform shader example:

```
; v1.xyz = position in the range -32767.0 to 32768.0 (integer only)
; v1.w = (compression matrix index * 4) in the range 0 to MAX_CHUNKS*4
; c0 = < 1.f, ?, ?, ?>
; array of decompression matrices from c1 up to MAX_CHUNKS*4
; i.e.,  c0 - c3 = Transpose of the 1st decompression matrix
;        c4 - c7 = Transpose of the 2nd decompression matrix
mov a0.x, v1.w              ; choose which decompression matrix to use
mov r0.xyz, v1.xyz          ; for replacing w
```

```
mov r0.w, c0.x              ; set w =1
m4x4 r0, r0 c[a0.x + 0]     ; decompress input vertex using selected matrix
```

Sliding Compression Transform

Rather than pack more data into the already used vector components, this time we put the extra "dummy" padding to good use. By encoding displacement values in the padding, we displace the entire compression matrix, allowing each vertex to slide the compression space to a better place for it.

The number and size of the spare padding ultimately decides how much extra precision is needed. Vertex shaders are not very good at extracting multiple numbers from a single padding, so it is best not to, but we can split values in the compressor and reconstruct the original value in the vertex shader.

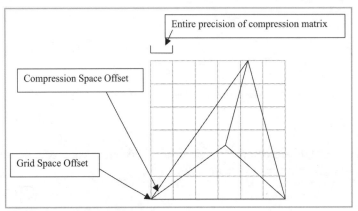

Figure 3: Sliding compression space example

Vertices store offset from local grid origin and store the grid number in the padding. This example has six times more precision along both world axes than the usual compression transform. The grid is aligned with the compression space, thus preserving maximum precision. Another way to look at it is that you break the range into discrete chunks and they are treated separately until decompression.

Compression

The first calculation is to decide how much extra precision you can get out of the padding. There is a different execution cost depending on how or what you have to extract, and this is likely to be the most important factor. The ideal situation is three padding values with enough range. The worst is to extract three values from a single padding. A typical case is one short pad and one byte pad (from a position and a normal); for this case, we can rearrange the data so we have three 8-bit values for extra precision.

In all cases, there is an extra precision that has to be factored into the compressor. This can be done by dividing the range that produces values greater than 1.f and then taking the integer components as the displacement scalars and the remainder as the compression values. The other method is to treat the slide as adding directly to the precision.

```
Sliding Compression Transform
{

    CalculateRotationMatrix()
    For Each Vertex v
    {
        v' = R⁻¹ * v
        LowerRange = Minimum (LowerRange, v')
        UpperRange = Maximum (UpperRange, v')

        O = TranslationMatrix( LowerRange )
        S = ScaleMatrix( UpperRange - LowerRange )
    }

    S = S / size of slide data-type
    C = R⁻¹ * O⁻¹ * S⁻¹

    For Each Vertex v
    {
        v" = C * v
        c = frac(v")
        g = floor(v")
        store FloatToInteger( c )
        store PackPadding ( g )
    }
}
```

The packing into a spare short and a byte is done by changing the four shorts into two lots of 4 bytes. The space used is the same, but we can access it differently.

Original stream definition:

```
D3DVSD_REG(0, D3DVSDT_SHORT4),
D3DVSD_REG(1, D3DVSDT_UBYTE4),
```

New stream definition:

```
D3DVSD_REG( 0, D3DVSDT_UBYTE4),
D3DVSD_REG( 1, D3DVSDT_UBYTE4),
D3DVSD_REG( 2, D3DVSDT_UBYTE4),
```

We place the lower 8 bits of each position component in register 0 and the upper 8 bits in register 1. This leaves the w component of each register for our slide value. One thing to watch for is the change from signed 16-bit values to unsigned 16-bit values caused by the split; this means the decompression matrix may have to change a little.

Decompression

To decompress, we recombine the position, get the slide values, and scale this by the grid size, which is then added to the compressed value.

```
Constants
{
    D = C⁻¹
    GridSize = size of data-type
    S = <255.0, 255.0, 255.0, 0.0>


}
```

```
Decompress( lowerVal, upperVal, slideVal )
{
    compressedVal = (IntegerToFloat(upperVal) * S) + IntegerToFloat( lowerVal )
    return ( compressedVal + (slideVal * GridSize)) * D)
}

; v1.xyz = lower half of position in the range 0 to 255.0 (integer only)
; v1.w = x slide
; v2.xyz = upper half of position in the range 0 to 255.0 (integer only)
; v2.w = y slide
; v3.xyz = normal in the range 0 to 255.0 (integer only)
; v3.w = z slide
; c1 = <255.0, 255.0, 255, 0.0>
; c2 = <65535.0, 1.0, 0.0, 0.0>
mov r1.xyz, v1.xyz                      ; due to 1 vertex register per instruction
mad r0.xyz, v2.xyz, c1.xyz, r1.xyz     ; r0.xyz = position (upper * 255.0) + lower
mad r0.x, v1.w, c2.x, r0.x             ; (x slide * 65535.0) + position x
mad r0.y, v2.w, c2.x, r0.y             ; (y slide * 65535.0) + position y
mad r0.z, v3.w, c2.x, r0.z             ; (z slide * 65535.0) + position z
mov r0.w, c2.y                         ; set w = 1
; now decompress using a compression matrix
```

A cost of six cycles has improved our precision 255 times in all axes by reusing the padding bytes. This effectively gives us 24 bits across the entire object, matching the precision (but not the range) of the original floating-point version.

Displacement Maps and Vector Fields

Displacements maps (and to a lesser degree their superset vector fields) are generally considered to be a good thing. It's likely that the future hardware and APIs will support this primitive directly, but by using vertex shaders, we can do a lot today.

First some background. What are displacement maps and vector fields? A displacement map is a texture with each texel representing distance along the surface normal. If that sounds a lot like a height field, it's because displacement maps are the superset of height fields (height fields always displace along the world up direction). Vector fields store a vector at each texel, with each component representing the distance along a basis vector.

Basic Displacement Maps

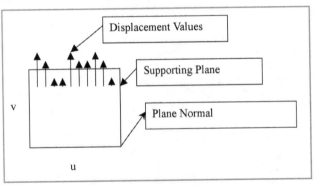

Figure 4: Displacement map example

We have a supporting plane which is constant for the entire displacement map and the displacement along the plane normal at every vertex. For true hardware support, that would be all that is needed, but we need more information.

To do displacement maps in a vertex shader requires an index list, whereas true displacement map hardware could deduce the index list from the rectilinear shape. Since the index data is constant for all displacement maps (only one index list per displacement map size is needed), the overhead is very small.

We also have to store the displacement along the u and v direction, as we can't carry information from one vertex to another. This is constant across all displacement maps of the same size, and can be passed in through a different stream. This makes the vector fields and displacement maps the same for a vertex shader program; the only difference is whether the u and v displacement is constant and stored in a separate stream (displacement maps) or arbitrarily changes per vertex (vector fields).

We can't automatically compute the normal and tangent (we would need per-primitive information), so we have to send them along with a displacement value (if needed; world space per-pixel lighting removes the need).

The easiest way (conceptually) is to store in vertex constants the three basis vectors representing the vector field. One basis vector is along the u edge, another the v edge, and the last is the normal. We also need to store maximum distance along each vector and a translation vector to the <0.0, 0.0, 0.0> corner of the displacement map.

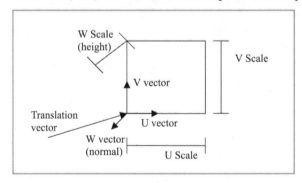

Figure 5: Displacement vector diagram

For each vertex, we take the displacement along each vector and multiply it by the appropriate scale and basis vector. We then add them to the translation vector to get our displaced point.

Basis displacement map/vector field shader example:

```
; v1.x = displacement w basis vector (normal) (dW)
; v2.xy = displacements along u and v basis vectors (dU and dV)
; c0.xyz = U basis vector (normalized) (U)
; c1.xyz = V basis vector (normalized) (V)
; c2.xyz = W basis vector (normalized) (W)
; c3.xyz = translation to <0.0, 0.0, 0.0> corner of map (T)
; c4.xyz = U V W scale
; c5 – c8 = world view projection matrix
; multiple normalized vectors
mul r0.xyz, c0.xyz, c4.x          ; scale U vector
mul r1.xyz, c1.xyz, c4.y          ; scale V vector
mul r2.xyz, c2.xyz, c4.z          ; scale W vector
; generate displaced point
mul r0.xyz, v2.x, r0.xyz          ; r0 = dU * U
```

```
mad r0.xyz, v2.y, r1.xyz, r0.xyz  ; r0 = dV * V + dU * U
mad r0.xyz, v1.x, r2.xyz, r0.xyz  ; r0 = dW * W + dV * V + dU * U
add r0.xyz, r0.xyz, c3.xyz        ; r0 = T + dW * W + dV * V + dU * U
; standard vector shader code
m4x4   oPos, r0, c5               ; transform position into HCLIP space
```

Hopefully, you can see this is just an alternative formulation of the compression matrix method (a rotate, scale, and translation transform). Rather than optimize it in the same way (pre-multiply the transform matrix by the compression transform), we follow it through in the other way, moving the displacement vector into HCLIP space.

Entering Hyperspace

Moving the displacement vector into HCLIP space involves understanding four-dimensional space. By using this 4D hyperspace, we can calculate a displacement vector that works directly in HCLIP space.

It sounds more difficult than it really is. HCLIP space is the space before perspective division. The non-linear transform of perspective is stored in the fourth dimension, and after the vertex shader is finished (and clipping has finished), the usual three dimensions will be divided by w.

The most important rule is that everything works as it does in 3D, just with an extra component. We treat it as we would any other coordinate space; it just has an extra axis.

All we have to do is transform (before entry into the vertex shader) the basis and translation vectors into HCLIP space and we use them as before (only we now use four components), and the displaced point is generated in HCLIP so we don't need to transform them again. We also pre-multiply the basis scales before transforming the basis vector into HCLIP space.

HCLIP displacement map/vector field shader example:

```
; v1.x = displacement w basis vector (normal) (dW)
; v2.xy = displacements along u and v basis vectors (dU and dV)
; c0.xyzw = Scaled U basis vector in HCLIP space (U)
; c1.xyzw = Scaled V basis vector in HCLIP space (V)
; c2.xyzw = Scaled W basis vector in HCLIP space (W)
; c3.xyzw = translation to <0.0, 0.0, 0.0> corner of map in HCLIP space (T)
; generate displaced point in HCLIP space
mul r0.xyzw, v2.x, c0.xyzw        ; r0 = dU * U
mad r0.xyzw, v2.y, c1.xyzw, r0.xyzw  ; r0 = dV * V + dU * U
mad r0.xyzw, v1.x, c2.xyzw, r0.xyzw  ; r0 = dW * W + dV * V + dU * U
add oPos, r0.xyzw, c3.xyzw        ; r0 = T + dW * W + dV * V + dU * U
```

This is a matrix transform. The only difference from the m4x4 (4 dp4) or the mul/mad methods is that the m4x4 is using the transpose of a matrix, whereas mul/mad uses the matrix directly. Clearly there is no instruction saving (if we could have two constants per instruction we could get down to three instructions) using vertex shaders for displacement mapping over compression transform, but we can reuse our index buffers and our u v displacements and make savings if we have lots of displacement maps.

This allows us to get down to only 4 bytes (either D3DVSDT_UBYTE4 or D3DVSDT_SHORT2) for every displacement position past the first map. For vector fields, the only savings we make over compression transform is reusing the index buffers.

Conclusion

I've demonstrated several methods for reducing the size of vertex data. The best method obviously depends on your particular situation, but you can expect a 50% reduction in size quite easily. That's good in many ways, as models will load faster (especially over slow paths, like modems), memory bandwidth is conserved, and memory footprint is kept low.

Acknowledgments

- S. Gottschalk, M.C. Lin, D. Manocha — "OBBTree: A Hierarchical Structure for Rapid Interference Detection," http://citeseer.nj.nec.com/gottschalk96obbtree.html.
- C. Gotsman — "Compression of 3D Mesh Geometry," http://www.cs.technion.ac.il/~gotsman/primus/Documents/primus-lecture-slides.pdf.
- Tom Forsyth — WGDC and Meltdown 2001 Displaced Subdivision
- Oscar Cooper — General sanity checking

Shadow Volume Extrusion Using a Vertex Shader

Chris Brennan

Introduction

The shadow volume technique of rendering real-time shadows involves drawing geometry that represents the volume of space that bounds what is in the shadow cast by an object. To calculate if a pixel being drawn is in or out of a shadow, shoot a ray from the eye through the shadow volume toward the point on the rendered object and count the number of times the shadow volume entered and exited. If the ray has entered more times than exited, the pixel being drawn is in shadow. The stencil buffer can be used to emulate this by rendering the back sides of the shadow volume triangles while incrementing the stencil buffer, followed by the front sides of the triangles, which decrement it. If the final result adds up to where it started, then you have entered and exited the shadow an equal number of times and are therefore outside the shadow; otherwise, you are inside the shadow. The next step is rendering a light pass that is masked out by a stencil test.

There are several other very different algorithms to doing shadows [Haines01]. Stencil shadow volumes have their benefits and drawbacks compared to other shadowing algorithms like depth buffers. The most important trade-off is that while shadow volumes have infinite precision and no artifacts, they have a hard edge and an uncertain render complexity, depending on object shape complexity and the viewer and light positions. Previous major drawbacks to shadow volumes were the CPU power required to compute the shadow geometry and the requirement that character animation must be done on the CPU so that a proper shadow geometry could be generated, but a clever vertex shader combined with some preprocessing removes the need for all CPU computations and therefore allows the GPU to do all the character animation. A brief comparison of CPU and GPU complexity and their drawbacks can be found in [Dietrich].

Another historical complexity of shadow volumes that has been solved is what to do if the viewer is inside the shadow. The problem arises that since the viewer starts in shadow, the stencil count begins off by one. Many solutions have been proposed [Haines02], and many are very computationally intensive, but a simple solution exists. Instead of incrementing and decrementing the stencil buffer with the visible portion of the shadow volume, modify the stencil buffer when the volume is hidden by another surface by setting the depth test to fail. This sounds counterintuitive, but what it does is exactly the same thing, except it counts how many times the ray from the eye to the pixel exits and enters the shadow volume <u>after</u> the visible point of the pixel. It still tests to see if the pixel is inside or outside of the shadow volume, but it eliminates the issues with testing to see if the viewer starts in shadow. It does, however, emphasize the need to make sure that all shadow volumes are complete and closed as opposed to previous algorithms, which did not require geometry to cap the front or back of the volume.

Creating Shadow Volumes

The time-consuming part of the algorithm is the detection of all the silhouette edges. These are normally found by taking a dot product with the light vector and each of the edge's two neighboring face normals. If one dot product is positive (toward the light) and one is negative (away from the light), then it is a silhouette edge. For each silhouette edge, create planes extending from the edge away from the light creating the minimum geometry needed for the shadow volume. Unfortunately, not only is it expensive to iterate across all of the edges, but it is also expensive to upload the new geometry to the video card every frame.

However, hardware vertex shaders can be used to do this work on the GPU. The general idea is to create geometry that can be modified by a vertex shader to properly create the shadow volume with any light position so that the geometry can reside on the GPU. At initialization or preprocess time, for each edge of the original object geometry, add a quad that has two sides consisting of copies of the original edge and two opposite sides of zero length. The pseudocode for this is as follows:

```
For each face
    Calculate face normal
    Create 3 new vertices for this face and face normal
    Insert the face into the draw list
    For each edge of face
        If (edge has been seen before)
            Insert degenerate quad into draw list
            Remove edge from checklist
        Else
            Insert edge into a checklist
If (any edges are left in checklist)
    flag an error because the geometry is not a closed volume.
```

Figure 1 shows the geometry with the quads inserted and spread apart slightly so that they can be seen. These quads will make up the extruded edges of the shadow volume when required. The original geometry is still present and is used to cap the extruded edges on the front and back to complete the volume. After the quad insertion, each vertex neighbors only one of the original faces and should include its face's normal. When rendering the volume, each vertex's face normal is dotted with the light vector. If the result is negative, the face is facing away from the light and should therefore be pushed out to the outer extent of the light along the light vector. Otherwise, it stays exactly where the original geometry lies.

Figure 1: Illustration of invisible quads inserted into the original geometry to create a new static geometry to be used with a shadow volume vertex shader

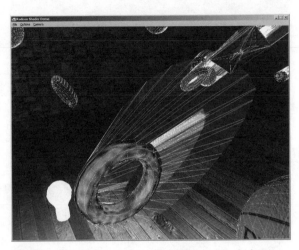

Figure 2: Shadow volumes after being extruded away from the light

After this pass is completed, the light pass is rendered using a stencil test to knock out the pixels that are in shadow.

Figure 3: The final pass completes the effect.

The shadowed room application with source code can be found on the companion CD and at http://www.ati.com/na/pages/resource_centre/dev_rel/sdk/RadeonSDK/Html/Samples/Direct-3D/RadeonShadowShader.html.

Effect File Code

```
matrix  mWVP;
matrix  mWV;
matrix  mP;
matrix  mWVt;
vector  cShd;
vector  pVL;

vertexshader vShd =
    decl
    {
        stream 0;
        float v0[3];  // Position
        float v1[3];  // FaceNormal
    }
    asm
    {
        ; Constants:
        ; 16..19 - Composite World*View*Proj Matrix
        ; 20..23 - Composite World*View Matrix
        ; 24..27 - Projection Matrix
        ; 28..31 - Inv Trans World*View
        ; 90     - {light range, debug visualization amount, z near, z far}
        ; 91     - View Space Light Position

        vs.1.0
        def c0, 0,0,0,1

        ; View Space
        m4x4  r0, v0, c20   ; World*View Transform of point P (pP)
        m3x3  r3, v1, c28   ; World*View Transform of normal (vN)

        sub   r1, r0, c91   ; Ray from light to the point (vLP)

        dp3   r11.x, r1, r1      ; length^2
        rsq   r11.y, r11.x       ; 1/length
        mul   r1, r1, r11.y      ; normalized

        rcp   r11.y, r11.y       ; length
        sub   r11.z, c90.x, r11.y  ; light.Range - len(vLP)
        max   r11.z, r11.z, c0.x   ; extrusion length = clamp0(light.Range -
                                   ; len(vLP))

        dp3   r10.z, r3, r1      ; vLP dot vN
        slt   r10.x, r10.z, c0.x ; if (vLP.vN < 0) (is pointing away from light)

        mad   r2, r1, r11.z, r0  ; extrude along vLP

        ; Projected Space
        m4x4  r3, r2, c24   ; Projected extruded position
        m4x4  r0, v0, c16   ; World*View*Proj Transform of original position

        ; Chose final result
        sub   r10.y, c0.w, r10.x  ; !(vLP.vN >= 0)
        mul   r1, r3, r10.y
        mad   oPos, r0, r10.x, r1
    };
```

```
technique ShadowVolumes
{
    pass P0
    {
        vertexshader = <vShd>;

        VertexShaderConstant[16] = <mWVP>;
        VertexShaderConstant[20] = <mWV>;
        VertexShaderConstant[24] = <mP>;
        VertexShaderConstant[28] = <mWVt>;
        VertexShaderConstant[90] = <cShd>;
        VertexShaderConstant[91] = <pVL>;

        ColorWriteEnable = 0;
        ZFunc            = Less;
        ZWriteEnable     = False;
        StencilEnable    = True;
        StencilFunc      = Always;
        StencilMask      = 0xffffffff;
        StencilWriteMask = 0xffffffff;

        CullMode = CCW;
        StencilZFail     = IncrSat;
    }

    pass P1
    {
        CullMode = CW;
        StencilZFail     = DecrSat;
    }
}
```

Using Shadow Volumes with Character Animation

The technique as described is for statically shaped objects and does not include characters that are skinned or tweened. The biggest advantage of doing shadow volume extrusion in a vertex shader is that the volumes can exist as static vertex buffers on the GPU and the updated geometry does not have to be uploaded every frame. Therefore, this technique needs to be extended to work on animated characters as well (see David Gosselin's "Character Animation with Direct3D Vertex Shaders" article in this book). Otherwise, if the animation of the shadow volume were to be done on the CPU, it would be possible to do the optimized shadow volume creation at the same time.

The most straightforward approach is to copy the vertex animation data to the shadow volume geometry and skin and/or tween the face normal as you would the vertex normal. Unfortunately, the face normals need to be very accurate and consistent across all vertices of a face; otherwise, objects will be split and extruded in inappropriate places, resulting in incorrect shadow volumes.

Figure 4: Artifacts caused by skinned face normals. Notice the notch in the shadow of the shoulder.

These artifacts are the result of the extrusion happening across a face of the original geometry as opposed to the inserted quads along the face edges. This is caused by the fact that each vertex has different weights for skinning, which yield a different face normal for each of the three vertices of a face. When that face becomes close to being a silhouette edge, it may have one or two vertices of the face moved away from the light, while the other one stays behind.

The ideal solution is to animate the positions and regenerate the face normals. However, generating face normals requires vertex neighbor information that is not normally available in a vertex shader. One possible solution is to make each vertex contain position information of its two neighbors, animate the vertex position as well as its two neighbors, and recalculate the face normal with a cross product. The regular vertex position data would need to be stored and animated three times. This can sometimes be very expensive, depending on the animation scheme and the size of the models.

An inexpensive way to fix the variation in face normals across a face is to calculate skinning weights per face in addition to per vertex and use the face weights for the face normal. This can be done by averaging all of the vertex weights or by extracting them directly from the original art. Using the same weight for each vertex of a face guarantees that the shadow volume can only be extruded along the edge quads.

Figure 5: Animated shadow volumes with face normals skinned by face weights

By using face weights for the face normals, the previously seen artifacts are not visible. This technique can be seen in the ATI Island demos on the companion CD, or at http://www.ati.com/na/pages/resource_ centre/dev_rel/demos.html.

References

[Dietrich] Sim Dietrich, "Practical Priority Buffer Shadows," *Game Programming Gems II*, Mark DeLoura, Ed. (Charles River Media, 2001), p. 482.

[Haines01] Eric Haines and Tomas Möller, "Real-Time Shadows," GDC 2001 Proceedings, http://www.gdconf.com/archives/proceedings/2001/haines.pdf.

[Haines02] Eric Haines and Tomas Akenine-Möller, *Real-Time Rendering*, 2nd edition (A.K. Peters Ltd., 2002).

Character Animation with Direct3D Vertex Shaders

David Gosselin

Introduction

With the introduction of vertex shaders to modern graphics hardware, we are able to move a large portion of the character animation processing from the CPU to the graphics hardware. Two common character animation techniques are *tweening* (also known as morphing) and *skinning* (also called skeletal animation). This article describes how both of these techniques and some related variations can be performed using vertex shaders. We will also cover how to combine animation with the per-pixel lighting techniques described in the articles by Wolfgang Engel in Part 1. We will conclude with a discussion of some geometry decompression techniques, which allow an application to minimize memory usage and memory bandwidth.

Tweening

Tweening is the technique of linearly interpolating between two (or more) "key" frames of animation. This technique is used in many popular games like *Quake*. The artwork consists of a character or object in a few poses spaced relatively close together in time. For example, the figure below shows a few frames of an animation stored as key frames.

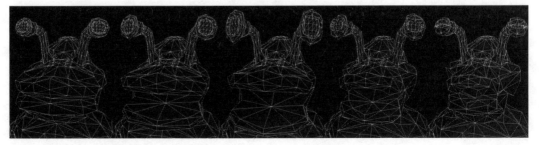

Figure 1: An object animated with tweening

In order to perform this type of animation, the object's position and normal data are stored for each frame of the animation. At run time, two frames are selected that represent the current state of the animation. The vertex buffers containing these two frames are loaded as separate streams of data. Typically, setting up the vertex streams looks something like:

```
d3dDevice->SetStreamSource (0, frame0VertexBuffer, frame0Stride);
d3dDevice->SetStreamSource (1, frame1VertexBuffer, frame1Stride);
```

Additionally, a tween factor is computed at run time. The tween factor represents the animation time between the two frames, with the value 0.0 corresponding to the first frame and the value 1.0 corresponding to the second frame. This value is used to perform the linear interpolation of the position data. One way to compute this value is shown below:

```
float t = time;
if (t < 0)
{
    t = (float)fmod ((float)(-t), TotalAnimationTime);
    t = TotalAnimationTime - t;
}
float tween = (float)fmod ((float64)t, TotalAnimationTime);
tween /= TotalAnimationTime;
tween *= (NumberOfAnimationFrames - 1);
which = (int32)floor ((float64)tween);
tween -= which;
```

The tween value and any lighting constants you may be using are loaded into the constant store. The vertex shader code then only needs to implement the following equation in order to perform the interpolation between the two frames:

```
A*(1-tween) + B*tween
```

Generally, the vertex shader should also multiply by the concatenated world, view, and projection matrix. The following vertex shader shows an implementation of tweening:

```
; position frame 0 in v0
; position frame 1 in v14
; tween in c0.x
; World/View/Projection matrix in c12-c15

; Figure out 1-tween constant
; use the 1.0 from position's w
sub r0, v0.wwww, c0

; Compute the tweened position
mul r1, v0, r0.xxxx
mad r1, v14, c0.xxxx, r1

; Multiply by the view/projection and pass it along
m4x4    oPos, r1, c12
```

To save some vertex shader instructions, the value of (1 – tween factor) can be computed by the application. Both of these values can be loaded into the constant store, in this case as part of the same constant vector. The z and w components of this constant register are also good places to stick handy constants like 1.0, 0.0, 2.0, 0.5, etc., if you happen to need them. The resulting vertex shader code looks like the following:

```
; position frame 0 in v0
; normal frame 0 in v3
```

```
; position frame 1 in v14
; normal frame 1 in v15
; tween in c0.x
; 1 - tween in c0.y
; View/Projection matrix in c12-c15

; Compute the tweened position
mul  r1, v0, c0.yyyy
mad  r1, v14, c0.xxxx, r1

; Multiply by the view/projection and pass it along
m4x4    oPos, r1, c12
```

In this section, we have explored an efficient tweening algorithm that can be easily computed within a vertex shader. It has the advantages of being very quick to compute and working well with higher order surface tessellation schemes such as N-Patches. Unfortunately, tweening has the downside of requiring quite a bit of data to be stored in memory for each animation. Another popular technique, which addresses the memory usage issue, is skinning. Skinning requires more vertex shader instructions but less data per frame of animation. We will explore skinning in more detail in the following section.

Skinning

Skinning is the process of blending the contributions from several matrices in order to find the final vertex position. Typically, the character modeling tool describes the matrices using a series of "bones." Figure 3 shows what this looks like in 3D Studio Max.

The diamond shapes in Figure 2 represent the various control matrices. The inner triangles represent the "bones." In this tool, the artist can move the joints, and the model's position is updated using inverse kinematics. During export of this data from Max, the triangles are grouped according to which matrices affect their position. Further preprocessing generates the vertex buffers used by the Direct3D API. The vertices created from the mesh have bone weights, which represent the amount of influence from the corresponding matrices (bones). These weights are used to blend the contributions of the corresponding matrices according to the following equation:

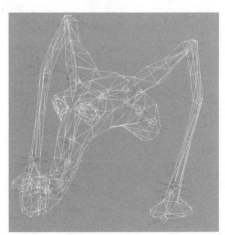

Figure 2: Skeleton of a skinned character with overlayed polygon mesh

```
Final Position = SUM (matrix[n]*position*weight[n])
```

Before the advent of vertex shading hardware, these computations took place on the CPU (typically referred to as "software skinning"). This approach has the benefit of being able to compute accurate normals after skinning a model, but typically it is fairly costly in terms of the amount of computation required. Some earlier graphics hardware had fixed-function hardware dedicated to performing these computations. The user specified a Flexible Vertex Format

(FVF), which contained the skinning weights and loaded two to four numbered world matrices to be blended. With vertex shaders, programmers have the ability to tailor the type of skinning to their own applications. In this section, we will explore two different kinds of skinning: a four-matrix skinned approach, which mirrors the functionality available from the fixed function pipeline, and a paletted approach, which allows for greater batching of drawing calls.

The following vertex shader shows how to perform four-matrix skinning. One common technique to reduce the amount of per-vertex data is to only store three vertex weights and compute a fourth one in the vertex shader by assuming that the weights sum to 1.0. At run time, the matrices for a particular group are loaded into the constant store, and the appropriate vertex buffers are loaded. The vertex shader code looks like the following:

```
; position in v0
; matrix weights in v1
; c0.z = 1.0
; View/Projection matrix in c12-c15
; World 0 matrix in c16-c19
; World 1 matrix in c20-c23
; World 2 matrix in c24-c27
; World 3 matrix in c28-31

; Multiply input position by matrix 0
m4x4    r0, v0, c16
mul     r1, r0, v1.xxxx

; Multiply input position by matrix 1 and sum
m4x4    r0, v0, c20
mad     r1, r0, v1.yyyy, r1

; Multiply input position by matrix 2 and sum
m4x4    r0, v0, c24
mad     r1, r0, v1.zzzz, r1

; Multiply input position by matrix 3
m4x4    r0, v0, c28

; Compute fourth weight
dp3     r10, v1, c0.zzzz
sub     r11, c0.zzzz, r10

; sum
mad     r1, r0, r11.wwww, r1

; Multiply by the view/projection matrix
m4x4    oPos, r1, c20
```

One variation on this technique is to store a palette of matrices in the constant store. During preprocessing, four indices are stored per-vertex. These indices determine which matrices from the palette are used in the blending process. Using this technique, a much larger set of triangles can be processed without changing constant store state (typically an expensive operation). Note that it is still worthwhile to sort the triangles by similar bone matrices to take advantage of pipelined hardware. The vertex shader code takes advantage of the indexing register in order to reach into the constant store to retrieve the correct matrices. The following vertex shader shows one way to implement this technique.

```
; position in v0
; matrix weights in v1
; matrix indices in v2
; c0.z = 1.0
; c10 = (16.0, 4.0, 1.0, 0.0)
; View/Projection matrix in c12-c15
; World 0 matrix in c16-c19
; World 1 matrix in c20-c23
; . . . Other world matrices follow

; figure out the last weight
dp3   r5, v1, c0.zzzz
sub   r5.w, c0.zzzz, r5

; First world matrix constant = index*4 + start index
mad     r7, v2.xyzw, c10.y, c10.x

; Skin by Matrix 0
mov     a0.x, r7.x
m4x4    r0, v0, c[a0.x]
mul     r1, r0, v1.xxxx

; Skin by Matrix 1 and sum
mov     a0.x, r7.y
m4x4    r0, v0, c[a0.x]
mad     r1, r0, v1.yyyy, r1

; Skin by Matrix 2 and sum
mov     a0.x, r7.z
m4x4    r0, v0, c[a0.x]
mad     r1, r0, v1.zzzz, r1

; Skin by Matrix 3 and sum
mov     a0.x, r7.w
m4x4    r0, v0, c[a0.x]
mad     r1, r0, r5.wwww, r1

; Multiply by the view/projection and pass it along
m4x4    oPos, r1, c12
```

One drawback to using the paletted skinning approach is that it doesn't work well with higher order surfaces. The issue stems from the fact that vertex shaders are computed post-tessellation and any vertex data other than positions and normals are linearly interpolated. Interpolating the index values for blend matrices is nonsensical.

Skinning and Tweening Together

It is also possible to blend skinning and tweening. There are cases where it makes sense to model a portion of a character using tweening, but you still want some basic movement controlled by bones. For example, you might want the face of a character to be tweened in order to capture some subtle movements that would require a large number of bones and would be difficult to manage within an art tool, but you want to use bones for the movement of the head and body. The following figures show this kind of example, where the mouth and claws of the character are tweened and skinned.

The following figure shows a few frames of animation using skinning alone.

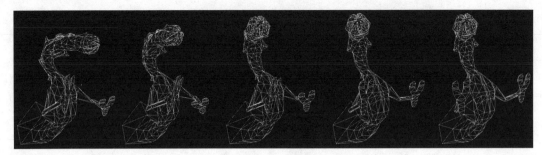

Figure 3

The next figure shows just the tweened portion of the animation. Note the complex animation of the mouth and claws.

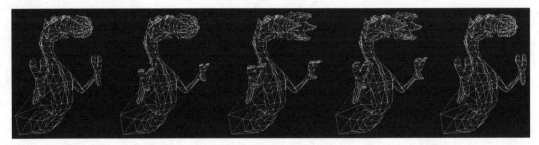

Figure 4

The final figure shows the skinning and tweening animations being performed simultaneously on the character.

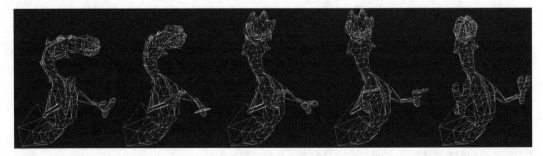

Figure 5

When performing this type of animation, the tween portion is computed first and then the resultant position is skinned. The following vertex shader shows one implementation of this technique.

```
; position frame 0 in v0
; position frame 1 in v14
; matrix weights in v1
; matrix indices in v2
```

```
; c0.z = 1.0
; tween in c9.x
; c10 = (16.0, 4.0, 1.0, 0.0)
; View/Projection matrix in c12-c15
; World 0 matrix in c16-c19
; World 1 matrix in c20-c23
; . . . Other world matrices follow

; Figure out tween constant
sub r9, v0.wwww, c9
mov r9.y, c9.x

; Compute the tweened position
mul r10, v0, r9.xxxx
mad r2, v14, r9.yyyy, r10

; figure out the last weight
mov   r5, v1
dp3   r3, v1, c0.zzzz
sub   r5.w, c0.zzzz, r3

; First world matrix constant = index*4 + start index
mad      r7, v2.xyzw, c10.y, c10.x

; Skin by Matrix 0
mov      a0.x, r7.x
m4x4     r0, r2, c[a0.x]
mul      r1, r0, v1.xxxx

; Skin by Matrix 1 and sum
mov      a0.x, r7.y
m4x4     r0, r2, c[a0.x]
mad      r1, r0, v1.yyyy, r1

; Skin by Matrix 2 and sum
mov      a0.x, r7.z
m4x4     r0, r2, c[a0.x]
mad      r1, r0, v1.zzzz, r1

; Skin by Matrix 3 and sum
mov      a0.x, r7.w
m4x4     r0, r2, c[a0.x]
mad      r1, r0, r5.wwww, r1

; Multiply by the projection and pass it along
m4x4     oPos, r1, c12
```

In this section, we explored one way to combine two different types of character animation. It is obviously just one way to mix the two types of animation. One benefit of vertex shaders is the ability to customize the vertex processing to get different effects that fit the needs of your particular application. Hopefully, this will provide you with some ideas for how to customize animation to suit your own needs.

So far, we have only discussed animation of vertex positions and normals. This is sufficient for vertex lighting of animated characters. Modern graphics chips provide very powerful pixel shading capabilities that allow lighting to be performed per-pixel. To do this, however, some care must be taken in the vertex shader to properly set up the per-pixel lighting computations. This will be discussed in the next section.

Animating Tangent Space for Per-Pixel Lighting

In order to reasonably light a character animated by these techniques, it is important to animate the normal as well as the position. In the case of tweening, this means storing a normal along with the position and interpolating the normal in the same way as the position. Getting the "right" normal isn't quite as simple in the case of skinning. Since skinning can potentially move each vertex in very different ways, the only way to get completely correct normals is to recompute the normal at each vertex once the mesh is reskinned. Typically, this tends to be a very expensive operation and would require a lot of additional information stored per-vertex. To top it off, there really isn't a way to index other vertices from within a vertex shader. The typical compromise, which gives "good enough" results, is to skin the normal using just the rotation part of the bone matrices.

Additionally, if you are doing per-pixel bump mapping or other effects requiring texture/tangent space discussed in the articles by Engel in Part 1, you also need to skin the basis vectors. The following shader shows the paletted matrix skinned version that also skins the tangent/texture space basis vectors.

```
; position in v0
; matrix weights in v1
; matrix indices in v2
; normal in v3
; tangent in v9
; binormal in v10
; c0.z = 1.0
; c10 = (16.0, 4.0, 1.0, 0.0)
; View/Projection matrix in c12-c15
; World 0 matrix in c16-c19
; World 1 matrix in c20-c23
; . . . Other world matrices follow


; figure out the last weight
dp3   r3, v1, c0.zzzz
sub   r5.w, c0.zzzz, r3

; First world matrix constant = index*4 + start index
mad     r7, v2.xyzw, c10.y, c10.x

; Skin by Matrix 0
mov     a0.x, r7.x
m4x4    r0, v0, c[a0.x]  ; Position
mul     r1, r0, v1.xxxx
m3x3    r0, v9, c[a0.x]  ; Tangent
mul     r2, r0, v1.xxxx
m3x3    r0, v10, c[a0.x] ; Bi-Normal
mul     r3, r0, v1.xxxx
m3x3    r0, v3, c[a0.x]  ; Normal
mul     r4, r0, v1.xxxx

; Skin by Matrix 1 and sum
mov     a0.x, r7.y
m4x4    r0, v0, c[a0.x]        ; Position
mad     r1, r0, v1.yyyy, r1
m3x3    r0, v9, c[a0.x]        ; Tangent
mad     r2, r0, v1.yyyy, r2
```

```
m3x3    r0, v10, c[a0.x]       ; Bi-Normal
mad     r3, r0, v1.yyyy, r3
m3x3    r0, v3, c[a0.x]        ; Normal
mad     r4, r0, v1.yyyy, r4

; Skin by Matrix 2 and sum
mov     a0.x, r7.z
m4x4    r0, v0, c[a0.x]        ; Position
mad     r1, r0, v1.zzzz, r1
m3x3    r0, v9, c[a0.x]        ; Tangent
mad     r2, r0, v1.zzzz, r2
m3x3    r0, v10, c[a0.x]       ; Bi-Normal
mad     r3, r0, v1.zzzz, r3
m3x3    r0, v3, c[a0.x]        ; Normal
mad     r4, r0, v1.zzzz, r4

; Skin by Matrix 3 and sum
mov     a0.x, r7.w
m4x4    r0, v0, c[a0.x]        ; Position
mad     r1, r0, r5.wwww, r1
m3x3    r0, v9, c[a0.x]        ; Tangent
mad     r2, r0, r5.wwww, r2
m3x3    r0, v10, c[a0.x]       ; Bi-Normal
mad     r3, r0, r5.wwww, r3
m3x3    r0, v3, c[a0.x]        ; Normal
mad     r4, r0, r5.wwww, r4

; Multiply by the projection and pass it along
m4x4    oPos, r1, c12

; >>>> At this point:
; >>>>>   r1 contains the skinned vertex position
; >>>>>   r2 contains the tangent   (v9)
; >>>>>   r3 contains the binormal (v10)
; >>>>>   r4 contains the normal    (v3)
```

Now, you might ask, what can we do with this basis vector? Well, one common usage is to perform per-pixel "Dot3" bump mapping. In order to compute this, two textures are needed. The first texture is the base map, which contains the color on the surface. The second texture is the bump map that contains the normal at each point in the original texture encoded into the red, green, and blue channels. Within the vertex shader, the vector from the light to the vertex is computed, normalized, and converted into tangent/texture space. This vector is then interpolated per-pixel before being sent to the pixel shader.

Per-Pixel Lighting

Additionally, within the vertex shader, you can compute a light falloff. This involves sending data about the light falloff values in the constant store. The three values sent to the vertex shader are the distance from the light when the falloff starts, the distance from the light where the falloff ends, and the difference between those two values. The following shader code builds upon the previous shader and performs the calculations for three bumped diffuse lights. If fewer lights are desired, the same shader can be used by setting the color of one or more of the lights to black (0,0,0,0).

```
; c0.z = 1.0
; c1 has the position of light 1
; c2 has the color of light 1
; c3.x has the start of the falloff for light 1
; c3.y has the end of the falloff for light 1
; c3.z has the difference between the end of the falloff and the
;             start of the falloff
; c4 has the position of light 2
; c5 has the color of light 2
; c6.x has the start of the falloff for light 2
; c6.y has the end of the falloff for light 2
; c6.z has the difference between the end of the falloff and the
;             start of the falloff
; c7 has the position of light 2
; c8 has the color of light 2
; c9.x has the start of the falloff for light 2
; c9.y has the end of the falloff for light 2
; c9.z has the difference between the end of the falloff and the
;             start of the falloff
;;;;;;;;;;;;;;;;;;;;;;;;;;;;;;;;;;;;;;;;;;;;;;;;;;;;;;;;;;;;;;;;;;;
; Compute vector for light 1
sub   r0, c1, r1        ; Ray from light to point
dp3   r5.x, r0, r0      ; length^2
rsq   r5.y, r5.x        ; 1/length
mul   r0, r0, r5.y      ; normalized
rcp   r5.z, r5.y        ; length

m3x3  r8, r0, r2        ; Convert to tangent space
dp3   r9.x, r8, r8      ; length^2
rsq   r9.y, r9.x        ; 1/length
mul   oT2.xyz, r8, r9.y ; normalized

sub   r7.x, c3.y, r5.z  ; fallEnd - length
mul   r7.y, c3.z, r7.x  ; (fallEnd - length)/
                        ; (fallEnd-fallStart)
min   r7.w, r7.y, c0.z  ; clamp
mul   oD0.xyz, r7.w, c2 ; falloff * light color


;;;;;;;;;;;;;;;;;;;;;;;;;;;;;;;;;;;;;;;;;;;;;;;;;;;;;;;;;;;;;;;;;;;
; Compute vector for light 2
sub   r0, c4, r1        ; Ray from light to the point
dp3   r5.x, r0, r0      ; length^2
rsq   r5.y, r5.x        ; 1/length
mul   r0, r0, r5.y      ; normalized
rcp   r5.z, r5.y        ; length

m3x3  r8, r0, r2        ; Convert to tangent space
dp3   r9.x, r8, r8      ; length^2
rsq   r9.y, r9.x        ; 1/length
mul   oT3.xyz, r8, r9.y ; normalized

sub   r7.x, c6.y, r5.z  ; fallEnd - length
mul   r7.y, c6.z, r7.x  ; (fallEnd - length)/
                        ; (fallEnd - fallStart)
min   r7.w, r7.y, c0.z  ; clamp
mul   oD1.xyz, r7.w, c5 ; falloff * light color


;;;;;;;;;;;;;;;;;;;;;;;;;;;;;;;;;;;;;;;;;;;;;;;;;;;;;;;;;;;;;;;;;;;
; Compute vector for light 3
sub   r0, c7, r1        ; Ray from light to the point
```

```
dp3   r5.x, r0, r0          ; length^2
rsq   r5.y, r5.x            ; 1/length
mul   r0, r0, r5.y          ; normalized
rcp   r5.z, r5.y            ; length

m3x3  r8, r0, r2            ; Convert to tangent space
dp3   r9.x, r8, r8          ; length^2
rsq   r9.y, r9.x            ; 1/length
mul   oT4.xyz, r8, r9.y     ; normalized

sub   r7.x, c9.y, r5.z      ; fallEnd - length
mul   r7.y, c9.z, r7.x      ; (fallEnd - length)/
                           ; (fallEnd- fallStart)
min   r7.w, r7.y, c0.z      ; clamp
mul   oT5.xyz, r7.w, c8     ; falloff * light color

;;;;;;;;;;;;;;;;;;;;;;;;;;;;;;;;;;;;;;;;;;;;;;;;;;;;;;;;;;;;;;;;;;;
; Pass along the texture coordinates.
mov   oT0.xy, v7.xy
mov   oT1.xy, v8.xy
```

In the pixel shader, we compute the dot products and sum up the contributions from all three lights. In addition, the light colors passed into the above shaders are pre-divided by two to allow a bigger range of light colors and allow the lights to over-brighten the base textures. Within the pixel shader, this range is re-expanded by using the _x2 modifier on the colors.

```
ps.1.4

; c2 - contains the ambient lighting color
texld r0, t0        ; DOT3 Bump Map Texture
texld r1, t1        ; Base Texture
texcrd r2.rgb, t2 ; L1 - light 1 vector
texcrd r3.rgb, t3 ; L2 - light 2 vector
texcrd r4.rgb, t4 ; L3 - light 3 vector
                  ; v0 - C1 color of light 1 (from above)
                  ; v1 - C1 color of light 2 (from above)
texcrd r5.rgb, t5 ; C3 - color of light 3
   dp3_sat r2, r0_bx2, r2_bx2      ; N.L1
   mul     r2, r2, v0_x2           ; (N.L1)*C1
   dp3_sat r3, r0_bx2, r3_bx2      ; N.L2
   mad     r2, r3, v1_x2, r2       ; ((N.L1)*C1) + ((N.L2)*C2)
   dp3_sat r4, r0_bx2, r4_bx2      ; N.L2
   mad     r2.rgb, r4, r5_x2, r2   ; ((N.L1)*C1) + ((N.L2)*C2) +
                                   ; ((N.L3)*C3)
   add     r2.rgb, r2, c2          ; add ambient
   mul     r0.rgb, r2, r1          ; ((N.L1)*C1) + ((N.L2)*C2) +
                                   ; ((N.L3)*C3)*base
```

The following figures show various pieces of this shader in action. The first three characters in Figure 6 show the contributions from each of the individual lights. The fourth character shows the summation of all the lighting contributions, and the fifth shows the base texture for the character.

Figure 6

The next figure shows a few frames of animation with the full shader in action.

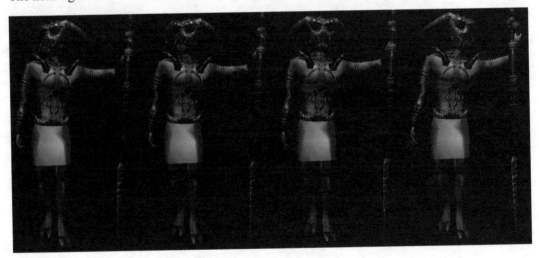

Figure 7

Compression

One downside of doing tweened animation is the large amount of storage space required to store each individual frame of animation data. Thus, it is desirable to reduce the amount of memory consumed in storing the character data as well as the amount of data that needs to be sent to the video card via the buses in the system. One compression technique is done by computing the bounding box of the character and specifying the position data as an integer offset from one of the corners of the box. The following example packs the position data into 16-bit shorts for x, y, and z, and pads with one short for w. The preprocessing code to do the packing looks something like this:

```
float half = (maxX - minX)/2.0f;
vertex.x = (short)(((x - minX - half)/half)*32767.5f)
half = (maxY - minY)/2.0f;
vertex.y = (short)(((y - minY - half)/half)*32767.5f)
half = (maxZ - minZ)/2.0f;
vertex.z = (short)(((z - minZ - half)/half)*32767.5f)
```

The vertex data can then be re-expanded within the vertex shader at a relatively low cost. The following vertex shader fragment shows how this is accomplished:

```
; position in v0
; c0.x = ((maxX - minX)/2)/32767.5
; c0.y = ((maxY - minY)/2)/32767.5
; c0.z = ((maxZ - minZ)/2)/32767.5
; c1.x = minX + (maxX - minX)/2
; c1.y = minY + (maxY - minY)/2
; c1.z = minZ + (maxZ - minZ)/2
; scale and bias position
mul r2, v0, c0
add r2, r2, c1
```

A similar technique can be applied to the weights for the skinning matrices. Again, here is a small bit of preprocessing code:

```
vertex.w1 = (unsigned char)((float)(w1)/255.0f);
vertex.w2 = (unsigned char)((float)(w2)/255.0f);
vertex.w3 = (unsigned char)((float)(w3)/255.0f);
```

A few vertex shader instructions can expand this data back into floating-point data to use for computing the skinned position.

```
; v1 contains the weights
; c0.x = 0.003921569 = 1/255
; c0.z = 1.0
; unpack the weights
mul    r9, v1, c0.x
dp3    r9.w, r9, c0.zzzz
sub    r9.w, c0.zzzz, r9.w
```

Normal data can also be compressed by sacrificing some quality by quantizing the normals into bytes or shorts and doing a similar unpacking process within the vertex shader. The following code shows how the data is packed within a preprocessing tool:

```
vertex.nx = (unsigned char)(nx*127.5 + 127.5);
vertex.ny = (unsigned char)(ny*127.5 + 127.5);
vertex.nz = (unsigned char)(nz*127.5 + 127.5);
```

A small bit of vertex shader code can be used to decompress the normals:

```
; v3 contains the normal
; c0.x = 0.007843137 = 1/127.5
; r2.w = 1.0
mad r3, v3, c0.x, -r2.w  ; scale and bias normal to -1 to 1 range
```

In this section, we showed a few ways to compress various vertex components. These techniques can be used to significantly reduce the amount of data required per character. They should, however, be used with some caution since they are lossy methods of compression and will not work with all data sets. For more on vertex compression, see the "Vertex Decompression Using Vertex Shaders" article in this book.

Summary

This chapter has discussed a few ways to perform character animation within a vertex shader. This should be considered a starting point for your exploration of character animation through vertex shaders. Vertex shaders give you the power to customize the graphics pipeline for your application, allowing you to free up the CPU to make a more engaging game.

Lighting a Single-Surface Object

Greg James

In this article, we'll explore how a programmable vertex shader can be used to light objects that expose both sides of their triangles to the viewer. Such objects can be problematic with fixed-function hardware lighting, but a few vertex shader instructions allow us to light such objects correctly from all points of view without having to modify vertex data, duplicate triangles, or make complex decisions based on the scene. We will also extend the basic technique to approximate the effect of light transmission through thin scattering objects.

Three-dimensional objects are often represented by single-surface geometry in 3D applications. Leaves, foliage, blades of grass, particle system objects, hair, and clothing are typically modeled as sheets of triangles where both sides of the sheet are potentially visible, and as such, these objects are rendered with back-face culling disabled. This approach is used widely in 3D games but presents a problem for hardware-accelerated lighting calculations. The problem stems from the restriction that each vertex is specified with only a single surface normal vector. This normal is correct when viewing the front faces of triangles but is not correct when the back faces are in view. When back faces are visible, this single normal vector points opposite the direction it should, so a lighting calculation based on this normal will give an incorrect result. Fortunately, we can use five instructions in an OpenGL or DirectX 8 vertex shader program to calculate the correct normal and pass it on to the lighting calculation so that a single-surface object is lit correctly from all orientations. This same correction will also light a twisted object correctly regardless of how the surface's front and back faces twist in and out of view. This approach of detecting the orientation of the normal and correcting it can also be used to enhance the lighting of thin objects by accounting for transmitted light. A realistic rendering of light shining through leaves or stained glass can be achieved without costly logic based on the positions of the objects in the scene.

The problem of lighting a single-surface object depends on the viewer's orientation relative to each face. Since surface normals are defined at each vertex, the surface facing is really a vertex facing defined by each vertex's normal vector. The four possible orientations of the vertex normal, viewer location, and light location are shown in Figure 1. In the first two cases, the front faces are visible and no correction of the normal is required. In the last two cases, the back faces are visible and the normal must be reversed to properly represent the face in view. Note that the position of the light is not relevant to the problem of selecting the proper normal. Only the eye position relative to the vertex normal matters. Correct illumination will result if the vertex normal is always chosen to face toward the viewer. The operation of guaranteeing that the normal always faces the viewer is easily accomplished in a vertex shader program.

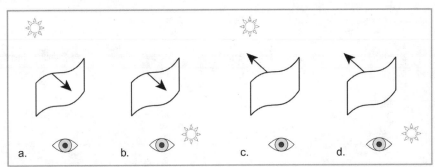

Figure 1: The four possible orientations of viewer, vertex normal, and light. The light position is irrelevant to selecting the proper vertex normal for lighting.

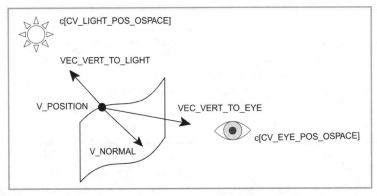

Figure 2: Illustration of variables calculated in Listing 1

Calculations for correcting the normal can be done in object space or world space. Since the vertex input position is in object space, and in a vertex shader this is typically transformed directly to homogeneous clip space (i.e., the world space position is never calculated), it is more efficient to perform the calculations in object space. If the calculations were done in world space, this would require extra vertex shader instructions to transform the vertex position and vertex normal to world space. On the other hand, working in object space requires us to transform the light position and viewer position from world space to object space. Since the light and viewer position in object space is constant for all vertices of the object being rendered, they should be calculated on the CPU and supplied as vertex shader constants. It would be wasteful to compute them in the vertex shader itself. To compute them, we will have to compute the inverse object-to-world transformation matrix, and this is simple if the world matrix consists only of rotation and translation without scaling [Foley94]. In that case, the inverse of the 4x4 transform is composed of the transpose of the 3x3 rotation portion along with the opposite amount of translation.

Vertex Shader Code

Figure 2 illustrates the values that we'll calculate, and Listing 1 shows the vertex shader instructions. The first step of the correction is to compute a vector from the vertex position to the viewer position. The viewer position in object space is computed on the CPU and supplied as a vertex shader constant: c[CV_EYE_POS_OSPACE]. The vector from the vertex to the eye is a simple subtraction. Next, we test whether the vertex normal is facing toward or away from the eye. The three component dot-product between the normal and the vector to the eye will give a value that is negative if the vertex normal points away from the eye or positive if the vertex normal points toward the eye. The result of the dot-product is written to the ALIGNED variable, which is positive if no correction is needed or negative if we have to flip the normal.

At this point, we must do one of two things based on the sign of the ALIGNED variable. The C equivalent of what we want to do is:

```
if ( ALIGNED < 0 )
    normal = -V_NORMAL;
else
    normal = V_NORMAL;
```

There are no "if" or "else" branch instructions in the vertex shader instruction set, so how can we perform this decision based on the sign of ALIGNED? The answer is to do one calculation for both cases which will result in a value as though a branch had been used. We use both the input normal (V_NORMAL) and the reversed normal (–V_NORMAL) in an expression in which either value can be masked out. Each value is multiplied by a mask and summed. If the value of "mask" is 1 or 0, then it can be used in the following equation to select either –V_NORMAL or V_NORMAL.

normal = mask * (–V_NORMAL) + (1 – mask) * V_NORMAL

In a vertex shader, we could compute mask and 1–mask, and this would be expressed as:

```
sub INV_MASK, c[ONE], MASK
mul COR_NORMAL, MASK, V_NORMAL
mad COR_NORMAL, INV_MASK, V_NORMAL, COR_NORMAL
```

For our case, the negative normal is computed from the positive normal as in the following equation, so we can skip the calculation of 1–mask and save one instruction in the vertex shader program.

–V_NORMAL = V_NORMAL – 2 * V_NORMAL

The vertex shader instructions are then:

```
mad COR_NORMAL, V_NORMAL, MASK, -V_NORMAL
mad COR_NORMAL, V_NORMAL, MASK, COR_NORMAL
```

The mask value is computed from ALIGNED using the sge (Set if Greater or Equal) instruction to compare ALIGNED to zero.

```
sge MASK,   ALIGNED,   c[ZERO]
```

MASK will be 0 if ALIGNED is less than c[ZERO], or it will be 1 if ALIGNED is greater or equal to c[ZERO].

The five instructions in the middle of Listing 1 (sub, dp3, sge, mad, mad) will always produce a vertex normal that faces toward the viewer. Lighting based on this normal will be correct for all light positions.

Performing the correction of the normal in a vertex shader lets us fill a scene with many single-surface objects with only a small cost for the added calculations. We can avoid more costly operations such as updating vertex data with the CPU or rendering in multiple passes to achieve the correct lighting. The single-surface objects may also be animated in the vertex shader and remain correctly lit. By performing all of the transform and lighting calculations in a hardware vertex shader, we can populate scenes with a large number of these objects.

Listing 1: Vertex shader for correcting the input vertex normal based on viewer position

```
// Include definitions of constant indices
#include "TwoSided.h"

// Define names for vertex input data
#define V_POSITION  v0
#define V_NORMAL    v1
#define V_DIFFUSE   v2
#define V_TEXTURE   v3

// Define names for temporaries
#define VEC_VERT_TO_EYE    r0
#define VEC_VERT_TO_LIGHT  r1
#define ALIGNED            r2
#define TEMP               r6
#define COR_NORMAL         r7

// Vertex shader version 1.1
vs.1.1

// Transform position to clip space and output it
dp4 oPos.x, V_POSITION, c[CV_WORLDVIEWPROJ_0]
dp4 oPos.y, V_POSITION, c[CV_WORLDVIEWPROJ_1]
dp4 oPos.z, V_POSITION, c[CV_WORLDVIEWPROJ_2]
dp4 oPos.w, V_POSITION, c[CV_WORLDVIEWPROJ_3]

//  Use eye position relative to the vertex to
//  determine the correct orientation of the
//  vertex normal.  Flip the normal if it is
//  pointed away from the camera.
//  Eye & light positions were transformed to
//  object space on the CPU and are supplied
//  as constants.

//  Make vector from vertex to the eye
sub  VEC_VERT_TO_EYE,   c[CV_EYE_POS_OSPACE],   V_POSITION

//  Dot product with the normal to see if they point
//  in the same direction or opposite
dp3 ALIGNED, V_NORMAL, VEC_VERT_TO_EYE

//  If aligned is positive, no correction is needed
//  If aligned is negative, we need to flip the normal
//  Do this with SGE to create a mask for a virtual
//  branch calculation
//  ALIGNED.x = ALIGNED.x >= 0 ? 1 : 0;
```

```
sge ALIGNED.x, ALIGNED, c[CV_ZERO]

mad COR_NORMAL, V_NORMAL, ALIGNED.x, -V_NORMAL
// now COR_NORMAL = 0  or  -V_NORMAL

mad COR_NORMAL, V_NORMAL, ALIGNED.x,  COR_NORMAL
// COR_NORMAL = V_NORMAL   or  -V_NORMAL

// Point lighting
// Vector from vertex to the light
add  VEC_VERT_TO_LIGHT, c[CV_LIGHT_POS_OSPACE], -V_POSITION

// Normalize it using 3 instructions
dp3 TEMP.w,    VEC_VERT_TO_LIGHT, VEC_VERT_TO_LIGHT
rsq TEMP.w,    TEMP.w
mul VEC_VERT_TO_LIGHT, VEC_VERT_TO_LIGHT, TEMP.w

// dp3 for lighting.  Point light is not attenuated
dp3 r4, VEC_VERT_TO_LIGHT, COR_NORMAL

// Use LIT to clamp to zero if r4 < 0
// r5 will have diffuse light value in y component
lit r5, r4

// Light color to output diffuse color
// c[CV_LIGHT_CONST].x  is ambient
add oD0, r5.y, c[CV_LIGHT_CONST].x

// Another lit for the light value from opposite normal
lit r5, -r4

// Square the value for more attenuation.  This
// represents transmitted light, which could fall
// off more sharply with angle of incidence
mul r5.y,   r5.y, r5.y

    // Attenuate it further and add transmitted ambient factor
mad oD1, r5.y, c[CV_LIGHT_CONST].z, c[CV_LIGHT_CONST].y

    // Output texture coordinates
mov oT0, V_TEXTURE
mov oT1, V_TEXTURE
```

Enhanced Lighting for Thin Objects

We can take this approach a step further by enhancing the lighting model for these thin objects. Ordinarily, we would most likely compute some function of the dot product of the light vector and normal vector (N·L) at each vertex and be done with it. This would account for light scattering off the surface but not for light shining through the surface. After all, these are thin objects, and thin objects tend to transmit light. Dramatic lighting effects are possible if we account for this transmission.

In this case, the transmission is not that of a clear object allowing light to pass directly through, but it is instead a diffuse scattering of transmitted light. Things behind the object are not visible, but bright light shining through the object is dispersed and scattered by the material. This reveals the inner details or thickness of the object, which have a different appearance than the surface illuminated by reflected light. Leaves, stained glass, and lamp shades show a good contrast between the transmitted and reflected light. Hold a leaf to the ground and it appears dark and waxy. Hold it up to the sun, and the veins and cells are revealed against a glowing green background. Stained glass viewed from the outside of a building is entirely dark, but viewing it from the inside with sunlight streaming through reveals brilliant colors. We can account for this transmitted light by supplying an additional texture for the object.

This additional texture is simply the colors we would see with bright light shining through the object. It is a texture representing light transmission. The standard lighting equation is applied to the ordinary diffuse reflective texture, and we add a new lighting calculation that will affect the diffuse transmission texture. The new lighting calculation is based on the normal pointing away from the viewer and should contribute no light when the light is positioned in front of the vertex in view. We use the vertex shader lit instruction to achieve this clamping to zero, just as we would for the front-facing lighting. When the front-facing reflective lighting clamps to zero, the transmissive lighting begins to show through.

The result of scattered reflected light can be placed in one vertex color, and the result of scattered transmitted light can be placed in the second specular color or any output which will be interpolated in rasterization. A pixel shader then fetches from each texture, applies the light contribution for transmission to the transmission texture and for reflection to the ordinary diffuse texture, and adds the results together. As each contribution is clamped to zero based on whether or not the light is in front or behind, the addition of each term results in correct lighting.

In this way, dramatic lighting effects are possible without requiring CPU processing or complex logic based on the placement of objects and lights. As the sun streams through leaves overhead, they appear different than leaves off in the distance, or as the viewer and lights move about a scene, fabrics and hair will change appropriately when lit from behind. Other effects like x-ray illumination or one-way mirrors could also be devised based on the vertex shader's determination of the correct normal.

About the Demo

Included on the companion CD is the NV Effects Browser demo "Two-Sided Lighting," which demonstrates this technique. To run, simply start the NVEffectsBrowser.exe and click the effect under the "Lighting (per-vertex)" section. Keyboard controls can be displayed by hitting the H or F1 keys. There are controls for twisting, scaling, and moving the object. Complete DirectX 8 source code is included.

References

[Foley94] James D. Foley, Andries van Dam, et. al., *Introduction to Computer Graphics* (Addison-Wesley Co., 1994), p. 182.

Optimizing Software Vertex Shaders

Kim Pallister

The introduction of the vertex shader technology in the DirectX APIs marked a significant milestone in the real-time graphics and gaming industries. It was significant not so much because it exposed any new capability, but rather because it put innovation back in the hands of the developer.

By making the pipeline programmable, developers were no longer limited to what the hardware and API had been explicitly designed to do. Conversely, hardware developers, and those designing the API, did not need to be clairvoyant in anticipating what game developers would want the pipeline to do over the coming years.

That's the good side of things. However, like most things, there's a cloud attached to this silver lining.

As is often the case with PC game development, developers are challenged to take advantage of new technologies while still supporting older systems. If programmable vertex shaders were only supported on the highest end of the PC performance spectrum, developers would have their work cut out for them, having to support multiple code paths for systems without support.

Thankfully, this isn't the case. Microsoft, with help from CPU vendors like Intel, has seen to it that software vertex shaders offer impressive performance and can be used in games today.

This is accomplished through a vertex shader compiler within the DirectX run-time that compiles the vertex shader code into CPU-optimal instruction streams (SSE and SSE2 instructions in the case of Pentium III and Pentium 4 processors).

Like with any compiler, properly designing and structuring the source code going into the compiler can improve the code that it generates. In this article, we'll look at some guidelines for writing vertex shaders to improve the performance of those shaders when running in software.

If you are simply interested in knowing a set of canonical rules to apply to your shaders, you can skip to the optimization guidelines in Table 1. However, if you are interested in some background about how the software emulation is done, we'll cover that beforehand. First we'll look at some details about the Pentium III and Pentium 4 processor architectures and then look at how the DirectX run-time compiler works. This is followed by a list of optimization guidelines and an explanation of why they help generate optimal code. Finally, we'll look at a sample vertex shader and how we can optimize it.

Introduction to Pentium 4 Processor Architecture

The Pentium II and Pentium III processors were both based on the same core architecture. This microarchitecture introduced speculative execution and out-of-order operation to Intel Architecture. The Pentium III processor made improvements over the Pentium II processor and added the Streaming SIMD Extensions (SSE).

The Pentium 4 processor introduced a new microarchitecture, the NetBurst™ microarchitecture. Like its predecessors, the Pentium 4 processor operates out of order and does speculative execution. However, it has a much deeper pipeline and boasts a number of other enhancements. For a more detailed explanation, see Figure 1.

Instructions are speculatively fetched by the Branch Predictor, the part of the diagram on the far left comprised of the Branch Target Buffer, or BTB, and the Instruction Translation Lookaside Buffer, or I-TLB. The logic in these units serves to make predictions about what instructions will be needed next, based on a branch history and some prediction rules.

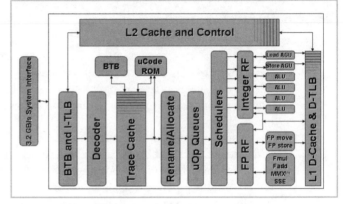

Figure 1: Pentium 4 processor architectural diagram

From there, the instructions are fed into the decoder. The Instruction Decoder receives the IA-32 opcode bytes delivered to it and breaks them into one or more simple micro-ops (µOps). These µOps are the operations that that core of the Pentium 4 processor executes.

The next stage is the Execution Trace Cache, an innovative microarchitecture redesign introduced as part of the NetBurst microarchitecture. The Trace Cache caches (i.e., remembers) the decoded µOps from the instruction decoder. The Trace Cache is the Pentium 4 processor's primary or L1 Instruction cache. It is capable of delivering up to three instructions per clock down the pipeline to the execution units. It has its own Branch Predictor, labeled here as BTB, that steers the Trace Cache to its next instruction locations. The micro-code ROM in the block below contains micro-code sequences for more complex operations like fault handling and string moves. The addition of the Trace Cache is significant because it means that often, previously executed instruction streams (e.g., a loop after its first iteration) will not need to go through the decoder stage, avoiding a possible stall.

The renaming stage maps logical IA-32 registers (see Figure 2) to the Pentium 4 processor's deep physical register file. This abstraction allows for a larger number of physical registers in the processor without changing the "front end" of the processor. The allocator stage assigns all the necessary hardware buffers in the machine for µOp execution, at which point the µOps go into some queues to await scheduling.

The scheduling stage that follows determines when an instruction is ready to execute. An instruction is ready to execute when both input operands (most instructions have two input sources) are ready, registers and an execution unit of the required type are free, etc. The scheduler is kind of like a restaurant host, only seating a party when all the party members have arrived and a table is free, thus ensuring maximum throughput of customers through the restaurant.

Once an instruction is ready to execute, execution takes place in the integer or floating-point units (depending on the type of instruction, of course). Having these many execution units operating at once is what makes the processor so highly parallelized and able to execute a number of integer and floating-point operations per clock cycle.

The Address Generation Units (labeled AGU) are used for doing loads and stores of data to the L1 data cache (the last block in Figure 1). Since programs have many loads and stores, having both a load port and a store port keeps this from being a bottleneck. The Pentium 4 processor also has an on-chip L2 cache that stores both code and data, along with a fast system bus to main memory.

In terms of maximizing performance of software running on this architecture, there are several goals to keep in mind, such as minimizing mis-predicted branches, minimizing stalls, maximizing cache usage, etc. We'll talk about how the vertex shader compiler aims to achieve some of these goals later on, but in order to understand that discussion, we must first look at some architectural features aimed at enhancing multimedia performance.

Introduction to the Streaming SIMD Extensions

As mentioned earlier, the Pentium III processor introduced the Streaming SIMD Extensions (better known as SSE), aimed at offering improved floating-point performance for multimedia applications. The Pentium 4 processor furthered the enhancements of SSE with the introduction of the SSE2 instructions. Since the vertex shader compiler uses these, a basic understanding of how these instructions operate will allow for a better understanding of how the vertex shader compiler works.

SIMD instructions (Single Instruction, Multiple Data) allow for an operation to be issued once and simultaneously performed on several pieces of data. This is extremely useful in multimedia applications using 3D graphics, video or audio, where an operation may be performed thousands of times on data (such as vertices, pixels, audio samples, etc.). Most of the SSE and SSE2 instructions utilize the eight 128-bit wide XMM registers, pictured on the far right of Figure 2.

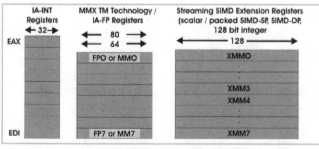

Figure 2: Pentium 4 processor register sets

These registers can be used in a number of ways. Depending on the instruction used, the data is read as four 32-bit single-precision floating-point numbers, two 64-bit double-precision floating-point numbers, eight 16-bit integers, or 16 single bytes. The following assembly example shows two of these usages:

```
MULPS XMM1, XMM2    // Multiply 4 single precision
                    // floating-point numbers in
                    // XMM1 by those in XMM2, place
                    // results in XMM1.
MULPD XMM1, XMM2    // Multiply 2 double-precision
                    // floating-point numbers in
                    // XMM1 by those in XMM2, place
                    // results in XMM1
```

In order to understand how the vertex shader compiler works, a full understanding of the SSE and SSE2 instruction set isn't necessary. However, those interested in learning how to use SSE instructions in their own code may refer to Intel's Developer Services web site (www.intel.com/IDS).

While the full SSE/SSE2 instruction set isn't covered here, there's one more subject that will give some insight into how the compiler functions: data arrangement.

Optimal Data Arrangement for SSE Instruction Usage

Often, execution can be hampered by memory bandwidth. This sometimes occurs when data is laid out in a format that is intuitive to the author of the code but can result in fragmented access to memory, unnecessary data being loaded into the cache, etc. This is best illustrated with an example.

Consider an array of vertices, each of which has of the following structure:

```
#define numverts 100

struct {
    float x, y, z;
    float nx, ny, nz ;
    float u,v;
} myvertex;

myvertex mVerts[numverts];
```

In this array-of-structures (AOS) layout, the array of these vertices would sit in memory as shown in Figure 3. The problem arises that as an operation is performed on all of the vertices, say doing transformations, only some of the elements are used in that operation, yet an entire cache line is loaded (anywhere from 32 to 128 bytes, depending on which processor is being used). This means that some elements of the vertex structure are being loaded into the cache and then not being used at all.

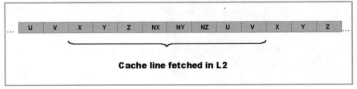

Figure 3: Ineffective cache line load with AOS data layout

A better approach is to use a structure-of-arrays (SOA) layout, as illustrated below:

```
#define numverts 100

struct {
    float x[numverts]; //x,x,x…
    float y[numverts]; //y,y,y…
    float z[numverts];
    float nx[numverts];
    float ny[numverts];
    float nz[numverts];
    float u[numverts];
    float v[numverts];

} myvertexarray;

myvertexarray mVerts;
```

While this type of an approach to structuring data may not be as intuitive, it has a couple of benefits. First, cache line loads consist of data that will be used for the given operation, with no unnecessary data being loaded into the cache. Secondly, applying SSE to the code becomes trivial.

Let's look at an example. Consider the following loop to do a simple animation to a vertex:

```
//assume variables of type float exist, called fTime and fVelocityX/Y/Z
for (n=0;n<numverts;n++)
{
    mVerts.x[n] += fTime * fVelocityX;
    mVerts.y[n] += fTime * fVelocityY;
    mVerts.z[n] += fTime * fVelocityZ;
}
```

Modifying this to use SSE becomes a matter of iterating through the loop differently. In the example below, the same loop has been modified slightly. Where we had our variables defined as floats before, we've now used a C++ class f32Vec4, which is just a container for four floats with overloaded operators that use the SSE instructions:

```
//assume variables of type f32Vec4 exist, called fTime and fVelocityX/Y/Z
for (n=0; n<numverts; n += 4)
{
    (m128*)(mVerts.x[n]) += fTime * fVelocityX;
    (m128*)(mVerts.y[n]) += fTime * fVelocityY;
    (m128*)(mVerts.z[n]) += fTime * fVelocityZ;
}
```

The online training resources available at http://developer.intel.com/software/products/college/ia32/sse2/ contain more detail about how to use these classes and instructions. We've just used them here to illustrate the structure-of-arrays data layout.

How the Vertex Shader Compiler Works

The DirectX 8 API describes a dedicated virtual machine known as the vertex virtual machine, or VVM, which does processing to a stream of incoming vertex data. This could be any kind of processing that can be performed autonomously on one vertex (see the articles by Wolfgang Engel in Part 1). The vertex shader mechanism was designed to run on dedicated hardware, but as we've been discussing, a software implementation exists. Actually, several software implementations exist and are invoked based on what processor is detected at run time.

When an Intel Pentium III or Pentium 4 processor is detected and software vertex processing is selected by the application, the vertex shader compiler is used. The compiler takes the vertex shader program and declaration at shader creation time (done with the IDirect3D-Device8::CreateVertexShader method) and compiles them to a sequence of Intel Architecture instructions. The compiler attempts to generate the most optimal sequence of IA instructions to emulate the functionality required. It does so by making use of the SSE and SSE2 instructions, minimizing memory traffic, rescheduling the generated assembly instructions, etc.

After this sequence of instructions is generated, it exists until destroyed (done with the IDirect3DDevice8::DeleteVertexShader method). Whenever any of the IDirect3DDevice8 ::Draw… methods are used after calling IDirect3DDevice8::SetVertexShader, execution will use the IA-32 code sequence generated by the compiler.

When following this path, a number of things happen. First, incoming vertex data is arranged into a structure-of-arrays format for more efficient processing. (As expected, there is a cost to doing this arrangement.) Vertices are then processed four at a time, taking advantage of the SIMD processing.

The way that the four-wide VVM registers are mapped to the SSE registers is by turning them on their side, so to speak. Each VVM register is mapped to four SSE registers. This mapping forms a 16-float block that is essentially a four-vertex deep VVM register. The illustration in Figure 4 shows what this looks like. The vertex shader then only needs to be executed one quarter as many times, with each iteration simultaneously processing four vertices.

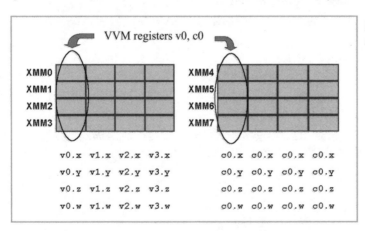

Figure 4: VVM to SSE register mapping

Vertex data is arranged back into the array-of-structures format on the way out to be sent on to the rendering engine. This also incurs a performance penalty.

Performance Expectations

As mentioned above, arranging incoming data from array-of-structures to structure-of-arrays, and then back again upon exit, incurs some performance penalty. However, this is countered by the fact that the shader need only be executed one quarter as many times. Additionally, processor clock speeds tend to be much higher than most graphics hardware.

In the end, the performance benefits depend on the complexity of the shader (as a more complex shader will amortize the cost of the data arrangement) and on how well the shader is written. The shader can be written in a way that lets the compiler best do its job of generating the assembly instructions.

Optimization Guidelines

The optimization guidelines listed below can help improve performance of vertex shaders running in software. What follows are some details on each one of the guidelines and why it can affect performance.

Guidelines for optimizing software vertex shaders

Rule
1. Write only the results you'll need.
2. Use macros whenever possible.
3. Squeeze dependency chains.
4. Write final arithmetic instructions directly to output registers.
5. Reuse the same temporary register if possible.
6. Don't implicitly saturate color and fog values.
7. When using exp and log functions, use the form with the lowest acceptable accuracy.
8. Avoid using the address register when possible.
9. If the address register must be used, try to order vertices in order of the address field.
10. Profile, profile, profile...

Write Only the Results You'll Need

In some cases, only a component of a register is needed. For example, the post-transform Z-value of a vertex might be used to calculate an alpha or fog value. As we discussed earlier, each of the components of the VVM registers maps to an individual SSE register. Any instruction performed on the VVM register will be performed to each of the four SSE registers; therefore, any unnecessary components of the VVM register that we can avoid using will save at least a few instructions on one of the SSE registers.

Let's look at an example:

	Vertex Shader Code	SSE Instruction Cost (for four vertices)
1	`mul r0, c8, r0`	Four SSE multiplies, 4 to 8 moves
2	`mul r0.z, c8.z, r0.z`	One SSE multiply, 1 to 2 moves

Use Macros Whenever Possible

Macros are traditionally thought of as a convenience more than an optimization technique. Indeed, in C code, macros are just a shorthand representation of a code sequence. In this case, however, they give the compiler some extraneous information about what a particular sequence of instructions is doing. In the m4x4 matrix multiplication macro, for example, the compiler is aware that the multiplies being executed will be followed by an add (since the matrix multiply is four dot product operations). Since the compiler is aware of this, it can retain results in registers, rather than moving them out and back in again.

This is illustrated in the following code sequence:

Before	After
`dp4 r0.x, v0, c2`	`m4x4 r0, v0, c2`
`dp4 r0.y, v0, c3`	`add r1, c6,-v0`
`dp4 r0.z, v0, c4`	`dp3 r2, r1, r1`
`dp4 r0.w, v0, c5`	`rsq r2, r2`
`add r1, c6,-v0`	`mov oT0, v2`
`dp3 r2, r1, r1`	`mul r1,r1,r2`
`rsq r2, r2`	`dp3 r3, v1, r1`
`mov oT0, v2`	`add r3, r3, c7`
`mul r1,r1,r2`	`mov oD0,r3`
`dp3 r3, v1, r1`	`mov oPos,r0`
`add r3, r3, c7`	
`mov oD0,r3`	
`mov oPos,r0`	

Squeeze Dependency Chains

Since four SSE registers are used to emulate a VVM register, and there are a total of eight SSE registers, data often gets moved in and out of registers to make room for the next instruction's operands.

In cases where an operation's result is going to be used in another operation, performing that operation soon afterward can often let the compiler use the registers containing the intermediate result without having to move that intermediate result to memory and back.

This is illustrated in the following example. The 4x4 matrix multiply result is stored in r0, and then r0 is not used again until the end of the code sequence, where it is moved into oPos. Therefore, bumping the mov instruction up in the code sequence is possible and can let the compiler save some instructions in the SSE code sequence.

Before	After
`m4x4 r0, v0, c2`	`m4x4 r0, v0, c2`
`add r1, c6,-v0`	`mov oPos,r0`
`dp3 r2, r1, r1`	`add r1, c6,-v0`

Before	After
| ```
rsq  r2, r2
mov  oT0, v2
mul  r1,r1,r2
dp3  r3, v1, r1
add  r3, r3, c7
mov  oD0,r3
mov  oPos,r0
``` | ```
dp3  r2, r1, r1
rsq  r2, r2
mul  r1,r1,r2
dp3  r3, v1, r1
add  r3, r3, c7
mov  oD0,r3
mov  oT0, v2
``` |

Write Final Arithmetic Instructions Directly to Output Registers

A keen eye may have looked at the previous code sequence and wondered why the result of the matrix multiplication wasn't written directly to the oPos register. Indeed, this is another opportunity to squeeze a few cycles out of the code sequence, as shown below.

Before	After
| ```
m4x4 r0, v0, c2
mov  oPos,r0
add  r1, c6,-v0
dp3  r2, r1, r1
rsq  r2, r2
mul  r1,r1,r2
dp3  r3, v1, r1
add  r3, r3, c7
mov  oD0,r3
mov  oT0, v2
``` | ```
m4x4 oPos, v0, c2
add  r1, c6,-v0
dp3  r2, r1, r1
rsq  r2, r2
mul  r1,r1,r2
dp3  r3, v1, r1
add  r3, r3, c7
mov  oD0,r3
mov  oT0, v2
``` |

Reuse the Same Temporary Register If Possible

When a temp register is used, there is some work the compiler does in terms of allocating SSE registers to map to the temp register and the like. Reusing the same temp registers can sometimes save the compiler some work in having to redo this.

Don't Implicitly Saturate Color and Fog Values

This is a simple rule to understand. The compiler saturates color and fog values. Any work done to saturate them by hand is wasted cycles.

Use the Lowest Acceptable Accuracy with exp and log Functions

The expp and logp instructions offer a variable level of precision. The modifier applied to the instruction determines the level of precision. As one would imagine, the lower the precision, the lower the amount of work required by the code sequence the compiler generates.

Avoid Using the Address Register When Possible

The address register allows for the addressing of different constant registers based on the value in the address register. This is a problem for the compiler generating the SIMD code, which is trying to process four vertices at a time. Each of the four vertices being processed may end up referencing a different constant register, in which case the compiler will have to revert to a scalar operation, processing each vertex one at a time.

Try to Order Vertices

Of course, the address register is there for a reason. Some vertex shaders may require its use. If that's the case, the next best thing is to order vertices in the order of the address field. Ordering by address field can result in "runs" of vertices with the same address value. The compiler will then use SIMD processing on blocks of four vertices with a shared address value.

Profile, Profile, Profile...

Less of an optimization guideline than a bit of advice, it should go without saying that optimizations need to be tested. The guidelines provided are a good start, but there's no substitute for good testing! Test your optimization changes before and after and under a variety of conditions and input data.

Testing the vertex shader performance can be a bit tricky. Some graphics vendors offer drivers that output performance statistics, but some do not. The DirectX 8 software vertex pipeline doesn't output performance statistics. The best place to start is to isolate the shader in a test harness so that performance differences will be amplified, as the shader will comprise a larger portion of what gets rendered in a frame.

A Detailed Example

The following vertex shader is the one used in the sample code provided on the companion CD with this book. It's simply a combination of a couple of well-known shaders, the matrix palette skinning shader and the reflection/refraction shader often used for "soap bubble" type effects. Combining these gives us a "glass character" type effects as shown in Figure 5. Additionally, a sine wave is propagated along the character's skin to provide a rippling effect.

Figure 5: Skinned mesh soap bubble shader example. Vertex shader is performing skinning, sinusoidal peturbation, reflection, and refraction calculations for texture coordinates.

Here's the shader before and after optimization:

Before	After
```vs.1.1```	```vs.1.1```
```; Section 1```	```; Section 1```
```; Matrix Palette Skinning```	```; Matrix Palette Skinning```
```mov a0.x, v3.x```	```mov a0.x, v3.x```
```;first bone and normal```	```;first bone and normal```
```dp4 r0.x, v0, c[a0.x + 50]```	```m4x3 r0.xyz, v0, c[a0.x + 50]```
```dp4 r0.y, v0, c[a0.x + 51]```	
```dp4 r0.z, v0, c[a0.x + 52]```	
```dp4 r0.w, v0, c[a0.x + 53]```	
```dp3 r1.x, v4, c[a0.x + 50]```	```m3x3 r1.xyz, v4, c[a0.x + 50]```
```dp3 r1.y, v4, c[a0.x + 51]```	
```dp3 r1.z, v4, c[a0.x + 52]```	
```mov r1.w, c4.y```	
```;second bone and normal```	```;second bone```
```mov a0.x, v3.y```	```mov a0.x, v3.y```
```dp4 r2.x, v0, c[a0.x + 50]```	```m4x3 r2.xyz, v0, c[a0.x + 50]```
```dp4 r2.y, v0, c[a0.x + 51]```	
```dp4 r2.z, v0, c[a0.x + 52]```	
```dp4 r2.w, v0, c[a0.x + 53]```	
```dp3 r3.x, v4, c[a0.x + 50]```	```m3x3 r3.xyz, v4, c[a0.x + 50]```
```dp3 r3.y, v4, c[a0.x + 51]```	```;blend between bones r0, r2```
```dp3 r3.z, v4, c[a0.x + 52]```	```mul r0.xyz, r0.xyz, v1.x```
```mov r3.w, c4.y```	```mad r2, r2.xyz, v2.x, r0.xyz```
	```mov r2.w, c4.w```
```;blend between r0, r2```	
```mul r0, r0, v1.x```	```;blend between r1, r3```
```mad r2, r2, v2.x, r0```	```mul r1.xyz, r1.xyz, v1.x mad```
```mov r2.w, c4.w```	```r3, r3.xyz, v2.x, r1.xyz```
	```mov r3.w, c4.y```
```;blend between r1, r3```	
```mul r1, r1, v1.x```	```; r2 contains final pos```
```mad r3, r3, v2.x, r1```	```; r3 contains final normal```
```; r2 contains final pos```	```; Sine-wave calculation```
```; r3 contains final normal```	
	```; Transform vert to```
```; Sine-wave calculation```	```; clip-space```
	```m4x4 r0, r2, c0```
```; Transform vert to```	
```; clip-space```	
```dp4 r0.x, r2, c0```	
```dp4 r0.y, r2, c1```	
```dp4 r0.z, r2, c2```	
```dp4 r0.w, r2, c3```	
	```; theta from distance & time```
```; theta from distance & time```	```mov r1.xyz, r0.xyz ; xyz```
```mov r1, r0 ; xyz```	```dp3 r1.x, r1, r1 ; d2```
```dp3 r1.x, r1, r1 ; d2```	

Before	After
| ```
rsq r1.x, r1.x
rcp r1.x, r1.x ; d
mul r1, r1, c4.x ; time

; Clamp theta to -pi..pi
add r1.x, r1.x, c7.x
mul r1.x, r1.x, c7.y
frc r1.xy, r1.x
mul r1.x, r1.x, c7.z
add r1.x, r1.x, -c7.x

; Compute 1st 4 series values
mul r4.x, r1.x, r1.x ; d^2
mul r1.y, r1.x, r4.x ; d^3
mul r1.z, r4.x, r1.y ; d^5
mul r1.w, r4.x, r1.z ; d^7

mul r1, r1, c10 ; sin
dp4 r1.x, r1, c4.w

; Move vertex sin(x)
mad r0, r1.x, c7.w, r0

mov oPos, r0

; Reflection/Refraction calc
; Trans. vert and normal
; to world-space
dp4 r0.x, r2, c12
dp4 r0.y, r2, c13
dp4 r0.z, r2, c14
dp4 r0.w, r2, c15

dp3 r1.x, r3, c12
dp3 r1.y, r3, c13
dp3 r1.z, r3, c14

; re-normalize normal
dp3 r1.w, r1, r1
rsq r1.w, r1.w
mul r1, r1, r1.w

; Get eye to vertex vector
sub r4, r0, c5
dp3 r3.w, r4, r4
rsq r3.w, r3.w
mul r3, r4, r3.w

; Calculate E - 2*(E dot N)*N
dp3 r4.x, r3, r1
add r4.x, r4.x, r4.x
mad oT0, r1, -r4.x, r3

; Get refraction normal
mul r1, r1, c6
``` | ```
rsq r1.x, r1.x
rcp r1.x, r1.x ; d
mul r1.xyz, r1, c4.x ; time

; Clamp theta to -pi..pi
add r1.x, r1.x, c7.x
mul r1.x, r1.x, c7.y
frc r1.xy, r1.x
mad r1.x, r1.x, c7.z, -c7.x

; Compute 1st 4 series values
mul r4.x, r1.x, r1.x ; d^2
mul r1.y, r1.x, r4.x ; d^3
mul r1.z, r4.x, r1.y ; d^5
mul r1.w, r4.x, r1.z ; d^7

dp4 r1.x, r1, c10 ; sin

; Move vertex sin(x)
mad oPos, r1.x, c7.w, r0

; Reflection/Refraction calc
; Trans. vert and normal
; to world-space
m4x4 r0, r2, c12




m3x3 r1, r3, c12


; re-normalize normal
dp3 r1.w, r1, r1
rsq r1.w, r1.w
mul r1, r1, r1.w

; Get eye to vertex vector
sub r4, r0, c5
dp3 r3.w, r4, r4
rsq r3.w, r3.w
mul r3, r4, r3.w

; Calculate E - 2*(E dot N)*N
dp3 r4.x, r3, r1
add r4.x, r4.x, r4.x
mad oT0.xyz, r1.xyz, -r4.x, r3.xyz

; Get refraction normal
mul r1.xyz, r1.xyz, c6.xyz
``` |

Before	After

```; Calculate E - 2*(E dot N)*N```
```dp3 r4.x, r3, r1```
```add r4.x, r4.x, r4.x```
```mad oT1, r1, -r4.x, r3```
	```; Calculate E - 2*(E dot N)*N```
	```dp3 r4.x, r3, r1```
	```add r4.x, r4.x, r4.x```
	```mad oT1.xyz, r1, -r4.x, r3```

A number of the optimization guidelines are used here, giving an improvement of about 15 percent. The vertex shader before optimization takes approximately 250 cycles per vertex. After optimization, this is reduced to approximately 220 cycles per vertex. The effect on the overall frame rate of the application will be less because there will usually be many more things going on, and the vertex shader comprises only a portion of the total execution time.

Hopefully, the details provided here have given some insight into how the software vertex shader compiler works and how to optimize code for it. The high performance available through the software implementation, especially when properly optimized, means that developers can take advantage of vertex shaders today, even if their games have to run on computers without vertex shader hardware.

Acknowledgments

I'd like to recognize a couple of individuals who contributed to this paper. First off, a large thanks is due Ronen Zohar at Intel. Ronen worked closely with Microsoft on optimizing the DirectX run-time and provided the optimization guidelines discussed in this article. Thanks as well to William Damon at Intel, who worked on the sample application referenced in the examples.

Compendium of Vertex Shader Tricks

Scott Le Grand

Introduction

There are a surprising number of procedural effects one can express with vertex shaders. As hardware speed increases, moving such effects from the CPU to the graphics hardware will free up more CPU time and memory bandwidth for other computations. In addition, a vertex shader-based approach to procedural rendering allows the use of static vertex buffers within procedural effects. This allows one to offload both the computation and the data for a procedural effect entirely into the graphics hardware.

However, the conversion of a procedural effect from a CPU-bound calculation to a vertex shader requires some thought: There is no flow control within a vertex shader, and data cannot be shared among the vertices. Fortunately, one can generate the equivalent of decision-based bit masks and use those to emulate flow control. This article will illustrate some of the tricks one can employ to move procedural effects into 3D hardware and provide a simple example of doing so.

Periodic Time

Vertex animation requires updating the positions of an effect's vertices over the time period of the effect. In a vertex shader, one wants to use static vertex buffers in order to minimize AGP bandwidth. So the first trick needed here is to calculate a periodic time value to drive vertex animation from within the vertex shader itself. The use of this periodic time allows the vertices to follow a calculated trajectory over the lifetime of an effect and then disappear at the end of one cycle of the period. If the effect is cyclic, the periodic nature of the calculated time value will allow each vertex to recycle itself and reappear as a seemingly new component of the effect during the next cycle of the time period. Mathematically, for this task we need an approximation to a fractional remainder function to calculate a fractional period. While the DirectX 8 specification supplies just such a function in the frc macro, there is a simpler approach. The y component of the destination register in an expp instruction returns the fractional part of the w component from the input register.

To derive a periodic time value for a vertex, first supply each vertex with a phase σ. Next, store the current absolute time, t, in a constant register and 1/period, μ, in another constant register. The fractional period, f, of any vertex can be calculated by passing $\mu*(t-\sigma)$ into an expp instruction as follows:

```
mov  r1, c0.xy          ; t is in c0.x, μ is in c0.y
sub  r1.w, c0.x, v0.x   ; σ is in v0.x
mul  r1.w, r1.w, c0.y
expp r1.y, r1.w         ; f is now in r1.y
```

Vertex phases can all be identical if you wish the vertices of the effect to move in tandem from an origin (such as a shockwave from an explosion), random if you wish the effect to always appear active (such as a particle fountain), or in groups of randomly generated but identical phases to generate clumps of vertices that are always at the same timepoint in their periodic trajectories (such as the rings emerging along the path of a railgun shot in *Quake*).

One-Shot Effect

A variant on the above involves skipping the expp instruction altogether, setting the phases of all the vertices to the same time as the creation of the effect, and only rendering the vertices up to the expiration of the time period. This is useful for a one-shot effect such as an explosion.

Random Numbers

While one can supply pregenerated random numbers as a vertex attribute, one will need to generate a new random number for every cycle of a periodic effect's period, or else the effect could look repetitive without an enormous number of vertices. Fortunately, one can use a simple equation (a linear congruence) and the aforementioned expp instruction to generate a pseudorandom number from a supplied seed (such as the phase used above if space is tight and it's random itself) and the integer part of the periodic time from above. To calculate a random number, store T, the integer part of the periodic time in a constant register, then pass $r=T\sigma$ into an expp instruction:

```
mov  r1.w, c0.z         ; T is in c0.z
mul  r1.w, r1.w, v0.x   ; σ
expp r2.y, r1.w         ; fractional time is in r2
sub  r1.w, r1.w, r2.y   ; a unit pseudo-random number is in r1.w
```

Such a random number will remain constant throughout a single period of an effect. This is useful for initializing a vertex's state. Since no calculated data is retained between invocations of a vertex shader, this pseudorandom value will be calculated upon every transformation of each vertex.

The above code fragment also demonstrates how to manipulate the vertex shader input and output masks. These masks are the register component (x, y, z, and w) sequences following the period in each input and output register in the above code fragment. While the expp instruction normally calculates four output values, we can indicate our interest in just the w component output by leaving out x, y, and z from the output register. The omission of unnecessary components of output registers can improve vertex shader performance, especially on machines that emulate vertex shaders in software. For input registers only, their four components can be collectively negated, and each component can be *swizzled*: replicated or permuted in any desired combination.

Flow Control

While there are no flow control instructions in the DirectX 8 vertex shader language, there are two instructions, sgt and sle, which will perform a greater than, equal, or a less than comparison between a pair of source registers and then set all of a destination register's components either to 1.0, if the comparison is true, or 0.0, if it is false. One can use a series of such tests to conditionally add in multiple components of an effect's trajectory.

Cross Products

When either constant or vertex attribute space is tight, one can use two instructions to calculate the cross product of two vectors in order to generate a vector orthogonal to an existing pair of normalized vectors. This is also handy for generating the third row of an orthonormal transformation matrix given only its first two rows. The cross product of two three-dimensional vectors v_1 and v_2 is defined as the determinant:

$$\begin{vmatrix} i & x_1 & x_2 \\ j & y_1 & y_2 \\ k & z_1 & z_2 \end{vmatrix} = \left(x_1 y_2 - y_1 x_2 \right) i + \left(z_1 x_2 - x_1 z_2 \right) j + \left(x_1 y_2 - y_1 x_2 \right) k$$

This sequence of two multiplies and one subtraction per vector component can be represented by:

```
mul r1.xzx, r2.yxy, r3.xyz
mad -r1.yxy, r2,xzx, r3.xyz
```

where v_1 is stored in r1 and v_2 is stored in r2. In this case, we have used the vertex mask swizzler on registers r1 and r2, along with negation of register r1 to reproduce the input terms of equation 1.

Examples

The first example for this article on the companion CD shows how to use periodic time to simulate and render a particle system entirely within a vertex shader. Each particle requires only four floating-point values. The first three of these values represent a three-dimensional heading vector, which the particle would follow in the absence of gravity. The fourth floating-point value is σ the phase, which is used to ensure the particle system effect is always in mid-stream, no matter when it is initiated. This shader only requires five constant registers, four of which hold the total transformation matrix. The fourth constant register contains, in order of component, the current time t, normalized by dividing it by T_p, the desired lifetime of a particle, followed by the launch speed of all particles, after which comes the total gravitational acceleration experienced by a particle during its lifetime, gT_p^2, where g is the gravitational acceleration, and finally, a constant, 1.0, which is used to convert the three-dimensional particle position into a four-dimensional homogeneous coordinate.

The second example makes more extensive use of random numbers to create a series of recurring procedural explosions similar to firework bursts. As in the first example, each particle has a phase value σ, which is used here to stagger the times of detonation of each individual explosion. However, there are two important differences here from the previous effect. First, each σ is shared by a group of particles so that the group animates synchronously. Second, there are three additional shared phase values for each of these particle groups, one for each spatial dimension. These three phases are used to pseudorandomize the position of each explosion. They each vary in range from 0.5 to 1.0. With each recurring explosion, the position of a particle is shifted in each dimension by the respective phase within a periodic box. The periodicity of the box is enforced, not surprisingly, by the use of the expp instruction.

Summary

Vertex shaders can perform much of the bookkeeping for special effects that is currently handled by the CPU. Converting a CPU-bound effect into a vertex shader effect requires thinking of the effect as either periodic or turning the effect on and off externally. The advantage of handling the effect inside a vertex shader is that the graphics hardware can render it entirely from static, pregenerated vertex buffers. The disadvantage is that if geometry bandwidth is tight, converting an effect to a vertex shader may slow things down. As with most processes, the only way to find out is to try each way.

Perlin Noise and Returning Results from Shader Programs

Steven Riddle and Oliver C. Zecha

Limitations of Shaders

The hardware-accelerated programmable shader is the most important advance in computer graphics today. Although early pixel shaders leave a few things to be desired, vertex shaders are proving to be a robust and versatile solution to many graphics problems. Together, pixel and vertex shaders allow a degree of realism on screen unprecedented in real-time animation. From particle systems to geometric deformations, their scope of application seems endless. The main reason for this is their vector processing capabilities, which allow complex lighting models and other visually stunning effects.

Currently, if you do not have a graphics card supporting vertex shaders, there are reasonable implementations that use the CPU to execute the vertex shader program. (The same is true for pixel shaders, but because the CPU must do all the texturing, it is painfully slow and renders the graphics processor useless.) However, at the rate with which graphics technology advances these days, it is difficult to believe that the CPU will be able to keep up with the GPU in the immediate future. This is due to the nature of the execution units.

A shader program does not allow branching or looping, and consequently, the GPU does not need to implement the hardware to make these possible. This fact alone allows the GPU to run much faster. Besides this, a GPU does not allow access to the data of other vertices, so they may be processed in parallel. Although CPU manufacturers have developed competing technologies to operate on multiple data with a single instruction, the GPU still has the advantage when working with larger sets of data. This becomes especially apparent when one considers all the other work the CPU must do, such as AI, collision detection, or whatever else your application requires.

Very soon, the number of vertices in average scenes will be so astronomically huge that performing the math to transform and light them on the CPU will be futile. Couple this with the memory bandwidth requirements for large meshes, and it becomes clear that the CPU's cycles are better spent on tasks other than vertex processing.

This leaves us with the vector math capabilities of the GPU. It can compute more vector operations faster than any PC hardware before it, and the numbers just keep getting bigger and better. Already, the number of vector operations feasible on a GPU exceeds that of a CPU, and there are no signs of going back. In fact, the trend seems to be that GPUs are doubling in power every six months, a full three times faster than Moore's Law predicts. Therefore, it seems reasonable that as much graphic computation as possible should be performed using the GPU. Not only this, but the GPU should be used for as much vector processing as possible.

What this really means, in terms of code, is that as much vector and graphic computation as achievable should be done using a programmable shader. Here we encounter the first major limitation of shaders, namely that we may use, at most, 128 instructions in the vertex pipeline and eight instructions plus four addressing instructions in the pixel pipeline. (Version 1.4 pixel shaders have increased to six addressing instructions but kept eight regular instructions in each phase; however, they allow two "phases" of 14 (8+6) instructions each.) "Well," you may think, "even if we are allowed only 140 instructions, at least the instructions themselves are relatively complicated mathematical operations, and using them we can do all sorts of neat things." Nevertheless, as graphics programmers, we are the type of people who like to push the limits, and so we ask, "What if we need more?" After all, 640K turned out to not be enough for everybody!

We have always been fascinated by computer graphics and physical simulation, so you can imagine how excited we were when given the opportunity to harness so much power for on-screen imaging and vector processing! One of the first applications we saw for vertex shaders was procedural deformation on a plane. We immediately noticed huge implications for landscapes and other generated meshes, but something was missing: There was no way of knowing the positions of the deformed vertices. As far as we were concerned, the objects had not changed. This presents a whole host of problems. Even doing collision detection with objects that have been transformed requires knowledge of the transformed vertices. In fact, it seems that there are many situations where getting results from the shader calculations is useful. Shortly after this, we discovered to our horror that the shader program outputs are write only. This marks the second major limitation of shaders: the difficulty in returning values.

The first identified limitation, the number of instructions, has been dealt with to some extent in several documents. The general idea, with which you are certainly familiar by now, is to utilize the costless modifiers. These consist of swizzle, mask, and negation for the vertex shader, a whole host of instruction modifiers, and instruction pairing for the pixel shader. This will allow you to group instructions for speed and possibly allow you to reduce the number of instructions used. Nevertheless, the gains you can make using these methods are minimal, in terms of decreasing the number of instructions used. The ideal solution would be to run two vertex shader programs sequentially, the second processing the output of the first. Unfortunately, this idea was not incorporated into the shader specification, which means that the best we can do is reduce the problem to getting output from the shader program. Interestingly enough, this coincides perfectly with the second limitation outlined earlier.

Finally, we have only one solution to discover, and fortunately it exists. Although we cannot get results directly from the shader program, they do give a sort of result. Generally, shader programs produce rendered output in memory, usually in video memory for display on screen. However, it is possible to render to texture. This is the technique used to return values from the shader program. The trick is to arrange everything so that the texture to which we render is used as an array of results for our computations. This may seem a bit strange at first, but the implications are vast. The ability to get values back from the shader pipeline lets us implement a variety of computation-intensive algorithms as fast shader programs which can run on the GPU.

In order to accomplish this, we need to add an extra piece of information to each vertex. This extra information represents the texture coordinate where the result will be stored. In order to justify moving this extra data across the AGP bus, we must be certain that the computations performed on each vertex are complex enough that doing them on the GPU is worthwhile. In this article, we use the vertex shader to generate three-dimensional Perlin noise. This is very intensive, since for each Perlin value, we need to do three cubic evaluations, eight dot products, and seven linear interpolations, plus a number of moduli, multiplications, and additions.

Perlin Noise and Fractional Brownian Motion

In general, computer graphics tend to have hard edges and appear "too perfect" to look real. To correct for this, noise is often added to give the impression of some blemishes and randomness. This noise may be added to lines to make them sketchy, textures to give them variation, character animation to make it more natural, or geometry to add some imperfections. In fact, there are countless applications of noise in computer imaging. Nevertheless, most noise is too random to look natural, unless you need a texture for TV static. For this reason, it is common to perform some smoothing on the noise, such as a Gaussian blur. There is a problem with this technique, however, when we consider real-time graphics. A Gaussian blur is quite slow. For this reason, Perlin noise was developed to approximate this smoothed noise.

Perlin noise, named for its creator Ken Perlin, is a technique for generating smooth pseudorandom noise. Smooth in this case means that the noise is defined at all real points in the domain. Pseudorandom means that it appears random, but is in fact a function. The most important feature of Perlin noise is that it is repeatable. This ensures that for any given point, the noise will be the same each time it is calculated. A Perlin noise function takes a value in $\Re^n$ and returns a value in $\Re$. In simpler terms, this means that it takes an n-dimensional point with real coordinates as input, and the result is a real number.

In order to produce smooth pseudorandom noise, we need a random number generator and a function for interpolation. The random number generator is used as a noise function, and the interpolation function is used to produce a continuous function from the noise.

Figure 1 shows an example of a one-dimensional random function. Given an integer, it generates a pseudorandom real number between zero and one. Each time it is used to compute a value for a given point, it gives us the same pseudorandom number, so it is repeatable. This is our noise function.

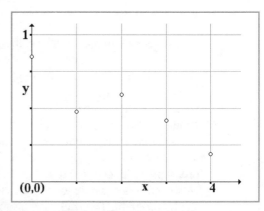

Figure 1: Random function

In Figure 2, you can see the results of cubic interpolation on our one-dimensional noise function. For the moment, don't worry about how this is done; I'll explain that later. This function is repeatable like the noise. However, unlike the noise function, this function is continuous, and consequently, it can be evaluated at any real point in the **x** domain. We call this smooth function our noise wave.

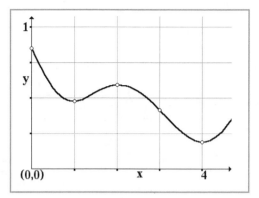

Figure 2: Cubic interpolation

It is sometimes helpful to think of the noise wave as a simple wave function, such as sine or cosine. You can see this analogy illustrated in Figure 3. The amplitude of a simple wave is the distance from valley to peak. Similarly, the amplitude (A) of the noise wave is the maximum possible distance from valley to peak (this is the range of the noise function). The wavelength (λ) is taken as the **x** distance between consecutive points. Since we know the wavelength (λ), we can calculate the frequency (f) by the following:

$$f = \frac{1}{\lambda}$$

Frequency is one way to describe Perlin noise waves and compare them with one another. When one noise wave has a frequency that is twice the frequency of another, its frequency is

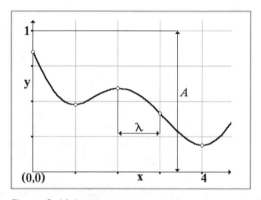

Figure 3: Noise wave

said to be one "octave" higher. This convention is borrowed from music, where notes exhibit the same property; if a note is one octave higher than another, it will have a frequency twice that of the lower note.

By varying the frequency and amplitude, we can create different sorts of Perlin noise. We scale the x-axis to alter the frequency; fewer points correspond to lower frequency. Additionally, dividing the output of the random number generator controls amplitude; larger divisors correspond to smaller amplitude. Below are some smooth noise functions; their range has been scaled to [–0.5,0.5]. In Figure 4, you can see the sum of the first five noise functions from Table 1.

Table 1: Perlin noise

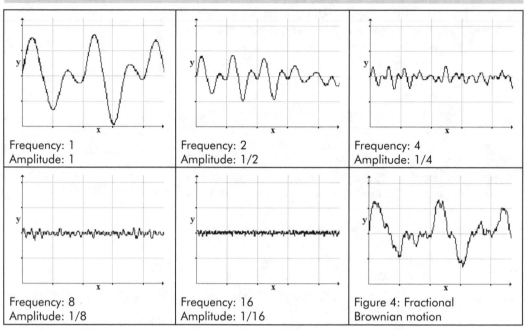

Frequency: 1 Amplitude: 1	Frequency: 2 Amplitude: 1/2	Frequency: 4 Amplitude: 1/4
Frequency: 8 Amplitude: 1/8	Frequency: 16 Amplitude: 1/16	Figure 4: Fractional Brownian motion

The intricate composite noise function in Figure 4 is called fractional Brownian motion (fBm), a fractal conceived by Ken Musgrave. The sum is simply a superposition of all the Perlin noise; this way, each wave's features are represented in the result. Summing successive octaves of Perlin noise is the most common approach to producing fBm noise. At each stage, the amplitude is divided by two to reduce the effect of the higher frequency. Benoit Mandelbrot coined the term "persistence" to describe the high-frequency component of a fractal. Low persistence leads to more high-frequency noise in the final product. In the case of our fractal, the persistence (p) is equivalent to the amplitude's divisor. Selecting a persistence value other than two is uncommon but can be used to create interesting effects. Reducing or increasing the persistence will roughen or smooth the noise, respectively. We have a similar value for calculating frequency; the harmonic interval (h) is the ratio of frequencies for consecutive octaves. Values between 1.0 and 2.0 really accentuate the fractal nature of the noise.

If n represents the nth octave, we can describe its frequency (f) and amplitude (A) as functions of the harmonic interval (h) and persistence (p):

$$f = h^n \qquad A = \frac{1}{p^n}$$

So far, all the noise functions we have seen are one-dimensional. The input is a real coordinate in one dimension, and the output is a real number. One-dimensional noise has its uses, but they are limited. Two-dimensional noise, on the other hand, has more applications since it can be used to texture surfaces or generate height maps. Two-dimensional noise takes a two-dimensional point with real coordinates as input and outputs a real number. Table 2 shows some examples of two-dimensional Perlin noise. Larger values are represented by darker regions and smaller values by lighter ones. The first row shows five octaves of noise with a persistence of one, so the noise functions are clearly visible. The second row shows the same five octaves of noise with a persistence of two; this is how they are added together.

Table 2: Two-dimensional Perlin noise

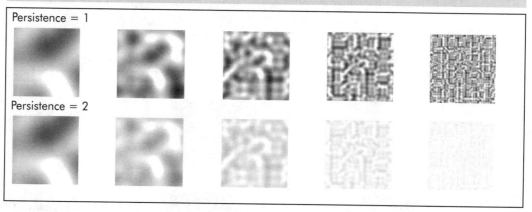

In Figure 5, you can see the fBm noise produced by the sum of the five Perlin noise waves from the second row of Table 2. Each Perlin noise wave still contributes some features to the sum just like one-dimensional fBm noise; however, we now use two dimensions to locate a given point. Since we are now working with multiple dimensions, it makes more sense if we think of fBm noise as taking a vector for input and producing a pseudorandom scalar as output. This thinking can be applied more easily to three- and higher-dimensional noise, which we will discuss shortly.

One important issue that has not yet been addressed is how many octaves of Perlin noise we should use to generate the fBm noise. Obviously, with a persistence of two, the amplitude of the Perlin noise quickly approaches zero. For this special case, Ken Musgrave suggests using no more than n octaves for noise with a resolution of res pixels, where n is given by:

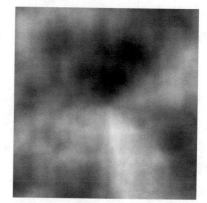

Figure 5: Two-dimensional fBm

$$n = \log_2 \left(res \right) - 2$$

This means that for noise with a 256 x 256 resolution, the recommendation is to use six octaves. Nevertheless, if you are using persistence values other than two or are concerned with speed, this rule of thumb may not apply. Ultimately, you're the judge. However, if the noise fluctuates faster than once about every two pixels, its features become too small to see.

Finally, before getting on to all the fun math stuff, we will take a brief look at three- and higher-dimensional fBm functions. This is where fBm becomes useful for solids and clouds. With three-dimensional noise, we can essentially carve out solid objects, which will still have continuous textures if cut in half. This technique is frequently used to simulate marble and looks quite good. With higher-dimensional noise, if we use one dimension to represent time, the object shows a beautiful morphing effect. This last technique is commonly used for cloud animation and looks incredible.

Table 3 shows how a marble texture would be generated using three-dimensional fractional Brownian motion for a cube and how a hole can be cut out of it. (These images were generated using Justin Legakis' Computer Graphics Gallery Marble Applet, which you can play with at http://graphics.lcs.mit.edu/~legakis/MarbleApplet/marbleapplet.html.) We do not bother to show how the fBm is composed of Perlin noise because by now you understand this already. What we do show is a form of procedural texturing.

Table 3: Volumetric textures

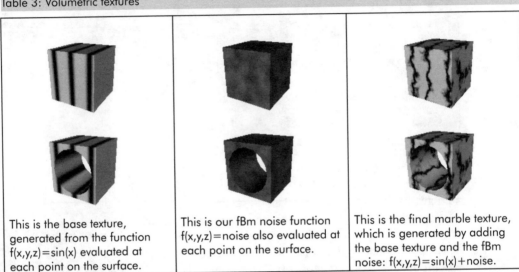

This is the base texture, generated from the function f(x,y,z)=sin(x) evaluated at each point on the surface.	This is our fBm noise function f(x,y,z)=noise also evaluated at each point on the surface.	This is the final marble texture, which is generated by adding the base texture and the fBm noise: f(x,y,z)=sin(x)+noise.

In our code (based on the Microsoft vertex shader sample), there are numerous examples outlining the ideas behind procedural textures using noise. The texture generator project (texturegenerator\ textureVS.dsw) on the companion CD shows two-dimensional cross sections of three-dimensional noise. In these particular cases, we do not use a base texture, although this is also common practice. Instead, for some of the algorithms, we use a function as a base, similar to the marble in Table 3. Other cases generate textures using only noise, such as the following:

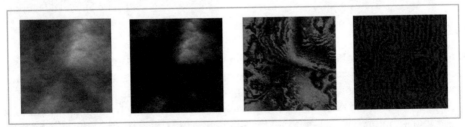

Figure 6: Textures using noise. From left: stone, clouds, marble, and wood

The manner in which our Perlin noise is returned is an important aspect of how we generate textures from it. Since the only outputs we are allowed are pixels, we must encode our results in colors. Our positive results are stored in the blue component, while the negative results are in the green component. Doing this allows us to return a greater range of values, since we effectively double the number of bits. In addition, the vertices are arranged in a grid, so finding a value corresponding to a vertex is just like looking up the value in a table by using (x, y) to locate it.

The stone texture is simply lit fractional Brownian motion. Each layer is an octave of Perlin noise with a persistence of two. Cloud is also a simple form of fBm. Each layer is again an octave of Perlin noise with a persistence of two, except this time the absolute value of the noise is taken before summation. This has the effect of adding sharp, defined edges and cusps. It does not yet look much like clouds because it still needs to drop off to zero faster. This will make the cloud less dense and more realistic. The cloud was left at its maximum size so that the divisions would be clearer. Since 1984, this formation has been called "turbulence" due to its flow-like appearance.

A good marble texture is much more complicated to generate. Marble is patchy in some areas and smooth in others. For this reason, we approached it slightly differently than the conventional method outlines in Table 3. For the patchy section, we calculate sin(positive noise && negative noise + **x**). For the smooth regions, we calculate cos(positive noise – negative noise + **x**) instead. To put these together, we check the value of the noise at each point. If that value is greater than 10, the patchy equation is used; otherwise, the smooth equation is used.

Wood is very similar to the smooth part of marble, except we add a small modifier in the sine equation: sin(positive noise – negative noise + smallconstant * (positive noise | negative noise) + **x**). The bitwise OR operation provides the imperfections in wood, and smallconstant ensures that their effect is on a small scale. The final thing to do once the texture has the correct "feel" is to adjust the color until it looks right. For the wood, we used a gradient from darker brown to lighter brown to simulate the appearance of grain in natural wood.

Another included project is a planet with a dynamic level of detail (planet\planetVS.dsw). Here you can see how noise is applied as a height map to a sphere, giving it a realistic terrain look. We calculate the value of the Perlin noise at each vertex in the mesh using the Perlin vertex shader. Once again, we are doing all the drawing using a separate vertex shader. Our technique for returning values is important to consider. Although it is not the ideal solution for all applications, it allows us to use the shader pipeline in very creative and unusual ways. Additionally, it allows us the versatility to implement both programs using the same shader.

The planet is an excellent example of the detail level possible using fBm. As you zoom in, the algorithm splits triangles and as a result, adds vertices. The main drawback to this technique is that we call the vertex shader for any vertex that is added. Ideally, we would put each vertex in a queue and process the queue every time it is filled. This would minimize the processing time required, since the vertex shader is a parallel unit and performs better with larger datasets.

In both pieces of example code, we use the same vertex shader. This is done to illustrate how flexible Perlin noise can be. Some performance improvements are possible if a specialized shader is written specifically for each application. Even so, if collision detection with a deformed surface is important, you will need to know the positions of the translated vertices.

Now let's get into the math of this whole problem. First, it is important to understand that we are trying to approximate cubic interpolation. Cubic interpolation returns a number between two known values, given four known values (two before and two after the desired point). We will label these heights V_1, V_2, V_3, V_4, in order from left to right, and assume that the x distance between consecutive V values is always 1. If we let x_1 represent the distance of the desired point from V_2 (where 0 means we are right on top of V_2, and 1 means we are right on top of V_3), we can calculate the height at A, as follows:

```
P   =    ( V4-V3 )-( V1-V2 )
Q   =    2( V1-V2 )-( V4-V3 )
R   =    V3 - V1
S   =    V2
A   =    Px1^3 + Qx1^2 + Rx1 + S
```

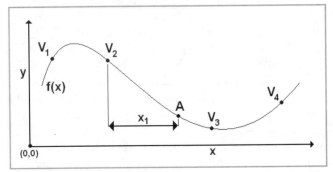

Figure 7: Cubic interpolation

Although the value at A will be exact if the function $f(x)$ is cubic, this computation is incredibly costly. For this reason, we use linear interpolation instead. In order to linearly interpolate, we only need to know two values, V_1 and V_2, on either side of A. Consequently, x_1 now represents the distance of the desired point from V_1. A is the value produced by the linear interpolation instead of the desired $f(x)$, where x represents the x value of the point in question.

```
A   =    V1*( 1-x1 ) + V2*x1
    =    V1 - x1*( V2 - V1)   ≈   f(x')
```

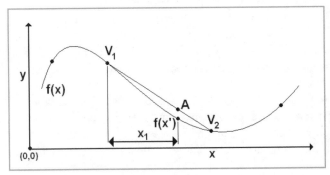

Figure 8: Linear interpolation

As you can see, this is much simpler and involves only a fraction of the computations required to interpolate cubically. The drawback is that linear interpolation does not produce as good of a result as cubic interpolation. In order to minimize this problem, we use a cubic filter prior to interpolation. The cubic filter that we use is called the ease curve, shown in Figure 9.

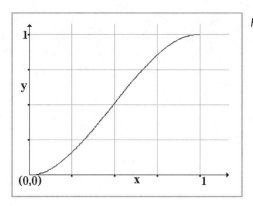

Figure 9: Ease curve

The ease curve brings us from 0 to 1 with a very gradual change in slope and is given by the function $e(x) = 3x^2 - 2x^3$ on the interval $0 \le x \le 1$. In order to utilize this function as a filter, we compute its value using x_1. This results in $e(x_1)$, which is approximately equal to x_1 for values of x_1 close to ½. If x_1 is close to either 0 or 1, $e(x_1)$ will be even closer to 0 or 1, respectively. We then proceed to use $e(x_1)$ in place of x_1 in the linear interpolation. The effects of applying this filter prior to interpolation are shown in Figure 10.

```
e(x₁)    =    3x₁² - 2x₁³
A        =    V₁*( 1-e(x₁) ) + V₂*e(x₁)
         =    V₁ - e(x₁)*( V₂ - V₁ )   ≈   f(x')
```

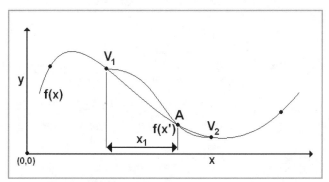

Figure 10: Ease interpolation

This added computation is slightly more costly than the simple linear interpolation shown in Figure 8 but produces much nicer results, as you can see in the comparison that follows. In addition to this, as we add dimensions to our noise, we only need to calculate one ease filter per axis. This added overhead is negligible relative to the exponential growth of the number of interpolations. Figures 11 and 12 show the results of cubic interpolation and linear interpolation, respectively. Figure 13 shows linear interpolation using the ease filter for comparison. Notice the improvement in smoothness over linear interpolation.

Now that you have a firm grasp on the interpolation that is used, we can continue to the generation of the actual Perlin noise. In order to compute the value of the noise at a given point, we need to linearly interpolate on each axis. The exact number of linear interpolations required is given by $(2^d)-1$, where **d** is the number of dimensions over which we want the noise. You may wonder what it is that we are interpolating between; the answer is that we are linearly interpolating between scalars, which represent the height at a given point. In one-dimensional noise, the scalar represents the height off the x-axis; in two-dimensional noise, the scalar represents the height off the x-y plane; in three-dimensional noise, the scalar represents the height out of the x-y-z space (into the fourth dimension). How we arrive at these scalars is explained later; for the moment, just take it for granted that each point with whole number coordinates has a scalar associated with it.

Figure 14 shows **(x)**, which is the point at which we would like to calculate the height. **n₁** and **n₂** represent the scalars associated with the two closest neighbors having whole number coordinates, and **dx** represents the distance from **n₁** to **x**.

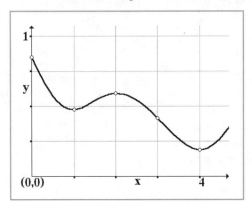

Figure 11: Cubic interpolation

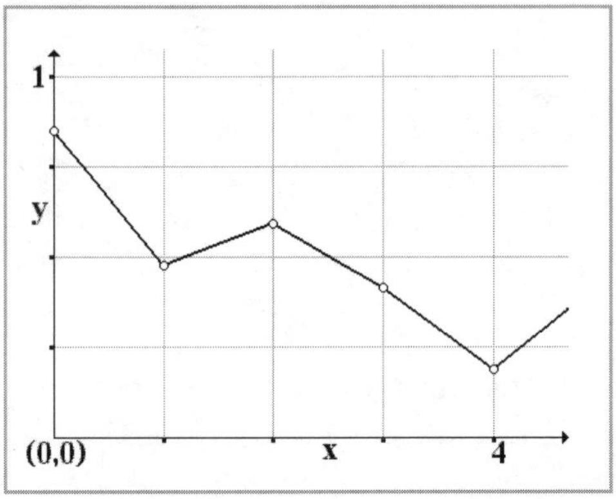

Figure 12: Linear interpolation

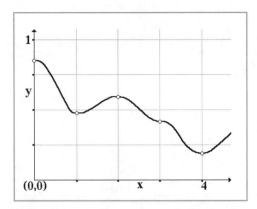

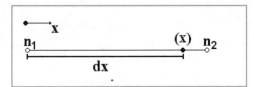

Figure 14: One-dimensional Perlin noise

Figure 13: Linear interpolation with ease filter

The scalar value at **x** is calculated in the following manner:

```
e(dx)   =   3*dx² - 2*dx³
(x)     =   n₁ - e(dx)*( n₂ - n₁)
```

Figure 15 shows exactly the same procedure for two dimensions. Now **(x,y)** represents the point for which we would like to calculate the height. **n₁**, **n₂**, **n₃**, and **n₄** represent the scalars associated with the four closest neighbors having whole number coordinates, **dx** represents the x distance from **n₁** to **(x,y)**, and **dy** represents the y distance from **n₁** to **(x,y)**. The two new variables **r₁** and **r₂** represent the intermediate interpolated values.

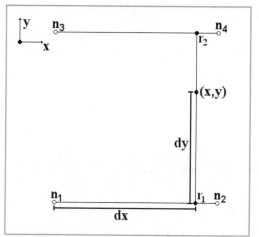

Figure 15: Two-dimensional Perlin noise

The scalar value at **(x,y)** is calculated in the following manner:

$$e(dx) = 3*dx^2 - 2*dx^3$$
$$r_1 = n_1 - e(dx)*(n_2 - n_1)$$
$$r_1 = n_3 - e(dx)*(n_4 - n_3)$$
$$e(dy) = 3*dy^2 - 2*dy^3$$
$$(x,y) = r_1 - e(dy)*(r_2 - r_1)$$

Finally, Figure 16 shows the same procedure again, for three dimensions. Now **(x,y,z)** represents the point for which we would like to calculate the height. n_1, n_2, n_3, n_4, n_5, n_6, n_7, and n_8 represent the scalars associated with the eight closest neighbors having whole number coordinates; **dx**, **dy**, and **dz** represent the x, y, and z distances respectively from n_1 to **(x,y,z)**. Lastly, the variables r_1, r_2, r_3, r_4, r_5, and r_6 represent the intermediate interpolated values.

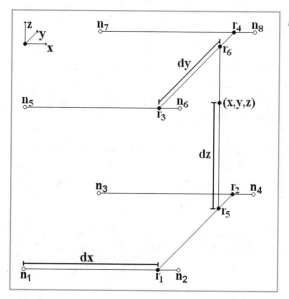

Figure 16: Three-dimensional Perlin noise

The scalar value at **(x,y,z)** is calculated in the following manner:

```
e(dx)    =    3*dx² - 2*dx³
r₁       =    n₁ - e(dx)*( n₂ - n₁)
r₂       =    n₃ - e(dx)*( n₄ - n₃)
r₃       =    n₅ - e(dx)*( n₆ - n₅)
r₄       =    n₇ - e(dx)*( n₈ - n₇)
e(dy)    =    3*dy² - 2*dy³
r₅       =    r₁ - e(dy)*( r₂ - r₁)
r₆       =    r₃ - e(dy)*( r₄ - r₃)
e(dz)    =    3*dz² - 2*dz³
(x,y,z)  =    r₅ - e(dz)*( r₆ - r₅)
```

Extending this technique into the fourth dimension and beyond is left as an exercise for the reader. As you may have guessed, it gets rather long but is not very hard.

Now, you lack only one piece of knowledge to make your own Perlin noise, and that is how to calculate the scalars at the neighboring points. In the case of Perlin noise, this value is found by taking the scalar product of the distance vectors and the gradients, as shown below. Our examples only cover two dimensions since three dimensions make the diagrams overly cluttered; however, the concepts are the same.

Figure 17 shows the distance vector from each neighbor point to **(x,y)** in two dimensions. We can take advantage of the fact that the neighbor points are regularly spaced to find these vectors easily. In our case, **dx** and **dy** are just the fractional components of **x** and **y**, since each **nₘ** is a point with integer coordinates.

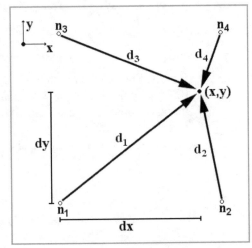

Figure 17: Distance vectors

```
d₁   =    (dx,dy)
d₂   =    (dx-1,dy)
d₃   =    (dx,dy-1)
d₄   =    (dx-1,dy-1)
```

Next, we need to look up the values for the pseudorandom gradients in a table of gradients, **gradient[t]**. In order to avoid symmetry about an axis, we use a shuffling table, **shuffle[t]**, to further randomize the gradients. The construction of the shuffling table is rather simple; each element contains a unique integer between zero and **t**, where **t** is the number of elements in the table. The value of **t** is also equal to the number of gradients. Building the table of gradients is equally easy. Select a number of random vectors with magnitudes less than one (|**gradient**| < 1) and normalize each one. This produces a uniform distribution of pseudorandom directions. Figure 18 on the following page shows the four neighbor points and the gradient associated with each.

Given the point **nₘ**, we know its coordinates, **(i,j,k)**. We use these coordinates and the shuffling table to choose a gradient **gₜ** for the point **nₘ**, in the following manner:

```
gₜ   =    gradient[ (k+shuffle[ (j+shuffle[ i ])%t ])%t ]
```

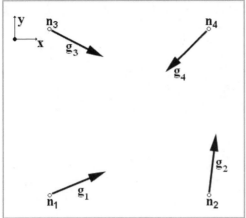

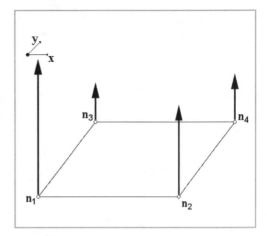

Figure 18: Pseudorandom gradients

Figure 19: Scalar product of distance and gradient shown as height

As you can see here, we do two shuffles, two moduli (represented by %), and three lookups. The shuffle makes the interval over which we repeat large, and the moduli are used here to ensure that we never try to read a value from outside the table.

We calculate the height by taking the scalar product of the gradient stored for each neighbor, and the distance vector from the neighbor to the point for which we want the noise. We could just as well use the magnitude of the cross product, since any continuous function will work. However this involves more effort and is not beneficial, so we shall stick to the dot product. The magnitudes of the vectors shown in Figure 19 represent the value of the scalar product at each neighbor, hence also the height out of the x-y plane.

$$n_1 = d_1 \cdot g_1$$
$$n_2 = d_2 \cdot g_2$$
$$n_3 = d_3 \cdot g_3$$
$$n_4 = d_4 \cdot g_4$$

Now that we know the scalar value at each neighbor, we can continue to interpolate, as described earlier, to find the scalar at any given point. For three-dimensional noise, we first perform four interpolations in the x-axis between the eight original points, which gives us the scalars at four new points. We then perform two interpolations in the y-axis, which results in the scalars for two new points. Finally, we interpolate between these two scalars in the z-axis to give us our final value, which is the scalar associated with the point in question. This process is performed exactly as shown in Figure 16.

To make it explicitly clear, you are interpolating linearly between values that are dependent on your position. As you move around in the domain, the scalars change smoothly and continuously, due to the smooth and continuous change in the direction vectors.

This concludes our discussion of how Perlin noise works and how to construct fBm. Next, we will illustrate the implemented algorithm in pseudocode, followed by a clarification of the actual shader program.

```
shuffle[2*(number of elements + 1)] is a table of integers
gradient[2*(number of elements + 1)][3] is a table of floats

Initialize Tables
  for i=0 to (number of elements - 1)
    shuffle[i] = i
    do
      for j=0 to 2 gradient[i][j] = random from -1.0 to 1.0
    while magnitude(gradient[i][j]) > 1.0
    normalize(gradient[i])
  end for
  for i=0 to (number of elements - 1)
    temp = shuffle[i]
    j = random from 0 and number of elements - 1
    shuffle[i] = shuffle[j]
    shuffle[j] = temp
  end for
  for i=0 to (number of elements + 2)
    shuffle[number of elements + i] = shuffle[i];
    for j=0 to 2 gradient[number of elements + i][j] = gradient[i][j];
  end for
End Initialize Tables
```

The first for loop in this section stores sequential numbers from zero to the number of elements less one in the shuffle table. Subsequently, another loop ensures that our table of pseudorandom gradients has a uniform distribution. This is done by continuing to select random points until one is found within the unit sphere. The vector from the origin to this point is then normalized and stored in the gradient list.

The second for loop does nothing other than mix up the shuffling table. It does this by randomly swapping values throughout the array. Randomizing these ensures that the shuffling table has no pattern, and as a result, the noise will have a large period.

The last for loop in the Initialize Tables section simply duplicates both the shuffle and the gradient tables. We do this so that we can avoid doing the two moduli when finding the gradient. This way, performing a lookup beyond the number of elements brings us back into the appropriate range. In our code, this is all done in C++; it is only the following section that is implemented as shader assembly.

The next section of pseudocode is implemented entirely in the vertex shader program, since this part is doing the heavy calculations. The shader assembly program does not follow the same sequence in order to make use of some optimizations; however, the main ideas are preserved.

```
Noise3d(vec[3] is a point in 3 dimensions) returns a float
    find 8 neighbor points
    look up gradient for each neighbor point, using shuffle
    compute distance vector for each neighbor point
    compute dot product of distance and gradient for each neighbor
    compute ease function for x,y,z (fractional components only)
    interpolate 4 times in x using e(x)
    interpolate 2 times in y using e(y)
    interpolate 1 time in z using e(z)
    return the value from the final interpolation
End Noise3d
```

To find the neighbor points, we must know the truncated position vector. We copy this vector and add one to each component. These two vectors provide the bounding box for the neighbor points, and all the **x,y,z** data we need to find their gradients. Finding the distance vectors for each neighbor point involves a similar technique. Beginning with the fractional component of the position, we copy it and subtract one. This results in the two sets of **x,y,z** data that we need. Once we know this, we can perform the dot products at each point. Finally, we get to the interpolation, for which we use the ease curve. The ease curve is simply calculated using the fractional component of the position from earlier. Subsequently, we do seven linear interpolations and arrive at a singular result.

Before we take a detailed look at the vertex shader program itself, we will build some of the more basic code that we will require later. First, we need a modulus function. The following is the only way we have found to do a modulus on the card, which unfortunately eats up many instructions.

$$v0 \bmod v1 = frc\left(\frac{v0}{v1}\right) \times v1$$

The frc macroinstruction actually counts as three instructions. Additionally, it can only compute the fractional components of **x** and **y**. Consequently, computing the fractional components of **x**, **y**, and **z** costs us six instructions. Carrying out the operation for all four components is done as follows:

```
mov    r0.xyzw,    v0.xyzw
mov    r1.xyzw,    v1.xyzw
rcp    r2.x,       v1.x
rcp    r2.y,       v1.y
rcp    r2.z,       v1.z
rcp    r2.w,       v1.w
mul    r3.xyzw,    r0.xyzw,    r2.xyzw
frc    r4.xy,      r3,xy
mov    r3.xy,      r3.zw
frc    r5.xy,      r3.xy
mov    r4.zw,      r5.xy
mul    r5.xyzw,    r4.xyzw,    r1.xyzw
```

Now r5 contains the result of v0 mod v1. We can simplify this slightly if we pass $\frac{1}{v1}$ in as v2, as shown in the following code:

```
mov    r0,         v0
mov    r1,         v1
mov    r2,         v2
mul    r3,         r0,         r2
frc    r4.xy,      r3,xy
mov    r3.xy,      r3.zw
frc    r5.xy,      r3.xy
mov    r4.zw,      r5.xy
mul    r5,         r4,         r1
```

We are required to do this modulus for each component of two vectors, the input vector and the input vector plus (1,1,1). We are now ready for the main assembly, so let's review our constants:

```
c[0].x = 0
c[0].y = 1
c[0].z = 2
c[0].w = 3

c[1].x = 1/42
c[1].y = 42
c[1].z = 1/frequency
c[1].w = frequency

c[2].x = x translation
c[2].y = y translation
c[2].z = z translation
c[2].w = 0.25

c[3-95].xyz gradient table
c[3-95].w    shuffling table
```

v3 is the input position in Perlin space; this is the point for which to find the noise. v0 is the texture space location; this is where the result of the noise function is written.

First, we calculate our Perlin space position after we have translated and adjusted the frequency of the noise for this octave. Then we make a backup of it in r5.

```
// r0 = vertex, then translate and scale
mov    r0,        v3
add    r0.xyz,    r0.xyz,    c[2].xyz
mul    r0.xyz,    r0.xyz,    c[1].www
// r5 = r0
mov    r5,        r0
```

Next, we take the translated point in r0 and find its fractional component. The value in r0 is then the value for calculating the cubic filter.

```
// r0 = frc(r5) = (dx,dy,dz)
mov    r2.xy,     r0.zw
frc    r2.xy,     r2.xy
frc    r0.xy,     r0.xy
mov    r0.z,      r2.x
```

Now we need to find the whole number component of the translated position by subtracting the fractional component in r0 from the translated position in r5. We have a copy of r5 stored in r4, to which we add one.

```
// trunc(r5) and r4 = r5
add    r4.xyz,    r5.xyz,    -r0.xyz
mov    r5.xyz,    r4.xyz
// r4 = r5 + (1,1,1,1)
add    r4.xyz,    r5.xyz,    c[0].yyy
```

The following are the moduli. They are found by dividing r4 and r5 by 42, finding the fractional component of the result, and multiplying that fraction by 42 to find the remainder.

```
// r4 = r4 * 1/42
// r4 = frc(r4)
mul     r4.xyz,     r4.xyz,     c[1].xxx
mov     r2.xy,      r4.zy
frc     r4.xy,      r4.xy
frc     r2.xy,      r2.xy
mov     r4.z,       r2.x
// r9 = r0+1 % 42
mul     r9.xyz,     r4.xyz,     c[1].yyy
// r4 = r5
// r4 = r4 * 1/42
// r4 = frc(r4)
mov     r4.xyz,     r5.xyz
mul     r4.xyz,     r4.xyz,     c[1].xxx
mov     r2.xy,      r4.zy
frc     r4.xy,      r4.xy
frc     r2.xy,      r2.xy
mov     r4.z,       r2.x
// r8 = r0 % 42
mul     r8.xyz,     r4.xyz,     c[1].yyy
```

Now r8 and r9 contain all the information we need to find the whole number neighbors. r8 and r9 contain all the possible **x,y,z** coordinates for the eight neighbors because r8 and r9 define the bounding box of the neighbors. Next, we use a similar technique to find all the values we need to construct our distance vectors. We subtract one from the fractional component of our position.

```
// r1 = r0-1 = (dx-1,dy-1,dz-1)
add     r1.xyz,     r0.xyz,     -c[0].yyy
```

Here we begin doing shuffle table lookups. First, we do a lookup for x and put the value in r10.x, and then we do a lookup for x+1 and put the result in r10.y.

```
// x lookup
mov     a0.x,       r8.x
mov     r10.x,      c[a0.x+3].w
// x+1 lookup
mov     a0.x,       r9.x
mov     r10.y,      c[a0.x+3].w
```

We add the values from the last lookups to our y and y+1 components. We use the resulting values for the next set of lookups into the table.

```
add     r5.xy,      r10.xy,     r8.yy
add     r6.xy,      r10.xy,     r9.yy
// x   + y
mov     a0.x,       r5.x
mov     r11.x,      c[a0.x+3].w
// x+1 + y
mov     a0.x,       r5.y
mov     r11.y,      c[a0.x+3].w
// x   + y+1
mov     a0.x,       r6.x
mov     r11.z,      c[a0.x+3].w
// x+1 + y+1
mov     a0.x,       r6.y
mov     r11.w,      c[a0.x+3].w
```

We can now add the z and z+1 values to the results from the preceding lookups. Then, we use these sums to look up the vectors for each neighbor in our table of gradients. Finally, we compute the dot product of the gradient and distance vectors at each neighbor, carefully arranging the results into r2 and r3 to ensure that the interpolation is as optimized as possible.

```
// + z
add     r5.xyzw,        r11.xyzw,       r8.zzzz
// + z+1
add     r6.xyzw,        r11.xyzw,       r9.zzzz
//lookup gradient, and compute dot product
//r2 = (n1,n5,n3,n7)
//r3 = (n2,n6,n4,n8)
mov     a0.x,           r5.x
dp3     r2.x,           r0.xyz,         c[a0.x+3].xyz
mov     a0.x,           r5.y
mov     r0.w,           r1.x
dp3     r3.x,           r0.wyz,         c[a0.x+3].xyz
mov     a0.x,           r5.z
mov     r0.w,           r1.y
dp3     r2.z,           r0.xwz,         c[a0.x+3].xyz
mov     a0.x,           r5.w
mov     r1.w,           r0.z
dp3     r3.z,           r1.xyw,         c[a0.x+3].xyz
mov     a0.x,           r6.x
mov     r0.w,           r1.z
dp3     r2.y,           r0.xyw,         c[a0.x+3].xyz
mov     a0.x,           r6.y
mov     r1.w,           r0.y
dp3     r3.y,           r1.xwz,         c[a0.x+3].xyz
mov     a0.x,           r6.z
mov     r1.w,           r0.x
dp3     r2.w,           r1.wyz,         c[a0.x+3].xyz
mov     a0.x,           r6.w
dp3     r3.w,           r1.xyz,         c[a0.x+3].xyz
```

It is almost time to do the linear interpolation, but first we need to calculate the ease function for each axis. This is done using the fractional component of the position.

```
// r4 = r0 * r0 * (-2*r0 +3) = e(r0)
mad     r7.xyz,         r0.xyz,         -c[0].zzz,
        c[0].www
mul     r7.xyz,         r7.xyz,         r0.xyz
mul     r4.xyz,         r7.xyz,         r0.xyz
```

Now we do the linear interpolations using the ease value for each axis. There are four x interpolations, two y interpolations, and one z interpolation.

```
// Linear interpolate along X
add     r5,             r3,             -r2
mul     r5,             r5,             r4.xxxx
add     r6,             r5,             r2
// Linear interpolate along Y
add     r5.xy,          r6.zw,          -r6.xy
mul     r5.xy,          r5.xy,          r4.yy
add     r7.xy,          r5.xy,          r6.xy
// Linear interpolate along Z
```

```
// r7.z = Noise(x,y,z)
add    r5.x,      r7.y,      -r7.x
mul    r5.x,      r5.x,      r4.z
add    r7.z,      r5.x,      r7.x
```

If Noise is positive, store the value in r7.y; otherwise, store –Noise in r7.z. Then move zero into r7.x and the alpha value into r7.w. The alpha value is used to compute the sum of the various Perlin noise layers. As the frequency of the noise increases, we decrease its alpha value to ensure the amplitude is scaled properly. Then we simply draw the layers we want to the same texture space with alpha enabled.

```
// r7.x = 0
// r7.y = Noise if Noise is +ve, otherwise its 0
// r7.z = -Noise if Noise is -ve, otherwise its 0
// r7.w = 1/frequency (alpha)
mov    r7.x,      c[0].x
max    r7.y,      r7.z,      c[0].x
max    r7.z,      -r7.z,     c[0].x
mov    r7.w,      c[1].z
```

The projected position is simply the x,y coordinates to which the results will be written in the texture. Remember that this is how we get back our results, using the green and blue components of the color for the positive and negative noise, respectively, and the alpha as our amplitude.

```
// x position = xy position on texture
mov    oPos,      v0
// Calculate color intensity
mov    oD0,       r7.xyzw
```

Final Thoughts

Our vertex consists of two vectors in an FVF, one for Perlin position, and one for texture position. This is acceptable, since the amount of data moving across the AGP bus is about 8 megabytes for a 128 x 128 mesh (around 16,384 points). This leaves space for 14 vectors of additional input. This is good since it allows a fair bit of extra data to be included in each vertex. Not only this, but no textures are used; these could be used for all sorts of data input. On the downside, 93 instruction spaces were used in the vertex pipeline. This is actually quite compressed, since we were able to do some major simplifications such as the linear interpolation in x, so there are still 35 instruction spaces remaining. In addition to this, the power of the pixel pipeline is completely untouched.

The following benchmarks were taken to give you some idea as to the effectiveness of the GPU vs. CPU. They were taken using slightly modified code without any drawing to screen in order to strictly test the Perlin throughput. The vertex programs run using an optimized vertex pipeline when executing in software. This makes vertex shaders a very hardware-independent method for taking advantage of streamlined CPU assembly instructions such as 3DNOW! and SSE.

Table 4: Shader benchmarks

Vertex shader running on CPU		
fps	CPU	GPU
5	750MHz PIII Coppermine (SSE)	GeForce256
11	1.2GHz Athlon Thunderbird (3DNOW!)	GeForce2
Vertex shader running on GPU		
fps	CPU	GPU
13	1.2GHz Athlon Thunderbird (3DNOW!)	GeForce3
(estimated) 25+	750MHz PIII Coppermine (SSE)	GeForce4

The technique for returning values is slow and may seem questionable, but as GPUs become faster, getting results back from them will become increasingly desirable. This, coupled with the simple fact that there is no alternative method to do so, makes this trick not only good to understand but very unique. In addition, returning values allows us a great deal of versatility in using the code, as illustrated by the two radically different test programs. Nevertheless, there is a major problem with the planet program, since it is not queued. Vertex shaders prefer bulk data; hence it would be much more efficient if we saved a list of added vertices and computed their noise values as a block.

Keep in mind that this is meant to be an experiment, or possibly a base for your own noise explorations, and not a production implementation. The constraint of needing to know the translated position, and thus the Noise value, for collision detection and surface interaction requires us to use a very inefficient process of writing to texture memory and then reading back from it. We have shown that this is possible and potentially useful; however, application-specific implementations are desirable, and further optimization is required. There is much room for improvement in the shader, particularly for texturing applications. Nonetheless, it clearly illustrates the relative power of the GPU vs. the CPU. After all, with the current product release cycle, it looks like we will see this single-pass Perlin noise vertex shader running at 100fps in about one year!

References

Paul Bourke, "Perlin Noise and Turbulence," http://astronomy.swin.edu.au/pbourke/texture/perlin/, January 2000.

David S. Ebert, F. Kenton Musgrave, Darwyn Peachey, Ken Perlin, and Steven Worley, *Texturing and Modeling, A Procedural Approach*, 2nd Ed. (AP Professional, Cambridge, 1998).

Hugo Elias, "Perlin Noise," http://freespace.virgin.net/hugo.elias/models/m_perlin.htm.

John C. Hart, "Perlin Noise Pixel Shaders," http://graphics.cs.uiuc.edu/~jch/papers/pixelnoise.pdf, University of Illinois, Urbana-Champaign.

Microsoft Corporation, "Vertex Shader Reference," http://msdn.microsoft.com/library/default.asp?url=/library/en-us/dx8_c/directx_cpp/Graphics/Reference/Shader/Vertex/Vertex.asp, 2002.

Sean O'Neil, "A Real-Time Procedural Universe, Part One: Generating Planetary Bodies," http://www.gamasutra.com/features/20010302/oneil_01.htm, March 2001.

Ken Perlin, "Noise and Turbulence," http://mrl.nyu.edu/~perlin/doc/oscar.html, MAKING NOISE, based on a talk presented at GDCHardCore, December 1999.

Matt Zucker, "The Perlin Noise Math FAQ," http://students.vassar.edu/mazucker/code/perlin-noise-math-faq.html, February 2001.

Part 3

Pixel Shader Tricks

Blending Textures for Terrain

Alex Vlachos

Historically, artists have had problems texturing terrain. Hiding texture seams and repetitive patterns is a difficult problem that most games suffer from. This shader shows how to programmatically interpolate between two textures based on their normal. The interpolation provides varying combinations of base textures when rendered as a combination of two textures. In the following figure, a brown rocky texture is biased toward polygons that are generally facing toward the sky. A strange blue texture is given to anything that is on an incline. For hills that are in-between, a blended combination of the two textures is used.

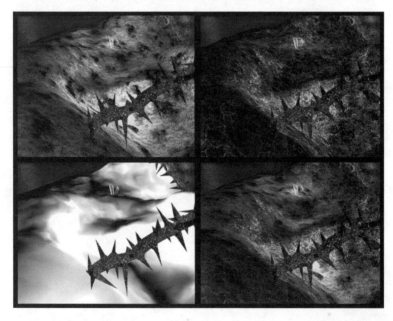

Ideally, using the angle of the normal from the ground plane should be used as the interpolation value to blend between the two textures. However, to simplify the math, an approximation can be implemented that simply uses the z-component of each vertex normal. In the example shown here, z^3 is used to get a sharper cross fade between the two terrain textures. When using just z, the blending is less harsh, which provides a slightly different look. Experimenting with different powers of z will be necessary to get the desired look given the surrounding scene.

The effect is achieved by computing the blend value in the vertex shader. The pixel shader will, at every pixel, use the interpolated blend value to blend between the two textures. In pre-shader hardware, these values can be precomputed and stored in the vertex. However, more complex schemes can be implemented in a vertex shader if the desired effect would be to blend four to six textures based on which direction the hill was facing. This technique could be used to simulate snow falling from a given direction and sticking to the side of a mountain. Over time, the intensity of the blend value could be increased to show the accumulation of snow.

A further enhancement could be to compute the blend value per-pixel instead of per-vertex. This could provide some very interesting results when used with a bump map. When computing the per-vertex values, the blend only varies linearly over the face of a polygon. A bump map could provide more interesting variation within polygons.

Vertex shader:

```
vs.1.1
m4x4 oPos, v0, c0  //Transform vertex by transformation matrix
mov oT0, v7        //Texture coordinates for texture 0
mov oT1, v8        //Texture coordinates for texture 1
mul r0, v3.z, v3.z //z^2 into temp register
mul oT2, r0, v3.z  //z^3 into third set of texture coordinates
```

Pixel shader:

```
ps.1.4
texld r0, t0       //Base texture 0
texld r1, t1       //Base texture 1
texcrd r2.rgb, t2 //Interpolation value
   lrp r0, r2.r, r1, r0 //Blend between the two textures
   //Lighting computations go here
```

Image Processing with 1.4 Pixel Shaders in Direct3D

Jason L. Mitchell

Introduction

With the ability to perform up to 16 ALU operations and 12 texture accesses in a single pass, Direct3D's pixel pipeline has begun to look like a powerful programmable 2D image processing machine. In this article, we will outline several techniques that utilize DirectX 8.1's 1.4 pixel shaders to perform 2D image processing effects such as *blurs*, *edge detection*, *transfer functions*, and *morphology*, and will point out applications of these 2D image operations to 3D game graphics. For an introduction to the structure and capabilities of 1.4 pixel shaders, please refer back to Wolfgang Engel's introductions to vertex and pixel shader programming.

As shown here and in "Non-Photorealistic Rendering with the Pixel and Vertex Shaders," post-processing of 3D frames and a general image-savvy mindset are fundamental to effectively utilizing 3D graphics processors to generate a variety of photorealistic and non-photorealistic effects [Saito90]. As shown in Figure 1, filtering an image with a GPU is done by using the image as a texture and drawing a screen-aligned quadrilateral into the *render target* (either the back buffer or another texture).

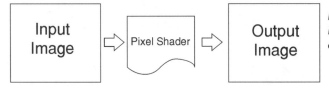

Figure 1: Using a pixel shader for image processing by rendering from one image to another

This results in the pixels of the render target being filled with the results of the pixel shader. With a very simple pixel shader that samples the source image and passes it directly to the destination without modification, this is equivalent to a Blt. In the simple Blt case, one source pixel determines the color of one destination pixel. In addition to merely copying the input image data, this operation can be useful for creating black-and-white or sepia tone images from the source image. We will illustrate these simple effects and more general transfer functions (like a heat signature) in the first part of this article.

Image processing becomes especially powerful when the color of the destination pixel is the result of computations done on multiple pixels sampled from the source image. In this case, we use a *filter kernel* to define how the different samples from the source image interact. Most of this chapter will be spent discussing the use of filter kernels to achieve different image processing effects, but first we will review basic 1.4 pixel shader syntax and the concept of a dependent texture read in the following section on simple transfer functions.

Simple Transfer Functions

For the purposes of this chapter, we define a *transfer function* to be a function (often one-dimensional) that is used to enhance or segment an input image. Transfer functions are often used in scientific visualization to enhance the understanding of complex datasets by making important details in the image clearly distinguishable. A transfer function might map a scalar such as heat, pressure, or density to a color to aid in understanding the phenomenon being visualized. This application of transfer functions is illustrated in "3D Textures and Pixel Shaders" by Evan Hart to apply pseudo-color to a dataset, which is a scalar density acquired from a medical imaging process.

Here, we show how to use transfer functions to stylize a whole rendered 3D frame or static 2D image. This allows us to take normal color images and cause them to become black and white or sepia toned, as was done for dramatic effect in recent films such as *Thirteen Days* and *Pleasantville*. We can also think of our frame buffer as containing heat and apply a heat signature transfer function to give an effect like that used in the films *Predator* and *Patriot Games*. The application of the following three transfer functions are shown in Color Plate 2 and illustrated at right for reference.

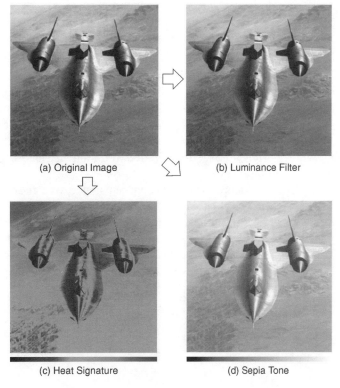

(a) Original Image

(b) Luminance Filter

(c) Heat Signature

(d) Sepia Tone

Figure 2: Three transfer functions

Black and White Transfer Function

As shown in Figure 2 and in Color Plate 2, we have applied three different transfer functions to the color input image of an SR-71 Blackbird. The first transfer function is a simple Luminance calculation which reads in the RGB color pixels from the source image and outputs them as RGB colors where R = G = B = Luminance. The Luminance operation is performed using a dot product operation to calculate Luminance = 0.3*red + 0.59*green + 0.11*blue. As shown in the pixel shader below, we define the constant {0.3f, 0.59f, 0.11f} with the def instruction and then sample texture 0 with the 0th set of texture coordinates using the texld instruction.

Listing 1: Simple Luminance shader for converting to black and white

```
ps.1.4
def c0, 0.30f, 0.59f, 0.11f, 1.0f
texld r0, t0
dp3 r0, r0, c0
```

The Luminance is calculated with the dp3 instruction and the final pixel color is stored in register r0. This is a very simple transfer function that is expressible in the pixel shader assembly language. Often, it is convenient to use a lookup table to apply a more arbitrary function to the input pixels. The next transfer function will use this technique by doing a dependent read.

Sepia Tone Transfer Function

An example of a transfer function that is implemented by using a dependent read is a sepia tone effect. In this example, we apply a 1D sepia map to the luminance of the input image to make it look like an old photograph. Cut scenes in a 3D game set in the Old West would be a good candidate for this effect. The bottom right image in Color Plate 2 shows the sepia tone version of the original image. The colored stripe beneath the sepia image is the 1D texture used to map from Luminance to Sepia tone. As shown in the shader code below, the color from the original image is converted to Luminance and then used as a texture coordinate to sample the 1D sepia tone transfer function.

Sampling this 1D texture using texture coordinates that were computed earlier in the shader is known as a dependent read and is one of the most powerful concepts in pixel shading. Many of the shaders in following chapters will use dependent reads. Some examples include application of transfer functions as shown in "3D Textures and Pixel Shaders," perturbation refraction rays as shown in "Accurate Reflections and Refractions by Adjusting for Object Distance," and indexing reflection and refraction maps as shown in "Rippling Refractive and Reflective Water" in this book.

Listing 2: Simple transfer function for sepia or heat signature effects

```
ps.1.4
def c0, 0.30f, 0.59f, 0.11f, 1.0f
texld r0, t0
dp3 r0, r0, c0 // Convert to Luminance
phase
texld r5, r0   // Dependent read
mov r0, r5
```

Heat Signature

Another example of a transfer function that is implemented by using a dependent read is a heat signature effect. In this example, we use the same shader as the sepia effect but use the 1D texture shown in the bottom left of Color Plate 2. This gives the look of an image used to visualize heat. This further illustrates the power of dependent texture reads: The same shader can produce radically different results based on simple modification of the texture used in the dependent read.

In future versions of Direct3D, we look forward to applying tone-mapping transfer functions to real-time high dynamic range scenes with this same technique.

While we have been able to perform some useful operations mapping one pixel in the input image to one pixel in the output image, we can perform even more useful tasks by sampling multiple pixels from the input image. We will explore filters with this property in the remainder of this article.

Filter Kernels

Filter kernels are a combination of the locations that the input image is sampled relative to a reference point and any coefficients which modulate those image samples. A Gaussian blur, for example, is designed to sample the source image in a radially symmetric way and weight the samples according to a Gaussian distribution. The coefficients of a Gaussian blur sum to one. The simple box filter used in this chapter weights all samples evenly, with the coefficients also summing to one. Edge filters such as the Roberts and Sobel filters shown later in this chapter have positive and negative lobes. The coefficients of edge filters (including Roberts and Sobel) typically sum to zero.

Texture Coordinates for Filter Kernels

When rendering the output image, it is necessary to take care when setting the texture coordinates of the quadrilateral that is texture mapped with the input image. To achieve a one-to-one mapping from input texels to output pixels, the naïve 0.0 to 1.0 texture coordinates do <u>not</u> give the correct mapping. The correct coordinates are $0.0+\varepsilon$ to $1.0+\varepsilon$, where ε is equal to 0.5 / image_dimension. Obviously, for non-square images ($h \neq w$), this will result in a separate $\varepsilon_h = 0.5 / h$ and $\varepsilon_w = 0.5 / w$. Filter samples that are offset from the one-to-one mapping must also take ε into account. The function ComputeImagePlacement() in the DX81_ImageFilter sample application on the companion CD illustrates the correct method of setting the texture coordinates on the quadrilateral texture mapped with the input image. Obviously, this texture coordinate perturbation could be done in a vertex shader [James01], thus saving the cost of storing and transferring the additional texture coordinates for a multi-tap filter kernel; this is left out of the sample application for clarity.

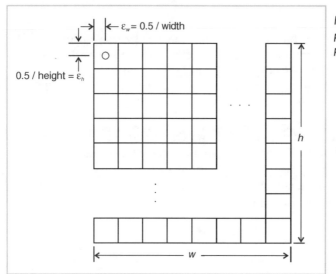

Figure 3: Correctly sampling textures for image processing

This may <u>seem</u> like a trivial detail and, indeed, getting this wrong may not introduce noticeable artifacts for some effects, but any ping-pong techniques that repeatedly render to and from a pair of textures can suffer massively from feedback artifacts if the texture coordinates are set up incorrectly. A ping-pong blur technique is implemented in the sample application.

Edge Detection

Edge detection is a very common operation performed in machine vision applications. In this section, we will illustrate two common edge detection filters and their applications to image processing. The use of image space methods for outlining of real-time non-photorealistic renderings will be explored further in "Non-Photorealistic Rendering with Pixel and Vertex Shaders" using the filters introduced here. A related gradient filter, the central-difference filter, is also discussed in "3D Textures and Pixel Shaders."

Roberts Cross Gradient Filters

One set of inexpensive filters that is commonly used for edge detection is the Roberts cross gradient. These 2×2 filters respond to diagonal edges in the input image and amount to doing a pair of 2-tap first-differences to approximate the image gradients in the diagonal directions.

−1	0
0	1

0	−1
1	0

Figure 4: Roberts cross gradient filters

Since the Roberts filters can be thought of as simply three taps (with one tap reused in both gradient calculations), it is easy to do the gradient magnitude calculation for both directions in the same pixel shader. The following pixel shader first computes luminance for all three taps, computes the luminance cross gradients, takes their absolute values, adds them together, and scales and inverts them before compositing them back over the original image.

Listing 3: Roberts cross gradient filter overlayed on original color image

```
// Roberts Cross Gradient Filter from color image
ps.1.4
Def c0, 0.30f, 0.59f, 0.11f, 1.0f
tex1d r0, t0   // Center Tap
tex1d r1, t1   // Down/Right
tex1d r2, t2   // Down/Left
dp3 r3, r0, c0
dp3 r1, r1, c0
dp3 r2, r1, c0
add r1, r3, -r1
add r2, r3, -r2
cmp r1, r1, r1, -r1
cmp r2, r2, r2, -r2
add_x4 r1, r1, r2
phase
mul r0.rgb, r0, 1-r1
+mov r0.a, c0.a
```

The result of this operation is black outlines layered over the original image in areas that have sharp luminance discontinuities, as shown in Figure 5.

Figure 5: Input image and image with overlayed edges computed with Roberts filters

Sobel Filter

A more robust and popular edge detection filter is the Sobel filter [Sobel90]. The Sobel filters are 6-tap 3×3 filters which detect horizontal and vertical edges. Like the Roberts filters, the Sobel filters are just 90° rotations of each other. The filter is shown below:

$$\delta u = \begin{array}{|c|c|c|} \hline -1 & 0 & 1 \\ \hline -2 & 0 & 2 \\ \hline -1 & 0 & 1 \\ \hline \end{array} \qquad \delta v = \begin{array}{|c|c|c|} \hline -1 & -2 & -1 \\ \hline 0 & 0 & 0 \\ \hline 1 & 2 & 1 \\ \hline \end{array}$$

Figure 6: The Sobel filter kernels

Because the Sobel filter for each direction, u and v, is a 6-tap filter and the 1.4 pixel shading model allows us to sample six textures, it is convenient to handle u and v gradients separately. This is not strictly necessary, as more taps can be sampled as dependent reads at texture coordinates which are derived from the other input texture coordinates. It should also be mentioned that it is possible to use the bilinear filtering capability of the hardware to approximate the double-weighting of the central samples. In order to keep this example manageable, however, we will avoid this and take a two-pass approach: one pass for $|\delta u|$ and one for $|\delta v|$. The two partial gradient magnitude images can then be composited to form a resulting gradient magnitude image, which highlights the edges. A Luminance-only version of the original SR-71 Blackbird image is shown in Figure 7, along with $|\delta u|$, $|\delta v|$, and $|\delta u|+|\delta v|$ images.

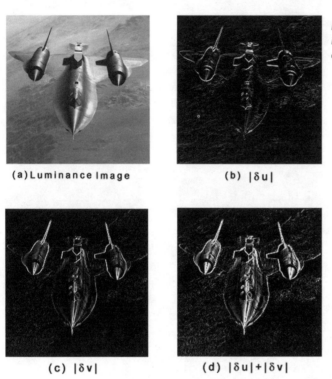

(a) Luminance Image

(b) $|\delta u|$

(c) $|\delta v|$

(d) $|\delta u|+|\delta v|$

Figure 7: Input image and gradient magnitude images for u and v directions

A given Sobel filter is easily handled in one rendering pass with the following pixel shader that samples all six taps, accumulates the samples, and takes the absolute value of the results. For a non-photorealistic object and shadow outlining effect like the one shown in "Non-Photorealistic Rendering with Pixel and Vertex Shaders," these white edges can be thresholded and inverted to produce clean, black outlines. The results of one such effect are shown in Color Plate 6 (see "Non-Photorealistic Rendering").

Listing 4: Sobel filter pixel shader

```
// Sobel Filter (use for U or V, perturbations control which)
ps.1.4
def c0, 0.1666f, 0.1666f, 0.1666f, 1.0f
tex1d r0, t0 // Expect samples in one of two layouts...doesn't matter which
tex1d r1, t1 //
tex1d r2, t2 // -t0    t3 -t0 -2t1 -t2
tex1d r3, t3 // -2t1 x 2t4or  x
tex1d r4, t4 // -t2    t5 t3 2t4 t5
tex1d r5, t5 //
add r0, -r0, -r2
```

```
add r0, -r0, -r1_x2
add r0, r0, r3
add r0, r0, r4_x2
add r0, r0, r5
cmp r0, r0, r0, -r0
```

Mathematical Morphology

Morphological operators are used in image processing applications that deal with the extraction, enhancement, or manipulation of region boundaries, skeletons, or convex hulls. In some sense, one can think of mathematical morphology as *set theory for images*. In general, mathematical morphology applies an arbitrary morphological operator to a source image. In the following discussion, we apply a limited set of morphological operators since we effectively hard-code them into the pixel shaders themselves. As such, the generality of the operators is limited by the instruction count of the pixel shaders and the expressiveness of the language. Nevertheless, morphology is an important area of image processing, and one can see how this will become even more useful in future generations of hardware, which can access more samples from the input image and even express the morphological operator as an image in a texture map. Even for the relatively small number of taps available to us in Direct3D's 1.4 pixel shaders, we can apply some interesting morphological operators.

Mathematical morphology is typically applied to binary (1-bit) images, but it can just as easily be applied to scalar (grayscale) images. In many cases, the input image is created from thresholding another image, often one which has been edge-filtered. This binary image is then operated on by a morphological operator and is either dilated or eroded by the operator. In this chapter, we will use morphology to enhance the edges used in the non-photorealistic rendering application discussed in "Non-Photorealistic Rendering." The image processing sample application on the companion CD and the non-photorealistic rendering sample application on the CD can both perform dilation on outline images.

The Definition of Dilation

Figure 8 illustrates a dilation operation. The image on the left is the original binary image. Each small cell in this figure represents one pixel. The small two-by-two black square in the center is the operator. The white square specifies which pixel is the origin of the operator—in this case, the top left pixel of the two-by-two operator.

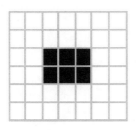

Original Binary Image

Operator

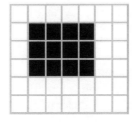

Dilated Binary Image

Figure 8: Dilation operation

To perform dilation of the original image, the operator is moved over the entire image. For every position of the operator, if any of the pixels of the operator cover a black pixel in the input image, then the pixel under the origin of the operator is set to black in the output image. This procedure results in the image on the right side of the figure where the black rectangle has been dilated up and to the left. The result of another dilation operation, with a 1×3 operator whose origin is centered vertically, is shown in Figure 9. Clearly, different dilation operators can enhance different features of an input image.

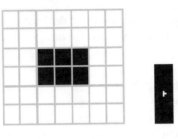 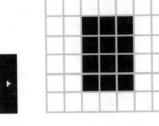

Figure 9: Dilation operation

| Original Binary Image | Operator | Dilated Binary Image |

A Dilation Shader

Once we have the binary input image, we apply the morphological operator in exactly the same way as the filters applied earlier, but the shader performs a different operation on the samples which lie under the kernel/operator. In the case of dilation, we use the cmp instruction to perform a threshold on the summation of the inverted samples. If the summation of the inverted samples exceeds a threshold, then part of the operator must cover some black pixels and we set the pixel to black. The source code for a 4-tap dilation operation is shown below:

Listing 5: Dilation shader

```
// Simple 4-tap dilation operator
ps.1.4
def c0, -0.2f, 1.0f, 0.0f, 0.0f
texld r0, t0              // Origin Tap
texld r1, t1
texld r2, t2
texld r3, t3

add r0, 1-r0, 1-r1        // Sum the inverted samples
add r0, r0, 1-r3
add r0, r0, 1-r2

add r0, r0, c0.r          // Subtract threshold
cmp r0, r0, c0.b, c0.g    // Set based on comparison with zero
```

Executing this shader on an image of object outlines thickens the outlines, as shown in Figure 10. Obviously, we could feed the dilated back through a dilation operation to thicken the lines further using a technique similar to the ping-pong blur in the image processing sample application on the companion CD. Application of dilation to non-photorealistic rendering is discussed further in "Non-Photorealistic Rendering."

Figure 10:- An edge image which has been dilated to thicken the edge lines

The Definition of Erosion

Where a dilation operation can "thicken" images, an erosion operation thins the structures present in an input binary image. This is often useful to clean up noise or thin down structures in an image for pattern recognition.

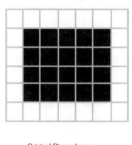 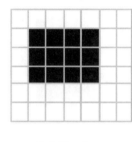

Figure 11: Erosion operation

Original Binary Image   Operator   Eroded Binary Image

An Erosion Shader

The erosion shader is very similar to the dilation shader. The 4-tap shader below applies a 2x2 box operator like the one shown in Figure 11. If any of the pixels under the box are white, then the pixel under the origin (upper left) is set to white.

Listing 6: Erosion shader

```
// Simple 4-tap erosion operator
ps.1.4
def c0, -0.05f, 1.0f, 0.0f, 0.0f
texld r0, t0              // Origin Tap
texld r1, t1              //
texld r2, t2              //
texld r3, t3              //

add r0, r0, r1            // Sum the samples
add r0, r0, r2
add r0, r0, r3

add r0, r0, c0.r          // Subtract threshold
cmp r0, r0, c0.g, c0.b    // If any pixels were white, set to white
```

Applying this operator to the original edge image, for example, thins down the lines and causes breaks in some places.

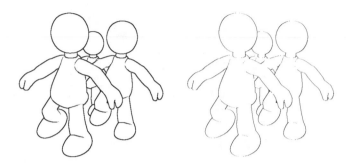

Figure 12: Original and eroded outlines

This erosion operator can also get rid of salt-and-pepper noise in a binary image. To illustrate this, we have added some small black areas (mostly smaller than 2x2 pixels) to the edge image and applied the erosion shader. The stray black pixels are all eliminated, and the original edges are thinned.

Figure 13: Noisy outline image, eroded noisy image, and opening of noisy image

Erosion can be followed by a dilation to eliminate salt-and-pepper noise while preserving larger structures in the input image. This is called the *opening* of the input image. Dilation followed by erosion is called the *closing* of the input image. Naturally, there is much more to mathematical morphology than just dilation and erosion, but these two operations form the building blocks of more advanced morphology techniques, including opening and closing.

Conclusion

We have provided an introduction to the concept of image processing in this chapter. This includes application of analytical and texture-based transfer functions, blurring and edge detection filters, and mathematical morphology. These filters have applications in data visualization, depth-of-field, non-photorealistic rendering, and general 3D frame post-processing. This chapter really only scratches the surface of image processing with pixel shaders but will hopefully serve as a reference for developers interested in post-processing their 3D scenes. For more on applying these filters to non-photorealistic rendering, see "Non-Photorealistic Rendering." For more on image processing in general, an excellent introduction to image processing concepts including those discussed here can be found in [Gonzalez92].

Hardware Support

At publication, only boards based on the ATI RADEON™ 8500 graphics processor support the 1.4 pixel shading model necessary to perform the image filters illustrated here. Any future hardware that supports the 1.4 pixel shader model or future pixel shader models such as ps.2.0 will be able to execute these shaders.

Sample Application

The DX81_ImageFilter sample on the companion CD illustrates image processing in Direct3D and implements all of the filtering examples shown here. Most of the shaders used require support for the 1.4 pixel shader model. Due to the simplicity of this application, it is reasonable to run this application on the reference rasterizer if you don't have a board that supports 1.4 pixel shaders. Rendered output images are also shown on the CD.

References

[Gonzalez92] Rafael C. Gonzalez and Richard E. Woods, *Digital Image Processing* (Addison-Wesley, 1992).

[James01] Greg James, "Operations for Hardware-Accelerated Procedural Texture Animation," *Game Programming Gems 2*, Mark DeLoura, Ed. (Charles River Media, 2001), pp. 497-509.

[Saito90] Takafumi Saito and Tokiichiro Takahashi, "Comprehensible Rendering of 3-D Shapes," SIGGRAPH Proceedings, 1990, pp. 197-206.

[Sobel90] Irvin Sobel, "An isotropic 3×3 image gradient operator," *Machine Vision for Three-Dimensional Scenes*, H. Freeman, Ed. (Academic Press, 1990), pp. 376-379.

Hallo World — Font Smoothing with Pixel Shaders

Steffen Bendel

Efficient programming is not tricky. A clear design is more important than the knowledge of special hacks. The shader described next is simple and demonstrates the main vertex shader principal. As the acronym T&L suggests, vertex shaders are built to transform and light a vertex. And much more is indeed not possible. All vertices are processed independent from each other and in the same way. Remember, modern CPUs have the same floating-point power as the vertex shader of current graphic cards. So, if some problems cannot be easily solved with the vertex shader, use the CPU. Examples of this include complex object construction like procedural trees or a view-dependent LOD.

An engine needs text output. To be independent from the OS, self-written routines are typically used. The standard way takes up three steps. First, print the text into a texture. Then upload the texture into video memory. Finally, render a quad with the text-texture. This allows full control, but if the texure is big, it will need a lot of texture memory and AGP-bandwidth for upload.

Because the theoretical triangle throughput is high enough, it is possible to render each char with an associated quad. If you do so, you save the cost of texture handling at the expense of vertex buffer upload. This can be an advantage in speed behavior or better handling.

Quads are often used in an engine. Different kinds of sprites are realized by it. In all these cases, they have the same characteristic. In principle, each quad is its own object, but rendering each quad with a single DirectX call is slow. Therefore, a vertex buffer is filled with data of many quads and rendered at once. This can be realized by triangle lists or indexed primitives. Index buffers are the best solution for most cases because they reduce the number of vertices used and increase the processing speed.

Since the index layout is the same for different quad buffers (quad 0: vertex 0-3, quad 1: vertex 4-7 ...), the index buffer can be reused. Some data, like quad corner position or texture coordinates, are equal for various buffers. To avoid double data in the buffers, it can be split into several vertex streams. One stream contains the generic data for all buffers, and the other has special values for each shader. In the samples in this book, the generic stream includes the corner position (0.0 or 1.0 for x, y coordinates) in register v0, indices for edge (0-3), and quad in register v1.

The char data and layout are in the second stream. It is identical for all vertices of a quad and must be duplicated in the C code. This cannot be done in the shader. The smallest data format that can be used is D3DVSDT_UBYTE4: two bytes for char position and two for the bitmap coordinates that select the char. The bitmap is organized in a 16*16 array. If one more byte of data is needed (for color selection), perhaps only the ASCII char must be transmitted by stream and the two bitmap indices can be calculated in the vertex shader. However, that is not as efficient as the preprocessing by CPU.

```
; v0        - 2d Position in quad
; v1.x      - vertex index in the quad
; v1.y      - current number of quad
; v2.xy     - char position
; v2.zw     - bitmap position for char
; c[0-3]    - transformation matrix (not transposed)
; c[4-7]    - bitmap : zw scaling, xy position-offset
; c[8-11]   - screen : zw scaling, xy position-offset

vs.1.1

; set index
mov a0.x, v1.x

; calculate bitmap position
mad oT0.xy, v2.zw, c[a0.x + 4].zw, c[a0.x + 4].xy

; calculate untransformed screen position
mad r0.xy, v2.xy, c[a0.x + 8].zw, c[a0.x + 8].xy

; transform from object to clip space
; (not complete matrix r0.z=0, r0.w=1)
mul r1, r0.xxxx, c0.xyzw
mad r1, r0.yyyy, c1.xyzw, r1.xyzw
add oPos, c3.xyzw, r1.xyzw
```

First in the shader, the corner index is set in the constant offset register. Then bitmap position is calculated. Both x and y indices are scaled by a factor and moved with an offset. The offset depends on which quad corner is currently used. Scaling factor is always the same, but in the vertex shader, only one constant can be used per instruction. So scaling and offset are combined in one register. The same is done for the char position. That is, the position is transformed to clip space. To reduce instruction count, an alternate form of matrix transformation is used instead of the typical construction with four dp4 commands. Here the matrix is not transposed. All lines of the matrix are multiplied separately with one coordinate of the vector, and the products are accumulated. Because the z-coordinate is explicit zero and the w-component is one, some calculations can be removed. The result is that one instruction slot is saved.

```
ps.1.0                ; Declare pixel shader version 1.0

tex    t0             ; Read texture

add r0.a, t0, c0      ; set and scale condition parameter
cnd r0, r0.a, c1, c2  ; set color dependend on condition
```

The pixel shader is not really interesting, but its functionality cannot be emulated by the old texture combiners in one rendering step. The alpha value of the bitmap is used to decide if font color or background color is drawn. Both colors are set as constants in the pixel shader. The alpha of the resulting color can be used for transparency. Before the compare is computed, the value is shifted. If the bitmap contains continuous alpha values instead of binary 0 or 1, the shift offset describes the boldness of the font. There is also another advantage, as smoothed alpha gives better interpolated data. The typical bilinear filtering artifacts are suppressed. Figure 1 shows a normal and a smoothed object. When it is interpolated and used in the shader above, you can see the result in Figure 2. Alpha values between 0.4 and 0.6 produce the best results.

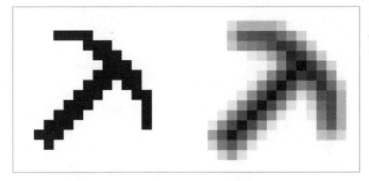

Figure 1: Normal (left) and smoothed object (right)

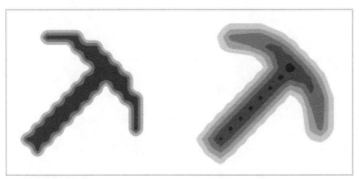

Figure 2: Contour lines for different values when interpolating Figure 1

Emulating Geometry with Shaders — Imposters

Steffen Bendel

The next shader demonstrates the ability to emulate geometry by pixel shader. Of course, real geometry details require a lot of triangles, but it must not be complex; it is sufficient if it looks complex. A digital picture consists of pixels. How it is created is not important and cannot be identified. A painted picture and a rendered image are the same in this manner. The difference is that a scene can be rendered from any view. The 3D data is easy to transform. To get more views for a non-3D object, they must be prepared and saved. That means a lot of memory consumption. It is a general rule that memory or CPU power can be reduced at the expense of the other.

Between the two extremes, there are some good compromises for special cases. Imposters are quads providing different views of the object. Before the age of real 3D graphics, this was the only way to draw complex objects in real time, but this allows no continuous turning. Previously, the quality was good enough relative to other algorithms (like drawing an object with ten untextured triangles). Now it is relatively bad because it scales bad with memory size. You need a lot of memory for the precomputed views to get a relatively smooth rotation. That memory is better used to increase the number of details in a triangle mesh. For general objects, imposters are only useful for "level of detail" if an object is far away and only a few pixels big.

A complete viewing description for an object is a five-dimensional array of ray-object intersection data. For every ray (three values for position and two for direction angles), the resulting color is saved. This array is too big for use. If the object is symmetric against transformation, the dimension number can be reduced by using alternate coordinates. These coordinates are computed from position and direction and have lower dimension. The body with the highest symmetry is the sphere. A point of the sphere rotated by origin is also on the sphere. The shape is the same, only texture coordinates must be transformed.

The presented algorithm calculates a textured and lighted sphere in the pixel shader. The sphere normal vector is used as alternate coordinate because it is easy to transform. Position and normal direction are equivalent and unique. These coordinates are computed by the first texture lookup. The bitmap contains normals that correlate to a front view. After that, the coordinates are transformed by matrix multiply to get a rotation. A cubemap lookup is done to get the color for the transformed sphere position.

The lighting is simple Gouraud shading with auxiliary ambient color. The dot product between normal vector and light vector is computed in the coordinates of the original normal vector.

Because texture values are always positive, the normal data must be compressed into the range [0.0, 1.0]. The _bx2 modifier expands it to [–1.0, 1.0].

The shape of the rendered quad is not a round. The alpha channel of the normal map contains data to mask the sphere. For quality improvement, it is smoothed as in the previous article.

Early versions of DirectX8 prohibited access to texture color if it was the source for a dependent texture read. This restriction was abolished in version 8.1.

```
; t0        - normal map
; t1,t2,t3 - bump matrix vectors
; t3       - cubemap

 ps.1.1                       ; Declare pixel shader version 1.1
; need DX8.1

 tex t0                       ; Read normal texture

 texm3x3pad t1, t0_bx2        ; transform normal vector and
 texm3x3pad t2, t0_bx2        ; look in cubemap
 texm3x3tex t3, t0_bx2        ;

 dp3_sat r0.rgb, t0_bx2, v0_bx2  ; scalar product for gouraud

 add r0.rgb, r0, c0           ; add ambient

 mul r0.rgb, r0, t3           ; mul light and color
+mov r0.a, t0.a               ; clip border
```

There are two input streams for the vertex shader, one containing general quad data (see previous article) and the other the position data for the sphere. This is the simple version; all spheres have the same radius and orientation. If the spheres differ here, the stream and shader must be extended.

The first part of the vertex shader performs typical billboard operations. The center position is transformed to view space, and then the corner scaled offset is added. Here the mad operation is used as mov for the z and w components by setting the product to zero. This saves one instruction, but a suitable constant setting in the registers is needed. The result is transformed to clip space and put into the output register.

Next, the matrix for the normal transformation in the pixel shader is computed. This is an approximation because perspective correction is not possible. The matrix is built of components of the eye vector. So if the sphere is rendered left on screen, you see more of the right side. The matrix vectors are normalized but not orthographic. At least, the vectors are transformed to world space. Normally, this is done by multiplying with the inverted view matrix, but in the shaders (pixel and vertex) the matrix must be transposed to realize a matrix multiply with the dot product operators. For orientation matrixes, inverting and transposing are equivalent operations. So all this can be done by multiplying with the view matrix: transpose(m*invert(view)) = transpose(m*transpose(view)) = m*view. If every sphere should have its own orientation, the resulting matrix needs to be transformed by an orientation matrix (not implemented in the example).

The light position is given in view space. In the shader, the object light vector is computed, normalized, and scaled by distance-dependent intensity. It is scaled into the range [0.0, 1.0] to pass through the vertex color register. Texture coordinates are 0.0 or 1.0 for each component. They are calculated by resizing the quad coordinates (−1.0 or 1.0).

```
;   oPos    -- the vertex's clip-space coordinates
;   oT0     -- the vertex's uv-coordinates
;   oD0     -- the light vector
;
;   v0      -- relative quad position
;   v1      -- quad indices
;   v2      -- position of billboard center

;   c0-c3   -- contains matrix to transform to view space
;   c4-c7   -- contains matrix to transform pespective
;   c8      -- 0.0, 0.5, 1.0, -1.0 constant
;   c9      -- radius, -radius, 0.0, 0.0
;   c10     -- light position in view space

; Declare vertex shader version 1.1
vs.1.1

; Transform to view coordinates
dp4 r0.x, v2, c0
dp4 r0.y, v2, c1
dp4 r0.z, v2, c2
dp4 r0.w, v2, c3

; perform billboard operation r1.xy = v0.xy + r0.xy and r1.zw = r0.zw
mad r1.xyzw, c9.xyzz, v0.xyzw, r0.xyzw

; Perform perspective transformation
dp4 oPos.x, r1, c4
dp4 oPos.y, r1, c5
dp4 oPos.z, r1, c6
dp4 oPos.w, r1, c7

; create bump matrix vector1 dependent an view position,
; r7.x = r0.z   r7.y = 0.0    r7.z = r0.x
mul r7.xyz, r0.zyx, c8.zxx

;normalize vector1
dp3 r1, r7, r7
rsq r1, r1
mul r7.xyz, r7.xyz, r1.xyz

; create bump matrix vector2 dependent an view position
; r8.x = 0.0    r8.y = r0.z   r8.z = r0.y
mul r8.xyz, r0.xzy, c8.xzz

;normalize vector2
dp3 r1, r8, r8
rsq r1, r1
mul r8.xyz, r8.xyz, r1.xyz

; create bump matrix vector3 dependent an view position
; r9.x = -r0.x   r9.y = -r0.y   r9.z = r0.z
mul r9.xyz, r0.xyz, c8.wwz

;normalize vector3
dp3 r1, r9, r9
rsq r1, r1
mul r9.xyz, r9.xyz, r1.xyz

; Put transform the bump mapping matrix with view and put in  T1, T2 and T3
dp3 oT1.x, r7, c0
dp3 oT1.y, r7, c1
```

```
dp3 oT1.z, r7, c2

dp3 oT2.x, r8, c0
dp3 oT2.y, r8, c1
dp3 oT2.z, r8, c2

dp3 oT3.x, r9, c0
dp3 oT3.y, r9, c1
dp3 oT3.z, r9, c2

; calculate light1 vector
sub r1, c10, r0

; resize by distance dependency
dp3 r2, r1, r1
rcp r2, r2
mul r1, r1, r2

; Shift the light vector and put in D0
mad oD0, r1, c8.yyyy, c8.yyyy

; Output texture coordinates
mad oT0.xy, v0.xy, c8.yy, c8.yy
```

The following figure demonstrates the pixel and vertex shaders discussed in this article.

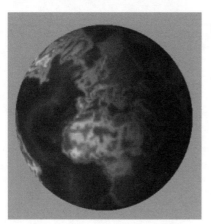

Figure 1

Smooth Lighting with ps.1.4

Steffen Bendel

Vertex lighting uses linear approximation between the vertices and causes visible artifacs. Exact lighting needs calculation per-pixel. This is the way of the future, but not all necessary operations can be calculated in the pixel shader, or they are too slow for current hardware.

This article describes how to create better lighting on a per-pixel basis. Only the light intensity calculation is discussed here. The material color is ignored in this rendering step.

What are the main components determining the brightness? The distance to the light source is one factor. If the object is farther away, it looks darker. The physical correct equation for a sphere light is proportional to the reciprocal of the squared distance (Figure 1). This function falls off too fast. Computer graphics have a smaller color representation range than the human eye can observe. If using the real equation, most scene parts are too dark or have maximum light intensity that can be represented. A more linear function, as in Figure 2, is a better solution for some cases.

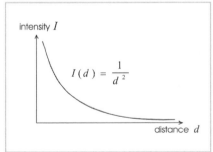

Figure 1

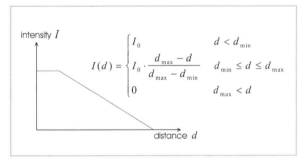

Figure 2

Because such operations are not possible in the pixel shader, a lookup table is required. All functions can be represented in this way. The distance dependency is a one-dimensional function, but the distance cannot be iterated or calculated in the pixel shader. A volume texture lookup is the easiest solution. The light vector is scaled and the result is used as coordinates for the texture that contains the distance function.

Another factor is the angle between normal vector, eye vector, and light vector. The reflected eye vector is often used instead of the original eye. Take a look at Figure 3 for notation.

277

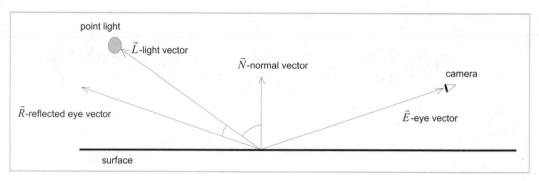

Figure 3

How are the vectors that are necessary for the lighting calculated? The normal vector is given by texture map (bump mapping). The light and eye vector are calculated in the vertex shader and transformed to the space of the normal map. If no world coordinates are needed in the pixel shader, a matrix transformation is avoided. The vectors are interated perspectively correct. They are normalized by cubemap lookups. Sometimes the precision (around 1% for an 8-bit per channel texture) is not enough because specular highlighting is very sensitive. A rough bump map can hide this problem.

The reflect eye vector is given by:

$$\vec{R} = \vec{E} - 2\vec{N}(\vec{N} \cdot \vec{E}) \qquad \vec{N}, \vec{N} \text{ are normalized}$$

In general, the intensity equation is separated into two parts, one for   and one for β.

$$I(\alpha, \beta) = I_{Diffuse}(\alpha) + I_{Specular}(\beta)$$

The diffuse α component is view independent. A typical function is $I_{Diffuse} = k_{Diffuse} \cos(\alpha)$. That is equal to the dot product between the normalized light and the normal vector. If the material is a mirror, this component vanishes. The specular highlight is decribed by β. This is an approximation for reflection and micro roughness of the surface. If the object is polished, the highlight is small and bright. A rough surface has a smooth highlight with low intensity. This is described by $I_{Specular} = k_{Specular} \cdot \cos(\beta)^n$. Metallic surfaces have values $n \approx 100$ for the exponent. The example uses a lookup table for the exponential function. The distance dependence is also encoded in this texture. Theoretically, this isn't urgent since both components are linearly independent and the result is a simple product. But texture values have a limited range. If one calculates with that, it comes to numeric inaccuracies. A combined texture for both values avoids the problems.

The same is done for the diffuse part. It is calculated by the multiplication of distance intensity and the dot product between $\vec{N}$ and $\vec{L}$ in a simpler variant. If the light source is near the surfaces, the normal vector changes strongly. As a result, the object looks too dark because the dot product is small and cannot be compensated for intensity. Here, a correction for small distances is precalculated in the lookup table.

There are a lot of improvements that are not included in the example, such as the lightsource has no color, the alpha channel of the bump map could contain a specular coefficient, and a spotlight or shadow map can be used instead of one of the lookup tables.

Pixel shader:

```
ps.1.4

texld r0, t0                        ; normal map N
texld r1, t1                        ; cubic normalization for light vector L
texld r2, t2                        ; cubic normalization for eye vector E
texld r3, t3                        ; volume table lookup for distance

dp3 r4, r0_bx2, r2_bx2              ; N*E
mad r4.rgb, r0_bx2, -r4_x2, r2_bx2  ; -N(2*N*E)+E

dp3_sat r5.xyz, r1_bx2, r4          ; L*Reflectted E
mov     r5.y, r3.r                  ; set distant value

dp3_sat r4.xyz, r1_bx2, r0_bx2      ; diffuse shading N*L
mov     r4.y, r3.r                  ; set distant value

phase

texld r4, r4                        ; table lookup for diffuse and distance
texld r5, r5                        ; table lookup for specular and distance

add r0, r4, r5                      ; add diffuse and specular
```

Vertex shader:

```
; v0        - 3d Position in quad
; v1-3      - face orientation matrix, v2 is normal
; v4        - bumpmap coordinates

; c[0-3]    - object to clip space matrix
; c4        - light position in object space
; c5        - camera position in object space
; c6.x      - inverse light range
; c6.y      - 0.5

vs.1.1
; calculate position for draw
dp4 oPos.x, v0, c0
dp4 oPos.y, v0, c1
dp4 oPos.z, v0, c2
dp4 oPos.w, v0, c3

; set bumpmap
mov oT0, v4

; calculate light vector in object space
sub r0.xyz, c4, v0

; transform light vector to object(normal) space
dp3 oT1.x, r0, v1
dp3 oT1.y, r0, v2
dp3 oT1.z, r0, v3

; set coordunates for distance lookup
mad oT3.xyz, r0, c6.xxx, c6.yyy

; calculate eye vector in object space
sub r1.xyz, v0, c5

; transform eye vector to object(normal) space
```

```
dp3 oT2.x, r1, v1
dp3 oT2.y, r1, v2
dp3 oT2.z, r1, v3
```

The following figure is an example using the pixel and vertex shaders in this article.

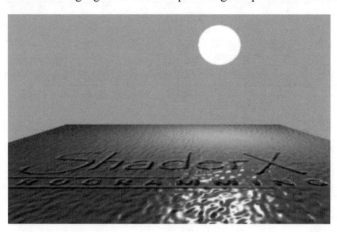

Figure 4

Per-Pixel Fresnel Term

Chris Brennan

Introduction

Common real-time environment mapping reflection techniques reflect the same amount of light no matter how the surface is oriented relative to the viewer, much like a mirror or chrome. Many real materials, such as water, skin, plastic, and ceramics, do not behave in this way. Due to their unique physical properties, these materials appear to be much more reflective edge-on than they are when viewed head-on. The change in reflectance as a function of the viewing angle is called the Fresnel effect, and the term in our lighting equation that we use to approximate this is called the Fresnel term.

Use of a Fresnel term can be somewhat subtle, but it is fundamental to photorealistic rendering of many materials, especially water. While this has been used as a per-vertex quantity in [Ts'o87] and [Vlachos00], we will show how to compute a per-pixel Fresnel term using 1.4 pixel shaders. In addition to photorealistic effects, we will show how this term can be used to generate some supernatural or just plain fun results as well.

In this chapter, we use a per-pixel Fresnel term in conjunction with cubic environment-mapped bump mapping. This is not a requirement, but it is a good illustrative example because a normal and reflection terms are readily available to experiment with.

Fresnel Effects

The Fresnel term is calculated with a simple dot product between the per-pixel normal N and a normalized eye vector E. The result of the dot product, $N \cdot E$, is then used as a parameter to a function, $F(x)$, to get a reflection intensity as seen in Figure 1, which uses an approximate Fresnel term of $F(x) = (1-x)^2$.

Figure 1: The Fresnel term, $(1-N \cdot E)^2$, which will be used as the intensity of the reflections

281

The following example shows the look of the ceramic statue with and without the Fresnel effect modulated into the reflection map:

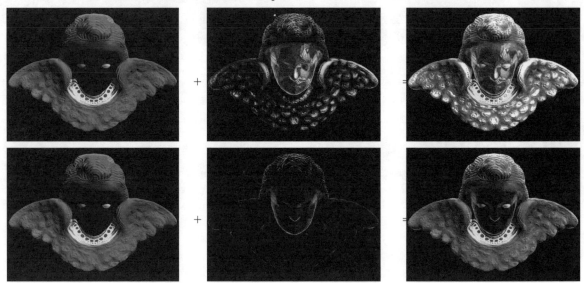

Figure 2: Diffuse + Reflections = final result with (bottom) and without (top) the Fresnel term

Some other effects can be achieved by using a Fresnel term in ways other than reflectance. In the following example, the Fresnel term is used as a transparency term. N·E is used in a dependent texture read to make F(x) completely arbitrary. This allows transparency to be soft along the silhouette edges of the skull, opaque just inside, and then transparent again when viewed straight on. When used with additive alpha blending, this gives a ghostly membrane effect similar to the alien creatures in the film *Final Fantasy: The Spirits Within*. Viewing F(x) = 1– N·E directly yields an effect that looks like an electron micrograph.

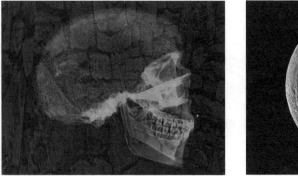
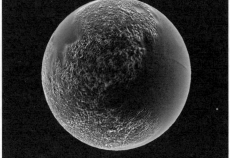

Figure 3: Ghostly effect and electron micrograph effect

Effect Code

```
matrix mW;        // World matrix
matrix mWVP;      // World*View*Projection matrix
matrix mWrt;      // Inverse Transpose World Rotation matrix
matrix mWVt;      // Inverse Transpose World*View matrix
vector pOV;       // Object space viewer position
vector cnst;
vector cHlf;

texture tBase;
texture tGloss;
texture tCube;
texture tDiffuseCube;
texture tNormal;
texture tNormalizer;

DWord dwCubeMipFilter = 2; // None = 0, Point = 1, Linear = 2

vertexshader vTexTangentmatrixViewLight =
    decl
    {
        stream 0;
        float     v0[3];  // Position
        D3DCOLOR v3;      // Normal
        float     v7[2];  // Tex coord 0
        D3DCOLOR v8;      // Binormal
        D3DCOLOR v9;      // Tangent
    }
    asm
    {
    ; Sample vertex shader which outputs a 3x3 orthogonal transform which
    ; takes you from world space to tangent space.  The result is stored in
    ; output tex coords 1,2,and 3. Tex coord 4 stores a view vector which
    ; can be used in a reflect operation.
    ;
    ; Tex coordinate 5 stores a scaled version of the centroid to vertex
    ; vector that is used as a correction factor for environment mapping.
    ;
    ; This sample expects the incoming vertex data to be set up as follows:
    ;
    ; v0     - Vertex Position
    ; v3     - Vertex Normal
    ; v7     - Vertex 2D Bumpmap Texture Coords
    ; v8     - Vertex Tangent (normalized assumed to be positive v direction for
    ;          tangent space)
    ; v9     - Vertex Tangent (normalized assumed to be positive u direction for
    ;          tangent space)
    ; This sample expects the constant store to be set up in the following manner:
    ;
    ; c1        - Color of material
    ; c12..c15 - World Matrix
    ; c16..c19 - Composite World-View-Projection Matrix
    ; c20..c23 - Env Transform Matrix   (object to world or view coord transform
    ;            (depends on type of env mapping you want to do) )
    ; c28       - ModelSpace Camera Position
    ; c95       - 0, .5, 1, 2
    vs.1.0
    def c94, 0.1f, 0.33f, 0.20f, 0.18f  ; Scalar for cube map adjustment
                                        ; = roughly 1/Radius of environment map.
```

```
        ; OutPos = ObjSpacePos * Composite World-View-Projection Matrix
        m4x4   oPos, v0, c16
        mov    oT0.xy, v7        ; passthrough texcoord 0 for bump map addressing

        ;derive per vertex eye vector using camera position
        add    r8, c28, -v0     ; view direction
        m3x3   r9, r8, c20      ; transform view vector from object space to env space
        dp3    r11.x, r9, r9    ; magnitude^2
        rsq    r11.y, r11.x     ; 1/mag
        mul    oT4.xyz, r9, r11.y ; normalize

        ;Expand from compressed D3DCOLOR to -1 to 1 range.
        mad  r3, v3, c95.wwwz, -c95.zzzx ; Normal = (v3*2.0)-1.0
        mad  r7, v8, c95.wwwz, -c95.zzzx ; TangentU = (v8*2.0)-1.0
        mad  r8, v9, c95.wwwz, -c95.zzzx ; TangentV = (v9*2.0)-1.0

        ; upper 3x3 of world matrix by upper tangent space transposed
        dp3    oT1.x, c20, r7
        dp3    oT1.y, c20, r8
        dp3    oT1.z, c20, r3

        dp3    oT2.x, c21, r7
        dp3    oT2.y, c21, r8
        dp3    oT2.z, c21, r3

        dp3    oT3.x, c22, r7
        dp3    oT3.y, c22, r8
        dp3    oT3.z, c22, r3

        ; Calculate adjustment amount to account for cube map center not being at this
           object's centroid.
        m3x3 r0, v0, c12
        mul oT5, r0, c94.w
        };

pixelshader ps14_Cube_Bump_Diff_Fresnel_Reflect = asm
{
    ps.1.4

    texld  r0, t0               ; Look up normal map.
    texld  r1, t4               ; Eye vector through normalizer cube map
    texcrd r4.rgb, t1           ; 1st row of environment matrix
    texcrd r2.rgb, t2           ; 2st row of environment matrix
    texcrd r3.rgb, t3           ; 3rd row of environment matrix
    texcrd r5.rgb, t5           ; Cube map position adjustment

    dp3    r4.r, r4, r0_bx2        ; 1st row of matrix multiply
    dp3    r4.g, r2, r0_bx2        ; 2nd row of matrix multiply
    dp3    r4.b, r3, r0_bx2        ; 3rd row of matrix multiply
    dp3    r0.rgb, r4, r1_bx2      ; (N.Eye)
    mad    r3.rgb, r4_x2, r0, r5   ; 2N(N.Eye) + adjustment for pos not being at
                                     center of cube map
    dp3    r2.rgb, r4, r4          ; N.N
    mad    r2.rgb, -r1_bx2, r2, r3 ; 2N(N.Eye) - Eye(N.N)
    mov_sat r0.rgb, 1-r0          ; Pass through 1-(N.Eye) for fresnal
                                     calculation

    phase

    ; texcrd r0, r0              ; N.Eye used for fresnel calculation
    texld  r2, r2               ; Sample cubic reflection map
    texld  r3, t0               ; Sample base map
    texld  r4, r4               ; Sample cubic diffuse map
    texld  r5, t0               ; Sample gloss map
```

```
    mul     r1.rgb, r5, r2          ; Specular = Gloss*Reflection
    +mul    r0.a, r0.b, r0.b        ; ^2
    mul     r0.rgb, r1, r0.b        ; Specular * Fresnel
    mad     r0.rgb, r3, r4_x2, r0   ; Base*Diffuse + Specular
};

technique ps14_Cube_Bump_Diff_Fresnel_Reflect
{
    pass P0
    {
        VertexShaderConstant[12] = <mW>;    // World
        VertexShaderConstant[16] = <mWVP>;  // World*View*Proj Matrix
        VertexShaderConstant[20] = <mWrt>;  // World Rotation Inv Transpose used
                                            // for Eye vector transform
        VertexShaderConstant[28] = <pOV>;   // Object space Viewer position
        VertexShaderConstant[95] = <cnst>;
        VertexShader = <vTexTangentmatrixViewLight>;

        Texture[0]    = <tNormal>;
        MagFilter[0] = Linear;
        MinFilter[0] = Linear;
        MipFilter[0] = Linear;

        Texture[1]    = <tNormalizer>;
        AddressU[1] = Clamp;
        AddressV[1] = Clamp;
        MagFilter[1] = Linear;
        MinFilter[1] = Linear;
        MipFilter[1] = Point;

        Texture[2]    = <tCube>;
        AddressU[2] = Clamp;
        AddressV[2] = Clamp;
        MagFilter[2] = Linear;
        MinFilter[2] = Linear;
        MipFilter[2] = <dwCubeMipFilter>;

        Texture[3]    = <tBase>;
        AddressU[3] = Wrap;
        AddressV[3] = Wrap;
        MagFilter[3] = Linear;
        MinFilter[3] = Linear;
        MipFilter[2] = Linear;

        Texture[4]    = <tDiffuseCube>;
        AddressU[4] = Clamp;
        AddressV[4] = Clamp;
        MagFilter[4] = Linear;
        MinFilter[4] = Linear;
        MipFilter[4] = <dwCubeMipFilter>;

        Texture[5]    = <tGloss>;
        AddressU[5] = Wrap;
        AddressV[5] = Wrap;
        MagFilter[5] = Linear;
        MinFilter[5] = Linear;
        MipFilter[5] = Linear;

        PixelShader  = <ps14_Cube_Bump_Diff_Fresnel_Reflect>;
    }
}
```

This technique, including shaders and source code, is used in the Treasure Chest demo available on the companion CD and also at http://www.ati.com/na/pages/resource_centre/dev_rel/Treasurechest.html. There are menus that can be accessed after going to windowed mode by pressing Alt+Enter.

References

[Ts'o87] Pauline Ts'o and Brian Barsky, "Modeling and Rendering Waves: Wave Tracing Using Beta-Splines and Reflective and Refractive Texture Mapping," *ACM Transactions on Graphics* (6) 1987, pp. 191-214.

[Vlachos00] Alex Vlachos and Jason L. Mitchell, "Refraction Mapping for Liquids in Containers," *Game Programming Gems*, Mark DeLoura, Ed. (Charles River Media, 2000).

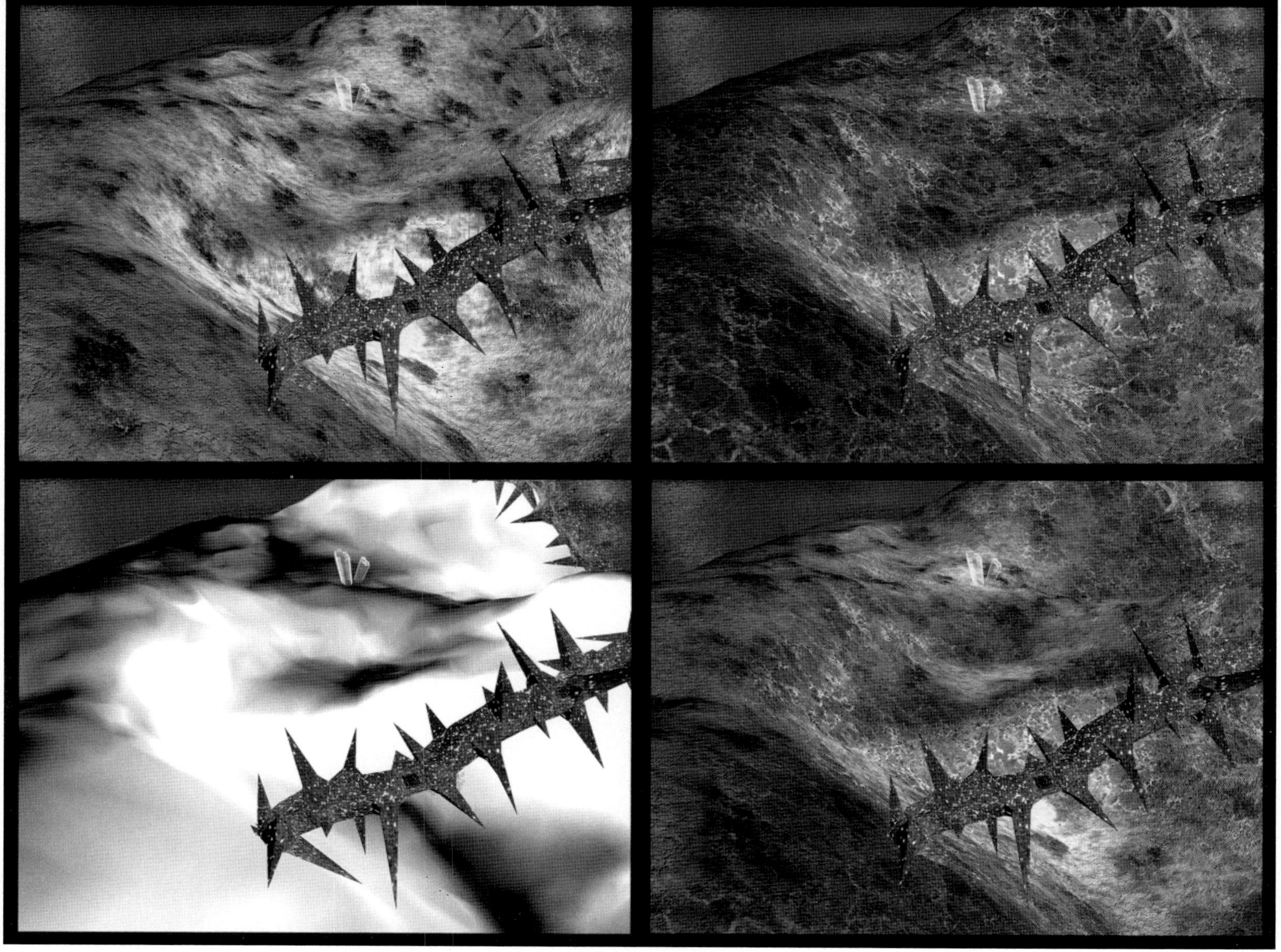

Color Plate 1

(a) Original Image

(b) Luminance Filter

(c) Heat Signature

(d) Sepia Tone

Color Plate 2

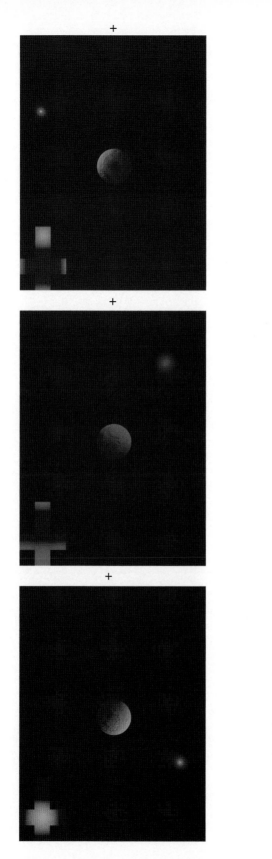

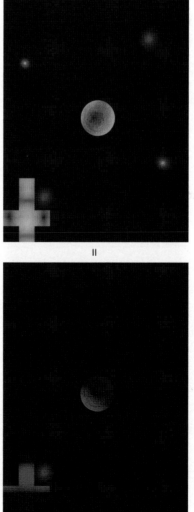

Color Plate 3

Color Plate 4

(a)

(b)

(c)

(d)

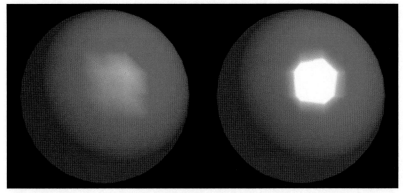

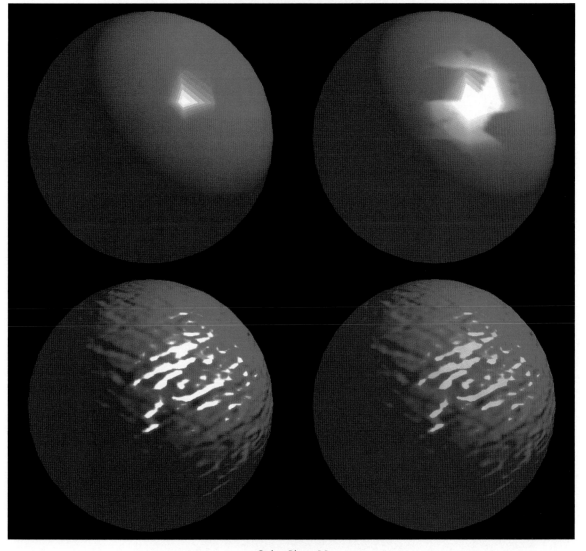

Color Plate 11

Color Plate 12

Diffuse Cube Mapping

Chris Brennan

Introduction

Cube mapping has become a common environment mapping technique for reflective objects. Typically, a reflection vector is calculated either per-vertex or per-pixel and is then used to index into a cube map that contains a picture of the world surrounding the object being drawn. To date, cube maps have been used primarily for specular effects that are layered on top of per-vertex diffuse lighting or static diffuse light maps. In this chapter, we present diffuse cube maps, which happen to come nearly for free when performing specular or environment mapping with a cube map. The main advantage of diffuse cube mapping is that an unlimited number of lights may be included in a single rendering pass. Diffuse cube maps can also be generated from light probes [Debevec98] acquired from a real environment to provide a diffuse or ambient term to really "place" an object in a scene.

Using Diffuse Cube Maps

Diffuse cube maps are different in usage from reflection maps only in that the surface normal is used to index into the map with the intention that it returns the total amount of light scattered from that direction. The reason it is free to use diffuse cube maps when using reflections is that a normal is required for doing the reflection operation given the normal (N) and eye vector (E):

$$R = 2N(N \cdot E) + E$$

or if the normal is not of unit length:

$$R = 2N(N \cdot E) + E(N \cdot N)$$

Even the unnormalized normal may be used in diffuse cube mapping without any additional pixel or vertex operations. The following is an example of per-pixel environment mapped bump mapping with the diffuse component added in bold:

```
ps.1.4
def c0, 1,1,1,1

texld   r0, t0              ; Look up normal map.
texcrd  r1.xyz, t4          ; Eye vector
texcrd  r4.xyz, t1          ; 1st row of environment matrix
texcrd  r2.xyz, t2          ; 2st row of environment matrix
texcrd  r3.xyz, t3          ; 3rd row of environment matrix
```

```
dp3      r4.x, r4, r0_bx2        ; N.x = 1st row of matrix multiply
dp3      r4.y, r2, r0_bx2        ; N.y = 2nd row of matrix multiply
dp3      r4.z, r3, r0_bx2        ; N.z = 3rd row of matrix multiply
dp3_x2   r3.xyz, r4, r1          ; 2(N.Eye)
mul      r3.xyz, r4, r3          ; 2N(N.Eye)
dp3      r2.xyz, r4, r4          ; N.N
mad      r2.xyz, -r1, r2, r3     ; 2N(N.Eye) - Eye(N.N)

phase

texld    r2, r2                  ; Sample cubic reflection map
texld    r3, t0                  ; Sample base map with gloss in alpha
texld    r4, r4                  ; Sample cubic diffuse map

mul      r1.rgb, r3.a, r2        ; Specular = Gloss*Reflection
mad      r0.rgb, r3, r4, r1      ; Base*Diffuse + Specular
+mov     r0.a, c0.a              ; Put 1.0 in alpha
```

The normal is calculated by looking up a normal map. However, the normal is in tangent space, which needs to be transformed into world space through a matrix multiply of the concatenation of the texture tangent matrix and the world matrix and stored in r4, which is used when sampling the diffuse map in the next phase. So with the addition of only one texture fetch and one instruction, an arbitrarily complex diffuse lighting component can be added.

Generating Dynamic Diffuse Cube Maps

The idea is that a cube map is generated dynamically every frame in the same way that a reflection cube map is generated, but instead of drawing actual world geometry from the point of view of the object into the six faces, a diffusely lit hemisphere around the object is accumulated into the cube map for each light. The following figure shows the corresponding diffuse and reflection maps for one light.

Figure 1: Diffuse cube map (right) and reflection cube map (left) for one light

So for four lights, the process would be to clear the cube map to the ambient color, and then for each light, add in its light component as shown below and in Color Plate 3.

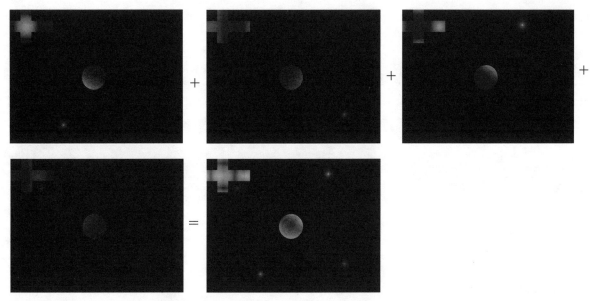

Figure 2: The accumulation of lights when generating a diffuse cube map

The resulting cube map can then be used to account for all light in the scene with one texture lookup. Generally, the cube maps do not need to be very large. 32x32 for each face is sufficient for not having any artifacts. Therefore, the cost of rendering a large number of lights into a cube map is much less than rendering many light passes per object when rendering the final image. This property makes diffuse cube mapping a logical choice when an object can be contained in an environment map and the lighting is complex or a reflection environment map is already being used.

This technique is used in the Treasure Chest demo available on the companion CD included in this book and also at http://www.ati.com/na/pages/resource_center/dev_rel/Treasurechest.html. There are menus to view the diffuse cube map that can be accessed after going to windowed mode by pressing Alt+Enter.

References

[Debevec98] Paul E. Debevec, "Rendering Synthetic Objects into Real Scenes: Bridging Traditional and Image-Based Graphics with Global Illumination and High Dynamic Range Photography," (SIGGRAPH Proceedings, July 1998).

Accurate Reflections and Refractions by Adjusting for Object Distance

Chris Brennan

Introduction

Environment mapping is a technique by which a texture map or maps contain the view of the environment from a particular point. The texture map is then addressed using a function of a reflection or refraction vector when rendering an object. There are several forms of environment mapping: spherical, dual paraboloid, and cubic, to name a few. They are all basically the same concept, differing only in what function is used to create and address the map. Cubic environment mapping is a method of sampling a texture consisting of six renderings of the world from the center of a cube out through each of its faces. The texture is addressed with a vector that indicates the direction from the center of the cube to the sample point on one of its faces. Therefore, a calculated reflection vector can be directly used as an address into the environment map. Because of these simple properties, cube maps lend themselves to dynamic real-time creation and addressing within pixel shaders. The following artifacts apply to all environment mapping, but this example is applied to cubic environment maps.

The Artifacts of Environment Mapping

One of the common problems seen when environment mapping is that flat surfaces do not render well. There is very little variation in the reflection vector direction itself, and because environment maps are indexed from the exact center, it does not take into account that a reflection vector can be originated off-center and therefore end up reflecting a different object. This deficiency would make a flat mirror appear to reflect all the same point. The result is that only a few texels are magnified and used in the final image. This artifact is worse the closer that reflected objects are relative to the viewer. The same artifact appears when using a refraction vector as opposed to a reflection vector, but it is more obvious where the transparent object meets the object behind. See Figure 1 for an example of the artifact as seen through a window using a refraction vector. Notice how the part of the chest seen through the window does not properly match the chest itself.

Figure 1: This example shows a windowpane with environment map artifacts that produce incorrect looking transparency.

Environment mapping based solely on the reflection vector direction acts as if the objects in the environment map are infinitely far away. *Advanced RenderMan* [Apodaca00] describes a way to alleviate this by adjusting the use of the environment map such that it has a finite radius that is close to the real proximity of the objects. The most precise way to do this is by intersecting the reflection or refraction ray with the environment map sphere and then using the vector from the center of the map to the intersection point (*CI*) to index the map. See Figure 2.

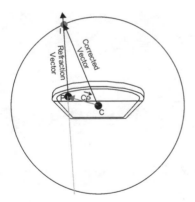 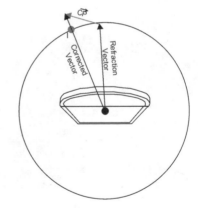

Figure 2: Corrected vector based on an intersection with a finite radius

Figure 3: Corrected vector adjusted by a vector based on the point's distance from center

Calculating the intersection of a circle and a vector is difficult in a pixel shader, but another approximation of the same goal can be achieved by adding a scaled version of the vector from the center point of the environment map to the point on the object being drawn (*CP*). Figure 3shows how the approximate corrected version of the vector intersects the same point *I* on the environment map. The scaling factor is 1/(environment map radius) and is derived from:

$$\vec{R'} = \vec{R} \cdot Radius + \overrightarrow{CP}$$

which when divided by the environment map radius changes to:

$$\vec{R''} = \vec{R} + \frac{\overrightarrow{CP}}{Radius}$$

The total correction factor of *CP*/*Radius* can be calculated in the vertex shader and interpolated for adding in after the per-pixel reflection calculation. The following figure illustrates the amount of correction applied.

Figure 4: The magnitude of the correction vector displayed as grayscale intensity.

The corrected version of Figure 1 is shown in Figure 5:

Figure 5: The adjusted version of the refraction vector shows the geometry behind at the correct scale at all viewing distances.

Notice how the refracted image now matches the geometry behind it. The correction can be applied per-pixel as seen in Figure 6 and Color Plate 4.

Figure 6: Stained glass color plate

The composite effect was rendered with the following shader:

```
; Sample vertex shader which outputs a 3x3 orthogonal transform which
; takes you from world space to tangent space.  The result is stored in
; output tex coords 1,2,and 3. Tex coord 4 stores a view vector which
; can be used in a reflect operation.
;
; Tex coordinate 5 stores a scaled version of the centroid to vertex
; vector that is used as a correction factor for environment mapping.
;
; This sample expects the incoming vertex data to be set up as follows:
;
; v0     - Vertex Position
; v3     - Vertex Normal
; v8     - Vertex Tangent U
; v9     - Vertex Tangent V
; This sample expects the constant store to be set up in the following manner:
;
; c1        - Color of material
; c12..c15 - World Matrix
; c16..c19 - Composite World-View-Projection Matrix
; c20..c23 - Env Transform Matrix  (object to world or view coord transform
;            (depends on type of env mapping you want to do) )
; c28       - ModelSpace Camera Position
; c95       - 0, .5, 1, 2
vs.1.0
def c94, 0.18f, 0.18f, 0.18f, 0.18f  ; Scalar for cube map adjustment
                                     ; = roughly 1/Radius of environment map.

; OutPos = ObjSpacePos * Composite World-View-Projection Matrix
m4x4    oPos, v0, c16
mov     oT0.xy, v7            ; passthrough texcoord 0 for bump map addressing

;derive per vertex eye vector using camera position
add     r8, c28, -v0         ; view direction
m3x3    r9, r8, c20          ; transform view vector from object space to env space
dp3     r11.x, r9, r9        ; magnitude^2
rsq     r11.y, r11.x         ; 1/mag
mul     oT4.xyz, r9, r11.y ; normalize

; upper 3x3 of world matrix by upper tangent space transposed
dp3     oT1.x, c20, v8
dp3     oT1.y, c20, v9
dp3     oT1.z, c20, v3

dp3     oT2.x, c21, v8
dp3     oT2.y, c21, v9
dp3     oT2.z, c21, v3

dp3     oT3.x, c22, v8
dp3     oT3.y, c22, v9
dp3     oT3.z, c22, v3

; Calculate an adjustment amount to account for cube map center not
; being at this object's center.
m3x3 r0, v0, c12     ; Object->World space position without translation.
mul  oT5, r0, c94.w ; Scale by 1/appoximate scene size

ps.1.4

def     c0, 0.9f, 0.0f, 0.0f, 0.0f
texld   r0, t0               ; Look up normal map.
texcrd  r1.rgb, t4           ; Eye vector
texcrd  r4.rgb, t1           ; t row of environment matrix
```

```
texcrd   r2.rgb, t2              ; 21sst row of environment matrix
texcrd   r3.rgb, t3              ; 3rd row of environment matrix
texcrd   r5.rgb, t5              ; Cube map position adjustment

dp3      r4.r, r4, r0_bx2        ; 1st row of matrix multiply
dp3      r4.g, r2, r0_bx2        ; 2nd row of matrix multiply
dp3      r4.b, r3, r0_bx2        ; 3rd row of matrix multiply
lrp      r2.rgb, c0.r, -r1, -r4  ; Refract by c0 = index of refraction fudge factor
add      r2.rgb, r5, r2          ; Adjust for cube map center
phase

texld    r2, r2                  ; Sample cubic reflection map
texld    r3, t0                  ; Sample base map
texld    r4, r4                  ; Sample cubic diffuse map
texld    r5, t0                  ; Sample gloss map

mul      r1.rgb, r5, r2          ; Specular = Gloss*Reflection
mad      r0.rgb, r3, r4_x2, r1   ; Base*Diffuse + Specular
+mov     r0.a, r3
```

The bold lines of the shader are the required lines for the environment map adjustment. This technique makes reflections look more accurate, but it also makes refraction possible because the eye is much more sensitive to the inaccuracies of refraction. This technique, including shaders and source code, is used in the Treasure Chest demo available on the companion CD and also at http://www. ati.com/na/pages/resource_centre/dev_rel/Treasurechest.html. There are menus to view the reflection cube map that can be accessed after going to windowed mode by pressing Alt+Enter.

References

[Apodaca00] Anthony A. Apodaca and Larry Gritz, *Advanced RenderMan* (Morgan Kaufmann Publishers, 1999), pp. 212-215.

UV Flipping Technique to Avoid Repetition

Alex Vlachos

A common problem exists among many shaders that rely on scrolling two copies of the same texture in slightly different directions. No matter what angle or speed the textures are scrolling, they will eventually line up exactly and cause a visual hiccup. This scrolling technique is commonly used to gain the effect of having random patterns, like water caustics. With caustics, the pattern appears to stop every once in a while even though it is scrolling at a constant speed.

This was also encountered when implementing the Ocean Water and Reflective and Refractive Water shaders when we scrolled two copies of the same bump map in opposite directions to produce high frequency waves (see "Rendering Ocean Water" and "Rippling Refractive and Reflective Water" later in this book). The method we used to solve this problem is to compute the two sets of texture coordinates like you normally would. Then immediately before using those texture coordinates to fetch from textures, choose one of the sets of texture coordinates and swap the U and V. This will effectively flip the texture along the diagonal.

Using this method, the intermittent hiccup that appears due to the two copies being perfectly aligned is now impossible since one of the textures is reflected about the diagonal of the texture.

Photorealistic Faces with Vertex and Pixel Shaders

Kenneth L. Hurley

Introduction

Achieving photorealistic faces in games has always been a goal of game developers. Today's DX8-compatible hardware allows the game programmer to use lots of polygons for characters. The developer can now use facial animation and facial shading as an important feature in today's games. This article introduces the reader to a technique using bump mapping and captured lighting to get more photorealistic-looking images. It includes instructions on how to use vertex and pixel shaders to use bump, diffuse, specular, and environment maps to achieve photorealistic-looking faces. This technique is based on an idea from an artist named Ulf Lundgren (see http://www.lost.com.tj/Ulf/artwork/3d/behind.html). There are some preprocessing steps that are necessary to use the vertex and pixel shaders for this technique, and they are explained in detail.

Software

Several commercial software packages were used for development of this technique. 3D Studio Max® 4.2 was used for the modeling portion. 2D image transformations were done in Adobe Photoshop® 5.5 and JASC® Paint Shop Pro™ 7.0. These two image-processing programs are used since neither one completely provides the functionality needed to accomplish separation of lighting conditions.

Additional software needed to reproduce this effect is contained on the companion CD. The software on the CD includes a diffuse cube map generator, a texture mapping cylindrical wrapper, and the vertex and pixel shaders. Other software that was used includes NVASM, the macro assembler from NVIDIA, DirectX 8.0, and Visual Studio 6.0. NVIDIA'S assembler (NVASM) was written by the author and is included on the CD for your convenience. NVASM has built-in #defines and macros and integrates easily into Visual Studio. The project files included on the CD include integration of the assembler into Visual Studio. You can click on output lines from the assembler and be taken right to the error.

The vertex and pixel shader code uses a left-handed coordinate system (Figure 1). The technique described can also be implemented using a right-handed system such as the one that OpenGL uses.

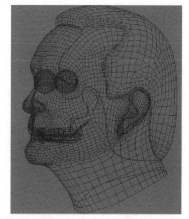

Figure 1

Resources

The author's face was used in the following figures. The reasoning behind the decision was one of scheduling. The facial hair makes the job that much harder. The photographs in Figure 2 are the starting point for this technique.

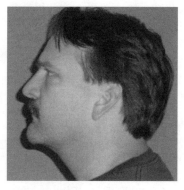

Figure 2: Front view (left) and side view (right)

3D Model

There are numerous ways to convert two photographs into a 3D model. The choice was made to use an artist named Stephen Burke, who was kind enough to take a mannequin model into 3DS Max and move the vertices to fit the photographs (see Figure 3). There are several other packages that allow you to take two photographs and change a "canonical" model of a face into the likeness of the subject. Most of these packages were not adequate for what is required for this technique. Additionally, most software packages cost money and do not export the data needed.

Most of the original work for converting a canonical model is based on the original ideas of Takaaki Akimoto, et al. [Akimoto]. There is also some good work that was done by Won-Sook Lee, et al [Lee]. One of the best ways to automatically fit a model to a set of photographs is to use DFFDS

Figure 3

(Dirichlet Free Form Deformations). This type of (FFD) Free Form Deformation shows the best results when transforming a "canonical" head. All the work on DFFDS is originally based on hand animation work by Laurent Moccozet, et al. [Moccozet].

Setup for Separation of Lighting Elements

Separating lighting equations from the photographs can be accomplished with a technique that starts out by separation of the diffuse, specular, and bump map components from photographs. Purists will probably point out that these techniques are not truly the lighting equations, but then most 3D graphics techniques aren't "exact." What really matters here is that the technique looks good.

The photographs in Figure 1 were taken in complete darkness with only the flash used for lighting. A digital camera with a flash attached was used. The green background was built from fabric purchased at a fabric store and glued onto some poster board. The color of the fabric isn't the same as the color used in "true" green screen movie settings, but it is sufficient for this technique. The digital camera was mounted to a tripod and placed about 4 feet in front of the subject. Two pictures are taken of the subject, one from the front and one from the side. The photographs were then cropped around the face and made into power of two textures.

Diffuse Lighting Component

There are a couple of assumptions that were made when trying to extract out the lighting characteristics of the subject's face. First off, the lighting direction is known, as is the flash from the camera. A complicated algorithm could have been used based on the normals of the 3D model and fitting a diffuse function to each pixel to extract the diffuse texture map, but a simpler approach was taken.

The diffuse part is a smattering of lights from all directions. For each pixel in the 3D model, the incoming light sources for that pixel are a result of the environment reflecting light and the face reflecting light. Skin absorbs most of the light that is being shone on it. Additional lighting on skin is very subtle. From any given point, the light reflectance can be considered coming mostly from the first reflection and direction illumination. The light energy falls off dramatically after first reflection because of the absorption properties of the skin. Some energy is deflected and the reflected light taken in these conditions is almost all being contributed from the face itself.

The transformations needed to get a diffuse cube map can be accomplished using imaging processing software. The extraction process will use Adobe Photoshop and JASC Paint Shop Pro. Start Adobe Photoshop and load the front-facing picture into it. Now choose Filters->Smart blur and set the radius to 50 and the threshold to 100. Select High in the Quality drop-down box. The smart blur filter keeps the general features of the face when blurring (see Figure 4). One additional preprocessing step is to paint out the shadows from the blurred picture. This processed picture will be used as the diffuse component. In the photographs, there are shadows below the chin (see Figure 4). It isn't really necessary to remove these manually, as the smart blur degrades these to such a degree that they won't be seen in the final rendering.

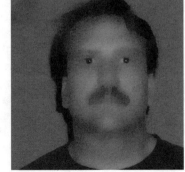

Figure 4

Extracting the Bump and Specular Map

Now switch over to JASC Paint Shop Pro. Paint Shop Pro is easier to work with in terms of its arithmetic operations on images. Load the original image and the blurred image into Paint Shop Pro. Now use the Image->Arithmetic menu and select the original and the diffuse for the two pictures to operate on. Use "Function Subtract" and make sure the operation is set to all channels by selecting the All channels check box. Unselect the clip color values and make sure

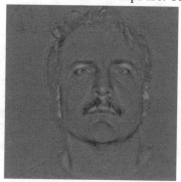

the divisor is set to 1 and the bias is set to 128 (see Figure 5a).

What this essentially does is take the blurred image out of the original and adjust the contrast/brightness back up to midrange values. The result should look like the picture in Figure 5b. If you zoom in on this image, you can see where the bumps are. You can also still see specular parts in the image. If you look closely at the tip of the nose, you will notice that there are specular highlights there.

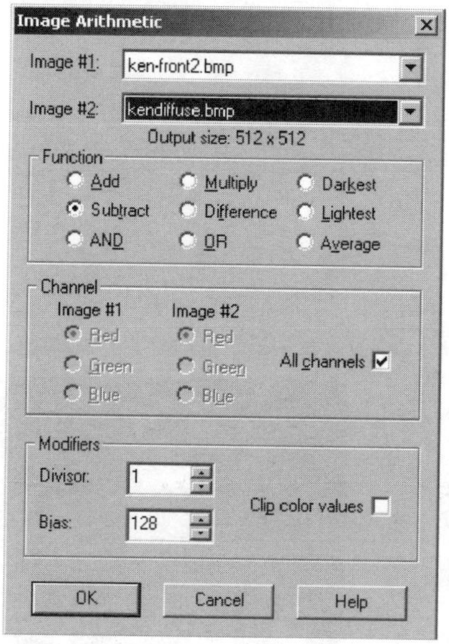

Figure 5a

Figure 5b

Separating Specular and Bump Maps

The separation of the specular portion of the texture map must be accomplished. Again, inside of Paint Shop Pro, press Ctrl+C and Ctrl+V to make a copy of the image in a new window. Now pick the menu item Colors->Histogram Functions->Histogram Adjustments. The trick to this portion of the extraction is to adjust the histogram to pull out the specular component of the face.

When the histogram adjustment window is opened, a spike in the center of the histogram window is visible. This spike is very similar to a specular lobe. This may have to be adjusted until the specular parts of the photograph show up in the final result. It isn't difficult to see the specular reflections in the photographs.

Using Figure 6a as a reference, move the black horizontal slider (triangle) to just before the spike. Then adjust the gray horizontal slider (triangle) to just inside the middle of the spike. Turn down the midtone compression slider to –50. Now, adjust the maximum output level to 147, which is about half way. The output level was reduced, since the specular component of the skin isn't very high. Hit the OK button, and you should have something very similar to Figure 6b.

Since the specular component is only a specular value and doesn't include color information, it can be put into the alpha channel of the diffuse map. Load the diffuse map that was created in Figure 4, and select the window for this image. Then use the Masks->New->From Image... menu item. Now select the specular image in the Source Window drop-down box. Make sure Source Luminance is checked and Invert Mask Data is unchecked. Don't worry about what the mask selection looks like, as it isn't really representative of what the alpha channel will look like. Now use Masks->Save to Alpha Channel and click OK. Rename this Alpha instead of the default Selection #1.

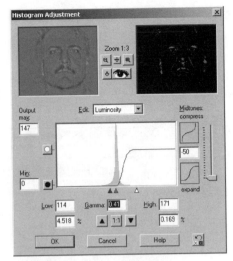

Figure 6a

Now the mask must be removed. Otherwise, when the image is being saved, it will "flatten" the mask onto your image layer, creating an unwanted masked diffuse image. It should now be saved into one of the formats that supports 32 bits of data. Targa (tga) files should be used, as the code included on the companion CD uses this format for 32-bit images. When the image is saved, Paint Shop Pro will give a warning that the image is being saved in .tga format and only one alpha channel will be saved. Click Yes and let it merge the layers; since there is no longer a mask, it will do the right thing with the rest of the channels, creating a 32-bit texture.

The pixel shaders use these 32-bit images to grab two images at once. One image is encoded in the RGB values, and the second image is encoded in the alpha component. The diffuse texture will be stored in the RGB, and the specular component will be stored in the A (alpha) channel.

Figure 6b

Normal Maps

Lastly, a normal map needs to be created for the face. Normal maps are a close relative to bump maps but are slightly different. Figure 5b was converted from the diffuse/original into what really constitutes a height map. This height map is biased from the value 128, since 128 was added to center the values in the arithmetic operation that was performed on the image.

NVIDIA's web site has a plug-in for Photoshop that converts a height map into a "normal map." Load in the image that was created similar to Figure 5b into Photoshop. Now use the Filter->nvTools->Normal Map Filter... menu

Figure 7

selection. The bias RGB radio button should be selected. Also, the scale of the bumps should be set to 5. The results can be seen in Figure 7. This image might be hard to see, as normals are encoded in color values in the texture map. Color plates for this chapter are included on the companion CD.

More on Normal Maps

Normals maps are not bump maps in the "Blinn" sense of the word. Jim Blinn [Blinn78] talked about how to perturb a normal. For instance, an interpolated vertex normal can be perturbed by some amount using a texture map lookup. Normal maps are a slight variation on this technique, as they don't use the normal in the calculation. Instead they encode the normal in the RGB color components of the texture map. RGB values are unsigned bytes, and normals are represented in the –1 to 1 range. We can use a technique to "scale" and "bias" a normal into the 0 to 255 range.

Since normals are used in dot product calculations, we want to encode the normals with a direction facing the light vector in order to get the correct result of the dot product. To encode these values, the sample vector {0, 0, –1}, which means 0 in the x direction, 0 in the y direction, and –1 in the z direction, is used. Encoding these values into the 0-255 ranges of each RGB value involves first scaling the values by multiplying by .5 (divide by 2). Now –1 becomes –.5 and 1 become .5. Then a bias is applied to the values so they fall into the 0 to 1 range. To do this, we add .5. Now –.5 becomes 0, 0 becomes .5, and .5 becomess 1.0.

This basically remapped the negative and positive ranged floating-point values into positive-only values. Finally, multiplying these values by 255 puts them into the 8 bits of precision of an RGB value. Since a normal will be used in the dot product calculation for the diffuse lighting computation, we can see that the {0, 0, –1} would be remapped to the {128, 128, 255} values, giving that kind of sky blue color seen in normal maps.

Since all the normals are defined in this flat 2D texture map, how can these normals be useful? The technique is very similar to texture mapping. Figure 8 shows how a triangle might be texture mapped with a texture. The flat plane represents a texture map. Only one triangle is shown on the texture map and one triangle on the sphere for clarity. The normals on the sphere are at each vertex.

These normals are usually used in calculating the diffuse lighting solution. Since the normals from the object are not being used, but the normals are being looked up instead from the texture map, some calculations will need to be done. The normals have to either be projected back onto the sphere for each pixel, which is computationally very expensive, or you need to do one other trick.

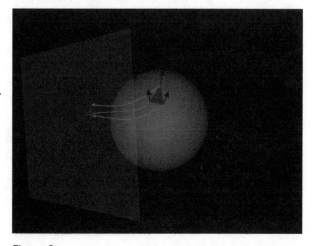

Figure 8

The following technique is useful to use when optimizing an application. Instead of transforming the texture-mapped normals, the light can be transformed at each of the vertices into the texture map plane to do the diffuse calculation. Basis vectors are used to transform the light at each vertex. Normal maps are used on a per-pixel basis, so there is one other thing to consider.

Texture mapping an object involves dividing by the W component to get perspective-correct texture mapping. This divide happens on a per-pixel basis. The basis vectors are calculations that take these divides by W into account when texture mapping or looking up the normal in the texture map.

Basically, a vector is used that encodes three things. The first component is the change in the U (S for OpenGL) texture coordinate (delta S) divided by the change in the polygon X value in object space (delta X). The next two components are the change in U with respect to the delta Y and delta Z.

The second basis vector is the change in the V (T for OpenGL) texture coordinate with respect to the three deltas in object space: X, Y, and Z. Of course, you need to have a third vector to have a rotation matrix. This third coordinate can be generated with a cross product of the first two vectors or the vertex normal can be used, as it is a very good close approximation.

These calculations create the basis vector at each vertex that rotates the light vector into texture mapping space, also known as texture space. These calculations are done in the vertex shader. There are a couple of caveats to be aware of when generating the basis vectors. 3D content creation applications such as 3DS Max allow the artist to create mirrored and duplicate texture coordinates, and this can be a problem when making the basis vector calculations. The calculated vector may also have to be flipped if the result of the cross product is pointing in the opposite direction of the face normal.

A Word About Optimizations

To save substantial amounts of vertex calculation work, a simple calculation on the CPU can be made. The CPU can be used to do an inverse transform of the light vector to object space. The vertex calculations rotate all the normals of an object by the object's matrix to put the normals in world space in order to do the diffuse lighting calculation. Depending on the number of normals, this can be quite a few rotations. Instead of rotating the normals, you can rotate the light into the object space and cut out all but one rotation. The first pass of the code presented in the vertex shader (Listing 1) doesn't use this optimization, but the second code listing (Listing 2) shows just how much time can be saved by utilizing this optimization.

Pixel shaders also have this notion of co-issue instructions that is documented in the DirectX 8.0 documentation. Basically, this means that you can have two instructions execute in one clock cycle on hardware that supports it. The pixel shader in this chapter uses that technique and will be described in that section.

Another way to optimize is to use NVIDIA's NVTune tool available on the NVIDIA web site. It is a free tool that registered developers can use to help optimize applications. It helps determine where your code is slowing down in terms of how the hardware is dealing with the data sent to it.

Half Angle

Half angles are used in the first few vertex shaders. A half angle vector in the context of these shaders is the vector that is exactly halfway between the light direction vector and the eye vector. This is really useful in calculating specular without having to use a reflection calculation. Jim Blinn discovered this information in 1977; consult [Blinn77] for further information.

Vertex Shader Explanation Pass 1 (Listing 1)

The following explanation describes the vertex and pixel shaders that use the maps described previously for this technique. This vertex shader sets up the pixel shader that will use a diffuse map, a specular map, and a bump map, all in the same pass. Throughout the code, the term "light direction" is used. This really means the opposite of the light direction for the reason that the arithmetic operations, such as the dot product, require this inverted vector to work correctly.

Line numbers have been added to the code for correlation between the explanations and the code snippets.

Lines 20-27 are definitions that allow organization of temporary register usage. Line 29 tells the assembler to expect a vertex shader and which version. In this case, version 1.0 of a vertex shader was chosen. Lines 32-35 of the code transform the vertex position by the concatenated "world->view->projection" matrix, which puts the vertex position in projection space for rasterizing.

Lines 38-44 transform the basis vectors to world space. Remember these lines, as they will play an important role in Listing 2, which is an optimized version of Listing 1. Lines 46-48 transform the normal into world space. Lines 50-51 scale the basis vector to increase or decrease the effect of the normal with respect to the light. Lines 53-56 transform the light direction vector by the world transformed basis vectors to put the light direction in texture space. Lines 59-61 normalize the light vector, which may or may not be necessary. If a bump scale value was not being used and the basis vectors were all normalized, then the light direction would only rotate around the unit sphere and the normalization would not be necessary.

Lines 71-73 transform the vertex position to world space so we can make a vertex position to eye position vector for calculating a half angle. Some of these lines will be optimized out in Listing 2. Line 82 does the calculation and lines 86-88 normalize the half angle vector. Lines 99-102 transform this vector by the world transformed basis vectors to put the half angle in texture space. Lines 108-109 output the texture space light direction to the texture coordinates for use in the pixel shader. Finally, lines 112-113 output the texture coordinates for looking up texels in the pixel shader for the diffuse and normal texture maps.

Listing 1: Vertex shader unoptimized

```
1:  /*******************************************************************
2:  Path: C:\Development\PhotoFace\
3:  File: dot3_directional.nvv
4:
5:  Copyright (C) 2001 Kenneth L. Hurley - Free for Any use whatsoever
6:  This file is provided without support, instruction, or implied warranty of any
7:  kind. Kenneth L. Hurley makes no guarantee of its fitness for a particular
    purpose
8:  and is not liable under any circumstances for any damages or loss whatsoever
9:  arising from the use or inability to use this file or items derived from it.
```

```
10:
11: Comments:
12: Kenneth Hurley - 10/15/2001
13:
14: ********************************************************************************/
15:
16:
17: #include "PF_Constants.h"
18:
19:
20: #define S_WORLD        r0
21: #define T_WORLD        r1
22: #define SxT_WORLD      r2
23: #define LIGHT_LOCAL    r3
24: #define VERTEX_WORLD   r4
25: #define EYE_VECTOR     r5
26:
27: #define HALF_ANGLE     r7
28:
29:         vs.1.0
30:
31: ; Transform position to clip space and output it
32:         dp4 oPos.x, V_POSITION, c[CV_WORLDVIEWPROJ_0]
33:         dp4 oPos.y, V_POSITION, c[CV_WORLDVIEWPROJ_1]
34:         dp4 oPos.z, V_POSITION, c[CV_WORLDVIEWPROJ_2]
35:         dp4 oPos.w, V_POSITION, c[CV_WORLDVIEWPROJ_3]
36:
37: ; Transform basis vectors to world space
38:         dp3 S_WORLD.x, V_S, c[CV_WORLD_0]
39:         dp3 S_WORLD.y, V_S, c[CV_WORLD_1]
40:         dp3 S_WORLD.z, V_S, c[CV_WORLD_2]
41:
42:         dp3 T_WORLD.x, V_T, c[CV_WORLD_0]
43:         dp3 T_WORLD.y, V_T, c[CV_WORLD_1]
44:         dp3 T_WORLD.z, V_T, c[CV_WORLD_2]
45:
46:         dp3 SxT_WORLD.x, V_NORMAL, c[CV_WORLD_0]
47:         dp3 SxT_WORLD.y, V_NORMAL, c[CV_WORLD_1]
48:         dp3 SxT_WORLD.z, V_NORMAL, c[CV_WORLD_2]
49:
50:         mul S_WORLD.xyz, S_WORLD.xyz, c[CV_BUMP_SCALE].w
51:         mul T_WORLD.xyz, T_WORLD.xyz, c[CV_BUMP_SCALE].w
52:
53: ; transform light by basis vectors to put it into texture space
54:         dp3 LIGHT_LOCAL.x, S_WORLD.xyz, c[CV_LIGHT_DIRECTION]
55:         dp3 LIGHT_LOCAL.y, T_WORLD.xyz, c[CV_LIGHT_DIRECTION]
56:         dp3 LIGHT_LOCAL.z, SxT_WORLD.xyz, c[CV_LIGHT_DIRECTION]
57:
58: ; Normalize the light vector
59:         dp3 LIGHT_LOCAL.w, LIGHT_LOCAL, LIGHT_LOCAL
60:         rsq LIGHT_LOCAL.w, LIGHT_LOCAL.w
61:         mul LIGHT_LOCAL, LIGHT_LOCAL, LIGHT_LOCAL.w
62:
63:
64: /////////////////////////////////////
65: // Calculate half angle vector
66:
67: // transform vertex position to world space
68: // to calculate V, vector to viewer in world
69: // space.
```

```
70:
71:          dp4 VERTEX_WORLD.x, V_POSITION, c[CV_WORLD_0]
72:          dp4 VERTEX_WORLD.y, V_POSITION, c[CV_WORLD_1]
73:          dp4 VERTEX_WORLD.z, V_POSITION, c[CV_WORLD_2]
74:
75: ; Half angle vector is (L+V)/||L+V|| or Normalize( L+V )
76: ; ||a|| is magnitude of a
77: ; L = vec to light from vertex point
78: ; V = vec to viewer from vertex point
79:
80: // vertex position - eye position
81: // eye position - vertex position
82:          add EYE_VECTOR, c[ CV_EYE_POS_WORLD ], -VERTEX_WORLD.xyz
83:
84:
85: ; Normalize eye vec
86:          dp3 EYE_VECTOR.w, EYE_VECTOR, EYE_VECTOR
87:          rsq EYE_VECTOR.w, EYE_VECTOR.w
88:          mul EYE_VECTOR, EYE_VECTOR, EYE_VECTOR.w
89:
90: // Add them to average & create half angle vector
91:          add HALF_ANGLE, c[CV_LIGHT_DIRECTION], EYE_VECTOR
92:
93:
94: ; Normalize it
95:          dp3 HALF_ANGLE.w, HALF_ANGLE, HALF_ANGLE
96:          rsq HALF_ANGLE.w, HALF_ANGLE.w
97:          mul HALF_ANGLE, HALF_ANGLE, HALF_ANGLE.w
98:
99:          dp3 oT3.x, HALF_ANGLE, S_WORLD
100:         dp3 oT3.y, HALF_ANGLE, T_WORLD
101:         dp3 oT3.z, HALF_ANGLE, SxT_WORLD
102:         mov oT3.w, c[ CV_ONE ]
103:
104:
105:      ////////////////////////////////////
106:      // move light vector to TC 2
107:
108:         mov oT2, LIGHT_LOCAL
109:         mov oT2.w, c[CV_ONE].w     // w to 0
110:
111:    ; output tex coords
112:         mov oT0, V_TEXTURE
113:         mov oT1, V_TEXTURE
```

Vertex Shader Explanation Pass 1 (Listing 2)

The following vertex shader is an optimized version of the one discussed in Listing 1. It does the rotation into object space on the CPU on a per-object basis instead of doing it on the GPU on a per-vertex basis.

Lines 1-35 haven't changed from Listing 1, so no further explanation is needed. Lines 38-39 scale the basis vectors that are in object space to increase the amount of bumpiness on the object. Lines 38-48 of Listing 1 have been completely eliminated. This is due to the fact that we rotate everything into object space in the C++ code, thereby eliminating the costly per-vertex calculations.

Lines 42-44 transform the light direction, which is in object space, directly into texture space. Lines 47-49 renormalize the light vector. Again, this might not have been necessary had there been no scale factor for the light direction to affect the bumps. Line 61 now uses the eye position in object space to do the calculation of vertex position to eye position, and calculations to transform the vertex position to world space have been eliminated. Lines 64-66 are the same and normalize this new eye vector.

Line 69 creates the half angle vector from the object space light vector and the object space eye vector. Lines 72-74 renormalize the half angle vector. Lines 77-80 transform this half angle vector by the basis vectors to put the half angle vector into texture space. Lines 86-91 are the same as the end of Listing 1.

With a little math on the CPU, the elimination of quite a few lines of code in the vertex shader was achieved. These calculations were being performed on a per-vertex basis. The instruction count was reduced from 40 instructions per vertex to 28 instructions per vertex, a reduction of 30%.

Listing 2: Vertex shader optimized

```
1.  /*****************************************************************************
2.  Path: C:\development\PhotoFace\
3.  File: dot3_directional.nvv
4.
5.  Copyright (C) 2001 Kenneth L. Hurley - Free for Any use whatsoever
5.  This file is provided without support, instruction, or implied warranty of any
6.  kind. Kenneth L. Hurley makes no guarantee of its fitness for a particular
    purpose
7.  and is not liable under any circumstances for any damages or loss whatsoever
8.  arising from the use or inability to use this file or items derived from it.
9.
10. Comments:
11.     Kenneth Hurley - 10/15/2001
12.
13. *****************************************************************************/
14.
15.
16. #include "PF_Constants.h"
17.
18.
19. #define S_OBJECT        r0
20. #define T_OBJECT        r1
21. #define SxT_OBJECT      r2
22. #define LIGHT_OBJECT    r3
23. #define VERTEX_WORLD    r4
24. #define EYE_VECTOR      r5
25.
26. #define HALF_ANGLE      r7
27.
28.     vs.1.0
29.
30. ; Transform position to clip space and output it
31.     dp4 oPos.x, V_POSITION, c[CV_WORLDVIEWPROJ_0]
32.     dp4 oPos.y, V_POSITION, c[CV_WORLDVIEWPROJ_1]
33.     dp4 oPos.z, V_POSITION, c[CV_WORLDVIEWPROJ_2]
34.     dp4 oPos.w, V_POSITION, c[CV_WORLDVIEWPROJ_3]
35.
36.     // scale bumps by amount requested
37.     mul S_OBJECT.xyz, V_S.xyz, c[CV_BUMP_SCALE].w
38.     mul T_OBJECT.xyz, V_T.xyz, c[CV_BUMP_SCALE].w
```

```
39. ; transform parallel light direction by basis vectors to put it into texture
    space
40.     dp3 LIGHT_OBJECT.x, S_OBJECT, c[CV_LIGHT_DIRECTION]
41.     dp3 LIGHT_OBJECT.y, T_OBJECT, c[CV_LIGHT_DIRECTION]
42.     dp3 LIGHT_OBJECT.z, V_SxT, c[CV_LIGHT_DIRECTION]
43.
44. ; Normalize the light vector
45.     dp3 LIGHT_OBJECT.w, LIGHT_OBJECT, LIGHT_OBJECT
46.     rsq LIGHT_OBJECT.w, LIGHT_OBJECT.w
47.     mul LIGHT_OBJECT, LIGHT_OBJECT, LIGHT_OBJECT.w
48.
49. ////////////////////////////////////
50. // Calculate half angle vector
51.
52. ; Half angle vector is (L+V)/||L+V|| or Normalize( L+V )
53. ; ||a|| is magnitude of a
54. ; L = vec to light from vertex point
55. ; V = vec to viewer from vertex point
56.
57. // vertex position - eye position
58. // eye position - vertex position
59.     add EYE_VECTOR, c[ CV_EYE_POS_OBJECT ], -V_POSITION.xyz
60.
61. ; Normalize eye vec
62.     dp3 EYE_VECTOR.w, EYE_VECTOR, EYE_VECTOR
63.     rsq EYE_VECTOR.w, EYE_VECTOR.w
64.     mul EYE_VECTOR, EYE_VECTOR, EYE_VECTOR.w
65.
66. // Add them to average & create half angle vector
67.     add HALF_ANGLE, c[CV_LIGHT_DIRECTION], EYE_VECTOR
68.
69. // Normalize it
70.     dp3 HALF_ANGLE.w, HALF_ANGLE, HALF_ANGLE
71.     rsq HALF_ANGLE.w, HALF_ANGLE.w
72.     mul HALF_ANGLE, HALF_ANGLE, HALF_ANGLE.w
73.
74. // transform half angle into normal map space
75.     dp3 oT3.x, HALF_ANGLE, V_S
76.     dp3 oT3.y, HALF_ANGLE, V_T
77.     dp3 oT3.z, HALF_ANGLE, V_SxT
78.     mov oT3.w, c[ CV_ONE ]
79.
80.
81. ////////////////////////////////////
82. // move light vector to TC 2
83.
84.     mov oT2.xyz, LIGHT_OBJECT.xyz
85.     mov oT2.w, c[CV_ONE].w     // w to 0
86.
87. ; output tex coords
88.     mov oT0, V_TEXTURE
89.     mov oT1, V_TEXTURE
```

Pixel Shader Explanation (Listing 3)

The following pixel shader modulates the specular map values with the base texture values and adds the diffuse color. Figure 9 is a texture map that was encoded with a diffuse lighting solution in the RGB components and a specular lighting solution in the A (alpha) component. This texture is selected into texture stage 3. Line 16 selects a pixel shader and a version of 1.1 for the assembler.

Figure 9

Diffuse map   Specular map

Line 18 takes the texture coordinates from the vertex shader and does a texture lookup into the diffuse or base texture of the face (see Figure 4 and Figure 6b). The RGB components contain the diffuse texture, and the alpha channel contains the specular map. Line 19 takes the texture coordinates from the vertex shader and does a texture lookup into the normal map texture (see Figure 7). Lines 20-21 do a 2x2 matrix calculation or two dot product calculations with the texture coordinates coming in from the vertex shader.

Texture coordinate set 2 is the light vector passed in by the vertex shader. There isn't a texture lookup for the texm3x2pad instruction. The texm3x2tex instruction first does a dot product and uses the calculation from the texm3x2 pad to look up a texture. It grabs a texel from the texture in Figure 9.

The C++ code sets the texture mode to clamp, so the result of the dot product will always be mapped into the texture map. The postfix "_bx2" modifier on the normal is necessary to bias and scale the value back into the –1 to 1 range before doing the dot product operation. Line 25 takes the result of N dot L (Normal * Light vector) and multiplies it by the base texture. The added "_x2" modifier makes the diffuse light act a little brighter in the calculation.

Line 26 uses the "+" prefix modifier to tell the assembler that this instruction is going to co-issue with the previous instruction. The pixel shader has the capability, when two adjacent instructions operate on the RGB and the alpha component separately, to execute the instructions in a one clock cycle. Line 26 also multiplies the specular lobe by the specular map associated with the face. Line 27 uses what is called a trinary operator. It multiplies the specular level with the diffuse color to get a specular color and then adds that value into the computed diffuse solution in one clock cycle.

Listing 3: Pixel shader

```
1.   /*******************************************************************
2.   Path: C:\Development\PhotoFace\
3.   File: ps_dot3.nvp
4.
5.   Copyright (C) 2001 Kenneth L. Hurley - Free for Any use whatsoever
6.   This file is provided without support, instruction, or implied warranty of any
7.   kind. Kenneth L. Hurley makes no guarantee of its fitness for a particular
     purpose
8.   and is not liable under any circumstances for any damages or loss whatsoever
9.   arising from the use or inability to use this file or items derived from it.
10.
11.  Comments:
12.      Kenneth Hurley - 10/15/2001
```

```
13.
14.  ************************************************************************/
15.
16.    ps.1.1
17.
18.    tex t0         // fetch base texture + specular in alpha
19.    tex t1         // fetch normal map
20.    texm3x2pad t2, t1_bx2      // u = ( t1=N ) dot ( t2=L )
21.    texm3x2tex t3, t1_bx2      // v = ( t1=N ) dot ( t3=H )
22.                              // fetch texture 4 at (u,v) rgb = (N dot L)
23.                              // alpha = (N dot H)
24.
25.    mul_x2  r1.rgb, t3, t0     // ( N dot L) * base texture
26.    +mul    r1.a, t0.a, t3.a   // ( N dot H) * specular map
27.    mad r0, r1.a, t0, r1       // (specular * base texture) + (diffuse Color)
```

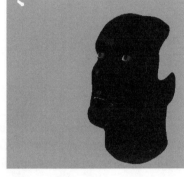

Figure 10: Technique 1 Results

Diffuse Lighting only

Specular Map

Normal Map

Diffuse + Specular + Normal Map

Full Head Mapping

The real challenge is to get a head mapped all the way around. Cylindrical mapping helps quite a bit. There are still problems with how to generate the textures. On the companion CD there is a plug-in for 3D Studio Max that will help generate a single unfolded texture. The source code for the plug-in is also on the CD, in case you would like to modify/enhance it. This software aids in merging two orthogonal photographs into one texture map.

Getting Started

For the plug-in to work, a specific setup of the material editor and mapping channels inside 3D Studio Max needs to be done. Create a Multi/Sub-Object in the Material Editor of 3D Studio Max. Set the number of sub-objects to four by clicking on the Set Number button. Next create four sub-materials that have textures. The first one should have its material ID set to 1. This one will be used for the cylindrical map that will be applied to the final stage. The plug-in uses the Material IDS to figure out which side of the head the 2D texture is being applied to. The IDS are preset in the plug-in as follows:

1 — Final Cylindrical Map

2 — Right Side

3 — Left Side

4 — Top Side

5 — Bottom Side

6 — Front Side

7 — Back Side

For the pictures that were used earlier, we will planar map these pictures on the left, right (for the side view), and front (for the front view). Here is how the material editor should have been set up.

Figure 11

Mapping the Photographs

Now use the UVW Mapping modifiers to map the photographs onto the head. For mapping the first material ID (1), just use cylindrical mapping with a dummy texture for now. Now map the two photographs by adding UVW Mapping modifiers for each of the faces. In this example, the left, right, and front were planar mapped onto the object. The companion CD contains a sample head named KenHeadTM_front-FINAL.max

Creating a Single Texture Map

Make sure you have installed the unwrap.dlu plug-in in your 3D Studio Max plug-ins directory. Now select the Utilities panel (the hammer). Next select the More button, and then scroll down until you find the utility named Unwrap Object Texture and click OK. Most of the defaults are acceptable, except the Spline Blending radio button should be selected. The differences between no spline blending and spline blending can be seen in Figure 13. The algorithm for selecting the triangles to render is based on using the normal of the triangle and doing a dot product with the direction of the unit cube. This then selects the texture map, which is most likely to contribute the "best" pixels to the triangle. There could have been some sort of simple blending done, but spline blending gives good results.

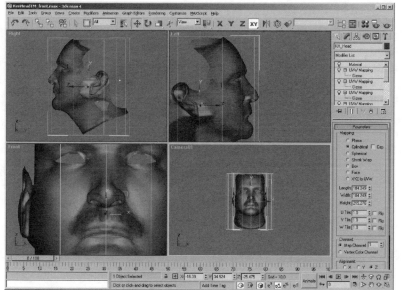

Figure 12

Peter Watje originally wrote the "unwrap" tool. The code has since been modified to include texture mapping and spline blending. The original texture mapping code was written by Chris Hecker and was modified to fit into the 3D Studio Max framework. The final processing code is based on [Burt]. The difficult part of the code was decomposing the images into Gaussian and Laplacian image pyramids. The code uses memory quite heavily and the plug-in will warn you that it can take a while to generate the images and then merge them all back together. On a Pentium III 500 MHz, it takes about 20 seconds. The time to generate the map is acceptable given the results of the blending. Save the generated image to disk by pressing on the disk icon.

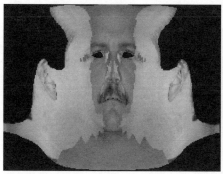

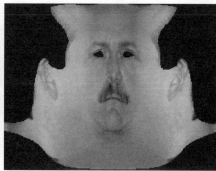

Figure 13

Normal Based

Normal Based with Spline Blending

Putting It All Together

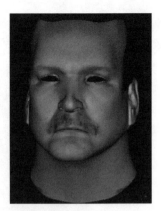

Figure 14

Now that a single texture map has been created, the process at the beginning of the chapter needs to be rerun. From this image, the diffuse, specular, and bump map needs to be generated. Before you export the file, you should remove the UVW mapping coordinates for the front, left, and right views, leaving the cylindrical map UVW mapping. Now change the map type to a normal bitmap and load in the image that was saved. Modification of the UVW coordinates is unnecessary because the image was generated from the cylindrical map and they should line up automatically. The 3D Studio Max rendering of the model can be seen in Figure 14.

What's Next?

3D Studio Max® does a pretty good job at rendering, but this chapter is aimed at putting this into a real-time application, like a game. There are several new techniques for getting environmental lighting that have been discussed on the web and in other publications [Lundgren][Blinn77][Blinn78] [Miller][Debevec]. Most are not practical for today's hardware. The next few sections will discuss some techniques that can be used with hardware that has pixel shaders, such as the GeForce 3.

Environmental Lighting

Environmental lighting simulates lighting of objects based on all incoming light in an area. This area can be outside, or it may be as small as one room. Radiosity has been used quite a bit, but so far it hasn't been done in real time, except for pre-computed light maps. Another technique that people have been using recently is called "High Dynamic Range" (HDR) image-based rendering (see [Debevec]). The HDR images are stored in floating-point format, which precludes them from being used in current hardware. There are some techniques that allow multiple passes with reduced precision to work on GeForce 2 class hardware. After looking at these sites, it was noticed that the lights could be broken up into three components — diffuse, specular, and directional diffuse. These terms are also used for "Bidirectional Reflection Distribution Functions" (BRDF). The next few sections will explain the techniques that can be used to recover these lights and how to possibly use them with today's 3D graphics hardware.

How to Get Diffusion Cube Maps

There is a program included on the CD with full source code that helps in making cube maps. It's under the DCM subdirectory which stands for "Diffusion Cube Maps." It aids in extraction of cube maps from digital pictures. The pictures are of a completely reflective ball. The program also allows you to draw an exclusion rectangle to remove the picture taker from the cube map. Since this technique doesn't use anything that is completely reflective in the scene, the exclusion rectangle can be ignored.

To extract the reflection maps, first load in the picture and then use the mouse to draw the ellipse enclosed in a rectangle. This rectangle should be stretched and moved so that the ellipse falls on the edges of the ball. Then set which direction is associated with the picture in the menu options. The pictures in the example use the negative X and negative Z direction (see Figure 15).

Figure 15 - Negative X sphere picture (left) and negative Z sphere picture (right).

Generating the Cube Maps

Now select the Generate menu option. After a few seconds, a window will come up with a cube map similar to the one in Figure 16a. Now if the window that contains the cube map is selected, the Generate menu item will generate a diffusion cube map like the one seen in Figure 16b. The image in 16b was gamma corrected in Paint Shop Pro since the diffusion routine reduces the gamma on the image.

(a)

For the specular component, the reflection map was taken into JASC Paint Shop Pro 7.0, and the Histogram Adjust was used as it was with the photographs of the faces. It wouldn't be hard to extract a specular map from the picture in Figure 16a running a convolution filter on the reflective map with the user inputting the specular component. These cube maps can now be used to do environmental lighting on the face.

(b)

(c)

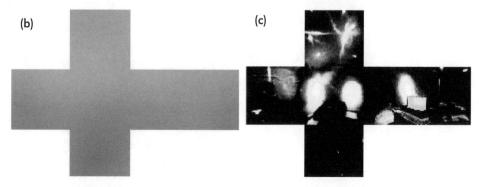

Figure 16: Reflection map(a), diffusion map(b), and specular map(c)

The Pixel Shader to Use All These Maps

The pixel shader in Listing 4 is quite interesting for a shader. It uses all the available texture units on a GeForce 3 and uses three instructions to combine everything. The vertex shader isn't included in the text, as it is very similar to Listing 5, which is described later. It uses the texture maps previously described to perform environmental lighting.

Lines 21-24 load up texture RGB values from the base (diffuse) texture from texture stage 0, a darkening map from texture stage 1, the diffusion map (see Figure 16b), and finally the specular map (see Figure 16c). The darkening map in this technique is similar to the one in Figure 6b with the specular component removed. This map simply uses the diffusion cube map and darkens the value, just like a dot product operation would do.

Line 26 multiplies the diffuse map by the environment diffusion cube map. Line 27 multiplies the specular map of the face by the environment map specular and adds in the values calculated in Line 26. Line 29 multiplies the "darkening" factor by the diffusion environment map and adds that to the result in line 27. All the operations add environmental lighting on the face.

Listing 4: Pixel shader

```
1.   /**************************************************************************
2.   Path: C:\Development\PhotoFace
3.   File: ps_EnvLight.nvp
4.
5.   Copyright (C) 2001 Kenneth L. Hurley
6.   This file is provided without support, instruction, or implied warranty of any
7.   kind. Kenneth L. Hurley makes no guarantee of its fitness for a particular
     purpose
8.   and is not liable under any circumstances for any damages or loss whatsoever
9.   arising from the use or inability to use this file or items derived from it.
10.
11.  Comments:
12.
13.  **************************************************************************/
14.
15.
16.  #include "PF_Constants.h"
17.
18.
19.      ps.1.1
20.
21.      tex t0          // fetch base texture
22.      tex t1          // fetch bump map
23.      tex t2          // fetch diffusion map using normal
24.      tex t3          // fetch specular using reflection vector
25.
26.      mul r0, t0, t2        // base map * diffusion map
27.      mad r1, t0.a, t3, r0  // specular environment cubemap * specular base map +
28.                            // previous
29.      mad r0, r0, t1, r1    // now use diffusion bump map * diffuse + previous
```

Environment Mapping for Eyes

Environment mapping for the eyes is very important. Someone once said, "The audience always watches the eyes." This is why the eyes are very important to achieving very realistic-looking faces. The outer portion of an eye is glossy in that it reflects a little bit of the environment, but it is also clear, showing the inner part of the eye. This visual effect can be reproduced in one pass on multitexturing hardware.

The vertex shader in Listing 5 sets up a couple of items. Lines 26-29 do the usual transforming of the position. Lines 34-40 calculate the vertex to eye position needed for a reflection calculation. Lines 45-47 calculate out 2 (N·E)N–E, which is the reflection vector calculation. The vertex shader then stores this value into texture coordinate T1 for input to the pixel shader.

Listing 5: Vertex shader

```
1.  /******************************************************************************
2.  Path: C:\Development\PhotoFaceFile: vs_glossy.nvv
3.
4.  Copyright (C) 2001 Kenneth L. Hurley - Free for Any use whatsoever
5.  This file is provided without support, instruction, or implied warranty of any
6.  kind. Kenneth L. Hurley makes no guarantee of its fitness for a particular
    purpose
7.  and is not liable under any circumstances for any damages or loss whatsoever
8.  arising from the use or inability to use this file or items derived from it.
9.
10. Comments:
11.     Kenneth Hurley - 10/15/2001
12.
13. ******************************************************************************/
14.
15.
16. #include "PF_Constants.h"
17.
18.
19. #define EYE_VECTOR          r1
20. #define REFLECTION_VECTOR   oT1
21.
22.     vs.1.0
23.
24. ; Transform position to clip space and output it
25.     dp4 oPos.x, V_POSITION, c[CV_WORLDVIEWPROJ_0]
26.     dp4 oPos.y, V_POSITION, c[CV_WORLDVIEWPROJ_1]
27.     dp4 oPos.z, V_POSITION, c[CV_WORLDVIEWPROJ_2]
28.     dp4 oPos.w, V_POSITION, c[CV_WORLDVIEWPROJ_3]
29.
30. ; output tex coords
31.     mov oT0, V_TEXTURE // for base texture lookup
32.
33. // vertex position - eye position
34. // eye position - vertex position
35.     add EYE_VECTOR, c[ CV_EYE_POS_OBJECT ], -V_POSITION.xyz
36. // Normalize eye vec
37.     dp3 EYE_VECTOR.w, EYE_VECTOR, EYE_VECTOR
38.     rsq EYE_VECTOR.w, EYE_VECTOR.w
39.     mul EYE_VECTOR, EYE_VECTOR, EYE_VECTOR.w
40.
41. ////////////////////////////////////
42. // Calculate reflection vector
43.
```

```
44.    dp3 r3, V_NORMAL, EYE_VECTOR
45.    mul r4, r3, V_NORMAL
46.    mad REFLECTION_VECTOR, r4, CV_TWO, -EYE_VECTOR
```

The pixel shader in Listing 6 is pretty simple. It is passed a reflection vector and the regular texture coordinates for the diffuse map. It then looks up the texture RGB values in lines 21 and 22. Texture stage 1 was set up with a cube map in the source code. Lines 24-26 simply use a blend factor to blend between the two maps with values specified in two pixel shader constant registers. These were also set up in the C++ code.

Listing 6: Pixel shader

```
1.    /********************************************************************
2.    Path: C:\Development\PhotoFace
3.    File: ps_Glossy.nvp
4.
5.    Copyright (C) 2001 Kenneth L. Hurley
6.    This file is provided without support, instruction, or implied warranty of any
7.    kind. Kenneth L. Hurley makes no guarantee of its fitness for a particular
      purpose
8.    and is not liable under any circumstances for any damages or loss whatsoever
9.    arising from the use or inability to use this file or items derived from it.
10.
11.   Comments:
12.
13.   ********************************************************************/
14.
15.
16.   #include "PF_Constants.h"
17.
18.
19.        ps.1.1
20.
21.        tex     t0      // fetch base texture
22.        tex     t1      // fetch specular using reflection vector
23.
24.        mul     r1, t0, c[CP_BLEND_DIFFUSE]
25.        mul     t3, t1, c[CP_BLEND_SPECULAR]
26.        add     r0, t3, r1
```

Final Result

Figure 17 and Color Plate 5 show the final result using the environmental effects. Another item that should eventually be tackled is hair. This addition of hair would visually enhance the rendering a great deal.

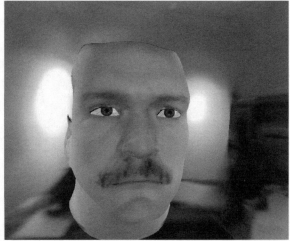

Figure 17

Facial Animation

Facial animation is a very important part to creating photorealistic faces. Frederic I. Parke and Keith Waters wrote an excellent book on facial animation [Parke]. They have released their public domain software for animating faces. The software requires that you type the data for the face and its corresponding muscles into a text file. There is another system for facial animation available at http://expression.sourceforge.net. This system allows you to attach the muscles to triangles using bones inside 3D Studio Max. To efficiently use this system, some code would have to be written in order to use vertex shaders. The code from Parke and Waters can easily be modified to use vertex shaders by simply putting the 18 muscle groups that they have defined in vertex shader constants. Each muscle requires ten floating-point values that can be stored in 45 vertex shader constants. The muscle.c file would need modification to be used as a vertex shader. This would then enable the vertex shader to move the vertices based on the original Parke and Waters code.

There are more utilities that would need to be written for this system to work well, as it is very difficult and cumbersome to extract out the exact data needed to tie triangles to the muscle. The jaw, eye, tongue, and teeth animation systems would need to be defined. Finally, in order to get speech hooked into the system, a speech system would have to be written or one of the publicly available ones could be used. Microsoft Speech API is a good choice. Another good choice is the University of Edinburgh free speech API, "The Festival Speech Synthesis System," available at http://www.cstr.ed.ac.uk/projects/festival/. This project is a free and open source, which might make it more attractive for some.

Another piece of the facial animation puzzle deals with animating the face for realistic-looking speech synchronization. Once the speech API is hooked up to the animation system, there might be anomalies in the animation. This visually represents itself as a "fluttering" effect between phoneme or word changes. One way to solve this problem is with the use of a coarticulation system. Cohen and Massaro developed a fairly robust system [Cohen]. Simply put, this is a system that blends lip sync positions based on a weighting value. More information on this system can be obtained from http://mambo.vcsc.edu/psl/ca93.html.

Conclusion

A lot of software was written for this chapter of the book. Some of it is unpolished, and the author would have liked to add some new features to the code. One good example is the DCM code. It does not use multi-resolution splines at the moment, and there are some artifacts in the cube maps, which would have easily been corrected with this code. Also, the DCM code could have used a specular convolution filter to automatically extract a specular map. The source code is included in case anyone wants to enhance the code.

Special thanks goes to Greg James at NVIDIA for the original idea of encoding the diffuse and specular maps into one 32-bit texture and for the basis of some of the code. Matthias Wloka deserves a special thank you for his help with some of the more difficult math problems and some ideas for recovering cube maps from photographs.

References

[Akimoto] Takaaki Akimoto, Yasuhito Suenaga, and Richard S. Wallace, "Automatic Creation of 3D Facial Models," IEEE Computer Graphics and Applications, 1993.

[Blinn77] Jim Blinn, "Models of Light Reflection for Computer Synthesized Pictures." *Computer Graphics* (SIGGRAPH Proceedings), July 1977, pp. 192-198.

[Blinn78] Jim Blinn, "Simulation of Wrinkled Surfaces," *Computer Graphics* (SIGGRAPH Proceedings), Vol. 12, No. 3, August 1978, pp. 286-292.

[Burt] Peter J. Burt and Edward H. Adelson, "A Multiresolution Spline with Application to Image Mosiacs," *ACM Transactions on Graphics*, Vol. 2. No 4, October 1983.

[Cohen] M. M. Cohen and D. W. Massaro, "Modeling coarticulation in synthetic visual speech." N. M. Thalmann and D. Thalmann (Eds.) *Models and Techniques in Computer Animation*. (Springer-Verlag, 1993).

[Debevec] Paul Debevec, Tim Hawkins, Chris Tchou, Haarm-Pieter Duiker, Westley Sarokin, and Mark Sagar, *Acquiring the Reflectance Field of a Human Face* (SIGGRAPH Proceedings), 2000.

[Lee] Won-Sook Lee, Prem Karla and Nadia Magnenat Thalmann, "Model Based Face Reconstruction for Animation," http://miralabwww.unige.ch/ARTICLES/ MMM97t.html, 1998.

[Lundgren] Ulf Lundgren, "3D Artwork Description," http://www.lost.com.tj/Ulf/artwork/3d/ behind.html, May 2001.

[Miller] Gene S. Miller and Robert C. Hoffman, *Illumination and Reflection Maps: Simulated Objects in Simulated and Real Environments*, Course Notes for Advanced Computer Graphics Animation, SIGGRAPH, 1984.

[Moccozet] L. Moccozet and N. Magnenat-Thalmann, "Dirichlet Free-Form Deformations and their Application to Hand Simulation," Computer Animation Proceedings, IEEE Computer Society, 1997, pp. 93-102.

[Parke] Frederic I. Parke and Keith Waters, *Computer Facial Animation* (AK Peters LTD, 1996).

Non-Photorealistic Rendering with Pixel and Vertex Shaders

Drew Card and Jason L. Mitchell

Introduction

Development of cutting-edge graphics techniques, like programmable pixel and vertex shaders, is often motivated by a desire to achieve photorealistic renderings for gaming or simulation. In this chapter, we apply vertex and pixel shaders to non-photorealistic rendering (NPR). In many types of images, such as cartoons and technical drawings, photorealism is not desirable. In the case of technical illustrations, non-photorealistic rendering techniques are used to enhance understanding of the scene or object being drawn without obscuring important features such as outlines. In other cases, we simply hope to simulate other media such as cel-shaded cartoons, wood-block prints, or hatched line drawings for stylistic purposes. In the following sections, we will apply Direct3D pixel and vertex shaders to implement and extend recent research efforts in non-photorealistic rendering.

Rendering Outlines

Rendering of object outlines is a common step in non-photorealistic rendering. In this section, we will present a geometric approach to outline rendering, which uses vertex shaders to determine silhouette edges. These outlines are used <u>with</u> the NPR shading techniques discussed in subsequent sections. An image space approach to outlining will be presented at the end of this article.

We consider the silhouette outline to be the minimum set of lines needed to represent the contour and shape of the object. Silhouette edges represent not only the outer edges of the object but also points of surface discontinuity (e.g., a sharp edge or crease in a surface).

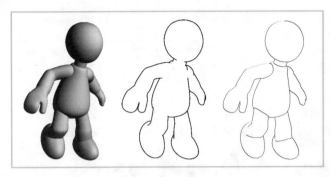

Figure 1: N L, silhouette outlines, image filtered outlines

The basic algorithm involves drawing every edge of an object as a quadrilateral fin and doing the silhouette determination in the vertex shader. This is very similar to the way that [Lengyel01] faded the "fins" used in fur rendering. The goal of this shader is very simple; if the edge is a silhouette, the vertex shader renders the quad fin; otherwise, the vertex shader renders a degenerate (unseen) fin.

The vertex shader determines if an edge is a silhouette by comparing the face normals of the triangles that share the edge (n_{face0} and n_{face1}). If one normal is front facing with respect to the viewer and the other is back facing, then the edge is a silhouette. This algorithm works perfectly except in the case of edges that are not shared by more than one triangle. These kinds of edges are considered "boundary edges" and need to be drawn all of the time. Boundary edges only have one face normal associated with them, so there is no second normal to be used in the comparison. In order to ensure that boundary edges are always drawn, the second shared normal is chosen so that it is the negation of the first normal ($n_{face1} = -n_{face0}$). This results in boundary edges always being drawn, since one normal will always be facing the viewer and the other will always be facing away from the viewer. With this organization of data, one vertex buffer and one rendering call can be used to draw all of the quad fins, and the vertex shader will handle both regular edges and boundary edges.

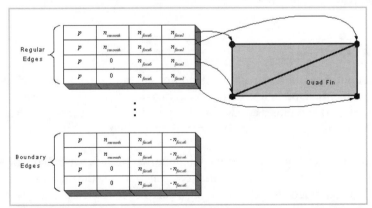

Figure 2: Vertex buffer organization for silhouette edge rendering

The data for drawing the object will typically be stored in memory in an organization similar to that shown in Figure 2. As shown, every vertex <u>of every edge</u> is composed of the vertex position (p), along with three normal values corresponding to the vertex's smooth normal (n_{smooth}) and the face normals of the triangles sharing the edge (n_{face0} and n_{face1}). The application should then render each edge quad fin, possibly passing the additional normal information in a separate data stream from the rest of the vertex. In order to reduce the memory bandwidth hit from reading in the "extra" data (n_{face0} and n_{face1}), one optimization would be to quantize the face normals to byte 4-tuples or short 4-tuples, as illustrated in "Character Animation with Direct3D Vertex Shaders" and "Vertex Decompression Using Vertex Shaders."

The vertex shader computes the view vector in camera space by multiplying the vertex by the view matrix and normalizing. The shader then transforms the face normals n_{face0} and n_{face1} into camera space and dots them with the view vector. If the edge is a silhouette edge, one of these dot products will be negative and the other will be positive. The shader checks for this condition by multiplying the two dot products together and checking for a value less than zero. If the value is less than zero, the vertex offset is set to zero (unchanged); otherwise, the vertex offset is set to one. The vertex offset is then multiplied by the smooth normal and added to the untransformed vertex position. Note that two of the four vertices for each quad fin have n_{smooth} = 0. This acts as a mask of the fin vertex displacement and causes two of the fin vertices to stick to the model while the other two are displaced to cause the fin to be visible.

Listing 1: Outline vertex shader

```
//NPR outline shader
// c0-3 view matrix
// c4-7 view projection matrix
// c8
// c9   (0.0, 0.0, 0.0, 1.0f)
// 10   line with scalar

vs 1.1
m4x4 r0, v0, c0        // compute the view vector
dp3  r1, r0, r0        // normalize the view vector
rsq  r1, r1
mul  r0, r0, r1

m3x3 r1, v7, c0        // multiply normal 1 by the view matrix
m3x3 r2, v8, c0        // multiply normal 2 by the view matrix
dp3  r3, r0, r1        // dot normal 1 with the view vector
dp3  r4, r0, r2        // dot normal 2 with the view vector
mul  r3, r3, r4        // multiply the dot products together
slt  r3, r3, c9        // check if less than zero

mov  oD, c9            // set the output color
dp4  r0, v0, c6        // compute the vertex depth
mul  r0, r0, c10       // multiply by a line thickness scalar
mul  r3, r3, r0        // multiply the thickness by the smooth normal

mul  r3, v3, r3        // multiply by the normal offset
add  r0, v0, r3        // add in the offset
mov  r0.w, c9.w        // swizzle in a one for the w value
m4x4 oPos, r0, c4      // transform the vertex by the model view projection
```

Hidden line removal is handled via the depth buffer. We assume that a shaded version of the model is rendered before the outlines to fill the z buffer with values that will cause hidden outlines to fail the z test. The following pseudocode outlines this process:

1. Preprocess the geometry into quad fins:
   a. For each vertex of each edge, store the edge vertex, the smooth surface normal, and the two face normals which share said edge; one should have the smooth normal, and the other should have the smooth normal field set to zero.
   b. If edge is unshared (only used in one face), store the negation of the one face normal as the second normal.

2. Render a shaded version of the geometry to fill the z-buffer.

3. Enable outline vertex shader and initialize the shader constant storage.

4. Set up stream mappings to pass in the additional normal data.

5. Render the edges as triangles.

6. Vertex shader breakdown:
   a. Compute the view vector by transforming the vertex into eye space (multiply by the view matrix) and normalize.
   b. Dot each face normal with the view vector.
   c. Multiply the resulting dot products together.
   d. Check for a value less than zero.
   e. Multiply the smooth normal by the result of the less than zero test.
   f. Compute the vertex depth (dot the vertex with the third row of the view projection matrix).
   g. Multiply the vertex depth by the line thickness factor to get a normal scale value.
   h. Multiply the smooth normal by the normal scale value.
   i. Add the smooth normal to the untransformed vertex.
   j. Transform the vertex and output.

There are some drawbacks associated with the previous algorithm. Along with the hassle of preprocessing the geometry and storing extra edge data, boundary edges may potentially be drawn incorrectly when a quad fin points straight at the viewer. This is because the algorithm currently only scales the edge along the smooth surface normal, thereby leaving no means to screen-align the quadrilateral edge. This could be addressed by reworking the algorithm to also screen-align the quad. Later in this article, we present an image space approach to rendering outlines, which requires no preprocessing and does not exhibit the same boundary edge issue.

In the next section, we will discuss methods for shading the interior of the object to achieve different stylized results.

Cartoon Lighting Model

One method of cartoon shading is to create banded regions of color to represent varying levels of lighting. Recent examples of 3D games using cel-shading techniques are *Cel Damage* by Pseudo Interactive and the *Jet Set Radio* games (called *Jet Grind Radio* in some markets) by Sega/Smilebit. A common technique illustrated in [Lake00] is a technique called *hard shading*, which shades an object with two colors that make a hard transition where N·L crosses zero. [Lake00] indexes into a 1D texture map to antialias the transition, while the method shown here computes the colors analytically. Figure 3 shows an approach that uses three colors to simulate ambient (unlit), diffuse (lit), and specular (highlight) illumination of the object.

This is accomplished using a vertex shader that computes the light vector at each vertex and passes it into the pixel shader as the first texture coordinate. The vertex shader also computes the half angle vector at each vertex and passes it into the pixel shader as the second texture coordinate. The pixel shader analytically computes the pixel color. As

Figure 3: Cartoon shaded with outlines

shown in Listing 2, the pixel shader first computes N·L and N·H. If the N·L term is above a specified threshold, the diffuse color is output; otherwise, the ambient color is output. If the N·H term is above a specified threshold, then the specular color replaces the color from the N·L term. This same analytical method could be expanded to use any number of banded regions.

Listing 2: Cartoon shading vertex shader code

```
// Cartoon vertex shader
// c9 is the light position
// c10 is the view projection matrix
// c14 is the view matrix
vs.1.1

// output the vertex multipled by the mvp matrix
m4x4 oPos, v0, c10

// compute the normal in eye space
m3x3 r0, v3, c14
mov  oT0, r0 // write the normal to tex coord 0

// compute the light vector
sub  r0, c9, v0
dp3  r1, r0, r0
rsq  r1, r1
mul  r0, r0, r1
m3x3 r1, r0, c14       // transform the light vector into eye space
mov  oT1, r1           // write the light vector to tex coord 1

// compute half vector
m4x4 r0, v0, c14       // transform the vertex position into eye space
dp3  r3, r0, r0        // normalize to get the view vector
rsq  r3, r3
mul  r0, r0, r3
add  r0, r1, -r0       //add the light vector and the view vector = half angle
dp3  r3, r0, r0        // normalize the half angle vector
rsq  r3, r3
r0, r0, r3
mov  oT2, r0           // write the half angle vector to tex coord 2
```

Listing 3: Cartoon shading pixel shader code

```
// Cartoon shading pixel shader
//
ps.1.4

def c0, 0.1f, 0.1f, 0.1f, 0.1f    // falloff 1
def c1, 0.8f, 0.8f, 0.8f, 0.8f    // falloff 2
def c2, 0.2f, 0.2f, 0.2f, 1.0f    // dark
def c3, 0.6f, 0.6f, 0.6f, 1.0f    // average
def c4, 0.9f, 0.9f, 1.0f, 1.0f    // bright

// get the normal and place it in register 0
texcrd r0.xyz, t0

// get the light vector and put it in register 1
texcrd r1.xyz, t1

// compute n dot 1 and place it in register 3
dp3 r3, r0, r1

// subtract falloff 1 from the n dot 1 computation
sub r4, r3, c0

// check if n dot 1 is greater than zero
```

```
                   if yes use average color otherwise use the darker color
                   cmp_sat r0, r4, c3, c2

                   // subtract falloff 2 from the n dot 1 computation
                   sub r4, r3, c1

                   // check if n dot 1 is greater than zero
                   // if yes use bright color otherwise use what's there
                   cmp_sat r0, r4, c4, r0
```

The ambient and diffuse bands help to visualize the shape of the object while the specular highlight gives insight into the properties of the surface of the object. If the goal of the cartoon shader is only to represent the object's shape, the shader could omit the specular portion and replace it with any number of additional diffuse regions.

Figure 4: Cartoon shaded object with specular and multiple diffuse regions

Hatching

Another method of NPR shading is *hatching*, which is commonly used in pen and ink drawings to show shape and differentiate between lit and unlit regions of an object. The density of the hatch pattern signifies how much light the surface is reflecting at that point. The current state of the art in real-time hatching is illustrated in [Praun01]. This technique uses an array of hatch patterns ranging from very sparse (well-lit) to very dense (unlit) hatching called *tonal art maps*. N·L is computed per-vertex and used to determine a weighted-average of the tones in the tonal art map. Per-pixel, the tonal art maps are blended together according to the weights interpolated from the vertices. The result is a hatched image that is well antialiased.

Figure 5: Hatched object

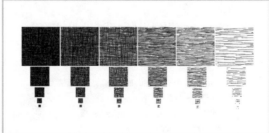

Figure 6: Tonal art map from [Praun01]

Listing 4: Hatching vertex shader

```
// Hatching vertex shader
//
// c0   0(0.0, 0.0, 0.0, 0.0)
// c1   1(1.0, 1.0, 1.0, 1.0)
// c2   2(2.0, 2.0, 2.0, 2.0)
// c3   3(3.0, 3.0, 3.0, 3.0)
// c4   4(4.0, 4.0, 4.0, 4.0)
// c5   5(5.0, 5.0, 5.0, 5.0)
// c6   6(6.0, 6.0, 6.0, 6.0)
// c7   7(7.0, 7.0, 7.0, 7.0)
// c8   brightness
// c9   light position
// c10  view projection matrix
// c14  view matrix
//
vs.1.1

m4x4    oPos, v0, c10    // output the vertex multiplied by the mvp matrix

mov     oT0, v7          // write out the texture coordinate
mov     oT1, v7

mov     r1, v3           //normalize the normal
mov     r1.w, c0
dp3     r2, r1, r1
rsq     r2, r2
mul     r1, r1, r2

sub     r2, c9, v0       // compute the light vector and normalize
dp3     r3, r2, r2
rsq     r3, r3
mul     r2, r2, r3

dp3     r3, r2, r1       // compute the light factor (n dot l) times six clamp at zero
mul     r3, r3, c8

mov     r5.x, c5.x       // seed the blend weights
mov     r5.y, c4.x
mov     r5.z, c3.x
mov     r5.w, c0.x

mov     r6.x, c2.x
mov     r6.y, c1.x
mov     r6.z, c0.x
mov     r6.w, c0.x

sub     r5, r3, r5       // sub each weight's initial value from the light factor
sub     r6, r3, r6

max     r5, r5, c0       // get rid of everything less than zero
sge     r7, c2, r5       // flag all weights that are <= 2
mul     r5, r5, r7       // zero out weights > 2
sge     r7, r5, c1       // flag all weights that are >= 1
mul     r7, r7, c2       // subtract all weights that are greater than or equal to one
                         //   from 2
sub     r5, r7, r5
slt     r7, r5, c0       // flag all weights that are < 0 and negate
sge     r8, r5, c0       // flag all spots that are >= 0
add     r7, -r7, r8      // add the flags
mul     r5, r5, r7       // should negate the negatives and leave the positives

max     r6, r6, c0       // same as above only on the second set of weights
sge     r7, c2, r6
```

```
mul     r6, r6, r7
sge     r7, r6, c1
mul     r7, r7, c2
sub     r6, r7, r6
slt     r7, r6, c0
sge     r8, r6, c0
add     r7, -r7, r8
mul     r6, r6, r7

sge     r8, c1, r3      // check for total shadow and clamp on the darkest texture
mov     r7, c0
mov     r7.z, r8.z
add     r6, r6, r7
min     r6, r6, c1

mov     oT2.xyz, r5     // write the 123 weights into tex coord 3
mov     oT3.xyz, r6     // write the 456 weights into tex coord 4
```

Listing 5: Hatching pixel shader

```
// Hatching pixel shader
ps.1.4

texld    r0, t0          // sample the first texture map
texld    r1, t1          // sample the second texture map
texcrd   r2.rgb, t2.xyz  // get the 123 texture weights and place it in register 2
texcrd   r3.rgb, t3.xyz  // get the 456 texture weights and place it in register 3
dp3_sat  r0, 1-r0, r2    // dot the reg0 (texture values) with reg2 (texture
                         //   weights)
dp3_sat  r1, 1-r1, r3    // dot the reg1 (texture values) with reg3 (texture
                         //   weights)
add_sat  r0, r0, r1      // add reg 0 and reg 1
mov_sat  r0, 1-r0        // complement and saturate
```

Gooch Lighting

The Gooch lighting model introduced in [Gooch98] is designed to provide lighting cues without obscuring the shape of the model, the edge lines, or specular highlights. This technique, designed to model techniques used by technical illustrators, maps the –1 to 1 range of the diffuse N·L term into a cool-to-warm color ramp. This results in diffuse lighting cues, which are shown as hue changes rather than color intensity changes. This diffuse lighting model is designed to work <u>with</u> the silhouette and feature-edge lines discussed earlier in this article. It essentially results in a reduction in the dynamic range of the diffuse shading so that the edge lines and specular highlights are never obscured. A similar technique is used in the game *Half-Life* by Valve Software [Birdwell01]. The *Half-Life* engine first computes a single approximate aggregate light direction. The –1 to 1 result of the per-vertex N·L from this aggregate light direction is then scaled and biased into the 0 to1 range rather than simply clamped at zero. This eliminates the flat look that would otherwise be apparent on the side of a game character that faces away from the light.

As shown in [Gooch98], the classic lighting equation illustrated in "Rippling Refractive and Reflective Water" can be generalized to the following, which allows us to experiment with cool-to-warm colors.

$$I = \left(\frac{(1+n\cdot l)}{2}\right) * k_{warm} + \left(1 - \frac{(1+n\cdot l)}{2}\right) * k_{cool}$$

$$k_{warm} = k_{yellow} + \beta * k_d$$

$$k_{cool} = k_{blue} + \alpha * k_d$$

Figure 7: Gooch lighting with outlining on a teapot and some cartoon characters

Listing 6: Gooch lighting vertex shader

```
// Gooch Lighting vertex shader
// c9 is the light position
// c10 is the view projection matrix
// c14 is the view matrix
vs.1.1

m4x4    oPos, v0, c10   // output the vertex multiplied by the vp matrix
sub     r0, c9, v0      // compute the light vector and normalize
dp3     r1, r0, r0
rsq     r1, r1
mul     r0, r0, r1
mov     r1, v3          // compute the normal
mov     oT0, r1         // write the normal to tex coord 0
mov     oT1, r0         // write the light vector to tex coord 1
```

Listing 7: Gooch lighting pixel shader

```
// Gooch Lighting pixel shader
// c0 is alpha (eg. {0.4, 0.4, 0.4, 1.0})
// c1 is beta (eg. {0.5, 0.5, 0.5, 1.0})
// c2 is kyellow (eg. {0.5, 0.5, 0.0, 1.0})
// c3 is kblue (eg. {0.0, 0.0, 0.4, 1.0})
// c4 is kd (eg. {0.0, 0.0, 0.4, 1.0})
// c5 is (1.0, 1.0, 1.0, 1.0)
ps.1.4

texcrd r0.xyz, t0        // get the normal and place it in register 0
texcrd r1.xyz, t1        // get the light vector and put it in register 1
dp3     r3, r0, r1       // compute n dot 1 and place it in register 3
add_d2  r3, r3, c5       // normalize the n dot 1 range

mul_sat r0, c4, c0       // compute the cool factor
add_sat r0, r0, c2
mul_sat r0, r0, r3

mul_sat r1, c4, c1       // compute the warm factor
add_sat r1, r1, c3
mad_sat r0, r1, 1-r3, r0 // add the warm and cool together and output
```

In the preceding sections, we have concentrated on shader techniques that render non-photorealistic images directly into the frame buffer. In the following section, we will look at image space techniques that require rendering into textures and subsequent processing of these rendered images to produce non-photorealistic images.

Image Space Techniques

As discussed in "Image Processing with Pixel Shaders in Direct3D," it is possible to render 3D scenes into textures for subsequent image processing. One technique developed in [Saito90] and refined in [Decaudin96] is to render the depth and world space normals of objects in a scene into a separate buffer. This rendered image is subsequently post-processed to extract edges which can be composited with a hatched, Gooch shaded, or cartoon shaded scene. We will show a Direct3D implementation of this technique as well as our own extension, which thickens the lines using morphological techniques discussed in "Image Processing." One advantage of an image space approach to determining outlines is that it is independent of the rendering primitives used to render the scene or even whether the models are particularly well-formed. A scene that contains N-Patch primitives [Vlachos01], for example, will work perfectly well with an image space approach, as will interpenetrating geometry such as the classic Utah teapot. This approach even works with user clip planes (or the front clip plane), correctly outlining areas of normal or depth discontinuity in the final image, without any application intervention at the modeling level. Another advantage is that this approach does not require the creation and storage of the auxiliary outline buffers discussed in the first section of this article.

The first step of this technique is to use a vertex shader to render the world space normals and depths of a scene into a texture map. The vertex shader scales and biases the world space normals from the -1 to 1 range into the 0 to 1 range and writes them to diffuse r, g and b (oD0.xyz). The eye-space depth is written into diffuse alpha (oD0.w). This interpolator is simply written out to the RGBA render target (i.e., a texture) by the pixel shader. One important detail is that the clear color for the scene should be set to world space $+z$, so the filter will interact properly with the objects at all orientations. An image of some cartoon characters rendered with this technique is shown in the following figures and in Color Plate 7. The RGBA texture containing world space normals and eye space depths is shown in Figure 8.

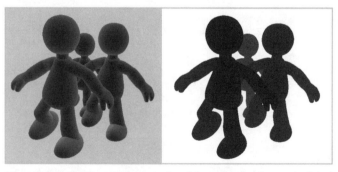

Figure 8: World space normals and eye space depth as in [Saito90] and [Decaudin96]. These are rendered to RGB and A of a renderable texture map.

The vertex shader used to render this scene is shown in Listing 8:

Listing 8: World space normals and eye space depth vertex shader

```
vs.1.1
m4x4 oPos, v0, c0
mov   r0, v3
mov   r0.w, c12.w
add   r0, c8, r0
mul   r0, r0, c9
m4x4 r1, v0, c4
```

```
sub  r1.w, r1.z, c10.x
mul  r0.w, r1.w, c11.x
mov  oD0, r0
```

The next step is to use image processing techniques like those shown in "Image Processing" to extract the desired outlines. The normals and depths are effectively processed independently to isolate different classes of edges. Discontinuities in the normals occur at internal creases of an object, while depth discontinuities occur at object silhouettes, as shown in Figure 9. Note that while the normal discontinuity filter picks up the edge at the top of the leg and the depth discontinuity filter does not, the union of the edge pixels from the two filters produces a reasonable outline for the object.

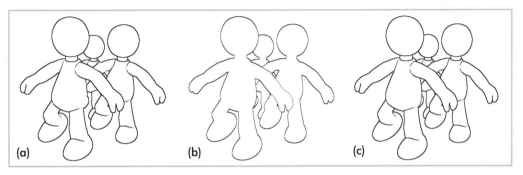

Figure 9: (a) Edges from world space normal discontinuities, (b) depth discontinuities, and (c) both together.

Listing 9: Determining edges from an image of a scene's world space normals

```
// Normal discontinuity filter for Non-Photorealistic Rendering
ps.1.4
def c0, 1.0f, 1.0f, 1.0f, 1.0f
def c1, -0.85f, 0.0f, 1.0f, 1.0f
def c2, 0.0f, 0.0f, 0.0f, 0.0f

// Sample the map five times
texld r0, t0    // Center Tap
texld r1, t1    // Down/Right
texld r2, t2    // Down/Left
texld r3, t3    // Up/Left
texld r4, t4    // Up/Right

dp3 r1.rgb, r0_bx2, r1_bx2    // Take dot products with center pixel (Signed result
                             //   -1 to 1)

dp3 r2.rgb, r0_bx2, r2_bx2
dp3 r3.rgb, r0_bx2, r3_bx2
dp3 r4.rgb, r0_bx2, r4_bx2

// Subtract threshold
add r1, r1, c1.r
add r2, r2, c1.r
add r3, r3, c1.r
add r4, r4, c1.r

phase

// Make black/white based on threshold
cmp  r1.rgb, r1, c0.r, c2.r
+mov r1.a, c0.a
cmp  r2.rgb, r2, c0.r, c2.r
```

```
+mov r2.a, c0.a
cmp  r3.rgb, r3, c0.r, c2.r
+mov r3.a, c0.a
cmp  r4.rgb, r4, c0.r, c2.r
+mov r4.a, c0.a

mul  r0.rgb, r1, r2
mul  r0.rgb, r0, r3
mul  r0.rgb, r0, r4
+mov r0.a, r0.r
```

Listing 10: Determining edges from an image of a scene's eye-space depth

```
// 5-tap depth-discontinuity filter
ps.1.4
def c0, -0.02f, 0.0f, 1.0f, 1.0f
texld r0, t0    // Center Tap
texld r1, t1    // Down/Right
texld r2, t2    // Down/Left
texld r3, t3    // Up/Left
texld r4, t4    // Up/Right

add r1, r0.a, -r1.a    // Take four deltas
add r2, r0.a, -r2.a
add r3, r0.a, -r3.a
add r4, r0.a, -r4.a

cmp r1, r1, r1, -r1    // Take absolute values
cmp r2, r2, r2, -r2
cmp r3, r3, r3, -r3
cmp r4, r4, r4, -r4

phase

add r0.rgb, r1, r2    // Accumulate the absolute values
add r0.rgb, r1, r3
add r0.rgb, r1, r4

add r0.rgb, r0, c0.r    // Substract threshold
cmp r0.rgb, r0, c0.g, c0.b
+mov r0.a, r0.r
```

Compositing the Edges

Once we have the image containing the world-space normals and depth, we composite the edge-filtered result with the frame buffer, which already contains a hatched, cartoon, or Gooch-shaded image. The output of the edge detection shader is either black or white, so we use a multiplicative blend (src*dst) with the image already in the frame buffer:

```
d3d->SetRenderState (D3DRS_ALPHABLENDENABLE,TRUE);
d3d->SetRenderState (D3DRS_SRCBLEND, D3DBLEND_DESTCOLOR);
d3d->SetRenderState (D3DRS_DESTBLEND, D3DBLEND_ZERO);
```

This frame buffer operation is nice because we can multi-pass edge filters with the frame buffer and get the aggregate edges. In the NPR sample on the companion CD, for example, we do one pass for normal discontinuities and one for depth discontinuities. It is worth noting that it would be possible to process both normal discontinuities and depth discontinuities using 1.4 pixel shaders and co-issue pixel shader instructions, but we chose to use a larger filter kernel (and thus more instructions) in the sample shown here.

Depth Precision

We have found that 8 bits of precision for eye-space depth works well for the simple scenes we have tested, but we expect this to be a problem for more aggressive NPR applications such as games with large environments. In scenes of large game environments, using only 8 bits of precision to represent eye space depth will cause some that are close to each other to "fuse" together if their world space normals are also similar. Because of this, it might be necessary to use techniques that spread the eye space depth across multiple channels or to simply rely upon future generations of hardware to provide higher precision pixels and texels.

Alpha Test for Efficiency

Since the black edge pixels are a very small subset of the total pixels in the scene, we can alpha test the edge image to save frame buffer bandwidth during the composite. Note that the last instruction in the depth and normal discontinuity shaders moves the red channel of the filter result into the alpha channel of the pixel. This is done so that the alpha test functionality which follows the pixel shader can be used to kill the pixel rather than composite it with the frame buffer, speeding up performance. Since we want to kill white pixels, we set an alpha reference value of something between white and black (0.5f) and use an alpha compare function of D3DCMP_GREATER:

```
d3d->SetRenderState(D3DRS_ALPHATESTENABLE, TRUE);
d3d->SetRenderState(D3DRS_ALPHAREF, (DWORD) 0.5f);
d3d->SetRenderState(D3DRS_ALPHAFUNC, D3DCMP_GREATER);
```

Shadow Outlines

In addition to outlining object silhouettes, it is also desirable to outline shadows in a scene. We have added this functionality to a stencil shadow application in the RADEON 8500 SDK on the ATI web site as shown in Figure 10 and Color Plate 8.

Figure 10a shows a scene using the hatching technique from [Praun01] alone. In addition to this, we use stencil shadows to generate an image in a texture which contains normals and depths similar to the preceding technique. The application renders the scene into the texture with world space normals and depths, using the stencil buffer to write to only pixels that are not in shadow. The application then re-renders the geometry to the pixels in shadow but negates the world space normals. This results in an image like the one shown in Figure 10b, where the alpha channel (not shown) contains depths. The same normal and depth discontinuity filters used above are applied to this image to determine both object and shadow edges in one pass. These edges are composited over a hatched scene that already contains areas in shadow which have been hatched with the densest hatching pattern to simulate shadow. Figure 10d shows this technique along with coloration of the TAMs and per-pixel TAM weight determination.

(a)

(b)

(c)

(d)

Figure 10: (a) A plain outlined hatched scene. (b) The renderable texture containing world space normals for non-shadowed pixels and negated normals for shadowed pixels. (c) A hatched scene with shadows, object outlines, and shadow outlines. (d) Adding base texture coloring and per-pixel TAM weight calculation.

Thickening Outlines with Morphology

The outlines generated by the above technique are a few pixels thick and look fine for many NPR applications, but some applications may want thicker lines. Rather than directly composite the edges onto a shaded image in the back buffer, we can render the edges into a separate texture and apply morphological operations as shown in "Image Processing." To thicken the lines, use dilation; to thin them or break them up, use erosion. To give a different style, we could thicken the lines by ping-pong rendering between renderable textures. After performing the desired number of dilations, composite the thickened edge image back onto the shaded frame buffer as discussed above.

Summary of Image Space Technique

Rendering a scene with the image space outlining technique shown here is done in the following steps:

1. Render shaded scene to back buffer
2. Render world space normals and depths to a texture map
3. If thickening lines using morphology,
    a. Clear renderable texture to white
    b. Draw quad into texture using world space normal discontinuity filter. Use alpha test and src*dst blending
    c. Draw quad into texture using depth discontinuity filter. Use alpha test and src*dst blending

     d. Dilate edges

     e. Composite with shaded scene in back buffer by drawing full screen quad using alpha test and src*dst blending

4. Else using edges directly,

     a. Draw full-screen quad over whole screen using world space normal discontinuity filter. Use alpha test and src*dst blending

     b. Draw full-screen quad over whole screen using depth discontinuity filter. Use alpha test and src*dst blending

Conclusion

We have presented Direct3D shader implementations of some recent developments in non-photorealistic rendering including outlines, cartoon shading, hatching, Gooch lighting, and image space techniques. For an excellent overview of these and many other NPR techniques, please refer to the recent book *Non-Photorealistic Rendering* by Gooch and Gooch. Gooch and Gooch also have an excellent online reference for NPR research: http://www.cs.utah.edu/npr/.

Acknowledgments

Thanks to Eli Turner for 3D modeling and Chris Brennan for implementing the shadow outlining technique.

References

[Birdwell01] Ken Birdwell, Valve Software, personal communication, 2001.

[Decaudin96] Philippe Decaudin, "Cartoon-looking rendering of 3D scenes," Technical Report INRIA 2919, Universite de Technologie de Compiegne, France, June 1996.

[Gooch98] Amy Gooch, Bruce Gooch, Peter Shirley, and Elaine Cohen, "A non-photorealistic lighting model for automatic technical illustration," (SIGGRAPH Proceedings, 1998), pp. 447-452.

[Lake00] Adam Lake, Carl Marshall, Mark Harris, and Marc Blackstein, "Stylized Rendering Techniques for Scalable Real-Time 3D Animations," Non-Photorealistic Animation and Rendering, 2000.

[Lengyel01] Jed Lengyel, Emil Praun, Adam Finkelstein, and Hugues Hoppe, "Real-time fur over arbitrary surfaces," ACM Symposium on Interactive 3D Graphics 2001, pp. 227-232.

[Praun01] Emil Praun, Hugues Hoppe, Matthew Webb, and Adam Finkelstein, "Real-time Hatching," (SIGGRAPH Proceedings, 2001), pp. 581-586. Figure 6 used with permission.

[Saito90] Saito, Takafumi, and Tokiichiro Takahashi, "Comprehensible Rendering of 3-D Shapes." (SIGGRAPH Proceedings, 1990), pp. 197-206.

[Vlachos01] Alex Vlachos, Jörg Peters, Chas Boyd, and Jason L. Mitchell, "Curved PN Triangles," ACM Symposium on Interactive 3D Graphics, 2001.

Animated Grass with Pixel and Vertex Shaders

John Isidoro and Drew Card

Introduction

The availability of programmable vertex and pixel shaders has allowed programmers to re-examine how they implement passive background scene geometry. Before the advent of programmable shaders, deformation animation was only used for characters and a select few scene objects due to the CPU overhead associated with it. With the ability to transfer this processing over to the GPU, previously static background objects can now be animated, adding life and realism to the scene. In this article, an approach is shown for realistically and inexpensively animating grass with a combination of vertex and pixel shaders.

Waving the Grass

The waving motion of the grass can be accomplished in a vertex shader. Using a traditional method, the grass is rendered with randomly placed intersecting quads. The quads are texture mapped and rendered with an alpha test. In a vertex shader, the top two vertices of each quad are animated using a combination of four sinusoidal waves. The waves are approximated using a Taylor Series approach laid out in "Rendering Ocean Water." This combination of sine waves using various different frequencies creates a natural waving that does not look like an animation or overly repetitious.

Lighting the Grass

When grass blades wave in the wind, they also turn and change their orientation with respect to the sunlight. Because this method involves using a textured quad to represent various blades of grass, it is impossible to change the lighting on individual grass blades. To simulate the change in color that would occur as the blades twisted in the wind, the same sine wave that was used to animate the grass is used to oscillate between two colors. In this case, the green channel of the color was changed to make the grass color change from intense green to a more yellowish-brown.

Figure 1: Grass texture

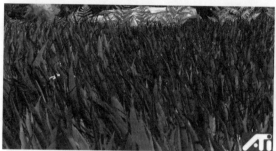

Figure 2: Results

Vertex shader code:

```
//vertex shader for grass..
//sinusoidal vertex motion for waving grass
//pos + sumOverI(wavedirI * texcoordy * sin( xdirI * (xpos+time)) + ydirI *
(ypos+time)))
SetVertexShaderConstant 0   commonConst
SetVertexShaderConstant 1   appConst
SetVertexShaderConstant 2   worldSpaceCamPos
SetVertexShaderConstant 4   wvp
SetVertexShaderConstant 8   sin9
SetVertexShaderConstant 10  frcFixup
SetVertexShaderConstant 11  waveDistortx
SetVertexShaderConstant 12  waveDistorty
SetVertexShaderConstant 13  waveDistortz
SetVertexShaderConstant 14  waveDirx
SetVertexShaderConstant 15  waveDiry
SetVertexShaderConstant 16  waveSpeed
SetVertexShaderConstant 17  piVector
SetVertexShaderConstant 18  lightingWaveScale
SetVertexShaderConstant 19  lightingScaleBias

StartVertexShader
  vs.1.1

  mul r0, c14, v0.x    // use vertex pos x as inputs to sinusoidal warp
  mad r0, c15, v0.y, r0 // use vertex pos y as inputs to sinusoidal warp

  mov r1, c1.x         // get current time
  mad r0, r1, c16, r0  // add scaled time to move bumps according to speed
  frc r0.xy, r0        // take frac of all 4 components
  frc r1.xy, r0.zwzw   //
  mov r0.zw, r1.xyxy   //
```

```
   mul r0, r0, c10.x      // multiply by fixup factor (due to inaccuracy of taylor
                          //     series)
   sub r0, r0, c0.y       // subtract 0.5
   mul r1, r0, c17.w      // *=2pi coords range from(-pi to pi)

   mul r2, r1, r1         // (wave vec)^2
   mul r3, r2, r1         // (wave vec)^3
   mul r5, r3, r2         // (wave vec)^5
   mul r7, r5, r2         // (wave vec)^7
   mul r9, r7, r2         // (wave vec)^9

   mad r0, r3, c8.x, r1   // (wave vec) − ((wave vec)^3)/3!
   mad r0, r5, c8.y, r0   // + ((wave vec)^5)/5!
   mad r0, r7, c8.z, r0   // − ((wave vec)^7)/7!
   mad r0, r9, c8.w, r0   // − ((wave vec)^9)/9!

   dp4 r3.x, r0, c11
   dp4 r3.y, r0, c12
   dp4 r3.zw, r0, c13

   mul r4, v7.y, v7.y     //
   mul r3, r3, v7.y       // attenuate sinusoidal warping by tex0.y^2

   mov r2.w, v0
   add r2.xyz, r3, v0     // add sinusoidal warping to grass position

   m4x4 oPos, r2, c4
   dp4  r1.x, r0, c18                 //scale and add sine waves together
   mad  oD0, c19.xzxz, −r1.x, c19.y   //scale and bias color values (green is scaled
                                      // more than red and blue)

   mov  oT0, v7
EndVertexShader
```

Pixel shader code:

```
StartPixelShader

ps.1.4
texld r0, t0
   mul_x2 r0, r0, v0

EndPixelShader
```

Texture Perturbation Effects

John Isidoro, Guennadi Riguer, and Chris Brennan

Introduction

The recent generation of graphics hardware has brought about a new level of per-pixel programmability for real-time graphics, especially with regard to dependent texture reads. With the ability to perform per-pixel math both before and after texture fetches, a variety of new texture-based effects are now possible. This article will focus on per-pixel texture perturbation effects, effects that use the results of a texture fetch to change the texture coordinates used to fetch another texel. Effects such as wispy clouds, billowing smoke, flickering fire, rippling water, and plasma can be rendered in real time using the techniques shown here.

Wispy Clouds

One of the easiest effects that can be achieved using texture perturbation is wispy clouds.

The idea is to scroll two tileable textures past each other in opposite directions. The first texture is the perturbation texture, which has u and v perturbations stored in the red and green channels of the texture.

Figure 1: Red channel of texture
(u perturbation)

Figure 2: Green channel of texture
(v perturbation)

The second texture is the cloud texture, which has its texture coordinates perturbed by the perturbation map. For this section, we use a grayscale cloud texture and pack it into the alpha channel of the perturbation map. Because of this packing, only one texture is needed for each layer of clouds. This texture is fetched from twice in the shader, first to obtain the perturbation values, then to read the perturbed texture.

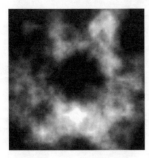

Figure 3: Cloud texture   Figure 4: Basic cloud shader in action

Here is the pixel shader code for the basic cloud shader:

```
ps.1.4
texld r0, t0
texcrd r1.rgb, t1

    mad r0, r0, c0, r1 //multiply perturbation by scale factor, and add texcoords

phase
texld r0,r0
    mov r0, r0
```

In order to make the clouds look much more realistic, however, it's best to use multiple layers of clouds. The layers can be combined in quite a few different ways. A straightforward approach to combining the layers is to linearly interpolate between them within the pixel shader. This gives the appearance of one layer of clouds on top of another. The cloud layers are scrolled past each other at different speeds to give the effect of depth through parallax.

The following shader is the result of combining two layers of clouds with a horizon.

In order to give the clouds a color gradient from a grayscale texture map, we use a multiply operation, which is scaled by two and then saturated. In the example, the color to be modulated with the clouds is orange (RGB values: 1.0, 0.7, 0.5). The gradient that results from the scale and modulation ranges between brown, orange, yellow, and white.

Cloud texture intensity	Color after modulation
0.00	(0.000, 0.000, 0.000) black
0.25	(0.500, 0.375, 0.250) brown
0.50	(1.000, 0.750, 0.500) orange
0.75	(1.000, 1.000, 0.750) yellow
1.00	(1.000, 1.000, 1.000) white

Because the same grayscale texture is used for both intensity and transparency, the black regions of the clouds are completely transparent. The two cloud layers are then linearly interpolated with the background. The background texture is just a gradient from purple to blue.

Figure 5: Scene using two-layer cloud shader with horizon

```
// SetPixelShaderConstant 0 psConstVec (0.0, 0.5, 1.0, 0.75)
// SetPixelShaderConstant 1 cloud0PerturbationFactor
// SetPixelShaderConstant 2 cloud0Color
// SetPixelShaderConstant 3 cloud1PerturbationFactor
// SetPixelShaderConstant 4 cloud1Color
ps.1.4
texld  r0, t1               //perturbation map 0
texld  r1, t3               //perturbation map 1
texcrd r2.rgb, t0           //cloud layer 0 tex coord
texcrd r3.rgb, t2           //cloud layer 1 tex coord
   mad r0.rgb, c1, r0_bx2, r2 //perturb base map coords by cloud coords
   mad r1.rgb, c3, r1_bx2, r3 //perturb base map coords by cloud coords

phase
texld r0, r0
texld r1, r1
texld r2, t4
   mul_x2_sat r4.rgb, r0.a, c2   //cloud layer 0, multiply by color
  +mul r4.a, r0.a, c2.a          //cloud layer 0, alpha scale
   mul_x2_sat r3.rgb, r1.a, c4   //cloud layer 1, multiply by color
  +mul r3.a, r1.a, c4.a          //cloud layer 1, alpha scale
   lrp r0.rgb, r1.a, r3, r4      //interpolate between layers 0 and 1
  +add_sat r0.a, r3.a, r4.a      //add transparency values for layer
   lrp_sat r0, r0.a, r0, r2      //interpolate between clouds and horizon
```

Cloud layers can be combined in ways other than simple linear interpolation. Another technique is to use the horizon texture to brighten the edges of the clouds around the moon to give a light halo effect. This shader is quite complex. The images below show each step of the shader.

Figure 6: Horizon map

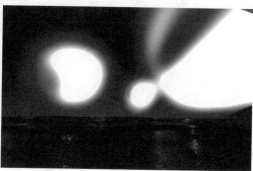

Figure 7: Alpha of horizon map (glow map)

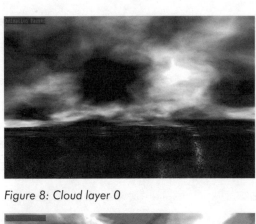

Figure 8: Cloud layer 0

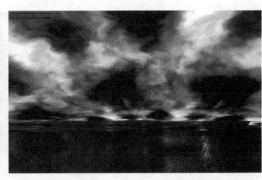

Figure 9: Cloud layer 1

Figure 10: Cloud edges of both maps combined extracted from cloud texture

Figure 11: Combined cloud layers

Figure 12: Combined cloud alphas (transparency map)

Figure 13: Cloud Edges * Glow

Figure 14: Two cloud layers combined with
Cloud Edges * Glow

Figure 15: Final result: Cloud layers with glowing edges blended with horizon

```
// SetPixelShaderConstant 0 psConstVec (0.0, 0.5, 1.0, 0.75)
// SetPixelShaderConstant 1 cloud0DistortionFactor
// SetPixelShaderConstant 2 cloud0Color
// SetPixelShaderConstant 3 cloud1DistortionFactor
// SetPixelShaderConstant 4 cloud1Color
// SetPixelShaderConstant 5 horizonBoost

ps.1.4
texld  r0, t1
texld  r1, t3
texcrd r2.rgb, t0
texcrd r3.rgb, t2
    mad r0.rgb, c1, r0_bx2, r2        //perturb base map coords by cloud coords
    mad r1.rgb, c3, r1_bx2, r3        //perturb base map coords by cloud coords
phase
texld r0, r0
texld r1, r1
texld r2, t4
    mov_x2 r3.rgb, r2.a               //alpha of horizon (glow map)
    +mul_sat r3.a, 1-r0.a, 1-r1.a     //mask edges for cloud glow

    mad_sat r0.rgb, 1-r0.a, c2, c2.a  //scale and bias inverted clouds layer 0
    +mov_x2_sat r0.a, r0.a            //boost cloud alpha 0

    mad_sat r1.rgb, 1-r1.a, c4, c4.a  //scale and bias inverted clouds layer 1
    +mov_x2_sat r1.a, r1.a            //boost cloud alpha 1

    lrp r0.rgb, r1.a, r1, r0          //combine cloud layers
    +mov r4.a, c5.a                   //

    mul_x2 r3, r3.a, r3               //multiply glow by edges of clouds
    mad_x2 r3, r3, c5, r4.a           //scale and bias glowing sections of clouds

    mul r0.rgb, r3, r0                //multiply glow by combination of cloud
                                      // layers
    +add_d2_sat r0.a, r0.a, r1.a      //add alphas of cloud layers

    lrp_sat r0, r0.a, r0, r2          //Lerp between clouds and horizon
```

Perturbation-Based Fire

Another interesting effect that can be created using texture perturbation is flickering fire. Traditionally, this was accomplished as either an animation, a texture feedback effect, or a particle system. However, each of these approaches has limitations.

Rendering fire as an animation has the disadvantages of looking unrealistic due to the cycling animation and requiring a lot of texture memory to store the frames of animation. In addition to this, if there are many flames in the scene and all use the same animation, the scene will look even more artificial. To capture the randomness of fire, cycling animations are not a good choice.

Another approach is to use a texture feedback. The basic idea is for each frame to generate a row of random pixels at the bottom of the texture, then blur and scroll the image upward in the texture. Although the visual effect of this is quite random, the repetitive blurring of the texture feedback process does not have the sharp edges that real fire has, and therefore looks very unrealistic.

Particle systems can also be used to create fire effects. Even though the fire effects they can produce are random in nature, calculating the physics for the particle system requires CPU time and can be prohibitive to perform for the amount of particles needed to create a realistic fire. In addition, particle fires tend not to have the opaqueness of real fire.

The technique described in this section for generating fire overcomes all of these shortcomings. Because it only requires two textures — a perturbation map and a base map — the technique requires much less texture memory than the animated fire. Also, due to the way we use the perturbation maps, the fire is both non-repetitive and preserves the sharp edges present in the base map. Also, the shader can be programmed to use vertex data to seed the offsets of the perturbation maps so that multiple flames in the same scene can have different appearances.

The idea behind this shader is to scroll three perturbation texture images (all three use the same texture) past each other vertically and add the results together to get a perturbation value. The three maps scroll at rates that are not integer multiples of the others, so the fire does not repeat as time advances. Using three maps ensures that repetition only happens after a very long time. When two of the perturbation maps line up, the third one is almost always offset from the other two. Giving the maps slightly different scroll speeds in the horizontal direction as well prevents the mechanical upward scrolling appearance of the fire.

The perturbation value is attenuated slightly based on the interpolated texture coordinate v value and then used to perform a perturbed fetch of a pixel in the base map. The attenuation is used to weaken the perturbation near the base of the fire in order to make the top of the fire flicker more than the base. After this, the perturbed fetch is performed in the same way as in the cloud shader, but both RGB components and alpha components are used from the fetched pixel.

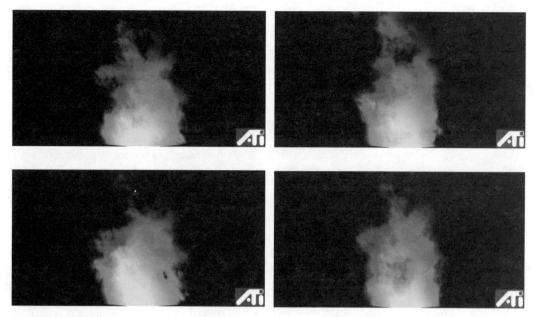

Figure 16: Fire effect in action

Figure 17: Base map
(rgb)

Figure 18: Opacity map
(alpha)

Figure 19: Distortion
texture

```
//SetPixelShaderConstant 0 texLerp
//SetPixelShaderConstant 1 distortAmount0
//SetPixelShaderConstant 2 distortAmount1
//SetPixelShaderConstant 3 distortAmount2
//SetPixelShaderConstant 4 heightAtten
//SetPixelShaderConstant 5 fireBoost

ps.1.4
texcrd r0.rgb, t0
texld  r2, t1
texld  r3, t2
texld  r4, t3
   mul r2.rgb, c1, r2_bx2       //noise0 * dis0
   mad r2.rgb, c2, r3_bx2, r2 //noise1 * dis1 + noise0 * dis0
   mad r2.rgb, c3, r4_bx2, r2 //noise2 * dis2 + noise1 * dis1 + noise0 * dis0
   +mad r0.a, r0.g, c4.x, c4.y //scale and bias y coord of base map
   mad r2.rgb, r2, r0.a,  r0  //mult distortion by scaled biased y coord
```

```
phase
texld  r0, r2
   mov r0, r0
```

Plasma Glass

In addition to the simulation of real-world phenomena, there are many other effects possible using texture perturbation. For instance, many science fiction movie-style special effects such as warping plasma are possible. The following technique produces something similar to the glass plasma spheres that emanate streams of plasma toward the surface of the glass when touched.

The concept behind the plasma effect is to use two scrolling textures again, but use each one as both a perturbation map and a base map. The base map is stored in the RGB components of the texture, and the perturbation map is stored in the alpha component. Each texture map perturbs the subsequent texel fetch of the other map. The following shader shows the basic plasma effect.

```
//SetPixelShaderConstant 1 Perturbation scaling
ps.1.4
texld  r1, t1                //Perturbation map 1 / base map 0
texld  r2, t2                //Perturbation map 0 / base map 1
texcrd r4.rgb, t1           //Base map coords 0
texcrd r5.rgb, t2           //Base map coords 1
   mad r4.rgb, c1, r2.a, r4 //Use alpha for Perturbation
   mad r5.rgb, c1, r1.a, r5 //Use alpha for Perturbation

phase
texld  r1, r5                //Base map 0
texld  r2, r4                //Base map 1
   add_d2 r0, r1, r2         //Add two perturbed textures together
```

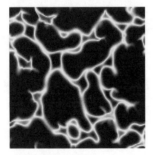

Figure 20: Base texture

Figure 21: Perturbation texture

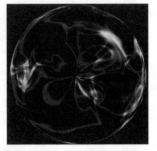

Figure 22: Simple plasma effect applied to a sphere

Mathematically, this effect is almost identical to the two-layer cloud effect, where the layers are added together, but the appearance of the effect is drastically different. Most of the difference in appearance can be attributed to using very different base and perturbation textures.

The plasma effect can be used as a building block to create more complex effects. For instance, the plasma effect can be combined with a glass effect to create a glass plasma sphere.

The first step is to use an environment cube map:

Figure 23: Environment map

To help give this a more glass-like appearance, the enviroment map is combined with a per-pixel Fresnel term. The per-pixel Fresnel term allows the glass to have a slightly bumpy appearance, which can be used to create a bumpy or a frosted glass appearance.

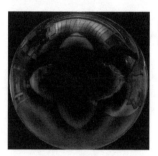

Figure 24: Environment map *
Per-pixel Fresnel term * glass color

The environment map is linearly interpolated with the plasma effect to produce the final result. For the final alpha value, the per-pixel Fresnel term and the plasma transparency value are added together.

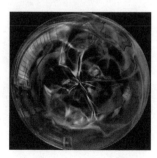

Figure 25: Final effect (interpolate
between environment and plasma)

Here is the pixel shader for the plasma glass effect.

```
//SetPixelShaderConstant 0 psConstVec (0.0, 0.5, 1.0, 0.75)
//SetPixelShaderConstant 1 psDistortScaleFactor
//SetPixelShaderConstant 2 glassColor
//SetPixelShaderConstant 3 plasmaColor
```

```
ps.1.4
texld r0, t0                        //bump map
texld r1, t1                        //perturbation map/ base map
texld r2, t2                        //perturbation map/ base map
texld r3, t3                        //tan space view vector lookup into
                                       normalization cube map
texcrd r4.rgb, t1                   //base map coords
texcrd r5.rgb, t2                   //base map coords
   dp3     r0, r3_bx2, r0_bx2       //V.N
   mad     r4.rgb, c1, r2.a, r4     //calc perturbed texture coords
   +cmp    r0.a, r0, r0, -r0        //abs(V.N)
   mad     r5.rgb, c1, r1.a, r5     //calc perturbed texture coords
   mov_sat r0, 1-r0.a               //1-abs(V.N)  (Fresnel term)

phase
texcrd r0, r0                       //pass through fresnel
texld r1, r5                        //perturbed base texture 0
texld r2, r4                        //perturbed base texture 1
texld r4, t4                        //env map reflective lookup.
   mul_x2 r4.rgb, r4, c2            //reflection map * glass color
   +add_d2_sat r1.a, r1.r, r2.r     //textures together
   mul r1.a, r1.a, r1.a             //square base texture (increases contrast)
   mul_x4_sat r1.rgb, r1.a, c3      //(plasma^n) * plasma color
   +mov r0.a, r0.r                  //fresnel term
   lrp r0.rgb, r0.a, r4, r1         //lerp plasma and environment map
   +mad_sat r0.a, r1.a, c3.a, r0.a //plasma * plasma alpha + fresnel
```

Summary

A variety of effects have been created using texture perturbation. Several other effects are also possible using a variation of the above shaders, such as rippling water or billowing smoke. By merely changing the base and perturbation textures, a vast array of new and interesting effects can be achieved. It is recommended that you experiment with these shaders yourself. More information on texture perturbation can be found in the references. The shaders described in this chapter can be seen in action in the video files included on the companion CD.

References

[Ebert98] David S. Ebert, F. Kenton Musgrave, Darwyn Peachey, Ken Perlin, and Steven Worley, *Texturing & Modeling: A Procedural Approach*, 2nd Ed., (AP Professional, July 1998).

Rendering Ocean Water

John Isidoro, Alex Vlachos, and Chris Brennan

Introduction

In computer graphics, simulating water has always been a topic of much research. In particular, ocean water is especially difficult due to the shape and combination of multiple waves, in addition to the sun in the sky and the reflection of the clouds.

The shader in this article is meant to simulate the appearance of ocean water using vertex and pixel shaders. The interesting part of this shader is that it runs completely in hardware in a single pass on recent graphics cards (Radeon 8500). This has the advantage of leaving the CPU free for other calculations, as well as allowing for a courser tessellation of the input geometry that can be tessellated using N-Patches or other higher order surface schemes. The input geometry is a grid of quads with one set of texture coordinates and tangent space, though in theory only a position is actually needed if assumptions are made about the orientation of the up vector and the scale of the ocean waves in the shader.

This shader is best explained by separating the vertex shader and the pixel shader while keeping in mind the final result, shown in Figure 1.

Figure 1

Figure 2

Sinusoidal Perturbation in a Vertex Shader

The vertex shader is responsible for generating the combination of sine waves that perturb the position and the cosine waves that perturb the tangent space vectors for the vertex. A Taylor series approximation is used to generate sine and cosine functions within the shader. Due to the SIMD nature of vertex shaders, four sine and cosine waves are calculated in parallel, and the results are weighted and combined using a single dp4.

Each sine wave has fully adjustable direction, frequency, speed, and offset that is configured in the constant store.

The first step is to compute each wave's starting phase into the sine or cosine function. The texture coordinates are multiplied by the direction and frequency of the four waves in parallel. $c14$ and $c15$ are the frequencies of the wave relative to S and T, respectively.

```
mul r0, c14, v7.x       //use tex coords as inputs to sinusoidal warp
mad r0, c15, v7.y, r0   //use tex coords as inputs to sinusoidal warp
```

Next, the time, which is stored in $c16.x$, is multiplied by the speed of the waves (in $c13$ and added to the wave offsets in $c12$):

```
mov r1, c16.x           //time...
mad r0, r1, c13, r0     //add scaled time to move bumps according to
                          frequency
add r0, r0, c12         //starting time offset
```

This computes the input to the cosine function. A Taylor approximation, however, is only accurate for the range it is created for, and more terms are needed the larger that range is. So for a repeating function like a cosine wave, the fractional portion of the wave phase can be extracted and then expanded to the $-\pi$ to π range before calculating the Taylor series expansion.

```
frc r0.xy, r0           //take frac of all 4 components
frc r1.xy, r0.zwzw      //
mov r0.zw, r1.xyxy      //
mul r0, r0, c10.x       //multiply by fixup factor (due to inaccuracy)
sub r0, r0, c0.y        //subtract .5
mul r0, r0, c1.w        //mult tex coords by 2pi  coords range from
                          (-pi to pi)
```

Calculate the Taylor series expansion of sine (r4) and cosine (r5):

```
mul r5, r0, r0          // (wave vec)^2
mul r1, r5, r0          // (wave vec)^3
mul r6, r1, r0          // (wave vec)^4
mul r2, r6, r0          // (wave vec)^5
mul r7, r2, r0          // (wave vec)^6
mul r3, r7, r0          // (wave vec)^7
mul r8, r3, r0          // (wave vec)^8

mad r4, r1, c2.y, r0    // (wave vec) - ((wave vec)^3)/3!
mad r4, r2, c2.z, r4    //+((wave vec)^5)/5!
mad r4, r3, c2.w, r4    //-((wave vec)^7)/7!

mov r0, c0.z            //1
mad r5, r5, c3.x ,r0    //-(wave vec)^2/2!
mad r5, r6, c3.y, r5    //+(wave vec)^4/4!
mad r5, r7, c3.z, r5    //-(wave vec)^6/6!
mad r5, r8, c3.w, r5    //+(wave vec)^8/8!
```

The results are modulated by relative heights of each of the waves and the scaled sine wave is used to perturb the position along the normal. The new object space position is then transformed to compute the final position. The vertex input, v5.x, is used to allow artist control of how high the waves are in different parts of the ocean. This can be useful for shorelines where the ocean waves will be smaller than those farther out to sea:

```
sub  r0, c0.z, v5.x        //... 1-wave scale
mul  r4, r4, r0            //scale sin
mul  r5, r5, r0            //scale cos

dp4  r0, r4, c11           //multiply wave heights by waves

mul  r0.xyz, v3, r0        //multiply wave magnitude at this vertex
                          //    by normal
add  r0.xyz, r0, v0        //add to position
mov  r0.w, c0.z            //homogenous component

m4x4    oPos, r0, c4       //OutPos = ObjSpacePos * World-View-Proj
                          //    Matrix
```

The tangent and normal vectors are perturbed in a similar manner using the cosine wave instead of the sine wave. This is done because the cosine is the first derivative of the sine and therefore perturbs the tangent and normal vectors by the slope of the wave. The following code makes the assumption that the source art is a plane along the Z axis.

It is worth mentioning that this vertex perturbation technique can be extended to sinusoidally warp almost any geometry. See "Bubble Shader" for more details.

```
mul    r1, r5, c11         //cos* waveheight
dp4    r9.x, -r1, c14      //normal x offset
dp4    r9.yzw, -r1, c15    //normal y offset and tangent offset
mov    r5, v3              //starting normal
mad    r5.xy, r9, c10.y, r5   //warped normal move nx, ny according to
                          //cos*wavedir*waveheight
mov    r4, v8             //tangent
mad    r4.z, -r9.x, c10.y, r4.z   //warped tangent vector

dp3    r10.x, r5, r5
rsq    r10.y, r10.x
mul    r5, r5, r10.y       //normalize normal

dp3    r10.x, r4, r4
rsq    r10.y, r10.x
mul    r4, r4, r10.y       //normalize tangent
```

The binormal is then calculated using a cross product of the warped normal and the warped tangent vector to create a tangent space basis matrix. This matrix will be used later to transform the bump map's tangent space normal into world space for cube-mapped environment-mapped bump mapping (CMEMBM).

```
mul    r3, r4.yzxw, r5.zxyw
mad    r3, r4.zxyw, -r5.yzxw, r3   //xprod to find binormal
```

CMEMBM needs the view vector to perform the reflection operation:

```
sub    r2, c8, r0          //view vector
dp3    r10.x, r2, r2
rsq    r10.y, r10.x
mul    r2, r2, r10.y                //normalized view vector
```

The height map shown in Figure 3 is used to create a normal map. The incoming texture coordinates are used as a starting point to create two sets of coordinates that are rotated and scroll across each other based on time. These coordinates are used to scroll two bump maps past each other to produce the smaller ripples in the ocean. One interesting trick used in this shader is to swap the u and v coordinates for the second texture before compositing them. This eliminates the visual artifacts that occur when the scrolling textures align with each other exactly and the ripples appear to stop for a moment. Swapping the texture coordinates ensure that the maps never align with each other (unless they are radially symmetric).

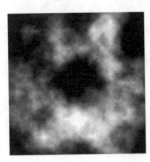

Figure 3: Height map used to create the normal map for the ocean shader

```
mov     r0, c16.x
mul     r0, r0, c17.xyxy
frc     r0.xy, r0          //frc of incoming time
add     r0, v7, r0         //add time to tex coords
mov     oT0, r0            //distorted tex coord 0

mov     r0, c16.x
mul     r0, r0, c17.zwzw
frc     r0.xy, r0          //frc of incoming time
add     r0, v7, r0         //add time to tex coords
mov     oT1, r0.yxzw       //distorted tex coord 1
```

The vertex shader is completed by the output of the remaining vectors used by the pixel shader. The pixel and vertex shader for the ocean water effect can be found in its entirety at the end of this article.

```
mov     oT2, r2            //pass in view vector (worldspace)
mov     oT3, r3            //tangent
mov     oT4, r4            //binormal
mov     oT5, r5            //normal
```

CMEMBM Pixel Shader with Fresnel Term

Once the vertex shader has completed, the pixel shader is responsible for producing the bump-mapped reflective ocean surface.

First, the pixel shader averages the two scrolling RGB normal bump maps to generate a composite normal. In this particular case, the bumps are softened further by dividing the x and y components in half. Next, it transforms the tangent space composite normal into world space and calculates a per-pixel reflection vector. The reflection vector is used to sample a skybox cubic environment map (Figure 4). The shader also calculates $2*N \cdot V$ and uses it to sample a Fresnel 1D texture (Figure 5). This Fresnel map gives the water a more greenish appearance when looking straight down into it and a more bluish appearance when looking edge on. The scale by two is used to expand the range of the Fresnel map.

```
texld r0, t0                        //bump map 0
texld r1, t1                        //sample bump map 1
texcrd r2.rgb, t2                   //View vector
texcrd r3.rgb, t3                   //Tangent
texcrd r4.rgb, t4                   //Binormal
texcrd r5.rgb, t5                   //Normal

  add_d4  r0.xy, r0_bx2, r1_bx2     //Scaled Average of 2 bumpmaps' xy
                                      offsets

  mul r1.rgb, r0.x, r3
  mad r1.rgb, r0.y, r4, r1
  mad r1.rgb, r0.z, r5, r1          //Transform bumpmap normal into world
                                      space

  dp3 r0.rgb, r1, r2                //V.N
  mad r2.rgb, r1, r0_x2, -r2        //R = 2N(V.N)-V

  mov_sat r1, r0_x2                 //2 * V.N  (sample over range of 1d
                                      map!)
```

Figure 4: Cubic environment map used for ocean water reflections

Figure 5: 1D texture used for the water color addressed by 1–N·V

The second phase composites the water color from the Fresnel map, the environment map, and other specular highlights extracted from the environment map. One trick we use is to square the environment map color values to make the colors brighter and to enhance the contrast for compositing. The advantage to doing this in the pixel shader instead of as a preprocessing step is so the same skybox environment map can be used for other objects in the scene. To get the specular light sparkles in the water, a specular component is derived from the green channel of the environment map. For this example, the choice is based on the environment map artwork. The desired effect is to have the highlights in the water correspond to bright spots in the sky, and in this case, the green channel seemed to work best. To make sure the specular peaks were only generated from the brightest areas of the environment map, the specular value extracted from the green channel was raised to the eighth power. This has the effect of darkening all but the brightest areas of the image.

Another approach for encoding specular highlights in an environment map is to have the artists specify a glow map as an alpha channel of the environment map. See "Bubble Shader" for more details.

```
texcrd r0.rgb, r0
texld r2, r2                  //cubic env map
texld r3, r1                  //Index fresnel map using 2*V.N

mul r2.rgb, r2, r2            //Square the environment map
+mul r2.a, r2.g, r2.g         //use green channel of env map as
                                  specular

mul r2.rgb, r2, 1-r0.r        //Fresnel Term
+mul r2.a, r2.a, r2.a         //Specular highlight ^4

add_d4_sat r2.rgb, r2, r3_x2  //+= Water color
+mul r2.a, r2.a, r2.a         //Specular highlight ^8

mad_sat r0, r2.a, c1, r2      //+= Specular highlight * highlight
                                  color
```

Ocean Water Shader Source Code

```
DefineParam texture rgbNormalBumpMap NULL
SetParamEnum rgbNormalBumpMap EP_TEX0

DefineParam texture waterGradientMap NULL
SetParamEnum waterGradientMap EP_TEX1

DefineParam texture cubeEnvMap NULL
SetParamEnum cubeEnvMap EP_TEX2

//Constant store
DefineParam vector4 commonConst (0.0, 0.5, 1.0, 2.0)

DefineParam vector4 appConst (0.0, 0.0, 0.0, 0.0) //Time, 1.0/lightFalloffDist
SetParamEnum appConst EP_VECTOR3

DefineParam vector4 worldSpaceCamPos (0, 0, 0, 0)
BindParamToState worldSpaceCamPos STATE_VECTOR_CAMERA_POSITION 0 WORLD_SPACE

DefineParam vector4 worldSpaceLightPos (-10000, -25000, 2000, 1)
SetParamEnum worldSpaceLightPos EP_VECTOR0

DefineParam matrix4x4 wvp [(1,0,0,0) (0,1,0,0) (0,0,1,0) (0,0,0,1)]
BindParamToState wvp STATE_MATRIX_PVW

//=========================================================================
//commonly used constants
//heights for waves 4 different fronts
DefineParam vector4 waveHeights (80.0, 100.0, 5.0, 5.0)

//offset in sine wave.. (ranges 0 to 1)
DefineParam vector4 waveOffset (0.0, 0.2, 0.0, 0.0)

//freqency of the waves (e.g., waves per unit time..)
DefineParam vector4 waveSpeed (0.2, 0.15, 0.4, 0.4)

//diection of waves in tangent space (also controls frequency in space)
DefineParam vector4 waveDirx (0.25, 0.0, -0.7, -0.8)
DefineParam vector4 waveDiry (0.0, 0.15, -0.7, 0.1)

//scale factor for distortion of base map coords
```

```
//bump map scroll speed
DefineParam vector4 bumpSpeed (0.031, 0.04, -0.03, 0.02)

DefineParam vector4 piVector (4.0, 1.57079632, 3.14159265, 6.28318530)

//Vectors for taylor's series expansion of sin and cos
DefineParam vector4 sin7 (1, -0.16161616, 0.0083333, -0.00019841)
DefineParam vector4 cos8 (-0.5, 0.041666666, -0.0013888889, 0.000024801587)

//frcFixup.x is a fixup to make the edges of the clamped sin wave match up again
due to // numerical inaccuracy
//frcFixup.y should be equal to the average of du/dx and dv/dy for the base texture
// coords.. this scales the warping of the normal

DefineParam vector4 frcFixup (1.02, 0.003, 0, 0)

DefineParam vector4 psCommonConst (0, 0.5, 1, 0.25)
DefineParam vector4 highlightColor (0.8, 0.76, 0.62, 1)

DefineParam vector4 waterColor (0.50, 0.6, 0.7, 1)

//===============================================================================
// 1 Pass
//===============================================================================
StartShader
   Requirement VERTEXSHADERVERSION 1.1
   Requirement PIXELSHADERVERSION 1.4
   StartPass
      SetTexture 0 rgbNormalBumpMap
      SetTextureFilter 0 BILINEAR
      SetTextureStageState 0 MIPMAPLODBIAS -1.0

      SetTexture 1 rgbNormalBumpMap
      SetTextureFilter 1 BILINEAR
      SetTextureStageState 1 MIPMAPLODBIAS -1.0

      SetTexture 2 cubeEnvMap
      SetTextureWrap 2 CLAMP CLAMP CLAMP
      SetTextureFilter 2 BILINEAR
      SetTextureStageState 2 MIPMAPLODBIAS 0.0

      SetTexture 3 waterGradientMap
      SetTextureWrap 3 CLAMP CLAMP CLAMP
      SetTextureFilter 3 LINEAR

      SetVertexShaderConstant 0 commonConst
      SetVertexShaderConstant 1 piVector
      SetVertexShaderConstant 2 sin7
      SetVertexShaderConstant 3 cos8

      SetVertexShaderConstant 4 wvp
      SetVertexShaderConstant 8 worldSpaceCamPos
      SetVertexShaderConstant 9 worldSpaceLightPos

      SetVertexShaderConstant 10 frcFixup
      SetVertexShaderConstant 11 waveHeights
      SetVertexShaderConstant 12 waveOffset
      SetVertexShaderConstant 13 waveSpeed
      SetVertexShaderConstant 14 waveDirx
      SetVertexShaderConstant 15 waveDiry
      SetVertexShaderConstant 16 appConst
      SetVertexShaderConstant 17 bumpSpeed

      StartVertexShader
         // v0   - Vertex Position
         // v3   - Vertex Normal
```

```
// v7      - Vertex Texture Data u,v
// v8      - Vertex Tangent (v direction)

// c0      - { 0.0,   0.5, 1.0, 2.0}
// c1      - { 4.0,  .5pi, pi, 2pi}
// c2      - {1, -1/3!, 1/5!, -1/7!  }  //for sin
// c3      - {1/2!, -1/4!, 1/6!, -1/8!  }  //for cos
// c4-7    - Composite World-View-Projection Matrix
// c8      - ModelSpace Camera Position
// c9      - ModelSpace Light Position
// c10     - {fixup factor for taylor series imprecision, }
// c11     - {waveHeight0, waveHeight1, waveHeight2, waveHeight3}
// c12     - {waveOffset0, waveOffset1, waveOffset2, waveOffset3}
// c13     - {waveSpeed0, waveSpeed1, waveSpeed2, waveSpeed3}
// c14     - {waveDirX0, waveDirX1, waveDirX2, waveDirX3}
// c15     - {waveDirY0, waveDirY1, waveDirY2, waveDirY3}
// c16     - { time, sin(time)}
// c17     - {basetexcoord distortion x0, y0, x1, y1}

vs.1.1

mul r0, c14, v7.x      //use tex coords as inputs to sinusoidal warp
mad r0, c15, v7.y, r0  //use tex coords as inputs to sinusoidal warp

mov r1, c16.x          //time...
mad r0, r1, c13, r0    //add scaled time to move bumps according to
                         frequency
add r0, r0, c12        //starting time offset
frc r0.xy, r0          //take frac of all 4 components
frc r1.xy, r0.zwzw     //
mov r0.zw, r1.xyxy     //

mul r0, r0, c10.x      //multiply by fixup factor (due to inaccuracy)
sub r0, r0, c0.y       //subtract .5
mul r0, r0, c1.w       //mult tex coords by 2pi  coords range from
                         (-pi to pi)

mul r5, r0, r0         //(wave vec)^2
mul r1, r5, r0         //(wave vec)^3
mul r6, r1, r0         //(wave vec)^4
mul r2, r6, r0         //(wave vec)^5
mul r7, r2, r0         //(wave vec)^6
mul r3, r7, r0         //(wave vec)^7
mul r8, r3, r0         //(wave vec)^8

mad r4, r1, c2.y, r0   //(wave vec) - ((wave vec)^3)/3!
mad r4, r2, c2.z, r4   //+ ((wave vec)^5)/5!
mad r4, r3, c2.w, r4   //- ((wave vec)^7)/7!

mov r0, c0.z           //1
mad r5, r5, c3.x ,r0   //-(wave vec)^2/2!
mad r5, r6, c3.y, r5   //+(wave vec)^4/4!
mad r5, r7, c3.z, r5   //-(wave vec)^6/6!
mad r5, r8, c3.w, r5   //+(wave vec)^8/8!

sub r0, c0.z, v5.x     //... 1-wave scale
mul r4, r4, r0         //scale sin
mul r5, r5, r0         //scale cos

dp4 r0, r4, c11        //multiply wave heights by waves

mul r0.xyz, v3, r0     //multiply wave magnitude at this vertex by normal
add r0.xyz, r0, v0     //add to position
mov r0.w, c0.z         //homogenous component
```

```
     m4x4     oPos, r0, c4     //OutPos = ObjSpacePos * World-View-Projection
                                     Matrix
     mul      r1, r5, c11              //cos* waveheight
     dp4      r9.x, -r1, c14           //normal x offset
     dp4      r9.yzw, -r1, c15         //normal y offset and tangent offset
     mov      r5, v3                   //starting normal
     mad      r5.xy, r9, c10.y, r5     //warped normal move nx, ny according to
                                       //cos*wavedir*waveheight
     mov      r4, v8                   //tangent
     mad      r4.z, -r9.x, c10.y, r4.z //warped tangent vector

     dp3      r10.x, r5, r5
     rsq      r10.y, r10.x
     mul      r5, r5, r10.y            //normalize normal
     dp3      r10.x, r4, r4
     rsq      r10.y, r10.x
     mul      r4, r4, r10.y            //normalize tangent

     mul      r3, r4.yzxw, r5.zxyw
     mad      r3, r4.zxyw, -r5.yzxw, r3 //xprod to find binormal

     sub      r2, c8, r0               //view vector
     dp3      r10.x, r2, r2
     rsq      r10.y, r10.x
     mul      r2, r2, r10.y            //normalized view vector

     mov      r0, c16.x
     mul      r0, r0, c17.xyxy
     frc      r0.xy, r0                //frc of incoming time
     add      r0, v7, r0               //add time to tex coords
     mov      oT0, r0                  //distorted tex coord 0

     mov      r0, c16.x
     mul      r0, r0, c17.zwzw
     frc      r0.xy, r0                //frc of incoming time
     add      r0, v7, r0               //add time to tex coords
     mov      oT1, r0.yxzw             //distorted tex coord 1

     mov      oT2, r2                  //pass in view vector (worldspace)
     mov      oT3, r3                  //tangent
     mov      oT4, r4                  //binormal
     mov      oT5, r5                  //normal
EndVertexShader

SetPixelShaderConstant 0 psCommonConst
SetPixelShaderConstant 1 highlightColor

StartPixelShader
   ps.1.4

   texld r0, t0                   //bump map 0
   texld r1, t1                   //sample bump map 1
   texcrd r2.rgb, t2              //View vector
   texcrd r3.rgb, t3              //Tangent
   texcrd r4.rgb, t4              //Binormal
   texcrd r5.rgb, t5              //Normal

     add_d4  r0.xy, r0_bx2, r1_bx2 //Scaled Average of 2 bumpmaps xy
                                       offsets

     mul r1.rgb, r0.x, r3
     mad r1.rgb, r0.y, r4, r1
     mad r1.rgb, r0.z, r5, r1      //Put bumpmap normal into world space

     dp3 r0.rgb, r1, r2            //V.N
```

```
            mad r2.rgb, r1, r0_x2, -r2      //R = 2N(V.N)-V

            mov_sat r1, r0_x2               //2 * V.N  (sample over range of 1d
                                                       map!)

        phase
            texcrd r0.rgb, r0
            texld r2, r2                    //cubic env map
            texld r3, r1                    //Index fresnel map using 2*V.N

            mul r2.rgb, r2, r2              //Square the environment map
   +mul r2.a, r2.g, r2.g                    //use green channel of env map as
                                              specular
     mul r2.rgb, r2, 1-r0.r                 //Fresnel Term
            +mul r2.a, r2.a, r2.a           //Specular highlight ^4

            add_d4_sat r2.rgb, r2, r3_x2    //+= Water color
            +mul r2.a, r2.a, r2.a           //Specular highlight ^8

            mad_sat r0, r2.a, c1, r2        //+= Specular highlight * highlight
                                              color

        EndPixelShader

    EndPass
EndShader
```

Sample Applications

This shader can be seen in the Island demos (http://www.ati.com/na/pages/resource_centre/
dev_rel/Demos.html) and the Ocean Screen Saver (http://www.ati.com/na/pages/resource_
centre/dev_rel/screensavers.html), as well as on the companion CD.

Rippling Reflective and Refractive Water

Alex Vlachos, John Isidoro, and Chris Oat

Introduction

One of the classic challenges of real-time computer graphics is to generate realistic-looking water. Because water can look very different depending on the context of the scene, it is important to define a few different categories of water effects. For example, techniques used to render ocean water (see "Rendering Ocean Water") may not produce realistic-looking puddle water. With this in mind, the shaders presented in this chapter will focus on highly realistic per-pixel lighting effects used to render real-time lake water. Unlike ocean water, lake water does not have large rolling swells. Instead, the surface geometry consists of high frequency, non-uniform perturbations that give the surface a subtle choppiness, resulting in slightly distorted reflections and refractions. Because of these surface characteristics, shallow water reflections and refractions, as shown in Figure 1, can be reasonably approximated with planar reflections and renderable textures.

Renderable textures allow the programmer to distort the reflection and refraction textures using a sum of scrolling bump maps to simulate the water surface ripples. One of the nice things about distorting these textures with a bump map is that the renderable textures can be of a much lower resolution than the screen resolution, and the end result will still look very compelling. The following example was rendered using two 512x256 renderable textures. Since the reflected and refracted geometry is drawn once for each renderable texture, rendering to these maps at a lower resolution provides a significant performance boost.

Figure 1: This scene was drawn using the reflection and refraction techniques described in this chapter.

357

Generating Reflection and Refraction Maps

When dealing with fairly flat water surfaces such as lake water, river water, or puddle water, reflections can be convincingly approximated with planar reflections. A reflection map is created by reflecting the scene geometry over the plane of the water's surface and rendering to a texture. It is important to utilize user clip planes in order to clip any geometry that is already below the plane of reflection, as this geometry is underwater and should not be included in the reflection map (see Figure 2).

Figure 2: Example of a reflection map created by reflecting scene geometry about the plane of the water's surface

As illustrated in Figure 3, the refraction map is generated by clipping all scene geometry above the plane of the water's surface. As with the reflection map, user clip planes are used to cull the geometry above the water's surface.

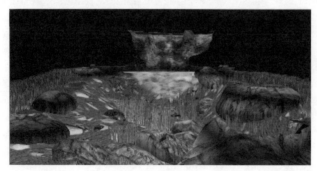

Figure 3: Example of a refraction map created by drawing only the geometry below the water's surface

Vertex Shader

A vertex shader is used to approximate sine and cosine waves to generate rippling water geometry as well as perturbing the tangent space vectors per vertex. This vertex shader is very similar to the vertex shader presented in "Rendering Ocean Water"; please refer to that article for a more detailed description of the vertex shader. The slightly altered ocean water vertex shader is presented below; the only difference is the value for wave height stored in c11.

```
StartVertexShader
    vs.1.1
    // v0    - Vertex Position
    // v7    - Vertex Texture Data u,v
    // v8    - Vertex Tangent (v direction)
```

```
//
// c0    - { 0.0,  0.5, 1.0, 2.0}
// c1    - { 4.0, .5pi, pi, 2pi}
// c2    - {1, -1/3!, 1/5!, -1/7!  }  //for sin
// c3    - {1/2!, -1/4!, 1/6!, -1/8!  }  //for cos
// c4-7  - Composite World-View-Projection Matrix
// c8    - ModelSpace Camera Position
// c9    - ModelSpace Light Position
// c10   - {fixup factor for taylor series imprecision, }
// c11   - {waveHeight0, waveHeight1, waveHeight2, waveHeight3}
// c12   - {waveOffset0, waveOffset1, waveOffset2, waveOffset3}
// c13   - {waveSpeed0, waveSpeed1, waveSpeed2, waveSpeed3}
// c14   - {waveDirX0, waveDirX1, waveDirX2, waveDirX3}
// c15   - {waveDirY0, waveDirY1, waveDirY2, waveDirY3}
// c16   - {time, sin(time)}
// c17   - {basetexcoord distortion x0, y0, x1, y1}

mul r0, c14, v7.x          // use tex coords as inputs to sinusoidal warp
mad r0, c15, v7.y, r0      // use tex coords as inputs to sinusoidal warp

mov r1, c16.x              // time...
mad r0, r1, c13, r0        // add scaled time to move bumps by frequency
add r0, r0, c12
frc r0.xy, r0              // take frac of all 4 components
frc r1.xy, r0.zwzw
mov r0.zw, r1.xyxy

mul r0, r0, c10.x          // multiply by fixup factor (fix taylor series
                           //    inaccuracy)
sub r0, r0, c0.y           // subtract .5
mul r0, r0, c1.w           // mult tex coords by 2pi  coords range from
                           //    (-pi to pi)

mul r5, r0, r0             // (wave vec)^2
mul r1, r5, r0             // (wave vec)^3
mul r6, r1, r0             // (wave vec)^4
mul r2, r6, r0             // (wave vec)^5
mul r7, r2, r0             // (wave vec)^6
mul r3, r7, r0             // (wave vec)^7
mul r8, r3, r0             // (wave vec)^8

mad r4, r1, c2.y, r0       // (wave vec) - ((wave vec)^3)/3!
mad r4, r2, c2.z, r4       //  + ((wave vec)^5)/5!
mad r4, r3, c2.w, r4       //  - ((wave vec)^7)/7!

mov r0, c0.z               // 1
mad r5, r5, c3.x ,r0       // -(wave vec)^2/2!
mad r5, r6, c3.y, r5       // +(wave vec)^4/4!
mad r5, r7, c3.z, r5       // -(wave vec)^6/6!
mad r5, r8, c3.w, r5       // +(wave vec)^8/8!

dp4 r0, r4, c11            // multiply wave heights by waves

mul r0.xyz, c0.xxzx, r0    // multiply wave magnitude at this vertex by normal
add r0.xyz, r0, v0         // add to position
mov r0.w, c0.z             // homogenous component

m4x4 oPos, r0, c4          // OutPos = ObjSpacePos * World-View-Projection
                           //    Matrix
mul r1, r5, c11            // cos* waveheight
dp4 r9.x, -r1, c14         // normal x offset
dp4 r9.yzw, -r1, c15       // normal y offset and tangent offset
mov r5, c0.xxzx
```

```
        mad r5.xy, r9, c10.y, r5    // warped normal move according to
                                            cos*wavedir*waveeheight
    mov r4, v9
    mad r4.z, -r9.x, c10.y, r4.z   // warped tangent vector
    dp3 r10.x, r5, r5
    rsq r10.y, r10.x
    mul r5, r5, r10.y              // normalize normal

    dp3 r10.x, r4, r4
    rsq r10.y, r10.x
    mul r4, r4, r10.y              // normalize tangent
    mul r3, r4.yzxw, r5.zxyw
    mad r3, r4.zxyw, -r5.yzxw, r3  // cross product to find binormal
    sub r1, c9, r0                 // light vector
    sub r2, c8, r0                 // view vector
    dp3 r10.x, r1, r1              // normalize light vector
    rsq r10.y, r10.x
    mul r1, r1, r10.y
    dp3 r6.x, r1, r3
    dp3 r6.y, r1, r4
    dp3 r6.z, r1, r5              // transform light vector into tangent space
    dp3 r10.x, r2, r2
    rsq r10.y, r10.x
    mul r2, r2, r10.y             // normalized view vector

    dp3 r7.x, r2, r3
    dp3 r7.y, r2, r4
    dp3 r7.z, r2, r5             // put view vector in tangent space

    mov r0, c16.x
    mul r0, r0, c24
    frc r0.xy, r0
    mul r1, v7, c26

    add oT0, r1, r0             // bump map coord1
    mov r0, c16.x
    mul r0, r0, c25
    frc r0.xy, r0
    mul r1, v7, c27

    add oT1, r1, r0            // bump map coord 2
    dp4 r0.x, v0, c20
    dp4 r0.y, v0, c21
    dp4 r0.zw, v0, c22

    mov oT2, r0               // projective tex coords for reflection/
                                    refreaction maps
    mov oT3, r7              // tan space view vec
    mov oT4, v7             // base map coords
    mov oT5, r6            // tan space light vec

EndVertexShader
```

Pixel Shader

The pixel shader used to render the water has a few novel features. When sampling from the renderable textures, the texture coordinates must be interpolated linearly in screen space. The reason for this is that the scene is already rendered from the point of view of the camera, and thus the contents of the renderable texture are already perspectively correct. To achieve this, the projection matrix must be altered in the following way:

```
Matrix M = { 0.5f,  0.0f,  0.0f,  0.0f,
             0.0f, -0.5f,  0.0f,  0.0f,
             0.0f,  0.0f,  0.0f,  0.0f,
             0.5f,  0.5f,  1.0f,  0.0f };
// row major element (1,4) is set to zero
projectionMatrix[11] = 0.0f;

// projection matrix uses scale and bias to get coordinates into
// [0.0, 1.0] range
projectionMatrix = M * projectionMatrix;
```

Now the projection matrix will move vertices into a normalized texture space for indexing into the pre-projected reflection and refraction maps. Given the linearly interpolated texture coordinates, the perturbations for the reflection and refraction maps can be performed on a per-pixel basis by simply adding a scaled and rotated version of the xy offsets from the scrolling bump maps. It is important to scale and rotate these offsets so that as the bump map scrolls, the perturbations move in the direction that the water is flowing. Another interesting trick is to sample the refraction map using the swapped texture coordinates used to index the reflection map (for example, index the reflection map using coordinates <u,v>, and then sample the refraction map using coordinates <v,u>). Swapping the coordinates in this way prevents the two scrolling bump maps from aligning. After sampling, the refractions are modulated with the water color, and the perturbed reflections are attenuated with a per-pixel Fresnel term and modulated with a reflection color. The per-pixel Fresnel term scales the reflections such that the strength of the reflection is dependent on the angle of the view vector with respect to the water surface normal. The full shader is shown below along with further comments.

```
StartPixelShader

    ps.1.4

    // T0 : Bump map 1 Coordinates
    // T1 : Bump map 2 Coordinates
    // T2 : Projective Texture Coordinates for Reflection/Refraction Maps
    // T3 : Tangent Space View Vector
    // T5 : Tangent Space Light Vector
    texld r0, t0
    texld r1, t1

    texcrd r2.xy, t2_dw.xyw     // renderable textures
    texcrd r4.xyz, t3           // tan space V
    texcrd r5.xyz, t5           // tan space L

    add_d2 r1.rgb, r0_bx2, r1_bx2

    mov r3.xy, r2

    dp3 r0.r, r4, r1            // V.N
    dp3 r0.g, r1, r5            // L.N

    mad_sat r5.rg, r1, c2, r3   // perturb refraction
    mad_sat r4.rg, r1, c1, r3   // perturb reflection

    phase

    texcrd r0.rgb, r0          // V.N, L.N, R.L

    texld r2, r4               // Reflection
    texld r3, r5               // Refraction

    mul_sat r2.rgb, r2, c3     // reflection color
    +mul r2.a, r0.g, r0.g
```

```
    mul_sat r3.rgb, r3, c4                    // refraction color
    +mul_sat r2.a, r2.a, r2.a

    mad_sat r0.rgb, 1-r0.r, r2, r3
    +mul_sat r2.a, r2.a, r2.a

    mad_sat r0.rgb, r2.a, c6, r0              // add specular highlights to reflection
    +mov r0.a, r0.r

EndPixelShader
```

Figure 4: Rippling reflective and refractive water

Note the perturbed refractions where the body of the fish is still underwater and the underwater vegetation. Perturbed reflections can be seen where the waterfall is reflected in the water's surface in the far right. Also note how the specular highlighting gives the water surface better definition.

Conclusion

This section focused on using vertex and pixel shaders to render realistic rippling water with realistic reflections and refractions by building on techniques described in other articles. The shaders presented here demonstrate the use of Taylor series approximations to compute sine and cosine waves in a vertex shader as well as the use of renderable textures to create rippling reflections and refractions.

The shaders described in this section, as well as the accompanying screen grabs, were taken from ATI's Nature demo. This real-time interactive graphics demo shows rippling reflective and refractive water in a complex natural environment and is available on the Internet as an executable program or compressed video in the Demos section of the ATI Developer's web site (www.ati.com/developer/).

Crystal/Candy Shader

John Isidoro and David Gosselin

Introduction

The goal of this article is to create a shader that gives the effect of a very shiny semi-transparent surface, such as crystal or a piece of hard candy. This is accomplished using a combination of vertex and pixel shaders. The shader combines a cubic environment map to provide the reflections, a bump map to provide some detail, a Fresnel term to control opacity, and a base map to provide the surface color.

Setup

This shader uses a model with one set of texture coordinates for both a base map (color) and bump map (normals encoded as colors). Additionally, the shader uses a cubic environment map. In this example, the environment map was prerendered using the ATI Sushi graphics engine and is shown in Figure 1.

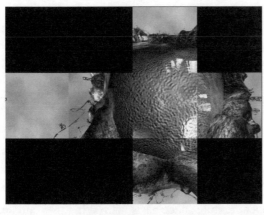

Figure 1: Cubic environment map

Since the object needs to be semi-transparent, it will be drawn in two passes, both blended into the frame buffer. The first pass will draw the back faces of the object. This can be accomplished by setting the cull mode to either clockwise or counterclockwise depending on how your application specifies back/front faces. This is accomplished by setting the Direct3D render state D3DRS_CULLMODE appropriately. The code for doing this is:

```
d3dDevice->SetRenderState (D3DRS_CULLMODE, D3DCULL_CCW);
```

The front faces are drawn by setting the opposite cull mode and drawing the model again:

```
d3dDevice->SetRenderState (D3DRS_CULLMODE, D3DCULL_CW);
```

For both passes, alpha blending is enabled in order to give the transparent effect. The code for setting this up is:

```
d3dDevice->SetRenderState (D3DRS_ALPHABLENDENABLE, TRUE);
d3dDevice->SetRenderState (D3DRS_SRCBLEND, D3DBLEND_SRCALPHA);
d3dDevice->SetRenderState (D3DRS_DSTBLEND, D3DBLEND_INVSRCALPHA);
```

Now that we have set these general render states, we will explore the specifics of the crystal/candy vertex and pixel shaders.

Vertex Shader

The vertex shader for this effect is centered on computing the view direction. Additionally, it will pass the tangent/texture space vectors along so that the bump map normal can be transformed into object space in the pixel shader. The first section of the vertex shader computes the transformed vertex position. The vertex shader code to perform this transformation follows:

```
// c0   - (0.125, 0.5, 1.0, 2.0)
// c2   - World Space Camera Position
// c4-c7- World/View/Projection Matrix
// v0   - Vertex Position
// v3   - Vertex Normal
// v7   - Vertex Texture Data u,v
// v8   - Vertex tangent Vector
vs.1.1
m4x4  oPos, v0, c4            // OutPos = ObjSpacePos * WVP Matrix
mov   oT0, v7                 // output basemap texcoords
```

The next section of the vertex shader computes the view vector in world space. This is accomplished by subtracting the world space camera position from the world space vertex position and then normalizing the result. Note that in this example, the world transform is identity and the input vertex position is used directly. If this is not the case in your application, you will need to transform the input position by the world matrix before performing this calculation.

```
sub   r8, c2, v0             // viewer direction
dp3   r10.x, r8, r8          // magnitude
rsq   r10.y, r10.x           // normalize
mul   r8, r8, r10.y          // V normalized view vector
mov   oT1, r8                // world space view vector
```

The next section passes along the tangent/texture space basis matrix. In this example, we compute the binormal by taking the cross product of the tangent and the normal. Note that this is not a general solution; it relies upon the fact that the texture coordinates for this model are not reversed on any triangles.

```
mov   r5, v3                 // normal (tZ)
mov   oT4, r5
mov   r3, v8                 // tangent (tY)
```

```
mov    oT2, r3
mul    r4, r5.yzxw, r3.zxyw       // compute binormal (tX) as being
mad    r4, r5.zxyw, -r3.yzxw, r4  // perpendicular to normal
mov    oT3, r4
```

The last section of this vertex shader transforms the view vector into tangent space. It also scales and biases the vector so that it can be passed to the pixel shader in one of the color interpolators.

```
m3x3   r6, r8, r3                 // xform view vec into tangent space
mad    oD0, r6, c0.y, c0.y        // tan space V vector
```

Now that the per-vertex computations are described, we can look at what happens at the pixel level to create the crystal look.

Pixel Shader

The pixel shader for this effect is accomplished in two shader phases. The first phase computes the reflection vector used for the cubic environment map, while the second phase composites the color from the dependent read with other maps. The full shader is shown below and a more detailed description of the various parts follows.

```
// c0 - (0.0, 0.5, 1.0, 0.75)
// c1 - base color (0.5, 0.0, 0.5, 1.0)
// c2 - reflection color (1.0, 1.0, 1.0, 1.0)
// c7 - (0.0, 0.0, 1.0, 0.4)
ps.1.4
texld r0, t0                      // bump map
texcrd r1.rgb, t1                 // view vec
texcrd r2.rgb, t2                 // tan x
texcrd r3.rgb, t3                 // tan y
texcrd r4.rgb, t4                 // tan z

    lrp r0.rgb, c7.a, r0, c7      // weaken bump map by lerping with 0,0,1
    mul r5.rgb, r0.x, r2          // move bump normal into obj space
    mad r5.rgb, r0.y, r3, r5      // move bump normal into obj space
    mad r5.rgb, r0.z, r4, r5      // move bump normal into obj space

    dp3 r3.rgb, r1, r5            // V.N
    mad r2.rgb, r3, r5_x2, -r1    // 2N(V.N)-V

phase
texld r1, t0                      // base map
texld r2, r2                      // fetch from environment map

    dp3 r0.a, v0_bx2, r0          // (N.V)fresnel term
    mul r1.rgb, r1, c1            // base map * base color
    +mov r0.a, 1-r0.a            // 1-(N.V)
    mul r2.rgb, r2, c2            // reflection map * reflection color

    mad r0.rgb, r2, r0.a, r1      // (1-(N.V)) * reflection map * reflection color
                                  //  + base map * base color
    +add_sat r0.a, r0.a, c0.y     // boost opacity: (1-(N.V)) + 0.5
```

At the core of the shader is the environment mapping, which is sampled as a dependent read at the top of the second phase. The following lines from the pixel shader compute the per-pixel reflection vector and sample the cube map:

```
    dp3 r3.rgb, r1, r5          // V.N
    mad r2.rgb, r3, r5_x2, -r1  // 2N(V.N)-V
phase
texld r2, r2                    // fetch from env map
```

If the shader was changed to just do this computation, the result would look like Figure 2. One thing to note is that in this picture, the top portion of the model has intentionally faceted normals to give the appearance of some kind of cut crystal, while the bottom part of the model has smooth normals.

To this effect, we now want to add bumpiness based on the normal map. In order for this to look correct, we take the sampled normal (r0) from the bump map and transform it into object space using the tangent space matrix that was computed in the vertex shader and interpolated across the polygon. The following lines show the part of the pixel shader where this computation takes place.

```
    mul r5.rgb, r0.x, r2        // move bump normal into obj space
    mad r5.rgb, r0.y, r3, r5    // move bump normal into obj space
    mad r5.rgb, r0.z, r4, r5    // move bump normal into obj space
```

If this is added to the environment mapping, you get something that looks like Figure 3.

Since this looks a little too bumpy for the effect we want, a small term is linearly interpolated with the bump map prior to doing the bump calculation. The following line of code from the shader performs this task:

```
    lrp r0.rgb, c7.a, r0, c7    // weaken bump map by lerping with 0,0,1
```

Figure 4 shows what this looks like on the above model.

Figure 2: Environment mapping only

Figure 3: Bumpy environment mapped

Figure 4: Weaker bumpy environment mapped

This basically wraps up the computation that occurs in the first phase of the pixel shader. In order to make the inner parts of the model (where you would see through more of the actual object) seem more opaque and the outer edges seem more transparent, a Fresnel term is used. (For more uses of the Fresnel term, see "Per-Pixel Fresnel Term.") The computation takes a few additional instructions, with one hidden in a co-issue alpha instruction. The following lines of code compute the Fresnel term used to give the impression of thicker crystal:

```
dp3 r0.a, v0_bx2, r0        // (N.V)fresnel term
+mov r0.a, 1-r0.a           // 1-(N.V)
```

Figure 5 shows what the model looks like with this term added to the shader.

Since we are going for a more solid-looking effect, the Fresnel term is tweaked a bit to make the model look more opaque. This is also done in a co-issued alpha instruction, shown below:

```
+add_sat r0.a, r0.a, c0.y   // boost opacity: (1-(N.V)) + 0.5
```

Figure 6 shows what the model looks like with this term applied.

Now we want to add some color to the model using the base map and base color. The following line in the pixel shader computes this contribution:

```
mul r1.rgb, r1, c1          // base map * base color
```

Figure 7 shows what this would look like on its own.

Figure 5: Fresnel term added

Figure 6: Tweaked Fresnel term

Figure 7: Base map and base color

The final step is to combine the terms together to create the final image. The following code performs this computation:

```
mul r2.rgb, r2, c2          // reflection map * reflection color
mad r0.rgb, r2, r0.a, r1    // (1-(N.V)) * reflection map * reflection color
                            // + base map * base color
```

This is what the final image looks like.

Figure 8: Putting it all together

Figure 9 shows what this looks like within an environment from the ATI Sushi engine.

Figure 9: The shader within a scene

Summary

This article has shown a method for creating a semi-transparent crystal/candy look on an object. It used cubic environment mapping for reflections and per-pixel bump mapping. Hopefully, this gives you some ideas and techniques that you can use within your applications.

Bubble Shader

John Isidoro and David Gosselin

Introduction

Some of the most visually interesting objects in the real world are soap bubbles. Their reflective and partially transparent nature, as well as the way they pulsate, makes them a key candidate for vertex and pixel shaders. Strangely enough, on a vertex and pixel shader level, they are implemented in a very similar manner to the ocean water shader described in "Rendering Ocean Water." There are a variety of different effects that make up the bubble shader.

Setup

As input, this shader uses a model with a position, a normal, the tangent vector (in *v* direction of texture coordinates), and one set of texture coordinates for a rainbow-like basemap (shown in the following figure).

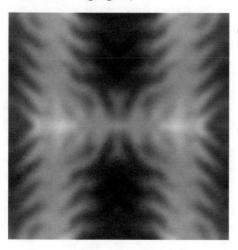

Figure 1: Base "rainbow" map

This shader, as in "Crystal/Candy Shader," uses a cubic enviroment map, shown below.

Figure 2: Cubic environment map color   Figure 3: Cubic environment map alpha

Also, like the candy shader, we want this object to be semi-transparent, which requires drawing the model in two passes: back faces first then front faces with alpha blending enabled.

Vertex Shader

The vertex shader uses four sine waves traveling in different directions over the surface of the bubble to perturb the vertex. The vertex is perturbed in the direction of the normal. In order to perturb the normal, cosine waves traveling in the same four directions are used. To provide a consistent-looking warping across vertices, the tangent and binormal are used to guide the direction of the sinusoidal warp. The first portion of the vertex shader looks almost identical to the ocean shader and is shown below.

```
// v0    - Vertex Position
// v3    - Vertex Normal
// v7    - Vertex Texture Data u,v
// v8    - Vertex Tangent (v direction of tex coords)
// c0    - { 0.0,  0.5, 1.0, 2.0}
// c1    - { 4.0, .5pi, pi, 2pi}
// c2    - {1, -1/3!, 1/5!, -1/7!} for sin
// c3    - {1/2!, -1/4!, 1/6!, -1/8!} for cos
// c4-7  - Composite World-View-Projection Matrix
// c8    - Model Space Camera Position
// c9    - Model Space Light Position
// c10   - {1.02, 0.04, 0, 0} fixup factor for Taylor series imprecision
// c11   - {0.5, 0.5, 0.25, 0.25} waveHeight0, waveHeight1, waveHeight2, waveHeight3
// c12   - {0.0, 0.0, 0.0, 0.0} waveOffset0, waveOffset1, waveOffset2, waveOffset3
// c13   - {0.6, 0.7, 1.2, 1.4} waveSpeed0, waveSpeed1, waveSpeed2, waveSpeed3
// c14   - {0.0, 2.0, 0.0, 4.0} waveDirX0, waveDirX1, waveDirX2, waveDirX3
// c15   - {2.0, 0.0, 4.0, 0.0} waveDirY0, waveDirY1, waveDirY2, waveDirY3
// c16   - { time, sin(time)}
// c17   - {-0.00015, 1.0, 0.0, 0.0} base texcoord distortion x0, y0, x1, y1
vs.1.1
mul r0, c14, v7.x      // use tex coords as inputs to sinusoidal warp
mad r0, c15, v7.y, r0  // use tex coords as inputs to sinusoidal warp
```

```
mov r1, c16.x          // time...
mad r0, r1, c13, r0    // add scaled time to move bumps according to frequency
add r0, r0, c12
frc r0.xy, r0          // take frac of all 4 components
frc r1.xy, r0.zwzw
mov r0.zw, r1.xyxy

mul r0, r0, c10.x      // multiply by fixup factor (due to inaccuracy of taylor
series)
sub r0, r0, c0.y       // subtract .5
mul r0, r0, c1.w       // mult tex coords by 2pi  coords range from(-pi to pi)

mul r5, r0, r0         // (wave vec)^2
mul r1, r5, r0         // (wave vec)^3
mul r6, r1, r0         // (wave vec)^4
mul r2, r6, r0         // (wave vec)^5
mul r7, r2, r0         // (wave vec)^6
mul r3, r7, r0         // (wave vec)^7
mul r8, r3, r0         // (wave vec)^8

mad r4, r1, c2.y, r0   //(wave vec) - ((wave vec)^3)/3!
mad r4, r2, c2.z, r4   //  + ((wave vec)^5)/5!
mad r4, r3, c2.w, r4   //  - ((wave vec)^7)/7!

mov r0, c0.z           //1
mad r5, r5, c3.x ,r0   //-(wave vec)^2/2!
mad r5, r6, c3.y, r5   //+(wave vec)^4/4!
mad r5, r7, c3.z, r5   //-(wave vec)^6/6!
mad r5, r8, c3.w, r5   //+(wave vec)^8/8!

dp4 r0, r4, c11        //multiply wave heights by waves

mul r0, r0, v3         //apply deformation in direction of normal

add r10.xyz, r0, v0    //add to position
mov r10.w, c0.z        //homogenous component

m4x4   oPos, r10, c4   // OutPos = WorldSpacePos * Composite View-Projection Matrix
mov    oT0, v7         // Pass along texture coordinates
```

This is where the shader starts to diverge a bit from the ocean shader. First the binormal is computed:

```
mov    r3, v3
mul    r4, v8.yzxw, r3.zxyw
mad    r4, v8.zxyw, -r3.yzxw, r4   //cross product to find binormal
```

Then the normal is warped based on the tangent space basis vectors (tangent and binormal):

```
mul    r1, r5, c11        //cos * waveheight
dp4    r9.x, -r1, c14     //amount of normal warping in direction of binormal
dp4    r9.y, -r1, c15     //amount of normal warping in direction of tangent
mul    r1, r4, r9.x       //normal warping in direction of binormal
mad    r1, v8, r9.y, r1   //normal warping in direction of tangent
mad    r5, r1, c10.y, v3  //warped normal move nx, ny: cos * wavedir * waveheight
```

The normal is then renormalized:

```
dp3    r10.x, r5, r5
rsq    r10.y, r10.x
mul    r5, r5, r10.y      //normalize warped normal
```

Next the view vector is computed:

```
sub     r2, c8, r0          //view vector
dp3     r10.x, r2, r2
rsq     r10.y, r10.x
mul     r2, r2, r10.y       //normalized view vector
```

Then the dot product of the view vector and the warped normal is computed:

```
dp3     r7, r5, r2          //N.V
mov     oT2, r7             //Pass along N.V
```

This is used to compute the reflection vector:

```
add     r6, r7, r7          //2N.V
mad     r6, r6, r5, -r2     //2N(N.V)-V
mov     oT1, r6             //reflection vector
```

Finally, the distance to the camera is computed:

```
rcp     r10.y, r10.y            //distance from camera
mad     oD0, r10.y, c17.x, c17.y //scale and bias distance
```

The vertex shader then passes along the texture coordinates of the base map, the reflection vector, the value of N·V, and the distance to the camera along to the pixel shader for further processing.

Pixel Shader

The pixel shader uses the brightly colored rainbow film map as a base texture. This texture map is meant to simulate the soap film appearance of a bubble. The environment map is modulated with this texture. The white highlights are stored in the alpha of the environment map as a glow map and are linearly interpolated into the result. The final alpha value used from blending with the frame buffer is the (1–abs(N·V)) + glow map. The full shader is shown below, and further descriptions follow.

```
// c0  - (0.0, 0.5, 1.0, -0.75)
// c1  - (0.6, 0.1, 0.0, 0.0) Alpha Scale and bias
ps.1.4
texld r0, t0
texld r1, t1
texcrd r2.rgb, t2

   cmp r2.r, r2.r, r2.r, -r2.r    // abs(V.N)
   +mad_x4_sat r1.a, r1.a, r1.a, c0.a

   mul_x2_sat r2.rgb, r0, r1      //  base * env (may change scale factor later)
   +mad r2.a, 1-r2.r, c1.x, c1.y  // alphascale * abs(V.N) + alphabias

   lrp r0.rgb, r1.a, r1, r2       // Lerp between Env and Base*Env based on glow map
   +add r0.a, r2.a, r1.a          // Add glow map to Fresnel term for alpha
```

The first thing that happens in this pixel shader is the sampling of the environment map. This happens in the following line of the pixel shader:

```
texld r1, t1
```

It produces the following image:

Figure 4: Cubic environment map only

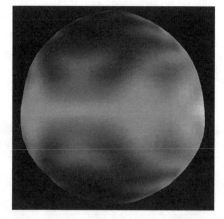

Figure 5: Base map

This is multiplied by the base texture color (shown in Figure 5) using the following code:

```
mul_x2_sat r2.rgb, r0, r1        //  base * env (may change scale factor later)
```

The results are shown in Figure 6.

Figure 6: Cubic environment map modulated with base map

Figure 7: Alpha for environment map

Now that the basic colors are computed, the opacity needs to be computed. The first step is to create strong specular lighting term. The alpha of the environment map (shown in Figure 7) is squared, multiplied by four, and given a bit of a bias. The following pixel shader co-issued instruction accomplishes this:

```
+mad_x4_sat r1.a, r1.a, r1.a, c0.a
```

The resulting image is shown in Figure 8.

Next, the Fresnel term is computed. This takes place in a few stages. First, take the absolute value of V·N, and then invert this value by computing 1–abs(V·N). This value is then scaled and biased. The following code shows how this is computed:

```
cmp r2.r, r2.r, r2.r, -r2.r      // abs(V.N)

+mad r2.a, 1-r2.r, c1.x, c1.y    // alphascale * abs(V.N) + alphabias
```

Figure 9 shows the result of this computation.

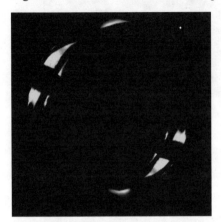

Figure 8: Alpha of the environment map squared and multiplied by four

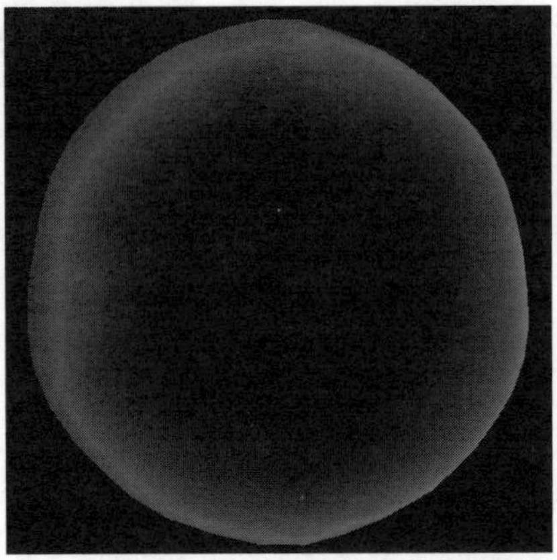

Figure 9: Scaled and biased Fresnel term

The next step is to add the Fresnel term with the glow map using the following code:

```
+add r0.a, r2.a, r1.a            // Add glowmap to Fresnel term for alpha
```

This produces the final alpha result used for blending and is shown in Figure 10.

Figure 10: Final alpha values

Figure 11: Final color values

Next, the glow map is used to linearly interpolate between just the environment map and the base multiplied by the environment map based on the alpha value in the environment map:

```
lrp r0.rgb, r1.a, r1, r2        // Lerp between Env and Base*Env based on glow map
```

This produces the final color values shown in Figure 11.

Figure 12 shows the blend produced by the alpha and color to create the final image.

See BubbleShadeTree.jpg on the companion CD for a graphic representation of all the above steps. Figure 13 shows what this shader creates within a scene produced by the ATI Sushi engine.

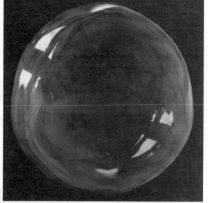

Figure 12: Final image

Figure 13: Bubble in an environment

Summary

This article has shown a technique to produce an interesting bubble effect built on top of some techniques described in other articles. It used sine waves computed within a vertex shader to produce an undulating shape and cubic environment mapping to give interesting reflections.

Per-Pixel Strand-Based Anisotropic Lighting

John Isidoro and Chris Brennan

Introduction

This technique uses Direct3D pixel shaders to implement a per-pixel version of the per-vertex anisotropic lighting technique presented in [Heidrich99]. An anisotropic lighting model is meant to simulate the effects of lighting on a grooved surface, like a record, a Christmas ornament, human hair, brushed metal, or some fabrics. The per-pixel nature of the shader uses a direction of an anisotropy map to determine the direction of the grooves. This allows us to be able to author many different anisotropic surface types by using standard image editing packages.

Strand-Based Illumination

The basic idea behind the strand-based illumination is the lighting of strands. These strands are modeled as having a circular cross section. When lighting them, we use the standard Phong illumination model but with a slight modification. The normal used in the Phong model is equal to the light vector projected into the normal plane of the strand at the point being lit and normalized. We call this strand normal vector N'. The modified Phong equation is:

$$I_o = k_a I_a + (k_d (L \cdot N') + k_s (V \cdot R')^n)I_i$$

The terms k_a, k_d, and k_s are material properties for the ambient, diffuse, and specular lighting, respectively. I_a is the ambient light color, and I_i is the incident light color. L is the light direction vector, V is the view direction vector, and n is the specular exponent. The reflection vector R' can be found using:

$$R' = 2N'(N' \cdot V) - V$$

As shown in [Banks94] and [Stalling97], using some trigonometric identities and the knowledge that L, T, and N' are coplanar, $L \cdot N'$ and $V \cdot R'$ can be expressed in terms of L, V, and T, the direction of the strand.

$$L \cdot N' = (1 - (L \cdot T)^2)^{0.5}$$
$$V \cdot R' = (1 - (L \cdot T)^2)^{0.5} (1 - (V \cdot T)^2))^{0.5} - (L \cdot T)(V \cdot T)$$

Luckily, these equations are a function of two dot products, $L \cdot T$ and $V \cdot T$. This allows us to use these dot products to index into a precomputed 2D texture map to compute the diffuse $L \cdot N'$ and specular $(V \cdot R')^n$ terms. Using the fact that L, T, and V are unit length vectors, it is known that the terms $L \cdot T$ and $V \cdot T$ range between $[-1,1]$. To use these terms to index into a texture lookup table, they first must be scaled and biased into the range of $[0,1]$.

Using this knowledge, building the texture lookup table tex(u,v) is straightforward. In the equations above, substitute $2u-1$ for $L \cdot T$ and $2v-1$ for $V \cdot T$. The diffuse component can be packed into the RGB component of the texture, and the specular component can be packed into the alpha channel of the texture.

This way both diffuse and specular lookups can be done with a single texture fetch per light source. Also, the specular exponent n can be pre-baked into the specular lookup table by computing $(V \cdot R')^n$ instead of just computing $(V \cdot R')$.

Figure 1: Diffuse texture lookup table

Figure 2: Specular texture lookup table

The rest of the math in the Phong model can be computed within the pixel shader.

Rendering Using the Texture Lookup Table

Depending on whether the technique is applied per-pixel or per-vertex, there are a few places where the dot products, scaling, and biasing can be computed. When rendering on a per-vertex basis, all the computation can easily be performed in a vertex shader or even in a traditional texture matrix. The tangent vector T can be stored with the vertex data as a per-vertex three-element texture coordinate. The light L and view V vectors can be stored as vertex shader constants. All vectors should be in object space if the texture matrix is used to perform the dot products. This is explained in more detail in [Heidrich99]. The main focus of this chapter is to illustrate the implementation of anisotropic lighting on a per-pixel basis and to present a unique orthonormalization technique that allows anisotropic lighting to be combined with bump mapping.

Per-Pixel Strand-Based Illumination

Per-pixel strand-based anisotropic lighting has a lot in common with standard per-pixel lighting (aka bump mapping). First off, all per-pixel computation is done in tangent space. The direction of anisotropy is stored in a texture map and, being in tangent space, has the advantage that the direction map is not coupled to the geometry. The same direction map can be applied to many different objects and in a way, can be thought of as part of the surface description in the same way a bump map is. The direction vectors T_t are encoded in the texture the same way normals are in a bump map, and the xyz direction is scaled by 0.5, biased by 0.5, and encoded as an RGB color. The light and view vectors are computed and transformed into tangent space in the vertex shader. The resulting vectors L_t and V_t are interpolated across the triangle.

Figure 3: Red channel of direction of anisotropy map

Figure 4: Green channel of direction of anisotropy map

In the pixel shader, two dot products need to be performed $(T_t \cdot L_t)$, and $(T_t \cdot V_t)$, and the resulting vector should be scaled and biased by 0.5 and used to fetch a texel in the texture lookup table. However, we can make a few optimizations here.

The first optimization is to perform the scale by 0.5 inside the vertex shader by multiplying L_t and V_t by 0.5 before outputting them. The second optimization is to offset the texture lookup table in u and v by half the texture width and height, respectively. By doing this and turning on texture wrapping in the texture stage containing the lookup map, this essentially gives us the bias by 0.5 for free. These optimizations save precious pixel shader instructions and in the case of 1.1 pixel shaders, make it possible to perform the anisotropic lighting at all.

Figure 5: Specular component shown offset by half of the texture width

Per-Pixel Strand-Based Illumination with Colored Light and Base Map

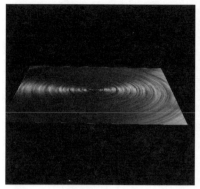

Figure 6   Figure 7   Figure 8: Result of per pixel anisotropic lighting (only two triangles!)

Here is a pixel shader that implements the anisotropic strand illumination:

```
ps.1.1
tex t0                      ; Contains direction of anisotropy in tangent space
tex t1                      ; base map
texm3x2pad t2, t0_bx2       ; Perform fist row of matrix multiply.
texm3x2tex t3, t0_bx2       ; Perform second row of matrix multiply to get a
                            ; 3-vector with which to sample texture 3, which is
                            ; a look-up table for aniso lighting
mad r0, t3, t1, t1.a        ; basemap * diffuse + specular
mul r0, r0, c0              ; color * basemap *diffuse
```

Per-Pixel Strand-Based Illumination with Four Colored Lights and Base Map in One Pass

Here is a pixel shader that implements the anisotropic strand shader with four colored lights:

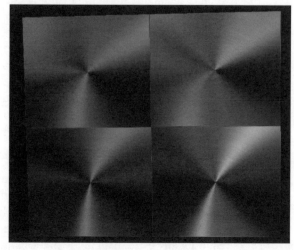

Figure 9: Anisotropic lighting with four colored lights. Also shown in Color Plate 9.

1.4 pixel shader:

```
ps.1.4
texld r0, t0        //sample bump map  (note alpha channel = 1)
texcrd r1, t1
texcrd r1, t2
texcrd r1, t3
texcrd r1, t4
texcrd r1, t5

dp3_d2 r1.rba, r1, r0_bx2       // .5 L0.T
dp3_d2 r2.rba, r2, r0_bx2       // .5 L1.T
dp3_d2 r3.rba, r3, r0_bx2       // .5 L2.T
dp3_d2 r4.rba, r4, r0_bx2       // .5 L3.T
dp3_d2 r1.g, r5, r0_bx2         // .5 V.T
mov r2.g, r1.g
mov r3.g, r1.g
mov r4.g, r1.g


phase
texld r1, r1       //aniso lookup 0
texld r2, r2       //aniso lookup 1
texld r3, r3       //aniso lookup 2
texld r4, r4       //aniso lookup 3
texld r5, t0       //sample base map

mad r1, r1, r5, r1.a // diffuse0 * base + specular
mad r2, r2, r5, r2.a // diffuse1 * base + specular
mad r3, r3, r5, r3.a // diffuse2 * base + specular
mad r4, r4, r5, r4.a // diffuse3 * base + specular
mul r0, r1, c1       // lightcolor0 * light0 effect
mad r0, r2, c2, r0   // lightcolor1 * light1 effect + previous
mad r0, r3, c3, r0   // lightcolor2 * light2 effect + previous
mad r0, r4, c4, r0   // lightcolor3 * light3 effect + previous
```

Per-Pixel Bump-Mapped Strand-Based Illumination Using Gram-Schmidt Orthonormalization

Another technique for bump mapping combines both anisotropic strand-based lighting and bump mapping at the same time. This has way more surface detail and can be added to objects using the anisotropic strand shader.

This shader uses the bump map to perturb the direction of anisotropy by using Gram-Schmidt orthonormalization. The basic idea is to make the direction of anisotropy orthogonal to the bump map normal by subtracting off the component of the tangent T vector projected onto the normal N and renormalizing the resulting vector:

$$T_{new} = || \, T - (N \cdot T) \, N \, ||$$

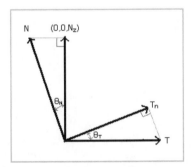

Figure 12

There are two possible places this math can be performed, either as a preprocessing step on the direction of anisotropy texture or inside the pixel shader. Doing the orthonormalization as a preprocessing step has the advantage of not requiring any extra math in the pixel shader. However, it has

Figure 10: Anisotropically lit chalice without bump mapping

Figure 11: Anisotropically lit chalice with bump mapping

the negative effect of tying the preprocessed direction map to the corresponding bump map. If the same direction map needs to be used with many different bump maps, additional textures need to be allocated. In addition, if the texture coordinates for the bump and direction maps are different, this preprocessing step is usually not possible.

The alternative is to do the orthonormalization in the pixel shader, as is done in the following example. All the math is fairly straightforward to perform in the pixel shader except for the vector normalization step. Luckily for us, this renormalization step has almost no visual impact due to the way the math works out. In the worst case, the lighting near the severe bumps may become slightly brighter. In addition, for most surfaces, the direction of anisotropy runs in the direction of the grooves in the bump map, thus making the bump map vectors perpendicular to the direction of anisotropy.

```
; t1 contains tangent-space L vector          ; Lx, Ly, Lz, 0
; t2 contains tangent-space reflection vector ; Vx, Vy, Vz, 0
; Map bound at stage 0 is a normal map
; Map bound at stage 3 is a T.L x T.V map as the z positive face of a cube map
ps.1.4

    texld  r0, t0              ; Contains direction of anisotropy in tangent space
    texcrd r2.rgb, t1          ; Light vector
    texcrd r3.rgb, t2          ; View vector
    texld  r4, t3              ; Bump map

    dp3 r5, r0_bx2, r4_bx2        ; T.N
    mad r0.xyz, r4_bx2, -r5, r0_bx2  ; Tn = T - N(T.N)

    ; Calculate V.T and L.T for looking up into function map.
    dp3_d2  r1.x, r2, r0          ; L.Tn
    dp3_d2  r1.y, r3, r0          ; V.Tn


phase

    texld  r2, r1                 ; Normalize Tn, and perform anisotropic lighting
                                  ; Function lookup
    texld  r3, t0                 ; Base map
```

```
mul_sat r0.rgb, r3, r2          ; aniso diffuse * basemap
mad_sat r0.rgb, r2.a, r3.a, r0  ; + glossmap * aniso specular
+mov r0.a, c0.b
```

Summary

A technique for per-pixel strand-based anisotropy was described in this article. This technique allows a per-texel direction of anisotropy vector as well as an optional per-texel bump map normal to be specified. Due to the efficiency of the math used, up to four lights per rendering pass can be achieved using DirectX 8.1 version 1.4 pixel shaders.

References

[Banks94] D. C. Banks, "Illumination in diverse codimensions," SIGGRAPH Proceedings, July 1994, pp. 327-334.

[Heidrich99] Heidrich Wolfgang and Hans-Peter Seidel, "Realistic, Hardware-accelerated Shading and Lighting," SIGGRAPH Proceedings, 1999.

[Stalling97] Stalling D., M. Zöckler, and H. C. Hege, "Fast Display of Illuminated Field Lines," *IEEE Transactions on Visualization and Computer Graphics*, 3(2), 1997, pp. 118-129.

A Non-Integer Power Function on the Pixel Shader

Philippe Beaudoin and Juan Guardado

Overview

Raising a variable to a non-integer power is an operation often encountered in computer graphics. It is required, for example, to compute the specular term in various shading schemes. It can also be used to produce a smooth conditional function useful in many pixel shaders. In most cases, the input variable falls between 0 and 1, while the exponent is greater than 1 and often quite large.

Like many other techniques, a quality gain can be achieved by computing the function per-pixel rather than per-vertex. This gain is very noticeable when using large exponents since the function varies a lot and sampling it at each vertex is bound to miss visually important details (see Figure 1 and Color Plate 10).

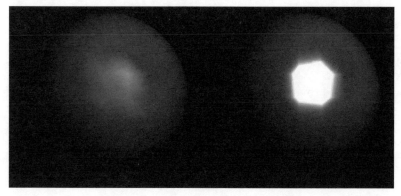

Figure 1: Gouraud shading (left) and Phong shading (right). (See also Color Plate 10.)

Therefore, we are particularly interested in finding a way to compute such a function on the pixel shader. Like any pixel shader trick, it is important to minimize the number of textures and blending stages since these are very limited resources. This article presents a simple shader trick that performs a good per-pixel approximation of a non-integer power function. The technique works for input values between 0 and 1 and supports large exponents. The presented

383

shader does not require any texture lookup and is scalable, making it possible to spend more instructions in order to decrease the error or to reach greater exponents.

We first consider and analyze two typical techniques used to compute a power function on the pixel shader. We then expose some mathematical background used throughout this article. Finally, we show how the algorithm can be used to perform smooth conditional functions and complex bump-mapped Phong shading. The actual implementation of the approximation as a pixel shader program is discussed in detail.

Traditional Techniques

When confronted with the problem of computing a power function on the pixel shader, two simple techniques come to mind. First, it seems possible to proceed through a 1D texture lookup, and second, applying successive multiplications looks promising.

Texture Lookup

Linearly interpolated textures can be thought of as piecewise linear functions. In particular, 1D textures with a linear filter are really a function taking a value between 0 and 1 and mapping it onto another value in the same range. (Actually, such a function can map the input onto four values, one for each of the R,G,B, and alpha channels. In the current case, however, we're only interested in one output value.). This looks promising for our problem since an input between 0 and 1 raised to any power greater than 0 yields a result between 0 and 1.

Listing 1 shows a piece of code that builds a 16-bit monochrome 1D texture of resolution Resi to compute x^n.

Listing 1: C function to create a 1D power texture

```
void ComputePowerTexture( int Resi, double n, unsigned short* Texture )
{
    int i;
    for( i=0; i<Resi; ++i )
        Texture[i] = (unsigned short)( pow( (double)i/Resi, n ) * USHRT_MAX );
}
```

Once this texture has been constructed, a simple texture lookup pixel shader can be used to perform the computation, provided that the value to raise to power n is placed in an interpolated texture coordinate. The pixel shader in Listing 2 shows how to apply the power function on the result of a dot product, as is often required. Note that this code only works for pixel shader versions 1.2 and 1.3. The code for version 1.4 is presented in Listing 3.

Listing 2: Code computing a power function using a 1D texture (pixel shader versions 1.2 and 1.3)

```
ps.1.2

tex t0              ; Texture #0 lookup a vector
texdp3tex t1, t0    ; Use texture coordinates #1 as a 3D vector,
                    ; performs dot product between this 3D vector and t0,
                    ; using the result, lookup power function in 1D texture #1

mov r0, t1          ; emit the result
```

Listing 3. Code computing a power function using a 1D texture (pixel shader version 1.4)

```
ps.1.4
texld r0, t0          ; Texture #0 look-up a vector
texcrd r1.rgb, t1     ; Load texture coordinates #1 as a 3D vector

dp3 r0, r0, r1        ; Performs dot product between this 3D vector and r0

phase

texld r1, r0.x        ; using the result, look-up power function in 1D texture #1

mov r0, r1            ; emit the result
```

Various problems exist with this particular technique:

- It uses up one texture stage, which may make it unfit for algorithms requiring many textures.

- Changing the value of the exponent n requires regenerating the texture, unless a 2D texture is used, in which case a limited number of predefined exponents can be used.

- For pixel shader versions before 1.4, a 1D texture lookup cannot be applied to intermediate computation results unless multiple passes are used.

This last limitation is often a major drawback since, usually, the power function must be preceded by a vector renormalization (such as with a cube map) and a dot product. With large exponents, the vector renormalization is especially important. This is due to the fact that the maximum value of a dot product is the product of the length of the two vectors. If one of these is not normalized, the dot product can never reach 1. When raised to a large exponent, a value smaller than 1 will rapidly move toward 0. This translates to visual details being washed out. Figure 2 shows a vector interpolated with and without normalization, followed by a dot product, and then raised to a high power. It is obvious that the detail (for example, a specular spot) is washed out in the second version.

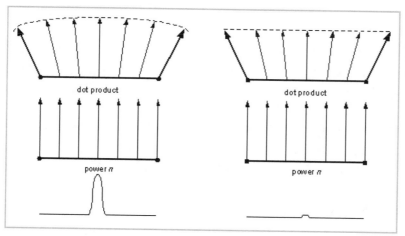

Figure 2: Result of not normalizing vectors before applying a power function

Successive Multiplications

Since raising a value to an integer power simply requires multiplying a value with itself a number of times, it seems possible to approximate a non-integer power function through successive multiplication steps.

For example, the pixel shader in Listing 4 shows how to raise t0 to power 16. Analyzing this scheme indicates that $\log_2 n$ multiplications are required to raise a variable to the power n, when n is a power of 2.

Listing 4: Power function using successive multiplications

```
ps.1.0
tex t0

mul r0, t0, t0        ; r0 = t0  *t0   = t0^2
mul r0, r0, r0        ; r0 = t0^2*t0^2 = t0^4
mul r0, r0, r0        ; r0 = t0^4*t0^4 = t0^8
mul r0, r0, r0        ; r0 = t0^8*t0^8 = t0^16
```

Listing 5 shows a pixel shader that raises t0 to power 31. Analyzing this shows that, in general, for n in the range $[2^a, 2^{a+1})$, the algorithm can require $2a$ multiplications and a temporary variables. (A step can be saved by combining a multiplication and an addition using the mad instruction.)

Listing 5: Power function with a non-power-of-2 exponent using successive multiplications

```
ps.1.1
tex t0

mul t1, t0, t0        ; t1 = t0^2
mul t2, t1, t1        ; t2 = t0^4
mul t3, t2, t2        ; t3 = t0^8
mul r0, t3, t3        ; r0 = t0^16
mul r0, r0, t3        ; r0 = t0^16 * t0^8 = t0^24
mul r0, r0, t2        ; r0 = t0^24 * t0^4 = t0^28
mul r0, r0, t1        ; r0 = t0^28 * t0^2 = t0^30
mul r0, r0, t0        ; r0 = t0^30 * t0   = t0^31
```

This technique has the following limitations:

- It only supports discrete changes in the exponent, making it impossible to change the value of n in a continuous fashion.
- It requires a lot of instructions for a large exponent.
- It requires a lot of instructions and temporary variables for non-power-of-2 exponents.

These last two problems often limit the usefulness of successive multiplications, since practical exponents have a tendency to be large and are usually not powers of 2.

The Need for a New Trick

Although the 1D texture lookup and the successive multiplications techniques have no limitations in common, both are too restrictive to be really useful in general cases. In particular, neither of them is suited to large exponents. In the case of 1D textures, the impossibility to perform a per-pixel renormalization before the lookup makes it unsuitable, and for successive multiplications, the number of instructions required for large exponents is prohibitive.

The power function approximation technique presented in the rest of this article addresses all of the preceding issues. Therefore we think it can often be used as an efficient alternative in pixel shaders that require a power function.

Mathematical Details

If we take x^n in the range from 0 to 1, and then for a large enough n, the function is very close to 0 on most of its domain and abruptly goes to 1 when x approaches 1. This is shown in Figure 3 for increasing values of n. This will be the basic concept used for developing our approximation.

It is interesting to note that the result x^n is greater than $1/256$ only for values of x greater than $256^{-1/n}$. For example, if we take $n = 16$, the function will be greater than $1/256$ only if x is over 0.707; with $n = 64$, this value becomes 0.917. Since $1/256$ is the smallest value displayable on 8-bits-per-channel hardware, approximating x^n with 0 will yield no perceptual error for values of x between 0 and $256^{-1/n}$.

Now, if we look at x^n for input values greater than $256^{-1/n}$, we can see that it looks pretty much like a scaled and offset power function of a lower degree. Figure 4 shows the function x^{16} being approximated by x^4 scaled and offset horizontally to reach 0 when $x = 256^{-1/16}$.

Therefore, using the null function from 0 to $256^{-1/n}$ and correctly scaling a lower degree power function for the rest of the range seems to constitute an adequate approximation. If our approximating function uses an exponent m, a scaled and offset version of the function can be written as $(Ax + B)^m$, where A is the scale and B is

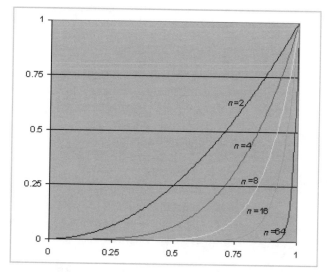

Figure 3: Shape of a power function with increasing exponents n = 2, 4, 8, 16, 64

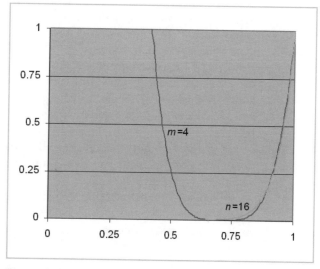

Figure 4: Approximating the right part of a power function with a lower degree exponent m

the offset. Now, naturally, we want this approximating function to be equal to 1 when x is 1. Also, we want it to reach 0 when $x = 256^{-1/n}$. Therefore, we can solve for A and B. We find that $A = 1 / (1 - 256^{-1/n})$ and $B = 1 - A$. The approximating function can be written as:

$$f(x) = \begin{cases} 0 & \text{if } x < 256^{-1/n} \\ (Ax + B)^m & \text{otherwise} \end{cases}$$

By noting that $x < 256^{-1/n}$ if and only if $Ax + B < 0$, the above function can be rewritten more concisely as:

$$f(x) = \max(Ax + B, 0)^m$$

Note that we will always consider $m \le n$ in the rest of the text. This is because we want the approximating function to have a lower degree than the original.

This technique can now be used with real examples. Figure 5 shows the result of approximating x^n with $\max(Ax + B, 0)^m$ for $n = 16$ and $m = 4$. In this case, A and B are computed as described earlier, and their value is $A = 3.4142$ and $B = -2.4142$. The graph displays both the original and approximated curves. The normalized error function is also plotted in order to show how the error is distributed to the left and right of the point where both curves cross.

A first analysis shows that the approximation gives good results for these values of A, B, n, and m. However, if we look more closely at the graph, we notice that the error is

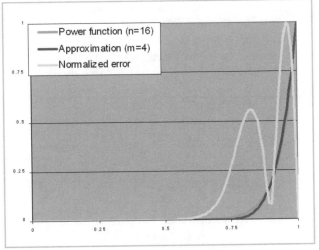

Figure 5: Approximation of a power function and normalized error

not distributed equally on each side of the crossing point. This leads us to think that the maximal approximation error could be lowered by adjusting A and B in order to move the crossing point.

In fact, for arbitrary values of n and m, the technique we've described to select A and B doesn't give any guarantee on the maximal approximation error. In practice, however, it may suit many applications.

In order to optimize the approximation error, one should seek values of A and B for which the maximal error on the left and right side are equal. We solve this problem using the numerical approach presented next.

First we need a function that, given approximate values of the optimal A and B, is able to compute the maximal error on the left and right side of the crossing point. To do so, we simply find the zero of the derivative of the error function on the left and right sides and evaluate the error function at these points. This is accomplished with the function EvaluateMaxError.

Then, we perform a binary search, changing our guess values for A and B in order to move the crossing point. When the left error is greater than the right error, the crossing point is moved to the left; otherwise, it is moved to the right. This is accomplished by the function FindAB.

For any value of n and m such that $1 \leq m \leq n$, the following algorithm is guaranted to pick values of A and B that minimize the maximal approximation error.

Listing 6: C code to determine optimal scale and offset for some approximation

```
const double Epsilon = 0.0001;
const double ThresholdError = 0.0001;

// Find values for A and B minimizing the maximal error given n and m
void FindAB( double n, double m, double &A, double &B )
{
    double k0 = 0;
    double k1 = 1;
    double k;
    double ErrorLeft, ErrorRight;

    // Binary search for optimal crossing point
    do
    {
        k = (k0 + k1)/2.0;
        A = ( pow( k, n/m ) - 1.0 ) / ( k - 1.0 );
        B = 1.0 - A;

        EvaluateMaxError( n, m, A, B, k, ErrorLeft, ErrorRight );

        if( ErrorLeft < ErrorRight )
            k0 = k;
        else
            k1 = k;


    } while( fabs( ErrorLeft - ErrorRight ) > ThresholdError );
}


// Evaluate the maximal error to the left and right of the crossing point
// for given values of A and B
// The crossing point k is given to reduce computation
void EvaluateMaxError( double n, double m, double A, double B, double k,
                       double &ErrorLeft, double &ErrorRight )
{
    double x;

    double DerErr;

    // Find maximal point of the error function on the left of the crossing point
    double x0 = 0;
    double x1 = k;
    do
    {
        x = (x0 + x1)/2.0;

        DerErr = DerError( x, n, m, A, B );
        if( DerErr < 0 )
            x0 = x;
        else
            x1 = x;
    } while( fabs( x0-x1 ) > Epsilon );
```

```
    // Evaluate the error at that point
    ErrorLeft = fabs( Error( x, n, m, A, B ) );


    x0 = k;
    x1 = 1;

    // Find maximal point of the error function on the right of the crossing point
    do
    {
        x = (x0 + x1)/2.0;

        DerErr = DerError( x, n, m, A, B );
        if( DerErr > 0 )
            x0 = x;
        else
            x1 = x;
    } while( fabs( x0-x1 ) > Epsilon );

    // Evaluate the error at that point
    ErrorRight = fabs( Error( x, n, m, A, B ) );

}


// Evaluate the approximation function
double Approx( double x, double m, double A, double B )
{
    if( x < -B/A )
        return 0;
    return pow( A * x + B, m );
}


// Evaluate the derivative of the approximation function
double DerApprox( double x, double m, double A, double B )
{
    if( x < -B/A )
        return 0;
    return A*m*pow( A * x + B, m-1 );
}


// Evaluate the error function
double Error( double x, double n, double m, double A, double B )
{
    return Approx( x, m, A, B ) - pow( x, n );
}


// Evaluate the derivative of the error function
double DerError( double x, double n, double m, double A, double B )
{
    return DerApprox( x, m, A, B ) - n*pow( x, n-1 );
}
```

Using this algorithm with the previous example, where $n = 16$ and $m = 4$, yields A = 3.525 and B = –2.525. This is illustrated in Figure 6. It can be seen that the error is equally distributed to the left and right of the crossing point, indicating that the maximal error has been minimized.

It should be noted that by selecting A and B through the algorithm of Listing 6, we lose the property that the $\max(Ax+B, 0)^m$ is equal to 0 only for values of $x^n < 1/256$. However, this doesn't hurt our approximation, since the maximal error has been lowered.

Table 1 shows the maximal approximation error for typical values of n and m. It also shows the optimal values of A and B for these values.

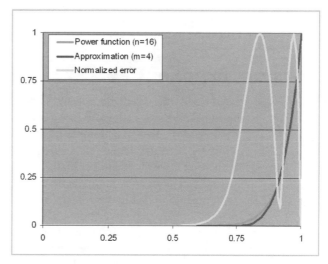

Figure 6: Approximation of a power function using optimized scale and offset

Table 1: Scale, offset, and maximal error for typical approximations

m	n	A	B	Max error	m	n	A	B	Max error
2	3	1.336	−0.336	0.025616	8	9	1.115	−0.115	0.001862
	4	1.683	−0.683	0.037531		10	1.229	−0.229	0.003314
	5	2.033	−1.033	0.044382		11	1.344	−0.344	0.004514
	6	2.385	−1.385	0.048856		12	1.459	−0.459	0.005527
	10	3.802	−2.802	0.057565		16	4.918	−0.918	0.008200
	18	6.645	−5.645	0.063146		24	2.838	−1.838	0.010886
4	5	1.208	−0.208	0.006984	16	17	1.060	−0.060	0.000491
	6	1.417	−0.417	0.011542		18	1.120	−0.120	0.000920
	7	1.628	−0.628	0.014761		19	1.180	−0.180	0.001321
	8	1.838	−0.838	0.017146		20	1.239	−0.239	0.001653
	12	2.681	−1.681	0.022635		24	1.479	−0.479	0.002682
	20	4.370	−3.370	0.026925		32	1.959	−0.959	0.004028

Power Function on the Pixel Shader

Approximating a power function on the pixel shader requires us to translate the preceding mathematical reasoning into the pixel shader assembly language. Doing so requires us to compute the function $\max(Ax+B, 0)^m$ through the set of available microcode instructions. We also need a way to specify the variables present in this equation, namely A, B, m, and x.

We can rule out a number of these variables easily: The input variable x will simply be stored in a general-purpose register, and the exponent m will be decided in advance. For variables A and B, we will consider two scenarios. At first, they will be fixed ahead of time and their content will be stored in constant registers. In the second scenario, we will show how A and B can be modified dynamically on a per-pixel basis.

Constant Exponent

Let's first study the case where A and B do not change per-pixel. In this scenario, A is placed in the constant register c0 while B is placed in c1. This means that the exponent n being approximated is constant as long as c0 and c1 remain unchanged.

Now we need to compute $\max(Ax+B, 0)^m$. First, the $\max(\ldots, 0)$ function is taken care of using the _sat modifier available on the pixel shader. Then, we pick m as a power of 2, selected to approximate with enough precision the target exponent n. We then perform a bias and scaling with mad, followed by $\log_2 m$ self-multiplications with mul. The result is the pixel shader in Listing 7, where the power function is applied to each element of the vector r0. It should be noted that $\log_2 m + 1$ is equal to the number of pixel shader stages required. Therefore, in an actual shader, the number of free instructions could limit m. (Note that if we want to compute the power function on a scalar rather than on a vector, we can co-issue the instructions, which could possibly help us gain a number of stages.)

Listing 7: Basic code for approximating a power function

```
ps.1.0

...                        ; Place input value x into r0

mad_sat r0, c0, r0, c1     ; r0 = max( Ax + B, 0 )
mul     r0, r0, r0         ; r0 = max( Ax + B, 0 )^2
mul     r0, r0, r0         ; r0 = max( Ax + B, 0 )^4
  .
  .                        ; repeat (log2 m) times the mul instruction
  .
mul     r0, r0, r0         ; r0 = max( Ax + B, 0 )^m
```

There is an important problem with the previous pixel shader. In fact, since all constant registers must be between −1 and 1, we have a very limited range of values for A and B. Table 1 shows that, for typical values of n and m, A is always greater than 1. Therefore, in practice, the proposed pixel shader is invalid.

To limit ourselves to scale and offset values in the allowed range, we first rewrite the approximation function as follows:

$$\max(Ax+B, 0)^m = k \max((Ax+B)k^{-1/m}, 0)^m = k \max(A'x+B', 0)^m$$

where we introduced variables A' and B' defined as:

$$A' = Ak^{-1/m} \qquad\qquad B' = Bk^{-1/m}$$

Therefore, A and B can be written:

$$A = A'k^{1/m} \qquad\qquad B = B'k^{1/m}$$

From these last two relations, we can see that with A' and B' between −1 and 1, we can obtain values of A and B between $-k^{1/m}$ and $k^{1/m}$. Given that k is greater than 1, this translates to an increased range for A and B.

The pixel shader lets us compute $k \max(A'x+B', 0)^m$ with k greater than 1 through its multiply instruction modifiers _x2 and _x4. If we take the program in Listing 7 and apply such modifiers to some or each of the mad or mul instructions, we will get a k greater than 1.

It is possible to compute k given a sequence of multiply instruction modifiers. This is performed by the function ComputeK in Listing 8. Before calling any function in this listing, make sure to correctly initialize the global array Multiplier so that it contains the correct multiply instruction modifier for each instruction (either 1, 2, or 4). If we want to know which value of A' and B' correspond to some values of A and B, we can use the computed k and the equation presented earlier; this is done with the function ComputeAB.

We go in the opposite direction and find the maximal values for A and B given k and m, as performed by the function MaxAB. This result can then be converted in a maximal value for n, as computed by MaxN.

Listing 8: C code for computing corrected scale and offset A' and B'

```
// Table containing multiply instruction modifier for each instruction (1, 2 or 4)
int Multiplier[] =  { 4, 4, 4, 4, 4, 4, 4, 4 };


// Compute value of k at instruction i given a table of multiply instruction
modifiers
double ComputeK( int i )
{
    if( i == 0 )
        return Multiplier[i];

    double Temp = ComputeK( i-1 );
    return Multiplier[i] * Temp * Temp;
}


// Compute values of A' and B' given A and B and a multiplier table
// LogM: log of m in base 2    (number of instructions - 1)
void ComputeApBp( int LogM, double A, double B, double &APrime, double &BPrime )
{
    double Temp = 1.0/MaxAB( LogM );   // Note that k -1/m = 1/MaxAB

    APrime = A * Temp;
    BPrime = B * Temp;
}


// Compute maximum absolute values for A and B given some m and a multiplier table
// LogM: log of m in base 2    (number of instructions - 1)
double MaxAB( int LogM )
{
    double m = pow( 2.0, LogM );   // Find the value of m
    double K = ComputeK( LogM );   // Compute K
    return pow( K, 1.0/m );
}


// Compute maximum possible exponent given some m and a multiplier table
// LogM: log of m in base 2    (number of instructions - 1)
double MaxN( int LogM )
{
    double m = pow( 2.0, LogM );   // Find the value of m
```

```
double Max = MaxAB( LogM );

double A;
double B;

double n0 = m;              // Lower bound for maximal exponent
double n1 = 5000;           // Upper bound for maximal exponent
double n;


do
{
    n = (n0 + n1)/2.0;

    FindAB( n, m, A, B );

    if( fabs(A) > Max || fabs(B) > Max )
        n1 = n;
    else
        n0 = n;

} while( fabs( n0 - n1 ) > Epsilon );

    return n;
}
```

It can be seen that the maximum value *n* is obtained when the modifier _x4 is used for each instruction in the code. Given that the value for A' and B' are stored in constant registers c0 and c1, respectively, the pixel shader in Listing 9 performs this approximation.

Listing 9: Corrected code for approximating a power function

```
ps.1.0

...                          ; Place input value x into r0

mad_x4_sat r0, c0, r0, c1 ; r0 = 4 * max( A'*x + B', 0 )
mul_x4     r0, r0, r0    ; r0 = 4 * (4*max( A'*x + B', 0 ))^2
mul_x4     r0, r0, r0    ; r0 = 4 * (4*(4*max( A'*x + B', 0 ))^2)^2
 .
 .                           ; repeat (log2 m) times the mul
 .
mul_x4     r0, r0, r0    ; r0 = 4^(2m-1) * max( A'*x + B', 0 )^m
```

Table 2 shows the maximal range for A and B and the maximal exponents *n* that can be obtained with the previous shader for various values of *m*.

Table 2: Maximal values of A, B, and n available, depending on approximation exponent m.

m	Range for A and B	Maximal *n*
2	[−8, 8]	21.81
4	[−11.314, 11.314]	52.87
8	[−13.454, 13.454]	116.34
16	[−14.672, 14.672]	244.08
32	[−15.322, 15.322]	499.99

Naturally, if for a given *m* we want to limit ourselves to exponents smaller than the maximal *n* listed in this table, we can remove some _x4 modifiers or replace them by _x2. When doing this, we figure the new maximal n by using the MaxN function with an updated Multiplier array.

Not using _x4 modifiers at each instruction is often a good idea since it can help reduce the numerical imprecision often present in pixel shaders. This lack of precision is mostly noticeable for small values of n since they translate to values of c0 and c1 close to zero. Such small numbers may suffer from an internal fixed-point representation and yield visual artifacts.

Per-Pixel Exponent

Until now, we have considered that the exponent to approximate n was fixed per-pixel and could be stored in constant registers. However, being able to vary the exponent based on the result of a texture lookup is sometimes required. The proposed pixel shader trick can be extended to support that. To do so, we must decide a value for m and a sequence of multiplication modifiers ahead of time. These must be chosen in order to cover all possible values of n, for $n \geq m$.

Once we have picked these values, we simply take a texture image of the desired n and translate each texel to their corresponding value of A. (Depending on its format, this texture can contain up to four different exponents n per pixel.) The texels are then translated to A' through a multiplication by $k^{-1/m}$. This time, however, instead of storing the result in a constant register, we update the texture. The program in Listing 10 executes the process.

Listing 10: C code to generate an approximation texture based on an exponent texture

```
// Translates a texture of exponents n into values that
// can be directly used by the pixel shader
// Texture: monochrome texture in custom format
// ResX: X resolution of the texture
// ResY: Y resolution of the texture
// LogM: log of m in base 2   (number of instructions - 1)
void TranslateTexture( double** Texture, int ResX, int ResY, int LogM )
{
    double A;
    double APrime;
    double Dummy;
    double m = pow( 2.0, LogM );        // Find the value of m

    for( int i=0; i<ResX; ++i )
        for( int j=0; j<ResY; ++j )
        {
            FindAB( Texture[i][j], m, A, Dummy );
            APrime = A/MaxAB( LogM );       // Compute A'. Note that k -1/m = 1/MaxAB
            assert( fabs(APrime) <= 1 );    // If assert fails select another m
                                            // or change the multipliers

            Texture[i][j] = APrime;         // Update the texture
        }

}
```

Once such a texture has been generated and placed in texture stage 0, we can easily extract A' inside a pixel shader. We can also extract B' by recalling that $B = 1 - A$. Since B' is the result of multiplying B by $k^{-1/m}$, we can write $B' = (1 - A)k^{-1/m} = k^{-1/m} - A'$. Since m is fixed, we store $k^{-1/m}$ in constant register c0 and perform a simple subtraction to extract B'.

The pixel shader of Listing 11 approximates a power function with n varying per pixel. This shader uses modifiers _x4 for each instruction; the texture and the constant register c0 should therefore be generated accordingly.

Listing 11: Code for approximating a power function with an exponent n varying per pixel

```
ps.1.0

tex t0                      ; Sample the value c0 for approximation

...                         ; Place input value x into r0

sub         r1, c0, t0      ; Compute B' = 1/MaxAB(LogM) - A'
mad_x4_sat  r0, t0, r0, r1  ; r0 = 4 * max( A'*x + B', 0 )
mul_x4      r0, r0, r0      ; r0 = 4 * 16 * max( A'*x + B', 0 )^2
mul_x4      r0, r0, r0      ; r0 = 4 * 16 * 256 * max( A'*x + B', 0 )^4
    .
    .                       ; repeat (log2 m) times the mul
    .
mul_x4      r0, r0, r0      ; r0 = 4^(2m-1) * max( A'*x + B', 0 )^m
```

This shader seems to show that one extra instruction is required to handle an exponent n varying per pixel. However, this is only true if we cannot spare additional texture space. In the case where a texture or a texture component is still available, we could precompute the value of B' and store it there. However, we believe that textures are often a more limited resource than pixel shader instructions; this is why we suggest you use the approach presented above.

As a last remark, note that the power function often only needs to be computed on a scalar. Therefore, provided that the input value x is placed in the alpha channel, the pixel shader can co-issue instructions. In such a case, we can also limit our usage of constant registers by using only the alpha channel of the constants. This technique is applied in the pixel shaders presented in the rest of this article.

Applications

The nature of the power function makes it very interesting for a number of applications in computer graphics. Any effect that should be visible at some point and fade out more or less rapidly for neighboring points can benefit from such a function. In this section we will present two techniques that require a per-pixel power function: smooth conditionals and specular Phong shading.

Smooth Conditional Function

Let's first start by studying the conditional instructions available in the pixel shader. We take cmp because it behaves similar to cnd while being more general:

```
cmp dest, src0, src1, scr2
```

This instruction loads dest with src1 or src2 depending on whether src0 is positive or not. If we consider this instruction with values of src1 = 1 and src2 = 0, we obtain the function illustrated in Figure 7.

Since conditional instructions can only take one of two values, they often produce jagged-edged artifacts. In fact, some neighboring pixels end up having very different colors because they sit on the threshold of the condition.

To overcome this problem, we can use the function illustrated in Figure 8. We call such a function a smooth conditional because it smoothly and rapidly goes from one value to the other as some threshold is crossed.

The function illustrated in Figure 8 corresponds to the following mathematical formula:

$$f(x) = \begin{cases} 1 - 0.5(1 - |x|)^n & \text{if } x > 0 \\ 0.5(1 - |x|)^n & \text{otherwise} \end{cases}$$

This formula can be computed on the pixel shader using the code in Listing 12. This code is similar to Listing 9. The difference is that it uses two extra cmp instructions, one for the absolute value and one for the condition $x > 0$. Also, note that the last mul has a _x2 multiply instruction modifier, although it should be considered as a 4 in the Multiplier table when generating A' and B'. This is done in order to account for the multiplicative factor in the term $0.5(1 - |x|)^n$ appearing in the formula.

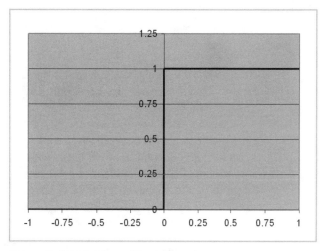

Figure 7: Standard conditional function

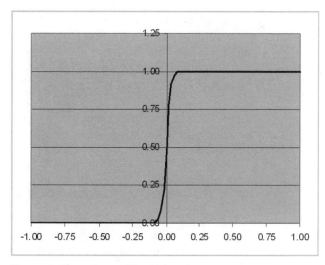

Figure 8: Smooth conditional function

Listing 12: Code to perform a smooth conditional function (pixel shader versions 1.2 and 1.3)

```
ps.1.2

; c2 = -1, -1, -1, -1            ; Used for the sign function

...                             ; Place input value x into r0

cmp         r1, r0, r0, -r0     ; r1 = |x|
mad_x4_sat  r1, c0, 1-r1, c1    ; r1 = k0 * max( A'*(1-|x|) + B', 0 )
mul_x4      r1, r1, r1          ; r1 = k1 * max( A'*(1-|x|) + B', 0 )^2
mul_x4      r1, r1, r1          ; r1 = k2 * max( A'*(1-|x|) + B', 0 )^4
  .
  .                             ; repeat (log2 m) times the mul
```

```
mul_x2      r1, r1, r1, c2      ; r1 = 0.5 * k * max( A'*(1-|x|)  + B', 0 )^m
cmp         r0, r0, 1-r1, r1    ; r0 = 1 - 0.5*(1-|x|)^n        if x > 0
                                ; r0 = 0.5*(1-|x|)^n            otherwise
```

We can use the above code to build a smooth conditional selection between two arbitrary values src1 and src2. To do so, we simply add a lrp instruction at the end of the previous pixel shader. This linear interpolation is made to map 0 to src1 and 1 to src2. The result is a function that mimics the standard cmp in a smooth fashion.

The presented code requires a lot of instructions; however, we can co-issue them if we want the smooth conditional to act only on the alpha channel. Moreover, the simplified asymmetric shape in Figure 9 often constitutes a good enough smooth conditional for $x > 0$. Given that the input x is saturated (greater or equal to 0), this function can be expressed as $1 - (1 - x)^n$. This is computed with minimal change to Listing 9. We simply need to use the invert source modifier at the input and output.

Other variations on the smooth conditional pixel shader code allows for various other arithmetic tests. In fact, the simple power function x^n can be considered as the smooth conditional for $x > 1$.

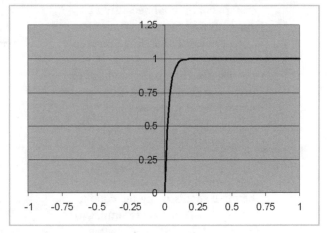

Figure 9: Simplified smooth conditional function

Volume Bounded Pixel Shader Effects

A problem that may arise with pixel shaders is that sometimes per-pixel effects need to occur only within a given volume. For example, say we have a magical spell that affects every pixel within a given radius of the casting point. If we want that spell to turn on a specific per-pixel effect, we need to find if each pixel is inside the spell radius using some pixel shader instructions. This can be done easily with a standard conditional instruction. However, if we do that, then we will most likely suffer from the jagged-edged artifacts mentioned earlier. Therefore, this is a good place where the smooth conditional function could be used.

So let's see how we can build a pixel shader that equals 1 for pixels within some radius r of a point P and smoothly goes to 0 for pixels outside this radius. First, for each vertex, we'll require a vector R that joins point P to the vertex. This vector needs to be scaled so that its length equals 1 for a vertex that is exactly at distance r from P. We place the vector P in texture coordinates 0. We will directly use this vector; therefore, no texture needs to be bound to stage 0.

We then select the approximation exponent m for the power function used in the smooth conditional. In the presented example, we take $m = 4$. The multiply instruction modifier _x4 was used with each instruction. Since we use a fixed exponent n for the shader, we place A' and B' in constant registers c0 and c1.

The pixel shader in Listing 13 uses this technique to apply a simple diffuse lighting equation to all pixels within some radius of a given point. The diffuse color is placed in interpolated color v0, texture 1 contains the decal texture to apply, and texture 2 holds an extra diffuse light map. A constant ambient factor is stored in constant register c2. More complex effects could use the same pixel shader trick in order to limit themselves to a volume. Also, more complex volumes could be devised by applying some per-vertex or per-pixel process on P.

Listing 13: Code to perform volume bounded pixel shader lighting

```
ps.1.0

; c0                            ; A'
; c1                            ; B'
; c2                            ; Ambient factor
; c7 = 1, 1, 1, 1               ; Uniform white, used in shader

; Texture address ops
 texcoord t0                    ; Pass on vector P
 tex t1                         ; Fetch decal texture

; Pixel ops
 dp3_sat    r0, t0, t0          ; r0 = max(0, P.P) = |P|^2

 add        r0.rgb, v0, t2      ; Compute diffuse lighting by adding v0 and t2
+mad_x4_sat r0.a, c0, r0, c1    ; r0.a = k0 * max( A'*x + B', 0 )

 mul        r0.rgb, r0, t1      ; Apply diffuse lighting to decal
+mul_x4     r0.a, r0, r0        ; r0.a = k1 * max( A'*x + B', 0 )^2

 mad        r0.rgb, c2, t1, r0  ; Add ambient contribution
+mul_x4     r0.a, r0, r0        ; r0.a = k  * max( A'*x + B', 0 )^4

 mul        r0.rgb, 1-r0.a, r0  ; 1-r0.a = SmoothConditional( |P|^2 < 1 )
                                ; Multiply by result of shading
+mov        r0.a, c7            ; Clear alpha
```

Phong Shading

One of the major problems of per-pixel lighting resides in computing the specular component of the final color. This component is due to the reflection of the light itself on a shiny material. It is easy to see that the reflection of a point light on a perfectly shiny sphere is a single point. Unfortunately, very few surfaces are perfectly shiny. To account for non-perfect reflections, sometimes called dull reflection, Phong (and Warnock before him) introduced a very popular model. This model relies on the use of a power function in which the exponent depends on the shininess of the material.

Pixel shader algorithms to perform Phong shading have been described before. However, they performed the per-pixel power function using the usual techniques described at the beginning and suffered from the problems of such techniques. This often leads to multipass algorithms or reduces the control over the shininess exponent.

We will now show how, using the power function algorithm exposed earlier, we can perform realistic per-pixel Phong shading including a normal map, a color diffuse texture map, a color specular texture map, and a shininess map.

Phong Equation with Blinn Half-Vector

First, we need to express our shading model mathematically. We suggest reading computer graphics textbooks for more information on the equations presented in this section.

Before we can express this equation, we need to detail the variables that are needed. First, the shading depends upon the light direction, described by unitary vector L. We also need to know the surface normal at the shading point, N. Finally, we need to use some vector to compute the specular component. As is often the case for per-pixel shading, we do not directly use the Phong equation. Instead we take the Blinn half-vector H, which is the unitary vector falling directly between the view direction V and the light direction L. Figure 10 illustrates these vectors.

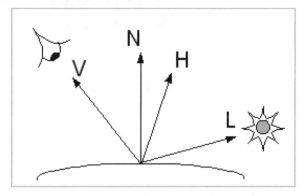

Figure 10: Vectors required for Phong shading

When using normal mapping, we distinguish between the perturbed normal used for lighting, N', and the real surface normal, N.

The scalar values that are needed for the computation are the ambient, diffuse, and specular coefficients: $MAmb_c$, $MDiff_c$, and $MSpec_c$ for the material and $LAmb_c$, $LDiff_c$, and $LSpec_c$ for the light. Here the index c is R, G, or B to indicate one of the color components.

The shading equation can now be written as:

$$I_c = MAmb_c\, LAmb_c + MDiff_c\, LDiff_c\, \max(0, \mathbf{L} \cdot \mathbf{N'})$$
$$+ MSpec_c\, LSpec_c\, \max(0, \mathbf{H} \cdot \mathbf{N'})^n$$

Expressing the Inputs

The Phong equation has a number of inputs that we need to be able to pass down to the pixel shader. We will first make a number of assumptions that reduce the number of inputs required for the above function.

First, we suppose that the ambient, diffuse, and specular coefficients do not vary from one pixel to the next. This means that the algorithm proposed cannot handle slide projectors or other kinds of textured lights.

We also suppose that the material ambient coefficients do not vary arbitrarily from pixel to pixel. Instead, these are linked to the material diffuse coefficients using the equation $MAmb_c = KAmb_c * MDiff_c$, with $KAmb_c$ constant within the shader. The equation states that the ambient color is always the same as the diffuse color up to some constant. This is not a very limiting assumption, since this relationship between material ambient and diffuse coefficients is often witnessed in practice.

The three coefficients $MDiff_c$ and exponent n can vary from pixel to pixel; therefore, they need to be expressed in a four-component, 2D texture map. Recall that we do not store n directly; instead we place the corresponding value A' in the texture's fourth component. Coefficients $MSpec_c$ can also vary at each pixel and can be placed in a separate three-component, 2D texture. These coefficients act as a color gloss map, effectively an extension of the traditional single-component specular gloss map.

The perturbed normal N' is expressed as a tangent-space normal map. We therefore use a 2D texture map containing color-encoded normalized vectors that can be accessed using a single 2D texture lookup. We refer the reader to other real-time shading texts to learn more on tangent space normal maps.

To effectively use a tangent-space normal map in our lighting equation, we need to have a normal map representation of the light vector L and halfway vector H. As discussed earlier, the halfway vector needs to be renormalized per pixel; otherwise, important visual artifacts will occur when the power function is applied. Therefore, we interpolate H through a texture coordinate and use a cube map lookup to renormalize it. A renormalization cube map, as illustrated in Figure 11, contains a color-encoded vector in each texel corresponding to the unitary vector pointing in the direction of that texel.

Since the light vector is only used in linear computations, not renormalizing it has almost no impact on the visual result. Therefore, we skip per-pixel renormalization in order to make the best usage out of our texture resources. This means that we can store the light vector L in an interpolated color.

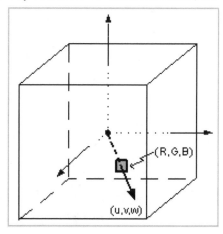

Figure 11: Renormalization cube map

The Pixel Shader

Let's put all this together into a single pixel shader. First, each texture stage and interpolated color is assigned as follows:

Table 3: Content of pixel shader interpolators and textures

Register	Vector	Texture Content
Texture 0	Diffuse u, v	$(MDiff_R, MDiff_G, MDiff_B, A')$
Texture 1	Normal map u, v	Normal map N'
Texture 2	Specular u, v	$(MSpec_R, MSpec_G, MSpec_B, 0)$
Texture 3	Halfway vector H	Renormalization cube map
Color 1	L' = Sign-corrected light vector L	—

Note that since interpolated colors do not support negative values, we place the sign corrected light vector in color 0. This can be written as L' = 0.5(L + (1,1,1)).

We need to have access to $KAmb_c$ and $LAmb_c$, which are constant within the shader. Due to the nature of the equation, we can precompute the product of these coefficients. Therefore, we store the resulting vector $(KAmb_R*LAmb_R, KAmb_G*LAmb_G, KAmb_B*LAmb_B)$ in the first three components of constant register c0.

We also need the values of constant coefficients $LDiff_c$ and $LSpec_c$. These are stored in the first three components of registers c1 and c2, respectively.

Finally, we need to pick the approximation exponent m used for the power function. In our example, we use $m = 8$. We also use _x4 as the multiply instruction modifier for each instruction of the power function approximation. Since we wish to use a value of n varying per pixel, we must precompute $k^{-1/m} = 0.074325$. We store this value in the alpha channel of constant register c0. Looking at Table 2, we find that the maximal n that can be achieved is 116.34. Also, using the function TranslateTexture in Listing 10, we can convert per-texel values of n into values of A' to be placed in the alpha component of texture 0.

The pixel shader that computes per-pixel Phong shading then becomes:

Listing 14: Code for Phong shading with various features (pixel shader versions 1.1, 1.2, and 1.3)

```
ps.1.1
; v1 RGB: light vector (L') (sign corrected)
; c0 RGB: ambient light (Kamb*Lamb), A: 1/MaxAB(logM) = 0.074325
; c1 RGB: diff light (Ldiff), A: 0
; c2 RGB: spec light (Lspec), A: 0
  tex t0     ; diffuse texture (Mdiff) + A' (exponent')
  tex t1     ; normal map (N')
  tex t2     ; specular texture (Mspec)
  tex t3     ; normalised halfway vector (H)

  dp3_sat    r0.rgb, v1_bx2, t1_bx2  ; L'.N'
+ sub        r0.a, c0.a, t0.a        ; B'

  dp3_sat    r1, t3_bx2, t1_bx2      ; H.N'

  mad        r0.rgb, r0, c1, c0      ; Kamb*Lamb + Ld*L'.N'
+ mad_x4_sat r1.a, t0.a, r1.a, r0.a  ; p0 = k0*max(A'x+B', 0)

  mul        r1.rgb, t2, c2         ; Ms*Ls
+ mul_x4     r1.a, r1.a, r1.a        ; p1 = p0*p0

  mul_x4     r1.a, r1.a, r1.a        ; p2 = p1*p1
  mul_x4     r1.a, r1.a, r1.a        ; p  = p2*p2 = H.N'^n

  mul r1.rgb, r1, r1.a               ; Ms*Ls*H.N'^n
  mad r0, r0, t0, r1                 ; Ma + Md*Ld*L'.N' + Ms*Ls*H.N'^n
```

Summary

We have presented a method of approximating a non-integer power function on a pixel shader by using as few texture stages as possible and gracefully degrading in accuracy depending on the desired exponent and available number of blend stages. Furthermore, the technique can be used for single or multiple channels, thus adapting nicely to individual shader requirements.

This method has several advantages over traditional exponentiation techniques that use either a texture lookup or a series of sequential multiplications. Texture lookups are only accurate for pixel shader versions 1.4 and greater, and even then they will require two phases. Sequential multiplications need a large number of stages to compute high power-of-two exponents and even more for non-power-of-two. Additionally, since the multiplications are inherently uniform during the entire shader, they do not allow for a smooth variation in power.

A couple of applications were suggested, and Phong shading in particular is covered in the results below. We believe such a useful technique can be applied to many other algorithms that require a power function, especially considering that it can be abstracted to any effect requiring a sharp yet smooth transition, such as a spotlight's cone falloff.

The per-pixel variation of the exponent, which is a handy extension to the basic principle, can provide important visual cues for surfaces whose specularity varies, such as for a material including both metallic and organic features. Its main disadvantages are that m constrains the lower bound of the specular exponent n, as explained in the mathematical details section, and that one component of a texture must be used to encode the exponent. The latter, however, is expected of any technique that varies the exponent per-pixel.

The shader code in Listing 14 was applied to red spheres with different properties, such as faceted per-pixel exponent maps, wrinkled normal maps, and orange specular maps. The results can be seen in Figure 12 and Color Plate 11. Due to the many iterative multiplications, there is a large accumulation of error that manifests itself as banding. Generally speaking, the greater the exponent, the more banding that will be evident; however, this is mostly noticeable on smooth surfaces, such as those expressed with uniform normal maps. The banding artifacts are less significant when using normal maps that contain some perturbation because the specular falloff is quite sharp due to the abrupt changes in the normal. Therefore, visual artifacts are reduced as detail in the normal map is increased.

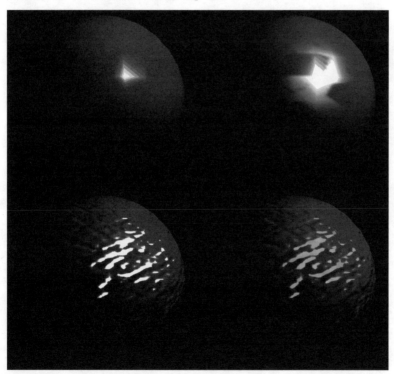

Figure 12: Per-pixel Phong shading on spheres. Clockwise from upper left: uniform normal and exponent maps, uniform normal map and faceted exponent map, noisy normal and exponent maps with uniform orange specular material, and noisy normal and exponent maps with uniform white specular material. (See also Color Plate 11.)

Banding can also result from reduced instruction counts. If additional instructions are available, we recommend using them to maximize precision. Note that since the Phong shading algorithm presented only requires exponentiation of a single component, the instructions easily fit into the scalar pipeline of the pixel shader, which reduces the number of dedicated stages. The shader code in Listing 14 consumes two stages purely for exponentiation purposes, but instructions in the vector pipeline can be co-issued at these stages if desired.

For example, the specular texture can be removed if the diffuse and specular materials are represented by a single texture. We can then use a cube map at that stage to represent the surrounding environment, even encoding a Fresnel term in the remaining color register. The math computations can easily be accommodated within the two remaining vector instructions.

Finally, the images in Figure 12 were rendered on hardware with 8 bits of fractional precision. Other hardware is available that has more than 8 bits of fractional precision and will suffer less from the banding artifacts.

We hope you found this trick helpful and that you will find many more uses for an approximating power function in your shading endeavors.

Bump Mapped BRDF Rendering

Ádám Moravánszky

Introduction

With this effect, we introduce the concept of the BRDF and show how they can be rendered efficiently by using vertex shaders. I will combine the BRDF technique with normal mapping to get a bumpy BRDF effect, taking full advantage of version 1.4 pixel shaders.

Figure 1: A teapot drawn with the BRDF effect and illuminated by four lights. The polygonal outline is caused by the self-shadowing algorithm, not the BRDF shader. (See also Color Plate 12.)

Bidirectional Reflectance Distribution Functions

Bidirectional Reflectance Distribution Functions (BRDFs) are a very important milestone along the road to photorealistic rendering. The BRDF is a generalization of all shading models, such as Lambert, Blinn, or Phong. A shading model is an analytic approximation of a surface's reflective properties; it describes how incoming light is reflected by a surface. The simplest shading model, Lambert shading, says that a surface reflects incoming light equally in all directions. Phong shading, on the other hand, has an additional additive specular term which permits a surface to reflect different amounts of light in different directions. Thus, each of these models is a formula which computes, for a given incoming and a given outgoing light direction, the portion of incoming light that gets reflected in the outgoing direction. Such functions are called BRDFs. Formally, the scalar valued BRDF is a five-dimensional function because the reflected light may not only depend on the incoming and outgoing direction vectors (which each have two degrees of freedom in three space) but also on the wavelength of the light. However, in computer graphics, we always decompose wavelengths into a sum of discrete color channels, like red, green, and blue. This way the BRDF becomes a 3D vector valued function with four parameters. Permitting the BRDF to be color dependent is important because some materials reflect certain colors differently than others: just look at the rainbow colored pattern on a CD. This pattern has another important property that neither Lambert nor Phong shading can capture, but it can be described by more general BRDFs: that of anisotropic reflection. The CD has tiny grooves, and light coming in orthogonally to them is in for a stronger reflection.

Perhaps the primary advantage of a BRDF is that it can be measured directly from real world objects; see [Marschner00] for a technique to do this via an inexpensive digital camera. There are also extensive databases of measured BRDF data available on the Internet. This data generally comes as a table of color values for a long list of incoming and outgoing directions (usually in polar coordinates).

With all the advantages, one has to be aware of the limitations: While BRDFs capture more lighting effects than any of the simple lighting models, even they cannot capture the effects of transmitted light (glass, water), subsurface light transport (marble, skin), or heterogeneous surfaces (wood). There are other, still more general concepts which can do these things, but they are beyond the scope of this article. On the other hand, BRDFs are great for rendering ceramics, metals, plastics, leathers, and a whole host of other common materials.

Because of its generality, a BRDF is not only convenient but also relatively expensive. For quite some time, BRDF rendering was beyond the scope of real-time graphics. In fact, it is still not sensible to render BRDFs directly, say, from a 4D lookup table; it would simply take too much memory for any reasonable sampling resolution. Instead, we are forced to go back and pick an analytic, parametric model that can do a good job at approximating the BRDF. The key idea is that we want to reduce the BRDF into a sum or product of two- or three-dimensional functions, so that we can store a lookup table to these functions in a texture map and then use additive or multiplicative blending to compute the result.

For this effect, I will use the parameterization presented by [McCool01]. The authors decided to represent BRDFs as a product of three factors, plus an optional additive term for very bright specular BRDFs: $f(\vec{u},\vec{v}) = p(\vec{u})q(\vec{h})p(\vec{v})+s(\vec{h})$, where $\vec{u}$ is the incoming direction, $\vec{v}$ the outgoing direction, and $\vec{h} = \frac{\vec{u}+\vec{v}}{\|\vec{u}+\vec{v}\|}$ the half-angle vector. The factors p, q, and s do not have any physical meaning; they are merely a way to factor the function. The full explanation for this factorization is found in [McCool01], but it suffices to say that this is an expressive formula (it approximates real BRDFs well), while using only three planar or cube map textures (so it is very economic).

Decomposing the Function

By now, you have either measured or, more likely, downloaded a 4D table of BRDF sample values for your favorite surface and would like to generate the texture maps we are going to use as lookup tables for rendering. While a program to do this is not included with this effect, writing the factorization code (especially in a matrix-oriented language like Matlab) based on the description in [McCool01] should be straightforward. If you would like to put that off until you have the real-time rendering portion, you can use the p, q, and s textures computed by the authors of that paper for a set of interesting BRDFs, which you can get from their web site as part of their OpenGL-based demo (http://www.cgl.waterloo.ca/Projects/rendering/Papers/ #homomorphic). I use a subset of these textures for my effect, which is implemented as an Effects Browser plug-in.

Note that the BRDF textures are scaled up by a factor of α to take full advantage of the limited 8-bit range of the images. This factor is saved along with the textures and will be needed during rendering to rescale the colors to the correct values.

Another trick is to use cube maps instead of simple planar textures. With cube maps, you can directly use the incident, exitant, and half-angle vectors as texture coordinates, without having to normalize them. Planar textures would require an additional transformation to project these 3D vectors into a 2D texture coordinate.

Reconstruction

Reconstruction is the process of taking the BRDF factors tabulated in the textures and, for a pair of given incident and exitant vectors, computing the value of the BRDF. While this is part of the rendering process, it is not all of it. You still need the incident light, which you will reflect. In the real world, various amounts of light are coming from all directions. Unfortunately, you would need to integrate over all these directions per-pixel to simulate this, which is clearly intractable. What you can do is only have a set of point lights illuminating your object. Thus, for each light, you have a single incident direction, for which you have to evaluate the BRDF once. The exitant direction is the only outgoing direction you are interested in: the direction toward the camera. You can then accumulate the light originating from the different lights L in the frame buffer via additive multipass blending by evaluating the sum:

$$\sum_{i}^{L} f(\vec{u}_i, \vec{v}) \frac{l_i}{r_i^2} (\vec{u}_i \cdot \vec{n})$$

The term after the BRDF is the incoming light at the surface. l is the intensity of your light source, which, in nature, falls off with the square of the distance r from the light to the surface. Finally, the dot product of the incident direction and the surface normal $\vec{n}$ models how the incoming light from the source gets distributed over a larger area of the surface (and thus less arrives per unit area) if the light is at a low angle relative to the surface.

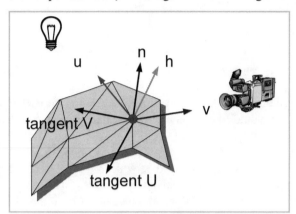

Figure 2: The tangent space vectors used in shading

Now we want to evaluate this lighting equation in Direct3D. We need to write a vertex and pixel shader, plus the setup code, which evaluates a light term in the sum, plus the routine which uses them to render a mesh. Then we can call this method repeatedly for different lights with additive blending turned on to get the final result.

Pseudocode for the single light rendering routine:

```
d3dDevice->SetTexture(0, P_Texture )
d3dDevice->SetTexture(1, Q_Texture )
d3dDevice->SetTexture(2, P_Texture )
if (BRDF has S texture)
    d3dDevice->SetTexture(3, S_Texture )

Set Pixel and Vertex Shader Constants
Set Pixel and Vertex Shader
Call DrawPrimitive() to render the mesh
```

The vertex shader is more interesting. Its job is to compute the per-vertex incoming (to_light) and outgoing (to_eye) vectors, which will be our texture coordinates. It is reproduced below, with each operation commented.

```
vs.1.0
; incoming vertex is [POS, TANGU, TANGV, NRML]
; Transform vertex position to homogenous clip space position
dp4 oPos.x, c[CMODVIEW0], POS
dp4 oPos.y, c[CMODVIEW1], POS
dp4 oPos.z, c[CMODVIEW2], POS
dp4 oPos.w, c[CMODVIEW3], POS

; compute to_light = normalize(light_position - vertex_position)
sub r1, c[LIGHTPOS], POS
dp3 r1.w, r1, r1
rsq r1.w, r1.w
mul r1.xyz, r1, r1.w

; compute to_eye = normalize(camera_position - vertex_position)
sub r2, c[CAMPOS], POS
dp3 r2.w, r2, r2
rsq r2.w, r2.w
mul r2.xyz, r2, r2.w
```

```
; compute (normal . to_light) * LCOLOR term.
; LCOLOR is the combined light color, and the texture scaling factor α.
dp3 r0, NRML, r1
mul oD0.xyz, r0, c[LCOLOR]

; texcoord0 = outgoing direction in the tangent space
dp3 r5.x, r2, TANGU
dp3 r5.y, r2, TANGV
dp3 r5.z, r2, NRML
mov oT0.xyz, r5.xyz

; texcoord2 = incoming direction in the tangent space
dp3 r6.x, r1, TANGU
dp3 r6.y, r1, TANGV
dp3 r6.z, r1, NRML
mov oT2.xyz, r6.xyz

; texcoord1 = texcoord3 = half-angle vector = outgoing + incoming,
; normalized implicitly by the cube map.
add r5.xyz, r5.xyz, r6.xyz
mov oT1.xyz, r5.xyz
mov oT3.xyz, r5.xyz
```

Note the way the vertex shader uses the same normal and tangent vectors to span a per-vertex tangent space as the "dot3" bump mapping techniques do. This means you will not have to generate any additional mesh attributes for this effect if your engine supports simple bump mapping. As for the constant registers, this shader needs the camera and light position in model space and a combined light color*α value. I left out the quadratic attenuation (it does not look good given the limited dynamic range of our lights), but it can easily be added by squaring the inverse light-vertex distance, which gets computed as part of the normalization of the to_light vector above.

An additional trick not shown here, but one I use in my production code, is to compute the normal vector from the two tangent vectors with a cross product, instead of passing it explicitly per-vertex. If you find that your normal is sometimes the negative of this cross product, you need to additionally encode its sign as the magnitude of one of your tangent vectors, which will then need renormalization as well.

The pixel shader is straightforward; it has to sample the textures and compute the product:

```
ps.1.0      ; out = diffuse*tex0(t0)*tex1(t1)*tex2(t2) + tex3(t3)
tex t0
tex t1
tex t2
tex t3

mul r0, v0, t0
mul r0, r0, t1
mul r0, r0, t2
add r0, r0, t3
```

Of course, you only need the final add if you used the optional additive S term.

Adding the Bumps

Unfortunately, applying a bump map to the BRDF is not as straightforward as one would hope. The reason is that the cube maps need their texture coordinates, the to_light, to_eye, and half-angle vectors, in the surface's tangent space. When there are no bumps, the basis of this tangent space is equivalent to the interpolated per-vertex basis from our vertex shader in the previous section. However, in the bumpy case, the tangent space is spanned by the per-pixel normal (read from a conventional normal map) and two tangent vectors orthogonal to it. Dot3 bump mapping also uses this exact normal, but in that case, it is only needed for a dot product operation, and the two tangent vectors are not used. We, on the other hand, have to transform our per-vertex vectors computed in the vertex shader into this space before doing the texture lookups. Fortunately, there are some corners that can be cut, but first we will make some changes to our vertex shader:

```
vs.1.0
; incoming vertex is [POS, TANGU, TANGV, NRML, TEXCOORD]
; Transform vertex position to homogenous clip space position
dp4 oPos.x, c[CMODVIEW0], POS
dp4 oPos.y, c[CMODVIEW1], POS
dp4 oPos.z, c[CMODVIEW2], POS
dp4 oPos.w, c[CMODVIEW3], POS

; compute to_light = normalize(light_position - vertex_position)
sub r1, c[LIGHTPOS], POS
dp3 r1.w, r1, r1
rsq r1.w, r1.w
mul r1.xyz, r1, r1.w

; compute to_eye = normalize(camera_position - vertex_position)
sub r2, c[CAMPOS], POS
dp3 r2.w, r2, r2
rsq r2.w, r2.w
mul r2.xyz, r2, r2.w

; conventional texture coordinate for the bump map
mov oT0.xy, TEXCOORD.xy

; texcoord1 = light direction
dp3 oT1.x, r1, TANGU
dp3 oT1.y, r1, TANGV
dp3 oT1.z, r1, NRML

; texcoord2 = eye direction
dp3 oT2.x, r2, TANGU
dp3 oT2.y, r2, TANGV
dp3 oT2.z, r2, NRML
```

We made two changes: First, we took out the code to compute the normal dependent diffuse color. Second, we no longer compute the half-angle sum here. Since the half-angle direction is the sum of the other two vectors, regardless of which space we are in, we can do the addition in the pixel shader. This way, we avoid having to transform it per-pixel along with the other two vectors. Finally, since we now use a bump map, we also have to pass texture coordinates for it along with each vertex. Of course, the texture bindings in the rendering routine have to be updated accordingly.

Now, on to the pixel shader:

```
def X_AXIS, 1.0f, 0.0f, 0.0f, 1.0f
def Y_AXIS, 0.0f, 1.0f, 0.0f, 1.0f


; PHASE1-TEXTUREADDRESS  1) fetch vertex space normal

texld r4, t0               ; look up the normal in the normal map
texcrd toLight_vs.xyz, t1  ; just grab the other vectors
texcrd toEye_vs.xyz,   t2  ; without using a texture map

; PHASE1  -  ARITHMETIC  2) create tangent space basis

; tangU_vs = X_AXIS - normal_vs *.DOT(X_AXIS,normal_vs)
mad tangU_vs, -normal_vs_bx2, normal_vs_bx2.x, X_AXIS
; same with y axis
mad tangV_vs, -normal_vs_bx2, normal_vs_bx2.y, Y_AXIS

; [tangU_vs, tangV_vs, normal_vs] now approximates an
; orthogonal basis


; transform toEye from the smooth tangent space to the
; bumpy one.

dp3 toEye_ts.x, tangU_vs , toEye_vs
dp3 toEye_ts.y, tangV_vs , toEye_vs
dp3 toEye_ts.z, normal_vs_bx2, toEye_vs

; not enough instructions available to do another
; full 3x3 multiplication: we just perturb one component

mov toLight_ts.xyz, toLight_vs
dp3 toLight_ts.z, normal_vs_bx2, toLight_vs

; compute the half angle vector as usual

add halfAngle_ts.xyz, toLight_ts, toEye_ts


phase
; PHASE2-TEXTUREADDRESS 4) sample cubemaps

texld r0, toLight_ts
texld r1, halfAngle_ts
texld r2, toEye_ts
texld r3, halfAngle_ts

; PHASE2  -  ARITHMETIC 5) do blending math
; compute LCOLOR * (toLight_vs . normal_vs)

dp3 normal_vs, toLight_vs, normal_vs_bx2
mul r4, normal_vs, c[LCOLOR]

mul     r0, normal_vs, r0
mul     r0, r0, r1
mul     r0, r0, r2
add     r0, r0, r3
```

What we are trying to do is totally hopeless in ps.1.3 and below and just about fits into the ps.1.4 spec. In the texture address part of phase 1, we retrieve the two vectors we computed in the vertex shader (they have since been interpolated across the triangle and may have been denormalized). We also look up the normal in the normal map. This normal is relative to the interpolated vertex basis, as are our other two vectors.

In the arithmetic phase, we need to construct the true surface's tangent space basis. To approximate that as compactly as possible, I separately orthogonalize the x and y axis to the normal. Full Gram-Schmidt orthogonalization would take too many instructions.

We immediately make use of this matrix by transforming the to_eye vector with it. We would like to do the same to the to_light vector, but due to the limited number of instructions available, we only succeed in transforming the z component. Fortunately, this approximation looks quite good regardless.

Finally, the half-angle vector is computed as the sum of the two transformed vectors. Phase 2 of the shader is the same as the one for the smooth case, with the exception that we also compute the color term using the perturbed normal.

Figure 3: Tori showing the bump mapped BRDF effect

Conclusion

We have presented a brief introduction to BRDFs and shown how the rendering technique of [McCool] can be extended to bumpy surfaces. This is only scratching the surface of the untapped possibilities of BRDF rendering. Other directions worth following are the combination of BRDF effects with color textures and environment maps.

Acknowledgments

Thanks to Jason Mitchell, Christoph Niederberger, and Tim Weyrich for help with different aspects of this effect.

References

[McCool01] Michael D. McCool, Jason Ang, and Anis Ahmad, "Homomorphic Factorizations of BRDFs for High-Performance Rendering," SIGGRAPH Proceedings, 2001, pp. 171-178.

[Marschner00] Stephen R. Marschner, Stephen H. Westin, Eric P. F. Lafortune, and Kenneth E. Torrance, "Image-based BRDF Measurement," *Applied Optics*, Vol. 39, No. 16, 2000.

Real-Time Simulation and Rendering of Particle Flows

Daniel Weiskopf and Matthias Hopf

In this article, we describe a pixel shader technique for simulating and rendering a 2D particle flow in real time. This physics-based approach allows the environment to affect the particles, leading to more realistically evolving scenes. Typical applications include water surfaces, lava streams, and waterfalls, etc.

Motivation

Computer games usually try to immerse the player in a realistic-looking environment. In most cases, you want the environment to be "alive" — there should be plenty of action in the background not directly related to the player's avatar or his or her friends and foes. For the most challenging effects, hundreds and thousands of moving elements have to be coordinated; these effects become time-critical features in the graphics engine.

Depending on the kind of action, either vertex-based or pixel-based approaches seem to be appropriate. Particle systems are a kind of vertex-based approach that is used for various effects that have to display many loosely coupled simple features and is already state of the art. Effects that can only be modeled with tightly coupled data and effects that are not closely related to distinguishable elements are inappropriate for particle systems. Here and in the case of 2D effects like TV screens, water surfaces, and clouds, animated textures are the way to go. Especially for water surfaces, a lot of techniques using bump maps (especially environment bump maps) already exist. The ideas in this article can be combined with these methods to achieve an optimal effect.

Even modern computer games do not feature a lot of static animated textures like movie screens or fire effects due to memory requirements. Dynamic animated textures for mirror effects and portal rendering are computationally expensive and thus rarely used as well. In contrast to particle systems, neither one can display changing surfaces that respond to external stimuli. For example, a water surface showing the flow of the underlying river should react to a rock that has been thrown into that river.

Procedural textures that are created on-the-fly can be used to incorporate a simulation process into the surface model. In the case of water, the resulting flow appears to be much more realistic; the process can create non-repeating texture animations, and it still does not need a lot of texture memory. The process can react to environmental changes, creating a kind of interaction with the environment unknown before.

Of course, there is a drawback. There always is.

You really don't want to use procedural textures in the form of textures created by the processor at run time, as you don't want to create and download a texture ten times a second or more. This would only be possible for small textures and very simple procedure models. Besides, we have to do some regular graphics, sound, AI, and user interaction, don't we?

With respect to 2D flows, we would like to offer a solution: We can use the GPU of modern graphics systems to solve some simple mathematical differential equations in order to simulate 2D particle transport. One could think of other equations and solving processes for different materials and effects, but for now, we will restrict ourselves to fluids. Using the GPU for the brute force mathematics, the processor just needs to work on the interaction model and set up the solving process.

Using these particle transport simulations, water surfaces, flowing lava, waterfalls, etc., can be rendered easily. We will now take a closer look at the underlying theory and how it can be implemented by using pixel shaders and texture render targets. Please refer to our technical description in [Weiskopf01] if you are interested in further details on the theoretical background of particle transport.

Ingredients

These are the benefits you get from physics-based simulation: Most phenomena look natural and convincing, they usually allow simple modeling by a few and physically meaningful parameters, and they provide a quite abstract definition of their dynamic behavior.

If we want to take a closer look at the simulation of moving fluid surfaces, the essential questions boil down to:

- What kind of motion is it? How do "objects" move?
- What "objects" are involved? What moves?

The answer to the first question is: The velocity of the flow governs the motion of "objects" within this flow. Note that velocity is a vector — it has a length (a speed) and a direction. Moreover, the velocity doesn't need to be constant across the flow. Rather, imagine a distinct velocity vector attached to each single point of the flow. See Figure 1 for a schematic sketch of such a velocity distribution.

The answer to the second question is: We are dealing with particles. These particles are negligible in size and mass (i.e., they are massless point-like objects). What's important is that particles carry further information such as color, temperature, and pressure. We can attach these or other properties to the particles according to our application. A particle keeps its attached properties along its way through the flow, making it easy to follow, or *trace*, the particle.

Particles are massless objects and can't withstand changes in velocity caused by an outside force. Therefore, a particle's velocity is identical to the velocity of the flow that surrounds the particle. This provides a link between the two main ingredients: the particles and the velocities in the flow.

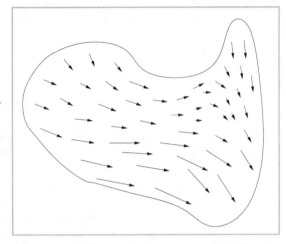

Figure 1: Distribution of velocities in a flow. The arrows show the different speeds and directions of motion at various points in the flow.

Now imagine that a large number of particles is spread across the surface of the fluid. The particles are stitched to the moving surface and are thus a direct means of showing the motion of the flow.

How Does a Single Particle Move?

Let's first consider the motion of a single particle. If you know how to trace one particle, you know how to follow all particles.

As a particle's velocity is identical to the velocity of the flow, we can directly relate a particle's motion to the behavior of the flow. Let's have a look at the definition of velocity v:

$$\frac{d\mathbf{r}}{dt} = \mathbf{v}$$

Note that velocity is a vector. In the current situation, we consider a two-dimensional flow. Therefore, velocity is a vector with two components (i.e., $\mathbf{v} = (v_x, v_y)$). Vector r describes a position and has two components as well (i.e., $\mathbf{r} = (x, y)$). The third quantity involved is time *t*.

The terms *dr* and *dt* are so-called *infinitesimal* quantities. Generally speaking, *dr* and *dt* are very tiny changes in position and time, respectively. As a good approximation, we can replace infinitesimal changes by small but finite changes Δr and Δt. This leads to the relationship:

$$\frac{\Delta \mathbf{r}}{\Delta t} = \mathbf{v}$$

Rewriting the above equation in a slightly different form yields:

$$\Delta \mathbf{r} = \Delta t \cdot \mathbf{v}$$

The same expression in explicit component-wise notation:

$$\Delta x = \Delta t \cdot v_x$$

$$\Delta y = \Delta t \cdot v_y$$

See Figure 2 for a graphical representation of this equation. A particle moves from a starting position r_0 to a subsequent position $r_1 + \Delta r$ within a time span Δt. The direction of the connection between the initial position and the subsequent position is, of course, identical to the direction of the particle's velocity. Note that the length of the displacement is the length of the velocity multiplied by the time span. How far we move in one time step depends on the time scale and the velocity.

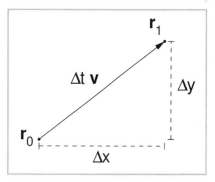

Figure 2: Relationship between velocity v and spatial displacement (x, y)

So far, we know how a particle moves from one position to a subsequent position during a small time step, but what happens for an extended time span? First, split this longer time span in small time intervals Δt, which usually are of equal length. Then apply the above displacement scheme for each single time step. Figure 3 shows this iterative process schematically. Starting at the initial position r_0, just add the displacement $\Delta t\ v_0$ to obtain the subsequent position r_1. In the next step, add the displacement $\Delta t\ v_1$. As the velocity may not be constant within the flow, you have to consider a different velocity at each step. If we perform this process step after step, we will finally obtain the complete motion of the particle.

This numerical method is called *Euler integration*. Please consult one of the numerous textbooks on numerical mathematics, such as [Press94], if you are interested in more background information on this or other related numerical techniques.

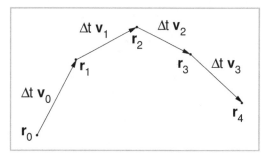

Figure 3: Motion of a particle for an extended time span

Basic Texture Advection: How Do a Bunch of Particles Move?

Since we would like to visualize a moving fluid surface by means of many different particles, we need to consider the motion of a large number of particles. We show how we can exploit the very fast texture and rasterization units offered by graphics chips to speed up tracing many particles.

Although the idea of point-like particles is conceptually beneficial, it is not directly applicable to graphics hardware. First, we have to transform point-like particles into a texture-based representation by means of sampling. Figure 4 shows such a sampling process. In this example, a grid cell of the texture takes the color of the particle contained in the cell (i.e., nearest neighbor sampling). If more than one particle is attached, the color of the cell is the sum of the particles' colors. Since this texture holds all information on particles, we call it a *particle texture*.

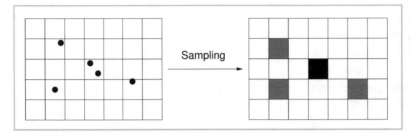

Figure 4: Sampling of point particles on a regular grid

After we spread all particles over the texture, we trace them by mapping the initial particle texture to the particle texture of the following time step. This approach is generally called *forward mapping*. Figure 5 illustrates the transformation of the particle texture for one time step. The arrows in the left part of the figure indicate the displacement of each particle, depending on the velocity of the underlying flow and on the step size Δt. The color information in each single cell of the old texture is transferred to another cell in the new texture, depending on the local displacement vector.

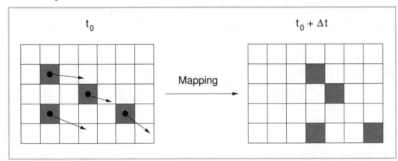

Figure 5: Propagating a particle texture one step forward in time

Unfortunately, this basic idea of *texture advection* suffers from two important problems. First, if the velocity or the step size is too small, particles may stay in a cell forever, even though, in fact, they should move slowly. This is caused by the finite size of a grid cell; by definition, we assume that particles are located at the center of a cell. If a displacement vector is too short to push a particle out of the cell, the new position of the particle lies inside the same cell. In the following step, we repeat the same procedure once again. We could iterate this process over and over without shifting the particle out of the cell.

The second problem is the possibility of gaps in the particle texture. If, for example, the flow diverges in some areas, neighboring cells might move into different directions in such a way that intermediate cells in the new particle texture don't receive any particles from the previous time step. These blank cells cause unpleasant visual artifacts. In general, gaps are an issue in forward mapping approaches.

We can overcome these two problems by replacing forward mapping by *backward mapping*. The basic idea remains the same: Just replace the mapping from time t to $t + \Delta t$ by a time-reversed mapping from t back to $t - \Delta t$. Figure 6 demonstrates backward mapping.

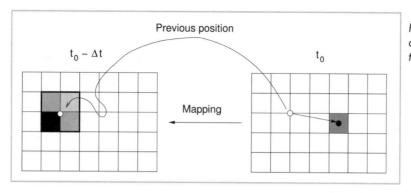

For the sake of simplicity, let us consider only a single cell in the right part of the figure. By inverting the direction of the displacement vector, we obtain the position from where this cell has originated:

$$x_{previous} = x_{new} - \Delta t \cdot v_x$$

$$y_{previous} = y_{new} - \Delta t \cdot v_y$$

Then, we use this position to determine the color of the original particle. As the previous position usually is not identical to the center of a cell, we apply a bilinear lookup: The actual color depends on the four surrounding cells. Finally, the complete texture advection approach consists of backward mappings for all cells in the new particle texture.

With this backward mapping approach, we overcome the two problems of forward mapping. First, bilinear interpolation guarantees that even small displacements affect the particle texture of the following time step. Secondly, all cells of the new particle texture receive new color values (i.e., no gaps can occur).

Based on the previous considerations, the graphics hardware-based approach to texture advection is as follows. The particle texture is represented by a standard 2D texture. The number of components in that texture depends on the type of application; normally, we use RGB values. The velocity field is stored in another 2D texture which has two components for (v_x, v_y).

The advection algorithm uses a dependent texture lookup in order to shift the particles along the velocity field. *Offset textures* are part of hardware-supported pixel operations. (In DirectX, offset textures are called texbem for bump environment-map transform.) See Figure 7 for a schematic diagram of a dependent texture lookup via an offset texture.

The offset texture functionality transforms signed components (du, dv) of a previous texture unit by a 2×2 matrix and then uses the result to offset the texture coordinates of the current stage. This process contains two texture fetch operations. The first step comprises a lookup in an offset texture based on texture coordinates (u_0, v_0). An offset texture is a signed 2D texture with two components describing the displacement of coordinates in the successive texture fetch operation. In the second step, a dependent texture lookup in a standard RGB texture is performed. Here, another pair of texture coordinates (u_1, v_1) is modified by the previously fetched offset values. We will discuss the scaling by a factor *mag* later in the section titled "How Can Particles Drop Out?"

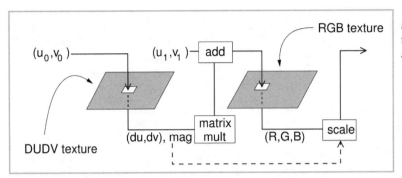

Figure 7: Dependent texture lookup via off-set texture

Based on offset textures, the pseudocode of the texture advection algorithm is:

```
// Texture tex1 holds information on particles
initialize tex1 with initial_particle_colors

// Texture tex0 is a signed texture holding
// the velocities
initialize tex0 with velocities

// Set initial time t to zero
t = 0

// Main simulation loop
while(simulation_running)  {

    // Load velocities as offset texture
    load_offset_texture tex0

    // Prepare dependent texture lookup
    // in particle texture tex1
    dependent_texture_look_up in tex1

    // Compute new particle information,
    // which is written into the intermediate
    // texture tex2
    draw_textured_rectangle into tex2

    // Update particle texture tex1 with
    // new data
    swap tex1 and tex2

    // Draw the actual part of the scene
    draw_textured_fluid_surface into framebuffer

    // Update time
    t = t + delta_t
}
```

During the advection process, the particles tend to bleed out, and sharp edges get smoother with every time step. This *diffusion* effect is intrinsic to our approach using discretized particle positions and thus can't be removed completely. You can use graphics hardware-based image sharpening filters or so-called morphological operators [Hopf00] to nearly compensate for this effect, but that is beyond the scope of this article.

Inflow: Where are the Particles Born?

The particles we are now able to trace in the texture have to come from somewhere. We call the incoming particles the *inflow*. Inflowing particles may be dropped into the texture at any time and any position if applicable. For instance, a leaf that falls into a river can now be projected onto the flow and rendered into the particle texture. However, in most cases, you do not want the particles to suddenly pop up in the middle of the flow.

Another possibility is to define an initial texture and leave it unchanged during run time. Texture coordinate wrapping prevents particles from flowing out of the texture at one of the edges. Instead, they are inserted on the opposing edge as you can see in Figure 8. You will realize soon that the texture gets blurry very fast, due to the diffusion effect, until you can no longer distinguish any features.

When we don't use texture wrap mode, texture elements near the rendered edges of the flow regularly address elements outside the texture boundaries during the advection step. As no texture is defined there, these texels get black, introducing very visible artifacts to the scene. However, when the used texture is a bit larger than the displayed portion, we can insert new particle blobs at the edges of the texture. During the advection, these new particles are sucked into the visible portion of the texture and retain the particle density. When the underlying flow has a

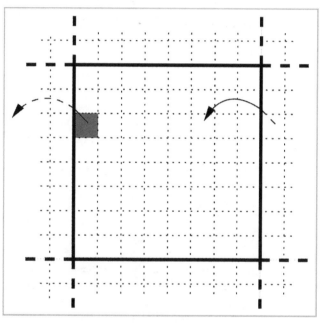

Figure 8: When using texture coordinate wrapping, an endless texture can be simulated and no lookups refer to areas outside the texture.

preferred flowing direction, we can remove or even cancel some of the non-displayed edges and concentrate on one or two edges as shown in Figure 9. Please keep in mind that the off-screen part of the texture must be large enough so that no off-boundary texels pop into the displayed part in a single time step. Additionally, they should be sharp-edged in the usual case, as they will smear out a bit during the flow due to the diffusion effect.

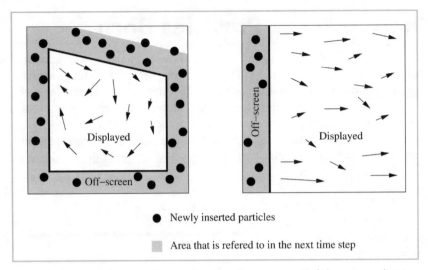

Figure 9: New particles are inserted in the off-screen part of the texture that is addressed in the next time step. The flow on the right side has a preferred direction; thus, only one edge has to be considered.

The design of the particle blobs, the used color palette, and the insertion pattern are as critical for achieving good-looking images as the flow pattern itself. Additionally, it largely depends on the kind of flow you want to render. For flows like lava streams, an interesting approach could be to completely fill the edge with a partially randomized flow color and add a few crack blobs of a completely different color afterward. For using the particle texture as a bump mapping texture (e.g., for water surfaces), the inserted blobs have to be much smoother. Always remember that it can be a good idea to add blobs inside the rendered part of the texture when something in the virtual environment interacts with the flow.

In the pseudocode of the texture advection algorithm, inflow is added just after the new particle information has been written to the target texture:

```
        ...

        // Main simulation loop
        while(simulation_running)  {

            ...

            // Compute new particle information,
            // which is written into the intermediate
            // texture tex2
            draw_textured_rectangle into tex2

+           // Add regular inflow
+           render_offscreen_inflow into tex2
+
+           // Add inflow that occurs due to
+           // interactions with the environment
+           render_interaction_inflow into tex2

            // Update particle texture tex1 with
            // new data
```

```
        swap tex1 and tex2

    ...
}
```

How Can Particles Drop Out?

Particles that enter the flow have to exit somewhere. We call the exiting particles the *outflow*. Of course, we do not trace particles individually but rather their concentration or features, so we can't really say that we have particles exiting the flow. However, the contents of texture cells that are not referred to by the offset texture addressing scheme do not contribute to the new texture contents. In this sense, the non-referred texels contain the outflow.

For flows with a preferred direction, natural outflow happens at the edge opposed to the inflow edge. Figure 9 depicts this situation. In some cases, with slow flow or additional blobs added to the flow, this may not be enough. For circular flows or textures using texture coordinate wrap mode, no natural outflow exists, and we have to apply other means to get the range of flowing particles into a steady state.

Similar to the inflow situation, you may want to remove particles at dedicated positions in the flow, for instance, when something is interacting with the flow. You could either subtract or weight a small part of the texture to remove or reduce the particles in this area. This can be done either explicitly after the advection process is completed or implicitly by choosing a luminance weighting at the end of the offset texture process. In the section on basic texture advection, we indicated that a scaling of fetched texels is possible. Each component of the final RGB triplet can be multiplied by a factor *mag*, which is part of the offset texture as an independent, third component. By choosing scaling values smaller than 1.0, you can specify arbitrarily shaped regions of outflow.

Implementation

Our implementation is based on DirectX 8.1 and ps.1.0. Let's start with the actual pixel shader program:

```
// Pixel shader 1.0
ps.1.0
// Load offset texture in stage 0
tex t0
// Dependent texture look-up in the particle
// texture t1. Texture coordinates are
// modified by the previous offset texture t0
texbem t1,t0
// Final color
mov r0, t1
```

First, we load the velocity field into texture stage 0. The velocity field t0 is a 2D texture whose components may have positive and negative values. A typical texture format is the signed format D3DFMT_V8U8. Then we perform a dependent texture lookup in the particle texture of the previous time step. The particle texture t1 is a standard 2D RGB texture. The name texbem stands for bump environment-map transform, indicating that its standard usage is in per-pixel bump mapping applications.

Before we can start the pixel shader program, we have to initialize the textures. The velocity field is stored as a signed 2D texture and can be defined by:

```
device->CreateTexture( width, height, 1, 0,
    D3DFMT_V8U8,
    D3DPOOL_MANAGED,
    &texture0);
```

The offset texture, in this case, is limited to 8 bits per component (i.e., the velocity is coded as signed bytes). It's a good idea to scale the actual velocity data to the maximum value range (from −128 to +127) in order to achieve the highest numerical accuracy. We can absorb this scaling in a later step, as described shortly.

The initial particle texture is a standard RGB texture. For example, we can use an RGB texture with 8 bits per color channel:

```
device->CreateTexture( width, height, 1, 0,
    D3DFMT_X8R8G8B8,
    D3DPOOL_MANAGED,
    &texture1);
```

The dependent texture lookup in texture stage 1 transforms the offset values (*du*, *dv*) before adding them to the texture coordinates of stage 1. Set the transformation matrix to a multiple of the identity matrix in order to uniformly scale the offset values:

```
float scale = -step_size;
device->SetTextureStageState
    (1, D3DTSS_BUMPENVMAT00, F2DW(scale));
device->SetTextureStageState
    (1, D3DTSS_BUMPENVMAT01, F2DW(0.0f) );
device->SetTextureStageState
    (1, D3DTSS_BUMPENVMAT10, F2DW(0.0f) );
device->SetTextureStageState
    (1, D3DTSS_BUMPENVMAT11, F2DW(scale));
```

The scaling takes care of the factor $-\Delta t$ in backward particle tracing. In this way, the step size can be changed without redefining the values of the velocity texture. In addition, scale absorbs the scaling of the original velocity values to the range of signed bytes, as introduced above.

In order to allow for outflow regions, you simply have to replace the texbem pixel shader operator with texbeml (which stands for bump environment-map transform with luminance correction) and use a three-component offset texture. For example, the texture format D3DFMT_V8U8 could be substituted by the signed format D3DFMT_W8Q8V8U8 or the mixed formats D3DFMT_X8L8V8U8 or D3DFMT_L6V5U5. The magnification coefficient L of the texture is multiplied with the texel color directly after lookup and can be set to values smaller than 1.0 for outflow regions.

The new particle texture of the current time step is the old particle texture of the subsequent time step. Therefore, we directly render the new particles into a texture by setting:

```
device->CreateTexture( width, height, 1,
    D3DUSAGE_RENDERTARGET,
    D3DFMT_X8R8G8B8,
    D3DPOOL_DEFAULT,
    &texture2));
```

and

```
renderBuffer->GetSurfaceLevel(0, &surface);
device->SetRenderTarget(surface, NULL);
```

Since the particle texture for the new time step is also a rectangular grid of the same size, as in the previous time step, we just have to render such a rectangle into the render target in order to obtain the new particles.

So far, we have accomplished the simulation of particle flow for one time step. After each time step, we swap the particle textures texture1 and texture2, so that texture1 holds the current state of the particle texture. (Note that both textures have to be defined as D3DUSAGE_RENDERTARGET, slightly changing the original definition of texture1.) In order to finally draw the surface of the fluid, we render the polygonal representation of the surface to the frame buffer, with the particle texture texture1 used as RGB texture.

Example code for simulating and rendering texture advection is contained on the companion CD.

Summary

We have described a method to simulate and render texture transport on a moving surface (for example, the surface of a liquid). This approach allows for dynamic interaction with the environment and on-the-fly inclusion of outside effects on the flow. For practical purposes, the design of both the flow pattern and the inflow procedures is critical. Particle advection can be used for enhancing liquid surfaces such as water surfaces, lava streams, or waterfalls.

References

[Hopf00] M. Hopf and T. Ertl, "Accelerating morphological analysis with graphics hardware," Workshop on Vision, Modeling, and Visualization VMV 2000 (infix, 2000), pp. 337-345.

[Press94] W. H. Press, S. A. Teukolsky, W. T. Vetterling, and B. P. Flannery, *Numerical Recipes in C*, 2nd Ed. (Cambridge University Press, 1994).

[Weiskopf01] D. Weiskopf, M. Hopf, and T. Ertl, "Hardware-accelerated visualization of time-varying 2D and 3D vector fields by texture advection via programmable per-pixel operations," Workshop on Vision, Modeling, and Visualization VMV 2001 (infix, 2001), pp. 439-446.

Part 4

3D Textures and Pixel Shaders

by Evan Hart

With the introduction of programmable pixel pipelines, graphics features that were once somewhat obscure are now finding additional uses. One example of this is 3D, or volumetric, textures. While 3D textures have been available for several years, few real applications have been created to take advantage of them. The reality is that real-time shading is still largely a discipline of pasting multiple 2D images onto 3D surfaces. In this article, we will define 3D textures and then present a variety of shaders which use them to achieve effects that are either awkward or impossible with 1D or 2D textures.

Using 3D Textures with Shaders

Truly Volumetric Effects

by Martin Kraus

This article presents several examples of ps.1.4 programming for volumetric effects, ranging from quite basic techniques to recent research results. These include volume visualization with transfer functions, animation of volume graphics by blending between different volume data sets, animation of transfer functions, and a recently developed rendering technique for real-time interactive, high-quality volume graphics, called *pre-integrated volume rendering*.

3D Textures and Pixel Shaders

Evan Hart

Introduction

With the introduction of programmable pixel pipelines, graphics features that were once somewhat obscure are now finding additional uses. One example of this is 3D or volumetric textures. While 3D textures have been in high-end graphics hardware for about a decade and appeared in consumer hardware nearly two years ago, few real applications have been created to take advantage of them. The reality is that real-time shading is still largely a discipline of pasting multiple 2D images onto 3D surfaces. Programmable pixel shaders have enabled a variety of unique algorithms, and 3D textures are a concise way to implement techniques that might be awkward or impossible with just 1D or 2D textures. In this article, we will define 3D textures and then present a variety of shaders which use them to achieve effects that are either awkward or impossible with 1D or 2D textures.

3D Textures

Since 3D textures have appeared relatively recently in consumer-level hardware, many people are unfamiliar with exactly what they are. The simplest way to think of a 3D texture is as a stack of 2D textures. There are multiple conventions for referring to the coordinates used to index a 3D texture; for this chapter, we will use s, t, r, and q. These are the width, height, depth, and projective coordinates, respectively. This is different from the terminology used in DirectX documentation, but it avoids confusion as to whether w is the depth component or the projective component of a texture.

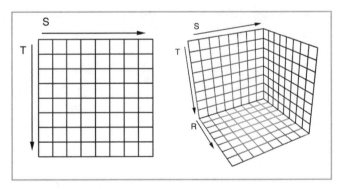

Figure 1: Relationship between 2D and 3D textures

Filtering

With the addition of an extra dimension, the filtering nomenclature changes a bit.

For a 3D texture, simple linear filtering of a single level of the mip map chain is referred to as *trilinear filtering*, as it performs linear filtering along all three axes of the texture, sampling colors from eight different texels. Most people automatically assume that trilinear filtering means that multiple mip maps are being blended together, but this is not the case with 3D textures. With 3D textures, this case is referred to as *quadrilinear filtering*, as it adds a linear filter along the fourth dimension of the volumetric mip maps, sampling from 16 different texels. As this change in nomenclature suggests, the filtering doubles in expense when moving from two-dimensional textures to three-dimensional textures. Additionally, anisotropic filtering becomes significantly more complex. With 2D textures, *anisotropic filtering* is thought of as a filter along a line across the texture with a width of two and length up to the maximum degree of anisotropy. This means that an anisotropic filter with a maximum level of anisotropy of 8 requires 16 texels. In three dimensions, this increases to a slab with width two extending in the other two dimensions up to the maximum degree of anisotropy. Now, our worst case for a maximum level of anisotropy becomes 8*8*2 = 128 texels. This is 32 times the cost of the bilinear fetch of a 2D texture that most programmers consider the basic unit of texture performance.

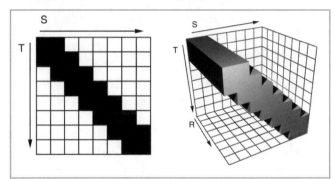

Figure 2: Anisotropic filtering in two and three dimensions

It is easily seen that anisotropic filtering of a 3D texture is something to avoid, unless the programmer has a very specific reason. Even if there is good justification, the programmer must understand that this sort of filtering may be impossible as current accelerators only handle a single direction of anisotropy at a time.

Storage

The only thing more expensive than filtering a 3D texture is storing it in memory. Three-dimensional textures grow extremely rapidly with increases in resolution. For example, a 32-bit 256×256×256 texture is 64 MB in size. While this is a significant hurdle to using volume textures, it can often be addressed with a few simple tricks. First, the number of channels used in a 3D texture should be kept to a minimum. If the data to be stored in the 3D texture represents a scalar quantity like density or intensity, it should be stored as a luminance or alpha texture rather than RGBA. Next, if the artifacts of DXTC style compression are not objectionable, the 3D texture may be compressed to conserve memory. Finally, mirroring and repeating offer a great way to compress 3D textures. Many of the examples in the following sections use textures that repeat or are symmetric. By using the wrapping and mirroring modes for the different dimensions, 2x to 8x compression can generally be achieved.

Applications

Despite the high storage and filtering costs, 3D textures do make a lot of tasks easier and can frequently be more efficient than using 2D textures to implement the same algorithm. Also, the two primary difficulties previously mentioned will become smaller issues over time. Memory on graphics accelerators has been doubling almost yearly, and the cost of the filtering operation is only as expensive as performing two texture fetches of the same quality. Modern cards that support 1.4 pixel shaders are capable of performing up to 12 2D fetches (which can each be trilinear, anisotropic, etc.) in a single pass.

Function of Three Independent Variables

The first and most obvious application for 3D textures in shaders is as lookup tables to provide piecewise linear approximations to arbitrary functions of three variables. Many of the following sections show specific examples of functions of three dimensions, but it is important to remember the general concept rather than particular examples. One simple example would be an implementation of the per-pixel calculation of Phong-style specular highlights. Note that this is an alternative to the technique proposed in "A Non-Integer Power Function on the Pixel Shader."

Since the half-angle (H) and reflection (R) vectors don't interpolate linearly across the surface of polygons, they must be recomputed per-pixel to obtain the best results. This leads to the creation of a vector of non-unit length, as graphics hardware is not yet able to perform a per-pixel square root. Naturally, the equation for specular highlights requires its inputs to be of unit length. The problem is that L·R or N·H, whichever you prefer, is not just $\cos(\theta)$, but $\cos(\theta) * |R|$ or $\cos(\theta) * |H|$. Clearly, this problem can be corrected by performing a normalizing divide prior to raising $\cos(\theta)$ to the kth power. Now, the function that needs to be evaluated is one of three variables: {N·H ($\cos(\theta) * |H|$), |H|, k} or {R·L ($\cos(\theta) * |R|$), |R|, k}. The equation actually implemented is shown below. The most important item to note about this particular algorithm is that it can be implemented much more efficiently as a projected 2D texture since the first operation is just a divide, but this example is good for illustrative purposes.

$$\left(\frac{N \circ H}{\sqrt{H \cdot H}} \right)^{k} \text{ where } N \circ H = 0 \text{ if } N \cdot H < 0$$

Pixel shader:

```
ps.1.4

texld r0.rgb, t0.xyz  //get normal from a texture lookup
texld r1.rgb, t1.xyz  //get light vector in same way
texld r2.rgb, t2.xyz  //get view vector in same way
texcrd r3.rgb, t3.xyz //pass in spec power in t3.x

//compute H as V+L/2
add_d2 r1.rgb, r1_bx2, r2_bx2
```

```
//compute N.H and store in r0.r
dot3 r0.r, r0_bx2, r1

//compute H.H and store in r0.g
dot3 r0.g, r1, r1

//copy in k
mov r0.b, r3.r

phase

texld r3, r0.rgb //fetch the 3D texture to compute specular

//move it to the output
mov_sat r0, r3
```

Noise and Procedural Texturing

Noise is a particular type of function texture that is extremely useful in pixel shading. The noise that is most interesting to us here is not white noise of random numbers, but Perlin noise that has smoothly varying characteristics [Perlin85]. Noise of this sort has been used for years in production quality 3D graphics for texture synthesis. It allows the creation of non-repeating fractal patterns like those found in wood, marble, or granite. This is especially interesting in that an effectively infinite texture can be created from finite texture memory. Other uses of 2D noise textures are discussed in "Texture Perturbation Effects."

The most classic example for using a 3D noise function is to create turbulence. Turbulence is an accumulation of multiple levels (octaves) of noise for the purpose of representing a turbulent flow. A great example of this is the appearance of marble. The veins flow through the material in a turbulent manner. The example we will use is an adaptation for real time of the Blue Marble shader in [Upstill89]. In this example, the shader uses six textures to create the effect. The textures are five occurrences of a noise map and a one-dimensional color table. (Note that this shader will work even better with more noise textures — six is just the limit for DirectX 8.1's 1.4 pixel shaders.) The noise textures are scaled and summed to create the turbulence, and the value of the turbulence is then used to index a 1D texture via a dependent read to map it to a color. The texture coordinates used to index into the noise maps are all procedurally generated in the same manner, and they are just different scales of each other.

Pixel shader code:

```
ps.1.4

//fetch noise maps
texld r0, t0.xyz
texld r1, t1.xyz
texld r2, t2.xyz
texld r3, t3.xyz
texld r4, t4.xyz

//accumulate multiple octaves of noise
// this sets r0 equal to:
// 1/2r0 + 1/4r1 + 1/8r2 + 1/16r3 + 1/32r4
add_d2 r3, r3_x2, r4
add_d2 r3, r2_x2, r3
add_d2 r3, r1_x2, r3
```

```
add_d4 r0, r0_x2, r3

phase

//fetch 1-D texture to remap
texld r5, r0.xyz

mov r0, r5
```

Realistically, the interactive 3D graphics field is just now on the edge of getting procedural noise textures to work. Noise textures tend to require several octaves of noise and dependent fetches just to implement something as simple as marble. This ignores the application of lighting and other effects one would also need to compute in the shader. As a result, it would be impractical to ship a game that relied upon noise textures of this sort today, but it still certainly applies as a technique to add that little bit of extra varying detail to help eliminate the repetitive look in many of today's interactive 3D applications. Finally, even if this technique is not immediately applicable, graphics hardware is evolving at such a pace that we expect this technique will be very common in a few years.

Figure 3: Marble shader using eight octaves of noise instead of five

Attenuation and Distance Measurement

Another procedural trick that 3D textures are useful for is attenuation. The attenuation can correspond to falloff proportional to the distance from a light source, or simply some distance measurement trick intended to create a cool effect. Typically, a distance measurement like this is implemented with a combination of pixel and vertex shaders, where the true distance is computed per-vertex and interpolated or a vector representing the distance is interpolated with its length being computed per-pixel. The deficiency in these methods is that they incorrectly linearly interpolate non-linear quantities or that they potentially force some of the computation to occur in lower precision, leading to poor quality. Additionally, these algorithmic solutions are only applicable to calculations based on simple primitives such as points, lines, and planes.

By using a 3D texture, the programmer is effectively embedding the object in a distance or attenuation field. Each element in the field can have arbitrary complexity in its computation since it is generated off-line. This allows the field to represent a distance from an arbitrary shape. On the downside, using a 3D texture can be reasonably expensive from a memory standpoint, and it relies on a piecewise linear approximation to the function from the filtering. The toughest portion of using a 3D texture to perform this sort of operation is defining the space used for the texture and the transform necessary to get the object into the space. Below is a general outline of the algorithm:

1. Define a texture space containing the area of interest.

2. For each texel in the space, compute the attenuation.

3. Apply the 3D attenuation texture to the object with appropriate texture coordinate generation.

The first step involves analyzing the data and understanding its symmetry and extents. If the data is symmetric along one of its axes, then one of the mirrored texturing modes, such as D3DTADDRESS_MIRRORONCE, can be used to double the resolution (per axis of symmetry) for a given amount of data. Additionally, an understanding of the extents of the data is necessary to optimally utilize the texture memory. If a function falls to a steady state, such as zero along an axis, then the texture address mode can be set to clamp to represent that portion of the data. Once the user has fit the data into a space that is efficient at representing the function, the function must be calculated for each texel. Below are a pair of pseudocode examples showing how to fill an attenuation field for a point. The first is naïve and computes all the attenuation values in the shape of a sphere; the second takes advantage of the symmetry of the sphere and only computes one octant. This can be done since the values all mirror against any plane through the center of the volume.

Complete sphere:

```
#define VOLUME_SIZE 32

unsigned char volume[VOLUME_SIZE][VOLUME_SIZE][VOLUME_SIZE];
float x, y, z;
float dist;

//walk the volume filling in the attenuation function,
// where the center is considered (0,0,0) and the
// edges of the volume are one unit away in parametric
// space (volume ranges from -1 to 1 in all dimensions
x = -1.0f + 1.0f/32.0f; //sample at texel center
for (int ii=0; ii<VOLUME_SIZE; ii++, x += 1.0f/16.0f)
{
   y = -1.0f + 1.0f/32.0f;
   for (int jj=0; jj<VOLUME_SIZE; jj++, y += 1.0f/16.0f)
   {
      z = -1.0f + 1.0f/32.0f;
      for (int kk=0; kk<VOLUME_SIZE; kk++, y += 1.0f/16.0f)
      {
         //compute distance squared
         dist = x*x + y*y + z*z;

         //compute the falloff and put it into the volume
         if (dist > 1.0f)
         {
            //outside the cutoff
            volume[ii][jj][kk] = 0;
         }
         else
         {
```

```
            //inside the cutoff
            volume[ii][jj][kk] = (unsigned char)
                ( 255.0f * (1.0f - dist));
        }
    }
}
```

Sphere octant, used with the `D3DTADDRESS_MIRRORONCE` texture address mode:

```
#define VOLUME_SIZE 16

unsigned char volume[VOLUME_SIZE][VOLUME_SIZE][VOLUME_SIZE];
float x, y, z;
float dist;

//walk the volume filling in the attenuation function,
// where the center of the volume is really (0,0,0) in
// texture space.
x = 1.0f/32.0f;
for (int ii=0; ii<VOLUME_SIZE; ii++, x += 1.0f/16.0f)
{
    y = 1.0f/32.0f;
    for (int jj=0; jj<VOLUME_SIZE; jj++, y += 1.0f/16.0f)
    {
        z = 1.0f/32.0f;
        for (int kk=0; kk<VOLUME_SIZE; kk++, y += 1.0f/16.0f)
        {
            //compute distance squared
            dist = x*x + y*y + z*z;

            //compute the falloff and put it into the volume
            if (dist > 1.0f)
            {
                //outside the cutoff
                volume[ii][jj][kk] = 0;
            }
            else
            {
                //inside the cutoff
                volume[ii][jj][kk] = (unsigned char)
                    ( 255.0f * (1.0f - dist));
            }
        }
    }
}
```

With the volume, the next step is to generate the coordinates in the space of the texture. This can be done with either a vertex shader or the texture transforms available in the fixed-function vertex processing. The basic algorithm involves two transformations. The first translates the coordinate space to be centered at the volume, rotates it to be properly aligned, then scales it so that the area effected by the volume falls into a cube ranging from –1 to 1. The second transformation is dependent on the symmetry being exploited. In the case of the sphere octant, no additional transformation is needed. With the full sphere, the transformation needs to map the entire –1 to 1 range to the 0 to 1 range of the texture. This is done by scaling the coordinates by one half and translating them by one half. All these transformations can be concatenated into a single matrix for efficiency. The only operation left to perform is the application of the distance or attenuation to the calculations being performed in the pixel shader.

Representation of Amorphous Volume

One of the original uses for 3D textures was in the visualization of scientific and medical data [Drebin88]. Direct volume visualization of 3D datasets using 2D textures has been in use for some time, but it requires three sets of textures, one for each of the axes of the data, and is unable to address filtering between slices without the use of multitexture. With 3D textures, a single texture can directly represent the dataset.

Although this article does not focus on scientific visualization, the implementation of this technique is useful in creating and debugging other effects using volume textures. Using this technique borrowed from medical volume visualization is invaluable in debugging the code that a developer might use to generate a 3D distance attenuation texture, for example. It allows the volume to be inspected for correctness, and the importance of this should not be underestimated, as presently an art tool for creating and manipulating volumes does not exist. Additionally, this topic is of great interest since a large amount of research is presently ongoing in the area of using pixel shaders to improve volume rendering. For more information on volumetric rendering, see "Truly Volumetric Effects."

Application

These general algorithms and techniques for 3D textures are great, but the really interesting part is the concrete applications. The following sections will discuss a few applications of the techniques described previously in this article. They range from potentially interesting spot effects to general improvements on local illumination.

Volumetric Fog and Other Atmospherics

One of the first problems that jumps into many programmers' minds as a candidate for volume texture is the rendering of more complex atmospherics. So far, no one has been able to get good variable density fog and smoke wafting through a scene, but many have thought of volume textures as a potential solution. The reality is that many of the rendering techniques that can produce the images at a good quality level burn enormous amounts of fill-rate. Imagine having to render an extra 50 to 100 passes over the majority of a 1024 x 768 screen to produce a nice fog effect. This is not going to happen quite yet. Naturally, hardware is accelerating its capabilities toward this sort of goal, and with the addition of a few recently discovered improvements, this sort of effect might be acceptable.

The basic algorithm driving the rendering of the atmospherics is based on the volume visualization shaders discussed earlier. The primary change is an optimization technique presented at the SIGGRAPH/Eurographics Workshop on Graphics Hardware in 2001 by Klaus Engel (http://wwwvis.informatik.uni-stuttgart.de/~engel/). The idea is that the accumulation of slices of the texture map is attempting to perform an integration operation. To speed the process up, the volume can be rendered in slabs instead. By having each slice sample the volume twice (at the front and rear of the slab), the algorithm approximates an integral as if the density varied linearly between those two values. This results in the slice taking the place of several slices with the same quality. This technique is better described in the following article, "Truly Volumetric Effects."

The first step in the algorithm is to draw the scene as normal, filling in the color values that the fog will attenuate and the depth values that will clip the slices appropriately. The atmospheric is next added to the scene by rendering screen-aligned slices with the shader described in the following article. When rendering something like fog that covers most of the view, this means generating full-screen quads from the present viewpoint. The quads must be rendered back to front to allow proper compositing using the alpha blender. The downside to the algorithm is in the coarseness of the planes intersecting with the scene. This will lead to the last section of fog before a surface to be dropped out. In general, this algorithm is best for a fog volume with relatively little detail, but that tends to be true of most fog volumes.

Light Falloff

A more attainable application of 3D textures and shaders on today's hardware is volumetric light attenuation. In its simplest form, this becomes the standard light-map algorithm that everyone knows. In more complex forms, it allows the implementation of per-pixel lighting derived from something as arbitrary as a fluorescent tube or a light saber.

In simple cases, the idea is to simply use the 3D texture as a ball of light that is modulated with the base environment to provide a simple lighting effect. Uses for this include the classic rocket flying down the dark hallway to kill some ugly monster shader. Ideally, that rocket should emit light from the flame. The light should roughly deteriorate as a sphere centered around the flame. This obviously oversimplifies the real lighting one might like to do, but it is likely to be much better than the projected flashes everyone is used to currently. Implementing this sort of lighting falloff is extremely simple; one only needs to create a coordinate frame centered around the source of the illumination and map texture coordinates from it. In practice, this means generating texture coordinates from world or eye-space locations and back, transforming them into this light-centered volume. The texture is then applied via modulation with the base texture. The wrap modes for the light map texture should be set as described in the earlier section on the general concept of attenuation.

Extending the simple glow technique to more advanced local lighting models brings in more complex shader operations. A simple lighting case that might spring to mind is to use this to implement a point light. This is not really a good use of this technique, as a point light needs to interpolate its light vector anyway to perform any of the standard lighting models. Once the light vector is available, the shader is only a dot product and a dependent texture fetch away from computing an arbitrary falloff function from that point. A more interesting example is to use a more complex light shape such as a fluorescent tube. A fluorescent tube is a great example. The light vector cannot be interpolated between vertices, so a different method needs to be found. Luckily, a 3D texture provides a great way to encode light vector and falloff data. The light vector can be encoded in the RGB channels, and the attenuation can simply fit into the alpha channel. Once the correct texel is fetched, the pixel shader must rotate the light vector from texture space to tangent space by performing three dot products. Finally, lighting can proceed as usual.

This algorithm uses the same logic for texture coordinate generation as the attenuation technique described earlier. The only real difference with respect to the application of the volume texture is that the light vector mentioned above is encoded in the texture in addition to the attenuation factor. The application of the light is computed in the following shader using the light vector encoded in the volume:

```
ps.1.4

texld r0.rgba, t0.xyz //sample the volume map
texld r1.rgb, t1.xyz  //sample the normal map
texcrd r2.rgb, t2.xyz //pass in row 0 of a rotation
texcrd r3.rgb, t3.xyz //pass in row 1 of a rotation
texcrd r4.rgb, t4.xyz //pass in row 2 of a rotation


//rotate Light vector into tangent space
dot3 r5.r, r0_bx2, r2
dot3 r5.g, r0_bx2, r3
dot3 r5.b, r0_bx2, r4

//compute N.L and store in r0
dot3_sat r0.rgb, r5, r1_bx2

//apply the attenuation
mul r0.rgb, r0, r0.a
```

The only tricky portion of this shader is the rotation into tangent space. The rotation matrix is stored in texture coordinate sets two through four. This matrix must rotate from texture space to surface space. This matrix is generated by concatenating the matrix composed of the tangent, binormal, and normal vectors (the one typically used in per-pixel lighting) with a matrix to rotate the texture-space light vector into object space. This matrix can easily be derived from the matrix used to transform object coordinates into texture space.

References

[Drebin88] Robert A. Drebin, Loren Carpenter, and Pat Hanrahan, "Volume Rendering," SIGGRAPH Proceedings, Vol. 22, No. 4, August 1988, pp. 65-74.

[Perlin85] Ken Perlin, "An Image Synthesizer," SIGGRAPH Proceedings, Vol. 19, No. 3, July 1985, pp. 287-296.

[Upstill89] Steve Upstill, *The RenderMan Companion* (Addison Wesley, 1989).

Truly Volumetric Effects

Martin Kraus

This article presents several examples of ps.1.4 programming for volumetric effects, ranging from quite basic techniques to recent research results; this includes volume visualization with transfer functions, animation of volume graphics by blending between different volume data sets, animation of transfer functions, and a recently developed rendering technique for real-time interactive, high-quality volume graphics, which is called *pre-integrated volume rendering*.

Volumetric effects have been part of computer graphics since transparency became popular, more than 20 years now. They include the rendering of common effects like explosions, fire, smoke, fog, clouds, dust, colored liquids, and all other kinds of semi-transparent materials. However, there are important differences. For example, noninteractive rendering for movie productions usually tries to achieve the highest possible quality by simulating the physics of volumetric effects, at least approximately. In contrast to this, graphics in computer games do not have the privilege of noninteractivity. Therefore, they usually have to fake volumetric effects, in particular by rendering polygons with precalculated, semi-transparent textures.

Nowadays, this necessity of faking volumetric effects becomes questionable, as modern graphics boards offer the required resources for real volume graphics. In fact, programmable pixel shading offers even more than is necessary, allowing us to increase the quality of interactive volume graphics and, maybe more importantly, to animate volumetric effects in ways that have not been possible in real time before.

The Role of Volume Visualization

One of the most valuable resources for programmers of interactive, truly volumetric effects is the literature on volume visualization. Since volume visualization is a branch of scientific data visualization, faking volumetric effects is not an option in this field; however, the demands for real-time interactivity and high visual quality come close to the demands in the entertainment industry. Moreover, in recent years, many applications of volume rendering techniques have emerged that are no longer within the strict limits of scientific visualization. All these technologies are now often subsumed under the more general term "volume graphics," which is a branch of computer graphics.

Apart from this growth of research topics, there is also a steady transition going on with respect to the employed hardware. In fact, PCs with OpenGL-capable graphics boards have been a common benchmark environment for algorithms in volume visualization for several years. Consequently, researchers have also started to make use of specific hardware features of new PC graphics boards. This transition from scientific volume visualization on high-end graphics workstations to volume graphics on off-the-shelf PCs in combination with the similarity of challenges is why recent research in volume visualization is so much more relevant for graphics and game programming than it was a few years ago. Therefore, it is worthwhile to take a closer look at the basic problem of volume visualization and the way researchers have solved it with the help of programmable pixel shading.

Note: Of course, there are many different algorithms for volume rendering (e.g., ray-casting, shear-warp, splatting, cell projection, axis-aligned slicing with two-dimensional textures, or viewplane-aligned slicing with three-dimensional textures). While this article only covers the latter, many of the presented ideas work exactly the same or in a similar way for other rendering algorithms.

Basic Volume Graphics

Volume visualization started with the task of generating pictures of three-dimensional scalar fields (i.e., volumes in which a real number is assigned to each point). This problem arose in medical imaging and many kinds of computer simulations. While one common way to view and represent this kind of data was a stack of two-dimensional grayscale images, the best suited representation on a modern graphics board is a three-dimensional texture with a single component. Note that this volume texture does not hold any colors or opacities, but only a single number per texel (or "voxel" in the terms of volume graphics). Although it might be convenient to store this number in the place of the red component of a texel, this in no way implies that all voxels have to be reddish.

If the volume texture does not specify colors, where do the colors come from? The answer of volume visualization is the concept of a transfer function. This function maps the numbers stored in the volume texture to colors and opacities (i.e., to red, green, blue, and alpha components). Thus, a transfer function works very much like a one-dimensional dependent texture, and this is in fact the way transfer functions are implemented with programmable pixel shading.

Note: If a specific graphics hardware does not support dependent textures or similar techniques, then the transfer function has to be applied to the volume data in a preprocessing step and the resulting colors and opacities are stored in an RGBA volume texture. (The technical term for this method is "preclassification.") Unfortunately, this alternative has many drawbacks. In particular, it needs four times more texture memory and does not usually permit modifications of the transfer function in real time—a feature that is crucial for both volume visualization and the programming of many volumetric effects.

Once we can color a single point of a volume texture, we can also render an arbitrary slice through it by assigning appropriate texture coordinates to the corners of the slicing polygon, as shown in Figure 1 for a volume texture, which resulted from a volume scan of a teddy bear. If we are able to render one slice, we can easily render the whole volume by rendering a stack of many slices parallel to the viewplane and compositing the slices in the frame buffer with the blending equation:

```
destColor = (1 - srcAlpha) * destColor + srcAlpha * srcColor
```

> **Note:** In many cases, srcColor is pre-multiplied with srcAlpha, thus the blending equation simplifies to:
>
> ```
> DestColor = (1 - srcAlpha) * destColor + srcColor
> ```

Figure 2 depicts a "coarse" rendering with too few slices, while an appropriate number of slices was chosen for Figure 3. In order to demonstrate the effect of transfer functions, Figure 4 depicts the same object with identical viewing parameters but a different transfer function.

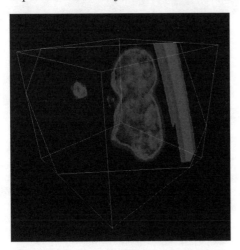

Figure 1: A textured slice through a volume texture

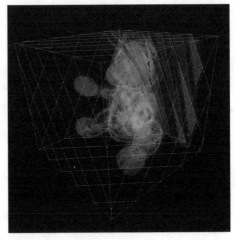

Figure 2: Several (but too few) composited slices

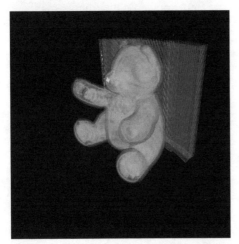

Figure 3: A volume rendering of a teddy bear

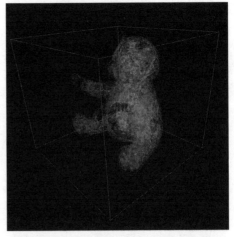

Figure 4: Same as Figure 3 with a more colorful transfer function

Here is a simple pixel shader 1.4 program that samples a volume texture, which is stored in texture stage 0, and applies a transfer function, which is specified in texture stage 1.

```
ps.1.4
texld r0, t0.xyz  // lookup in volume texture
phase
texld r1, r0      // lookup for transfer function
mov r0, r1        // move result to output register
```

Rendering a stack of viewplane-parallel slices that are textured this way is straightforward. In fact, it is much more challenging to come up with interesting volume data sets and appropriate transfer functions for particular volumetric effects.

> **Tip:** A common technique to reduce the screen area of the slicing polygons is to clip them in the space of texture coordinates, such that all fragments have texture coordinates within the limits of the volume texture and no time is wasted with the rasterization of superfluous fragments. This technique is demonstrated in Figures 1 to 4.

Animation of Volume Graphics

While animations of faked volumetric effects often require too many resources, texture memory in particular, or do not offer a satisfying visual quality, there are several ways to animate true volume graphics without additional costs.

Rotating Volume Graphics

Perhaps the most important advantage of truly volumetric graphics is the ability to rotate them easily. In order to do this, we may, however, not rotate the geometric positions of the slices but rather the texture coordinates. This may seem awkward at first glance, but it becomes clear when you remember that the slices are parallel to the viewplane all the time. (See the source code for the simple volume renderer on the book's companion CD for more details.)

Animated Transfer Functions

In some sense, transfer functions are just the three-dimensional analog of color palettes or indexed colors for images. Many applications of animated color palettes exist in two-dimensional computer graphics; similarly, the animation of transfer functions has a special importance for volume graphics and volumetric effects in particular.

While color palettes are often animated by modifying single entries or setting a new palette, there is a different, very efficient and general way to animate transfer functions that are implemented by dependent textures. The idea is to store a set of one-dimensional textures as the rows of a two-dimensional texture. When accessing this two-dimensional dependent texture, we just need to set a second texture coordinate (with the same value for all fragments), which selects a specific row of the texture and corresponds to a time parameter. We can easily implement this idea by extending the previous code example. The volume texture is again set in texture stage 0, texture stage 2 specifies the texture containing the transfer functions, and the green component of the constant vector c0 represents a time parameter.

```
ps.1.4
texld r0, t0.xyz // lookup in volume texture
mov r0.g, c1.r   // copy time parameter
phase
texld r2, r0     // lookup for transfer functions
mov r0, r2       // move result to output register
```

Tip: One additional advantage of this implementation is the linear interpolation in the dependent texture lookup (i.e., the possibility to choose the time parameter continuously). This results in a smooth blending between successive transfer functions, which permits smoother animations.

Blending of Volume Graphics

While blending between images is definitely not a spectacular effect, blending between volume data can lead to rather surprising and dramatic results. This is partially due to the effect of transfer functions and can be further enhanced by blending between more than two volume data sets, especially volume data sets with a complicated structure (e.g. noise or turbulence).

An example is given in Figures 5 to 8. Figure 5 depicts a volume rendering of the radial distance field of a point, while Figure 6 shows a volume data set consisting of noise. Blending between these two volumes with different pairs of weights results in Figures 7 and 8.

Tip: As indicated in Figures 7 and 8, we cannot only blend smoothly from one volume texture to another, but we can also distort, warp, or twist volumes by blending with an appropriate second volume texture.

Figure 5: Volume rendering of a sphere

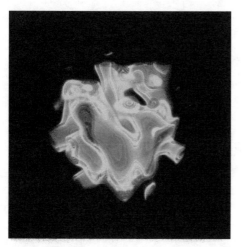

Figure 6: Volume rendering of some noise

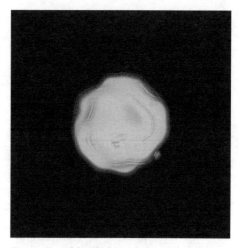

Figure 7: A blended combination of the volumes of Figure 5 and 6

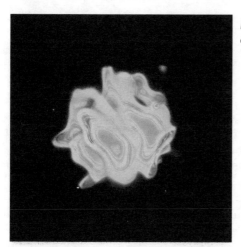

Figure 8: Same as Figure 7 with an increased weight of Figure 6

The following implementation stores four independent volume data sets in the red, green, blue, and alpha components of an RGBA volume texture. After the texture lookup, a dot product with a constant vector of weights is performed in order to blend between the four data sets. Finally, we apply the transfer function and move the result to the output register. The volume data is again associated with texture stage 0, time-dependent weights are stored in c0, and texture stage 1 specifies the transfer function.

```
ps.1.4
texld r0, t0.xyz // lookup in RGBA volume texture
dp4 r0, r0, c0   // blend components with c0
phase
texld r1, r0     // lookup for transfer function
mov r0, r1       // move result to output register
```

> **Tip:** Depending on the particular data sets, the vector of weights does not necessarily have to be normalized. In fact, a sum of weights unequal to 1 offers another degree of freedom for volumetric effects. Another way of enhancing this example is the animation of transfer functions, as discussed before.

High-Quality but Fast Volume Rendering

Presumably, the most important drawback of volume rendering is the required rasterization performance necessary to achieve a satisfying visual quality by rendering a sufficient number of slices. How many slices are necessary? A first guess is to render enough slices to match the resolution of the volume texture. This is, in fact, very acceptable for small volume textures. Unfortunately, the application of transfer functions usually adds further fine structures to the original volume texture, which leads to visible artifacts if the number of slices is not increased appropriately. Thus, our dilemma is that we do not want to abandon transfer functions, but we also do not want to render additional slices.

Fortunately, the literature on volume graphics suggests a solution to this problem, called "pre-integrated volume rendering." In the context of textured slices, this technique actually requires programmable pixel shading. Its features include full support for transfer functions and a much higher visual quality than the simple composition of slices, in particular for transfer functions with jumps and sharp peaks. For a detailed description of this algorithm, see [EKE2001].

Pre-integrated volume rendering reduces the number of slices by rendering slabs instead of slices. A slab is simply the space between two successive slices. For a single fragment, the problem reduces to the computation of the color contributed by a ray segment between the two slices; see Figure 9. If a linear interpolation of the volume data along this ray segment is assumed, the color will only depend on three numbers: the value on the front slice (at point F in Figure 9), the value on the back slice (at point B), and the distance between the two slices. If the slice distance is also assumed to be constant, the color of the ray segment will only depend on the two values of the volume data, and a two-dimensional lookup table is already enough to hold this dependency.

In the context of pixel shading, this table is implemented as a two-dimensional dependent texture, which is generated in a preprocessing step by computing the ray integrals for all possible pairs of values at the start and end points F and B. (The precomputation of this integral is the reason for the name "pre-integrated volume rendering.")

A corresponding ps. 1.4 program has to fetch the value of a volume texture on the front slice and the value on the back slice (i.e., on the next slice in the stack of slices). Then these two values are used as texture coordinates in a dependent texture fetch, which corresponds to the lookup of the precalculated colors of ray segments.

In the following code example, texture stage 0 specifies the volume texture on the front slice, while texture stage 3 specifies the volume texture on the back slice (i.e., both refer to the same volume texture data but use different texture coordinates). The lookup table for the precomputed ray integrals is specified in texture stage 4.

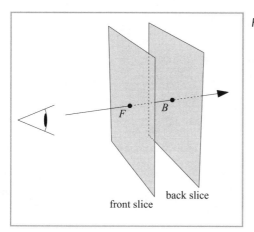

Figure 9: A slab of the volume between two slices

```
ps.1.4
texld r0, t0.xyz // lookup for front slice
texld r3, t3.xyz // lookup for back slice
mov r0.g, r3.r   // merge texture coordinates
phase
texld r4, r0     // lookup for transfer function
mov r0, r4       // move result to output register
```

Note that an additional mov command is necessary in the first phase in order to merge the two slice values in register r0, which holds the texture coordinates of the dependent texture lookup in the second phase.

The following code shows one possibility for the computation of a lookup texture for pre-integrated volume rendering of slabs of a specified thickness. The RGBA transfer function with premultiplied colors is stored in an array of floats called tfunc[TABLE_SIZE][4]. Note that the color and alpha components in this transfer function specify color and opacity densities (i.e., color and opacity per unit length). The resulting RGBA lookup table is returned in lutable[TABLE_SIZE][TABLE_SIZE][4].

```
void createLookupTable(float thickness,
  float tfunc[TABLE_SIZE][4],
  float lutable[TABLE_SIZE][TABLE_SIZE][4])
{
  for (int x = 0; x < TABLE_SIZE; x++)
  {
    for (int y = 0; y < TABLE_SIZE; y++)
    {
      int n = 10 + 2 * abs(x-y);
      double step = thickness / n;
      double dr = 0.0, dg = 0.0, db = 0.0,
        dtau = 0.0;
      for (int i = 0; i < n; i++)
      {
        double w = x + (y-x)*(double)i/n;
        if ((int)(w + 1) >= TABLE_SIZE)
          w = (double)(TABLE_SIZE - 1) - 0.5 / n;
        double tau = step *
          (tfunc[(int)w][3]*(w-floor(w))+
          tfunc[(int)(w+1)][3]*(1.0-w+floor(w)));
        double r = exp(-dtau)*step*(
          tfunc[(int)w][0]*(s-floor(w))+
```

```
            tfunc[(int)(w+1)][0]*(1.0-w+floor(w)));
        double g = exp(-dtau)*step*(
          tfunc[(int)w][1]*(w-floor(w))+
          tfunc[(int)(w+1)][1]*(1.0-w+floor(w)));
        double b = exp(-dtau)*step*(
          tfunc[(int)w][2]*(w-floor(w))+
          tfunc[(int)(w+1)][2]*(1.0-w+floor(w)));
        dr += r;
        dg += g;
        db += b;
        dtau += tau;
      }
    }
    lutable[x][y][0] =
      (dr > 1.0 ? 1.0f : (float)dr);
    lutable[x][y][1] =
      (dg > 1.0 ? 1.0f : (float)dg);
    lutable[x][y][2] =
      (db > 1.0 ? 1.0f : (float)db);
    lutable[x][y][3] =
      (1.- exp(-dtau));
  }
}
```

Tip: There are many ways to accelerate the computation of the pre-integrated lookup table; some of them are discussed in [EKE2001]. However, for static transfer functions, the best solution is probably to save this table to a file and load it from disk when it is needed.

Where to Go from Here

Programmable pixel shading offers a whole world of new possibilities for volumetric effects, and only a small fraction of them have been actually implemented and described. This article covers an even smaller fraction of these ideas, focusing on the pixel shader programming. Thus, there are many paths to take from here, for example:

■ Play with the code! The book's companion CD contains a simple volume renderer, which includes all the code snippets presented and discussed in this chapter. It also displays and lets you modify the pixel shader programs.

■ Design your own volumetric effects: Try to play with different volume textures and transfer functions.

■ Look for other applications of volume graphics. The research literature about volume visualization and volume graphics is full of interesting applications (e.g., shape modeling, terrain rendering, simulation of natural phenomena, etc.).

Acknowledgments

The author would like to thank Klaus Engel, who generated Figures 1 to 8 and programmed earlier versions of several code samples.

References

[EKE2001] Klaus Engel, Martin Kraus, and Thomas Ertl, "High-Quality Pre-Integrated Volume Rendering Using Hardware-Accelerated Pixel Shading," SIGGRAPH Proceedings/Eurographics Workshop on Graphics Hardware, August 2001, pp. 9-16 (http://wwwvis.informatik.uni-stuttgart.de/~engel/pre-integrated/).

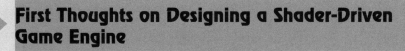

Part 5

First Thoughts on Designing a Shader-Driven Game Engine

by Steffen Bendel

When you design a game engine, you have to think about the usage of effects before writing even one line of code. Otherwise, it is possible that your initial engine design might be trashed by the addition of a new effect. A single effect is easy to realize, but an engine is more than the sum of its components. The topics in this article focus on issues that need to be taken into consideration when designing an engine that uses shaders.

Engine Design with Shaders

▶ Visualization with the Krass Game Engine

by Ingo Frick

The objective of this article is to present selected visualization techniques that have been applied in a successful game engine. The structure of these techniques is demonstrated and motivated by their developmental history, the further requirements in the foreseeable future, and the main design goal of the entire engine.

▶ Designing a Vertex Shader-Driven 3D Engine for the Quake III Format

by Bart Sekura

This article explains how vertex programs can be used to implement real game engine algorithms, in addition to great-looking effects and demos. Rather than showing a particular trick, my goal is to provide the reader with the display of applicability which, for the current vertex shader capable hardware, provides easier coding paths and visible performance benefits compared to CPU-based implementations of the same effects.

First Thoughts on Designing a Shader-Driven Game Engine

Steffen Bendel

When you design a game engine, you have to think about the usage of effects before writing even one line of code. Otherwise, it is possible that your initial engine design might be trashed by the addition of a new effect. A single effect is easy to realize, but an engine is more than the sum of its components. An engine includes a concept and a lot of compromises. It must share the resources in a meaningful way. Some of the effects described in this book are too expensive to incorporate into a real-time game engine. In case of an already existing game engine, they might be too difficult because the overall engine design is not prepared for that. The perfect engine does not exist, but there is a good engine for a special purpose and for a defined hardware basis. Try to focus on the things that are most important for you and optimize your design for that.

I would like to present a few thoughts on specific topics that have to be considered while designing a engine that uses shaders.

Bump Mapping

Bump mapping is futile without real dynamic lighting. If there is no moving light source, you see no effect and the effort is wasted. So bump mapping is not an isolated effect. It needs a complete engine infrastructure, not only for light. Objects using bump mapping require additional tangent space vectors, which must be supported by the rendering pipeline. The enormous effort is the reason why it is so seldom used.

Real-time Lighting

Real-time lighting is one of the most important things in engine design today. It is not a post-rendering effect that changes the brightness of the picture; it is a calculation which connects material properties and light intensity. If you decide to use real-time lighting, you have to implement it into every shader you use. Whereas per-vertex lighting is an easy way to implement lighting, it is very inaccurate. It works only with specifically optimized meshes because you get artifacts with big triangles. You can't use an LOD system with per-vertex lights, as lower LOD levels will produce artifacts because of the bigger triangles.

Precalculation is only possible for static lights. Dynamic lightmaps can be calculated only in real time if there is a simple projection algorithm for the texture coordinates. This is especially suitable for flat landscapes. One of the big challenges is to give the user a consistent impression of the lighting in the engine. Using different types of lighting for objects and landscape doesn't seem to work. Try to avoid an artifical look here. When using dynamic lights in the engine, sometimes a very simple lighting model is used. The resulting picture of such a simple lighting model will be too clear and too easy to analyze for the human brain, which is confusing. To make it more dusty, a preprocessed part of light might be a good idea. You might use radiosity, which could be too slow, or precalculated lightmaps to make it more dusty.

Use Detail Textures

In the real world, there are numerous details all the way down to the microscopic level. In computer graphics, the user should not realize an end to details. Geometry is limited by hardware polygon throughput, but for textures, multilayer detail textures are a good solution. Approximately one texel of the highest resolution texture should be mapped onto one screen pixel.

Use Anisotropic Filtering

Blurring is no longer state of the art. If hardware supports it, anisotropic texture filtering can increase quality in some cases. Without either, the picture is smooth or flickers. The difference between anisotropic and trilinear filtering is amazing.

Split Up Rendering into Independent Passes

The more complex the rendering model gets, the more important a clear structure of the engine will get. Two elements determine the color of the object: material and light. The product of both is the visible color. In the simplest version, this is premodulated in a single texture:

$$Color = \left(\sum_i \alpha_i(\vec{r}) \cdot Material_i(\vec{r}) \right) \left(\sum_j Light_j(\vec{r}) \right) \left(1.0 - Fog \text{ intensity}(\vec{r}, \vec{r}_{Camera}) \right) +$$

$$Fog \text{ intensity}(\vec{r}, \vec{r}_{Camera}) \cdot Fogcolor\vec{r} - Worldposition$$

If you use a different algorithm to render material and light, then there are many combinations.

To reduce the count of vertex and pixel shaders, it makes sense to split the rendering into independent passes. The speed increase by using two textures instead of one is noticeable. More than two textures per pass amount is not so noticeable and is not compatible with older hardware. Thus, it is not necessary if the feature does not request it. A separation of the material, light, and fog part allows the combination of every material shader with any light shader.

A compact shader is, of course, the better solution if there is only one material map and one or no lightmap, but these are a limited number of cases.

Two solutions are possible. First, the material color is accumulated in the frame buffer and the result is blended with the light calculated by the following pass, or the light is rendered and modulated by material. The best solution depends on your specification. The component that is rendered second must fit into one pass.

Use _x2

Most rendering values are only in a range between zero and one. This means the light factor is limited and the product of a color multiply is darker than the original values. To get a brighter picture, the result of light and material blending should be scaled by a factor of 2. This is processed by using the pixel shader _x2 modifier in the single pass solution. If the blending is done in the frame buffer, SourceBlendingFactor is set to DestColor and DestBlendingFactor is set to SourceColor to realize the doubled modulation.

Visualization with the Krass Game Engine

Ingo Frick

Introduction

The objective of this article is to present selected visualization techniques that have been applied in a successful game engine. The structure of these techniques is demonstrated and motivated by their developmental history, the further requirements in the foreseeable future, and the main design goal of the entire engine.

Apart from the theoretical discussion, the practical suitability will also be demonstrated, as all techniques were used without modification in *AquaNox™*, the recently published game from Massive Development GmbH in Germany.

We will present techniques which offer a good balance between the current state of technology, practical usability, and the application in a real game engine. All the techniques are part of the krass™ engine, a European game engine that powers some high-end 3D games. It is important to see the historical development of this engine, as it didn't take place in an ivory tower with the only focus on technical details. Instead, it originated in the context of gaming and was first used about six years ago in a game called *Archimedean Dynasty*. Because of its origins, its software patterns are mainly designed to solve the problems that arise during the creation of computer games.

General Structure of the Krass Engine

To explain the location of the rendering systems within the main structure, we will begin with a short description of the engine's architecture. The entire system offers an extensive functionality covering the areas of visualization, networking, simulation, collision, mathematics, physics, and more. The top structure consists of three separated layers. The topmost layer, the so-called *application layer*, holds the game-specific code. It is intended to exchange this layer while moving to another project. The second layer, the *component layer*, aggregates functionality, which had been identified as reusable units and can be shared between different games; for instance, here you find systems like particle systems, collision systems, animation systems, and more. The third and lowest layer is the *system layer*. It offers basic system functionality like I/O, timing, rendering, etc.

Developmental History of the Rendering Component

The rendering component is implemented in the system and component layers. The basic functionalities, like textures, vertex buffers, frame buffers, and depth buffers, are located in the system layer. More specific effects, like "render object with fogmap, static- and dynamic lightmap," are located in the component layer. The best way to understand the structural architecture is to follow its historical development.

Regarding the development of visualization techniques over the past five years, the development of specialized hardware was the biggest change. This specialization led to higher graphics quality and an unloading of the main CPU. This shift made a lot of reorganization necessary. Some of them negatively affected the software design and the downstream production processes. In earlier (software-driven) rendering systems, it was usually easier to design the algorithms and data structures regarding flexibility and controllability. Accessing data structures like triangles, vertices, and materials using the consistent and powerful programming language of the main CPU (C++, Assembler) often led to data structures that were more object oriented than process oriented. Beyond this, the overall production efficiency was very high. This meant that the evolution of specialized hardware had to pass through many steps to regain these initial advantages.

Considered a simple model, the generation of a picture with the rendering approach requires at least the following data structures:

- Vertex
- Triangle (constructed from vertices)
- Triangle's pixel (fragment, generated from color(s), texture(s), etc.)
- Frame's pixel (composed of triangle pixel and frame pixel)

The enumeration above is not complete, but it should be sufficient for the following thoughts. In the following table, you will find a brief overview of the chronological shift of these data structures from software to specialized hardware. The data structures that came along with each shift are labeled with a "D" and the respective processes are labeled with "AP." "SW-" means software and "HW-" means hardware.

Table 1

Period	Vertex	Triangle	Trianglepixel	Framepixel
0 Software-Rendering	D: SW-Vertex (arbitrary layout) P: SW-Processing (programmable)	D: SW-Triangle (arbitrary layout) P: SW-Processing (programmable)	D: SW-Texture (arbitrary layout) P: SW-Processing (programmable)	D: HW-FrameBuffer (selection) P: SW-BlendingMode (programmable)

Period	Vertex	Triangle	Trianglepixel	Framepixel
1 "Glide"	D: SW-Vertex (predefined) P: SW-Processing (programmable)	unchanged	D: HW-Texture (selection) P: HW-RenderState (selection)	D: HW-FrameBuffer (selection) P: HW-BlendingMode (selection)
2 Hardware (T/T&L)	D: HW-VertexBuffer (selection / (FVF)) P: HW-Processing (selection (T/T&L))	D: HW-IndexBuffer (selection) P: HW-Processing (selection)	unchanged	unchanged
3 Vertex Shader	D: HW-VertexStream (selection) P: HW-VertexShader (programmable)	unchanged	unchanged	unchanged
4 Pixel Shader	unchanged	unchanged	D: HW-Texture+Data (selection) P: HW-PixelShader (programmable)	unchanged
5 Pixel Shader++	unchanged	unchanged	D: HW-Texture+Data (arbitrary layout) P: HW-PixelShader (programmable)	D: HW-FrameBuffer (arbitrary layout) P: HW-PixelShader (programmable)

Comparing period 0 (pure software rendering) with period 5 (maximum hardware support) shows a nearly equivalent flexibility for the individual organization and interpretation of the data structures and processes. This closes the evolution circle mentioned above.

Previous Drawbacks of Hardware Development

The main objective of visualization in computer games is the creation of individual effects. They are the unique selling points over the competitors and show a definite influence on the success of a product. Restrictions caused by the current hardware technology normally result in a drastic reduction of the possible amount of individual effects. This consequence could clearly be noticed right after the introduction of graphics hardware with T&L capabilities. Though the game developer could configure the T&L pipeline for the standard cases, every aberrant feature caused serious problems. The "Character Skinning" problem, for instance, is well suited to demonstrate this effect. From today's point of view, the approach to solve this problem using the standard path (e.g., transformation matrix palettes) seems curious. The resulting lack of individuality caused all 3D games of this period to look nearly the same.

Current Drawbacks

With the return of flexibility (e.g., vertex and pixel shaders), this problem can be avoided. The variety of visual effects is again determined by the imagination of the developer instead of the hardware capabilities. Instead, now you have to face another problem, which unfortunately gets overlooked many times. The programming of individual vertex and pixel shader effects only leads to a local flexibility (assembly-syntax, unrestricted data layout). In a larger context, you catch a global inflexibility, as we went back to the development of "effects." Effects very often tend to interact with each other, which makes it difficult to recombine simple effects to more complex ones. Take a simple vertex shader implementing some effects like skinning and mapping texture coordinates and try to combine it with a second vertex shader doing the illumination. This usually very common and basic combination becomes difficult.

Consequently, you have to implement the skinning shader for each number of possible light sources. This example seems to be more of a technical shortcoming of the current hardware technology, but it demonstrates the general problem.

Ordering Effects in the *Krass Engine*

Modeling the rendering process through an accumulation of a sufficient amount of "effects" seems to be a reasonable method. It disengages the rendering techniques from using parameterized standard methods and enters the terrain of individually designed rendering effects. These thoughts also stood at the beginning of the current *krass* revision. The next question is how to define and associate the effects to the overall structure.

Considering commercial and traditional rendering systems for the non-real-time range of use (3DSMax, Maya), you will usually not find effects in terms of our definition. In fact, these applications use standard rendering methods on a per material basis and combine these with a multipass approach to emulate "quasi-effects." Apart from that, some effect-oriented concepts have been realized, such as the shading concept of the RenderMan systems. Here as well, the visualization is done by the individual programming of a pixel effect (→material) rather than by the combination of generic texture parameter sets.

In our case (real time, hardware accelerated), it makes no sense to take something like a material as the only criterion of organization. In most of the cases, we don't have a material in the common sense (e.g., terrain rendering) or the effect is determined more by a geometric characteristic (e.g., plankton, skinning, morphing).

In our latest game, *AquaNox*, it turned out to be very useful to order the effects directly by the different game entities. Each effect is created by some subeffects combined in a very special way to ensure flexibility and recombination. The effects themselves are labeled as *render pipeline* (RP) because they can be interpreted as a specialized encapsulation of the global render pipeline for a single effect.

The following table contains a short description of some render pipelines together with a qualitative description of the effect and the related main elements:

Table 2

Render Pipeline	Elements of Effect
Building RP for all fixed objects like buildings	■ Caustic texture (animated) ■ Light texture (prelighted) ■ Dynamic lighting ■ Detail texture ■ Diffuse texture ■ Fog texture

Render Pipeline	Elements of Effect
Terrain RP for generating the terrain visualization from given level-of-detail (LOD) geometry	▓ Caustic texture (animated) ▓ Light texture (prelighted) ▓ Dynamic lighting ▓ Detail texture ▓ One to six material textures ▓ One material selection texture ▓ Fog texture
Plankton RP for translation, rotation, wrapping, and visualization of individual particles	▓ Diffuse texture ▓ Fog texture ▓ Translation with vertex shader ▓ Rotation with vertex shader ▓ Wrapping in view space with vertex shader

At that point, it is appropriate to return to the above-mentioned problem of recombining effects with one another (light source difficulty). To solve this problem in an elegant way, we only have to unify the advantages of both approaches (recombination through multipass rendering and individual effect programming for each pass). Reconsidering the Aquanox render pipelines reveals an interesting strategy. Instead of combining the individual render passes in one "inflexible" vertex and/or pixel shader, it makes sense to assign the individual passes to larger function blocks.

We identified the following blocks:

▓ Illumination (lightmap, caustic map, vertex-/pixel light, bump map)
▓ Material (diffuse map, detail map)
▓ Global effects (fog map, environment map)

That settles the matter for the larger group of effects. Creating the three function blocks — illumination, material, and global effects — seems to be a sensitive concept, which has been demonstrated in the krass engine and *AquaNox* for the first time. (In the following, this approach will be abbreviated as IMG = Illumination, Material, Global Effects). This reorganization gives you the opportunity to implement each individual pass with the highest flexibility and also to recombine these blocks with each other. In this context, it makes sense to reintroduce the multipass concept. So far, this concept has mainly been used as an emergency solution in the case of an insufficient number of texture stages.

If you assume that the frame buffer stores arbitrary values instead of traditional pixels, you can interpret the IMG technique as calling subroutines for specialized tasks (illumination, material generation, global effects). If it was possible to call (non-trivial) subroutines within the vertex and pixel shaders, the multipass IMG system could easily be collapsed to a single pass concept.

Application of the IMG Concept for Terrain Rendering

The proposed function block organization particularly makes sense, as the first block (illumination) can be constructed from independent individual passes. This block finally results in the summation of all lights. As shadow is the absence of light, even shadow passes fall within this block. In the *AquaNox* terrain system, the summation of all lights originates in the following sources:

1. **Illumination Stage (I)**
   - Light texture (prelighted)
   - Caustic texture (animated)
   - Dynamic lights (rendertarget)

The next stage (material) is composed of a predefined number of materials. Each material is assembled from a material texture, a fine detail texture, and a coarser color texture.

2. **Material Stage (M)**
   - Material texture (sand)
   - Color texture (color)
   - Detail texture (sand crystals)

The last stage (global) handles the fog which is realized by using a procedurally generated and dynamically mapped fog texture.

3. **Global Stage (G)**
   - Fog texture (procedural, volumetric fog)

Figure 1 shows an overview of the entire process. The three frames show the clearly separated IMG stages. The interconnections between the different stages are indicated by the arrows. The combining operations are displayed as well.

We can now go into detail regarding the global stage. *AquaNox* here uses a volumetric fog system which allows us to define multiple planes of constant height with real fog density. Interestingly enough, this feature is not only a visual effect but also offers a gameplay-relevant element (e.g., hiding). We do not generate the fog itself with the graphics hardware in the standard manner (vertex and pixel fog), but instead we use the vertex shader to map a real-time generated texture onto the geometry (in view space). This method doesn't show the annoying artifacts that normally accompany the use of standard fog in combination with transparent textures. It also avoids the appearance of the popping effects that always happen when vertex-related calculations are carried out on the basis of a real-time LOD geometry system. The 3D texture is generated in a preprocessing step. The generator solves the equation of light transport for a predefined parameter range through a numerical integration. The integrated values for fog density (α) and fog color (r,g,b) are stored in the 3D texture array. The texture mapping itself corresponds more to a parameterized solution lookup of the equation of light transport.

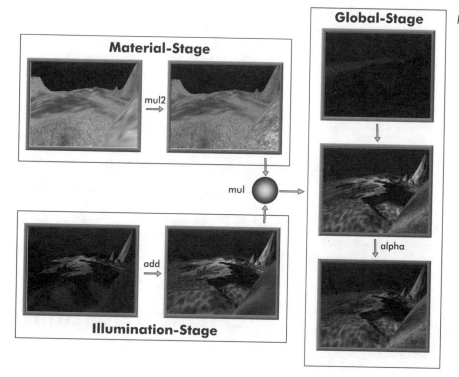

Figure 1

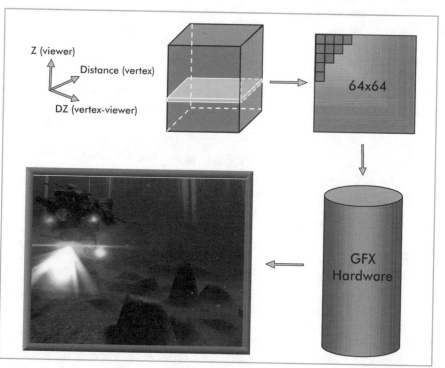

Figure 2

Unfortunately, the major part of the customers' presently installed hardwarebase does not support hardware-accelerated volume textures. To meet this challenge, we had to think of a small work-around: We put the texture data set into the CPU main memory and extract one fog texture slice for each rendered frame. This slice is uploaded to the hardware and used as a standard 2D texture. The restrictive condition for this method is to find one fixed texture coordinate for the entire frame which could be achieved by a well-defined texture parameterization. In the model we use here, the fog parameters are determined by the following values:

- Height of the observer (origin of camera in world space)
- Height difference between vertex and observer
- Distance between camera and vertex (linear norm is sufficient)

Together with the information about the maximum distance (far plane) and the maximum height and depth of the covered game world, it becomes possible to map the three values to the 3D texture coordinates (u,v,w). Because the height of the observer remains constant for the entire frame, this parameter is used as the fixed coordinate (w). The texture slice (u,v) is extracted from the 3D data array exactly at this coordinate (linear interpolation). Figure 2 demonstrates this process:

Particle Rendering to Exemplify a Specialized Effect Shader

Beside the shaders operating according to the introduced stage concept, we have developed other shaders for *AquaNox*, which show the character of an effect shader. As an example for these shaders, we will now take a look at the so-called particle shader: Its render pipeline allows you to translate, rotate, wrap, and display a dense field of individual polygons in the near range of the observer. At first glance, this sounds similar to the hardware-accelerated point-primitive. The point-primitive had been invented to render huge amounts of quads with an identical texture map. Up to now, they still show some serious shortcomings which challenge their use; for example, they are restricted in their maximum size, and they cannot be rotated. These problems have been solved with the particle shader. We also additionally satisfied the following requirements:

- Minimum vertex and pixel demand for individual particle
- Translation of individual particle with graphics hardware
- Rotation of individual particle with graphics hardware
- 3D position wrapping with graphics hardware ("classic star scroller")

In order to minimize the area (pixel demand) and the number of vertices (vertex demand) of an individual particle, we build up each particle from a single triangle. This avoids a second triangle setup for the graphics hardware, and the amount of rasterized pixels is reduced (depends on particle shape on texture). The vertex shader also has to process only three vertices per particle instead of four. This is important because the vertex shader turned out to be the bottleneck ("complex" vertex program).

The individual translation and rotation could be achieved by a sophisticated vertex stream data layout. In contrast to the standard data, each vertex holds not only the position of the triangle's center, but also its relative position with regard to this center. The individual rotation is controlled by a rotational velocity of this relative position around the center. The wrapping functionality has been realized with the help of the expp vertex shader instruction. For this purpose, we first carried out the translation in a unit particle cube (0 to 1) and later eliminated the integer part of the position with the instruction mentioned above. In the sequencing step, the unit cube particle position is transformed into world space coordinate system and the rotated relative vertex position is added. The correct location (origin, dimension) of the unit cube in the world space (required to create the cubeworld transformation) is illustrated in Figure 3.

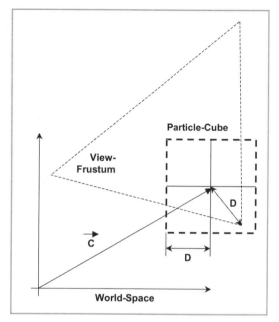

Figure 3

The center of the cube (C) is determined by adding the camera position to the viewing direction vector which is normalized to a half cube edge length in world space (D). The entire vertex shader process is demonstrated in Figure 4.

Operation	Space
Translation ($P_{ABS} + V_{ABS} * t$)	Unit Space
Wrapping (fmodf(P,1.0f))	Unit Space
Transform (U→W→V)	View Space
Attenuation ($\sim$D)	View Space
Rotate ($P_{ABS} + V\alpha * t * P_{REL}$)	View Space
Transform (V→C)	Clip Space

Figure 4

Summary

In this article, we presented selected visualization techniques that we have actually used in a shipped game engine. The structure of these techniques is demonstrated by their developmental history. We showed that the techniques passed the real-world game test successfully with *AquaNox*. The mixture of procedural and classic texture generation (fog), as well as the procedural geometry handling (particle), proved to be adequate procedures. Introducing the IMG concept offers an interesting alternative to reduce the huge amount of shader permutations (>100) that game developers need for their games.

Concluding Remarks and Outlook

The techniques presented here only demonstrate the current state of development. Regarding the foreseeable developments in hardware evolution, you can deduce tendencies which will become important in the near future:

- The pixel shader will advance to be the most important instrument for rendering effects.
- The complexity of vertex and pixel shader language will increase and new instructions will be added (jumps, subroutine calls).
- The size of programs, as well as the related data, will increase.
- The hardware internal data formats will develop to a complete 32-bit floating-point representation.
- The classic pixel will only be used for input/output purposes.

Eventually, if you compare the graphics hardware processors (GPU) with the normal main processors (CPU), the differences will appear rather small. Just like the main processors, the graphics processors will need continually increasing assembly programs. This development will finally force people to introduce a higher level programming language. Perhaps one of the already existing higher level languages can be used, which might also be the one you used to write the "rest" of the application.

So we're back to square one. The only difference lies within ourselves: We have gained a much more comprehensive rendering knowledge, and we can look forward to the next hardware evolution in the realm of the remaining global rendering techniques, such as raytracing or radiosity.

Designing a Vertex Shader-Driven 3D Engine for the Quake III Format

Bart Sekura

Some time ago, I developed a Quake III Arena level viewer for the purpose of trying out various algorithms and techniques using an industry standard engine format and an abundance of tools and shading techniques. When DirectX 8.0 came out, I immediately decided to port my viewer to this API and in particular, take advantage of new programmable pipelines available for developers. The result was a Quake III Arena level viewer, which runs various effects, described in a shader script as a vertex program and thus on vertex shader capable cards in hardware. In this article, I will present the vertex program translation process, which I think is also very useful outside of the Quake level viewer context, as it introduces some nice tricks and effects that can be implemented in vertex programs. The reader can find the Quake III Arena viewer and its full source code on the companion CD. Please consult the viewer documentation included on the CD for instructions on how to run and compile it.

I have chosen this particular platform to demonstrate how vertex programs can be used to implement real game engine algorithms, in addition to great looking effects and demos. Rather than showing this or that particular trick, my goal is to provide the reader with the display of applicability which, for the current vertex shader capable hardware, provides easier coding path and visible performance benefits compared to CPU-based implementation of the same effects.

Quake III Arena Shaders

Quake III Arena allows level designers to create shader scripts for a specific brush/surface during mapping process. This shader is then used by the renderer to draw the faces associated with it. The shader in Quake III Arena is a text script that describes how the surface should be rendered and is preprocessed by the game engine upon startup. In general, the shader scripts can be complex and can contain information not relevant for the rendering process (such as hints or commands for the level editor). A description of the full capabilities of the shader system is beyond the scope of this article. Useful documentation is provided by the game developer, id software, and is included on the companion CD with this book.

463

Basically, at the beginning of the shader script, general parameters are provided, such as culling or geometry deformation functions. Consecutive layers are then specified, where each layer is usually a texture, along with its blending function and various parameters, such as:

- Texture coordinates function (e.g., deformation function or a specific type of coordinate generation, such as environment mapping)
- Diffuse color and alpha source — vertex, periodic function, fixed
- Depth and alpha test parameters

We will focus on some of the most common shader effects that can be easily translated to vertex programs. First, the description of the shader setup in the viewer is presented to give the reader an idea of how things are organized. Next, we will follow the translation process and look at some specific shader effects as they are translated into vertex programs. Finally, we will put it all together and see the whole rendering process.

To minimize confusion, I will refer to Quake III Arena shader scripts as "Quake III shaders" and DirectX 8.1 vertex shaders as simply "vertex shaders."

Vertex Program Setup in the Viewer

Quake III Arena stores the game data in a package file, which is basically a zipped archive containing all art content as well as Quake III shaders. The collection of shader scripts resides in the scripts subdirectory inside the package and each of the text files usually contains many Quake III shaders.

When the viewer initializes, it scans the package file for any Quake III shader scripts and parses them into the internal format, represented as C++ classes, which contain shader parameters and a collection of passes, each with specific material properties. Below is a C++ representation of Quake III shaders (reformatted for clarity):

```
struct shader_t
{
    // shader pass definition
    struct pass_t
    {
        pass_t() : flags(0), map_ref(0), vsh_ref(0), tcgen(0) {}

        int flags;          // misc flags
        std::string map;    // texture name applied for this pass
        int map_ref;        // internal renderer reference to texture
        int vsh_ref;        // internal vertex shader reference

        int blend_src;      // blend operation (source)
        int blend_dst;      // blend operation (destination)
        int alpha_func;     // alpha test function
        int alpha_ref;      // alpha test reference value
        int depth_func;     // depth test function

        int tcgen;          // texture generation type

        // texture coordinate modification functions
        std::vector<tcmod_t> tcmods;
        // concatenated matrix of texture coordination modifications
        matrix_t tcmod_mat;
```

```
        // color (RGB) generation function
        struct rgbgen_t {
            rgbgen_t() : type(0), color(vec4_t(1,1,1,1)) {}
            int type;
            wave_func_t func;
            vec4_t color;
        }
        rgbgen;

        // animated textures collection
        struct anim_t {
            // helper to determine current texture from the collection
            // based on current time and FPS settings
            int frame(double time) const {
                int i = (int)(time*fps)%maps.size();
                return map_refs[i];
            }

            float fps;              // animation speed
            std::vector<std::string> maps;
// textures collection
            std::vector<int> map_refs;
// renderer refs
        }
        anim;
    };

    // the shader itself
public:
    shader_t() : flags(0), type(0), stride(0) {}

    std::string name;              // name of the shader
    std::vector<pass_t> passes;    // collection of passes
    int stride;                    // stride in vertex stream
    int flags;
    int type;

    int vertex_base;
    int vertex_count;

    // vertex deformation function
    struct deform_t {
        float div;
        wave_func_t func;
    }
    deform;

    // parsing function - translates text script representation
    // into this class internal representation suitable for
    // rendering pipeline
    static void parse(const byte* data,
                      int size,
                      std::vector<shader_t>& shaders);
};
```

This C++ object is created per the Quake III shader and used during the rendering phase. It makes it easy to traverse the shader passes and apply various parameters that directly influence the rendering process. One additional thing that is performed during the setup phase is setting up all the textures used by Quake III shaders (loading them up and uploading to the card) and translating of various passes into corresponding vertex shaders. I will describe the latter process in greater detail now.

Many of the surfaces inside the game level reference Quake III shaders that don't exist in the form of the script. This is just a handy shortcut for default Quake III shaders that use only a base texture and lightmap with no additional rendering passes or special parameters. Whenever the Quake III shader that is referenced from within the level is not found among the parsed scripts, the viewer will create a default Quake III shader with two passes: default texture, looked up by the shader's name, and a lightmap.

To facilitate the setup code as well as provide easier and more optimized code paths for rendering, I divided the shaders into the following categories:

Table 1: Shader categories

Shader Category/Type	Description
SHADER_SIMPLE	This is the default Quake III shader that uses base texture, lightmap texture, and constant diffuse. There is no vertex or texture coordinate deformation, and diffuse color is not coming from vertex stream data. This is by far the majority of shaders, also known as default shaders, automatically created when there is no explicit script code. Primarily, it is used for basic world geometry.
SHADER_DIFFUSE	This category is very similar to the above shader type, the difference being that diffuse color is coming from the vertex stream. It also uses base texture and lightmap. It is used primarily for mesh models embedded in world geometry.
SHADER_CUSTOM	All non-standard shaders fall into this category, which represents arbitrarily complex shaders with one or many passes, various vertex and texture coordinate deformation functions, etc.

The category that the Quake III shader belongs to is stored in a type member variable of shader_t class. The default vertex shaders, SHADER_SIMPLE and SHADER_DIFFUSE, are set up in world_t::upload_default_vertex_shaders() method. These never change and are uploaded when the viewer starts. In addition, I have added one more default vertex shader, which is not a result of Quake III shader script translation process but is set up to facilitate all screen space rendering operations (heads-up display, 2D window interface, etc.) and is represented as SHADER_FONT type. This shader uses one texture and expects the coordinates in normalized device range (–1.0 to +1.0). The primary use of this shader can be found in font_t class.

The Quake III shaders that fall into the SHADER_SIMPLE, SHADER_DIFFUSE, and SHADER_FONT categories are hard-coded, since they never change. All SHADER_CUSTOM shaders are dynamically constructed depending on the number of passes, their parameters, etc. This process is constructed from consecutive steps that result in final vertex shader source code, which is then compiled by DirectX runtime and uploaded to the card. The basic steps are as follows:

Table 2: Constructing custom shaders

Step	Description
Vertex coordinates	These are either set up as coming unchanged from the vertex stream or as a result of a deformation function. In the second case, the vertex deformation function, sinus, is evaluated using a Taylor series.
Vertex diffuse color	The vertex color can be constant, come from the vertex stream, or be evaluated as a result of a periodic function. In any case, the actual evaluation happens in CPU, and the vertex program code merely loads the appropriate value from constant memory or vertex stream data.
Texture coordinates	Texture coordinates either come unchanged from the vertex stream or are computed using a simplified environment mapping function. The texture unit used depends on whether we're dealing with base texture or lightmap.
Texture coordinates modification	Texture coordinates computed in the previous step can be optionally changed, depending on shader pass parameters. If that is the case, they are multiplied by a concatenated texture coordinate modification matrix in the vertex shader. The matrix is prepared by CPU.

As you can see, various Quake III shader script effects are translated into the corresponding vertex shader source. As it turns out, the final vertex shader code is very often identical for many different Quake III shader scripts, and it would be a waste of resources to upload identical vertex shaders many times. I have employed a simple string comparison mechanism to prevent this. Whenever a vertex shader is generated from the Quake III shader definition, after it is compiled by the DirectX run-time, its source code is put on a map to allow for easy lookup later on. The source code (a string) becomes a key for the collection and the value is the ID of the already compiled vertex shader, as it was returned by the DirectX run-time after successful compilation. Then, whenever the vertex shader source is generated and it is time to compile it, first the map is consulted to see whether there was previously an identical vertex shader already compiled. If there were, the same ID is used; otherwise, it is compiled and put on the source code map.

Vertex Shader Effects

We will now look in more detail at some of the effects that can be created.

Deformable Geometry

One of the simple things that you can do in Quake III shader is deformable geometry. Basically, you can specify a periodic function such as sin() and provide the parameters, and the geometry is then deformed during the rendering process and parameterized by time. This is, for example, how all those waving banners are done in Quake levels. It would be great to do that in a vertex shader, especially since it involves recomputing the vertex position, something we'd rather avoid. So we need to evaluate the sin function from within vertex shader.

There is no direct way to do this; that is, there is no sin instruction similar to the C library function that is available from within vertex shader. Therefore, we have to simulate one. This becomes possible thanks to Taylor series, which allows us to generate approximate sinus values using available vertex shader instructions.

The theory behind Taylor series is beyond the scope of this article. What is interesting to us is how to generate approximate sinus values using Taylor series. Here are the approximation formulas:

```
sin(x) = x - (x^3)/3! + (x^5)/5! + (x^7)/7! + ...
sin(x) ~= x*(1-(x^2)*(1/3!-(x^2)(1/5!-(x^2)/7!)))
```

To compute sinus from within vertex shader using Tayor series, we need to set up some magic numbers in vertex shader constant memory. These numbers are:

```
1.0 1/3! 1/5! 1/7!
```

Additionally, since Taylor series will only work accurately with the input range of {–PI, PI}, we need to prepare our input variable accordingly. This is done in the following way:

```
// r0.x - x
// r1.y - temp
expp r1.y, r0.x
// r1.y=x-floor(x)
mad  r0.x, r1.y, c[12].y, -c[12].x
// r0.x=x*2PI-PI
```

As you see, we also need to add 2*PI and PI to vertex shader constant memory. During translation of shader scripts into vertex shader, we generate vertex shader code with the following:

```
if(shader.flags&SHF_DEFORM)
{
    // vertex deformation code
    vsh    << "dp3 r1.x, v0, c15.w\n"
           << "add r0.x, r1.x, c14.y\n" // r0.x=off+phase
           << "add r0.x, r0.x, c15.x\n" // r0.x=off+phase+time
           << "mul r0.x, r0.x, c14.w\n" // r0.x=(off+phase+time)*freq
           << "expp r1.y, r0.x\n"       // r1.y=x-floor(x)
           //r0.x=x*TWO_PI-PI
           << "mad  r0.x, r1.y, c12.y, -c12.x\n"
           // fast sin
           // r0.x=sin(r0.x)
           << "dst   r2.xy, r0.x, r0.x\n"
           << "mul   r2.z,  r2.y, r2.y\n"
           << "mul   r2.w,  r2.y, r2.z\n"
           << "mul   r0,    r2,   r0.x\n"
           << "dp4   r0.x,  r0,   c13\n"
           // r1=y*amp+base
           << "mad r1.xyz, r0.xxx, c14.zzz, c14.xxx\n"
           << "mov r0,v0\n"
           << "mad r0.xyz, v1.xyz, r1.xyz, r0.xyz\n"
           << "mov r0.w, c10.x\n"  // w=1.0f
           // transform to clip space
           << "dp4 oPos.x,r0,c0\n"
           << "dp4 oPos.y,r0,c1\n"
           << "dp4 oPos.z,r0,c2\n"
           << "dp4 oPos.w,r0,c3\n";
}
```

This vertex shader section takes vertex position in world space and deforms in time using the sinus function. All parameters (particularly current time) are passed in using vertex shader constant memory. The shader computes a new vertex world position and then transforms it to clip space.

Texture Coordinate Generation

One particular effect that is often used is environment mapping. The exact way this is done in the Quake III Arena engine is, of course, not public knowledge, so the effect we will show here is an approximation. It has to be noted that even the Q3A engine does not implement real environment mapping (e.g., using cubemaps), but rather a crude approximation that uses skillfully prepared texture and generats texture coordinates based on the viewing angle. This simple effect is pretty nice and especially useful for implementing all kinds of chrome effects.

Our approximation works like this: Based on the viewing position, referred to as "eye," and the vertex position in world space, we compute the reflection vector; based on the result, we generate texture coordinates dynamically. This gives the effect of shiny or chrome-like surfaces, which change along with the position of the player and the viewing angle.

The C++ code to compute the texture coordinates for our "fake" environment mapping is something like this:

```
vec3_t dir = cam->eye-vec3_t(vertex_pos);
dir.normalize();
st[0]=dir[0]+normal[0];
st[1]=dir[1]+normal[1];
```

We basically take the direction vector from the vertex to the eye (camera position) in world space, normalize it, and generate the texture coordinates by adding the normal of the surface to the direction vector.

In the vertex shader setup phase, we process the custom shader definition and attempt to generate the corresponding fragment of vertex shader code. In case of the environment mapping texture coordinate generation, we construct the code in the following way:

```
if((pass.flags & SPF_TCGEN) && pass.tcgen == SP_TCGEN_ENVIRONMENT)
{
    vsh      << "add r0, r0, -c11\n"    // r0=vertex-eye
             << "dp3 r0.w,r0,r0\n"      // normalize(r0)
             << "rsq r0.w,r0.w\n"
             << "mul r0,r0,r0.w\n"      // r0=normalize(vertex-eye)
             << "add r1.x,r0.x,v1.x\n"
             << "add r1.y,r0.y,v1.y\n"
             << "mov r1.zw, c10.zw\n";
}
```

Note that this can be easily extended to support full environment mapping using cubemaps on hardware that supports it. We would need to compute the reflection vector from within the vertex shader and use it to generate the texture coordinates for the cubemap.

Texture Matrix Manipulation

The texture coordinates can be deformed to produce nice-looking effects. With the Quake shader script, one can specify multiple texture coordinate modification steps, each applied on top of another. These modification functions are usually time-based periodic functions with various parameters controlling amplitude, frequency, etc. In our viewer, during the rendering phase, we evaluate all these functions based on the current time value, producing a single matrix per step. So if, for example, we had two modification steps specified in a shader script, one that does the scaling and another that rotates the texture, we would end up with two matrices for each step: a scaling matrix and a rotation matrix. These matrices are then concatenated to produce one texture coordinates deformation matrix, which is then loaded to the vertex shader. The actual modification of texture coordinates takes place inside the vertex program, when we simply multiply original texture coordinates by the tcmod matrix, thus producing the final effect.

Let's look at this in more detail. The following function is called once per frame per shader pass, which involves texture coordinate modification:

```
static void
eval_tcmod(shader_t::pass_t& pass, const float time)
{
    matrix_t t;
    t.translate(+0.5f,+0.5f,0);
    for(int i = pass.tcmods.size()-1; i >= 0; --i)
    {
        pass.tcmods[i].eval(time);
        t*=pass.tcmods[i].mat;
    }
    t.translate(-0.5f,-0.5f,0);
    matrix_t::transpose(t,pass.tcmod_mat);
}
```

This function moves through all the texture modification steps for a particular shader pass and produces a single concatenated matrix. The matrix is transposed in order to be used from within the vertex shader. Later in the rendering process, when it comes to the actual drawing of batched geometry data that uses this particular shader, the following piece of code updates the constant memory of the vertex shader with the final texture modification matrix produced above, prior to the actual DrawIndexedPrimitive() call:

```
const int pass_count=s.passes.size();
for(int i=0; i<pass_count; ++i)
{
    const shader_t::pass_t& pass = s.passes[i];

    [ omitted for clarity ]

    // set vertex shader for this pass
    d3dev->SetVertexShader(pass.vsh_ref);

    // set tcmod matrix if needed
    if(pass.flags&SPF_TCMOD)
    {
        d3dev->SetVertexShaderConstant(4,pass.tcmod_mat,4);
    }

    [ omitted for clarity ]
}
```

To put it all together, let's step back to the setup code, which creates a vertex shader for each shader script. During the translation process, whenever we encounter the pass that involves texture coordinate modification, we add the following piece of vertex shader code:

```
if(pass.flags&SPF_TCMOD)
{
    vsh     << "dp4 " << unit << ".x,r1,c4\n"
            << "dp4 " << unit << ".y,r1,c5\n";
}
```

This generates the code to transform the texture coordinates of the vertex by our matrix (actually, the first two vectors from it), which had been set up at constant memory locations 4 through 8. So the final vertex shader code looks like this, assuming we're dealing with the first texture unit:

```
dp4 oT0.x, r1, c4
dp4 oT0.y, r1, c5
```

This results in transforming the texture coordinates by our concatenated texture modification matrix. This is similar to setting the texture matrix when using a fixed programmable pipeline and letting DirectX 8.0 handle the transformation.

Rendering Process

We will now describe the rendering pipeline of our level viewer, which is greatly simplified thanks to vertex shaders. Normally, all kinds of effects require the CPU to touch each vertex and modify the stream accordingly, which makes the code path rather complicated. Since we are using vertex shaders to do that on GPU instead of CPU, our lower level pipeline boils down to preparing the vertex stream, managing the rotating dynamic index buffer, and setting up vertex constant memory.

The rendering process is divided roughly into higher and lower level pipeline code. Table 3 shows a summary of which tasks and functions belong to higher and lower level rendering code:

Table 3: Rendering code levels

Level	Main Functions
Higher level rendering pipeline code Implementation in: world.cpp	▪ Traverses BSP tree ▪ Culls BSP nodes and leaves to view frustrum ▪ Culls faces to view frustrum ▪ Culls faces according to PVS tables ▪ Sorts faces by shader and lightmap ▪ Arranges faces by solid and translucent ▪ Walks sorted, batched shader faces list and prepares vertex constant memory data
Lower level rendering pipeline code DirectX 8.0 specific driver Implementation in: d3dev.cpp	▪ Device initialization/shutdown ▪ Texture upload management ▪ Static/dynamic vertex and index buffer management ▪ Batch rendering and device state setup according to shader pass parameters

The higher level rendering pipeline code is traversing the BSP tree and performing some gross culling using the view frustrum and bounding boxes for the BSP nodes. At a finer level, each face is tested using PVS data when it is considered a candidate for drawing. The result of the higher level rendering pipeline code is a sorted list of faces, batched by shader and lightmap, and the shader hash map is sorted by shader solidity and translucency. This is performed in world_t::process_faces() function. The higher level rendering begins in world_t::render_faces()

function, where the sorted shader batches are visited and vertex constant memory data is prepared, if needed. This includes texture coordinate modification matrix, RGB generation functions, etc. When the current batch is ready to be rendered, the control is passed to the lower level rendering code.

The lower level code is a DirectX 8.0 driver that does the actual rendering of the triangles. Its main rendering loop consists of managing vertex and index buffers and making low-level calls for drawing primitives. A single dynamic index buffer is used to prepare batched up vertices for drawing, according to the list passed in from the higher level rendering code. For hardware vertex processing, all level geometry is uploaded into one static vertex buffer. This gives significant performance benefits, since the data is effectively cached on GPU and does not need to travel across the bus. For software vertex processing, this is not possible due to performance reasons, so I have provided a fallback mechanism, where a fixed-size dynamic vertex buffer is managed and vertex stream data is uploaded dynamically prior to rendering calls. The reason behind this stems from the fact that when calling the DrawIndexedPrimitive() API of DirectX, the range of vertices that needs to be processed is interpreted differently depending on whether we're using hardware or software vertex processing. In hardware mode, vertices are transformed and lit according to the indices passed to the call, so the range of vertices specified does not influence the process. We can therefore use a single static vertex buffer that is spatially addressed by indices from our dynamic index buffer. In software mode, however, the optimized processor-specific pipeline transforms exactly the range of vertices that were specified during the call. Thus, it is significantly more beneficial for software vertex processing pipeline to batch vertices for drawing using a single dynamic vertex buffer so that the range of vertices is continuous and always corresponds exactly to the number of vertices actually being drawn.

Assuming hardware vertex processing and a single static vertex buffer with level geometry uploaded, the actual rendering loop is extremely simple. All the low-level driver does is manage the index buffer by filling it up with the current batch triangle indices, set up device state according to shader pass parameters (culling, blending, z-buffering writes), set up vertex program constant memory, initialize texture units with textures, set up current vertex shader, and make actual calls to DrawIndexedPrimitive. All this is performed in the d3dev_t::render_faces() function.

Summary

It should be noted that the vertex shaders that result from the translation process do not provide the full implementation of the Quake III shader scripts in a way that no CPU work is required for their implementation during rendering process. Because of the great amount of combinations of vertex shaders that are possible as a result of a single Quake III shader script, as well as size limitations imposed on the current vertex shader implementation, the ideal situation of having vertex shaders that implement the Quake III shader script in its entirety (sometimes involving evaluation of a couple of sin functions) is extremely hard to achieve, if not impossible. For performance reasons, the intention was to eliminate the need for CPU to touch every vertex in order to perform given shader script functions, such as texture coordinate modification or vertex deformation. This was required in the traditional model, before vertex shaders were available. The fixed rendering pipeline of DirectX does not allow developers to customize vertex processing according to their needs. Thanks to programmable pipeline and vertex shaders resulting from translation process, geometry data once uploaded to the card never needs to be touched by the CPU again, as the GPU makes all the changes to it. The geometry can therefore be treated as "static," even though we are doing changes to individual components of the vertex stream. Using vertex shaders implemented in hardware, the stream data does not need to travel across the bus. The balance was achieved in such a way that the CPU performs more complicated tasks, such as evaluation time-based periodic functions, and simply updates the constant memory of the vertex shader in each frame, greatly reducing the complexity of the vertex shader.

Glossary

anisotropic – Exhibiting different properties when measured from different directions. Directional dependence. For instance, anisotropic lighting takes into account direction with respect to the surface of incoming and/or outgoing light when illuminating a surface.

anisotropic filtering – With 2D textures, anisotropic filtering is thought of as a filter along a line across the texture with a width of two and length up to the maximum degree of anisotropy. In three dimensions, this increases to a slab with width two extending in the other two dimensions up to the maximum degree of anisotropy. 3D anisotropy is not supported by current accelerators.

anisotropic lighting – *See* anisotropic.

basis vectors – A (complete) set of line or row vectors for a matrix; these might be the three vectors that represent a rotation matrix.

bilerping/bilinear filtering – An image interpolation technique that is based on the averaging of the four nearest pixels in a digital image. It first computes a texel address, which is usually not an integer address, and then finds the texel whose integer address is closest to the computed address. After that, it computes a weighted average of the texels that are immediately above, below, to the left of, and to the right of the nearest sample point.

binormal – To realize per-pixel lighting, a texture space coordinate system is established at each vertex of a mesh. With the help of this texture space coordinate system, a light vector or any other vector can be transformed into texture space. The axes of the texture space coordinate system are called tangent, binormal, and normal.

BRDF – Bidirectional Reflectance Distribution Functions. The BRDF is a generalization of all shading models, such as Lambert, Blinn, or Phong. A shading model is an analytic approximation of a surface's reflective properties: It describes how incoming light is reflected by a surface. The simplest shading model, Lambert shading, says that a surface reflects incoming light equally in all directions. Phong shading (*see* Phong shading), on the other hand, has an additional additive specular term, which permits a surface to reflect different amounts of light in different directions. Thus, each of these models is a formula which computes, for a given incoming and a given outgoing light direction, the portion of incoming light that gets reflected in the outgoing direction. Such functions are called BRDFs.

bump map – Bump mapping adds surface detail (bumpiness) to objects in 3D scenes without adding more geometry than already exists. It does so by varying the lighting of each pixel according to values in a bump map texture. As each pixel of a triangle is rendered, a lookup is done into a texture depicting the surface relief (aka the bump map). The values in the bump map are then used to perturb the normals for that pixel. The new bumped-and-wiggled normal is then used during the subsequent color calculation, and the end result is a flat surface that looks like it has bumps or depressions in it. Usually a normal map (*see* normal map) contains the already perturbed normals. In this case, an additional bump map is not necessary.

canonical – Very common. With respect to faces, it means a face with very common features.

cartoon shading – The use of any class of rendering approaches that are designed to mimic hand-drawn cartoon artwork. Examples include pen-and-inking, pencil sketch, pastel, etc.

convex hull – The smallest convex region that can enclose a defined group of points.

cube map – Cube mapping has becoming a common environment mapping technique for reflective objects. Typically, a reflection vector is calculated either per-vertex or per-pixel and is then used to index into a cube map that contains a picture of the world surrounding the object being drawn. Cube maps are made up of six square textures of the same size, representing a cube centered at the origin. Each cube face represents a set of directions along each major axis (+X, –X, +Y, –Y, +Z, –Z). Think of a unit cube centered about the origin. Each texel on the cube represents what can be "seen" from the origin in that direction.

The cube map is accessed via vectors expressed as 3D texture coordinates (S, T, R or U, V, W). The greatest magnitude component, S, T, or R, is used to select the cube face. The other two components are used to select a texel from that face.

Cube mapping is also used for vector normalization with the light vector placed in the texture coordinates.

dependent read – A read from a texture map using a texture coordinate that was calculated earlier in the pixel shader, often by looking up the coordinate in another texture. This concept is fundamental to many of the advanced effects that use textures as transfer functions or complex functions like power functions.

diffuse lighting – Diffuse lighting simulates the emission of an object by a particular light source. Therefore, you are able to see that the light falls onto the surface of an object from a particular direction by using the diffuse lighting model.

It is based on the assumption that light is reflected equally well in all directions, so the appearance of the reflection does not depend on the position of the observer. The intensity of the light reflected in any direction depends only on how much light falls onto the surface.

If the surface of the object is facing the light source, which means it is perpendicular to the direction of the light, the density of the incident light is the highest. If the surface is facing the light source under some angle smaller than 90 degrees, the density is proportionally smaller.

The diffuse reflection model is based on a law of physics called Lambert's Law, which states that for ideally diffuse (totally matte) surfaces, the reflected light is determined by the cosine between the surface normal N and the light vector L.

directional light – A directional light is a light source in an infinite distance. This simulates the long distance the light beams have to travel from the sun. In game programming, these light beams are treated as being parallel.

displacement map – A texture that stores a single value at every texel, representing the distance to move the surface point along the surface normal.

edge detection – A type of filter that has a strong response at edges in the input image and a weak response in areas of the image with little change. This kind of filter is often used as the first step in machine vision tasks which must segment an image to identify its contents.

EMBM – Environment Mapped Bump Mapping. Introduced with DirectX6, this is a specific kind of dependent lookup (*see* dependent read) allowing values of texels in one texture to offset the fetching of texels in another texture, often an environment map. There is spherical, dual paraboloid, and cubic environment mapping.

Fresnel term – Common real time environment mapping reflection techniques reflect the same amount of light on matter depending how the surface is oriented relative to the viewer, much like a mirror or chrome. Many real materials, such as water, skin, plastic, and ceramics, do not behave in this way. Due to their unique physical properties, these materials appear to be much more reflective edge-on than they are when viewed head-on. The change in reflectance as a function of the viewing angle is called the Fresnel effect.

Gram-Schmidt orthonormalization – Given a set of vectors making up a vector space, Gram-Schmidt orthonormalization creates a new set of vectors which span the same vector space, but are unit length and orthogonal to each other.

half vector – The half-way vector H is useful to calculate specular reflections (*see* specular lighting). It was invented by James F. Blinn to prevent the expensive calculation of a reflection vector (mirror of light incidence around the surface normal). The H vector is defined as halfway between L and V. H is therefore:

$$H = (L + V) / 2$$

When H coincides with N, the direction of the reflection coincides with the viewing direction V and a specular highlight is observed. This specular reflection model is called the Blinn-Phong model.

isotropic – Exhibiting the same properties when measured from different directions. Directional independence.

Lambert model – *See* diffuse lighting.

light reflection vector – A vector, usually called R, that describes the direction of the reflection of light.

light vector – A vector that describes the light direction.

LUT – Look-up table. A precomputed array of values used to replace a function evaluation often for the sake of performance. Many pixel shader techniques use 1D and 2D textures as lookup tables to calculate functions that are prohibitive or even impossible to calculate given the limited size and scope of the pixel shader instruction set and size.

mip mapping – Mip maps consist of a series of textures, each containing a progressively lower resolution of an image that represents the texture. Each level in the mip map sequence has a height and a width that is half of the height and width of the previous level. The levels could be either square or rectangular. Using mip maps ensures that textures retain their realism and quality as you move closer or further away.

normal map – A normal map stores vectors that represents the direction in which the normal vector (*see* normal vector) points. A normal map is typically constructed by extracting normal vectors from a height map whose contents represent the height of a flat surface at each pixel.

normal vector – Normals are vectors that define the direction that a face is pointing or the visible side of a face.

orthonormal – Two vectors are considered to be orthonormal if both vectors are unit length and have a dot product of 0 between them.

per-pixel lighting – For example, diffuse (*see* diffuse lighting) or specular (*see* specular lighting) reflection models calculated on a per-pixel level are called per-pixel lighting. Per-pixel lighting gets the per-pixel data usually from a normal map, which stores vectors representing the direction in which the normal vector (*see* normal vector) points. The additional needed light (*see* light vector) and/or half angle vector(s) (*see* half vector) are usually transformed via a texture space coordinates system, that is, build per-vertex into texture space so that the normal vector provided by the normal map and these vectors are in the same space.

per-vertex lighting – Per-vertex lighting means that the actual lighting calculations are done for each vertex of a triangle, as opposed to each pixel that gets rendered (*see* per-pixel lighting). In some cases, per-vertex lighting produces noticeable artifacts. Think of a large triangle with a light source close to the surface. As long as the light is close to one of the vertices of the triangle, you can see the lighting effect on the triangle. When the light moves toward the center of the triangle, then the triangle gradually loses the lighting effect. In the worst case, the light is directly in the middle of the triangle and there is nearly no light visible on the triangle, instead of a triangle with a bright spot in the middle.

That means that a smooth-looking object needs a lot of vertices or in other words, a high level of tessellation; otherwise, the coarseness of the underlying geometry is visible.

Phong shading – Phong shading is done by interpolating the vertex normals across the surface of a polygon or triangle and illuminating the pixel at each point, usually using the phong lighting model. At each pixel, you need to re-normalize the normal vector and also calculate the reflection vector.

point light – A point light source has color and position within a scene but no single direction. All light rays originate from one point and illuminate equally in all directions. The intensity of the rays will remain constant regardless of their distance from the point source, unless a falloff value is explicitly stated. A point light is useful to simulate light bulb.

post-classification (in volume graphics) – The mapping of volume data to RGBA tuples after interpolating, filtering, and/or sampling of the volume data.

power of 2 texture – A texture that has dimensions that fall into the set 1, 2, 4, 8, 16, 32, 64, 128, 256, 512, 1024, 2048, 4096. Some hardware have these limitation, or it may be more efficient for hardware to deal with these dimensions.

pre-classification (in volume graphics) – The mapping of volume data to RGBA tuples before interpolating, filtering, and/or sampling of the volume data.

pre-integrated classification (in volume graphics) – The mapping of (small) line segments of volume data to RGBA tuples with the help of a pre-computed look-up table.

quadrilinear filtering – Adds a linear filter along the fourth dimension of the volumetric mip maps consisting of 3D textures, sampling from 16 different texels.

reflection – The return of light from a surface.

reflection vector – The mirror of a vector around a surface normal. In lighting equations, often substituted by the half-vector (*see* half-vector).

refraction – Refraction is a phenomenon that simulates the bending of light rays through semi-transparent objects. There are several properties defined with refraction, Snell's law, and the critical angle. Snell's law states that for a light ray going from a less dense medium to a higher dense medium, the light ray will bend in one direction, and going from a higher density medium to a lower density medium, it will bend in the other direction. These properties are known as the refraction index, and it is a ratio of the speed of light through one medium divided by the speed of light through the other medium.

render target – The buffer in memory to which a graphics processor writes pixels. A render target may be a displayable surface in memory, like the front or back buffer, or the render target may be a texture.

renderable texture – The render target (*see* render target) is a texture.

scientific data visualization – The branch of computer graphics that is concerned with the (interactive) generation of comprehensible, informative, accurate, and reliable images from scientific or technical data.

shadow volume – The volume of space that forms a shadow for a given object and light. Objects inside this volume of space are in shadow. Rapidly determining whether something is in shadow can be done by using the stencil buffer and a vertex shader.

skinning – A technique for blending several bone matrices at a vertex level to produce a smooth animation.

slab (in volume graphics) – The space between two consecutive slices through volume data. The interior of the slab is considered to be filled with the volume data.

slice (in volume graphics) – A flat subset of volume data, often implemented as a polygon that is textured with a three-dimensional texture.

specular lighting – Compared to the diffuse reflection (*see* diffuse lighting) model, the appearance of the reflection depends on the specular reflection model on the position of the viewer. When the direction of the viewing coincides, or nearly coincides, with the direction of specular reflection, a bright highlight is observed. This simulates the reflection of a light source by a smooth, shiny, and polished surface. To describe reflection from shiny surfaces, an approximation is commonly used, which is called the Phong illumination model (not to be confused with Phong shading), named after its creator Phong Bui Tong. According to this model, a specular highlight is seen when the viewer is close to the direction of reflection. The intensity of light falls off sharply when the viewer moves away from the direction of the specular reflection.

spotlight – A light source in which all light rays illuminate in the shape of a cone. The falloff (the attenuation in the intensity of a light source as the distance increases), spread (the parameter that controls the width of the cone of light produced by the spotlight), and dropoff (the parameter that controls the way the light intensity fades based on its distance from the center of the light cone) of a spotlight are adjustable.

SSE – Streaming SIMD Extensions. A set of registers and instructions in Pentium III and Pentium 4 processors for processing multiple floating-point numbers per instruction.

tangent space – Tangent space is a 3D coordinate system defined for every point on the surface of an object. It can be thought of as a transform from object space into texture space. The x and y axes are tangent to the surface at the point and are equal to the u and v directions of the texture coordinates, respectively. The z-axis is equal to the surface normal. Tangent space is used for a variety of per pixel shaders due to the fact that most bump maps and other types of maps are defined in tangent space. Tangent space is sometimes called the Frenet Frame or a Surface Normal Coordinate Frame.

tap – Each sample that contributes to a filter result.

Taylor series – A Taylor series allows the generation of approximate sinus and cosinus values without being computationally as expensive as the sinus and cosinus functions.

texels – Abbreviation for texture elements, usually meaning 1 RGB or ARGB component of the texture.

texture perturbation – With the ability to perform per-pixel math both before and after texture fetches, a variety of new texture-based effects are possible. Per-pixel texture perturbation effects, effects that use the results of a texture fetch to change the texture coordinates used to fetch another texel (*see* dependent read).

texture space – *See* tangent space.

topology – The arrangement in which the nodes of a 3D object are connected to each other.

transfer function – A function (often one-dimensional) which is used to enhance or segment an input image. Transfer functions are often used in scientific visualization to enhance the understanding of complex datasets. A transfer function might map a scalar, such as heat, pressure, or density, to a color to aid in understanding the phenomenon being drawn. In games, transfer functions can be used on images to stylize them or to simulate effects like night-vision goggles or heat-sensitive displays. In volume graphics, this is the mapping of a number to an RGBA tuple; it is used in volume visualization and volume graphics to assign colors to numeric data.

trilinear filtering – In case of 2D textures, this means that multiple linear filtered mip maps are being blended together. In case of a 3D texture, trilinear filtering performs a linear filtering along all three axes of the texture, sampling colors from eight different texels. The filtering method that is called trilinear filtering in conjunction with 2D textures is called quadrilinear filtering for 3D textures.

trinary operator – Operation that can use three components and do two operations simultaneously.

tweening – A technique for interpolating between two or more key frames to produce a smooth animation.

unit vector – A unit vector is a vector with the length 1. To calculate a unit vector, divide the vector by its magnitude or length. The magnitude of vectors is calculated by using the Pythagorean theorem:
$$x^2 + y^2 + z^2 = m^2$$
The length of the vector is retrieved by:
$$\|A\| = sqrt(x^2 + y^2 + z^2)$$
The magnitude of a vector has a special symbol in mathematics. It is a capital letter designated with two vertical bars: $\|A\|$. So dividing the vector by its magnitude is:
$$UnitVector = Vector / sqrt(x^2 + y^2 + z^2)$$

vector field map – A texture that stores a vector at every texel to move the surface point.

volume data – A data set that is indexed by three coordinates, often implemented as three-dimensional textures (volume textures).

volume graphics – The branch of computer graphics that is concerned with the rendering of volumetric (as opposed to polygonal) primitives.

volume visualization – The branch of scientific data visualization that is concerned with the visualization of volume data.

About the Authors

Philippe Beaudoin (pBeaudoin@digital-fiction.com)

Philippe recently completed a masters thesis in computer graphics at the University of Montreal where he developed algorithms for the spreading and rendering of 3D fire effects. As part of his job as a hardware architect at Matrox Graphics, he studied and developed various vertex and pixel shader technologies. He is currently employed at Digital Fiction where he develops games for various next-generation consoles.

Steffen Bendel (bendel@massive.de)

Steffen started his career as a game programmer in 1996 at a company called BlueByte. After that, he studied physics with a specialty in quantum optics at the university in Rostock. While studying, he worked as a freelancer for Massive Development where he wrote some parts of the 3D engine of the underwater game *AquaNox*.

Chris Brennan (cbrennan@ati.com)

Chris graduated with a BS degree in Computer Science and another BS degree in Electrical Engineering from Worcester Polytechnic Institute in '97 and joined Digital Equipment Corp's Workstation Graphics group doing hardware design and verification. When Digital died, Chris joined ATI as a 3D ASIC designer for the RADEON line of graphics chips and then moved over to the 3D Application Research Group where he tries to get those chips to do things that were not originally thought possible.

Dean Calver (deano@rattie.demon.co.uk)

Games are fun; Dean figured that out at age 2 and has spent the following years working out how to make better games. For the last five years, people have even paid him to do it. Having no real preference for console or PC has meant a mixed career flipping between them for every project. Professionally, he started on a war game, did three years of a racing game, followed by an X-COM style game and arcade classic updates. Currently he's doing a 3D graphic adventure. He still studies various subjects including optics, mathematics, and other geeky things for fun. This preoccupation with learning means that he has been taking exams every year for over half his life. At least he'll be ready to write the first game for a quantum computer.

Drew Card (dcard@ati.com)

Drew is currently a software engineer in the 3D Application Research Group at ATI Research where he is focusing on the application of shader-based rendering techniques. He has worked on SDK applications as well as helped out with the demo engine. Drew is a graduate of the University of South Carolina.

Wolfgang F. Engel (wolfgang.engel@shaderx.com)

Wolfgang is the author of *Beginning Direct3D Game Programming* and a co-author of *OS/2 in Team*, for which he contributed the introductory chapters on OpenGL and DIVE. Wolfgang has written several articles in German journals on game programming and many online tutorials that have been published on www.gamedev.net and his own web site, www.direct3d.net. During his career in the game industry, he built two game development units from scratch with four and five people that published, for example, six online games for the biggest European TV show "Wetten das..?" As a member of the board or as a CEO in different companies, he has been responsible for several game projects.

Ingo Frick (ficke@massive.de)

Ingo is co-founder and technical director of Massive Development GmbH. He has played a leading role in the development of the Krass engine, *Archimedean Dynasty* (*Schleichfahrt*), and *AquaNox*. In the mid-80s he developed several games (C64, Amiga, PC) that were mainly distributed by smaller publishers and magazines. His first successful commercial product was the conversion of *The Settlers* from the Commodore Amiga. Ingo has a PhD in the area of numerical simulation of the motion of granular media.

David Gosselin (gosselin@ati.com)

Dave is currently a software engineer in the 3D Application Research Group at ATI Research. He is involved in various demo and SDK work, focusing mainly on character animation. Previously, he worked at several companies, including Oracle, Spacetec IMC, Xyplex, and MIT Lincoln Laboratory on varied projects from low-level networking and web technologies to image processing and 3D input devices.

Juan Guardado (jguardad@matrox.com)

Juan currently works at Matrox as a graphics architect. He started as the first developer support engineer in the days before DirectX. Later, his focus shifted to better understanding the requirements of next-generation games and APIs, using this analysis to direct research projects and argue with his boss.

Evan Hart (ehart@ati.com)

Evan is presently a software engineer with ATI's Application Research Group. He works with new hardware features on all levels from API specification to implementation in applications. He has been working in real-time 3D for the past four years. He is a graduate of Ohio State University.

Matthias Hopf

Matthias graduated with a degree in computer science from the FAU Erlangen in Germany. Right now, he is a PhD student in the Visualization and Interactive Systems Group at the University of Stuttgart. Despite all his research on adaptive and hierarchical algorithms as well as on hardware-based filters, he is still interested in highly tuned low-level software and hardware. He is mainly known for still being the maintainer of the Aminet archive mirror at the FAU Erlangen, collecting gigabytes of Amiga software.

Kenneth L. Hurley (khurley@nvidia.com)

Kenneth started his career in the games industry in 1985 with a company called Dynamix. He has also worked for Activision, Electronic Arts, and Intel and now works in developer relations at NVIDIA Corp. His current job includes research and development and instructing developers how to use new technology from NVIDIA. His credits in the game industry include *Sword of Kadash* (Atari ST), *Rampage* (PC, Amiga, Apple II),

Copy II ST, *Chuck Yeager's Air Combat Simulator* (PC), *The Immortal* (PC), and *Wing Commander III* (Playstation). While at NVIDIA, he has contributed the following packages/demos: NVASM (GeForce3 vertex/pixel shader assembler), NVTune (NVIDIA's performance analysis tool set), DX7 Refract demo, Minnaert Lighting demo, Particle Physics demo, and the Brushed Metal effect.

John Isidoro (jisidoro@ati.com)

John is a member of the 3D Application Research Group at ATI Technologies and a graduate student at Boston University. His research interests are in the areas of real-time graphics, image-based rendering, and machine vision.

Greg James (GJames@nvidia.com)

Greg is a software engineer with NVIDIA's technical developer relations group where he develops tools and demos for real-time 3D graphics. Prior to this, he worked for a small game company and as a research assistant in a high-energy physics laboratory. He is very glad to have avoided graduate school and even happier to be working in computer graphics, which he picked up as a hobby after his father brought home a strange beige Amiga 1000.

Martin Kraus (Martin.Kraus@informatick.uni-stuttgart.de)

Since graduating in physics, Martin is a PhD student in the Visualization and Interactive Systems Group at the University of Stuttgart in Germany. In recent years he has published several papers on volume visualization, but he is still best known for his Java applet LiveGraphics3D. Martin started programming on a C64 in his early teens and quickly became addicted to computer graphics. Major goals in his life include a long vacation after receiving his PhD and achieving a basic understanding of quantum mechanics.

Scott Le Grand (SLeGrand@nvidia.com)

Scott is a senior engineer on the Direct3D driver team at NVIDIA. His previous commercial projects include *BattleSphere* for the Atari Jaguar and *Genesis* for the Atari ST. Scott has been writing video games since 1971 when he played a Star Trek game on a mainframe and was instantly hooked. In a former life, he picked up a BS in biology from Siena College and a PhD in biochemistry from Pennsylvania State University. Scott's current interests are his wife, Stephanie, and developing techniques to render planets in real time.

Jason L. Mitchell (v-jmitch@microsoft.com)

Jason is the team lead of the 3D Application Research Group at ATI Research, makers of the RADEON family of graphics processors. Working on the Microsoft campus in Redmond, Jason has worked with Microsoft to define new Direct3D features, such as the 1.4 pixel shader model in DirectX 8.1. Prior to working at ATI, Jason did work in human eye tracking for human interface applications at the University of Cincinnati where he received his master's degree in Electrical Engineering. He received a BS in Computer Engineering from Case Western Reserve University. In addition to several articles for this book, Jason has written for the *Game Programming Gems* books, *Game Developer Magazine*, Gamasutra.com, and academic publications on graphics and image processing.

Ádám Moravánszky (amoravanszky@dplanet.ch or http://n.ethz.ch/student/adammo/)

Adam is a computer science student at the Swiss Federal Institute of Technology. He is looking forward to receiving his master's degree in April 2002, after finishing his thesis on real-time 3D graphics.

Christopher Oat (coat@ati.com)

Christopher is a software engineer in the 3D Application Research Group at ATI Research where he explores novel rendering techniques for real-time 3D graphics applications. His current focus is on pixel and vertex shader development in the realm of PC gaming.

Kim Pallister (kim.pallister@intel.com)

Kim is a technical marketing manager and processor evangelist with Intel's Software and Solutions Group. He is currently focused on real-time 3D graphics technologies and game development.

Steven Riddle (sriddle314@hotmail.com)

Steven is an independent contractor developing various web and 3D applications. Since he started programming on the C64, his main interest has been graphics. It has taken him from writing the first Sega Genesis emulator to writing his own rendering engine in C and Assembly. Currently, he is focusing on using vertex and pixel shaders to create a virtual universe.

Guennadi Riguer (griguer@ati.com)

Guennadi is a software developer at ATI Technologies, where he is helping game engine developers to adopt new graphics technologies. Guennadi holds a degree in Computer Science from York University and has previously studied at Belorussian State University of Computing and Electronics. He began programming in the mid-80s and worked on a wide variety of software development projects prior to joining ATI.

John Schwab (johns@shaderstudio.com, www.shaderstudio.com)

John has been programming for the better part of his life. He is the creator of Shader Studio, but in the past ten years, he has been developing games professionally and has worked for Psygnosis and Microsoft. His specialty is computer graphics, and he is always trying to do what others don't think is possible. Currently, he is software engineer at Electronic Arts. In his spare time, he builds robots and designs electronic devices.

Bart Sekura (bsekura@acn.waw.pl)

Bart is a software developer with over seven years of professional experience. He loves computer games and enjoys writing 3D graphics-related code. He spends most of his time tinkering with DirectX, locking and unlocking vertex buffers, and transposing matrices. Bart is currently a senior developer for People Can Fly working on *Painkiller*, a next-generation technology action shooter.

Alex Vlachos (Alex@Vlachos.com or http://alex.vlachos.com)

Alex is currently part of the 3D Application Research Group at ATI Research, where he has worked since 1998 focusing on 3D engine development. Alex is one of the lead developers for ATI's graphics demos and screen savers, and he continues to write 3D engines that showcase next-generation hardware features. In addition, he has developed N-Patches (a curved surface representation which is part of Microsoft's DirectX 8). Prior to working at ATI, he worked at Spacetec IMC as a software engineer for the SpaceOrb 360, a six degrees-of-freedom game controller. He has also been published in *Game Programming Gems 1, 2*, and *3* and ACM's *I3DG*. Alex is a graduate of Boston University.

Daniel Weiskopf (weiskopf@informatik.uni-stuttgart.de)

Daniel is a researcher at the Visualization and Interactive Systems Group at the University of Stuttgart. His scientific interests range from figuring out how the latest graphics boards can be used to speed up scientific visualization to rather crazy things like visualizing general relativistic faster-than-light travel in a warp spaceship. Daniel received a PhD in Theoretical Astrophysics from the University of Tuebingen.

Oliver C. Zecha (ozecha@hotmail.com)

Oliver is an independent consultant with five years experience in the real-time 3D graphics field. His primary focus is dynamic physical simulation, for which he has received several awards and accolades. Recently, he migrated from OpenGL to Direct3D in order to utilize programmable hardware shaders. At the time of publication, his research involves the design of new algorithms that utilize consumer grade graphics hardware in creative and unconventional ways, as well as implementing them for the X-Box console.

Index

Gamedev.net

The most comprehensive game development resource

- The latest news in game development
- The most active forums and chatrooms anywhere, with insights and tips from experienced game developers
- Links to thousands of additional game development resources
- Thorough book and product reviews
- Over 1000 game development articles!
  Game design
  Graphics
  DirectX
  OpenGL
  AI
  Art
  Music
  Physics
  Source Code
  Sound
  Assembly
  And More!

 Gamedev.net

nVSDK

developer.nvidia.com

www.GameInstitute.com
A Superior Way to Learn Computer Game Development

The Game Institute provides a convenient, high-quality game development curriculum at a very affordable tuition. Our expert faculty has developed a series of courses designed to teach you fundamental and advanced game programming techniques so that you can design and develop your own computer games. Best of all, in our unique virtual classrooms you can interact with instructors and fellow students in ways that will ensure you get a firm grasp of the material. Whether you are a beginner or a game development professional, the Game Institute is the superior choice for your game development education.

Quality Courses at a Great Price

○ **Weekly Online Voice Lectures** delivered by your instructor with accompanying slides and other visuals.

○ **Downloadable Electronic Textbook** provides in-depth coverage of the entire curriculum with additional voice-overs from instructors.

○ **Student-Teacher Interaction** both live in weekly chat sessions and via message boards where you can post your questions and solutions to exercises.

○ **Downloadable Certificates** suitable for printing and framing indicate successful completion of your coursework.

○ **Source Code** and sample applications for study and integration into your own gaming projects.

"The leap in required knowledge from competent general-purpose coder to games coder has grown significantly. The Game Institute provides an enormous advantage with a focused curriculum and attention to detail."

—Tom Forsyth
Lead Developer
Muckyfoot Productions, Ltd.

3D Graphics Programming With Direct3D

Examines the premier 3D graphics programming API on the Microsoft Windows platform. Create a complete 3D game engine with animated characters, light maps, special effects, and more.

3D Graphics Programming With OpenGL

An excellent course for newcomers to 3D graphics programming. Also includes advanced topics like shadows, curved surfaces, environment mapping, particle systems, and more.

Advanced BSP/PVS/CSG Techniques

A strong understanding of spatial partitioning algorithms is important for 3D graphics programmers. Learn how to leverage the BSP tree data structure for fast visibility processing and collision detection as well as powerful CSG algorithms.

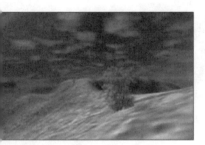

Real-Time 3D Terrain Rendering

Take your 3D engine into the great outdoors. This course takes a serious look at popular terrain generation and rendering algorithms including ROAM, Rottger, and Lindstrom.

Path Finding Algorithms

Study the fundamental art of maneuver in 2D and 3D environments. Course covers the most popular academic algorithms in use today. Also includes an in-depth look at the venerable A*.

Network Game Programming With DirectPlay

Microsoft DirectPlay takes your games online quickly. Course includes coverage of basic networking, lobbies, matchmaking and session management.

MORE COURSES AVAILABLE AT

www.GameInstitute.com

THIS
CHANGES
EVERYTHING™

NOW WITH
128 MB
OF DDR MEMORY!

Brand yourself a warrior
with the groundbreaking,
high-resolution 3D graphics
of RADEON™ 8500 now with
128MB of memory for
lightning fast 3D gaming.
Get the most out of today's
hottest 3D games and
experience the most
immersive 3D gaming
imaginable. RADEON™ 8500
changes everything.

ATI.COM

About the CD

The companion CD contains vertex and pixel shader code along with a variety of programs demonstrating the concepts presented throughout the book. When you unzip the CD files, they will be organized into directories named for the articles.

See the individual readme files for more information.

Additional resources are available at www.shaderx.com

WARNING: By opening the CD package, you accept the terms and conditions of the CD/Source Code Usage License Agreement.

Additionally, opening the CD package makes this book non-returnable.

CD/Source Code Usage License Agreement

Please read the following CD/Source Code usage license agreement before opening the CD and using the contents therein:

1. By opening the accompanying software package, you are indicating that you have read and agree to be bound by all terms and conditions of this CD/Source Code usage license agreement.

2. The compilation of code and utilities contained on the CD and in the book are copyrighted and protected by both U.S. copyright law and international copyright treaties, and is owned by Wordware Publishing, Inc. Individual source code, example programs, help files, freeware, shareware, utilities, and evaluation packages, including their copyrights, are owned by the respective authors.

3. No part of the enclosed CD or this book, including all source code, help files, shareware, freeware, utilities, example programs, or evaluation programs, may be made available on a public forum (such as a World Wide Web page, FTP site, bulletin board, or Internet news group) without the express written permission of Wordware Publishing, Inc. or the author of the respective source code, help files, shareware, freeware, utilities, example programs, or evaluation programs.

4. You may not decompile, reverse engineer, disassemble, create a derivative work, or otherwise use the enclosed programs, help files, freeware, shareware, utilities, or evaluation programs except as stated in this agreement.

5. The software, contained on the CD and/or as source code in this book, is sold without warranty of any kind. Wordware Publishing, Inc. and the authors specifically disclaim all other warranties, express or implied, including but not limited to implied warranties of merchantability and fitness for a particular purpose with respect to defects in the disk, the program, source code, sample files, help files, freeware, shareware, utilities, and evaluation programs contained therein, and/or the techniques described in the book and implemented in the example programs. In no event shall Wordware Publishing, Inc., its dealers, its distributors, or the authors be liable or held responsible for any loss of profit or any other alleged or actual private or commercial damage, including but not limited to special, incidental, consequential, or other damages.

6. One (1) copy of the CD or any source code therein may be created for backup purposes. The CD and all accompanying source code, sample files, help files, freeware, shareware, utilities, and evaluation programs may be copied to your hard drive. With the exception of freeware and shareware programs, at no time can any part of the contents of this CD reside on more than one computer at one time. The contents of the CD can be copied to another computer, as long as the contents of the CD contained on the original computer are deleted.

7. You may not include any part of the CD contents, including all source code, example programs, shareware, freeware, help files, utilities, or evaluation programs in any compilation of source code, utilities, help files, example programs, freeware, shareware, or evaluation programs on any media, including but not limited to CD, disk, or Internet distribution, without the express written permission of Wordware Publishing, Inc. or the owner of the individual source code, utilities, help files, example programs, freeware, shareware, or evaluation programs.

8. You may use the source code, techniques, and example programs in your own commercial or private applications unless otherwise noted by additional usage agreements as found on the CD.

Warning: By opening the CD package, you accept the terms and conditions of the CD/Source Code Usage License Agreement.

Additionally, opening the CD package makes this book non-returnable.